D0773044

SOMETHING ABOUT THE AUTHOR®

Something about the Author *was named an* ***"Outstanding Reference Source"*** *the highest honor given by the American Library Association Reference and Adult Services Division.*

ISSN 0276-816X

SOMETHING ABOUT THE AUTHOR®

Facts and Pictures about Authors and Illustrators of Books for Young People

EDITED BY
KEVIN S. HILE

VOLUME 82

Gale Research Inc.
An International Thomson Publishing Company

Changing the Way the World Learns

NEW YORK • LONDON • BONN • BOSTON • DETROIT • MADRID
MELBOURNE • MEXICO CITY • PARIS • SINGAPORE • TOKYO
TORONTO • WASHINGTON • ALBANY NY • BELMONT CA • CINCINNATI OH

∞™ This book is printed on acid-free paper that meets the minimum requirements of American National Standard for Information Sciences—Permanence Paper for Printed Library Materials, ANSI Z39.48-1984.

Library of Congress Catalog Card Number 72-27107

ISBN 0-8103-2292-7 ISSN 0276-816X

Printed in the United States of America

I(T)P™ Gale Research Inc., an International Thomson Publishing Company.
ITP logo is a trademark under license.

10 9 8 7 6 5 4 3 2 1

Contents

J

K

L

M

N

O

P

R

S

T

V

W

Authors in Forthcoming Volumes

Below are some of the authors and illustrators that will be featured in upcoming volumes of *SATA*. These include new entries on the swiftly-rising stars of the field, as well as completely revised and updated entries (indicated with *) on some of the most notable and best-loved creators of books for children.

Piers Anthony: While best known for his adventures set in the magical land of ''Xanth,'' this prolific writer has also garnered numerous laurels for his many other science fiction and fantasy titles.

***Glenn Balch:** Published between the 1930s and the 1970s, Balch's poignant novels about horses and dogs feature sympathetic portrayals of Native American characters.

Orson Scott Card: The first writer to earn consecutive Nebula and Hugo Awards, Card combines traditional science fiction concepts with issues of morality and religion in *Ender's Game* and *Speaker for the Dead.*

Mary Peace Finley: In Finley's applauded historical novel, *Soaring Eagle,* a Mexican boy finds his true identity and a new name when he journeys to Bent's Fort, Colorado.

***Douglas Florian:** Florian, a seasoned author and illustrator, has received special attention for his recent nonsense verse collections, including *Beast Feast* and *Monster Motel.*

***Joe Lasker:** An accomplished painter, Lasker showcases both his artistic training and a sensitive writing style in historical picture books such as *Merry Ever After,* a tale of two very different medieval weddings.

Dom Lee: Using an original technique of scratching images onto beeswax, this Korean-born artist captured the somber mood of Ken Mochizuki's *Baseball Saved Us,* a story about young Japanese Americans interned in a war camp.

Gareth Owen: A British poet, novelist, and playwright, Owen deals with friendship, growing up, and everyday situations with humor and unique insight.

Rosa Parks: The civil rights activist who sparked the movement to end segregation for African Americans describes her life and struggles in *Rosa Parks: My Story.*

***Susan Beth Pfeffer:** Highly popular among young adults for her explorations of problems ranging from fear of public speaking to teen suicide, Pfeffer has won awards for such novels as *The Year without Michael* and *About David.*

Marcus Pfister: This Swiss author/illustrator incorporates emotional subject matter, as well as eye-catching creative innovations, in *The Rainbow Fish* and other picture books about animals.

J. Otto Seibold: With campy, computer-generated illustrations, Seibold and wife Vivian Walsh's zany stories of the bird-chasing dog, Mr. Lunch, have been widely praised in both the United States and Japan. (Entry contains exclusive interview.)

***Theodore Taylor:** Famed for his award-winning and controversial 1969 novel, *The Cay,* in which a white boy and a black man are stranded on an island, Taylor has recently revisited the characters in his critically acclaimed prequel/sequel, *Timothy of the Cay.*

***Maia Wojciechowska:** Wojciechowska earned the 1965 Newbery Medal for *Shadow of a Bull,* in which a boy grapples with questions of belonging, and is currently at work on her ''Dreams of ...'' series, concerning sports and other pastimes.

Introduction

Something about the Author (*SATA*) is an ongoing reference series that deals with the lives and works of authors and illustrators of children's books. *SATA* includes not only well-known authors and illustrators whose books are widely read, but also those less prominent people whose works are just coming to be recognized. This series is often the only readily available information source on emerging writers or artists. You'll find *SATA* informative and entertaining whether you are a student, a librarian, an English teacher, a parent, or simply an adult who enjoys children's literature for its own sake.

What's Inside SATA

SATA provides detailed information about authors and illustrators who span the full time range of children's literature, from early figures like John Newbery and L. Frank Baum to contemporary figures like Judy Blume and Richard Peck. Authors in the series represent primarily English-speaking countries, particularly the United States, Canada, and the United Kingdom. Also included, however, are authors from around the world whose works are available in English translation. The writings represented in *SATA* include those created intentionally for children and young adults as well as those written for a general audience and known to interest younger readers. These writings cover the entire spectrum of children's literature, including picture books, humor, folk and fairy tales, animal stories, mystery and adventure, science fiction and fantasy, historical fiction, poetry and nonsense verse, drama, biography, and nonfiction.

Obituaries are also included in *SATA* and are intended not only as death notices but also as concise overviews of people's lives and work. Additionally, each edition features newly revised and updated entries for a selection of *SATA* listees who remain of interest to today's readers and who have been active enough to require extensive revisions of their earlier biographies.

Two Convenient Indexes

In response to suggestions from librarians, *SATA* indexes no longer appear in every volume but are included in alternate (odd-numbered) volumes of the series, beginning with Volume 57.

SATA continues to include two indexes that cumulate with each alternate volume: the Illustrations Index, arranged by the name of the illustrator, gives the number of the volume and page where the illustrator's work appears in the current volume as well as all preceding volumes in the series; the Author Index gives the number of the volume in which a person's Biographical Sketch or Obituary appears in the current volume as well as all preceding volumes in the series.

These indexes also include references to authors and illustrators who appear in Gale's *Yesterday's Authors of Books for Children, Children's Literature Review,* and the *Something about the Author Autobiography Series.*

Easy-to-Use Entry Format

Whether you're already familiar with the *SATA* series or just getting acquainted, you will want to be aware of the kind of information that an entry provides. In every *SATA* entry the editors attempt to give as complete a picture of the person's life and work as possible. A typical entry in *SATA* includes the following clearly labeled information sections:

- *PERSONAL:* date and place of birth and death, parents' names and occupations, name of spouse, date of marriage, and names of children, educational institutions attended, degrees received, religious and political affiliations, hobbies and other interests.

- *ADDRESSES:* complete home, office, and agent addresses.

- *CAREER:* name of employer, position, and dates for each career post; military service; memberships and offices held in professional and civic organizations.

- *AWARDS, HONORS:* literary and professional awards received.

- *WRITINGS:* title-by-title chronological bibliography of books written and/or illustrated, listed by genre when known; lists of other notable publications, such as plays, screenplays, and periodical contributions.

- *ADAPTATIONS:* a list of films, television programs, plays, and other media presentations that have been adapted from the author's work.

- *WORK IN PROGRESS:* description of projects in progress.

- *SIDELIGHTS:* a biographical portrait of the author or illustrator's development, either directly from the person—and often written specifically for the *SATA* entry—or gathered from diaries, letters, interviews, or other published sources.

- *FOR MORE INFORMATION SEE:* references for further reading.

- *EXTENSIVE ILLUSTRATIONS:* photographs, movie stills, book covers, and other interesting visual materials supplement the text.

How a SATA Entry Is Compiled

A *SATA* entry progresses through a series of steps. If the biographee is living, the *SATA* editors try to secure information directly from him or her through a questionnaire. From the information that the biographee supplies, the editors prepare an entry, filling in any essential missing details with research and/or telephone interviews. When necessary, the author or illustrator is sent a copy of the entry to check for accuracy and completeness.

If the biographee is deceased or cannot be reached by questionnaire, the *SATA* editors examine a wide variety of published sources to gather information for an entry. Biographical and bibliographic sources are consulted, as are book reviews, feature articles, published interviews, and material sometimes obtained from the biographee's family, publishers, agent, or other associates.

Entries that have not been verified by the biographees or their representatives are marked with an asterisk (*).

We Welcome Your Suggestions

We invite you to examine the entire *SATA* series, starting with this volume. Please write and tell us if we can make *SATA* even more helpful to you. Send comments and suggestions to: The Editor, *Something about the Author,* Gale Research Inc., 835 Penobscot Bldg., 645 Griswold St., Detroit, MI 48226-4094.

Acknowledgments

Grateful acknowledgment is made to the following publishers, authors, and artists whose works appear in this volume.

RICHARD E. ALBERT. Photograph courtesy of Richard E. Albert.

MARY ANDERSON. Jacket of ***Catch Me, I'm Falling in Love,*** by Mary Anderson. Jacket illustration copyright © 1985 by David Henderson. Reprinted by permission of Delacorte Press, a division of Bantam Doubleday Dell Publishing Group, Inc./ Jacket of ***FTC Superstar,*** by Mary Anderson. Atheneum, 1976. Copyright © 1976 by Mary Anderson. Illustrations by Gail Owens. Reprinted by permission of Gail Owens./ Photograph by Marc Romanelli.

CHRISTY HALE APOSTOLOU. Photograph courtesy of Christy Hale Apostolou.

KATYA ARNOLD. Photograph courtesy of Katya Arnold.

MIRIAM AROMER. Photograph courtesy of Miriam Aromer.

SUSAN AVISHAI. Photograph courtesy of Susan Avishai.

MIRIAM BAT-AMI. Jacket of ***When the Frost Is Gone,*** by Miriam Bat-Ami. Jacket illustration copyright © 1994 by March Dunn Ramsey. Reprinted by permission of Atheneum Books for Young Readers, an imprint of Simon & Schuster Children's Publishing Division./ Photograph courtesy of Miriam Bat-Ami.

MARYJANE BEGIN. Illustration by Maryjane Begin from ***Little Mouse's Painting,*** by Diane Wolkstein. Illustrations copyright © 1992 by Maryjane Begin. Reprinted by permission of Morrow Junior Books, a division of William Morrow & Company, Inc./ Photograph courtesy of Maryjane Begin.

NORMAN A. BERT. Photograph by Deb Bert, courtesy of Norman A. Bert.

NANCY BOND. Cover of ***A String in the Harp,*** by Nancy Bond. Copyright © 1987 by The Viking Press, Inc. Cover illustration by Maureen Hyde. Reprinted by permission of Puffin Books, a division Penguin Books USA, Inc./ Jacket of ***Another Shore,*** by Nancy Bond. Jacket illustration copyright © 1988 by Glenn Harrington. Reprinted by permission of Glenn Harrington./ Jacket of ***Truth to Tell,*** by Nancy Bond. Jacket illustration copyright © 1994 by Michael Dooling. Reprinted by permission of Michael Dooling.

C. DALE BRITTAIN. Cover of ***Mage Quest,*** by C. Dale Brittain. Copyright © 1993 by C. Dale Brittain. Cover art by Laurence Schwinger. Reprinted by permission of Baen Publishing Enterprises./ Photograph courtesy of C. Dale Brittain.

DEBBY AND KEN BUCHANAN. Cover from ***This House Is Made of Mud,*** by Ken Buchanan. Illustrations copyright © 1991 by Libba Tracy. Reprinted by permission of Northland Publishing./ Photograph courtesy of Edward McCain.

MARILEE ROBIN BURTON. Photograph courtesy of Marilee Robin Burton.

ELIZABETH CATLETT. Illustration by Elizabeth Catlett from ***Lift Every Voice and Sing,*** by James Weldon Johnson. Illustrations copyright © 1993 by Elizabeth Catlett. Reprinted by permission of Walker and Company./ Photograph, AP/Wide World Photos.

BONNIE CHRISTENSEN. Photograph by Owen Stayner.

ANN NOLAN CLARK. Cover of ***Little Boy with Three Names: Stories of Taos Pueblo,*** by Ann Nolan Clark. Copyright © 1990 by Ancient City Press. Cover design and illustration by Ellen Fox. Reprinted by permission of Ancient City Press./ Cover of ***Little Herder in Autumn,*** by Ann Nolan Clark. Copyright © 1988 by Ancient City Press. Cover design and illustration by Janice St. Marie. Reprinted by permission of Ancient City Press./ Cover of ***Secret of the Andes,*** by Ann Nolan Clark. Cover illustration copyright © 1987 by Viking Penguin Inc. Cover illustration by Robert Barrett. Reprinted by permission of Puffin Books, a division of Penguin Books USA, Inc./ Cover of ***There Still Are Buffalo,*** by Ann Nolan Clark. Copyright © 1992 inclusive of all art work, by Ancient City Press. Cover illustration by Timothy Green. Cover design by Mary Powell. Reprinted by permission of Ancient City Press./ Photograph by Jack Sheaffer.

MARGARET GOFF CLARK. Cover of ***Death at Their Heels,*** by Margaret Goff Clark. Copyright © 1975 by Margaret Goff Clark. Jacket painting by John Floherty, Jr./ Photograph by Ed Jarrett, courtesy of Margaret Goff Clark.

ACE COLLINS. Movie still taken from ***Lassie: A Dog's Life: The First Fifty Years,*** by Ace Collins. Movie still from ***Lassie Come Home*** copyright © 1943, Turner Entertainment Co., all rights reserved. Reprinted by permission of Turner Entertainment Co./ Photograph courtesy of Ace Collins.

GEORGE CRESPO. Photograph by Dario Acosta, courtesy of George Crespo.

STEPHEN CURRIE. Photograph courtesy of Stephen Currie.

MARGUERITE W. DAVOL. Cover of ***Black, White, Just Right!,*** by Marguerite W. Davol. Illustrations copyright © 1993 by Irene Trivas. Reprinted by permission of Albert Whitman & Company./ Photograph by Ellen Augarten, courtesy of Marguerite Davol.

CHRIS L. DEMAREST. Illustration by Chris L. Demarest from ***The Butterfly Jar,*** by Jeff Moss. Illustrations copyright © 1989 by Chris L. Demarest. Reprinted by permission of Bantam Books, a division of Bantam Doubleday Dell Publishing Division./ Illustration by Chris L. Demarest from his ***Clemens' Kingdom.*** Copyright © by Chris L. Demarest. Reprinted by permission of Lothrop, Lee & Shepard Books, a division of William Morrow & Company, Inc./ Self-portrait, courtesy of Chris L. Demarest.

CARL DEUKER. Cover of ***On the Devil's Court,*** by Carl Deuker. Copyright © 1988 by Carl Deuker. Reprinted by permission of Avon Books.

JULIA DONALDSON. Photograph courtesy of Julia Donaldson.

JANE DRAKE. Cover of ***Take Action: An Environmental Book for Kids,*** by Jane Drake and Ann Love. Illustrations copyright © 1992 by Pat Cupples. Reprinted in the United States by permission of Beech Tree Books, an imprint of William Morrow & Company, Inc. Reprinted in Canada and the British Commonwealth by permission of Kids Can Press Ltd., Toronto, Canada./ Photograph courtesy of Jane Drake.

TERRY FARISH. Photograph courtesy of Beth Bergman.

DIANA FARR. Photograph by Dennis Farr, courtesy of Diane Farr.

ZLATA FILIPOVIC. Jacket of ***Zlata's Diary,*** by Zlata Filipovic. Translation copyright © 1994 Editions Robert Laffont/Fixot. Jacket design by Neil Stuart. Jacket photograph by Paul Lowe/Magnum Photos. Jacket photo reprinted by permission of Paul Lowe/Magnum Photos. Cover design reprinted by permission of Viking Penguin, a division of Penguin Books USA Inc.

ALICE SULLIVAN FINLAY. Cover of ***A Gift from the Sea for Laura Lee,*** by Alice Sullivan Finlay. Illustration copyright © 1993 by Julie Durrell. Reprinted by permission of Zondervan Publishing House.

ROBERT L. FORWARD. Cover of ***Return to Rocheworld,*** by Robert L. Forward and Julie Forward Fuller. Copyright © 1993 by Robert L. Forward and Julie Forward. Cover art by David Mattingly. Reprinted by permission of Baen Publishing Enterprises./ Photograph by Claudia Kunin, courtesy of Robert L. Forward.

PAIGE FRAILEY. Photograph courtesy of Paige Frailey.

RICHARD GARRETT. Photograph courtesy of Richard Garrett.

SARA GILBERT. Cover of ***How to Live with a Single Parent,*** by Sara Gilbert. Copyright © 1982 by Sara Gilbert. Reprinted by permission of Lothrop, Lee & Shepard Books, a division of William Morrow & Company, Inc./ Jacket of ***You Can Speak Up in Class,*** by Sara Gilbert. Cover illustration copyright © 1991 by Roy Doty. Reprinted by permission of Morrow Junior Books, a division of William Morrow & Company, Inc./ Photograph by Harry Heleotis, courtesy of Sara Gilbert.

LIBBY GLEESON. Jacket of ***I Am Susannah,*** by Libby Gleeson. Cover illustration copyright © 1992 by Patricia Raine. Reprinted by permission of Beech Tree Books, an imprint of William Morrow & Company, Inc./ Photograph by Evan Touey, courtesy of Libby Gleeson.

LES GRAY. Illustration by Les Gray from ***Max and Felix,*** by Larry Dane Brimner. Copyright © 1993 by Les Gray. Reprinted by permission of Boyds Mills Press, Inc./ Photograph courtesy of Les Gray.

VALISKA GREGORY. Illustration from ***Babysitting for Benjamin,*** by Valiska Gregory. Text copyright © 1993 by Valiska Gregory. Illustration copyright © 1993 by Lynn Munsinger. Reprinted by permission of Little, Brown and Company./ Illustration from ***Through the Mickle Woods,*** by Valiska Gregory. Text copyright © 1991 by Valiska Gregory. Illustration copyright © 1991 by Barry Moser. Reprinted by permission of Little, Brown and Company./ Photograph by Robert Stalcup.

JAMES HAMILTON-PATERSON. Photograph by Jane Brown, courtesy of James Hamilton-Paterson.

ROSIE HARLOW. Photograph courtesy of Rosie Harlow.

ROSEMARY HARRIS. Cover of ***The Bright and Morning Star,*** by Rosemary Harris. Copyright © 1972 by Rosemary Harris. Cover illustration by Ant Parker. Reprinted by permission of Faber & Faber Limited./ Cover of ***The Moon in the Cloud,*** by Rosemary Harris. Copyright © 1968 by Rosemary Harris. Reprinted by permission of Faber & Faber Ltd./ Cover of ***The Shadow on the Sun,*** by Rosemary Harris. Copyright © 1970 by Rosemary Harris. Cover illustration by Ant Parker. Reprinted by permission of Faber & Faber Limited./ Jacket of ***Zed,*** by Rosemary Harris. Copyright © 1982 by Rosemary Harris. Cover illustration by Brian Grimwood. Reprinted by permission of Faber & Faber Limited./ Photograph © Jerry Bauer.

PETER MURRAY HAUTMAN. Photograph by Tim Francisco.

CONNIE K. HECKERT. Jacket of ***Dribbles,*** by Connie Heckert. Jacket illustration copyright © 1993 by Elizabeth Sayles. Reprinted by permission of Houghton Mifflin Company./ Photograph courtesy of Connie K. Heckert.

JANE PENELOPE JOSEPHINE HELYAR. Jacket of ***Moon Eyes,*** by Josephine Poole. Copyright © 1965, 1967 by Josephine Poole. Reprinted by permission of Trina Schart Hyman./ Photograph courtesy of Vincent Helyar.

JULIET HESLEWOOD. Jacket of ***Earth, Air, Fire & Water,*** by Juliet Heslewood. Copyright © Juliet Hesslewood 1985. Front and spine illustrations by Jane Lydbury. Copyright © by Oxford University Press. Reprinted by permission of Oxford University Press./ Photograph courtesy of Juliet Heslewood.

AMY HEST. Cover of ***The Midnight Eaters,*** by Amy Hest. Illustrations copyright © 1989 by Karen Gundersheimer. Reprinted by permission of Simon & Schuster Books for Young Readers, an imprint of Simon & Schuster Children's Publishing Division./ Cover of ***The Purple Coat,*** by Amy Hest. Illustrations copyright © 1986 by Amy Schwartz. Reprinted by permission of Simon & Schuster Books for Young Readers, an imprint of Simon & Schuster Children's Publishing Division./ Jacket of ***Nannies for Hire,*** by Amy Hest. Jacket illustrations © 1994 by Irene Trivas. Illustration copyright © 1994 by Irene Trivas. Reprinted by permission of Morrow Junior Books, a division of William Morrow & Company, Inc.

THOMAS HILL. Photograph courtesy of Thomas Hill.

FELICE HOLMAN. Cover of ***Slake's Limbo,*** by Felice Holman. Cover illustration © 1986 by Jon Weiman. Reprinted by permission of Aladdin Paperbacks, an imprint of Simon & Schuster Children's Publishing Division./ Illustration from ***Professor Diggins' Dragons,*** by Felice Holman. Copyright © 1966 by Felice Holman. Reprinted by permission of Atheneum Books for Young Readers, an imprint of Simon & Schuster Children's Publishing Division./ Jacket of ***Elisabeth the Treasure Hunter,*** by Felice Holman. Illustrations copyright © 1964 by Erik Blegvad. Reprinted by permission of Atheneum Books for Young Readers, an imprint of Simon & Schuster Children's Publishing Division./ Photograph courtesy of Felice Holman.

CHARLOTTE HUCK. Cover of ***Princess Furball,*** retold by Charlotte Huck. Illustrations copyright © 1989 by Anita Lobel. Reprinted by permission of Greenwillow Books, a division of William Morrow & Company, Inc./ Photograph by Barbara Critchlow, courtesy of Charlotte Huck.

ANN JAMES. Illustration by Ann James from ***Dial-a-Croc,*** by Mike Dumbleton. Illustrations copyright © 1991 by Ann James. Reprinted by permission of Orchard Books, New York.

ADRIENNE JONES. Jacket of ***Sail, Calypso!,*** by Adrienne Jones. Copyright © 1968 by Adrienne Jones. Jacket and illustrations by Adolf Le Moult./ Photograph by Gwen Rinehart, courtesy of Adrienne Jones.

KATHLEEN KARR. Jacket of ***Oh, Those Harper Girls!,*** by Kathleen Karr. Jacket art copyright © 1992 by Ellen Eagle. Reprinted by permission of Farrar, Straus & Giroux, Inc./ Photograph by James Goodman Smith, courtesy of Kathleen Karr.

CHARLES KELLER. Cover of ***Belly Laughs!: Food Jokes & Riddles,*** by Charles Keller. Illustrations copyright © 1990 by Ronald Fritz. Reprinted by permission of Simon & Schuster Books for Young Readers./ Jacket of ***Colossal Fossils: Dinosaur Riddles,*** compiled by Charles Keller. Illustrations copyright © 1987 by Leonard Kessler. Reprinted by permission of Simon & Schuster Books for Young Readers./ Photograph courtesy of Charles Keller.

MICHAEL KERSHEN. Photograph courtesy of Michael Kershen.

PATRICE KINDL. Photograph courtesy of Patrice Kindl.

JOAN KNIGHT. Jacket of ***Bon Appetit, Bertie!,*** by Joan Knight. Illustrations copyright © 1993 by Penny Dann. Reprinted by permission of Dorling Kindersley./ Photograph courtesy of Joan Knight.

CAROL KOFFINKE. Photograph courtesy of Bel-Air Studio.

ROBERT CLEMENT KRAY. Photograph courtesy of Robert Clement Kray.

SIGMUND A. LAVINE. Cover of ***Wonders of Animal Architecture,*** by Sigmund A. Lavine. Copyright © 1964 by Sigmund A. Lavine. Illustrations by Margaret Cosgrove. Reprinted by permission of Margaret Cosgrove./ Photograph from ***Wonders of Badgers,*** by Sigmund A. Lavine. Copyright © 1985 by Sigmund A. Lavine. Reprinted by permission of The Forest Life Picture Library./ Photograph courtesy of Sigmund Lavine.

MARY PRICE AND RICHARD S. LEE. Photograph courtesy of Mary Price Lee and Richard S. Lee.

ROBERT LEVY. Jacket cover of ***Clan of the Shape-Changers,*** by Robert Levy. Jacket art copyright © 1994 by N. Taylor Blanchard. Reprinted by permission of Houghton Mifflin Company.

SHARON LINNEA. Photograph by Thomas Veres.

IRMGARD LUCHT. Illustration by Irmgard Lucht from her ***In This Night.*** Text and illustrations copyright © 1993 by Ravensburger Buchverlag Otto Maier GmbH, Germany. Reprinted by permission of Hyperion Books for Children./ Photograph by Anne Lucht, courtesy of Imgard Lucht.

ROSS MARTIN MADSEN. Photograph courtesy of Ross Martin Madsen.

KEVIN MAJOR. Cover of ***Blood Red Ochre,*** by Kevin Major. Copyright © 1989 by Kevin Major. Reprinted by permission of Dell Books, a division of Bantam Doubleday Dell Publishing Group, Inc./ Jacket of ***Far from Shore,*** by Kevin Major. Jacket illustration copyright © 1981 by Fran Stiles. Reprinted by Delacorte Press, a division of Bantam Doubleday Dell Publishing Group./ Jacket of ***Hold Fast,*** by Kevin Major. Jacket painting copyright © 1980 by Michael Dudash. Reprinted by permission of Delacorte Press, a division of Bantam Doubleday Dell Publishing Group, Inc./ Photograph by Ann Crawford.

PAUL MARCUS. Photograph courtesy of Paul Marcus.

LINDA MARTIN. Photograph by Pat Hillenius, courtesy of Linda Martin.

WILLIAM D. McCANTS. Photograph courtesy of William D. McCants.

KAREN KAWAMOTO McCOY. Photograph courtesy of Karen Kawamoto McCoy.

MICHAEL McCURDY. Jacket by Michael McCurdy from his ***The Old Man and the Fiddle.*** Jacket art copyright © 1992 by Michael McCurdy. Reprinted by permission of G. P. Putnam's Sons, a division of The Putnam & Grosset Book Group./ Jacket by Michael McCurdy from his ***The Devils Who Learned to Be Good.*** Copyright © 1987 by Michael McCurdy. Jacket design by Jeanne Abboud. Reprinted by permission of Little, Brown and Company./ Photograph by Gerard Malanga, courtesy of Michael McCurdy.

JEAN MERRILL. Cover of ***The Pushcart War,*** by Jean Merrill. Text copyright © 1964 by Ronni Solbert. Cover illustration by Carl Cassler. Reprinted by permission of Dell Books, a division of Bantam Doubleday Dell Publishing Group, Inc./ Cover of ***The Toothpaste Millionaire,*** by Jean Merrill. Copyright © 1972 by Houghton Mifflin Company. Cover illustration by Jan Palmer. Reprinted by permission of Houghton Mifflin Company. All rights reserved. Photograph courtesy of Jean Merrill.

CHARLES MICUCCI. Jacket by Charles Micucci from his ***The Life and Times of the Apple.*** Jacket illustration copyright © 1992 by Charles Micucci. Reprinted by permission of Orchard Books, New York.

KYOKO MORI. Jacket of ***Shizuko's Daughter,*** by Mari Kyoko. Copyright © 1993 by Kyoko Mori. Jacket illustration copyright © 1993 by Mary Jo Mazzella. Jacket design copyright © 1993 by Louise Fili. Reprinted by permission of Henry Holt and Company, Inc./ Jacket of ***The Dream of Water,*** by Kyoka Mori. Copyright © 1995 by Kyoko Mori. Jacket design by Darlene Barbaria. Reprinted by permission of Henry Holt and Co, Inc./ Photograph courtesy of Katherine A. McCabe.

DAVID NEEL. Photograph courtesy of David Neel.

SALLY NOLL. Cover by Sally Noll from her ***Jiggle Wiggle Prance.*** Copyright © 1987 by Sally Noll. Reprinted by permission of Greenwillow Books, a division of William Morrow & Company, Inc./ Photograph courtesy of Sally Noll.

ELIZABETH ONEAL. Cover of ***The Language of Goldfish,*** by Zibby Oneal. Cover illustration copyright © 1990 by Neil Waldman. Cover design by Rebecca Laughlin. Reprinted by permission of Puffin Books, a division of Penguin Books USA, Inc./ Jacket of ***In Summer Light,*** by Zibby Oneal. Jacket illustration by Bob Dacey. Copyright © 1985 Viking Penguin Inc. Reprinted by permission of Viking Penguin, a division of Penguin Books USA, Inc./ Photograph courtesy of Zibby Oneal.

JOANNE OPPENHEIM. Cover from ***Have You Seen Birds?,*** by Joanne Oppenheim. Illustrations copyright © 1986 by Barbara Reid. Reprinted by permission of Scholastic Canada Ltd./ Jacket of ***You Can't Catch Me!,*** by Joanne Oppenheim. Jacket painting copyright © by Andrew Schachat. Reprinted by permission of Houghton Mifflin Company./ Photograph courtesy of Joanne Oppenheim.

DONNA PAPE. Illustration from ***The Mouse at the Show,*** by Donna Lugg Pape. Copyright © 1981 by Daniel Weiner. Reprinted by permission of Daniel Weiner. Photograph courtesy of the Sheboygan Press.

MARILYN PARKE. Photograph courtesy of Marilyn Parke.

JULIE ANNE PETERS. Photograph courtesy of Julie Anne Peters.

CHRISTINE POPESCU. Jacket of ***The Long Search,*** by Christine Pullein-Thompson. Jacket illustration copyright © 1993 by Joe Baker. Reprinted by permission of Joe Baker./ Photograph courtesy of Christine Popescu.

TERRY PRATCHETT. Cover of ***Witches Abroad,*** by Terry Pratchett. Copyright © 1991 by Terry and Lyn Pratchett. Cover illustration by Darrell K. Sweet. Reprinted by permission of Darrell K. Sweet./ Illustration derived from Terry Pratchett's Discworld characters. Copyright © 1994 by Mamelok Press Ltd. Illustration by Stephen Player. Reprinted by permission of Clarecraft Design./ Photograph courtesy of Terry Pratchett.

JOSEPHINE PULLEIN-THOMPSON. Photograph courtesy of Josephine Pullein-Thompson.

INDIRA HIGHAM RANA. Cover of ***The Roller Birds of Rampur,*** by Indi Rana. Copyright © 1993 by Indi Rana. Reprinted by permission of Ballantine Books, a division of Random House, Inc./ Photograph by Madan Mahatta, New Delhi.

MIRA REISBERG. Photograph courtesy of Mira Reisberg.

ENID RICHEMONT. Jacket of ***The Time Tree,*** by Enid Richemont. Copyright © 1989 by Enid Richemont. Jacket illustration by Jennifer Eachus. Reprinted by permission of Little, Brown and Company./ Photograph by Sydna Younson, courtesy of Enid Richemont.

EDWINA RIDDELL. Photograph courtesy of Edwina Riddell.

CATHERINE RIPLEY. Photograph courtesy of Catherine Ripley.

CRISTINA SALAT. Photograph courtesy of Cristina Salat.

LINDA SAYLOR-MARCHANT. Photograph couresy of Linda Saylor-Marchant.

ELEANOR SCHICK. Illustration by Eleanor from her ***City in the Summer.*** Copyright © 1969 by Eleanor Schick. Reprinted by permission of Atheneum Books for Young Readers, an imprint of Simon & Schuster Children's Publishing Division./ Jacket by Eleanor Schick from her ***I Have Another Language: The Language Is Dance.*** Jacket illustration copyright © 1992 by Eleanor Schick. Reprinted by permission of Atheneum Books for Young Readers, an imprint of Simon & Schuster Children's Publishing Division./ Photograph courtesy of Cary Herz.

MARY SERFOZO. Cover of ***Who Said Red?,*** by Mary Serfozo. Illustrations copyright © 1988 by Keiko Narahashi. Reprinted by permission of Margaret K. McElderry Books, an imprint of Simon & Schuster Children's Publishing Division./ Photograph courtesy of Mary Serfozo.

TRES SEYMOUR. Jacket of ***Life in the Desert,*** by Tres Seymour. Text copyright © 1992 by Tres Seymour. Copyright © 1992 by Andrew Radcliffe. Jacket: a detail from Desert Scene #4 by Andrew Radcliffe. Copyright © 1992 by Andrew Radcliffe. Reprinted by permission of Orchard Books, New York./ Photograph courtesy of Tres Seymour.

CATHERINE SIRACUSA. Illustration by Catherine Siracusa from her ***The Giant Zucchini.*** Text and illustrations copyright © 1993 by Catherine Siracusa. Reprinted by permission of Hyperion Books for Children. Photograph by Denise Demarest, courtesy of Catherine Siracusa.

BRENDA SMITH. Photograph courtesy of Brenda Smith.

DOROTHY GLADYS SMITH. Movie still from ***101 Dalmations,*** story by Dorothy Gladys Smith. Copyright © 1961 The Walt Disney Company. Reprinted from ***Encyclopedia of Walt Disney's Animated Characters,*** by John Grant. Copyright © 1993. Published by Hyperion. Reprinted by permission of the publisher.

SHARON SMITH. Photograph courtesy of Sharon Smith.

SHERWOOD SMITH. Cover of ***Wren to the Rescue,*** by Sherwood Smith. Copyright © 1972 by Robb White. Cover illustration by Jody Lee. Reprinted by permission of Dell Books, a division of Bantam Doubleday Dell Publishing Group, Inc./ Jacket of ***Wren's Quest,*** by Sherwood Smith. Jacket illustration copyright © 1993 by Dennis Nolan. Jacket design by Calilla Filancia. Reprinted by permission of Dennis Nolan.

SHERI COBB SOUTH. Photograph by Glamour Shots.

ROBIN SPOWART. Illustration by Robin Spowart from ***Vegetable Soup,*** by Jeanne Modesitt. Illustrations copyright © 1988 by Robin Spowart. Reprinted by permission of Atheneum Books for Young Readers, an imprint of Simon & Schuster Children's Publishing Division./ Photograph courtesy of Robin Spowart.

R. CONRAD STEIN. Cover of ***America The Beautiful: Oregon,*** by R. Conrad Stein. Copyright © 1989 by Childrens Press, Inc. Cover photo reprinted by permission of Steve Terrill. Cover design reprinted by permission of Childrens Press, Inc./ Cover of ***Cornerstones of Freedom: The Story of the Golden Spike,*** by R. Conrad Stein. Copyright © 1978 by Regensteiner Publishing Enterprises, Inc. Illustrations by Tom Dunnington. Reprinted by permission of Childrens Press, Inc./ Photograph courtesy of R. Conrad Stein.

JILL STOVER. Jacket by Jill Stover from her ***Alamo Across Texas.*** Jacket illustrations © 1992 by Jill Stover. Reprinted by permission of Lothrop, Lee & Shepard Books, a division of William Morrow & Company, Inc./ Photograph by Walter Silver, courtesy of Jill Stover.

JENNY STOW. Photograph courtesy of Jenny Stow.

K. DYBLE THOMPSON. Photograph courtesy of K. Dyble Thompson.

TOBI TOBIAS. Cover of ***The Quitting Deal,*** by Tobi Tobias. Copyright © 1975 by Tobi Tobias. Illustrations copyright © 1975 by Trina Schart Hyman. Reprinted by permission of Viking Penguin, a division of Penguin Books USA Inc./ Jacket of ***Pot Luck,*** by Tobi Tobias. Jacket illustration copyright © 1993 by Nola Langner Malone. Reprinted by permission of Lothrop, Lee & Shepard Books, a division of William Morrow and Company, Inc.

RUTH TURK. Photograph courtesy of Ruth Turk.

KATHY TYERS. Photograph by Kathy Wierda Photography, courtesy of Kathy Tyers.

JEAN VAN LEEUWEN. Cover of ***Tales of Amanda Pig,*** by Jean Van Leeuwen. Illustrations copyright © Ann Schweninger, 1983. Reprinted in the United States and Canada by permission of Dial Books for Young Readers, a division of Penguin Books USA, Inc. Reprinted in the British Commonwealth by permission of William Heinemann Ltd./ Illustration from ***More Tales Of Oliver Pig,*** by Jean Van Leeuwen. Pictures copyright © 1981 by Arnold Lobel. Reprinted in the United States and Canada by permission of Dial Books for Young Readers, a division of Penguin Books USA Inc. Reprinted in the British Commonwealth by permission of The Bodley Head./ Illustration from ***The Great Rescue Operation,*** by Jean Van Leeuwen. Pictures copyright © 1982 by Margot Apple. Reprinted by permission of Dial Books for Young Readers, a division of Penguin Books USA./ Jacket of ***Dear Mom, You're Ruining My Life,*** by Jean Van Leeuwen. Copyright © 1989 by Jean Van Leeuwen Gavril. Cover design reprinted by permission of Dial Books for Young Readers, a division of Penguin Books USA Inc. Cover illustration reprinted by permission of Deborah Chabrian./ Jacket of ***Going West,*** by Jean Van Leeuwen. Illustrations copyright © 1992 by Thomas B. Allen. Reprinted by permission of Dial Books for Young Readers./ Photograph by Elizabeth Gavril, courtesy of Jean Van Leeuwen.

DIANNE MARIE CATHERINE WALKER. Jacket of ***Peter,*** by Kate Walker. Jacket art copyright © 1991 by Vivienne Goodman. Reprinted by permission of Houghton Mifflin Company./ Photograph courtesy of Dianne Marie Catherine Walker.

ELIZABETH E. WEIN. Cover of ***The Winter Prince,*** by Elizabeth E. Wein. Copyright © 1993 by Elizabeth E. Wein. Cover art by Darrell K. Sweet. Reprinted by permission of Baen Publishing Enterprises./ Photograph by Amanda Banks, courtesy of Elizabeth E. Wein.

ROGER L. WELSCH. Jacket of ***Uncle Smoke Stories: Nehawaka Tales of Coyote the Trickster,*** by Roger Welsch. Jacket art copyright © 1994 by Richard Mantel. Reprinted by permission of Alfred A. Knopf, Inc./ Photograph courtesy of Roger Welsch.

JOANNA WEZYK. Photograph courtesy of Joanna Wezyk.

NATASHA WING. Photograph by Daniel B. Wing, courtesy of Natasha Wing.

DIANE WOLKSTEIN. Cover of ***The Banza,*** by Diane Wolkstein. Pictures copyright © 1981 by Marc Brown. Reprinted by permission of Dial Books for Young Readers, a division of Penguin Books USA Inc. Cover of ***The Magic Orange Tree, and Other Haitian Folktales,*** collected by Diane Wolkstein. Illustrations copyright © 1978 by Alfred A. Knopf, Inc. Reprinted by permission of Diane Wolkstein./ Photograph by Rachel C. Zucker, courtesy of Diane Wolkstein.

MARJORY WUNSCH. Photograph courtesy of Marjory Wunsch.

SOMETHING ABOUT THE AUTHOR®

ADAMS, Nicholas
See SMITH, Sherwood

* * *

ALBERT, Richard E. 1909-

■ Personal

Born March 8, 1909, in Halstead, KS; son of Elwood (a merchant) and Marie (a homemaker; maiden name, Babcock) Albert; married Marijane (a homemaker; maiden name, Eager), August 27, 1938 (deceased); children: Richard, Earl. *Education:* Attended Pittsburg State College and Kansas State University; University of Southern California, B.S., 1936. *Politics:* Democrat. *Religion:* Christian.

■ Addresses

Home—1764 Oakwood Ave., Arcadia, CA 91006.

■ Career

Southern California Gas Company, CA, engineer, 1935-45, design and development engineer for gas fired equipment, 1945-70. *Member:* American Society of Gas Engineers (past president of local chapter), Boy Scouts of America, YMCA.

■ Writings

Alejandro's Gift, illustrated by Sylvia Long, Chronicle Books, 1994.

RICHARD E. ALBERT

Has also written numerous "pulp westerns" and stories for children's magazines.

■ Sidelights

Though Richard E. Albert sold numerous "pulp westerns" from the 1930s to the 1950s and wrote many stories for children's magazines after retirement, *Alejan-*

dro's Gift is his first published book. He told *SATA* that he is currently "working on others."

■ For More Information See

PERIODICALS

Kirkus Reviews, February 15, 1994, p. 221.
Publishers Weekly, February 14, 1994, p. 87.

* * *

ANDERSON, Mary 1939-

■ Personal

Born January 20, 1939, in New York, NY; daughter of Andrew Joseph and Nellie (DeHaan) Quirk; married Carl Anderson (a commercial artist), March 1, 1958; children: Lisa, Maja, Chersteen. *Education:* Attended Hunter College of the City University of New York and New School for Social Research.

■ Addresses

Home—270 Riverside Dr., New York, NY 10025.

■ Career

Writer. Actress in Off-Broadway productions, New York City, 1956-58; secretary in advertising and television fields, New York City, 1958-59; teacher of creative writing in New York schools in conjunction with Teachers and Writers Collaborative. Lecturer; guest on television and radio programs.

MARY ANDERSON

■ Awards, Honors

New York Public Library Best Books of the Year, 1973, 1978, and 1984; Sequoyah Children's Book Award nomination, 1978, for *F.T.C. Superstar!;* Dorothy Canfield Fisher Award nominations, 1979, for *Step on a Crack,* and 1980; South Carolina Young Adult Book Award nomination, 1981, for *Step on a Crack.*

■ Writings

(With Hope Campbell, pseudonym of Geraldine Wallis) *There's a Pizza Back in Cleveland,* Four Winds, 1972.
Emma's Search for Something, illustrated by Peter Parnall, Atheneum, 1973.
Matilda Investigates, illustrated by Carl Anderson, Atheneum, 1973.
I'm Nobody! Who Are You?, Atheneum, 1974.
Just the Two of Them, illustrated by Carl Anderson, Atheneum, 1974.
F.T.C. Superstar!, illustrated by Gail Owens, Atheneum, 1976.
Matilda's Masterpiece, illustrated by Sal Murdorca, Atheneum, 1977.
The Mystery of the Missing Painting, Scholastic, 1977.
Step on a Crack, Atheneum, 1978.
F.T.C. and Company, illustrated by Don Sibley, Atheneum, 1979.
The Rise and Fall of a Teen-age Wacko, Atheneum, 1980.
Forever, Ahbra, Atheneum, 1981.
You Can't Get There from Here, Atheneum, 1982.
That's Not My Style, Atheneum, 1983.
R.I.S.K., Atheneum, 1983.
Tune in Tomorrow, Atheneum, 1984.
Catch Me, I'm Falling in Love, Delacorte, 1985.
Do You Call That a Dream Date?, Delacorte, 1987.
Who Says Nobody's Perfect?, Delacorte, 1987.
The Catnapping Caper, Dell, 1987.
The Unsinkable Molly Malone, Harcourt, 1991.
Suzy's Secret Snoop Society, Avon, 1991.

Also contributor to *The New York Kid's Book,* Doubleday, 1979. Author of libretto, "Sara Crewe: The Orphan Princess" (musical adaptation of Frances Hodgson Burnett's classic, *A Little Princess*), produced by Performing Arts Repertory Theatre (now Theatre Works). Excerpts from Anderson's books have appeared in textbooks by Scott, Foresman; Ginn; and the Economy Company.

"MOSTLY GHOSTS" SERIES

The Haunting of Hillcrest, Dell, 1987.
The Leipzig Vampire, Dell, 1987.
The Three Spirits of Vandermeer Manor, Dell, 1987.

"MOSTLY MONSTERS" SERIES

The Hairy Beast in the Woods, Dell, 1989.
The Missing Movie Creature, Dell, 1989.

The Terrible Thing in the Bottle, Dell, 1989.
The Curse of the Demon, Dell, 1989.

■ Work in Progress

An adult historical mystery thriller.

■ Sidelights

Mary Anderson once told *SATA:* "The main motivation behind my work is to recreate for others (and myself) the pleasure I received from reading as a child. Children's books are one of the last strongholds in literature where optimism, joy, compassion, and a sheer wonder for the world are still being portrayed successfully." She has also commented, "I believe the primary function of a novel for young people is to *entertain.* Beyond that, I like my books to have main characters, who, in spite of problems, find some way to control their own destinies and discover the unique assets they individually possess." Anderson's numerous light mysteries for middle-grade readers and young adult novels have garnered attention for the humorous banter exchanged by the characters, their realistic problems, and the author's successful resolution of their difficulties.

Anderson began her career writing light mysteries with comical touches and strong female characters for middle-grade readers. *Emma's Search for Something* centers on Emma Pigeon, who, through her ability to read, discovers the world's disdain for her kind and sets about trying to rectify the situation. *Publishers Weekly* contributor Jean F. Mercier dubbed this "an original and interesting bit of make-believe." Virginia Haviland described *Matilda Investigates,* Anderson's first book to feature a young girl who dreams of being a detective, as "a light, bantering story of crime sleuthing" in her *Horn Book* review. In this work, Mattie pursues her goal of becoming New York's first female detective by uncovering the culprit in a string of jewelry thefts. Critics noted the author's emphasis on female equality as asserted through the voice of her main character. Later, Anderson published a sequel, *Matilda's Masterpiece,* in which Mattie's determination to prove her sleuthing ability to her skeptical father coincides with the discovery of the theft of a valuable painting. Mattie's initial suspect turns out to be innocent, but she accidentally finds the real culprits and wins a reward. Although a *Bulletin of the Center for Children's Books* reviewer faulted the story line as "both lightweight and protracted," Barbara Elleman, writing in *Booklist,* declared that critical readers will nonetheless "be swept along by Anderson's acute dialogue and brisk pace."

For slightly older adolescents Anderson next published *I'm Nobody! Who Are You?,* which relates the unlikely friendship that springs up between two boarding school girls who discover time-travelling as a way to escape their unhappiness. Though reviews of this work were generally less favorable, Mercier allowed that "some good suspense provides the book's best moments." Also for this age group is *Just the Two of Them,* Anderson's next effort, which portrays the lonely Luis, recently immigrated from Puerto Rico, who finds friendship in New York's Central Park by helping an elderly woman take care of the animals in the zoo. Anderson returned to animal stories with two books intended for middle-grade readers: *F.T.C. Superstar!* and *F.T.C. and Company,* which center on the adventures of a group of neighborhood animals and their experiences acting on stage and in television commercials. Helen Gregory dubbed *F.T.C. Superstar!* a "fast-moving, funny story" in her *School Library Journal* review, and Denise M. Wilms remarked in *Booklist:* "Deft character sketches plus a knack for dialogue make [*F.T.C. and Company*] hum along nicely."

In Anderson's award-winning work for middle schoolers, a New York City alley cat is trained by a neighborhood pigeon to become a Broadway star. (Cover illustartion by Gail Owens.)

Step on a Crack, Anderson's next young adult novel, inaugurated a string of works aimed at primarily female junior high and high school readers. *Horn Book* dubbed this work, which focuses on Sarah's attempts to uncover the source of a recurring nightmare in which she kills her mother, "a suspenseful psychodrama." While several critics faulted the novel's psychological insights, a *Bulletin of the Center for Children's Books* writer found Sarah's story "fascinating," "deftly structured," and "well written." Anderson followed this success with *The*

Rise and Fall of a Teen-age Wacko, the story of Laura, whose artistic ambitions lean toward acting, although the rest of her family is more interested in the fine arts. Alone in New York for two weeks one summer, Laura indulges her love of shopping and becomes an extra in a Woody Allen film before disaster strikes. Steve Matthews, writing in *School Library Journal,* found the scenes set in New York "well drawn and essentially believable," and a *Bulletin of the Center for Children's Books* contributor commented: "The writing style is smooth and is consistently that of an adolescent."

Forever, Ahbra is a romantic mystery set in the High School of Music and Art in Manhattan. In this work, Larry becomes intrigued with a mysterious young woman when she faints in front of their lockers and then again at the Metropolitan Museum of Art. Though several critics, including one for *Kirkus Reviews,* found the novel's premise "pretty silly," *Voice of Youth Advocates* reviewer John R. Lord felt that "with a good class of perceptive students," *Forever, Ahbra* would easily form the basis for productive discussions about ancient Egypt. In *You Can't Get There from Here,* a young woman becomes involved with a charismatic acting teacher after her home life is destroyed when her parents divorce. Critics compared the atmosphere in Anderson's acting school to depictions of a religious cult, and predicted that that element alone would, in the words of *Booklist* writer Sally Estes, "hold and involve readers." Also for older adolescents is Anderson's *That's Not My Style,* about a boy's singleminded ambition to be a writer and how it blinds him to the real stories and emotions of those around him. Critics praised the humor with which this story is portrayed. "Deft characterization and sharp-edged humor make this a winner," concluded Anne Connor in *School Library Journal.*

An unhappy young woman with a broken ankle ends up falling in love with her much older chiropractor in this humorous tale. (Cover illustration by David Henderson.)

Critics also praised the lighthearted elements in Anderson's next work, *Tune in Tomorrow,* in which two teenage girls trail the stars of their favorite soap opera while vacationing on Fire Island. Kate M. Flanagan in *Horn Book* noted: "[The narrator's] first-person musings about herself, her mother, and the meaning of life are both comical and insightful and always ring true." Similarly, "Anderson's latest refreshes the reader like an unpolluted breeze blowing through fiction for young adults," enthused critic Mercier of *Catch Me, I'm Falling in Love.* Andrea Davidson, writing in *Voice of Youth Advocates,* found this novel about a young woman who falls in love with her chiropractor after breaking her ankle "very funny, written with a light, tongue-in-cheek manner." Anderson has also written *Do You Call That a Dream Date?* and *Who Says Nobody's Perfect?,* both featuring Jenny Beaumont, whose worst problem is that she is too ordinary. In *Do You Call That a Dream Date?,* Jenny plagiarizes her older sister's essay in order to win a date with a rock star and be popular in her school. Elizabeth S. Watson remarked in a *Horn Book* review: "Jenny's conflict with her sister is strong and really bitter but consistent and believable." The sisters' relationship is also a focal point in the novel's sequel, *Who Says Nobody's Perfect?,* in which Jenny duplicates her competitive relationship with her sibling with the seemingly perfect Norwegian exchange student who takes her place. Catherine Clancy in *Voice of Youth Advocates* dubbed this "another sure winner from Anderson."

Anderson often emphasizes the humor in the dilemmas in which she places her characters. Though she writes light mysteries for middle-grade readers, her young adult novels often center on commonplace problems—such as divorcing parents, loneliness, unpopularity, and a feeling of not fitting in—that many adolescents face. While Anderson is sometimes criticized for resolving her characters' problems too easily, critics also praise her realistic settings, sympathetic characters, and engaging dialogue.

■ Works Cited

Clancy, Catherine, review of *Who Says Nobody's Perfect?, Voice of Youth Advocates,* December, 1987, p. 46.

Connor, Anne, review of *That's Not My Style, School Library Journal,* April, 1983, p. 120.

Davidson, Andrea, review of *Catch Me, I'm Falling in Love, Voice of Youth Advocates,* April, 1986, p. 26.

Elleman, Barbara, review of *Matilda's Masterpiece, Booklist,* June 15, 1977, p. 1572.
Estes, Sally, review of *You Can't Get There from Here, Booklist,* April 15, 1982, p. 1082.
Flanagan, Kate M., review of *Tune in Tomorrow, Horn Book,* April, 1984, p. 199.
Review of *Forever, Ahbra, Kirkus Reviews,* October 15, 1981, p. 1299.
Gregory, Helen, review of *F.T.C. Superstar!, School Library Journal,* April, 1976, p. 68.
Haviland, Virginia, review of *Matilda Investigates, Horn Book,* June, 1973, p. 268.
Lord, John R., review of *Forever, Ahbra, Voice of Youth Advocates,* February, 1982, p. 28.
Review of *Matilda's Masterpiece, Bulletin of the Center for Children's Books,* September, 1977.
Matthews, Steve, review of *The Rise and Fall of a Teen-age Wacko, School Library Journal,* November, 1980, p. 81.
Mercier, Jean F., review of *Emma's Search for Something, Publishers Weekly,* January 7, 1974, p. 54.
Mercier, review of *I'm Nobody! Who Are You?, Publishers Weekly,* July 1, 1974, p. 82.
Mercier, review of *Catch Me, I'm Falling in Love, Publishers Weekly,* October 4, 1985, p. 77.
Review of *The Rise and Fall of a Teen-age Wacko, Bulletin of the Center for Children's Books,* January, 1981, p. 86.
Review of *Step on a Crack, Bulletin of the Center for Children's Books,* September, 1978.
Review of *Step on a Crack, Horn Book,* June, 1978.
Watson, Elizabeth S., review of *Do You Call That a Dream Date?, Horn Book,* May-June, 1987, p. 345.
Wilms, Denise M., review of *F.T.C. and Company, Booklist,* April 1, 1979, p. 1216.

■ For More Information See

BOOKS

Contemporary Authors, New Revision Series, Volume 16, Gale, 1986.

PERIODICALS

Bulletin of the Center for Children's Books, February, 1975, p. 89; May, 1982; December, 1985.
Horn Book, June, 1982, pp. 295-96; June, 1983, p. 307.
Kirkus Reviews, February 1, 1973, p. 113; July 15, 1973, pp. 752-53; March 1, 1974, p. 242; February 15, 1977, p. 165; February 15, 1978; July 1, 1979, p. 739; October 1, 1980, pp. 1301-2; January 1, 1983, p. 6; December 1, 1986, pp. 1796-97.
New York Times Book Review, May 5, 1974, p. 26.
Publishers Weekly, July 29, 1974, p. 56; February 13, 1987, p. 94.
School Library Journal, May, 1977; April, 1978; September, 1979, p. 126; December, 1981, p. 70; April, 1984, p. 121; October, 1985; November, 1987, p. 112.
Voice of Youth Advocates, August, 1982, p. 27; August, 1984, p. 143; October, 1987, p. 105.

—*Sketch by Mary Gillis*

ANTHONY, C. L.
See SMITH, Dorothy Gladys

* * *

APOSTOLOU, Christine Hale 1955-
(Christy Hale)

■ Personal

Born January 21, 1955, in Southbridge, MA; daughter of Harold Charles (a mechanical engineer) and Eunice Sherman (a draftsperson) Hale; married Scott Julian Apostolou, August 31, 1991. *Education:* Lewis and Clark College, B.A., 1977, M.A.T., 1980; Pratt Institute, B.F.A., 1986. *Politics:* Democrat. *Religion:* Protestant. *Hobbies and other interests:* Letterpress printing, playing guitar, traveling, and speaking Spanish.

■ Addresses

Home—1 Second Place, Apt. 2, Brooklyn, NY 11231.

■ Career

Willamette Middle School, West Linn, OR, art instructor, 1978-84; freelance designer and illustrator, 1986—; E. P. Dutton, New York City, art assistant, 1986-87; Aperture, New York City, designer, 1987-88; Putnam/Philomel, New York City, senior designer, 1987-89; Bradbury Press, New York City, interim art director, 1989; Macmillan, New York City, interim art director, 1989-90; Four Winds Press, art director, 1990-94.

CHRISTINE HALE APOSTOLOU

Awards, Honors

Award of Excellence, AIGA Cover Show, 1988; two Merit Awards for photo design, 1988-89; first place, Bookbinder's Guild, 1989, for special trade book; honorable mention, How Magazine, 1990, for illustration.

Illustrator

UNDER NAME CHRISTY HALE

William Stafford, *How to Hold Your Arms When It Rains,* Confluence Press, 1990.

Felix Pitre, reteller, *Juan Bobo and the Pig,* Lodestar, 1993.

May Swenson, *The Complete Poems to Solve,* Macmillan, 1993.

T. Obinkaram Echewa, *The Ancestor Tree,* Lodestar, 1994.

Pitre, reteller, *Paco and the Witch,* Lodestar, 1995.

Work in Progress

Crows Can Only Count to Seven (working title), for Simon & Schuster for Young Readers, 1996.

Sidelights

"I have been interested in 'making books' since I can remember," Christy Hale told *SATA.* "I decided at ten to become a writer and illustrator; although, the writer part hasn't happened yet. I entered into book design through letterpress printing, fine print editioning, paper making, and book binding and am just getting started on my illustration career. From the printer's need to make multiples, I have worked mainly in linoleum and woodcut. I have worked with poets on small chapbooks, and this medium (linocut) has allowed me to become the publisher of limited edition books along with several small books of poetry and illustration.

"I enjoy the research involved in illustration. My picture books have been set in other cultures with great riches for me to draw from."

* * *

ARNOLD, Katya 1947-

Personal

Born August 6, 1947, in Moscow, USSR (now Russia); daughter of Igor (a professor of mathematics) and Nina (an art historian) Arnold; married Alexander Melamid (an artist), August 6, 1968; children: Andrey Arnold, Daniel Melamid. *Education:* Received degree, 1965; Moscow Polygraph Institute, M.A., 1971. *Politics:* "Hate all." *Religion:* None. *Hobbies and other interests:* Mushrooms, reading, hiking, cooking, gardening.

Addresses

Home and office—126 Mercer St., Jersey City, NJ 07302.

Career

Painter, 1960—; illustrator for a children's magazine and for Moscow publishing houses, 1970—. Art teacher, 1965—. Makes frequent school visits. *Member:* Society of Children's Book Writers and Illustrators.

Awards, Honors

Baba Yaga was named to the American Folklore Society Aesop Accolade List, 1994.

Writings

(Reteller and illustrator) *Baba Yaga: A Russian Folktale,* North-South Books, 1993.

(Reteller and illustrator) *Baba Yaga and the Little Girl: A Russian Folktale,* North-South Books, 1994.

(Adapter and illustrator) *Knock, Knock, Teremok!: A Traditional Russian Tale,* North-South Books, 1994.

(Self-illustrated) *Home Sweet Home,* North-South Books, 1995.

(Illustrator) Eric A. Kimmel, reteller, *The Red Valiant Rooster: A Story from Hungary,* Holt, 1995.

Katya's Book of Mushrooms, Holt, 1996.

KATYA ARNOLD

Also illustrator for "The Wise Man's Solution," retold by Jean Casella. Some of Arnold's works have been translated into French and Dutch.

■ Adaptations

Knock, Knock, Teremok! was performed on *Storytime,* PBS, 1995.

■ Work in Progress

Adapting and illustrating *Who Said "MIAW"?*

■ Sidelights

Katya Arnold, the reteller and illustrator of *Baba Yaga* and *Baba Yaga and the Little Girl,* has contributed to multicultural children's literature with her retellings of traditional Russian and Eastern European folktales. *Baba Yaga* is a retelling of an old Russian folktale collected by Aleksandr Afanas'ev in the nineteenth century. It begins when an elderly, childless couple bundle up a piece of wood like a baby, place it in a cradle, and rock it to sleep. Magically, the wood becomes a real boy, Tishka, and he is raised as the couple's own son. When Baba Yaga kidnaps the little boy, Tishka tricks the witch's daughter into climbing in the oven, and Baba Yaga eats her own daughter. Baba Yaga finds Tishka hiding in a tree and tries to gnaw her way through it, but a goose rescues him from the witch's wrath. According to Denise Anton Wright in *School Library Journal,* this book "presents a slice of Russian folklore in an authentic and masterful style." A reviewer for *Junior Bookshelf* appreciated the "splendidly colourful" illustrations in the "style of early woodcuts." These gouache illustrations are "a fitting match for this retelling," concluded a *Publishers Weekly* critic.

Although Arnold grew up in a house full of books, she was not allowed to touch them and didn't discover their beauty until she was four years old. As she wrote in a publicity release for North-South Books, she was sick in bed when her mother read to her "from the first illustrated edition of Lewis Carroll's *Alice in Wonderland*" and "illuminated the drawings in the book with brilliant" blue and red paint. "I watched the story come to life with her brush," the author recalled. "Ever since that time, I have been stunned by the magic of color, the magic of creating a new world, and the different worlds, real and imagined, that people can live in."

Arnold has been creating new worlds of her own since she decided to become an artist at the age of twelve. The examples of her grandmother, an artist, sculptor, and writer, and her uncle, a children's book author, inspired her. She studied at the Moscow Polygraph Institute, taught art at Moscow University, lived in Jerusalem, and visited various countries around the world before settling in New Jersey with her husband. As Arnold wrote in the North-South publicity release, "The admiration and enthusiasm of my students ... led me" to become a children's author.

As a teacher in Brooklyn, New York, Arnold shares her talent for painting and illustration with children. She enjoys visiting schools to read her books, discuss folklore, and explain how she creates her books.

■ Works Cited

Arnold, Katya, "Katya Arnold" (publicity release), North-South Books, 1994.

Review of *Baba Yaga, Junior Bookshelf,* December, 1993, p. 224.

Review of *Baba Yaga, Publishers Weekly,* August 9, 1993, p. 478.

Wright, Denise Anton, review of *Baba Yaga, School Library Journal,* January, 1994, p. 103.

■ For More Information See

PERIODICALS

Booklist, April 1, 1994, p. 1536.

New York Times Book Review, March 13, 1994, p. 20.

* * *

ARONER, Miriam

■ Personal

Born in Chicago, IL; daughter of William and Rose Aroner; children: Sarah, Jonathan (twins). *Education:* University of Michigan, B.A.; San Francisco State University, M.A.; San Jose State University, M.L.S. *Hobbies and other interests:* Reading, classical music, nature.

■ Addresses

Home—El Cerrito, CA.

■ Career

Librarian, Wiener Library, Tel Aviv University, Tel Aviv, Israel; Project Associate and Photo Archivist, Magnes Museum, Berkeley, CA. *Member:* Society of Children's Book Writers and Illustrators.

■ Writings

The Kingdom of Singing Birds (picture book), illustrated by Shelly O. Haas, Kar-Ben, 1993.

Giraffes Aren't Half as Fat (nonfiction), Millbrook Press, 1994.

■ Work in Progress

Several fiction and nonfiction books for young children about baby animals and their dads, a bear who loves hats, and a man who is searching for his "life's work."

■ Sidelights

"My inspiration for *The Kingdom of Singing Birds* came from a few lines in a book of Jewish legends about a simple but wise historical figure," Miriam Aroner told *SATA.* "There are many accounts of Susya, the main character in my book. One particular account, in which Susya frees an innkeeper's birds, resonated in my imagination for a number of years. My book is not a retelling of the legend but an original story. I hope to write other stories that reflect the life-affirming values found in the Jewish tradition.

"I began reading and writing children's books after my twins were born. Previously I'd published several poems and humorous articles. I find that writing for children gives me a lot of freedom to play with poetry and humor, and to use these genres to express my ideas and values. I try to observe the world with a child's imagination, influenced of course by an adult's knowledge.

"I worked for many years as a library researcher and I'm trained as a librarian. I enjoy digging for information. Recently I have been working on nonfiction for very young children. My second book, *Giraffes Aren't Half as Fat,* gave me an opportunity to combine my enjoyment of research and learning with my love of poetry and humor. I have finished a nonfiction picture book about kangaroos and a story about peacocks. I am currently working on several new picture book manuscripts, fiction and nonfiction."

MIRIAM ARONER

■ For More Information See

PERIODICALS

Publishers Weekly, June 14, 1993, p. 70.

School Library Journal, September, 1993, p. 222; April, 1995, p. 121.

* * *

AVISHAI, Susan 1949-

■ Personal

Surname pronounced "A-vee-*shy*"; born March 18, 1949, in Montreal, Quebec, Canada; daughter of Maurice (an automotive parts salesperson) and Alice (an enamelist; maiden name, Weigensberg) Cheifetz; married Bernard Avishai (a writer and consultant), June 8, 1969; children: Benjamin, Elisheva, Tamar. *Education:* Sir George Williams University, Montreal, B.F.A., 1971; attended Ontario College of Art, Toronto, and Academie Julien, Paris. *Politics:* Democrat. *Religion:* Jewish. *Hobbies and other interests:* Canoeing, camping, participating in the Outward Bound wilderness training program.

■ Addresses

Home and office—28 Marlboro St., Newton, MA 02158.

■ Career

Freelance illustrator, Boston, MA, 1981—. Fine artist exhibiting silverpoint and colored pencil drawings in group and solo shows throughout the United States. Has also published and commissioned artwork, illustrated text books, and worked within the advertising industry. *Exhibitions:* Numerous exhibits spanning over twenty years, including Women Illustrators in New England, Schlesinger Library, Radcliffe College, Cambridge, 1991; Francesca Anderson Fine Art, Lexington, MA, 1993; Boston Center for the Arts, drawing show, 1993; Andrea Marquit Fine Arts, Boston, 1994. *Member:* Graphic Artists Guild.

■ Awards, Honors

Drawing prize, Cornerstone Gallery, first national open juried exhibition, 1991; Springfield Art League Merit Award, 73rd national juried exhibition, 1992; Gallery Affiliates Award, Colored Pencil Society Exhibition, 1993; second place award, Other Media in Lake Worth Art League, 52nd anniversary national juried competition, 1993; second place award, *Realism '94,* Parkersberg Art Center, West Virginia, 1994.

■ Illustrator

Janet Gallant, *My Brother's Bar Mitzvah,* Kar-Ben, 1990.

SUSAN AVISHAI

Charlotte Herman, *The House on Walenska Street,* Dutton, 1990.

Earl Grollman, *Talking About Death, A Dialogue Between Parent and Child,* Beacon Press, 1990.

Ruth Horowitz, *Bat Time,* Four Winds, 1991.

Stephanie Tolan, *Sophie and The Sidewalk Man,* Four Winds, 1992.

Oliver Butterworth, *A Visit to the Big House,* Houghton, 1993.

Susan Nessim, *A Friend for Life,* Cancervive Inc., 1994.

Contributor to *Figure Drawing,* by Nathan Goldstein, Prentice-Hall, 1992, *The Best of Colored Pencil,* Colored Pencil Society of America, 1993, and *Discovering Drawing,* by Ted Rose, Davis Publications Inc., 1994. Illustrator of book covers, including young adult series for Recorded Books.

■ Work in Progress

Series of egg tempera paintings entitled "Scapes of the Clothed Figure," which will be exhibited in Boston, Lexington, MA, and Florida.

■ Sidelights

"I'm at my best when drawing children who express poignancy with their faces and body language," Susan Avishai told *SATA.* "Children feel so much that often goes unsaid—sometimes because they cannot yet articulate their feelings, sometimes because we adults just don't let them. But I'd like to think a child can speak through my drawings.

"I work from photos I take of children and always let them take the lead once I've described the character to portray. I often find that a child can come up with a far better expression than I could ever suggest.

"I've illustrated some very powerful stories about kids facing hard situations or making tough decisions, and I'd like to think these books have accompanied children through similarly difficult times. As always, though, it's the kids I work with that are my best inspiration."

B

MIRIAM BAT-AMI

BAT-AMI, Miriam 1950-

■ Personal

Surname pronounced "Bott a-*me*"; born June 26, 1950, in Scranton, PA; daughter of Simon H. (a rabbi) and Huddie (a violinist; maiden name, Weinstein) Shoop; married Ronald Rubens (a builder), April 11, 1976; children: Aaron Rubens, Daniel Rubens. *Education:* Hebrew University, Jerusalem, B.A., 1974; California State University, Los Angeles, M.A., 1980; University of Pittsburgh, Ph.D., 1989. *Religion:* Jewish. *Hobbies and other interests:* Research on multiple perspectives in American historical fiction and nonfiction for children, downhill skiing, gardening.

■ Addresses

Home—3709 South Park St., Kalamazoo, MI 49001. *Office*—Dept. of English, Western Michigan University, Kalamazoo, MI 49008. *Agent*—Barbara Kouts, P.O. Box 558, Bellport, NY 11713.

■ Career

University of Pittsburgh, Pittsburgh, PA, teaching fellow in English, 1980-84; Southwest Missouri State University, Springfield, instructor in English, 1984-89; Western Michigan University, Kalamazoo, assistant professor, 1989-94, associate professor of English, 1994—. Has also worked as a tutor for Special Services at California State University, team taught English as a Second Language at Los Angeles City College, worked as an executive assistant at the Israeli Consulate in Los Angeles, and consulted on college texts and multicultural literature for Harcourt Brace Jovanovich and Simon & Schuster publishers. *Member:* Modern Language Association, Children's Literature Association, National Council of Teachers of English, Society of Children's Book Writers and Illustrators, Michigan Council of Teachers of English.

■ Awards, Honors

First prize, CELERY Short Story Award, Western Michigan University, 1982, for "Nielah"; John Gilmore Emerging Artists' Grant, 1991, for completion of *When the Frost Is Gone;* Faculty Research and Creative Arts Support Grant (FRACAS), Western Michigan University, 1993, for completion of *Punctuation Porpoises and Other Space People;* Highlights Awards Foundation Scholarship, 1993.

Natalie finds both hope and tragedy in her community in the course of her thirteenth summer. (Cover illustration by Marcy Dunn Ramsey.)

■ Writings

Sea, Salt, and Air, illustrated by Mary O'Keefe Young, Macmillan, 1993.
When the Frost Is Gone, illustrated by Marcy Dunn Ramsey, Macmillan, 1994.
Dear Elijah, Farrar, Straus, 1995.
All Day Long with Dad, Orchard Books, in press.
The Practicing Sunflower (sequel to *All Day Long with Dad*), Orchard Books, in press.

Contributor of critical essays to journals, including *Beacham's Guide to Literature for Young Adults, Children's Literature in Education, Children's Literature Association Quarterly,* and *Language Arts Journal of Michigan,* among others. Contributor of short stories and poetry to periodicals, including *Voices: A Magazine for English Poetry in Israel, Response, Davka, Tree, Gargoyle,* and *Statement: California State University Journal.*

■ Work in Progress

Dancing Ghosts, a picture book illustrated by Dan Andreasen, completed and awaiting production; *As a Frog in Winter,* a historical fiction for adolescents based on the experiences of refugees housed at Ft. Ontario, NY, from 1944-46, in which "a girl from town has a special relationship with a boy who attends the same public school and lives at the fort with his family"; *Punctuation Porpoises and Other Space People,* a poetry manuscript playing with grammar rules and hypothetical personalities; *All the Changing Things,* poetry.

■ Sidelights

Miriam Bat-Ami told *SATA:* "I have always wanted to move people. I love to hear children laugh. I love to see them laugh when I'm reading to them. I suppose I get this from my father, who would stand on the pulpit and move us all to laughter and tears. I love the tears, too, that come after the laughter when suddenly the world opens, and we see something new, something perhaps that's always been there.

"I think I've always had a gift for voice, for remembering how people say things. Dialogue is very important to me, even when I write picture books. I find that, in speech, I reach down into what my characters are about. I also have a flair for the dramatic; and my years working in the theatre have influenced the way I write.

"In many respects teaching is very important to me. I don't want to tell people what to think, but I love posing questions and guiding my students into new thoughts.

"As a child, I often felt somehow different. Given my background, I was different, and so I find my characters to be sensitive to difference—slightly outside looking in on many worlds. I've also thought it very important to have an empathetic imagination. I want children to feel worlds that aren't necessarily their own and yet, also, to delight in worlds they have.

"My second book grew out of my experiences on what one might call a 'marginal' block. On that block, though, I found deep community, and so I wanted to tell children how what is outside (poverty) sometimes masks a real richness of people pulling together. This book, *When the Frost Is Gone,* was written because I needed to believe in harmony. I still do. I also want my literature to sometimes address action. Children will read it and feel optimistic about what they can do in the world.

"My first, third, and fourth books came from personal feelings about my own past. *Sea, Salt, and Air,* my first picture book, deals with the yearly summer trips my family took to the beach: how we packed for the trip, the long ride, our feelings of freedom when we swam in the ocean, and the whole sense of timelessness one feels at the beach. It also deals with my love for my grandparents, who welcomed us into their summer cottage. Mary O'Keefe Young, working in vibrant pastels, wonderfully captured that sense of freedom and love.

"*Dear Elijah,* a middle grade novel, explores a young Jewish girl's feelings about God. Rebecca's father has had a heart attack; Passover is coming; and no one in her house is doing anything to get ready. She writes to the prophet Elijah; and, in the writing, begins to understand herself. She needs to find her own route to prayer: it isn't her father's. She also needs to find her own place in the world. In this sense, she is not only a Jewish girl coming to terms with faith; she is every girl exploring female identity. Her questions are closely tied to ones I had at her age, ones which have no easy answers and which, sometimes, I still ask. In this sense, *Dear Elijah* was a particularly painful book for me to write. Painful, too, was the fact that my own father died of a heart attack. Rebecca's father does not die, though the reader doesn't know what will ultimately happen. I don't think I could have made him die. It would have been too painful.

"*Dancing Ghosts,* my second picture book, is all about the ghosts I thought lived in my growing-up house. It also addresses my sense of what happens to memories and how families, particularly the female members of a family, are bound together. Here the daughter, mother, and grandmother delight in a yearly ghost search. I love spook stories. When I was a child, I loved getting scared; I love telling my own children spooky stories—scaring them just a little. With *Dancing Ghosts* I play this same game with my readers. Of course, Dan Andreasen's illustrations beautifully reveal that other world—the world of half shadows and unknown things which children think inhabit corners of their homes.

"*All Day Long with Dad,* to be released by Orchard, is my simplest work for pre-schoolers. I love it for its simplicity; because I can read it to very young children; and because it's about my husband and my younger son. Its sequel, *The Practicing Sunflower,* is my most ridiculously humorous picture book. It is also touchingly real and came out of the fears my son had when he was about to enter kindergarten. One night he asked me if he could go back to pre-school, not just to visit but to stay. The young child in this book asks the same question. He also wonders why the sunflower which he has planted doesn't have to practice like he does: it just grows and grows.

"My older son wants to see himself in a book. I've promised to write one—just for him."

■ For More Information See

PERIODICALS

Booklist, May 15, 1993, p. 1695.
Publishers Weekly, March 7, 1994, p. 72; January 16, 1995, p. 455.
School Library Journal, June, 1993, p. 70.

BEGIN, Maryjane 1963-
(Maryjane Begin-Callanan)

■ Personal

Born January 28, 1963, in Pawtucket, RI; married Brian Callanan (an editorial and advertising illustrator), October 29, 1988. *Education:* Rhode Island School of Design, B.F.A., 1985.

■ Addresses

Home and office—3 Hidden St., Providence, RI 02906.

■ Career

Illustrator. Rhode Island School of Design, part-time instructor. Former art editor. *Exhibitions:* Faber Biron Art Association, Stamford, CT, 1985; Springfield Art Association, Springfield, IL, 1989; Museum of Art, Rhode Island School of Design, Providence, RI, 1992; Books of Wonder Gallery, Beverly Hills, CA, 1992; Central Piedmont College, Charlotte, NC, 1993; Elizabeth Stone Gallery, Birmingham, MI, 1993; Mazza Collection Gallery, Finlay, OH; and Society of Illustrators Gallery, New York City. *Member:* Society of Illustrators.

■ Awards, Honors

Merit Award, Art Directors' Club, 1986; Certificates of Merit, Society of Illustrators, 1986, 1988, 1989, 1991, and 1992; Awards of Excellence, *Communication Arts Magazine,* 1986, 1988, 1989, 1991, and 1992; Certificate of Excellence, American Institute of Graphic Arts Book Show, 1988; Irma Simonton Black Award, Bank Street College, 1989, for *The Porcupine Mouse;* First Place, New York Book Show—juvenile trade, 1992, and

MARYJANE BEGIN

Critics applauded the engaging creatures Begin depicted in Diane Wolkstein's award-winning *Little Mouse's Painting.*

Critici in Erba Prize, Bologna Book Fair, 1993, both for *Little Mouse's Painting.*

Illustrator

Bonnie Pryor, *The Porcupine Mouse,* Morrow, 1988.
(As Maryjane Begin-Callanan) Thomas Hood, *Before I Go to Sleep,* Putnam, 1990.
Diane Wolkstein, *Little Mouse's Painting,* Morrow, 1992.

Work in Progress

Illustrations for *Mouse Told His Mother;* text and illustrations for *Annoying Fred.*

Sidelights

Maryjane Begin's early ambitions included becoming a teacher, an archeologist, and a veterinarian. However, drawing was her first love, and after high school she studied under children's book illustrator Chris Van Allsburg at the Rhode Island School of Design, and received her first illustration assignment in 1985, the year she graduated from the school. Begin has won several awards for her book illustration, and credits such early influences as Dr. Seuss, Garth Williams's illustrations of Laura Ingalls Wilder's "Little House" series, and Van Allsburg. Of the latter, Begin told *Art and Design News:* "His work made me more aware of the potential for creating a reality that only exists on the page, but is so convincing that you believe it might really exist somewhere else."

Begin's illustrations are noted for their realistic detail and humorous, often whimsical, commentary on the text. Her first book, *The Porcupine Mouse* by Bonnie Pryor, was well received by critics, who praised the warmth with which the artist depicts the book's main characters, Dan and Louie, two mouse brothers who discover all sorts of things about the world when they set off on their own. Begin remarked to *Art and Design News:* "*The Porcupine Mouse* had very rich, believable characters who defined the story they were in, and in some ways dictated the atmosphere of the book." Reviewers praised Begin's dramatic illustration of the story's climax, a frightening confrontation between Dan and a cat whom Louie cleverly outwits. A *Booklist* critic characterized Begin's illustrations as "so alive that the cat and mouse brothers seem ready to spring off the pages." "The snug, miniature world of the mice is created as much by an illusionist as by a skillful artist," a *Publishers Weekly* contributor commented.

Begin's next project, a modern edition of Thomas Hood's *Before I Go to Sleep,* a poem originally published in the nineteenth century, provided different challenges for the artist. As Begin told *Art and Design News:* "*Before I Go to Sleep* has no characters; it is a poem with 'scenes' of activity and no main character or 'players' of any kind. What I had to create from the poetry was a sense of 'the child,' any child, as the main character, choosing what his personality would be based on the type of scenes the author had written." The poem describes a child imagining ten animals he would like to be as he tries to fall asleep. Marianne Pilla, writing in *School Library Journal,* praised Begin's "exquisite illustrations," adding, "her interpretations [of Hood's verses], in full-color, are clever and creative."

Begin again earned the accolade "exquisite," this time from *Kirkus Reviews,* for the illustrations for her next work, *Little Mouse's Painting* by Diane Wolkstein. Critics praised the charm and unusual message of this story, which focuses on the various interpretations of an artist's work. Writing in *Booklist,* Ilene Cooper singled out Begin's "attention-grabbing art" in her review of the work. "With almost photographic clarity," Cooper continued, "[Begin] creates an animal world that is richly detailed." Lisa Dennis, writing in *School Library Journal,* concluded: "Wolkstein's expressive, straightforward narrative and Begin's beautiful, luminous watercolor and acrylic illustrations combine to produce an appealing, insightful look at friendship and creativity."

Works Cited

Art and Design News, November-December, 1991, pp. 18-19.
Cooper, Ilene, review of *Little Mouse's Painting, Booklist,* April 1, 1992, p. 1450.
Dennis, Lisa, review of *Little Mouse's Painting, School Library Journal,* June, 1992.
Review of *Little Mouse's Painting, Kirkus Reviews,* May 1, 1992.
Pilla, Marianne, review of *Before I Go to Sleep, School Library Journal,* March, 1990.
Review of *The Porcupine Mouse, Booklist,* March 1, 1988.

Review of *The Porcupine Mouse, Publishers Weekly,* March 18, 1988.

■ For More Information See

PERIODICALS

Money, August, 1991, p. 34.

* * *

BEGIN-CALLANAN, Maryjane
See BEGIN, Maryjane

* * *

BERT, Norman A(llen) 1942-

■ Personal

Born June 6, 1942, in Upland, CA; son of Eldon F. (in business) and Harriet B. (a homemaker; maiden name, Bohen) Bert; married Barbara K. Spring (a realtor), August 15, 1964 (divorced, 1989); married Deb Martin (a writer), September 1, 1990; children: Tabitha, Jeremy. *Education:* Upland College, B.A., 1964; Goshen College Biblical Seminary, B.D., 1967; Kansas State University, M.A., 1972; Indiana University, Ph.D., 1975. *Politics:* Democrat. *Religion:* Quaker. *Hobbies and other interests:* Reading, writing, and cooking.

■ Addresses

Home—2936 Millice Ave., Billings, MT 59102-6642. *Office*—Communication Arts/Theatre, Montana State University-Billings, 1500 North 30th St., Billings, Montana 59101-0298.

■ Career

Choma Secondary School, Choma, Zambia, teacher and deputy headmaster, 1969-70; Messiah College, Grantham, PA, assistant professor of Drama, 1975-81; Eastern Montana College, Billings, 1981—, began as assistant professor, became associate professor, then professor, also member of the Graduate Faculty, for Communication Arts/Theatre Department, chair, Communication Arts Department, 1991—. Has also been an artistic consultant, director, and actor for various productions. *Member:* Association for Theatre in Higher Education (Playwrights Program Vice President for Projects, 1990—), Dramatists Guild (associate member), Authors League of America, Rocky Mountain Theatre Association (ex-officio member of the Board of Directors, 1984-87), Montana State Theatre Association (founding member of the Board of Directors, 1986; secretary of the Board of Directors, 1987-89).

■ Awards, Honors

Semi-Finalist, Competition of the Christian Theatre Artists Guild, 1978, and National Search for Plays on Christian or Jewish Themes selection, Anchorage Press

NORMAN A. BERT

and the Religion and Theatre Project of the American Theatre Association, 1978, both for *Jeremiah of Anathoth;* Second Runner Up, Competition of the Christian Theatre Artists Guild, 1979, for *Woolman;* Playwriting Fellowship, Pennsylvania Council on the Arts, 1979-80; First Prize, Goshen College Peace Play Competition, 1982; Eastern Montana College, Merit Award for Faculty Excellence, 1984-85, 1985-86, 1989-90, 1991-92, and 1992-93, Faculty Achievement Award in Scholarship and Creative Endeavor, 1992; finalist, Burlington Northern Faculty Achievement Award in Scholarship/Creativity, 1991. Has also received numerous grants for professional development.

■ Writings

(And editor) *One-Act Plays for Acting Students,* Meriwether Publishing (Colorado Springs), 1987.

A History and Genealogy of Peter Bert, Triangle Press, 1987

(And editor) *The Scenebook for Actors: Great Monologs and Dialogs from Contemporary and Classical Theatre,* Meriwether Publishing, 1990.

(And editor) *Theatre Alive!,* Meriwether Publishing, 1991.

(And editor) *Scenes from Classic Plays,* Smith & Kraus, 1993.

(With wife, Deb Bert) *Play It Again: More One-Act Plays for Acting Students,* Meriwether Publishing, 1993.

Founder and editor of *Montana Theater Connection,* 1983-89. Contributor of articles to journals, including *Theatre Journal, Brethren in Christ History and Life, Religious Communication Today, Christianity and Literature, Kansas Speech Journal, Southwest Theatre Topics,* and *Gestus: A Quarterly Journal of Brechtian Studies.* Also author of two filmscripts, *And They Shall Be Mine,* and *The Planting of the Lord,* both produced by the Brethren in Christ Board for Missions, both 1972.

PLAYS

The Planting of the Lord, produced by Brethren in Christ Board for Missions, 1972.
And They Shall Be Mine, produced by Brethren in Christ Board for Missions, 1972.
Dayspring, produced by the United Methodist Church of Bloomington, IN, 1974.
The Bottsologuing of Miss Jones, produced by Indiana University's Theatre Department in Bloomington, IN, 1975.
(And director) *Woolman,* produced by Messiah College Players in Grantham, PA, 1976.
Jeremiah of Anathoth, produced by Kansas State University's Department of Speech in Manhattan, KS, 1978.
(And director) *Shake the Country,* production by Lamb's Players in San Diego, 1981.
Post Office, produced by Eastern Montana College's Katoya Players, 1982.
Cat Games, produced by Western Illinois University's Theatre Department, 1982, new version titled *Happy Hour at Velma's Place,* 1989.
Yellowstone, Hurrah!, produced by METRA in Billings, 1982.
The Dove, The Hawk, and the Phoenix, produced by Goshen College in Goshen, IN, 1983.
Mixed Doubles, produced by Eastern Montana College's Communication Arts Department in Billings, 1986.
A Visit From Harry, produced by Yellowstone County Democratic Club in Billings, 1987.
(And director) *Pilgrimage,* Evangel Press, 1988.
(And director) *Breakfast* (produced by Eastern Montana College's Katoya Players in Billings, 1988), Meriwether Publishing, 1993.
(And director) *The Montana Times* (produced by centennial organizations at Glendive and Cut Bank, MT, 1989), KEMC public radio, 1989.
(And director) *Cowboy Serenade, or Duck Riders on the Sly,* produced by Chuck & Norm's Good Time Show and Musical Emporium in Billings, 1990.
(With Madeleine Martin) *Uncross Junction,* public reading by Moving Arts in Los Angeles, 1993.
(And director) *Dr. Dixie Duzzett's Delight,* produced by Eastern Montana College's Communication Arts Department in Billings, 1993.

Also author of *Phonecall from Sunkist,* published in *Quarry 4,* Spring, 1974, and *When the Bough Breaks,* 1989.

■ Work in Progress

Best New Plays for Directors, with Judith Royer, expected 1995.*

* * *

BLAKELY, Roger K. 1922-

■ Personal

Born May 13, 1922, in Barnum, MN; son of Clement C. (a physician) and Florence K. (a teacher and homemaker) Blakely. *Education:* Macalester College, B.A.; University of Minnesota, M.A. *Politics:* Democrat. *Religion:* Presbyterian. *Hobbies and other interests:* Photography, music.

■ Addresses

Home—1368 Asbury, St. Paul, MN 55108. *Office*—c/o English Department, Macalester College, St. Paul, MN 55105.

■ Career

Macalester College, St. Paul, MN, began as college teacher, became professor, 1946—. *Military service:* Army H/R Corps cryptographer, India and Western Pacific, 1943-45. *Member:* Phi Beta Kappa.

■ Awards, Honors

Burlington Northern Teaching Award; Distinguished Alumni Citation.

■ Writings

North from Duluth, New Rivers Press, 1981.
Wolfgang Amadeus Mozart, Lucent Books, 1993.

Coeditor of *Border Crossings,* New Rivers Press, 1981, and *Stiller's Pond II* (with Jonis Agee and Susan Welch), New Rivers Press, 1990. Author of article, "Letter of Sinclair Lewis," *Minnesota History,* 1985.

■ Work in Progress

Schubert's Daughter, a novel; *The Green Girl,* a novella; short stories and photography with poems.

■ Sidelights

Roger K. Blakely told *SATA:* "My writing has taken a back seat to teaching during my forty years of college employment. Now, semi-retired, I am scribbling away on two long novels and various short stories. I got into pedagogical work with the biographical study of Mozart for Lucent Books—a challenging but enjoyable project that entailed much research."

■ For More Information See

PERIODICALS

Horn Book Guide, fall, 1993, p. 374.
School Library Journal, August, 1993, p. 192.*

* * *

BLOCH, Robert (Albert) 1917-1994

OBITUARY NOTICE—See index for *SATA* sketch: Born April 5, 1917, in Chicago, IL; died of cancer, September 23, 1994, in Los Angeles, CA. Author. Bloch, a prolific spinner of horror, mystery, and fantasy tales, is the author of the 1959 novel *Psycho,* which filmmaker Alfred Hitchcock adapted into the suspense movie of the same name. Based on Bloch's research into the life of an actual Wisconsin serial killer, *Psycho* became the work with which the author became most closely associated. Later in his career, however, Bloch expressed concern about the graphic violence routinely depicted in modern film and television productions that *Psycho* had helped spawn. He began his career in the 1930s creating lurid stories for such pulp magazines as *Weird Tales.* For a time he worked as a copywriter in advertising, but he moved to California in the 1950s to work in the film and television industry. Using a variety of pseudonyms, he also penned hundreds of short stories, among them the tale of the Victorian-era English murderer Jack the Ripper that was produced on radio and television numerous times. Bloch's television writing credits include episodes of *Alfred Hitchcock Presents, Star Trek,* and *Night Gallery;* his screenwriting work has been seen in the films *Strait-Jacket, The Psychopath, The House That Dripped Blood,* and *Twilight Zone—The Movie.* He was also the author of over twenty novels, such as *The Scarf, Firebug, It's All in Your Mind, American Gothic,* and *Strange Eons;* his later books include *Midnight Pleasures, Fear and Trembling, Psycho House,* and *The Jekyll Legacy.* Bloch and his immense contribution to the genre were honored in 1991 with the Bram Stoker Award from the Horror Writers of America.

OBITUARIES AND OTHER SOURCES:

BOOKS

Contemporary Theater, Film, and Television, Volume 2, Gale, 1986.
Who's Who in America, 47th edition, Marquis, 1992.

PERIODICALS

Chicago Tribune, September 25, 1994, Section 2, p. 6.
New York Times, September 25, 1994, p. 48.
Times (London), September 26, 1994, p. 21.
Washington Post, September 25, 1994, p. B6.

BOND, Nancy (Barbara) 1945-

■ Personal

Born January 8, 1945, in Bethesda, MD; daughter of William H. (a librarian) and Helen L. (an elementary school teacher; maiden name, Lynch) Bond. *Education:* Mount Holyoke College, B.A., 1966; College of Librarianship, Aberystwyth, Dyfed, Wales, Dip.Lib., 1972. *Politics:* Independent. *Religion:* "Informal."

■ Addresses

Home—109 Valley Rd., Concord, MA 01742.

■ Career

Oxford University Press, London, England, member of promotional staff, 1967-68; Lincoln Public Library, Lincoln, MA, assistant children's librarian, 1969-71; Gardner Public Library, Gardner, MA, director, 1973-75; Massachusetts Audubon Society, Lincoln, administrative assistant, 1976-77; Simmons College, Center for the Study of Children's Literature, Boston, MA, instructor in children's literature, 1978—; Barrow Book Store, Concord, MA, salesperson, 1980—. *Member:* Wildlife Preservation Trust International, Authors Guild, Massachusetts Audubon Society.

■ Awards, Honors

Newbery Honor Book, American Library Association, *Boston Globe/Horn Book* honor book citation, International Reading Association award, and Tir na n'Og citation, Welsh Arts Council, all 1977, all for *A String in the Harp; Boston Globe/Horn Book* honor book citations, 1981, for *The Voyage Begun,* and 1985, for *A*

NANCY BOND

Place to Come Back To; Parents' Choice honor citation, 1994, for *Truth to Tell.*

■ Writings

FOR CHILDREN

A String in the Harp, Atheneum, 1976.
The Best of Enemies, Atheneum, 1978.
Country of Broken Stone, Atheneum, 1980.
The Voyage Begun, Atheneum, 1981.
A Place to Come Back To, Atheneum, 1984.
Another Shore, Macmillan, 1988.
Truth to Tell, Macmillan, 1994.

■ Sidelights

Nancy Bond is a respected and award-winning author of novels for adolescents. Noted and admired for writing books that portray realistic characters dealing with major change and conflict, Bond has explored such dilemmas as accepting responsibility, upholding principles, family breakups, stepfamilies, and death. Bond has also been praised for her sensitivity, insight, and originality in presenting her characters and their lives using memorable settings and skillful writing. "As a writer, I want more than anything to achieve with some reader somewhere [a] sense of sharing...," Bond wrote in *Catholic Library World.* "The kind of fiction I write aims to be about people; about relationships, feelings, understandings, misunderstandings, mistakes, choices, fears, and triumphs—all kinds of human things."

Although born in Bethesda, Maryland, Bond has lived in Concord, Massachusetts most of her life. "I had a fairly ordinary, undramatic childhood," Bond related in *Something about the Author Autobiography Series* (*SAAS*), occasionally complicated by quarrels with her sister and a tumultuous three-way friendship with two other girls. Books were a constant in her life, providing entertainment alone and with her family, and serving as the inspiration for outdoor games where she joined the characters from her favorite stories. Later, she recalled, "I wrote stories for myself on paper, as well as in my head. They were mostly beginnings and mostly slavish imitations of the books I admired." Nevertheless, she added, "I would have been incredulous if anyone had said to me, 'One day, child, you'll be a writer.'"

As a child, Bond spent a year in England with her family—"enough to fall passionately and permanently in love with Britain"—so after graduating from Mt. Holyoke College and spending a year in an undemanding publishing job, she and a friend travelled to London to look for work. While at Oxford University Press, Bond discovered the works of Rosemary Sutcliff in the company's children department. "I read *The Lantern Bearer* out of curiosity and was hooked," the author related in her autobiographical essay. "That's when it first penetrated my consciousness that there were people who earned their living from children's literature—not writing it, that realization was still some years off—publishing, selling, distributing children's books." After returning home to Concord, Bond found a job as an assistant librarian, and spent her days reading, discussing, and recommending children's books. To further her career, Bond decided to go to library school, this time spending a year in Wales studying and exploring the country.

After obtaining her library science degree Bond had trouble finding work near her Concord home. "I distracted myself in the meantime by thinking about Wales and reading everything I could get my hands on," the author recalled in *SAAS.* In addition, "I began playing with the idea of writing a full-length novel. I'd never written anything long before, only poems and short stories that I could finish in a few days or a week at most. I had no idea if I'd have the patience and persistence needed to get all the way to the end of a novel *once,* let alone several times." Bond kept working away, however, even after finding a job as a library director, and in 1976 *A String in the Harp* was published. The books follows the three Morgan children as they move from the United States to Wales, where their newly widowed father has obtained a teaching post. The family tries to adjust to a new life while the middle child, Peter, discovers a magical key that allows him to

The Morgan children's magical discoveries ease the strain of losing their mother and moving to Wales in this 1977 Newbery honor book. (Cover illustration by Maureen Hyde.)

experience events in the life of the legendary Welsh bard Taliesin. "Although *A String in the Harp* is considered a fantasy" because of this aspect of the book, Bond noted, "the heart of the book for me has always been the 'real' story of the Morgans and how they find each other."

Bond's first novel has earned much critical praise, as well as a Newbery Honor citation. *A String in the Harp* "masterfully integrates a Welsh legend into the story of young Peter Morgan," *School Library Journal* contributor Susan Davie states, making for a "tightly written book." *Horn Book* reviewer Virginia Haviland similarly hails Bond's "polished, descriptive writing" that gives her Welsh settings "a vitality of their own, a background for the mood and the action." "Bond has squeezed a solid, readable story out of this nearly exhausted [fantasy] tradition," a *Kirkus Reviews* critic notes, praising the author's characters and setting. This "most impressive first novel," Zena Sutherland remarks in the *Bulletin of the Center for Children's Books,* has characters that "are drawn with depth, changing and growing in their maturity and in their understanding of each other."

Bond followed *A String in the Harp* with 1978's *The Best of Enemies,* which has twelve-year-old Charlotte adjusting to family changes at the same time she uncovers a plot to sabotage Concord's annual Patriot's Day celebration. As with her first book, "Bond successfully interweaves a two-level plot," Barbara Elleman observes in *Booklist,* while Paul Heins in *Horn Book* notes that the work "again shows [Bond's] skill in delineating family relationships and in creating individual characters." *Washington Post Book World* critic Brigitte Weeks qualified her praise for the author's handling of Charlotte's family relationships by faulting the "long digressions and top-heavy descriptions" for slowing the book. A *Publishers Weekly* writer, however, concludes that the work is "an intricate story that keeps its hold on the reader long after one closes the book."

Country of Broken Stone similarly demonstrates Bond's ability to capture her readers' attention with a balance of interesting characters, fascinating plots, and intriguing locations. In this novel an American family is once again relocated to England, where a blended family's mother is directing an archaeological dig. Fourteen-year-old Penelope is able to make friends with a local child, Randall, but his family is opposed to the expedition. As conflicts arise, Bond creates "a nice balance ... between the brooding, mysterious atmosphere and the day-to-day life of the family," Marilyn Kaye states in *School Library Journal,* a balance enhanced by the author's "rich, evocative descriptions." In her *Christian Science Monitor* review, Christine McDonnell comments that *Country of Broken Stone* "is a many-layered story with complex, believable characters and strong personal relationships. It is enriched by lively dialogue ... and by luxurious detail: descriptions of the countryside, its weather and its people.... It is a long book with room for local color, character development, and mounting suspense." The result, according to *Horn Book* writer Ann A. Flowers, is "a beautifully written

In Bond's 1988 work, a teenager taking part in a living history exhibit finds herself transported to the year 1744 and meets others from her own time who have suffered the same fate. (Cover illustration by Glenn Harrington.)

novel, dealing in various ways with the theme of conflict and resolution."

Bond's next novel, *The Voyage Begun,* "owes a great deal to the summers we spent on Nantucket Island when I was young," the author related in *SAAS.* Set in Cape Cod of the near future, *The Voyage Begun* "ties a subtle plea for conservation into an involving story of two young people who come together," Stephanie Zvirin describes in *Booklist.* As newcomer Paul, the son of a government scientist, works with his local friend Mickey to help the elderly Walter regain his independence, he also sees the effects of a wasteful society on the environment and economy of areas like the Cape. Despite Bond's portrayal of natural ruin, "she rarely preaches," Alice Digilio, writing in the *Washington Post Book World,* states; "she's too good a storyteller. An environment spoiled by man simply provides a backdrop for the rich collection of characters." "With its well-developed characters and strongly defined, passionately felt theme," Mary M. Burns writes in *Horn Book,* "the book is a provocative novel which probes personalities and interweaves many threads into a carefully wrought fabric." As the *Bulletin of the Center for Children's Books* critic Sutherland concludes: "[It's] hard to say which is the more impressive, the merging of characters and story line, or the convincingly bleak context for the events."

In *A Place to Come Back To,* which *Horn Book* writer Ethel L. Heins describes as Bond's "fifth, and perhaps finest, novel," the author returns to the characters from *The Best of Enemies.* Now a high school sophomore, Charlotte finds her friendships with Oliver and twins Kath and Andy becoming complicated by stronger feelings, especially after the great-uncle Oliver is living with dies and Oliver learns he must leave Concord. *A Place to Come Back To* has the same strong setting, "fine characterization," and "insight into the confusion of adolescence" as its predecessor, writes Anne Connor in *School Library Journal.* As Ethel L. Heins explains, "Respecting the reader as she does her characters, [Bond] has written a quietly powerful novel of friendship, love, and responsibility." Because of the author's skill in creating details, Elleman similarly concludes in *Booklist,* "the story flows out fully, leaving a richly encountered experience that echoes long after."

When she and her mother move from England to New Zealand, Alice becomes caught up in a mystery concerning her family and her mother's new employer. (Cover illustration by Michael Dooling.)

Bond returns to fantasy in 1988's *Another Shore,* but "uses the genre to entirely different effect here," *School Library Journal* contributor Barbara Chatton notes. After taking a job with a historical park in which she recreates an inhabitant of an eighteenth-century town, seventeen-year-old Lyn awakes one day to find she is actually living in 1744. As Lyn struggles to adjust to the morals and standards of a different time, she discovers other twentieth-century time travellers living around her—travellers who have not been able to find a way back home. "This intense twist of the time fantasy genre forces readers not only to learn from the past but to accept its reality," Chatton observes. "The contrast between eighteenth- and twentieth-century social mores is particularly well developed through detailed description, obviously the result of painstaking research," Burns remarks in *Horn Book,* "carefully integrated into the development of Lyn's character." With its unexpected ending and exploration of "such rich, timeless themes as identity, loyalty and the ambiguity of many necessary choices," a *Publishers Weekly* critic concludes, "the book's power will not easily [be] forgotten."

In 1994's *Truth to Tell,* Bond returns to the more realistic, if foreign, setting of New Zealand. The year is 1958, and fourteen-year-old Alice is puzzled and unhappy with her mother's decision to move the family from England to New Zealand, leaving Alice's stepfather to join them when he can. As Alice tries to adjust to her new situation, she also explores secrets in her background and that of her mother's imperious employer. "What the novel demonstrates . . . is an intense concern with relationships, with what people say to each other while trying to find their places in the world," Roger Sutton notes in the *Bulletin of the Center for Children's Books.* This "sense of belonging—or not belonging—is a matter that has preoccupied me most of my life," Bond wrote in her *SAAS* essay. "I find myself writing about it over and over again in my books."

The author also explained her persistence in her work: "I write my books in order to *find out*. . . . There have been times during the writing of each book when its difficulties seemed so great, and my ability to solve them so insufficient, that I've been tempted to give up. What drives me back each time is knowing that the story and the characters will exist *only* in my mind if I don't finish. No one else will ever have the chance to know them." In addition, she once told *SATA,* "Children's books are one of my greatest loves and always have been. I was much encouraged to find more than twenty years ago that I did not in fact ever have to outgrow them. But it took me rather a long time to realize I could do more than simply read them. There is a lot of very exciting fiction being written and published for children! Good stories belong to readers of all ages to relish and pass along. I wage a constant campaign to introduce my favorite books and authors to other adults as well as children.

"My other deep interest is natural history. I am involved with organizations active in conservation, but more fundamental, I have a real conviction that human beings are only a part of the natural pattern and that much of what we do to the environment is senseless, thoughtless, and tragic. Only by pausing to look and make ourselves truly aware that all the parts fit, even though we may not understand how, can we preserve and protect the balance of the whole. It is therefore essential to me that we encourage by word and deed attention to minutiae, wonder at detail, and respect [for] life in all forms.

"I believe that where we live has a tremendous influence on who we are. This accounts for my particular interest in the settings for my stories. I need to know where my characters are, to place them in their world, as I write about them."

■ Works Cited

Review of *Another Shore, Publishers Weekly,* September 30, 1988, pp. 70-71.

Review of *The Best of Enemies, Publishers Weekly,* April 3, 1978, p. 81.

Bond, Nancy, "A Writer's Freedom," *Catholic Library World,* November, 1984, pp. 169-71.

Bond, Nancy, essay in *Something about the Author Autobiography Series,* Volume 13, Gale, 1991, pp. 37-53.

Burns, Mary M., review of *The Voyage Begun, Horn Book,* February, 1981, p. 50.

Burns, Mary M., review of *Another Shore, Horn Book,* March/April, 1989, p. 214.

Chatton, Barbara, review of *Another Shore, School Library Journal,* October, 1988, pp. 159-60.

Connor, Anne, review of *A Place to Come Back To, School Library Journal,* April, 1984, p. 122.

Davie, Susan, review of *A String in the Harp, School Library Journal,* April, 1976, p. 84.

Digilio, Alice, review of *The Voyage Begun, Washington Post Book World,* February 14, 1982, p. 11.

Elleman, Barbara, review of *The Best of Enemies, Booklist,* March 15, 1978, p. 1185.

Elleman, Barbara, review of *A Place to Come Back To, Booklist,* March 15, 1984, pp. 1053, 1055.

Flowers, Ann A., review of *Country of Broken Stone, Horn Book,* June, 1980, pp. 303-4.

Haviland, Virginia, review of *A String in the Harp, Horn Book,* June, 1976, p. 287.

Heins, Ethel L., review of *A Place to Come Back To, Horn Book,* June, 1984, pp. 335-36.

Heins, Paul, review of *The Best of Enemies, Horn Book,* June, 1978, pp. 273-74.

Kaye, Marilyn, review of *Country of Broken Stone, School Library Journal,* April, 1980, p. 120.

McDonnell, Christine, review of *Country of Broken Stone, Christian Science Monitor,* May 12, 1980.

Review of *A String in the Harp, Kirkus Reviews,* March 1, 1976, p. 255.

Sutherland, Zena, review of *A String in the Harp, Bulletin of the Center for Children's Books,* July-August, 1976, p. 171.

Sutherland, Zena, review of *The Voyage Begun, Bulletin of the Center for Children's Books,* November, 1981, p. 42.

Sutton, Roger, review of *Truth to Tell, Bulletin of the Center for Children's Books,* June, 1994, pp. 313-14.

Weeks, Brigitte, review of *The Best of Enemies, Washington Post Book World,* August 13, 1978, p. E4.

Zvirin, Stephanie, review of *The Voyage Begun, Booklist,* September 15, 1981, p. 98.

■ For More Information See

BOOKS

Children's Literature Review, Volume 11, Gale, 1986, pp. 21-31.

PERIODICALS

Bulletin of the Center for Children's Books, July/August, 1980, p. 207-8.

Horn Book, June, 1984, pp. 297-306.

School Library Journal, April, 1978, p. 91; September, 1981, p. 132; June, 1994, p. 144.

Voice of Youth Advocates, April, 1982, p. 38; August, 1994, p. 142.

Washington Post Book World, May 2, 1976, p. L1.

—Sketch by Diane Telgen

* * *

BRITTAIN, C. Dale 1948-

■ Personal

Born May 17, 1948. *Education:* Middlebury College, A.B., 1970; University of Chicago, A.M., 1973, Ph.D., 1976.

■ Addresses

Home—2006 Blair Blvd., Wooster, OH 44691.

■ Career

Professor of medieval history and writer. *Member:* Science Fiction and Fantasy Writers of America.

■ Writings

A Bad Spell in Yurt, Baen, 1991.

The Wood Nymph and the Cranky Saint, Baen, 1993.

Mage Quest, Baen, 1993.

Voima, Baen, 1995.

The Witch and the Cathedral, Baen, 1995.

■ Work in Progress

Another fantasy novel set in the Yurt universe, tentatively titled *Daughter of Magic.*

■ Sidelights

"I've loved fantasy and wanted to write it ever since I first read J. R. R. Tolkien's *Lord of the Rings* in ninth grade," C. Dale Brittain told *SATA.* "In high school and college I wrote a number of fantasy stories, mostly for myself, but in the meantime I also became very interest-

C. DALE BRITTAIN

ed in the real Middle Ages. So I went on to get a Ph.D. in medieval history and became a college professor, putting my creative energy into scholarship rather than fiction for over fifteen years.

"But then a few years ago the characters and situations that form the heart of *A Bad Spell in Yurt* came to me quite literally in a dream and took over my thoughts, insisting I write their story," Brittain added. "Doing so was enormous fun, but just when I was finished (and thinking I might get my brain back!), the characters told me they had lots *more* adventures I should write about, and I've been doing so ever since."

Brittain's first novel, *A Bad Spell in Yurt,* introduced readers to a fantasy world in which wizards learn spell casting as a college course of study. Just out of school, Daimbert is offered the job of Royal Wizard by the diminutive kingdom of Yurt. Upon his arrival, however, Daimbert finds himself ill-prepared to assume the responsibilities of his station. At the queen's request he struggles with the magic necessary to create a telephone network, and, facing failure, Daimbert enlists the help of a retired wizard. Under the wizard's tutelage, Daimbert increases both in knowledge and wisdom, and with the aid and guidance of a priest, the young Royal Wizard uncovers a menace threatening the kingdom.

In a *Locus* review, Carolyn Cushman called the world of *A Bad Spell in Yurt* "delightful, with its magic-based modern conveniences and organized wizards in amiable rivalry with the medieval church." A *Kliatt* reviewer found Brittain's cast of characters convincing, and noted that they "quickly involve the reader."

Brittain continued to focus on Daimbert and his companions in subsequent works. In *The Wood Nymph and the Cranky Saint* Daimbert is left in charge of the kingdom while the king is away on vacation. In the king's absence, several minor crises arise, including a plague of enchanted, horned rabbits. These episodes hint at some larger magical disturbance, which it falls upon Daimbert to discover and control. In a *Voice of Youth Advocates* review, Susan Rice asserted that this adventure would not disappoint curious readers. *Dragon* reviewer John C. Bunnell noted the comic similarities between Brittain's first and second novels, but added that *The Wood Nymph and the Cranky Saint* contains "some real chills as the climax approaches."

Daimbert's exploits continued in *Mage Quest.* In this tale, Daimbert journeys with the king into the mysteri-

The third installment of Brittain's fantasy series finds the wizard Daimbert testing his powers as he and the king search for a legendary blue rose.

ous Eastern Kingdoms, in search of a legendary blue rose. The trip is fraught with peril, however, and Daimbert must finally acknowledge the limits of his powers as a wizard. *Voice of Youth Advocates* reviewer Gladys Hardcastle speculated that Brittain's humor might be too understated to reach a young audience, but characterized the work as a whole as "imaginative and entertaining."

Brittain's most recent novels are *Voima,* a different sort of fantasy with a grittier edge, incorporating elements of Norse legend, and *The Witch and the Cathedral,* another story about the Royal Wizard of Yurt, in which Daimbert discovers that love and magic don't mix.

"I've written these stories as the kind that I would enjoy reading myself and have been very pleased that a number of other people, teenagers through adults, seem to have enjoyed them just as much," Brittain concluded. "They can be read purely for fun, for the adventure and the humor and characters, but I also have put in some more serious questions about the way people interact with each other and indeed about the nature of life and death."

■ Works Cited

Review of *A Bad Spell in Yurt, Kliatt,* September, 1991, p. 20.

Bunnell, John C., reviews of *The Wood Nymph and the Cranky Saint* and *Mage Quest, Dragon,* July, 1993.

Cushman, Carolyn, review of *A Bad Spell in Yurt, Locus,* August, 1991, p. 55.

Hardcastle, Gladys, review of *Mage Quest, Voice of Youth Advocates,* October, 1993, p. 224.

Rice, Susan, review of *The Wood Nymph and the Cranky Saint, Voice of Youth Advocates,* August, 1993, p. 160.

■ For More Information See

PERIODICALS

Kliatt, July, 1993.

Locus, January, 1995; February, 1995.

* * *

BRITTON, Rick 1952-

■ Personal

Born November 17, 1952, in Richmond, VA; son of Hughes (a business executive) and Catalina Del Carmen (a homemaker; maiden name, Romano) Britton. *Education:* Attended University of Virginia, 1971-72, and Piedmont Virginia Community College, 1975-76.

■ Addresses

Home—1002 Linden Ave., No. 212, Charlottesville, VA 22902.

■ Career

Iron Crown Enterprises (publishing firm), vice president and advertising director, 1980-89; Studio 500 (commercial design), Charlottesville, VA, senior designer and owner, 1989—; *Times Dispatch,* Richmond, VA, desk editor and broadcast journalist, 1994—. *Member:* Company of Military Historians, Northern Virginia Reenactment Unit, Young Men's Christian Association.

■ Illustrator

Susan Beller, *Cadets at War,* Betterway, 1990.

Genevieve A. O'Conner, *The Admiral and the Deck Boy: One Boy's Journey with Christopher Columbus,* Shoe Tree Press, 1991.

Christina Ashton, *Codes and Ciphers,* Betterway, 1992.

■ Work in Progress

Illustrating maps for *To Hold This Ground* by Susan Beller, for Simon & Schuster.

■ Sidelights

Rick Britton told *SATA:* "I enjoy illustrating maps and technical and spot illustrations."

* * *

BUCHANAN, Debby 1952-

■ Personal

Born February 25, 1952, in Detroit, MI; daughter of Ken (an electrician) and Adabelle (a registered nurse; maiden name, Beyette) Rossman; married Ken Buchanan (a writer), June 24, 1979; children: Joshua, Elijah. *Education:* Attended University of Arizona, 1970-71, Central Arizona College, Pima Community College, and St. Lawrence University. *Politics:* "Human rights and equality." *Religion:* Non-denominational.

■ Addresses

Office—P.O. Box 344, Madrid, NY 13660-0344.

■ Career

Writer; public speaker at schools, libraries, and educator's conferences. Active in a variety of community services.

■ Awards, Honors

Southwest Book Award, Border Regional Library Association, 1994, and Reading Rainbow selection, 1995, both for *It Rained on the Desert Today.*

■ Writings

(With husband, Ken Buchanan) *Lizards on the Wall,* illustrated by Betty Schweitzer-Johnson, Harbinger House, 1992.

(With K. Buchanan) *It Rained on the Desert Today,* illustrated by Libba Tracy, Northland Publishers, 1994.

Author of "Stirring the Stew" column in *The Connection.*

■ Work in Progress

The Garden Girl, a picture book; two screenplays, including *Dolphin Bay* (proposed title), with Ken Buchanan; a children's book about imagination.

■ Sidelights

"Something in me has always known I was born to teach," Debby Buchanan told *SATA.* "To achieve this, I was given the gift of language, a natural ability to write. I take this responsibility very seriously and work hard to produce works that will teach my fellow humans to respect one another and treat the environment with reverence and care. I believe we are at a critical time in the evolution of humankind, and I hope that through my writings, I may help to illuminate the dark, fearful places within each of us, and help to make the world a more peaceful place. I believe in the power of imagination and that we are each responsible for what we manifest into our lives, and I think it is very important that we teach this principal to children while their imaginations are fresh and unfettered. Few things give me greater pleasure than speaking to school children about creativity and love."

* * *

BUCHANAN, Ken 1952-

■ Personal

Born December 10, 1952, in Sacramento, CA; son of John Buchanan (a construction worker) and Rosalie May Shields (a homemaker; maiden name, Andree); married Deborah Leevonne Rossman (a writer), June 24, 1979; children: Joshua, Elijah. *Education:* Attended Santa Rosa Junior College, 1981-82. *Politics:* Green Party of Arizona. *Religion:* "Child of God."

■ Addresses

Home and office—P.O. Box 344, Madrid, NY 13660-0344.

■ Career

Writer; public speaker in schools, libraries, and educator's conferences.

■ Awards, Honors

Author of the Year, Children's Books, Arizona Library Association, 1992, and Reading Rainbow selection, 1992, both for *This House Is Made of Mud;* Southwest Book Award, Border Regional Library Association, 1994, and Reading Rainbow selection, 1995, both for *It Rained on the Desert Today.*

DEBBY AND KEN BUCHANAN

■ Writings

This House Is Made of Mud, Northland Publishers, 1991.

(With wife, Debby Buchanan) *Lizards on the Wall,* illustrated by Betty Schweitzer-Johnson, Harbinger House, 1992.

(With D. Buchanan) *It Rained on the Desert Today,* illustrated by Libba Tracy, Northland Publishers, 1994.

Author of humor column in *The Connection.*

■ Work in Progress

Screenplay about the first meeting of the Spanish and the Maya, completion expected early 1995; *Dolphin Bay* (proposed title), a screenplay, with D. Buchanan; researching Spanish and Mayan cultures; *The Dawning of the King* (seeking publication), a picture book about sunrise in the desert; two children's manuscripts (untitled).

■ Sidelights

"All of my life I knew that my role to play was that of a writer," Ken Buchanan told *SATA.* "Early on I discov-

Ken Buchanan's gentle story describes the beauty and simplicity of life in the Sonoran Desert. (Cover illustration by Libba Tracy.)

ered that in order to write, I needed a clear understanding of what it was to be a human being. What was reality? What made us laugh or cry? What made us love or hate?

"The more I discovered, the more questions arose. I did not even try to publish anything in my twenties; I didn't know enough yet. In my late twenties I married and had two sons; more than anything else, this provided me with the knowledge necessary to become a writer. Finally in my late thirties I succeeded (with tremendous help from my wife) in getting my first children's book published.

"Now, after nearly forty years of studying the human condition, I've concluded that 'reality' is a state of mind! In other words, it's all in your imagination! In children's books I try to avoid the standard 'conflict that gets resolved' theme, and concentrate on presenting a world that is not in conflict, but instead, is harmonious and loving. If, indeed, the world is made of imagination, then let us teach our children to imagine love!"

* * *

BURTON, Marilee Robin 1950-

■ Personal

Born December 27, 1950, in Los Angeles, CA; daughter of Joe (a chemical engineer) and Lillian (an adult education teacher; maiden name, Weisman) Burton. *Education:* California State College, Sonoma (now Sonoma State University), B.A., 1973; Pacific Oaks College, M.A., 1979. *Hobbies and other interests:* Ballroom and swing dancing, photography, writing long letters.

■ Addresses

Home—c/o Burton, 4624 Varna Ave., Sherman Oaks, CA 91423.

■ Career

Kindergarten teacher in Encino, CA, 1978-80; kindergarten and first grade teacher in New York City, 1981-84; substitute teacher for kindergarten through seventh grades, New York City Public School System and Los Angeles Unified School District, 1985-88; Midtown West School, New York City, language arts teacher, 1988-92; freelance editor, 1993—. *Member:* Society of Children's Book Writers and Illustrators, Teachers and Writer's Collaborative, Child Study Children's Book Committee (Bank Street College), Pacific Oaks College Alumnae Association.

■ Writings

FOR CHILDREN; SELF-ILLUSTRATED

The Elephant's Nest: Four Wordless Stories, Harper, 1979.
Aaron Awoke: An Alphabet Story, Harper, 1982.
Oliver's Birthday, Harper, 1986.
Tails Toes Eyes Ears Nose, Harper, 1988.

OTHER

(Illustrator) Leslie Kimmelman, *Me and Nana,* Harper, 1990.
My Best Shoes, illustrated by James E. Ransome, Tambourine Books, 1994.
One Little Chickadee, illustrated by Janet Street, Tambourine Books, 1994.

■ Work in Progress

Writing and illustrating *Moonlight Festival,* a children's book about a shy elephant whose friends like to dance; two books for juveniles, *Sam* and *Owls Stay Up All Night.*

■ Sidelights

"I've been a private artist my whole life, always painting, drawing, making things all around me without ever thinking much about it," author and illustrator Marilee Robin Burton told *SATA.* "As a child I never questioned that I would grow up, get married, have children, and work as an artist. But along the way, one discovers that things don't always work out exactly as (or in the order) one expects.

"Strangely, and due to many turns of events, I graduated from college with a degree in psychology and history (my present interest in history lies firmly in Trotsky's dog—the illusive, legendary one) and set out to make a living teaching meditation. This livelihood was fulfilling, but not lucrative; I went back to school to earn a teaching degree, dreaming that the short teaching day would give me luxurious hours to pursue art.

MARILEE ROBIN BURTON

"My first book, *The Elephant's Nest*, came about as a result of a language arts project I was working on with kindergartners during my graduate study. I was interested in wordless stories and had drawn twelve and asked the children to title and tell them. Pleased with the results, I chose my four favorites and submitted them to Harper & Row; they were accepted on first submission. (I have never in my publishing history had this experience a second time.) When I completed the final artwork for *The Elephant's Nest* my editor asked me what I was planning for my second book. There was the budding of the idea of myself as a writer, an idea that continues to grow stronger over time."

In a *School Library Journal* review, Mary B. Nickerson characterized the stories in *The Elephant's Nest* as "gentle, imaginative, and silly," noting that these qualities "are hard to beat for children." *Publishers Weekly* reviewer Jean F. Mercier found the tales "easy to follow" and the illustrations "inspired." Other commentators responded favorably to Burton's wordless format; Jane Langton, writing for the *New York Times Book Review*, suggested that *The Elephant's Nest* might engage the imagination of a young child by allowing him or her to create stories in the margins around the illustrations.

In Burton's second book, *Aaron Awoke: An Alphabet Story,* alliterative phrases describe in alphabetical order the activities comprising Aaron's day, while the illustrations incorporate many small objects that begin with the letter being considered. A reviewer for the *New York Times Book Review* praised the illustrations for their "charming simplicity." More than one critic, however, questioned Burton's depiction of Aaron's day, contending that his routine of adult responsibilities—managing his own farm and household—should have been more realistically childlike. Others were charmed by Aaron the farmer; Mercier, in a review for *Publishers Weekly*, maintained that *Aaron Awoke* "fills the bill and then some as a starter on reading for little kids."

Burton's next work, *Oliver's Birthday*, features a young ostrich who eagerly awaits the arrival of his friends on his birthday. Oliver is disheartened when no one shows, but he later finds that his friends have gathered at another location to surprise him with a party. Critics have commended the reassuring message of this story, in which the all-too-familiar pain of being left out is supplanted by the joy of a happy ending. *Publishers Weekly* reviewer Mercier described Burton's illustrations for this tale as "soothing and unambiguous." "Beginning readers will easily manage the simple text," observed Pamela T. Childs in a *School Library Journal* review.

Tail Toes Eyes Ears Nose explores a format similar to that of *The Elephant's Nest,* but here the illustrations present a series of visual riddles rather than a narrative. Children are encouraged to identify an animal through the recognition of its parts as presented by Burton's drawings. On the following page, the animal is shown in its entirety. In a *School Library Journal* review, Nancy Gifford noted that the large format of the drawings make for easy identification, and added that the book would certainly "keep young children guessing and entertained." Nancy B. Cardozo, writing in the *New York Times Book Review,* held high praise for the book, calling it an "exercise in humor, visualization, concentration and memory, and a pleasant activity for parent and child."

■ Works Cited

Review of *Aaron Awoke, New York Times Book Review,* September 26, 1982, p. 31.

Cardozo, Nancy B., review of *Tails Toes Eyes Ears Nose, New York Times Book Review,* January 29, 1989, p. 39.

Childs, Pamela T., review of *Oliver's Birthday, School Library Journal,* December, 1986, p. 81.

Gifford, Nancy A., review of *Tails Toes Eyes Ears Nose, School Library Journal,* January, 1989, pp. 60, 62.

Langton, Jane, review of *The Elephant's Nest: Four Wordless Stories, New York Times Book Review,* August 19, 1979, pp. 20-21.

Mercier, Jean F., review of *The Elephant's Nest, Publishers Weekly,* June 4, 1979, p. 61.

Mercier, Jean F., review of *Aaron Awoke: An Alphabet Story, Publishers Weekly,* August 27, 1982, p. 358.

Mercier, Jean F., review of *Oliver's Birthday, Publishers Weekly,* November 28, 1986, p. 72.

Nickerson, Mary B., review of *The Elephant's Nest, School Library Journal,* April, 1979, pp. 40-41.

■ For More Information See

PERIODICALS

Bulletin of the Center for Children's Books, October, 1979, p. 23; October, 1982, p. 22; November, 1988, p. 66.

Children's Book Review Service, December, 1986, p. 35.

Publishers Weekly, February 24, 1992, p. 56; May 2, 1994, p. 306.

School Library Journal, September, 1982, pp. 104-5.

C

CANNAN, Joanna (Maxwell) 1896-1961

■ Personal

Born May 27, 1896, in Oxford, England; died April 22, 1961; daughter of Charles and Mary (Wedderburn) Cannan; married H. J. Pullein-Thompson, 1918 (died, 1957); children: Denis, Josephine, Diana and Christine (twins). *Education:* Attended Wychwood School, Oxford, and schools in Paris.

■ Career

Writer.

■ Writings

FOR CHILDREN

A Pony for Jean, illustrated by Anne Bullen, Lane, 1936, Scribner, 1937.
We Met Our Cousins, illustrated by Bullen, Collins, 1937, Dodd, Mead, 1938.
Another Pony for Jean, illustrated by Bullen, Collins, 1938.
London Pride, illustrated by Bullen, Collins, 1939.
More Ponies for Jean, illustrated by Bullen, Collins, 1943.
They Bought Her a Pony, illustrated by Rosemary Robertson, Collins, 1944.
Hamish: The Story of a Shetland Pony, illustrated by Bullen, Penguin, 1944.
I Wrote a Pony Book, Collins, 1950.
Gaze at the Moon, illustrated by Sheila Rose, Collins, 1957.

ADULT NOVELS

The Misty Valley, First Novel Library, 1922, Doran, 1924.
Wild Berry Wine, Stokes, 1925.
The Lady of the Heights, Unwin, 1926.
Sheila Both-Ways, Benn, 1928, Stokes, 1939.
The Simple Pass On, Benn, 1929, published as *Orphan of Mars,* Bobbs Merrill, 1930.
No Walls of Jasper, Benn, 1930, Doubleday, 1931.
Ithuriel's Hour, Hodder & Stoughton, 1931, Doubleday, 1932.
High Table, Doubleday, 1931.
Snow in Harvest, Hodder & Stoughton, 1932.
North Wall, Hodder & Stoughton, 1933.
Under Proof, Hodder & Stoughton, 1934.
The Hills Sleep On, Hodder & Stoughton, 1935.
A Hand to Burn, Hodder & Stoughton, 1936.
Frightened Angels, Harper, 1936.
Pray Do Not Venture, Gollancz, 1937.
Princes in the Land, Gollancz, 1938.
They Rang up the Police, Gollancz, 1939.
Death at the Dog, Gollancz, 1940, Reynal, 1941.
Idle Apprentice, Gollancz, 1940.
Blind Messenger, Gollancz, 1941.
Little I Understood, Gollancz, 1948.
The Hour of the Angel; Ithuriel's Hour, Pan, 1949.
Murder Included, Gollancz, 1950, published as *Poisonous Relations,* Morrow, 1950, published as *The Taste of Murder,* Dell, 1951.
Body in the Beck, Gollancz, 1952, Garland, 1983.
And All I Learned, Gollancz, 1952.
Long Shadows, Gollancz, 1955.
People to Be Found, Gollancz, 1956.
And Be a Villain, Gollancz, 1958.
All Is Discovered, Gollancz, 1962.

OTHER

(Editor, with M. D. and May W. Cannan) *The Tripled Crown: A Book of English, Scotch and Irish Verse for the Age of Six to Sixteen,* Frowde, 1908.

Also author of *Oxfordshire,* Robert Hale, an undated wartime edition of the County Books series.

■ Sidelights

British novelist Joanna Cannan pioneered the popular genre of the "pony story" which has been continued by her daughters Josephine, Diana, and Christine Pullein-Thompson. Cannan's first children's book, *A Pony for Jean,* follows young Jean Leslie as she moves to the countryside from her London home. There she meets a neglected pony nicknamed "The Toastrack"; through perseverance, Jean brings her pony—renamed Cavalier—back to health and begins to ride and train him. Eventually, the pair win several honors at a local competition. While Cavalier "is a dream pony," according to Angela Bull in *Twentieth-Century Children's Writers,* he "is always second in interest. Jean—passionate, resolute, brave, but lighthearted—dominates the book." Jean's story has a spirit that is "true and natural," according to *New York Times Book Review* writer Ellen Lewis Buell, and is told with "a sparkle of humor."

It was Cannan's focus on rider, rather than horse, that revitalized a genre whose popularity endures today. As Bull noted, prior to *A Pony for Jean,* children's books about horses were a "procession of blameless animals scarred by humanity [that] had become tediously repetitive.... 'Pony books,' after Cannan, meant 'rider books': stories of heroines struggling with ponies who may at first seem difficult but who, through schooling and cherishing, become winners in the last chapter." As Bull concluded, by creating the character of Jean, "the first fanatical pony addict to appear in a book," Cannan "left a lasting mark on children's literature."

■ Works Cited

Buell, Ellen Lewis, review of *A Pony for Jean, New York Times Book Review,* October 24, 1937, p. 9.

Bull, Angela, "Joanna Cannan," *Twentieth-Century Children's Writers,* 4th edition, St. James Press, 1995, pp. 181-82.

■ For More Information See

PERIODICALS

Growing Point, January, 1977, p. 3039.

New York Times, April 5, 1925, p. 14; April 21, 1929, p. 9; March 23, 1930, p. 25; April 10, 1932, p. 7; January 15, 1939, p. 12; March 2, 1941, p. 26; July 31, 1950, p. 11.

Saturday Review of Literature, April 6, 1929, p. 853; July 11, 1936, p. 18.

Times Literary Supplement, April 16, 1925, p. 269; October 31, 1929, p. 876; May 1, 1930, p. 368; November 21, 1936, p. 966.

[Sketch reviewed by daughter, Josephine Pullein-Thompson.]

* * *

CATLETT, Elizabeth 1919(?)-

■ Personal

Born April 15, c. 1919, in Washington, DC; became naturalized citizen of Mexico, 1963; daughter of John H. (a professor of mathematics) and Mary (a truant officer; maiden name, Carson) Catlett; married Francisco Mora (a painter and printmaker), May 31, 1946; children: Francisco, Juan, David. *Education:* Howard University, B.S. (cum laude), 1935; State University of Iowa, M.F.A., 1940; attended Art Institute of Chicago, 1941; attended Art Students' League, 1942-43; attended Escuela de Pintura y Escultura, 1947-48.

ELIZABETH CATLETT

■ Addresses

Home—375 South End Ave., Apt. 20t, New York, NY 10280.

■ Career

Sculptor and printmaker, 1940—. Teacher in Texas, Louisiana, Virginia, and New York City, 1940-45; National School of Fine Arts, National Autonomous University of Mexico, professor of sculpture, 1959-73, department head, 1959-76. *Exhibitions:* Solo Exhibitions include "Paintings, Sculptures and Prints," Barnett-Arden Gallery, Washington, DC, 1947-48; "Black Experience" (sculpture and prints), Modern Art Museum, Mexico City, 1970; "Sculpture and Prints," Studio Museum in Harlem, New York City, 1971-72; Scripps College, Claremont, CA, 1975; New Orleans Museum of Art, 1983; Howard University, Washington, DC, 1984; Spelman College, Atlanta, GA, 1985; Museum Diego Rivera, Guanajuato, Guan, Mexico, 1987; "Elizabeth Catlett: Print Retrospective," Jamaica Arts Center, Queens, NY, 1989; Montgomery Museum of Art, Montgomery, AL, 1991; "Sculpture," June Kelly Gallery,

Catlett's inspirational linoleum prints portraying events in the African American experience underscore James Weldon Johnson's powerful anthem, *Lift Every Voice and Sing.*

NY, 1993. Group exhibitions include: "The Art of the American Negro (1851-1940)," Tanner Art Galleries, Chicago, IL, 1940; "Tenth Anniversary of Exhibitions of Paintings, Sculpture and Prints by Negro Artists," Atlanta University, Atlanta, GA, 1951; "Francisco Mora and Elizabeth Catlett," Altes Schloss der Prinzen von Sachsen, Dresden, Germany, 1973; "Forever Free: Art by African-American Women 1862-1980," Center for the Visual Arts Gallery, Illinois State University, Normal, IL (and traveling), 1981; "African-American Artists 1880-1987: Selections from the Evans-Tibbs Collection," organized by the Smithsonian Institution Traveling Exhibition Service, 1989; "A Courtyard Apart: The Art of Elizabeth Catlett and Francisco Mora," Mississippi Museum of Art, Jackson, MS, and Museum of African-American Art, Detroit, MI, 1991; "Free Within Ourselves; African-American Art from the National Museum of American Art," IBM Gallery of Science and Art, NY, organized by the National Museum of American Art, Smithsonian Institution (traveling), 1993. *Member:* Women's Caucus for Art (honorary life member), Salon de La Plastica Mexicana, Delta Sigma Theta.

■ Awards, Honors

First Prize, American Negro Exposition, 1941, for sculpture, *Mother and Child;* Julius Rosenwald Foundation fellow, 1945-47; Second Prize (sculpture), Atlanta University National Exhibition, 1946; Atlanta University Annual, Second Prize (sculpture), 1956, First Prize (sculpture), 1965; Tlatilco Prize, First Sculpture Biennial (Mexico), 1962; Honorable Mention, Second Latin American Print Exhibition (Cuba), 1963; First Purchase Prize, National Print Salon (Mexico), 1969; study and travel prize, Intergrafic Exhibition (Berlin), 1970; Alumni Award, Howard University, 1979; Women's Caucus for Art award, National Congress, 1981; Brandywine Workshop Award, Philadelphia Museum of Art, 1982; Purchase Prize, Salon de la Plastica Mexicana, Drawing Salon (Mexico), 1985; Honoree, National Sculpture Conference—Works by Women, 1987; Art Award, Amistad Research Center, 1990; Candace Award for Art, National Coalition of 100 Black Women, 1991; Artist of the Year, New York City Art Teachers Association, UFT, 1991; honorary doctorate from Morgan State University, 1993; honorary doctorates from Spelman College, Tulane University, and New School for Social Research, all 1995; and numerous additional awards.

■ Illustrator

Margaret Walker, *For My People,* Limited Editions, 1992.

James Weldon Johnson, *Lift Every Voice and Sing,* introduction by Jim Haskins, Walker, 1993.

■ Work in Progress

A hanging woodcarving for a Chicago library, contracted by Chicago Council for the Arts.

■ Sidelights

Internationally acclaimed sculptor and printmaker Elizabeth Catlett continually renews her commitment to making art accessible. According to Theresa A. Leininger in *Epic Lives: One Hundred Black Women Who Made a Difference,* during the 1960s and 1970s Catlett joined numerous other African American artists and "sought to educate the public with her portrayals of great figures in black history." In the 1990s, Catlett provided the illustrations for James Weldon Johnson's *Lift Every Voice and Sing,* a textual version of the song that many consider to be the African American national anthem, as well as Margaret Walker's *For My People.* "Art can't be the exclusive domain of the [elite]," Catlett explained to *Ebony* writer Lynn Norment in 1993. "It belongs to everyone.... Artists should work to the end that love, peace, justice and equal opportunity prevail all over the world."

Catlett, whose grandparents were slaves, was born in Washington, D.C., to a middle-class family. Her father, a mathematics professor at Tuskegee University, died before she was born. Her mother raised Catlett and encouraged her to follow her dream of becoming an artist. Catlett had known that she wanted to be an artist since the age of thirteen, and she did not let a race-based rejection from the Carnegie Institute of Technology in Pittsburgh deter her. She studied design, printmaking, drawing, and art history at Howard University in Washington, and earned a B.S. degree with honors from that institution.

Inspired by the murals and public art of Diego Rivera, Catlett was employed by the Public Works of Art Project. This inspiration was to shape Catlett's future. After teaching school and studying in Iowa, Chicago, and Harlem, Catlett accepted a Julius Rosenwald Foundation fellowship and traveled to Mexico to produce works dedicated to black women. There she married Mexican painter and printmaker Francisco Mora and taught at the National Autonomous University of Mexico's National School of Fine Arts. Her work as a printmaker, exemplified by her "Black Woman" series of 1946 to 1947, blossomed. Catlett was appointed professor of sculpture at the National School of Fine Arts in 1959, and she became a Mexican citizen in 1963.

By 1971, the United States government had listed Catlett as an undesirable alien, and when the artist tried to return to the United States for a retrospective exhibition of her work in New York, her admirers had to pressure the government to allow her into the country. Nevertheless, Catlett maintained the public spirit in her political activities and artwork. Sculptures featuring Catlett's characteristic mother and child theme (including the famous black marble *Maternity*) and solo female figures, and prints like *In Harriet Tubman, I Helped Hundreds to Freedom,* are displayed in museums and galleries throughout the United States. Catlett has also received scores of prizes, awards, and commissions. In addition, according to Norment in *Ebony,* Catlett "continues to create with fervor."

Catlett told *SATA:* "I try to interest our people in art by creating dignified works of art that can interest them. It is my aim to bring them and their children to major museums and art galleries."

■ Works Cited

Leininger, Theresa A., "Elizabeth Catlett," *Epic Lives: One Hundred Black Women Who Made A Difference,* Visible Ink Press, 1993.

Norment, Lynn, "Elizabeth Catlett: Dean of Women Artists," *Ebony,* April, 1993, pp. 46, 48, 50.

■ For More Information See

BOOKS

Elizabeth Catlett: Sculpture and Graphics 1946-79, Your Heritage House, 1979.

Fax, Elton C., *Seventeen Black Artists,* Dodd, Mead, 1971.

Haab, Armin, *Mexican Graphic Art,* Arthur Niggli, 1957.

Lewis, Samella, *The Art of Elizabeth Catlett,* Handcraft Studios, 1984.

Rubinstein, Charlotte, *American Women Artists,* G. K. Hall, 1982.

PERIODICALS

Art in America, March, 1990.

Essence, June, 1985.

School Arts, December, 1992.

* * *

CHRISTENSEN, Bonnie 1951-

■ Personal

Born January 23, 1951, in Saranac Lake, NY; daughter of Wallace (a forester) and Theo (a homemaker; maiden name, Cole) Christensen; married Jan Herder (a theatre technical director), December 19, 1987; children: Emily. *Education:* Attended the Center for Book Arts and Parsons School of Design; University of Vermont, B.A., 1973. *Politics:* Democrat. *Religion:* Unitarian. *Hobbies and other interests:* Letterpress printing and book arts.

■ Addresses

Home—P.O. Box 143, Bakersfield, VT 05441.

■ Career

Has taught classes at Church Street Center, University of Vermont, Burlington, and Shelburne Museum, Shelburne, VT; artist/educator for "Arts in Education," Vermont Council on the Arts, 1991-1995; artist and illustrator. *Exhibitions:* "Art '89," T. W. Wood Gallery,

BONNIE CHRISTENSEN

Montpelier, VT; Annual Print Show, T. W. Wood Gallery, Montpelier; "Creativity '93," Art Direction Magazine Annual; "The Original Art," Society of Illustrators, New York City, 1994. *Member:* Society of Children's Book Writers and Illustrators, Typophiles, New England Letterpress Guild.

■ Awards, Honors

Artist Development Grant, Vermont Council on the Arts, 1992; Ezra Jack Keats Mini Grant, 1995.

■ Writings

FOR CHILDREN

(Self-illustrated) *An Edible Alphabet,* Dial Books for Young Readers, 1994.
(Illustrator) Shelley Moore Thomas, *Putting the World to Sleep,* Houghton, 1995.
(Illustrator) Stephen Krensky, *Breaking into Print,* Little, Brown, in press.

FOR ADULTS

(Illustrator) Joe Citro, *Green Mountain Ghosts, Ghouls and Unsolved Mysteries,* Chapters/Vermont Life Publishing, 1994.
(Illustrator) Margaret MacArthur, *Vermont Heritage Songbook,* Vermont Folklife Center, 1994.

Contributor of illustrations to *Endgrain: Contemporary Wood Engraving in North America,* Barbarian Press, 1994. Illustrations have appeared in periodicals, including *Ladybug, Vermont Life, National Gardening,* and *Vermont.* Works include posters for the Champlain Valley Festival, Open Stage (*A Christmas Carol*), Burlington Friends of Music, the University of Vermont, and the Shelburne Museum.

■ Sidelights

Bonnie Christensen told *SATA:* "I love books, both for children and adults, antique and new, short and long, with or without illustrations, and so I've come to love the book arts, which include printing, papermaking, book-binding and wood engraving. My first book contract came about as a result of two interests—letterpress printing/wood engraving and gardening. My plan was to do an alphabet book using large antique wood type interwoven with a fruit or vegetable wood engraving. I was going to print the book myself, on fine paper, by hand, on a printing press over 170 years old. Fortunately a wonderful editor was taken with the one such sample in my portfolio, and *An Edible Alphabet* was molded as a children's book. The illustrations reflect real scenes from life in rural Vermont (we press cider and make about 180 gallons of maple syrup a year!) as well as memories from all the different places I've lived."

■ For More Information See

PERIODICALS

Booklist, January 15, 1994, p. 932.
Kirkus Reviews, March 15, 1994, p. 394.
Publishers Weekly, December 13, 1993, p. 69.
School Library Journal, May, 1994, p. 107.
Smithsonian, November, 1994, p. 34.

* * *

CLARK, Ann Nolan 1896-
(Marie Dunne)

■ Personal

Born December 5, 1896, in Las Vegas, NM; daughter of Patrick Frances (a merchant) and Mary (a teacher; maiden name, Dunne) Nolan; married Thomas Patrick Clark, August 6, 1919 (deceased); children: Thomas Patrick, Jr. (pilot, killed in World War II). *Education:* New Mexico Normal School (now New Mexico Highlands University), B.A., 1919. *Politics:* Democrat. *Religion:* Catholic.

■ Addresses

Home—2500 North Rosemont Blvd., No. 603, Tucson, AZ 85712.

■ Career

Teacher in New Mexico, c. 1916-19, 1923-30; Bureau of Indian Affairs, Washington, DC, education specialist working in many states, including New Mexico, Arizona, North and South Dakota, and Utah, 1930-62; International Cooperation Administration, Washington,

ANN NOLAN CLARK

This 1942 tale traces the life of a buffalo from its birth among the Sioux to its eventual leadership of the herd. (Cover illustration by Stephen Tongier.)

DC, education consultant, Latin-American Bureau, 1945-50. Former material specialist, Institute of Inter-America Affairs; U.S. delegate to UNESCO conference, Brazil. *Member:* International Council of Women, PEN, National Council of Women, Alpha Delta Kappa, Altrusa International.

■ Awards, Honors

New York Herald Tribune Spring Festival Awards, 1941, for *In My Mother's House,* 1952, for *Looking-for-Something* and *Secret of the Andes,* and 1955, for *Santiago;* Newbery Medal, American Library Association, 1953, for *Secret of the Andes;* Distinguished Service Award, U.S. Department of the Interior, 1962; Regina Medal for lifetime achievement, Catholic Library Association, 1963; Daughter of Mark Twain Honor, *Mark Twain Journal,* 1971; named "outstanding Arizona author," 1984. Some of Clark's books have been Junior Literary Guild selections, including *In My Mother's House* and *Secret of the Andes.*

■ Writings

Handmade Tales, privately printed, 1932.

Who Wants to Be a Prairie Dog?, illustrated by Van Tishnahjinnie, U.S. Office of Indian Affairs, 1940.

Little Herder in Spring (also see below), illustrated by Hoke Denetsosie, U.S. Office of Indian Affairs, 1940.

Little Herder in Autumn (also see below), illustrated by Denetsosie, U.S. Office of Indian Affairs, 1940.

Little Boy with Three Names: Stories of Taos Pueblo, illustrated by Tonita Lujan, U.S. Office of Indian Affairs, 1940, 2nd edition, Ancient City Press, 1990.

The Pine Ridge Porcupine, illustrated by Andrew Standing Soldier, U.S. Office of Indian Affairs, 1941.

In My Mother's House (earlier version privately printed as *Third Grade Home Geography*), illustrated by Velino Herrera, Viking, 1941.

(With Frances Carey) *A Child's Story of New Mexico,* University Publishing, 1941, 3rd edition, 1960.

About the Slim Butte Raccoon, illustrated by Andrew Standing Soldier, U.S. Department of the Interior, Bureau of Indian Affairs, 1942.

Little Herder in Winter (also see below), illustrated by Denetsosie, U.S. Office of Indian Affairs, 1942.

Little Herder in Summer (also see below), illustrated by Denetsosie, U.S. Office of Indian Affairs, 1942.

Buffalo Caller: The Story of a Young Sioux Boy of the Early 1700's, Before the Coming of the Horse, illustrated by Marian Hulsizer, Row, Peterson, 1942.

There Still Are Buffalo, illustrated by Standing Soldier, U.S. Office of Indian Affairs, 1942, Haskell, 1958.

About the Grass Mountain Mouse, illustrated by Standing Soldier, U.S. Office of Indian Affairs, 1942.

About the Hen of Wahpeton, illustrated by Standing Soldier, U.S. Office of Indian Affairs, 1942.

Young Hunter of Picuris, illustrated by Herrera, U.S. Office of Indian Affairs, 1943.

Little Navajo Bluebird, illustrated by Paul Lantz, Viking, 1943.

Bringer of the Mystery Dog, illustrated by Oscar Howe, Department of the Interior, Bureau of Indian Affairs, 1943.

Brave against the Enemy: A Story of Three Generations—of the Day Before Yesterday, of Yesterday, and of Tomorrow, illustrated by Helen Post, U.S. Bureau of Indian Affairs, 1944.

Sun Journey: A Story of the Zuni Pueblo, illustrated by Percy T. Sandy, U.S. Bureau of Indian Affairs, 1945, 2nd edition, Ancient City Press, 1988.

Singing Sioux Cowboy Primer, illustrated by Standing Soldier, U.S. Indian Service, 1945.

Singing Sioux Cowboy Reader, illustrated by Standing Soldier, U.S. Indian Service, 1947.

Linda Rita, Government Printing Office, 1948.

Magic Money, illustrated by Leo Politi, Viking, 1950.

Little Herder in Spring, in Summer (includes *Little Herder in Spring and Little Herder in Summer*), U.S. Indian Service, 1950.

Little Herder in Autumn, in Winter (includes *Little Herder in Autumn* and *Little Herder in Winter*), U.S. Indian Service, 1950.

Little Navajo Herder (compilation of *Little Herder in Spring, Little Herder in Summer, Little Herder in Autumn,* and *Little Herder in Winter*), U.S. Indian Service, 1951.

Secret of the Andes, illustrated by Jean Charlot, Viking, 1952.

Looking-for-Something, illustrated by Politi, Viking, 1952.

Blue Canyon Horse, illustrated by Allan Houser, Viking, 1954.

Santiago, illustrated by Lynd Ward, Viking, 1955.

The Little Indian Pottery Maker, illustrated by Don Perceval, Melmont, 1955.

Third Monkey, illustrated by Don Freeman, Viking, 1956.

The Little Indian Basket Maker, illustrated by Harrison Begay, Melmont, 1957.

A Santo for Pasqualita, illustrated by Mary Villarejo, Viking, 1959.

World Song, illustrated by Kurt Wiese, Viking, 1960.

Paco's Miracle, illustrated by Agnes Tait, Farrar, Straus, 1962.

The Desert People, illustrated by Houser, Viking, 1962.

Tia Maria's Garden, illustrated by Ezra Jack Keats, Viking, 1963.

Medicine Man's Daughter, illustrated by Don Bolognese, Farrar, Straus, 1963.

Father Kino: Priest to the Pimas, illustrated by H. Lawrence Hoffman, Farrar, Straus, 1963.

Bear Cub, illustrated by Charles Frace, Viking, 1965.

This for That, illustrated by Freeman, Golden Gate, 1965.

Brother Andre of Montreal, illustrated by Harold Lang, Farrar, Straus, 1967.

Summer Is for Growing, illustrated by Tait, Farrar, Straus, 1967.

(With Glenna Craw) *Arizona Is for Young People,* Nebraska University Publishing, 1968.

A Child's Story of New Mexico, Nebraska University Publishing, 1968.

Along Sandy Trails, illustrated by Alfred A. Cohn, Viking, 1969.

Journey to the People, Viking, 1969.

These Were the Valiant: A Collection of New Mexico Profiles, Calvin Horn, 1969.

Circle of the Seasons, illustrated by W. T. Mars, Farrar, Straus, 1970.

Hoofprint on the Wind, illustrated by Robert Andrew Parker, Viking, 1972.

Year Walk, Viking, 1975.

All This Wild Land, Viking, 1976.

To Stand against the Wind, Viking, 1978.

(With Dang Manh Kha) *In the Land of Small Dragon: A Vietnamese Folktale* illustrated by Tony Chen, Viking, 1979.

Also author of pamphlet *Writers and Writing of New Mexico,* Writers' Round Table of Las Vegas, NM, 1935, and *Local Government,* United Pueblo Agency. Supervised the preparation of materials for adult literacy, Bureau of Indian Affairs, and reading texts for several countries in Latin America, including Guatemala, Costa Rica, Ecuador, Honduras, Panama, and Peru. Contributor of articles to *New Mexico* magazine under name Ann Nolan Clark and pseudonym Marie Dunne, 1935-37.

■ Sidelights

Ann Nolan Clark is an American of Irish descent who has spent much of her life writing books for Native American and Hispanic American children. Clark was one of the first non-Indian educators to realize that Indian children needed books they could relate to, with stories reflecting their own rich heritages. The author began on a small scale, writing easy primers for her own Indian students. Eventually, these primers—and later Clark's more sophisticated stories—became favorites among white children as well. As Claire Huchet Bishop wrote in *Catholic Library World:* "Ann Nolan Clark's books are a joy to the Indians, both young and old, who recognize themselves, their traditions, their sense of values, their suffering and their hopes. Also, her books introduce the Indians to what is relevant for them in the White man's culture and which they can assimilate without betraying their own ways." Clark's books generally relate day-to-day events in Indian society rather than focusing on myth or unusual adventure. *New York Times Book Review* contributor Anne T. Eaton claimed that such an approach "gives to [all] little children ... a sense of knowing Indian boys and girls and the feeling of experiences shared."

Ann Nolan was born in 1896 in Las Vegas, New Mexico. Her own parents and grandparents were Irish, but she grew up with an Indian nurse and knew people of Indian, Spanish, and French backgrounds. In an essay for *Horn Book* magazine, the author noted that New Mexico gave her "understanding, a tolerance and acceptance and appreciation and ease with different peoples who have other ways of thinking and other ways of living. New Mexico gave that to all her early children, and for me it has made my life-way rich and warm and wide." As she further explained in her *Something about the Author Autobiography Series* (*SAAS*) entry, "I do not remember how Las Vegas looked as a town, whether it was large or small, attractive or ugly, but only that it was a happy place and that I belonged there."

Young Ann was raised by strict parents who expected responsible behavior; nevertheless, her childhood was filled with books, picnics, riding, and many family

A Taos Pueblo boy with three names—Anglo, Hispanic, and Native American—is the subject of these heartfelt summertime stories. (Cover illustration by Tonita Lujan.)

Clark's experience as a teacher of Native American children informs her "Little Herder" books, which have remained in print long after their original publication in the 1940s. (Cover illustration by Hoke Denetsosie.)

activities. "When I look back on my childhood," she revealed in *SAAS,* "it seems to me that we were a loving family among loving people in a lovely land." She recalled having a poem published in the local paper on the occasion of New Mexico's statehood, and although her brothers later teased her that it was only printed because her uncle owned the paper, she was undaunted in her desire to write: "Since I could remember, I had always wanted to be a writer; dreamed, planned, talked about the days that I would spend writing and writing and writing." A Catholic, she attended convent day school and then the public high school in Las Vegas, where she became the first female editor of the school paper. After graduating from high school she took courses at New Mexico Normal School (which later became New Mexico Highlands University), helping to pay her tuition by serving as an assistant English instructor.

During this time the United States became involved in World War I, and Clark looked for a way to contribute to the fight against Germany. Because of her talents driving the family car, she recalled in *SAAS,* "I was certain I was qualified to drive any ambulance in France. Why was I not permitted to drive an ambulance in France and help win the war as my brothers were?" Instead, the young teacher was given an assignment in a German community near her home. The wide range of student abilities, lack of materials, and fanatically pro-German stance of her neighbors proved a bitter experience for her, and she was happy to leave after only seven months when funds for her salary ran out. To occupy her time for the rest of the school year, she accepted a post in the Indian pueblo of Tesuque, intrigued by a supervisor's description of the Indians' lives as "beautiful." "If they were poor, if they lived in a simple manner, how could their lives be beautiful, I wondered. I thought beautiful was the kind of life that actors lived in the motion picture shows. Could it be found here in a mud-walled town?"

The decision proved to be a pivotal event in her life. Although the conditions were primitive, with no running water and few school supplies, the children were eager learners. At the end of the term, Clark recalled in *SAAS,* "I was sorry that my two months were over and I had to go.... It was my time to leave, but in my heart I never left Tesuque." After working the summer near her brother in Tacoma, Washington, at a series of factory jobs, she returned to New Mexico, taking a teaching post at a mining school. Many of the children there were Mexican, speaking no English, and "it was discovered that I had a 'flair' for teaching English to those who could not speak it," Clark recalled. "I did not know I had a 'flair' for anything, but I had felt sorry all year for the poor frightened children who had newly come from Mexico, standing in little groups or alone looking at the other Mexican children who, because they could speak the English, were treated as if they belonged." In 1919, however, she left teaching when she married Thomas Patrick Clark, and in 1920 her only child, Thomas, Jr., was born.

By 1923, Clark was a widow with a young son to support. For several years she taught at county schools and mining camps, until she decided to move closer to her family. She recalled her experience at Tesuque Pueblo, and determined to take the examination for permanent employment in the Indian Service. She took the test and passed. Her first assignment was at the Santa Fe Boarding School for Indian children, a large and well-maintained facility. Then a new opportunity arose. As Clark once related to *SATA:* "After several years teaching older Indian children, the Tesuque Pueblo people asked ... if I could come to them—a one-room school from pre-school to fourth grade. I was delighted because by this time I wanted to follow the development of an Indian child from pre-school to boarding school age. The superintendent of the Santa Fe Indian School where I was teaching said I could go, but if I went from a large boarding school to a tiny one-room school my career as an Indian educator would be ended." That superintendent was wrong. Clark's experience in that tiny school led directly to her long and fruitful writing career.

Clark quickly discovered that the young Indian children faced an extremely difficult task. They had to learn a new language—English—as well as new ways of thinking and living. Very little emphasis was put on their own culture. Instead, they were expected to learn "American" ways. "They followed a pattern of ancient tradition.... My culture pattern was different," Clark explained in *SAAS.* "My people changed as the wind changed. Which way was better? The question had no answer, at least that I could give; but I could do something about the problem. Using their own culture as a foundation, respecting it, strengthening it, I could slowly and naturally build our culture upon it. When my pupils grew to adulthood they could, I hoped, face the world securely and proudly as Indians at home and at peace in two worlds." To address this situation, Clark began to write easy-to-read primers about the Pueblo way of life, using poetic language that translated easily from English into the Tesuque dialect.

"At first these books were about Indians and for Indians," Clark told *SATA*. "But there soon became a demand for books about Indians for Indian and also non-Indian children." A primer that Clark had produced with her class made its way to Washington, and several months later, the author recalled in *SAAS,* she received a letter stating that "I was the only one in the Indian Bureau who did not know that the Viking Publishing Company wanted to publish my *Third Grade Home Geography.*" This book was published in 1941 as *In My Mother's House* and quickly earned widespread acclaim. Eaton called it "a rare achievement and one very welcome in the field of children's books about the Indians," while May Lamberton Becker observed in the *New York Herald Tribune Books* that it "would be hard to find use of words—call it poetry or prose as you prefer—carrying a beautiful meaning more clearly to a young mind: what life means to a . . . community, close to earth and sky." "Most important," Ophelia Gilbert asserted in the *Dictionary of Literary Biography,* "*In My Mother's House* was the first children's book written about American Indian children from their point of view."

Due to her book's success with her students, Clark became a specialist in teaching children to read and write English through stories about their own familiar traditions. The resulting books not only helped Indian children to learn a second language, they also gave non-Indian children a glimpse of everyday Indian life. In *Elementary English,* Evelyn Wenzel described Clark's primers, such as *In My Mother's House* and the Navajo "Little Herder" series: "These are truly delightful stories telling of familiar details of the everyday living of the Navajo, Sioux, and Pueblo children; revealing humor and sensitive understanding of these people as individual personalities as well as a minority culture with its problems; and written in simple, often poetic language which has an Indian 'flavor' even in English." Many of these easy-to-understand "Indian Life Readers" remain in print, even though they were written in the 1940s and 1950s.

Eventually Clark left teaching and became a full-time writer and educational specialist with the Bureau of Indian Affairs. Her work took her through Latin America and South America as well, where she taught local school administrators how to reach their minority students. Clark's travels enriched her imagination, and soon she found herself writing stories about the children she encountered in such places as Guatemala, Peru, and Mexico. These stories, meant for a slightly older audience, often revolve around the conflict an Indian child feels between the traditional ways of his or her people and the demands of the alien majority culture. Wenzel noted that Clark "feels a strong responsibility: to help Indian children understand their own problems of growing-up and to interpret to children of other cultures these people she knows and loves so well." In works such as *Secret of the Andes, Santiago,* and *Little Navajo Bluebird,* the critic continued, "Clark's artistry is at its best, for only a teacher who knows and loves children and a person who has lived and felt with these people could deal with such problems so simply and effectively."

In the Newbery-winner *Secret of the Andes,* for instance, an Inca boy in modern Peru becomes heir to a four-hundred-year-old secret dating to the days before the Spaniards overtook the region. The boy must choose to become guardian of the secret in his turn or forever lose the path of the ancient Inca peoples. A *New York Herald Tribune Book Review* critic called the work "another of [Clark's] thoughtful, deeply felt books, giving children a sympathetic sense of far-away Indian life," praising her tone as "one of beauty and mystery." In noting the author's background in her subject, *Horn Book* critic Anne Carroll Moore observed that Clark "has been able to translate personal knowledge and experience into

Clark received the 1953 Newbery Medal for her story of an Inca boy who learns a four-hundred-year-old secret of his people and must prove that he can be trusted with it. (Cover illustration by Robert Barrett.)

memorable words with a universal appeal," and she termed *Secret of the Andes* "one of the most beautiful and original books for children and young people of our time." "To my mind," Bishop similarly stated, "*Secret of the Andes* is one of the summits of American literature for the young."

A similar choice between the life of the tribe and the life of the "modern" world lies at the heart of 1955's *Santiago,* another highly praised work that "adds another cubit to Mrs. Clark's stature as a writer," as Moore noted in another *Horn Book* review. Santiago's cultural conflict arises when he is returned to his Guatemalan Indian village after having been accepted into a North American family. After living in the impoverished village for several years, Santiago declines an invitation to return to the material comfort of his American friends, instead becoming a teacher among his own people. "The book's distinction derives from [Clark's] power to express her ideas, to create a varied array of characters and re-create actual scenes in prose that is rich and beautiful," Virginia Haviland noted in the *New York Herald Tribune Book Review. Library Journal* contributor Siddie Joe Johnson found *Santiago* the best of Clark's work, noting that "not even in *Secret of the Andes* is the boy's reaction to life so poignant, the feeling of race so strong, the conception of beauty and mysticism so clarified."

Clark's later books include more accounts of Native Americans as well as stories about Irish islanders, Basque immigrants of Spain, Finnish settlers in Minnesota, and Vietnamese youngsters caught in the dangers of war. In his review of *Year Walk, Christian Science Monitor* writer Marvin S. Sharpe commented that this tale of Basque sheepherders in Idaho "is well up to her high standard," and added that "Clark doesn't just sit down and write a story—she does her homework thoroughly before she writes." *All This Wild Land,* which portrays a conflict between Finnish settlers and Native Americans, similarly earned praise for its characterization. Wendy Moorhead observed in another *Christian Science Monitor* article that Clark's characters "are people we quickly get to know and care about." The quality of her books has made them popular with children decades after being published. Their longevity "suggests that Ann Nolan Clark is not only a builder of bridges of cultural understanding," Arnold A. Griese concluded in *Elementary English,* "but a literary artist whose status as a writer for children will not be diminished by the passing years."

Named an "outstanding Arizona author" in 1984 by the state to which she retired, Clark told *Horn Book:* "I have worked with Spanish children from New Mexico to Central and South America, with Indian children from Canada to Peru. I have worked with them because I like them. I write about them because their stories need to be told. All children need understanding, but children of segregated racial groups need even more. All children need someone to make a bridge from their world to the world of the adults who surround them. Indian children need this; they have the child problems of growing up, but also they have racial problems, the problems of conflicting interracial patterns between groups, and the conflicts of changing racial patterns within the group. Anyway you look at it, it's rugged to be a child. Often I think more of us did not survive the experiences than meets the eye." The author concluded, "If the children like what I write, that's a gift to me from my grandfather's fairies in Ireland."

■ Works Cited

Becker, May Lamberton, "Three Prize Winning Books, Spring 1941," *New York Herald Tribune Books,* May 11, 1941, p. 8.

Bishop, Claire Huchet, "Ann Nolan Clark," *Catholic Library World,* February, 1963, pp. 280-86, 333.

Clark, Ann Nolan, "Newbery Award Acceptance," *Horn Book,* August, 1953, pp. 249-57.

Clark, Ann Nolan, essay in *Something about the Author Autobiography Series,* Volume 16, Gale, 1993, pp. 33-109.

Eaton, Anne T., review of *In My Mother's House, New York Times Book Review,* May 4, 1941, p. 11.

Gilbert, Ophelia, "Ann Nolan Clark," *Dictionary of Literary Biography,* Volume 52: *American Writers for Children since 1960: Fiction,* Gale, 1986, pp. 75-84.

Griese, Arnold A., "Ann Nolan Clark—Building Bridges of Cultural Understanding," *Elementary English,* May, 1972, pp. 648-58.

Haviland, Virginia, review of *Santiago, New York Herald Tribune Book Review,* May 15, 1955, p. 6.

Johnson, Siddie Joe, review of *Santiago, Library Journal,* June 15, 1955, p. 1510.

Moore, Anne Carroll, review of *Secret of the Andes, Horn Book,* June, 1952, pp. 160-61.

Moore, Anne Carroll, review of *Santiago, Horn Book,* June, 1955, pp. 177-78.

Moorhead, Wendy, "From Appalachia to Chinatown—Adventures in Americana," *Christian Science Monitor,* May 4, 1977, p. B2.

Review of *Secret of the Andes, New York Herald Tribune Book Review,* May 11, 1952, p. 7.

Sharpe, Marvin S., "Basque Boy Tends Flock in Idaho Wilds," *Christian Science Monitor,* May 7, 1975, p. B2.

Wenzel, Evelyn, "Ann Nolan Clark: 1953 Newbery Award Winner," *Elementary English,* October, 1953, pp. 327-32.

■ For More Information See

BOOKS

Arbuthnot, May Hill, "Here and Now: Ann Nolan Clark," *Children and Books,* 3rd edition, Scott, Foresman, 1964, pp. 452-53.

Children's Literature Review, Volume 16, Gale, 1989.

Sadker, Myra Pollack, and David Miller Sadker, *Now Upon a Time: A Contemporary View of Children's Literature,* Harper, 1977, pp. 180-181.

PERIODICALS

Books, September 2, 1952, p. 10.

Bulletin of the Center for Children's Books, April, 1979, p. 132.
Catholic Library World, September, 1963, pp. 14-17.
Horn Book, May-June, 1943, p. 169; August, 1953, pp. 258-62; October, 1954, p. 330.
Kirkus Reviews, September 15, 1969, p. 995; May 15, 1970, p. 561; August 15, 1976, p. 906; May 15, 1979, p. 572.
Library Journal, May 1, 1952, p. 799; March 15, 1953, pp. 475-77.
New York Herald Tribune Book Review, April 4, 1943, p. 8; May 11, 1952, p. 6.
New York Times, April 19, 1959, p. 30.
New York Times Book Review, May 16, 1943, p. 16; July 10, 1960, p. 24; May 12, 1963, p. 29.
Virginia Kirkus' Bookshop Service, February 1, 1952, p. 70; February 15, 1952, p. 123.*

* * *

CLARK, Margaret Goff 1913-

■ Personal

Born March 7, 1913, in Oklahoma City, OK; daughter of Raymond Finla and Fanny (Church) Goff; married Charles Robert Clark, 1937; children: Robert Allen, Marcia Clark Noel. *Education:* Attended Columbia University, 1934; New York State College for Teachers (now State University of New York at Buffalo), B.S., 1936. *Hobbies and other interests:* Archaeology, square dancing, swimming, travel, history, bridge, helping endangered animals.

■ Addresses

Home—334 Shoreland Dr., Ft. Myers, FL 33905. *Agent*—Dorothy Markinko, McIntosh & Otis, Inc., 310 Madison Ave., New York, NY 10017.

■ Career

Elementary school teacher in Niagara, NY, 1933-34, and Buffalo, NY, 1934-39; teacher of creative writing in adult education programs, 1960-61; Georgian College Summer School of the Arts, Huntsville, Ontario, Canada, teacher of creative writing, 1974-78. Former deputy town clerk, Niagara. *Member:* National League of American Pen Women (Southwest Florida branch), Association of Professional Women Writers (president, 1960-61), Mystery Writers of America, Authors Guild, Authors League of America, Delta Sigma Epsilon, Delta Kappa Gamma (honorary member), Alpha Delta Kappa (honorary member).

■ Awards, Honors

Distinguished Alumnus Award, State University of New York at Buffalo, 1979; Children's Choice Award, 1980, for *Who Stole Kathy Young?; The Vanishing Manatee* was named to a list of best science trade books for young readers, 1990.

MARGARET GOFF CLARK

■ Writings

The Mystery of Seneca Hill, F. Watts, 1961.
The Mystery of the Buried Indian Mask, F. Watts, 1962.
Mystery of the Marble Zoo, Funk, 1964.
Mystery at Star Lake, Funk, 1965.
Adirondack Mountain Mystery, Funk, 1966.
The Mystery of the Missing Stamps, Funk, 1967.
Danger at Niagara, Funk, 1968.
Freedom Crossing, Funk, 1969.
Benjamin Banneker, Garrard, 1971.
Mystery Horse, Dodd, 1972.
Their Eyes on the Stars: Four Black Writers, Garrard, 1973.
John Muir, Garrard, 1974.
Death at Their Heels, Dodd, 1975.
Mystery of Sebastian Island, Dodd, 1976.
Mystery in the Flooded Museum, Dodd, 1978.
Barney and the UFO, Dodd, 1979.
Who Stole Kathy Young?, Dodd, 1980.
Barney in Space, Dodd, 1981.
The Boy from the UFO, Scholastic, 1981.
Barney on Mars, Dodd, 1983.
The Latchkey Mystery, Dodd, 1985.
The Vanishing Manatee, Dutton, 1990.
The Endangered Florida Panther, Dutton, 1993.
The Threatened Florida Black Bear, Dutton, 1995.

Clark uses her knowledge of nature and ecology in this suspenseful tale about two boys chased by a killer in Canada's Algonquin Park.

Also author of *The Mysterious Hole* (a talking book), International Learning Co., 1975. Author of twenty-five one-act plays and numerous poems. Contributor of more than two hundred short stories to American and Canadian magazines, including *American Girl, Ingenue, Teen Talk,* and *Instructor.* Contributor to anthologies, including *The New People and Progress,* 1955, *Stories to Live By,* 1960, *Time of Starting Out,* 1962, *Pressing Onward,* 1964, and *They Loved the Land,* 1974.

■ Work in Progress

Researching and writing a nonfiction book about the Florida black bear.

■ Sidelights

Although Margaret Goff Clark has delighted young people with her work in mystery, suspense, science, and historical fiction, she has also enlightened them with her nonfiction books about endangered species. While Clark knew in the fourth grade that she wanted to be a writer, "I had no idea it was a career possibility," she stated in a Dodd, Mead, publicity release. She wrote throughout her childhood and adolescence, and finally began to write seriously when she joined an adult writing club.

Clark began her career writing for young people with *The Mystery of Seneca Hill. The Mystery of the Buried Indian Mask* and *Mystery of the Marble Zoo* soon followed, and Clark had begun to establish her reputation as a mystery writer. In *Canadian Children's Literature,* Dave Jenkinson writes that Clark's mysteries follow a similar plot: an adolescent away from his or her parents for the summer is "suddenly confronted by a mysterious occurrence which may have been criminally motivated." With the clever persistence of this adolescent, the guilty parties are "exposed and punished." After reviewing *Mystery at Star Lake* and *Mystery in the Flooded Museum,* Jenkinson concluded that "Clark's fast-paced mysteries, with their mix of male and female protagonists and their effective use of chapter ending narrative hooks, will make good reading for upper elementary and early junior high readers."

Clark's historical novels include *Danger at Niagara* and *Freedom Crossing. Danger at Niagara* is set during the War of 1812. A fifteen-year-old orphan assists his neighbors, serves in the army, and eludes the British. Normakay Marthinson writes in *Library Journal* that Clark has "well integrated good background material" of the period into her story. *Freedom Crossing* involves the Underground Railroad before the Civil War. A fifteen-year-old girl who has spent time in the south is disturbed when she finds that her family helps former slaves escape to Canada. Nevertheless, when her brother is arrested, Laura takes his place and helps an eleven year old escape to freedom. Sister Rita Angerman in *Library Journal* concludes that the "story is fast-moving and will hold readers' interest."

Death at Their Heels and *Who Stole Kathy Young?* are examples of Clark's other suspense stories. In *Death at Their Heels,* Denny and his older stepbrother Rick are chased on a camping trip by a killer against whom Rick had testified in court. Denny and his new brother learn to respect each other after Denny saves Rick from the murderer. Throughout the book, which is set in Algonquin Park in Canada, Clark's knowledge of nature and ecology is apparent. As she once told *SATA,* "After several years of canoeing, fishing and camping in the park, the background was a part of me. I had to write a story about the park and the creatures who inhabit it." Myra Silver in *School Library Journal* concludes that the book is "very readable" and that the "wilderness experiences are realistically handled." *Who Stole Kathy Young?* is set on the Gulf Coast of Texas and begins when a teenager witnesses the kidnapping of her deaf friend. The stories of the kidnapped girl and her friend are both told in this book, and according to a reviewer for *School Library Journal,* "Clark knows how to keep the action moving." *Who Stole Kathy Young?* earned a Children's Choice Award in 1980.

As Clark stated in her publicity release, it was after she met a teenager who was excited about UFOs—unidentified flying objects—that she wrote *Barney and the UFO.*

In this book, an orphan decides that leaving the planet on a UFO would be better than staying with his adoptive parents, who he believes do not want him. Just in time, Barney's parents persuade him that they do want him and convince his alien friend that Barney must stay where he belongs. Carolyn Caywood in *School Library Journal* notes that "the suspense will pull older reluctant readers along." *Barney in Space* relates the further adventures of Barney as a renegade space creature attempts to kidnap him to keep Barney from telling about the existence of his fellow Garks. According to Barbara Elleman in *Booklist,* this book "will appeal" to readers because of "fast pace and lots of dialogue." *Barney on Mars,* Clark's third Barney book, begins when Barney's space friend tries to warn him about a flood on earth and ends as Barney and his friends retrieve a dog from the Garks.

Clark's interest in nature and environmental issues has moved her to produce nonfiction works for children about endangered species. As the author once remarked, "Seeing a manatee swimming in the Caloosahatchee River behind our mobile home in Ft. Myers, Florida, sent me to the library for information about this enormous marine animal. When the librarian said she had no books on the subject and begged that I write about it, I began a long and interesting research." In *The Vanishing Manatee,* Clark discusses these fascinating animals and explains how humans have threatened their survival by spoiling the manatees' habitat and accidentally killing them. Frances E. Millhouser in *School Library Journal* writes that this "well-organized" book "will be a useful addition to most collections." In 1990, *The Vanishing Manatee* was named to a list of best science trade books for young readers.

Clark related that "my interest in endangered animals [also] led to ... *The Endangered Florida Panther.*" In this book, Clark discusses the elusive panther and the destruction of its home in the Everglades. As in *The Vanishing Manatee,* the efforts of those trying to save the animals, along with anecdotes, are included. Betsy Hearne in the *Bulletin of the Center for Children's Books* writes that "Clark has done her homework here," and praises the author's "good sense of story" in presenting her material. Readers who have enjoyed Clark's books about endangered species may also be interested in *John Muir,* a biography which provides readers with the life story of one of the founders of the environmental movement in the United States.

Clark continues to write and give talks in schools about her books. "My subjects are based on current books," she once remarked: "on how the book developed, how I researched it, how to get started in writing, and so on." The Seneca Indians, who have adopted Clark, have fittingly named her Deh-yi-sto-esh, or "She Who Writes and Publishes."

■ Works Cited

Angerman, Sister Rita, review of *Freedom Crossing, Library Journal,* February 15, 1970, p. 778.

Caywood, Carolyn, review of *Barney and the UFO, School Library Journal,* November, 1979, p. 74.

Clark, Margaret Goff, publicity release from Dodd, Mead, c. 1985.

Elleman, Barbara, review of *Barney in Space, Booklist,* October 15, 1981, p. 298.

Hearne, Betsy, review of *The Endangered Florida Panther, Bulletin of the Center for Children's Books,* May, 1993, p. 279.

Jenkinson, Dave, review of *Mystery at Star Lake* and *Mystery in the Flooded Museum, Canadian Children's Literature,* Number 12, 1978, pp. 37-39.

Marthinson, Normakay, review of *Danger at Niagara, Library Journal,* October 15, 1968, p. 3976.

Millhouser, Frances E., review of *The Vanishing Manatee, School Library Journal,* July, 1990, p. 83.

Silver, Myra, review of *Death at Their Heels, School Library Journal,* March, 1975, p. 104.

Review of *Who Stole Kathy Young?, School Library Journal,* December, 1980, p. 72.

■ For More Information See

PERIODICALS

Christian Science Monitor, November 7, 1968, p. B10.

New York Times Book Review, September 7, 1975, p. 20.

School Library Journal, November, 1981, pp. 88-89; February, 1984, p. 67; October, 1985, p. 169; December, 1993, p. 122.*

* * *

COLLINS, Ace 1953-
(Andrew J. Collins)

■ Personal

Born August 17, 1953, in Rantoul, IL; son of Doyle E. (a teacher) and Charlene (a teacher; maiden name, Shell) Collins; married Kathy Chapman (a teacher), 1975; children: Clint, Rance. *Education:* Baylor University, B.A., 1975. *Politics:* Independent. *Religion:* Baptist. *Hobbies and other interests:* Running, training collie dogs, restoring cars.

■ Addresses

Home and office—P.O. Box 644, Hillsboro, TX 76645. *Agent*—Evan Fogelman, Fogelman Literary Agency, 7515 Greenville Ave., Suite 712, Dallas, TX 75231.

■ Career

Free-lance writer. *Member:* Media Action Research Center; Baylor University Women's Athletic Cabinet; Country Music Association.

■ Awards, Honors

America's Award; Angel Award of Excellence; Golden Quill.

Writings

"YOU CAN DO IT" SERIES; FOR CHILDREN; PUBLISHED BY THE SUMMIT GROUP

You Can Do It Running, 1993.
You Can Do It Dog Training, 1993.
You Can Do It Juggling, 1993.
You Can Do It Sidewalk Art and Games, 1993.
You Can Do It Balloon Shapes and Animals, 1993.

"HOLIDAY ADVENTURE" SERIES; FOR CHILDREN; WITH LOUISE MANDRELL; PUBLISHED BY THE SUMMIT GROUP

Runaway Thanksgiving, illustrated by Paige Frailey, 1992.
Jonathan's Gifts, illustrated by Mark Gale, 1992.
Peril in Evans Woods, illustrated by Frailey, 1993.
All in a Day's Work, illustrated by Don Morris, 1993.
Eddie Finds a Hero, illustrated by Steve Grey, 1993.
Best Man for the Job, illustrated by Morris, 1993.
A Mission for Jenny, illustrated by Leslie Stall, 1993.
Sunrise over the Harbor, illustrated by Gale, 1993.

Also author of *Bond of Trust, Kimi's American Dream, Candy's Frog Prince, Abe's Hard Lesson, The End of the Rainbow, Twin Disasters, The Eyes of an Eagle,* and *The Parade.*

Ace Collins with Lassie

ADULT NONFICTION

(With Mandrell) *The Mandrell Family Album,* Thomas Nelson, 1983.
The Christian Executive, Word, Inc., 1984.
(With Lauren Chapin; under name Andrew Collins) *Father Does Know Best,* Thomas Nelson, 1989.
Bette Midler, St. Martin's, 1989.
Sigourney Weaver, St. Martin's, 1989.
After the Storm, Starsong Press, 1992.
I Saw Him in Your Eyes, Vision Press, Volume I, 1993, Volume II, 1995, Volume III, 1995.
Lassie, a Dog's Life: The First Fifty Years, Penguin Books, 1993.
Tanya Tucker: A Biography, St. Martin's, 1994.

ADULT FICTION

Darkness before Dawn, Vision Press, 1994.
The Cutting Edge, Vision Press, 1994.
Saving Grace, Vision Press, 1995.
The Image of Truth, Vision Press, 1995.

OTHER

Also wrote the 1940s segment of *The Spirit of Christmas,* scripted the play *American Spirit,* and wrote script and original song lyrics for *A Christian Carol.*

Work in Progress

Eighty Years in Hollywood, the Life and Times of Director Jack Hively; The 100 Greatest Songs in the History of Country Music and the Stories Behind Them; Hi O'Silver—The Lone Ranger; Top Dog—The Rudd Weatherwax Story.

Sidelights

Ace Collins told *SATA:* "I am a firm believer that every person changes the world in a dramatic fashion. By simply being born, we redefine in some way every person and everything we touch. Hence, if we do have so much creative power in our hands each day, we must decide how we want to use it. Many people fail to consider that we have a right to choose if we are to have a negative or positive influence in our life and work. Over the course of the years I have always tried through my writings for both children and adults to make some type of positive statement.

"When I write, I first consider the audience. I want to meet them where they live. If I compose an award-winning book that is not read, then I have failed and the award means nothing. So, before I write a word, I want to visualize those who will read the book. After I have defined my audience, I outline my story. The first thing the story must do is to entertain. If I bore my audience, then I will lose them before I can have a chance to touch them. Once the plot line has developed entertainment value, then I consider where and how to drop in my lesson or moral. Finally, in dealing with adults or children, I try to sneak in a bit of educational value as well.

"The book I wrote covering Lassie's first fifty years provided me with a special opportunity as a writer and a person. Lassie is a genuine superstar whose stardom crosses several generations. In that sense this dog is an important character in entertainment history. Lassie is also one of the world's most successful marketing tools. In one facet or another, he (all eight Lassies have been males) has made billions for various companies. Lassie has also transcended film to become a worldwide icon and hero. In a sense, he walked off the pages of a fiction book and became real to billions of people.

"Lassie's success was created through eight generations of dogs and one family of dog trainers. How Lassie became so smart, how he was trained, and what makes those eight generations of dog actors so special is another important element of this story. Finally, a host of famous people worked with the dog over the years. Their stories have to blend with all the other elements into a flowing and interesting work.

"Because the book *Lassie, a Dog's Life* was written about a subject that meant so much to me as a baby boomer, the project also allowed me to experience again the emotions of my youth. By combining all of these separate elements, the real and complete story of Lassie was told, and in the process it became a book which crossed all age and cultural boundaries. In other words, the book was able to reach and touch the same demographics as its subject had for five decades.

"I wouldn't be making my living without the pushing and prodding of Louise Mandrell. This fabulous friend and entertainer convinced me to use my talents and give free-lance a try. Every time I wanted to give up, she was there either to find me another job or to urge me on. She believed in me so strongly, she wouldn't let me quit. In that sense, the awards I have won and the books I have sold have her fingerprints all over them.

"I love being a writer. I love doing research. I love being able to use my career to reach people in a positive way. I

***Lassie: A Dog's Life* covers the world-renowned collie's first fifty years, including her stardom in hit films such as *Lassie Come Home,* with Roddy McDowall, in 1943.**

guess I love everything about writing but the hard work that goes into it. I often dread sitting down in front of the computer and putting my ideas into motion. Yet, once I get started, it is so hard to stop. In the final evaluation, I must be the luckiest man on earth!"

* * *

COLLINS, Andrew J.
See COLLINS, Ace

* * *

COOPER, Lettice (Ulpha) 1897-1994

OBITUARY NOTICE—See index for *SATA* sketch: Born September 3, 1897, in Eccles, England; died July 24, 1994, in Coltishall, England. Author. Cooper first gained popularity as a novelist in 1925 with the publication of *The Lighted Room.* Her subsequent works of the 1920s and 1930s, praised for their stylistic simplicity and perceptive characterizations, were well received by critics and the public. During the 1960s and early 1970s, she wrote a number of successful children's stories, including *Blackberry's Kitten, The Bear Who Was Too Big,* and *Robert, the Spy Hunter.* In the 1980s her early works became the focus of renewed interest when they were reissued by her publisher. Cooper was also active in a variety of professional and social causes—she was a member of both PEN and the Writer's Action Group—and many of her works reflect her liberal political ideals. Her writings include the novels *National Provincial, Fenny, Snow and Roses,* and *Unusual Behavior,* as well as children's biographies of Queen Victoria, Florence Nightingale, and Edgar Allan Poe.

OBITUARIES AND OTHER SOURCES:

BOOKS

The Writers Directory: 1992-1994, St. James Press, 1991.

PERIODICALS

Times (London), July 26, 1994, p. 17.

* * *

CRESPO, George 1962-

■ Personal

Born September 23, 1962, in Yonkers, NY; son of Jorge Luis (a restaurateur) and Maria A. (a homemaker; maiden name, Nunez) Crespo; married Mercy N. Litardo (a computer operator), April 19, 1984; children: Ivan Perdomo, Mercy Christine. *Education:* Parsons School of Design, B.F.A., 1984.

■ Addresses

Home—14 East 2nd St., Apt. #2, Mineola, NY 11501. *Office*—479 West 146th Street, New York, NY 10031.

GEORGE CRESPO

■ Career

Sculptor in New York City, 1985—. Has also appeared on local television and lectured at middle and high schools. Spanish interpreter for the Supreme Court in Mineola, NY. *Exhibitions:* Numerous exhibits since 1985, including *Sculpture in a Box,* solo show, New York University, 1987; *Syncretic Myths,* solo show, Museum of Contemporary Hispanic Art, New York City, 1990; *First Invasion: Contemporary Artists of Cuba and Puerto Rico,* group show, Galeria de la Raza, San Francisco, CA, 1992.

■ Awards, Honors

Travel grant, Grupo de Empressarios Pro Arte, 1989; Pollock-Krasner Foundation Grant, 1992, for sculpting.

■ Writings

RETELLER AND ILLUSTRATOR

How the Sea Began: A Taino Myth, Clarion Books, 1993.

How Iwariwa the Cayman Learned to Share: A Yanomamo Myth, Clarion Books, 1994.

■ Work in Progress

Illustrations for *The Village Basket Weaver,* Dutton; *Flor Canera,* a Snow White story from Puerto Rico; *How Matu the Manatee Saved the Day,* a Taino myth from Haiti; a series of Puerto Rican folk tales that will include *Cofresi: A Real Life Pirate;* a series on the Afro-

Cuban turtle trickster, Jicotea; *Maria Cenicienta: A Cinderella Story from Puerto Rico,* for Dutton.

■ Sidelights

"After graduating from Parsons School of Design's illustration program, I decided to become a full-time sculptor," George Crespo told *SATA.* "My sculptural work brought me through a search for a personal spirituality to look at my own ancestors, the native Taino people of Puerto Rico. I wrote and illustrated my first book, *How the Sea Began: A Taino Myth,* to tell people about my ancestry. My second book, a Yanomami story from Brazil, will benefit the Yanomami Health Fund. This fund provides health care to the Yanomami by protecting them against disease brought in by invading gold miners.

"I am presently telling stories from other indigenous peoples of Latin America. My interest in other cultures, particularly Caribbean, has led me to traveling. I just returned from a seventeen-day trip to the Carib people's territory in the commonwealth of Dominica. I was there to research the illustrations for a book entitled *The Village Basket Weaver,* to be published by Dutton. At the territory, I learned basket weaving from a master basket maker.

"I collected two stories from a Caribbean couple that I hope will be published. To illustrate this book, I would return to the territory and collaborate with local artists on the art."

■ For More Information See

PERIODICALS

Bulletin of the Center for Children's Books, June, 1993.
Horn Book Guide, fall, 1993, p. 325.
Publishers Weekly, March 8, 1993, p. 78.
School Library Journal, July, 1993, p. 76.

* * *

CURRIE, Stephen 1960-

STEPHEN CURRIE

■ Personal

Born September 29, 1960, in New York, NY; son of David Park (a law professor) and Barbara Suzanne (an Illinois state legislator; maiden name, Flynn) Currie; married Amity Elizabeth Smith (a teacher), July 3, 1983; children: Irene Elizabeth, Nicholas David. *Education:* Williams College, B.A. (magna cum laude), 1982. *Hobbies and other interests:* Swimming, music, playing with his children, baseball.

■ Addresses

Office—Poughkeepsie Day School, 39 New Hackensack Rd, Poughkeepsie, NY 12603.

■ Career

Poughkeepsie Day School, Poughkeepsie, NY, teacher, 1982—. Korean Enrichment Program, language enrichment teacher, 1989-91; Dutchess Community College, Saturday Enrichment Program teacher, 1986-89. Has cataloged and annotated maps for the Adriance Memorial Library, 1982-83; editorial referee for National Council of Teachers of Mathematics journals, 1993-94; served as counselor for art- and sports-related camps. *Member:* National Association for the Education of Young Children.

■ Writings

Music in the Civil War, Betterway Books, 1992.
Problem Play, Dale Seymour, 1993.
A Birthday-a-Day Easel, GoodYear Books, 1995.
The March of the Mill Children, Lerner Publications, 1995.

Also author of *Problem Play Poster Set,* Dale Seymour, 1994. Contributor to periodicals, including *Cobblestone, Cricket, Teaching K-8, Independent School, Civil War History, Chicago Tribune,* and *Baseball Hobby News;* author of math materials for Curriculum Concepts, Inc.; consultant and author of teacher's guide for "Eleanor Roosevelt's Wallet," Franklin and Eleanor Roosevelt Library; author of juvenile series fiction.

■ Work in Progress

An untitled picture book on the invention of the potato chip; researching the history of food, showboats, and flagpole sitting.

■ Sidelights

"As a teacher, I've found that children in my class love to study history if it's presented as a story," Stephen Currie told *SATA,* "and that's what I try to achieve in my nonfiction books. Social history in particular works well for this kind of 'storytelling.' Anything from songs to the lives of real people can help bring a time and event to life for a child. Kids especially like scandal, and they enjoy hearing about grown-ups who behave in silly ways. My students, for instance, appreciate and respect such great men and women as Thomas Jefferson, Marie Curie, and Martin Luther King, but their attention really springs to life when they hear about someone like Shipwreck Kelly, who spent weeks sitting on flagpoles during the 1920s, or such flamboyant personalities as Carry Nation, Milton Hershey, and Mother Jones. Nicholas, my five-year-old son, knows nothing about battles and very little about presidents. Yet he loves to hear the story of how a cook named George Crum invented potato chips by accident. Through stories like these, he's gaining an appreciation for history and its people. My books are not designed to 'make history fun'; history is *already* fun. Just ask Nick."

■ For More Information See

PERIODICALS

Arithmetic Teacher, March, 1994, p. 424.
Come-All-Ye, summer, 1993, p. 3.
School Library Journal, May, 1993, p. 114.

D

MARGUERITE W. DAVOL

DAVOL, Marguerite W. 1928-

■ Personal

Born July 2, 1928, in East Peoria, IL; daughter of Eugene P. Welcher (a real estate broker) and Vera Ruth Peteit (maiden name, Huber); married Stephen H. Davol (a psychology professor), March 19, 1950 (deceased July 8, 1982); married Robert L. Greenberg (an engineer), September 12, 1992; children: Susan M. Carlson, Jonathan Davol, Sarah R. Davol-Kelley. *Education:* University of Colorado, B.A., 1951; graduate work at Kansas State University, 1953-54, and University of Rochester, 1955-56. *Politics:* Democrat. *Hobbies and other interests:* Music, children's theater.

■ Addresses

Home—124 College Street #19, South Hadley, MA 01075-1413. *Agent*—Virginia Knowlton, Curtis Brown, Ltd., 10 Astor Place, New York, NY 10002.

■ Career

Rocky Ford Junior High School, Rocky Ford, CO, teacher, 1952-53; various part-time town and school library jobs, 1953-64; Gorse Child Study Center, Mount Holyoke College, South Hadley, MA, preschool teacher, 1964-92. Active in local Parent-Teacher Associations and Know Your Town. *Member:* Society of Children's Book Writers and Illustrators (national and New England chapters), Pioneer Valley Folklore Society, League for the Advancement of New England Storytelling, National Storytelling Association.

■ Writings

PICTURE BOOKS

The Heart of the Wood, illustrated by Sheila Hamanaka, Simon & Schuster, 1992.
Black, White, Just Right!, Whitman, 1993.

OTHER

Papa Alonzo Leatherby (fiction), Simon & Schuster, 1995.

Contributor of short story "Flesh and Blood" to *Werewolves,* Harper, 1988.

■ Work in Progress

A middle-grade novel tentatively titled *Barney by Any Other Name;* picture books *How Snake Got His Hiss* and *Bat Wings and the Curtain of Night* for Orchard Books and *The Paper Dragon* for Atheneum; a middle-grade novel set partly in South America; and research for nonfiction articles related to recent travels in Central and South America.

Sidelights

"I've had a long apprenticeship—over twenty-five years—in learning to write children's books," Marguerite W. Davol told *SATA*. "And I am still learning!

"As a preschool teacher in a college laboratory school with excellent library facilities, I was able to choose from an extensive collection of books, books which we read every day. I soon learned from experience those which appealed, those which failed to capture the interest and imagination of young children. I learned which books were too old or too young, too long or too dull, and those with unappealing illustrations. And why were some books literally worn out from children's choosing to look at them over and over and others not given a second glance? I worked at sharpening my critical sense of what a child's book should be.

"Throughout all my years of teaching, I often could not find just the right story or poem or song to fit whatever themes or ideas I wished to explore with the children. I began to write my own stories, songs, and poems, often with input from the children themselves. Searching for just the right word, the appropriate metaphor, was a challenge and a struggle. No less difficult was learning to hear with an inner ear the rhythm and texture and sound of my words. I learned from my successes and failures. (A wiggling four year old announcing loudly, 'I'm tired!' is a most honest critic!)"

Davol brought this experience to her first book, *The Heart of the Wood.* The cumulative tale follows a sycamore tree from the forest, where it is felled by a woodcutter, to the sawmill, then to a craftsman's table, where the lumber is made into a fiddle, and finally, into a musician's hands, where the fiddle makes joyous music. "Davol sheds some gentle light on the interconnected worlds of art and nature in her first picture book," wrote *Publishers Weekly* reviewers Diane Roback and Richard Donahue. *Bulletin of the Center for Children's Books* writer Betsy Hearne found the book's success in its "merging of a subject—singing and dancing—with a style that sings and dances." Critics also commended Sheila Hamanaka's illustrations, which Lisa Dennis described as "rich and vivid" in a *School Library Journal* review.

In *Black, White, Just Right!,* Davol gives voice to the child of a mixed-race marriage who cheerfully expresses her parents' differences and proudly declares herself, "Just right!" Hazel Rochman, writing in *Booklist,* lauded the book for highlighting the individuality of the family members, as each cultivates tastes and pursues interests that are not limited by stereotype or convention. Dad, who is white, dances to rap, while Mom, who is black, prefers ballet. *Publishers Weekly* critics Diane Roback and Elizabeth Devereaux expressed concern that the book failed to address any of the problems a child in this situation might face outside the family, but added, "The book's upbeat tone is welcoming and refreshing."

The child of an interracial couple celebrates the family members' similarities and differences in Davol's upbeat 1993 picture book. (Cover illustration by Irene Trivas.)

"Today, besides picture books for the preschool child, I also write novels for older children and young adults," Davol told *SATA*. "I still search for the exact word and metaphor, still try to sense the rhythm and sound. My years of apprenticeship have helped me shape my writing, whatever the level."

Works Cited

Davol, Marguerite W., *Black, White, Just Right!,* Whitman, 1993.

Dennis, Lisa, review of *The Heart of the Wood, School Library Journal,* October, 1992, p. 86.

Hearne, Betsy, review of *The Heart of the Wood, Bulletin of the Center for Children's Books,* February, 1993, p. 173.

Roback, Diane, and Elizabeth Devereaux, review of *Black, White, Just Right!, Publishers Weekly,* October 25, 1993, p. 62.

Roback and Richard Donahue, review of *The Heart of the Wood, Publishers Weekly,* August 10, 1992, p. 69.

Rochman, Hazel, review of *Black, White, Just Right!, Booklist,* November 1, 1993, p. 528.

For More Information See

PERIODICALS

Booklist, December 1, 1992, p. 674.

Children's Book Review Service, winter supplement, 1993, p. 62.

Kirkus Reviews, November 15, 1993, p. 1460.

* * *

DEMAREST, Chris(topher) L(ynn) 1951-

Personal

Born April 18, 1951, in Hartford, CT; son of Robert (a salesperson) and Shirley (a librarian; maiden name, Johnston) Demarest; married Larkin Dorsey Upson (a finish carpenter), February 2, 1982 (divorced); married Laura L. Gillespie (a travel/tour director), September 26, 1992. *Education:* University of Massachusetts, B.F.A., 1976. *Hobbies and other interests:* Sailing, cycling, music/rock 'n' roll, tennis, horseback riding.

Addresses

Home and office—P.O. Box 86, East Thetford, VT 05043. *Agent*—Liza Pulitzer Voges, Kirchoff/Wohlberg, Inc., 866 United Nations Plaza, New York, NY 10017.

Career

Cartoonist, author, and illustrator of books for children. House painter in Seattle, WA, 1976-77. *Member:* Society of Children's Book Writers and Illustrators.

Awards, Honors

Ford Foundation Grant, 1975; Junior Guild selections, 1982, for *Benedict Finds a Home,* and 1983, for *Clemens' Kingdom;* Kentucky Bluegrass Awards, 1991, for *The Butterfly Jar,* and 1994, for *Bob and Jack;* Colorado Children's Book Award nomination, 1991, for *No Peas for Nellie;* Parents' Choice Award, 1992, for *My Little Red Car; School Library Journal* Best Book, 1994, for *Lindbergh;* Children's Choice Award and Reading Rainbow selection, both 1994, for *Smart Dog.*

Self portrait by Chris L. Demarest

Writings

FOR CHILDREN; SELF-ILLUSTRATED

Benedict Finds a Home, Lothrop, 1982.
Clemens' Kingdom, Lothrop, 1983.
Orville's Odyssey, Simon & Schuster, 1986.
Morton and Sidney, Macmillan, 1987.
No Peas for Nellie, Macmillan, 1988.
The Lunatic Adventure of Kitman and Willy, Simon & Schuster, 1988.
Kitman and Willy at Sea, Simon & Schuster, 1991.
My Little Red Car, Caroline House, 1992.
Lindbergh (biography), Crown, 1993.
My Blue Boat, Harcourt, 1995.

ILLUSTRATOR

Rose Greydanus, *Tree House Fun,* Troll, 1980.
Elizabeth Isele, *Pooks,* Lippincott, 1983.
Betty Jo Stanovich, *Hedgehog and Friends,* Lothrop, 1983.
Stanovich, *Hedgehog Adventures,* Lothrop, 1983.
Sue Alexander, *World Famous Muriel,* Little, Brown, 1984.
Stanovich, *Hedgehog Surprises,* Lothrop, 1984.
Alexander, *World Famous Muriel and the Dragon,* Little, Brown, 1985.
Jeff Moss, *The Butterfly Jar* (poems), Bantam, 1989.
Joanne Oppenheim, *"Not Now!" Said the Cow,* Bantam, 1989.
Andrew Sharmat, *Smedge,* Macmillan, 1989.
Marvin Varori, *I've Got Goose Pimples: And Other Great Expressions,* Morrow, 1990.
(With others) Joanna Cole and Stephanie Calmenson, compilers, *The Scary Book* (stories, poems, and riddles), Morrow, 1991.
David Kirby and Allen Woodman, *The Cows Are Going to Paris,* Caroline House, 1991.
Stephen Krensky, *The Missing Mother Goose,* Doubleday, 1991.
Moss, *The Other Side of the Door* (poems), Bantam, 1991.
Oppenheim, *The Donkey's Tale,* Bantam, 1991.
Bobbye S. Goldstein (editor), *What's on the Menu?* (poems), Viking, 1992.
Jeffie Ross Gordon, *Two Badd Babies,* Boyds Mills Press, 1992.
Moss, *Bob and Jack: A Boy and His Yak,* Bantam, 1992.
Diana Klemin, *How Do You Wrap a Horse?,* Boyds Mills Press, 1993.
Ralph Leemis, *Smart Dog,* Caroline House, 1993.
Oppenheim, *"Uh-oh!" Cawed the Crow,* Bantam, 1993.
N. L. Sharp, *Today I'm Going Fishing With My Dad,* Boyds Mills Press, 1993.
David L. Harrison, *When Cows Come Home,* Boyds Mills Press, 1994.
Susan Karnovsky, *Billy and the Magic String,* Troll, 1994.
Thomas McKean, *Hooray for Grandma Jo!,* Crown, 1994.

Moss, *Hieronymus White: A Bird Who Believed That He Was Always Right,* Ballantine, 1994.

Marvin Terban, *Time to Rhyme: A Rhyming Dictionary,* Boyds Mills Press, 1994.

Nancy Lee Charlton, *Derek's Dog Days,* Harcourt, 1995.

Cynthia DeFelice, *Casey in the Bath,* Farrar, Straus, 1995.

Also illustrator of greeting cards. Contributor to *Atlantic Monthly, Travel and Leisure, Woman's Day, Town and Country, Reader's Digest, Yankee, Highlights for Children,* the *New York Times, New York Daily News,* and the *Boston Globe.* An illustrator of *Free to Be ... a Family,* edited by Marlo Thomas with Christopher Cerf and Letty Cottin Pogrebin.

■ Sidelights

Chris L. Demarest's talents as a children's book author and illustrator have been noted ever since the creator of the greeting-card bird named Benedict produced his first children's book, *Benedict Finds a Home.* Whether it is expressed in text or wordless watercolors, gentle humor is the hallmark of Demarest's work. Demarest once commented that his "motive is pure entertainment" and that he attempts to leave his "readers with a warm smile and the feeling they've been included in the joke."

Demarest's success is the result of years of practice as well as talent and enthusiasm. As a boy growing up in Connecticut and Massachusetts, Demarest loved cartoons and animation. He once told *SATA* that when he "started drawing, the first images were of many of my cartoon heroes." Demarest earned a painting degree from the University of Massachusetts, but, as he has commented, he decided to stop painting seriously because he realized that he "found more enjoyment in dashing off a drawing in minutes than in slaving for weeks over one painting, and even then questioning the result." With his training as a painter and his interest in the human form to guide him, Demarest began to develop his cartooning skills.

A lion statue outside a library becomes curious about what goes on inside the building—and decides to find out—in Demarest's self-illustrated story, *Clemens' Kingdom.*

Demarest launched his career as a cartoonist by creating greeting cards and contributing illustrations to *Town and Country, Reader's Digest, Yankee, Highlights for Children,* the *New York Times, New York Daily News,* and the *Boston Globe.* In his first book, *Benedict Finds a Home,* a bird leaves his crowded nest in search of a new place to live. After trying out a shoe in the park, a trumpet, a statue, and a weathervane, Benedict ends up in his old nest. A critic for *Publishers Weekly* admired the "scenes of unusual beauty" and Benedict's "comic adventures." However Kristi L. Thomas, writing in *School Library Journal,* decided that the book "never quite takes flight."

Clemens' Kingdom tells the story of Clemens, a lion statue who wonders what he is guarding. Clemens leaves his pedestal and ambles inside what turns out to be the library. He settles down in the sunny children's room and reads every book on the shelves. Louise L. Sherman in *School Library Journal* noted that the "whimsical watercolor illustrations" and "simple text" create a "pleasant picture book fantasy." In another imaginative tale, *Orville's Odyssey,* young Orville drops his fishing line into a puddle in the sidewalk while waiting for the bus. A large fish pulls him underwater, and after being snapped at by a crab and nudged by a sea horse, Orville escapes back to the surface in an enormous air bubble and even manages to catch his bus. According to *School Library Journal* contributor Lisa Castillo, the characters in this wordless work "radiate with life."

"Children will delight" in *Morton and Sidney,* wrote Jennifer Smith in *School Library Journal.* Morton is a little boy who finds that the monsters in his closet have evicted Sidney, a pink monster with green horns. Morton tries to find Sidney a new home under a chair and in the laundry basket, but he soon realizes that the monster is too big. When Morton and Sidney dress up as a large, scary monster, Sidney is finally allowed back into the closet. A critic for *Publishers Weekly* enjoyed the moral of the story: "Think twice before rejecting something—what takes its place may be worse."

No Peas for Nellie begins when Nellie refuses to eat her peas. As she tells her mother what she would rather eat—a spider, a hunk of wart hog, and even an elephant, Demarest's illustrations show her stalking these animals and preparing to eat them. Ants on these pages carry peas away, and by the end of the book, readers find that Nellie has eaten up her peas! Ann A. Flowers, a reviewer for *Horn Book,* described the illustrations as "ridiculously funny" and enjoyed the "horrified" expressions of the animals as Nellie confronts them.

The Lunatic Adventure of Kitman and Willy and *Kitman and Willy at Sea* feature Kitman, a cat, and Willy, a mouse. In the second book, the pair improvise a boat and sail to an island where a hunter is rounding up all the animals. The cat and mouse come up with a plan to rescue the animals and manage to teach the hunter a lesson. Debra S. Gold noted in *School Library Journal* that "each page is full of captivating details" and recommended the book as "a prize selection for summertime story hours." In the opinion of a critic for *Publishers Weekly,* "children will want to cast off again with this beguiling crew."

With his red toy car in hand, a little boy imagines future adventures in *My Little Red Car.* He motors up mountains, lunches in Paris, and drives to the North Pole. According to a *Publishers Weekly* critic, the "charmingly skewed vision" of *My Little Red Car* is "illustrated with warm zippiness." At the end of the book, the boy cuddles up with his car to sleep.

Demarest has written and illustrated one work of nonfiction for children, *Lindbergh.* This biography describes Charles Lindbergh's youth with text and watercolor pictures. Readers learn how Lindbergh becomes an excellent mechanic, walks on the wings of airplanes, and flies dangerous U.S. airmail routes. In the words of Barbara Peklo Abrahams in *School Library Journal,* "The clear prose relates the pertinent facts briefly and with verve," and the illustrations are "crisp and light filled." Notes about Lindbergh's later life along with sources for more information are included in this book.

Children who wonder how Demarest develops his stories will want to know that "the visuals are worked out first—usually in storyboard fashion to allow an overall view." As Demarest once explained to *SATA,* "Seldom is the ending known. What happens is a character is born and sent upon an adventure which keeps developing from page to page. In other words the story line is very much a puzzle which has to be assembled before the story works."

Demarest emphasizes the role of physical activity in his work. He once explained to *SATA* that sports and "cartooning go hand-in-hand" because his work "involves moving figures," and "having an understanding of body motion helps to translate that to paper. Most of my cartoons are captionless so this too is where motion comes in handy." Demarest also told *SATA* that sports are important because they provide a "physical release.... The longer I'm stationary, the shorter my attention-span and thus my work becomes demented."

■ Works Cited

Abrahams, Barbara Peklo, review of *Lindbergh, School Library Journal,* October, 1993, p. 117.

Review of *Benedict Finds a Home, Publishers Weekly,* February 19, 1982, p. 65.

Castillo, Lisa, review of *Orville's Odyssey, School Library Journal,* January, 1987, pp. 61-62.

Demarest's simple, carefree drawings complement Jeff Moss's *The Butterfly Jar,* a goofy yet perceptive verse collection about the lighter side of childhood.

Flowers, Ann A., review of *No Peas for Nellie, Horn Book,* July/August, 1988, p. 478.

Gold, Debra S., review of *Kitman and Willy at Sea, School Library Journal,* August, 1991, p. 144.

Review of *Kitman and Willy at Sea, Publishers Weekly,* May 31, 1991, pp. 74-75.

Review of *Morton and Sidney, Publishers Weekly,* March 13, 1987, p. 82.

Review of *My Little Red Car, Publishers Weekly,* August 17, 1992, p. 498.

Sherman, Louise L., review of *Clemens' Kingdom, School Library Journal,* September, 1983, p. 104.

Smith, Jennifer, review of *Morton and Sidney, School Library Journal,* April, 1987, p. 80.

Thomas, Kristi L., review of *Benedict Finds a Home, School Library Journal,* August, 1982, p. 96.

■ For More Information See

PERIODICALS

Publishers Weekly, May 20, 1983, p. 236; January 16, 1987, p. 73; January 16, 1995, p. 454.

School Library Journal, November, 1992, pp. 68-69.

* * *

DEUKER, Carl 1950-

■ Personal

Born October 26, 1950, in San Francisco, CA; son of John and Marie (maiden name, Milligan) Deuker; married Anne Mitchell (a teacher), 1978; children: Marian. *Education:* University of California at Berkeley, B.A., 1972; University of Washington, M.A., 1974;

University of California at Los Angeles, teaching certificate, 1976. *Politics:* Democrat.

■ Addresses

Home—2827 Northwest 62nd St., Seattle, WA 98107.

■ Career

Saint Luke School, Seattle, WA, teacher, 1977-90; Northshore School District, Botzell, WA, teacher, 1991—. *Seattle Sun* (daily newspaper), film and book critic, 1980-85. *Member:* Authors Guild, Authors League of America, Phi Beta Kappa.

■ Awards, Honors

South Carolina Young Adult Book Award, 1992, for *On the Devil's Court; Heart of a Champion* and *On the Devil's Court* were both named to ALA Best Books for Young Adults list.

■ Writings

On the Devil's Court, Little, Brown, 1988.
Heart of a Champion, Little, Brown, 1993.

Also author of *Playing Games,* 1995.

■ Sidelights

Carl Deuker told *SATA* that he is often asked by his readers if he writes sports novels for young adults because he was an outstanding athlete. "The answer is—not really," he confessed. "As a high school student, I made a few teams, but I did more sitting on the bench than playing. In college I played on intramural teams. But it wasn't those experiences that laid the groundwork for my becoming a writer.

"Instead I think I was on my way to becoming a writer with the imaginary games I played alone between the ages of eight and twelve. For hour after hour, the dart board in my garage was the strike zone, and I was Juan Marichal baffling the Dodgers. Or the pillow on the sofa was the basketball hoop, the walnut was the basketball, and I was Rick Barry, draining twenty-footers to beat the Lakers. I played football games with marbles, baseball games with clothespins, golf with hula hoops. But really I played those games—literally thousands of them—in my mind."

In Deuker's first book, *On the Devil's Court,* Joe Faust, a high school student with a nearly obsessive interest in basketball, moves with his family from the East Coast to the West. Believing that the move will further his basketball career, Joe convinces his parents to let him attend a large public school with a strong sports program. However, Joe's attendance at a drunken party leads to a run-in with police, after which his parents insist that he enroll at a small private school. One evening in the gym, an angry Joe, who has just been demoted to the junior varsity, hits every shot he takes.

A high school basketball player fears that the Devil is responsible for his success on the court in Carl Deuker's first novel.

Inspired by his recent reading of Christopher Marlowe's *Dr. Faustus,* Joe offers himself to the Devil in exchange for continued prowess and a perfect season. No sooner is the promise made than does Joe begin to star on the varsity team, leading his school to the state finals. With each victory, Joe becomes increasingly anxious about his fate. Has he really sold himself to the Devil? In light of his success, Joe wonders if his father's untimely heart attack isn't an early payment exacted by the Devil. Not until Joe's team wins without him does he realize that the season belongs to his team, and that he has made a bargain with no one but himself.

In a *School Library Journal* review, Gerry Larson called *On the Devil's Court* a "fine addition to sports fiction," and praised Deuker's engaging mixture of suspense, family drama, and athletic competition. *Publishers Weekly* reviewers Kimberly Olsen Fakih and Diane Roback considered Deuker's characters "well-rounded" and concluded that the book was a "vivid contemporary morality play." *Horn Book* reviewer Nancy Vasilakis asserted that young readers will enjoy both the story and

Joe's ability to deal squarely with his parents by the book's end, "whether or not they fully comprehend what developmental steps were taken to achicve this measure of independence."

In *Heart of a Champion,* Deuker used the sport of baseball to examine the lives of two adolescent boys. Seth has yet to come to terms with his father's death when he meets Jimmy, a budding young baseball star. Inspired by Jimmy's intense pursuit of the game, Seth begins playing baseball, and the competitive nature of the game increases his confidence in other aspects of his life. Seth's grades improve, and, with his mother's help, he begins to address his father's death. Behind their shared success in baseball, however, is Jimmy's father, an alcoholic who drives his son toward perfection on the diamond. He proves a tragic role-model for Jimmy, who, as high school baseball star, dies in an alcohol-related traffic accident. Seth must then deal with the loss of his closest friend, as well as the complexity of the father-son relationship that foreshadowed Jimmy's death.

A *Horn Book* reviewer described the book as a "sensitive, moving portrait of adolescence combined with dramatic sports action." *Bulletin of the Center for Children's Books* reviewer Betsy Hearne praised the detailed relationship between the boys, but found the book's examination of the "balance between talent and discipline" even more strikingly realistic. Jack Forman speculated that the "well-paced novel will involve many readers" in a *School Library Journal* review.

"There's a big difference between being alone and being lonely," Deuker concluded. "I was alone often as a child, rarely lonely. Those imaginary games and all that time I 'wasted' playing them—in those hours I was becoming a writer."

■ Works Cited

Fakih, Kimberly Olsen, and Diane Roback, review of *On the Devil's Court, Publishers Weekly,* November 11, 1988, p. 60.

Forman, Jack, review of *Heart of a Champion, School Library Journal,* June, 1993, p. 126.

Hearne, Betsy, review of *Heart of a Champion, Bulletin of the Center for Children's Books,* September, 1993, p. 7.

Review of *Heart of a Champion, Horn Book,* May/June, 1993, p. 337.

Larson, Gerry, review of *On the Devil's Court, School Library Journal,* January, 1989, p. 92.

Vasilakis, Nancy, review of *On the Devil's Court, Horn Book,* March/April, 1989, p. 216.

■ For More Information See

PERIODICALS

Booktalker, September, 1989, p. 11.

Kirkus Reviews, January 1, 1989, pp. 47-48.

Publishers Weekly, May 31, 1993, pp. 56-57.

Voice of Youth Advocates, April, 1989, p. 27.

DONALDSON, Julia 1948-

■ Personal

Born September 16, 1948, in London, England; daughter of James (a geneticist) and Elizabeth (Ede) Shields; married Malcolm Donaldson (a pediatrician), September 30, 1972; children: Hamish, Alastair, Jesse. *Education:* Bristol University, degree in drama and French, 1970. *Politics:* "Labour voter." *Religion:* Agnostic.

■ Addresses

Home—2 Chapelton Ave., Glasgow G61 2RE, Scotland.

■ Career

Writer.

■ Writings

A Squash and a Squeeze, illustrated by Axel Scheffler, McElderry, 1993.

Birthday Surprise (play), Ginn (London), 1994.

Names and Games (play), Ginn, 1995.

Author of songs, scripts, and stories for BBC television and radio (mainly children's programs). Author of unpublished musicals, *King Grunt's Cake* and *Pirate on the Pier.*

JULIA DONALDSON

Sidelights

Julia Donaldson told *SATA:* "I am principally a songwriter, performing my own material (for adults and children) with my guitar-playing husband, Malcolm, and also writing songs for other performers on children's T.V. and radio. My book *A Squash and a Squeeze* started life as a song on a television programme. I also visit a lot of schools and libraries (doing songs, drama, and storytelling), and have written two musicals for children (unpublished but often performed), *King Grunt's Cake* and *Pirate on the Pier. Birthday Surprise* and *Names and Games* are both short plays for schoolchildren to read and/or perform."

For More Information See

PERIODICALS

Children's Book Review Service, August, 1993, p. 158.
Horn Book Guide, fall, 1993, p. 325.
London Times, November, 1993, p. 45.
Los Angeles Times Book Review, May 2, 1993, p. 7.
Publishers Weekly, April 26, 1993, p. 78.
School Library Journal, April, 1993, p. 95.*

* * *

DRAKE, Jane 1954-

JANE DRAKE

Personal

Born April 19, 1954, in Toronto, Ontario, Canada; daughter of H. J. M. (a physician) and Kay (a nurse and homemaker; maiden name, Gourlay) Barnett; married Jim Drake (a neurosurgeon), September 11, 1976; children: Stephanie, Brian, Madeline. *Education:* University of Western Ontario, B.A. (with honors), 1976.

Addresses

Home—125 Rose Park Dr., Toronto, Ontario, Canada M4T 1R6.

Career

Author of nonfiction books for children. *Member:* Canadian Society of Children's Authors, Illustrators, and Performers.

Writings

(With sister, Ann Love) *Take Action: An Environmental Book for Kids,* illustrated by Pat Cupples, Kids Can Press, 1992, Tambourine Books, 1993.

(With Ann Love) *The Kids' Cottage Book,* illustrated by Heather Collins, Kids Can Press, 1993, published as *The Kids' Summer Handbook,* Ticknor & Fields, 1994.

Work in Progress

A series of four first information books on the resource industries: mining, forestry, fishing, and farming, coauthored with Ann Love; *The Kids' Campfire and Song Book,* coauthored with Love.

Sidelights

Jane Drake told *SATA:* "I grew up as the third child in a Toronto family. With an older sister and sandwiched between two brothers, I couldn't be spoiled. There was nothing very unconventional about my parents or their approach to child rearing, but they were unusual and, inadvertently, gave me a different sort of upbringing.

"My mother is a wonderful storyteller. She spent many evenings creating elaborate stories for me and my brother Ian. We would impatiently say, 'get reading, Mom' when she paused to think, and howl in protest when it was time to go to sleep. I became intrigued with the details that made the story interesting. I started to observe people and situations and often saw the humour or the novelty in an event. In grade seven I prowled the Toronto subways with my friend Stephanie, eavesdropping and imitating the characters I saw. Real life was not enough and, from a young age, I dabbled in musicals and theatre—having roles as diverse as Mary Poppins, Lady Macbeth, and even Janis Joplin.

"My father is a naturalist and adventurer. He has a rich fund of scientific knowledge that he shares either in the field or around the supper table. I learned from him by osmosis, a love of nature slowly seeping into my blood. He made me aware of the changing of seasons, especially the coming of spring. A walk never gets me just from one place to another. There is always something to be on the lookout for: a moth egg case, a wood duck, or a deer.

My father also passed on his love of literature to me. There is a constant flow of books between our homes.

"I spent the summers of my youth exploring North America with my family. I never went to Disneyland or to conventional attractions but saw my first wolverine in the garbage dump at Lake Louise, Alberta. I also explored the Labrador coast by boat looking for whales, rescued beached squid by moonlight, slept in a fishing shack and sought the elusive puffin on the islands off Witless Bay, Newfoundland. Each trip's success was graded according to what wildlife was seen and the novelty of the accommodation.

"When I was five my parents bought a cabin in the woods north of Toronto. Here I and my brother made our own fun. We constructed forts in the goldenrod fields or made them out of snow; caught salamanders and frogs; went berry picking to make pies; swam in the pond along with leeches and snapping turtles; tramped through the woods looking for orchids; chopped and carted wood for the woodstove or fireplace; followed game trails and identified tracks or scat in the snow; raised vegetables and monarch butterflies; etc. Not every child's dream—no T.V. or wild parties—but grist for the mill for a future writer (especially when it came to writing *The Kids' Cottage Book*).

"I attended the University of Western Ontario in the early 70s. I applied to the English department but when I got a blank timetable, crossed the road to the Social Science Building and ended up with an honours history degree, with options in English. It was a lucky mistake—I spent my third and fourth years working in the Social Science Computing Laboratory as a research assistant for one of my history professors. Here I was exposed to the wonders of the computer and learned how to use a library. Both skills have been very useful in my writing career.

"I married at twenty-two and joined my husband for three years in Ireland where he pursued his medical training. I was designated an 'alien' by the immigration authorities but was able to get a work permit through my heritage—my grandfather was born in Bray, outside Dublin. I found work in the storeroom of an Irish handicraft store for twenty pounds a week ($40.00) where the tourists objected to my lack of Irish accent. I then became an accounting clerk where my salary varied depending on how well my boss did on the horses. In both jobs I delighted in meeting Irish people, found their local customs and dialects intriguing, and made some lifelong friends. Together with my husband, Jim, I travelled all over the island in an old banger of a car nicknamed the 'ogre.' Every day someone asked me what part of America I came from, to which I would reply I was not American, but Canadian. The ensuing argument was finally resolved by suggesting it was like calling an Irishman 'English.' I recorded my observations in long diary-like letters that I sent home to my family.

Written with Drake's sister, Ann Love, this book uses an energetic approach to help kids find ways to improve the environment.

"I returned to Canada expecting our first child and spent the next ten years on a travelling roadshow, moving from London to Kingston, to Toronto, to Paris, and finally settling in Toronto. Each stop provided opportunities for making new friends and for study. I always took night classes to provide a change of scene from the diaper pail at home. Among others I took tyoping (oops), tailoring, writing for the children's market, and in Paris, the Cordon Bleu cooking course.

"I made a very conscious decision to remain the prime caregiver for my kids. With my husband immersed in a gruelling post-graduate residency I remained at home. Here began my interest in childhood education. I was a founding parent of the local nursery and daycare centre. As president I negotiated grants to raise the salaries of the teachers, initiated the use of the computer in an enrichment program, and struggled through the exponential growth of the centre. I was active as a fundraiser—even hula danced to help raise funds for a new playground.

"I was first published in 1972 in the Whitehorse *Star.* Between babies I free-lanced for McLean Hunter but never enjoyed journalistic writing.

"I and my sister, Ann Love, joined forces in 1989 to become a writing team. Together we wrote *Take Action,* published in February 1992. After the initial brainstorming, we divided the book in half and retreated to our separate computers to write. Each weekend we got together with between three and six children, three dogs, two cats, and a coffee pot and reviewed each other's work. I have been asked repeatedly how I manage to write with my sister. The answer is to be friends, to know each other's strengths, and to have a sense of humour. I never take offense at my sister's red ink nor does Ann object to my standard comment of 'wool' in the margin of the manuscript.

"When not writing, I enjoy giving book talks about the writing process or the content of *Take Action* in schools and libraries. I also volunteer in my kids' school as a fundraiser, slowpitch coach, library assistant, giver of nature walks, chauffeur to soccer games, and coordinator of special interest groups and events such as Terry Fox Run. My husband is trying, unsuccessfully, to train me to say NO."

■ For More Information See

PERIODICALS

Booklist, April 1, 1994, p. 1438.
Children's Book Review Service, June, 1994, p. 128.
Five Owls, May, 1994, pp. 99, 101.
Kirkus Reviews, May 15, 1994, p. 697.
Publishers Weekly, May 30, 1994, p. 58.
School Library Journal, June, 1994, p. 137.

* * *

DUNCOMBE, Frances (Riker) 1900-1994

OBITUARY NOTICE—See index for *SATA* sketch: Born July 11, 1900, in Bernardsville, NJ; died after a long illness, June 27, 1994, in Briarcliff Manor, NY. Author and community activist. Duncombe was educated at Bryn Mawr College and the New York School of Fine and Applied Arts before she married and began raising a family. A longtime resident of the suburban New York county of Westchester, she was active in civic affairs there. She belonged to the Katonah Women's Civic Club and the Bedford Historical Society, and in 1975 bestowed forty-eight acres of land to the Mount Holly Nature Preserve. Her first two children's books, *Hoo De Witt* and *High Hurdles,* were published in 1941, followed by several more over the next few decades, including *Eemi, the Story of a Clown, The Quetzal Feather,* and *Summer of the Burning.* Duncombe was also a contributor to a local history of her area called *Katonah: A History of a New York Village and Its People.*

OBITUARIES AND OTHER SOURCES:

PERIODICALS

New York Times, July 7, 1994, p. D19.

* * *

DUNNE, Marie
See CLARK, Ann Nolan

F

TERRY FARISH

FARISH, Terry 1947-

■ Personal

Born June 8, 1947, in Waterbury, CT; daughter of Clifford and Eleanor (Bronson) Dickerson; married Stephen Farish (a U.S. Air Force officer), 1970; children: Elizabeth. *Education:* Texas Woman's University, B.S., 1969; California State University, M.L.S., 1976; Antioch University, M.A., 1985. *Politics:* Democrat.

■ Addresses

Home—10 Courtland St., Nashua, NH 03060. *Agent*—Marilyn Marlow, Curtis Brown Ltd., 10 Astor Place, New York, NY 10003.

■ Career

Ralston Public Library, Ralston, NE, director, 1976-82; Leominster Public Library, Leominster, MA, head of children's services, 1986-90; Cambodian Mutual Assistance Association, Lowell, MA, director of Young Parent Program, 1990-91; *Choice* magazine, political science editor, 1993—. Worked for American Red Cross in Vietnam, 1969-70. *Member:* Society of Children's Book Writers and Illustrators, National Writers Union, American Library Association.

■ Writings

Why I'm Already Blue (young adult novel), Greenwillow, 1989.
Shelter for a Seabird (young adult novel), Greenwillow, 1990.
Flower Shadows (adult novel), Morrow, 1992.
If the Tiger (adult novel), Steerforth, 1995.

■ Work in Progress

Be Kind to Animals, a young adult novel.

■ Sidelights

Terry Farish's first novel, *Why I'm Already Blue,* examines the complex feelings of an adolescent girl whose parents are on the verge of divorce. Feeling as if the burden of family stability lies on her shoulders, Lucy Purcell begins to retreat into herself when her older sister leaves for nursing school. She also distances herself from her closest childhood friend, Gus, who has muscular dystrophy. When Lucy's sister brings a baby from the hospital to the family cottage, Lucy begins to assume some responsibilities for the child's care. Finally, the entire family, along with Gus and his mother, meet at the cabin to celebrate Thanksgiving. At the meal's conclusion Lucy's parents announce their separation, but a newly mature, independent Lucy takes the news in stride, and looks forward to new beginnings.

School Library Journal contributor Bonnie L. Raasch noted that the novel's mood is occasionally quite serious, but that Lucy's reaction to her parents' break-up shows that "sometimes separation is better than staying together." A *Publishers Weekly* reviewer concluded that mood figures more importantly than plot in the novel, which "is about the collision of emotions rather than a simple coming-of-age tale."

With *Shelter for a Seabird* Farish addresses a range of issues, including teen pregnancy, loss of community, and the desire for sympathetic companionship. Sixteen-year-old Andrea has just given up her baby for adoption when she returns to her parents' home. Despite the radical changes that have taken place in her life, Andrea's family refuses to acknowledge her past, and act as if nothing has happened. Andrea faces a similar crisis of understanding among her friends, who are ill-prepared to appreciate the emotional depth of her recent experiences. Then Andrea meets Swede, an AWOL soldier who listens without judgment to Andrea's account of her life. Together, Andrea and Swede come to share a caring relationship that transcends both their histories and the eroding quality of the life surrounding them.

Contemplative readers will appreciate the novel's realism, asserted a *Publishers Weekly* reviewer. "The writing is flawless," wrote Judie Porter in a *School Library Journal* review, "but the mood is sustained almost to the point of sullenness." Porter concluded, however, that the book would be valued by teens in situations similar to Andrea's.

Farish is also the author of an adult novel, *Flower Shadows,* about the horrors faced by female Red Cross volunteers during the Vietnam War. The main character's "breathless innocence makes this story a particularly heartbreaking and memorable one," declared a *Kirkus Reviews* critic.

Farish commented: "*Shelter for a Seabird* chronicles a young girl's grieving and healing after she gives a baby up for adoption. The novel is set on Shelter Island off Long Island, which is my family's home. *Flower Shadows* draws on a murder which occurred in Cu Chi, Vietnam, where I was stationed for a time with the American Red Cross."

"*If the Tiger* is the story of the impact of war on two young women—one Cambodian, one American—whose fathers fought in Asia. I have been very interested in the Asian-American experience and began collecting Asian-American children's stories when I was a children's librarian in Leominster, Massachusetts.

"I am currently writing a dog story with all the love for a dog named Spy that I could not have as a girl. It is also a story about political issues concerning rights and class in a small New England town, seen through the eyes of twelve-year-old Siobhan Hannah."

Works Cited

Review of *Flower Shadows, Kirkus Reviews,* October 15, 1991, pp. 1303-1304.

Porter, Judie, review of *Shelter for a Seabird, School Library Journal,* November, 1990, p. 138.

Raasch, Bonnie L., review of *Why I'm Already Blue, School Library Journal,* October, 1989, p. 117.

Review of *Shelter for a Seabird, Publishers Weekly,* September 14, 1990, p. 128.

Review of *Why I'm Already Blue, Publishers Weekly,* July 14, 1989, p. 80.

For More Information See

PERIODICALS

Booklist, October 1, 1989, p. 347; November 15, 1990, p. 654; January 1, 1992, p. 810.

Book Report, January, 1990, p. 46; March, 1991, p. 42.

Children's Book Review Service, February, 1990, p. 78; January, 1991, p. 57.

Horn Book Guide, July, 1989, p. 77; July, 1990, p. 87.

Junior Bookshelf, April, 1990, p. 97.

Kirkus Reviews, November 1, 1989, p. 1591.

Library Journal, May 1, 1992, p. 144.

Publishers Weekly, October 18, 1991, p. 54.

Times (London), April 14, 1990.

Voice of Youth Advocates, April, 1989, p. 29; October, 1989, p. 212.

* * *

FARR, Diana 1930-
(Diana Pullein-Thompson)

Personal

Born October 1, 1930, in Wimbledon, Surrey, England; daughter of Harold James (an army officer; later secretary to Headmasters' Conference) and Joanna (an author; maiden name, Cannan) Pullein-Thompson; married Dennis Larry Ashwell Farr, CBE (an author and former art gallery director), 1959; children: Benedict Edward, Joanna Helen. *Education:* Educated privately and at Wychwood School, Oxford, England. *Religion:* Church of England.

Addresses

Home—Orchard Hill, Swan Barn Rd., Haslemere, Surrey GU27 2HY, England.

Career

Writer. Worked variously as a breaker and schooler of horses, a riding teacher, a literary agent, and a publishers' reader; Rosica Colin Ltd. (literary agency), London, England, staff member, 1950-52; Faith Press, London, part-time editor, 1957-59; Grove Riding Schools, Oxfordshire, England, director for fifteen years. *Member:* PEN, Society of Authors (London), Authors and Publishers Lending Right Association (committee member,

DIANA FARR

1959-65), Children's Writer's Group (founding member).

Writings

FOR CHILDREN; FICTION; UNDER NAME DIANA PULLEIN-THOMPSON

(With sisters, Christine and Josephine Pullein-Thompson) *It Began with Picotee,* illustrated by Rosemary Robinson, A. & C. Black, 1946.
I Wanted a Pony, illustrated by Anne Bullen, Collins, 1946.
Three Ponies and Shannan, illustrated by Bullen, Collins, 1947.
The Pennyfields, Collins, 1949.
A Pony to School, illustrated by Bullen, Collins, 1950.
A Pony for Sale, illustrated by Sheila Rose, Collins, 1951.
Janet Must Ride, illustrated by Mary Gernat, Collins, 1953.
Horses at Home, and Friends Must Part, illustrated by Rose, Collins, 1954.
Riding with the Lyntons, illustrated by Rose, Collins, 1956.
The Boy and the Donkey, illustrated by Shirley Hughes, Criterion, 1958, published as *The Donkey Race,* Armada, 1970.
The Secret Dog, illustrated by Geraldine Spence, Collins, 1959.
The Hidden River, illustrated by Rose, Hamish Hamilton, 1960.
The Boy Who Came to Stay, illustrated by Alan Breese, Faith Press, 1960.
The Battle of Clapham Common, Parrish, 1962.
Bindi Must Go, illustrated by Rose, Harrap, 1962.
The Hermit's Horse, Collins, 1974.
(With C. and J. Pullein-Thompson) *Black Beauty's Clan,* Brockhampton Press, 1975, McGraw, 1980.
Ponies in the Valley, Collins, 1976.
(With C. and J. Pullein-Thompson) *Black Beauty's Family,* illustrated by Elisabeth Grant, Hodder & Stoughton, 1978, McGraw, 1980.
Ponies on the Trail, Collins, 1979.
Ponies in Peril, Armada, 1979.
Cassidy in Danger, Dent, 1979, revised edition published as *This Pony Is Dangerous,* 1990.
Only a Pony, Collins, 1980.
The Pony Seekers, Severn House, 1981.
A Foal for Candy, Severn House, 1982.
(With C. and J. Pullein-Thompson) *Black Beauty's Family Two,* Beaver, 1982.
A Pony Found, Severn House, 1983.

FOR CHILDREN; NONFICTION; UNDER NAME DIANA PULLEIN-THOMPSON

Riding for Children, Foyle, 1957.
(Editor) *True Horse and Pony Stories,* Armada, 1976.
Dear Pup: Letters to a Young Dog (humor), illustrated by William Rushton, Barrie & Jenkins, 1988.

OTHER; UNDER NAME DIANA FARR

Gilbert Cannan: A Georgian Prodigy, Chatto & Windus, 1978.
Five at Ten: Prime Ministers' Consorts since 1957, Deutsch, 1985.
Choosing (adult novel), Bodley Head, 1988.

Contributor to *Daily Telegraph, Bookseller, Author, Library World, Young Elizabethan, Riding, Good Housekeeping, Writers' Monthly,* and other periodicals. Several of her works have been published in foreign editions.

Work in Progress

A joint memoir of her childhood, with sisters Christine and Josephine Pullein-Thompson.

Sidelights

Diana Farr was born into a family of writers. Her mother, father, and siblings wrote, and, as she once commented: "Sometimes when I was growing up four of us might be sitting around the same table working on our books." Farr began writing stories for children when she was just fourteen years old. Since Farr and her sisters Christine and Josephine published *It Began with Picotee* in 1946, she has provided young horse-lovers with a variety of novels, written under the name Diana Pullein-Thompson. The first published novel she wrote on her own, *I Wanted a Pony,* combines her knowledge of horses with a keen grasp of family dynamics, and has been popular with readers for many years.

Cassidy in Danger exemplifies Farr's best later fiction for young people. When Katerina's mother departs for

Russia to visit the father Katie has never met, the girl has adventures of her own. Katie stays with her godmother and befriends a pony in a nearby field. When she finds out that the pony bucks, injures potential riders, and is to be killed, she works to save him. As she discovers the history of the ex-circus pony, she begins to resolve her own family problems. B. Clark in *Junior Bookshelf* states that *Cassidy in Danger* is "quite an enjoyable story," especially for "mad-about-pony" teenagers, while Linda Yeatman writes in *Twentieth-Century Children's Writers* that the book "is perhaps [the author's] best."

Readers who have enjoyed Farr's pony stories will appreciate the books in the *Black Beauty* series (based on Anna Sewell's *Black Beauty*), written with Farr's sisters. These anthologies follow up on Sewell's 1877 classic by telling the stories of various relations of Sewell's mistreated horse. The historical details the horses relate make the stories interesting, according to *Growing Point* critic Margery Fisher, and the authors "use the animal autobiography confidently and without self-consciousness." In addition, the observations of the horses "paint an interesting picture of the social conditions of the time," *Junior Bookshelf* writer D. A. Young notes. While *School Library Journal* contributor Wendy Delett finds the narratives do "a fairly good job of continuing the technique of horse-as-author," she feels that the stories "do not measure up to the much stronger original" due to some overly human observations. But Fisher concludes in another *Growing Point* review that by using the horse's point of view to narrate their tales, the Pullein-Thompsons "invoke the spirit and intention of Anna Sewell."

Fans should know, however, that Farr is known for more than her horse stories. *The Hidden River, The Secret Dog,* and *The Boy and the Donkey* are fine examples of Farr's other work for young people, involving themes of loneliness, peer pressure, and dealing with poverty, and often set in an urban landscape. A novel for adults, *Choosing,* has been described by *Times Literary Supplement* reviewer Frances Sellers as retaining "some of the pleasing features of children's fiction: a gripping plot and sympathetic protagonist." As Yeatman notes, "For those who have read her books . . . the story tends to live on for a while after it has been finished, as is the way with all good books. This is because she really writes about people, and people situations, not just about ponies and riding situations."

Farr continues to write. As she once remarked, "Writing is a lonely profession, but for me it is almost as necessary as breathing. So I must go on. There is no way out. And often when my imagination runs ahead of me it can bring hours of great happiness."

■ Works Cited

Clark, B., review of *Cassidy in Danger, Junior Bookshelf,* June, 1980, p. 146.

Delett, Wendy, review of *Black Beauty's Family, School Library Journal,* April, 1981, p. 130.

Fisher, Margery, review of *Black Beauty's Clan, Growing Point,* November, 1975, p. 2749.

Fisher, Margery, review of *Black Beauty's Family, Growing Point,* November, 1978, pp. 3407-3408.

Sellers, Frances, "Between the Wars," *Times Literary Supplement,* February 5, 1988, p. 133.

Yeatman, Linda, "Diana Pullein-Thompson," *Twentieth-Century Children's Writers,* 3rd edition, St. James Press, 1989, pp. 802-803.

Young, D. A., review of *Black Beauty's Family, Junior Bookshelf,* February, 1979, pp. 58-59.

■ For More Information See

PERIODICALS

New Statesman, February 3, 1978, pp. 157-8.

Times Educational Supplement, December 23, 1988, p. 20.

Times Literary Supplement, February 10, 1978.

* * *

FILIPOVIC, Zlata 1980-

■ Personal

Born December 3, 1980; daughter of Malik (a lawyer) and Alica (a chemist) Filipovic. *Education:* Attends school in Paris. *Hobbies and other interests:* Piano, tennis.

■ Addresses

Home—Paris, France. *Agent*—Susanna Lea, Editions Robert Laffont/Fixot, 24 Avenue Marceau, Paris 75008, France.

■ Career

Student and diarist. Has given numerous interviews and made television appearances.

■ Awards, Honors

Person of the Week, ABC News, 1993.

■ Writings

Zlata's Diary: A Child's Life in Sarajevo, introduction by Janine di Giovanni, translated with notes by Christina Pribichevich-Zoric, Viking, 1994 (revised from the original, published in Croatia by UNICEF, 1993).

Zlata's Diary has been translated into numerous languages.

■ Adaptations

Film rights for *Zlata's Diary* have been sold to Universal Pictures.

■ Sidelights

When eleven-year-old Zlata Filipovic first began to keep a diary in late 1991, she had no idea that the world would be invited to read it or that it would create controversy. Within a few months, however, Zlata's "normal" life as a Bosnian girl of mixed ethnic heritage in Sarajevo was destroyed by a war no one could seem to stop, and the entries in her diary described violence, death, and suffering. After UNICEF and a French publisher discovered her diary, it was published and Zlata's family was evacuated to Paris. Although Zlata was just thirteen years old, *Zlata's Diary* was an international bestseller and she was interviewed by American television networks. Comparisons were made between her life and the life of Anne Frank, the Dutch Jewish Nazi victim and author of *The Diary of a Young Girl.*

These comparisons angered many people who felt that Zlata's writing was not in the same league as Anne Frank's. They also pointed out that the latter died in a concentration camp, and criticized the advertising promotions that drove the comparisons between the two. Judith Viorst, writing in *Washington Post Book World,* felt that, despite the controversy, *Zlata's Diary* should be taken seriously. Anne Frank's diary, the reviewer explained, "has become a classic not because she suffered but because she transmuted that suffering into art." Viorst asserted that we should read *Zlata's Diary* "not as literature but as a reminder—it seems we still need one—of the toll war exacts on the world's most vulnerable citizens."

Zlata began her diary in the fall of 1991 before Sarajevo was besieged. Her life at that time was relatively calm. As the only child of a well-to-do family, her days were filled with school, piano lessons, tennis, parties, and occasional holidays. Like many young people in the United States, she enjoyed MTV, *Murphy Brown,* and Madonna. Although the threat of war began to cast a shadow over Sarajevo, Zlata did not worry about politics. It was not until the city of Dubrovnik was destroyed, her father served time in the peace reserve, and a gas shortage ensued that she realized something was seriously wrong. Remembering how Anne Frank, who lived in hiding with her family for two years in Amsterdam before the Nazis sent them to a death camp, called her diary "Kitty," Zlata decided to give her diary a name: "I've decided to call you Mimmy."

By early April, Zlata's world of school, parties, and tennis was vanishing. She couldn't concentrate on her homework because she could hear gunfire and felt that "something" was coming, "something very bad." By the end of April, she began to lose friends who fled by bus for distant towns. "Everybody has gone. I'm left with no friends." Then a storm of shelling and gunfire began

Zlata Filipovic with her parents

pounding Zlata's neighborhood. The family was forced to hide in the cellar, which was "ugly, dark, smelly," and listen to "the pounding shells, the shooting, the thundering noise overhead." Zlata realized that the "awful cellar was the only place that could save our lives. Suddenly, it started to look almost warm and nice."

Zlata's new world was one in which "no one and nothing" was "normal." She witnessed the destruction of her city on the television and often first-hand. Friends and neighbors who had remained in Sarajevo began to die. She wrote on May 7, 1992, "Today a shell fell on the park in front of my house, the park where I used to play and sit with my girlfriends. A lot of people were hurt. AND NINA IS DEAD. A piece of shrapnel lodged in her brain and she died.... I cry and wonder why."

It was June when the electricity went out. The television went black, the food in the freezer began to defrost, and the stove was useless. Zlata was forced to stay at home and live "in misery." Zlata wrote to Mimmy that she was a "schoolgirl without a school," a "child without games, without friends, without the sun, without birds, without nature, without fruit, without chocolate or sweets, with just a little powdered milk." During the two years she wrote, Zlata faced other hardships. She outgrew her clothes and had to search the deserted apartments of her friends to find things to fit her. She watched the trees in the park fall as they were cut for firewood. The canary and cat she depended on for companionship died. Her father developed a hernia, and her cousin was shot and killed by a sniper.

Zlata, however, was fortunate among children in Sarajevo. In October, 1992, UNICEF (the United Nations Children's Fund) discovered Zlata's diary. Zlata explained to Mimmy that she had heard that UNICEF wanted to publish a child's diary: "And so I copied part of you into another notebook and you went to the City Assembly to be looked at. And I've just heard that you're going to be published! You're coming out for the UNICEF Week! SUPER!" For the next year, Zlata wrote her entries in her diary knowing that others would read it.

Despite the happy news about her diary, Zlata became increasingly depressed and wondered if the war would ever end. "Gone will be my childhood, gone my youth, gone my life. And I'll die and this war still won't be over." Zlata wrote about politics and the stupidity of the war. She could not understand why being a Serb, Croat, or Muslim made a difference. Her friends and family made up a "mixed group" and she had never paid attention to "who was a Serb, a Croat or a Muslim. Now politics has started meddling around ... it wants to separate them. And to do so it has chosen the worst, blackest pencil of all—the pencil of war which spells only misery and death."

As Zlata's frustration grew, so did her fame. On July 17, 1993, she spoke at a book promotion for her diary. After that, "journalists, reporters, cameramen" from Spain,

A young Bosnian girl's personal reactions to the mounting conflict in Sarajevo, Filipovic's diary has become a worldwide bestseller that some have inevitably compared to *The Diary of Anne Frank.*

France, England, and the U.S. interviewed her. ABC News featured her as the "Person of the Week." Zlata realized the irony of the fact that others were watching her on television and living in "bright light" while she lived in "darkness." "Just as I can't see myself on TV tonight, so the rest of the world probably can't see the darkness I'm looking at. We're at two ends of the world."

Zlata wrote the last entry in the diary on October 17, 1993. She reported that six people had been killed and fifty-six wounded after a day of five hundred and ninety shells. She was angry and sad after spending hours in the dark cellar. "I am convinced now that it [the shooting] will never end. Because some people don't want it to, some evil people who hate children and ordinary folk. We haven't done anything. We're innocent. But helpless!" This hopelessness was shortlived. Fortunately for Zlata and her family, the efforts to get them out of Sarajevo had succeeded, and they were transported to Paris.

Once again, Zlata found herself in the world of "light" that she had remembered. Her book became a bestseller in France and the rights to publish it in America were sold to Viking Penguin for $565,000 in early 1994.

Ironically, the light that she had so longed for was soon transformed into the spotlight's glare. When *Zlata's Diary* was published in the United States, many critics discussed the book's promotion and questioned the appropriateness of comparing Zlata to Anne Frank. Christopher Lehmann-Haupt, writing in the *New York Times,* felt that it was "to be counted as yet another aspect of the tragedy there [Bosnia and Herzegovina] that a child could have been exploited as Zlata has been."

Looking at the diary from a different angle, *New York Times Book Review* critic Francine Prose commented, "One wishes this book and its author so well that one also wishes it came unencumbered by the machinery of publicity at its most tasteless and gruesome. If only the French publishers of 'Zlata's Diary' had never thought or spoken the phrase 'the Anne Frank of Sarajevo'!" "When critics write ... 'Zlata Filipovic is no Anne Frank,'" stated Jack Miles in the *Los Angeles Times Book Review,* "they will be right. And yet the voice heard here, impotently and angrily repeating the word *stupid,* is the recognizable voice of a little girl pushed past her limit and about to burst into tears."

In March, 1994, Zlata went on a five-city tour of the United States to promote *Zlata's Diary* and appeared on television talk shows on NBC and PBS. Ginia Bellafante in *Time* observed Zlata's composure during an interview on NBC's *Today Show* and noted that Zlata had "become adept at answering painful questions about her tragically abbreviated childhood." Zlata has also answered questions about her responsibility to those she left behind in Sarajevo. According to Bettina Drew in Chicago *Tribune Books,* the thirteen-year-old girl "hopes to use her new fame to help the 70,000 children still in Sarajevo." "In this regard," Drew wrote, "and as historical document," Zlata's "diary has indisputable meaning and value."

■ Works Cited

Bellafante, Ginia, "Are You There, NBC? It's Me, Zlata," *Time,* March 21, 1994, p. 24.

Drew, Bettina, "Nothing Here Is Normal," *Tribune Books* (Chicago), March 13, 1994.

Filipovic, Zlata, *Zlata's Diary: A Child's Life in Sarajevo,* translated by Christina Pribichevich-Zoric, Viking, 1994.

Lehmann-Haupt, Christopher, "Another Diary of a Young Girl," *New York Times,* February 28, 1994, p. C15.

Miles, Jack, "Will the Shelling Never Stop: A Bosnian Girl Bears Witness," *Los Angeles Times Book Review,* February 27, 1994, pp. 1, 15.

Prose, Francine, "A Little Girl's War," *New York Times Book Review,* March 6, 1994, p. 7.

Viorst, Judith, "Girl in the Crossfire," *Washington Post Book World,* March 20, 1994, p. 2.

■ For More Information See

PERIODICALS

Bulletin of the Center for Children's Books, May, 1994, p. 285.

Kirkus Reviews, February 15, 1994, p. 217.

New Republic, March 28, 1994, pp. 31-34.

Newsweek, February 28, 1994, pp. 25-27.

Publishers Weekly, February 21, 1994, p. 245.*

* * *

FINLAY, Alice Sullivan 1946-

■ Personal

Born September 10, 1946, in Philadelphia, PA; daughter of James Neely Johnston (a writer and advertiser; died 1947) and Alice (a writer and teacher; maiden name, McLaughlin) Sullivan; stepdaughter of Timothy F. X. Sullivan (a certified public accountant); married Richard A. Finlay (a banker and retired U.S. Army sergeant), 1976; stepchildren: Angalene, Joanna, Valerie. *Education:* Gwynedd-Mercy College, B.A., 1968; New York University, M.A., 1974; University of Kansas, postgraduate study, 1975-76. *Hobbies and other interests:* Photography, nature, stained glass, travel.

ALICE SULLIVAN FINLAY

■ Addresses

Office—c/o Zondervan Publishing House, 5300 Patterson Ave. SE, Grand Rapids, MI 49530. *Agent*—Bruce W. Zabel, The Curtis Bruce Agency, P.O. Box 16406, Seattle, WA 98126.

■ Career

Free-lance writer. Literary Guild, New York City, member of editorial staff for book clubs, 1969-70; E. P. Dutton, New York City, assistant editor in juvenile publishing department, 1970-72; Fifteenth Street School, New York City, assistant to director, teacher of reading, drama and puppetry workshop leader, 1972-74; University of New Mexico, developed and taught a short-story writing course, 1986-93. Taught creative writing to writers' groups, 1985-86; speaks to schoolchildren about writing; appears on television and radio stations, 1987—. *Member:* National League of American Pen Women (president of Albuquerque branch, 1992-94), Society of Children's Book Writers, Mystery Writers of America, Southwest Writers Workshop (secretary and member of board of directors, 1986-87), American Legion Auxiliary.

■ Awards, Honors

Southwest Writers Workshop awards—juvenile mystery novel, third place, 1986, for *The Mystery of Treasure Cove,* juvenile short story, second place, 1990, for "The Silent, Patient Shell"; Gold Medallion Award nomination, Evangelical Christian Publishers Association, 1994, for the "Laura Lee" series; National League of American Penwomen's National Biennial Letters Competition, Merit Award in the Children's Picture Book Category, for *Laura Lee and the Monster Sea,* Honorable Mention award in the Children's Picture Book Category, for *A Victory for Laura Lee* and *A Gift from the Sea for Laura Lee,* and Honorable Mention in the Juvenile Novel Category, for *Laura Lee and the Little Pine Tree,* all 1994.

■ Writings

"LAURA LEE" SERIES; ILLUSTRATED BY JULIE DURRELL

Laura Lee and the Monster Sea, Zondervan, 1994.
A Victory for Laura Lee, Zondervan, 1994.
Laura Lee and the Little Pine Tree, Zondervan, 1994.
A Gift from the Sea for Laura Lee, Zondervan, 1994.

OTHER

Author of *The Mystery of Treasure Cove* and the short story, "The Silent, Patient Shell." Contributor to anthologies, including *The Christian Family Christmas Book,* edited by Ron and Lyn Klug, Augsburg, 1987, *The Christian Family Easter Book,* edited by Ron and Lyn Klug, Augsburg, 1989, and *The Favorites Anthology,* by the Institute of Children's Literature, 1991. Has also contributed poetry to such anthologies as *Touch with Love,* edited by Louis M. Savary, Association Press, 1971, and *Passages,* edited by Marianne S. Andersen and Louis M. Savary, Harper & Row, 1972. Contributor to periodicals, including *Discoveries, The Friend, Clubhouse Magazine, Grit, Capper's Weekly,* and *Mature Living.*

Finlay explores the meaning of friendship in a Florida setting in this "Laura Lee" story. (Cover illustration by Julie Durrell.)

■ Work in Progress

Easy-to-read books; a mystery chapter book for the middle grades; more series ideas.

■ Sidelights

Alice Sullivan Finlay told *SATA:* "I grew up in a big family of seven children. My mother and father had good senses of humor, so we had quite a bit of family fun. Since there were so many of us, there was always something going on. I often draw on incidents from my childhood for my writing. The humor and the family warmth carry over. I've always been a storyteller. My first grade teacher and cousins have told me I used to tell them stories. I really think I developed this ability in our large family.

"I loved to read at an early age. I wanted to write easy-to-reads to help children learn to enjoy reading. I liked emotional books about animals. When I was older, I would spend long hours in our school library or our attic, reading series. The *Nancy Drew, Hardy Boys,* and *Bobbsey Twin* series got me hooked on reading. I wanted to read more and more about each character. In my writing now, I seem to want to write more about each character I develop, as if visiting them in each book.

"I decided to be a writer when I was fifteen. My birth father was a writer and my mother had studied journalism. I'm sure they helped cultivate in us a love of writing and reading. My mother remarried an Irishman from Boston. Our grandmother had come over as an immigrant to make a better life for herself and her children. Their stories always inspired me.

"Being around famous authors also inspired me. My hometown is in Bucks County, which was the home of twentieth-century authors Pearl S. Buck and James A. Michener. I heard them talk and was really inspired. My mother had a tea for Mr. Michener one day, and my sisters and I were elated to be meeting a real author.

"I often get story ideas from settings. I love to camp out and spend time in nature, or go walking in the mountains. My Laura Lee character also loves nature and animals. One of the best ways to think of ideas is to pretend. I might take a drive and see trucks on a freeway. I might pretend to be a truck driver for a few minutes. Or maybe I see interesting people in a restaurant. I try to imagine what their lives and families are like. If I think of a problem for them, that is the start of the story. If I think of the solution to the problem, that is the end. Then I fill in the incidents when I write.

"I wrote the first Laura Lee book over a period of five years. At first, my writing was not vivid enough. Then the character developed. Finally, the character really came to life, and a friend told me to send it to my publisher. They bought not one but four books. I wrote the other three books within a year, due to deadlines.

"I owe a lot to my teachers who encouraged me. I loved penmanship exercises and spelling. In fifth grade, I wrote an emotional story about baby birds falling out of a nest. My teacher judged the story to be the best in the class. In college, when I started to write poetry, my teachers had me do poetry readings and published some of my poems. This made me change my course to study literature. I wrote poetry for many years. In graduate school, I studied education and theatre. I read and wrote plays and learned about atmosphere and dialogue. Nothing you write is ever wasted. Writing and reading poetry gave me the ability to create vivid word pictures. Writing and reading drama gave me a sense of plot and dialogue. Studying the classics in literature gave me a sense of rhythm. I feel a certain rhythm whenever I write.

"The late sixties was a vivid time in our country's history, and there were many opportunities for women. I moved to New York to work in publishing, where I did editing and copywriting. Working with children's book authors made me decide to write for children. When I started to write to sell, I wrote and published fillers, nostalgia articles, and children's stories for magazines. Then I branched out into children's book writing. Here's how I developed ideas for the Laura Lee books:

"In *Laura Lee and the Monster Sea,* Laura Lee goes to the seashore but is afraid to swim in the sea. This story idea came from the time we spent at the seashore. I had swimming lessons, but the ferocious ocean scared me. Our neighbor, who swam beyond the waves every day, taught me confidence. In the story, Laura Lee learns to swim in the sea.

"Once we spent the whole school year in Florida. I had a hard time making friends, but I loved the monkeys and parrots and collecting shells. I combined these scenes with the theme of friendship in *A Gift from the Sea for Laura Lee. Laura Lee and the Little Pine Tree* is also based on my childhood. When I was little, my father rented us a rustic cabin in the mountains that did not even have running water. Laura Lee arrives at the cabin and discovers that there is no electricity or running water, and only an outhouse. Someone is taking their food and a snowstorm threatens. Laura Lee learns not to worry and even has fun.

"We always fed ducks as a family. We also rescued injured birds and animals. I saw a news story about ducks getting stuck in plastic rings. In *A Victory for Laura Lee,* Laura Lee and her brother rescue a duck and organize a protest and campaign to clean up the duck pond. Laura Lee learns that children can make a difference."

* * *

FLEISCHER, Jane
See OPPENHEIM, Joanne

* * *

FORWARD, Robert L(ull) 1932-

■ Personal

Born August 15, 1932, in Geneva, NY; son of Robert T. and Mildred (a teacher; maiden name, Lull) Forward; married Martha Neil Dodson, August 29, 1954; children: Robert D., Mary Lois Mattlin, Eve Laurel, Julie Elizabeth Fuller. *Education:* University of Maryland, B.S., 1954, Ph.D., 1965; University of California, Los Angeles, M.S., 1958. *Religion:* Congregational.

■ Addresses

Office—Forward Unlimited, P.O. Box 2783, Malibu, CA 90265. *Agent*—Scott Meredith Literary Agency, 845 Third Ave., New York, NY 10022.

ROBERT L. FORWARD

Career

Hughes Research Laboratories, Malibu, CA, technical staff member, 1956-66, associate manager in theoretical studies department, 1966-67, manager in exploratory studies department, 1967-74, senior scientist, 1974-87; Forward Unlimited, Malibu, science consultant, 1987—. *Military service:* U.S. Air Force, 1954-56; became captain. *Member:* Science Fiction and Fantasy Writers of America, American Institute of Aeronautics and Astronautics (associate fellow), American Astronomical Society, Institute of Electrical and Electronic Engineers, American Physical Society, British Interplanetary Society (fellow), Sigma Xi, Sigma Pi Sigma.

Awards, Honors

Award for outstanding achievement in the field of gravity, Gravity Research Foundation, 1965; research award, Ventura Branch of the Scientific Research Society of America, 1969.

Writings

SCIENCE FICTION

Dragon's Egg, Ballantine, 1980.
The Flight of the Dragonfly, Pocket Books, 1984, enlarged version as *Rocheworld,* Baen, 1990.
Starquake (sequel to *Dragon's Egg*), Ballantine, 1985.
Martian Rainbow, Ballantine, 1991.
(With daughter, Julie Forward Fuller) *Return to Rocheworld,* Baen, 1992.
Timemaster, Tor, 1992.
(With wife, Martha Dodson Forward) *Marooned on Eden,* Baen, 1993.
Camelot 30K, Tor, 1993.
(With M. D. Forward) *Ocean under the Ice,* Baen, 1994.
(With J. F. Fuller) *Rescued from Paradise,* Baen, 1995.

OTHER

Future Magic (nonfiction), Avon, 1988.
(With Joel Davis) *Mirror Matter: Pioneering Antimatter Physics* (nonfiction), Wiley, 1988.
Indistinguishable from Magic (nonfiction), Baen, 1995.

Also contributor to *Hard Science Fiction,* edited by George E. Slusser and Eric S. Rabkin, Southern Illinois University Press, 1985; contributor of numerous articles and stories to periodicals, including *Analog, Galaxy, Galileo, Omni,* and *Science 80.*

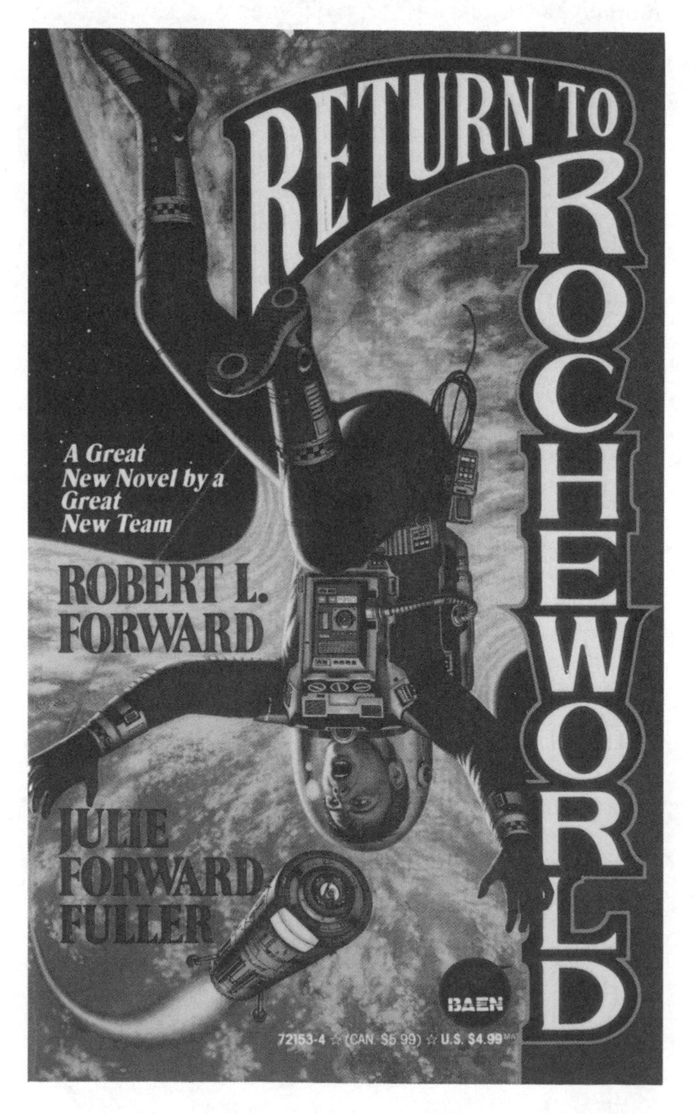

This science fiction work, written with Forward's daughter, Julie Forward Fuller, continues the saga set on the double planet, Rocheworld. (Cover illustration by David Mattingly.)

Sidelights

Robert L. Forward is a hard science fiction writer who has translated years of experience as a gravitational physicist at the Hughes Aircraft Company Research Laboratories into novels that stretch scientific facts to highly imaginative limits. His first novel, *Dragon's Egg,* described life on a neutron star, where the force of gravity is sixty-seven billion times stronger than it is on Earth. One critic praised Forward's scientifically accurate details in a *Publishers Weekly* review, writing that Forward "does an exemplary job of rigorously developing his premise in the tradition of Hal Clement."

Continuing his predilection for creating out-of-the-ordinary worlds, Forward set his next novel, *The Flight of the Dragonfly,* on the double planet, Rocheworld, orbiting Barnard's Star. The two planetary bodies of Rocheworld circle each other at a distance of a mere eighty kilometers and share the same atmosphere. Critics admired the creativity Forward demonstrated in his story. A *Publishers Weekly* reviewer wrote: "Nothing is more exciting than a good idea beautifully developed," concluding that the book is a "must" for lovers of hardcore science fiction. When *The Flight of the Dragonfly* was to be published in paperback, the paperback editor Jim Baen requested that the heavily edited hardcover be restored to its original manuscript version. The new book, renamed *Rocheworld,* was 50,000 words longer that the original version. Forward has written—both by himself and with his wife, Martha, and daughter, Julie—four more books set on Rocheworld, including *Return to Rocheworld, Ocean under the Ice, Marooned on Eden,* and *Rescued from Paradise.*

More recently, Forward made a new addition to his increasing collection of bizarre, alien worlds with *Camelot 30K.* The premise involves Earth scientists making contact with intelligent, shrimp-like aliens who inhabit a frozen planetoid beyond Pluto. The "keracks" have developed a complex society resembling medieval Europe. The humans make contact with a wizard named Merlene and discover that their wicked queen is genetically programmed to develop a hydrogen bomb with devastating consequences for keracks and humans alike.

A few critics of Forward's work have complained that his characters lack depth and his plots are short on imagination. One *Kirkus Reviews* contributor, for example, described the plot of *The Flight of the Dragonfly* as "humdrum," and a *Publishers Weekly* reviewer felt the characters in *Camelot 30K* were "interchangeable." However, other critics have found much to praise in Forward's work, and Susan L. Nickerson in *Library Journal* called the author "one of the foremost writers of 'hard' sf."

Works Cited

Review of *Camelot 30K, Publishers Weekly,* August 2, 1993, p. 66.

Review of *Dragon's Egg, Publishers Weekly,* March 14, 1980, pp. 70-71.

Review of *The Flight of the Dragonfly, Kirkus Reviews,* January 1, 1984, p. 19.

Review of *The Flight of the Dragonfly, Publishers Weekly,* January 13, 1984, p. 65.

Nickerson, Susan L., review of *The Flight of the Dragonfly, Library Journal,* February 15, 1993, p. 390.

For More Information See

PERIODICALS

Kirkus Reviews, July 15, 1993, pp. 897-98.

* * *

FRAILEY, Paige (Menefee) 1965-

Personal

Born January 28, 1965, in Beaumont, TX; daughter of Lindy (a small business owner) and Glenda (a homemaker; maiden name, Wheeler) Menefee; married James A. Frailey (an aerospace engineer), May 4, 1991; children: Hannah. *Education:* Lamar University, B.F.A., 1987; Texas Christian University, M.F.A., 1990. *Politics:* Republican. *Religion:* Christian. *Hobbies and other interests:* Painting, sewing, antiquing, church involvement, spending time with husband and daughter.

Addresses

Home—3421 Worth Hills Dr., Fort Worth, TX 76109.

Career

Freelance illustrator, 1990—; Tarrant County Junior College, Fort Worth, TX, Painting I and II instructor, 1990-91. *Exhibitions:* Exhibitor at Southwest Regional

PAIGE FRAILEY

Juried Exhibition, 1990; Trammell Crow Lower West Pavilion, Dallas, TX, 1990; Master of Fine Arts Thesis Exhibition (solo), Texas Christian University, Fort Worth, TX, 1990; Dishman Art Gallery Three Person Exhibition, Beaumont, TX, 1991.

■ Illustrator

Louise Mandrell and Ace Collins, *Runaway Thanksgiving,* Summit Group, 1992.
Mandrell and Collins, *Peril in Evans Woods,* Summit Group, 1993.

Also contributor to the cover illustration for *The Battle for the Worlds,* by Harold B. Bullock, Summit Group, 1990, and *Nolan Ryan: The Authorized Pictorial History,* edited by D. Kent Pingel, Summit Group, 1991.

■ Sidelights

Paige Frailey explained to *SATA:* "Instead of a difficult search to begin my illustration career, I feel very fortunate to have had it come to me. Having just graduated from Texas Christian University, I was looking toward a career as a painter and art instructor, when a friend working at an advertising agency needed an illustrator to fill in on a job for someone who was getting married. I was thrilled to have my first job be a four-color illustration for the cover of the children's book *The Battle for the Worlds.* That job led to several small illustration contracts and recently, the opportunity to illustrate the children's books *Runaway Thanksgiving* and *Peril in Evans Woods,* both in pastels.

"Children's illustration seems like a natural avenue for me. Since my childhood, I have loved visual arts, and as a new mother, I have become an avid reader of children's books. In elementary school I often entered the state fair art competitions. My first blue ribbon was for a drawing of my second grade class with the teacher working at the chalkboard and all the students in their desks looking at her.

"I began working in pastels in college. The pastel medium suits my style of painting as I am able to use both color and line in an aggressive, gestural manner. In *The Art Spirit,* Robert Henri said, 'A work of art is the trace of a magnificent struggle.' Many times in my painting I have identified with this principle. I was hoping that with illustration it would be different. I found, however, that I experience the same struggle and go through the same processes with illustration as I do in my painting. I often begin a project with an initial period of excitement but soon find myself frustrated, unsure of where the work is really going. Sometimes I use water to smear the pastels on the paper, which often form new subtleties of color and abstract forms that suggest a new direction or a slightly different composition. I enjoy allowing these surprises to give the illustration life and energy, and keep it from being forced.

"The concept of a rescue is a theme that I have dealt with extensively in my paintings. One aspect of *Peril in Evans Woods* that I appreciate is that it is a rescue story. It was enjoyable to have the continuity of the rescue theme extended from my earlier paintings into the illustrations in the book. My goal in illustrating *Peril in Evans Woods* was to create the story visually in a way that would not just support the storyline but become inseparable from it."

G

GAMBRELL, Jamey

■ Personal

Born in New York, NY. *Education:* University of Texas, B.A., 1975; graduate work at Columbia University.

■ Addresses

Office—Art in America, 575 Broadway, New York, NY 10012. *Agent*—Deborah Karl, Wylie, Aitken & Stone, 250 West 57th St., New York, NY 10107.

■ Career

Art in America, New York City, contributing editor and staff writer, 1983—; freelance art crtic, essayist, and translator from Russian.

■ Awards, Honors

Translation fellowship, National Endowment for the Arts, 1993.

■ Writings

TRANSLATOR

(And editor and author of introduction) Andrei Honchalovsky and Alexander Lipkov, *The Inner Circle: An Inside View of Soviet Life Under Stalin,* Newmarket, 1991.

Tatyana Tolstaya, *Sleepwalker in a Fog,* Knopf, 1992.

Daniil Kharms, *The Story of a Boy Named Will,* North-South, 1993.

Also author of essays on Russian art, literature, media, and culture in *New York Review of Books* and *Harper's.*

■ Work in Progress

Translating Kornei Chukovsky's *Telephone,* with illustrations by Vladimir Radunsky, for North-South.*

GARRETT, Richard 1920-

■ Personal

Born January 15, 1920, in London, England; son of Victor (in business) and Gladys (Fisher) Garrett; married Anne Selves, August 20, 1945; children: Anthony, Simon, Jane. *Education:* Attended school in Berkshire, England. *Politics:* "Middle of the road." *Religion:* Christian. *Hobbies and other interests:* Walking, the countryside, watching the sea.

■ Addresses

Home—White Cottage, 27-A Broadwater Down, Tunbridge Wells, Kent TN2 5NL, England.

■ Career

Freelance writer, 1969—. Worked previously in journalism, public relations, and advertising. Owner of industrial book and magazine publishing company in England, 1958-69. Broadcaster of weekly general interest shows for British Broadcasting Corp. (BBC); guest on radio and television programs. *Military service:* British Army, 1939-45; served as officer in Norway; prisoner-of-war in Italy and Germany, 1943-45; became captain; staff writer for *Soldier. Member:* Society of Authors.

■ Writings

FOR CHILDREN

Great Sea Mysteries, Piccolo, 1971.
Atlantic Jet, Hutchinson, 1971.
Hoaxes and Swindles, Piccolo, 1972.
True Tales of Detection, Piccolo, 1972.
Narrow Squeaks, Piccolo, 1973.
Heroines, Piccolo, 1974.
Queen Victoria, Hutchinson, 1974.
They Must Have Been Crazy, Piccolo, 1977.
Kaiser Bill, Wayland, 1978.
Dangerous Journeys, Piccolo, 1978.
(Compiler) *Great Air Adventures,* Piccolo, 1978.

RICHARD GARRETT

In the Nick of Time, Piccolo, 1979.
File on Spies, Granada, 1981.
File on Forgers, Granada, 1982.
Jailbreakers, Granada, 1983.
Aliens from Outer Space, Piccolo, 1983.
The Story of Britain, Granada, 1983, revised edition, HarperCollins, 1991.

FOR ADULTS

Fast and Furious: The Story of the World Championship of Drivers, foreword by Graham Hill, Stanley Paul, 1968, Arco, 1969.
The Motor Racing Story, Stanley Paul, 1969, A. S. Barnes, 1970.
Anatomy of a Grand Prix Driver, Arthur Barker, 1970.
The Rally-Go-Round: The Story of International Rallying, Stanley Paul, 1970.
Motoring and the Mighty, Motorbooks International, 1971.
Cross-Channel, Hutchinson, 1972.
The Search for Prosperity: Emigration from Britain, 1815-1830, Wayland, 1973.
Stories of Famous Ships, Arthur Barker, 1974.
General Gordon, Arthur Barker, 1974.
The British Sailor, Wayland, 1974.
General Wolfe, Arthur Barker, 1975.
Famous Characters of the Wild West, Arthur Barker, 1975, St. Martin's, 1977.
Stories of Famous Natural Disasters, Arthur Barker, 1976.
Clash of Arms: The World's Great Land Battles, Weidenfeld & Nicolson, 1976.
Robert Clive, Arthur Barker, 1976.
Submarines, Little, Brown, 1977.
Famous Rescues at Sea, Arthur Barker, 1977.
Scharnhorst and Gneisenau: The Elusive Sisters, Hippocrene, 1977.
Mrs. Simpson, St. Martin's, 1979.
The Raiders, Van Nostrand, 1980.
P.O.W., Hippocrene, 1981.
Royal Travel, Blanford, 1982.
Royal Quiz, Longman, 1985.
Atlantic Disaster: The "Titanic" and Other Victims of the North Atlantic, Buchan & Enright, 1986.
Flight into Mystery: Reports from the Dark Side of the Sky, Weidenfeld & Nicolson, 1986.
Voyage into Mystery: Reports from the Sinister Side of the Sea, Weidenfeld & Nicolson, 1987.
Great Escapes of World War II, Weidenfeld & Nicolson, 1989.
The Final Betrayal: Armistice 1918 . . . and Afterwards, Buchan & Enright, 1989.
Sky High: Heroic Pilots of the Second World War, Weidenfeld & Nicolson, 1991.

■ Sidelights

Whether they have been written for children or adults, the products of Richard Garrett's writing career have made many aspects of sports, technology, and history more accessible and enjoyable. *Fast and Furious: The Story of the World Championship of Drivers,* for one example, explains racing and the technology that permits it while providing intriguing inside information about car designers, racers, and mechanics. Garrett's "absorbing" details make the story smell "of racing oil . . . and dangerous glory," according to *Publishers Weekly* writer Albert Johnston.

Atlantic Jet takes the reader through the history of air travel. A reviewer for *Times Literary Supplement* notes the discussion of the training and careers of civil aviators and suggests that those who "feel this is the life for them" will gain a more realistic understanding of the work. *Great Air Adventures,* compiled by Garrett, provides a historical, biographical, and sometimes technical account of exciting air adventure stories from the invention of the airplane to World War II. This book is spiced with an "occasional touch of suspense or drama," as a reviewer for *Growing Point* notes. *Submarines* relates the history of submersibles from their conception and creation through the two World Wars. While Roger E. Bilstein in *Library Journal* laments the "sketchy coverage of postwar Russian activity," he recommends the book.

Garrett has also crafted works which focus more specifically on English personalities and history. According to *Times Literary Supplement* critic Keith Harling, Garrett's *General Wolfe* is "one of a familiar kind retelling the lives of great Englishmen, with the emphasis on a good yarn rather than on biography." *The Story of Britain* is an attempt to relate the history of Britain from five thousand years ago to the early 1980s. Peter Sanderson, writing in *School Librarian*, criticizes the work for presenting "traditional tales and rumours" as fact. Nevertheless, the readers for whom this was intended seem to enjoy it. *The Story of Britain* is still in print eleven years after its original publication and other of Garrett's books for children have been translated into German, Norwegian, Swedish, Italian, and Japanese.

Garrett once explained his writing: "My basic aim is to tell a story (I suspect a novelist screaming to get out, but since I have no talent in this area, he remains inside). I attempt to explore history, to experience the feeling of the times, and, in the case of children's books, to pass on this excitement. I suspect that history is taught without much imagination in the schools—there is little attempt to show what tremendous stories history contains. My books concentrate on entertainment—easy to read books which could happily occupy a long train journey."

■ Works Cited

Review of *Atlantic Jet*, *Times Literary Supplement*, October 22, 1971, p. 1344.

Bilstein, Roger E., review of *Submarines*, *Library Journal*, May 1, 1978, p. 979.

Review of *Great Air Adventures*, *Growing Point*, November, 1978, p. 3421.

Harling, Keith, review of *General Wolfe*, *Times Literary Supplement*, January 16, 1976, p. 60.

Johnston, Albert, review of *Fast and Furious*, *Publishers Weekly*, January 27, 1969, p. 97.

Sanderson, Peter, review of *The Story of Britain*, *The School Librarian*, March, 1984, p. 82.

■ For More Information See

PERIODICALS

Booklist, March 1, 1978, p. 1093.
Books & Bookmen, February, 1980, pp. 27-28.
Publishers Weekly, November 26, 1979, p. 45.
School Library Journal, March, 1980, p. 55.

* * *

GILBERT, Sara (Dulaney) 1943-

■ Personal

Born October 5, 1943, in Washington, DC; daughter of Ben Bane (a journalist) and Jean (an editor; maiden name, Brownell) Dulaney; married Ian R. Gilbert (a lawyer), August 31, 1963 (marriage ended); children: Sean Dulaney Gilbert. *Education:* Attended Pembroke College, 1961-63; Barnard College, B.A. (with honors), 1966; New York University, master's candidate. *Hobbies and other interests:* Gardening, travel.

■ Addresses

Home—New York, NY. *Agent*—Bert Holtje, James Peter Associates, Box 772, Tenafly, NJ 07670.

■ Career

American Broadcasting Corp., Washington, DC, staff aide for "ABC News," 1963-64; Cowles Communications, New York City, encyclopedia editor and writer, 1966-68; free-lance writer, 1968—; New York University School of Continuing Education, New York City, public relations manager, 1984—. *Member:* American Society of Journalists and Authors, Authors Guild, Public Relations Society of America.

■ Awards, Honors

Mr. Freedom Award, Religious Liberty Association, 1972, for articles; New York Public Library citation, for *Go for It—Get Organized;* Children's Books of the Year citation, Library of Congress, for *You Are What You Eat;* Outstanding Book citation, National Science Teachers Association, for *Fat Free.*

■ Writings

NONFICTION FOR CHILDREN

Fat Free: Common Sense for Young Weight Worriers, Macmillan, 1975.

SARA GILBERT

You Are What You Eat: A Commonsense Guide to the Modern American Diet, Macmillan, 1977.
Feeling Good: A Book About You and Your Body, Four Winds, 1978.
Ready, Set, Go: How to Find the Career That's Right for You, Four Winds, 1979.
Trouble at Home, Lothrop, 1981.
What Happens in Therapy, Lothrop, 1982.
How to Live With a Single Parent, foreword by Scott Hurlbert and Evelyn Hurlbert, Lothrop, 1982.
How to Take Tests, Morrow, 1983.
By Yourself: A Kid's Book on Coping, illustrated by Heidi Johanna Selig, Lothrop, 1983.
Using Your Head: The Many Ways of Being Smart, Macmillan, 1984.
Lend a Hand: The How, Where, and Why of Volunteering, Morrow, 1988.
Get Help: Solving the Problems in Your Life, Morrow, 1989.
Go for It—Get Organized, Morrow, 1990.
You Can Speak Up in Class, illustrated by Roy Doty, Morrow, 1991.

NONFICTION FOR ADULTS

Three Years to Grow: Guidance for Your Child's First Three Years, Parents' Magazine Press, 1972.
What's a Father For?, Parents' Magazine Press, 1975.
The Career Training Sourcebook: Where to Get Free, Low-cost, and Salaried Job Training, McGraw-Hill, 1993.
Arco Guide to Internships: A Directory for Career-Finders, Macmillan, 1995.

Contributor to periodicals, including *Baby Care, Ms., Good Housekeeping, Travel, Careers, Bridal Guide, Campfire Girl, Liberty, Metrolines, Writers Digest,* and *National Businesswoman.* Also author of filmstrips, newsletters, speeches, and pamphlets.

■ Work in Progress

Studying for her master's degree in leisure studies at New York University; more books.

■ Sidelights

Sara Dulaney Gilbert has spent much of her writing career providing young people with valuable information about their bodies and lifestyles. The "usual with Gilbert's advice books," writes a *Kirkus Reviews* critic, is an "overall tone [that] is reassuring—geared to making kids feel comfortable with the idea of getting help." Gilbert's first two books made advice about eating accessible to teenagers. In *Fat Free: Common Sense for Young Weight Worriers,* Gilbert discusses fat sources and fat storage, and explains various methods of dealing with fat. In the process, she debunks many assumptions about fat and exposes the faults of many popular diets. A calorie-carbohydrate chart, a list of suggested readings, and an index are included. According to Jean F. Mercier in *Publishers Weekly,* this "lucid and helpful book" could be useful for adults as well as adolescents, while *Bulletin of the Center for Children's Books* writer Zena Sutherland terms it an "excellent book" with a "brisk, informal, and sensible text." *You Are What You Eat: A Commonsense Guide to the Modern American Diet* discusses mass production and advertising and their effect on American eating habits. Joan W. Paul in *School Library Journal* describes the book as "carefully written and thought-provoking" and notes that Gilbert encourages young people to "think before they eat."

Gilbert breaks the silence surrounding single parenthood, offering problem-solving tips for both parents and children in this 1982 volume.

Feeling Good: A Book About You and Your Body provides information about the physical changes that come with adolescence, ways to maintain a healthy body, and dealing with drugs, alcohol, and tobacco. Gilbert branched out into mental health and psychological issues with *Trouble at Home,* which covers death, divorce, remarriage, drug addiction, alcoholism, child abuse, and sibling rivalry. A chapter on determining whether problems are minor or major, and when and how to get help ends the book. "The discussion of each situation is brief, realistic . . . and constructive," Gale Eaton comments in *School Library Journal,* noting that a long list of suggested readings (both nonfiction and fiction), hotlines, and addresses of helpful organizations is also included. Joan Jestel in *Voice of Youth Advocates* describes *Trouble at Home* as a "little gem" and recommends it as a "MUST for school and YA libraries" as well as for "youth workers."

Other of Gilbert's books focus on more specific family situations and encourage young people to speak out about their problems. In *How to Live With a Single Parent,* Gilbert addresses the needs of adolescents finding themselves in such a situation. This work, based on questionnaire results from single parent kids and Gilbert's own experience as the daughter of a single parent, dwells on finances, visitation schedules, dating, remarriage, and incest. One chapter of the book is devoted to parents. Included are a list of helpful books and organizations, as well as an index. *School Library Journal* contributor Marsha Hartos praises Gilbert for "her understanding and caring [that] show through," while Sally Estes in *Booklist* concludes that the book is "full of commonsensical and reassuring advice." In *By Yourself,* a book *Publishers Weekly* critic Mercier calls "a winner," Gilbert deals with latchkey children by focusing on anticipating problems and offering safe and enjoyable solutions and suggestions. A chapter for parents is also included.

Gilbert's works have also presented information about intellect and performance in school. *How to Take Tests* provides information on types of tests (including the standardized PSAT, SAT, and GRE), as well as step-by-step methods of preparation. A bibliography is included. Virginia W. Marr in *Voice of Youth Advocates* recommended this "highly useful" book as an "essential purchase for school libraries." Test scores don't always reveal intelligence, however, and *Using Your Head: The Many Ways of Being Smart* encourages young people to understand that everyone has different talents (from book smarts to street smarts). The book enables readers to evaluate their own intellectual strengths with various questions, provides suggestions on caring for the brain, and includes a glossary and bibliography. While Fran Wolfe in *School Library Journal* finds the writing "awkward" and "unclear," *Voice of Youth Advocates* contributor Susan Hopkins states that the work is "fun and easy to read," and will be "extremely valuable" for students with skills that don't test well. Another guide to enhancing classroom performance is *You Can Speak Up in Class,* which lists concerns and offers suggestions for those afraid to ask questions, volunteer answers, or make a presentation in class. Doris A. Fong in *School Library Journal* recommends buying "more than one copy" of this "clear concise guide."

A more general guide is *Get Help: Solving the Problems in Your Life,* which Sutherland in *Bulletin of the Center for Children's Books* calls a "tremendously useful, wide ranging, and well-organized compendium" that facilitates the process of finding help. After asserting that teens need to recognize when they need help and then seek it, Gilbert provides descriptions, addresses, and telephone numbers of sources of assistance in separate chapters for problems ranging from abuse and eating disorders to employment and college scholarships. She provides information on what to expect once an agency has been contacted, as well as what to expect in response. All of the services featured are inexpensive or free, and one hundred national organizations are listed. Beverly Robertson in *Voice of Youth Advocates* advises: "Talk it up, take it into the schools, and make it as visible as you can."

In addition to advising young people and showing them how to find help in her books, Gilbert has demonstrated how teens can help others. In *Lend a Hand: The How, Where, and Why of Volunteering,* Gilbert helps readers determine which volunteer jobs may be right for them. After a discussion of the use of volunteering and then a list of one hundred nonprofit organizations which accept young volunteers, Gilbert explains what might be expected from such organizations. Suggestions for adults on enlisting young volunteers are included. Steve Matthews in *School Library Journal* concluded that *Lend a Hand*'s "spirit and enthusiasm . . . should bolster the converted and convince the undecided."

While young people may gain a better understanding of how to care for their minds and bodies from Gilbert's books, Gilbert herself benefits from writing them. As she once told *SATA,* "I tend, perhaps naturally, to write about topics that directly concern me, and find that I learn a lot from what I write, which is the point." She

This book provides support and suggestions for students who are uncomfortable answering questions or making presentations in class. (Cover illustration by Roy Doty.)

later commented: "I find that the major interest in my life is the 'why' of people, and that the qualities I value most in other people, no matter what their superficial characteristics, are the ability to and interest in exploring and understanding the motivations for behavior and the underlying emotional forces in themselves and in others. In a sense, it is through my writing that I've become aware of this interest, and in my writing, past, present and future, I pursue it.

"More recently, with my books for adults, my work in continuing education, and my studies in leisure education, I am equally concerned with the 'how' of making the most of one's life at any age. And I'm still learning from the projects I choose to write on."

■ Works Cited

Eaton, Gale, review of *Trouble at Home, School Library Journal,* August, 1981, p. 74.
Estes, Sally, review of *How to Live With a Single Parent, Booklist,* February 15, 1982, p. 753.
Fong, Doris A., review of *You Can Speak Up in Class, School Library Journal,* June, 1991, p. 116.
Hartos, Marsha, review of *How to Live With a Single Parent, School Library Journal,* May, 1982, p. 69.
Hopkins, Susan, review of *Using Your Head, Voice of Youth Advocates,* June, 1985, p. 145.
Jestel, Joan, review of *Trouble at Home, Voice of Youth Advocates,* December, 1981, p. 42.
Marr, Virginia W., review of *How to Take Tests, Voice of Youth Advocates,* June, 1984, p. 109.
Matthews, Steve, review of *Lend a Hand, School Library Journal,* May, 1988, pp. 116-117.
Mercier, Jean F., review of *Fat Free, Publishers Weekly,* May 26, 1975, p. 60.
Mercier, Jean F., review of *By Yourself, Publishers Weekly,* September 30, 1983, p. 116.
Paul, Joan W., review of *You Are What You Eat, School Library Journal,* February, 1977, p. 71.
Robertson, Beverly, review of *Get Help, Voice of Youth Advocates,* June, 1989, p. 124.
Sutherland, Zena, review of *Fat Free, Bulletin of the Center for Children's Books,* October, 1975, p. 27.
Sutherland, Zena, review of *Get Help, Bulletin of the Center for Children's Books,* April, 1989, p. 195.
Review of *What Happens in Therapy, Kirkus Reviews,* July 15, 1982, p. 803.
Wolfe, Fran, review of *Using Your Head, School Library Journal,* January, 1985, p. 85.

■ For More Information See

PERIODICALS

Bulletin of the Center for Children's Books, September, 1981, p. 171; May, 1982, p. 168.
Horn Book, January/February, 1985, pp. 67-68.
Kirkus Reviews, September 1, 1978, pp. 954-55; December 1, 1979, p. 1381.
School Library Journal, September, 1978, p. 157; October, 1982, p. 160; June, 1989, p. 128.
Voice of Youth Advocates, October, 1982, p. 54.
Wilson Library Bulletin, May, 1989, pp. 110-11.

GLEESON, Libby 1950-

■ Personal

Born September 19, 1950, in Young, New South Wales, Australia; daughter of Norman John (a teacher) and Gwynneth (a homemaker; maiden name, Whitten) Gleeson; married Euan Tovey (a scientist); children: Amelia, Josephine, Jessica. *Education:* University of Sydney, B.A., 1973; New South Wales Department of Education, teaching certification, 1975. *Hobbies and other interests:* Family, reading, swimming, tennis, community arts.

■ Addresses

Home—11 Oxford St., Petersham, N.S.W. 2049, Australia. *Agent*—Hickson Associates, P.O. Box 271, Woollahra, N.S.W. 2025, Australia.

■ Career

Instructor in secondary school and university, 1974-86; visiting lecturer at various universities, 1985—; full-time writer, 1989—. Has also been a consultant for teaching English as a second language, 1986-90. Authors' representative on Public Lending Right Committee of Australia. *Member:* Australian Society of Authors.

■ Awards, Honors

Angus & Robertson Award for Writers for Young Readers, 1984, highly commended, Australian Chil-

LIBBY GLEESON

dren's Book of the Year, 1985, shortlisted for New South Wales Premier's Award, 1985, South Australia Premier's Award, 1985, and Guardian Newspaper's Award for Children, all for *Eleanor, Elizabeth;* Honor Book, Australian Children's Book of the Year, 1988, and shortlisted for Victorian Premier's Award, 1988, both for *I Am Susannah;* Children's Literature Peace Prize, 1991, and International Board on Books for Young People (IBBY) Award, 1992, both for *Dodger;* Prime Minister's Multicultural Award, 1991, for *Big Dog;* Honor Book, CBC Picture Book of the Year, 1993, for *Where's Mum?;* shortlisted for Australian Children's Book of the Year, 1994, for *Love Me, Love Me Not.*

■ Writings

Eleanor, Elizabeth, Holiday House, 1984.
I Am Susannah, Holiday House, 1987.
One Sunday, illustrated by John Winch, Angus & Robertson, 1988.
The Great Big Scary Dog, illustrated by Armin Greder, Tambourine Books, 1991.
Dodger, Turton & Chambers, 1991, Puffin, 1993.
Uncle David, illustrated by Greder, Tambourine Books, 1992.
Hurry Up!, illustrated by Mitch Vane, SRA School Group, 1992.
Where's Mum?, illustrated by Craig Smith, Omnibus Books, 1993.
Mum Goes to Work, illustrated by Penny Azar, Ashton Scholastic, 1993.
Love Me, Love Me Not, Viking, 1993.
Sleeptime, Ashton Scholastic, 1993.
Walking to School, illustrated by Linda McClelland, SRA School Group, 1994.
Skating on Sand, illustrated by Ann James, Viking, 1994.
The Princess and the Perfect Dish, illustrated by Greder, Ashton Scholastic, 1995.

Also author of numerous short stories, including "The Boy Who Wouldn't Get Out of Bed," "Bedtime Story," "Farewell," "In the Swim," and "Her Room." Gleeson's works have been translated into Swedish, Dutch, German, and Italian.

■ Sidelights

Award-winning Australian children's author Libby Gleeson grew up in rural New South Wales. During her childhood, her family moved quite often due to her father's teaching career. "There were six children and no television," Gleeson told *SATA.* "That meant family entertainment was usually reading. I read everything I could get my hands on. I think I decided then that to be a writer and to make books would be a most wonderful occupation. I didn't set out to do this straight away. I studied at the University of Sydney and became a secondary school teacher.

"After two years teaching I set out to see the world. I spent five years traveling and working in western Europe, England, and America. At the same time, I wrote constantly—determined to become a writer. I began my first novel, *Eleanor, Elizabeth,* while I was living in London. I joined a group of writers who met regularly and discussed work-in-progress. That experience helped me shape the text and develop my own critical skills. It is a novel that grew out of my bush childhood, with historical material of the last century largely taken from the childhood of my grandparents. It is fiction, not autobiography."

The story centers around a young girl named Eleanor who has just moved to a new town. In the course of the move, Eleanor discovers her grandmother's diary, written in 1895 when her grandmother was twelve. The diary helps Eleanor come to terms with her new home, and, as Connie Tyrrell Burns wrote in *School Library Journal,* "to appreciate her own concerns in the light of her grandmother's." The diary also helps save the lives of Eleanor, her brother, and a friend when they escape from a raging brush fire by finding her grandmother's secret cave.

In *I Am Susannah,* it is the main character's best friend who moves away, leaving Susannah to deal with her self-involved mother, making new friends, and her first encounter with adolescent kissing games. At the same time, a mysterious woman with a supposedly tragic past, known as the "Blue Lady," moves into her best friend's old house. When Susannah, an aspiring artist, spies the Blue Lady's artistic talents, the two begin a friendship of their own. Nancy Vasilakis praised *I Am Susannah* in *Horn Book* for its "excellent characterizations and an exploration of pertinent contemporary themes."

In 1991, Gleeson published two works of very different natures, *The Great Big Scary Dog* and *Dodger.* The first, called an "unusual and engaging book" by *School Library Journal* reviewer Lisa Dennis, moved Gleeson's focus from adolescent angst to the typical fears of a preschooler. *The Great Big Scary Dog* is the story of how three young children, using their imaginations and some very colorful costumes, help a little girl overcome her fear of a neighborhood dog. The second book, *Dodger,* returns to themes of adolescent anxieties and adjustments. Mick Jamieson is a troubled student of thirteen who has a lot to deal with. Since his mother's recent death, Mick has had to move from a small Australian country town to suburban Campbelltown to live with his grandmother. His father, a truck driver, is away all the time, although Mick is constantly hoping for his return. *Dodger* is also the story of Penny, a first-year teacher who sees enough in Mick to cast him as the Artful Dodger in the school production of *Oliver Twist,* despite the resistance of several other teachers. In a review for *Magpies,* Stephanie Owen Reeder noted the sensitive handling of the relationship between the two characters, as well as Gleeson's portrayal of "young adolescents dealing with life in believable settings, and in a way which captures the emotions of the reader." Following *Dodger,* Gleeson returned to books for younger children, including *Uncle David,* about a young child's tendency to exaggerate, and *Mum Goes to Work,* which compares

A young aspiring artist confronts changes in family members and friends in Gleeson's award-winning novel. (Cover illustration by Patricia Raine.)

mothers' work with that of their children's in the day care center.

Gleeson's own three children have had considerable influence on her work. "I am constantly observing them and being reminded of my own experiences as a child," she told *SATA*. "I try to bring to the reader the feelings of those real experiences so that they can identify with the characters—whether they be kids from the bush as in *Eleanor, Elizabeth,* the city as in *I am Susannah,* or suburbia as in *Dodger.*"

Works Cited

Burns, Connie Tyrrell, review of *Eleanor, Elizabeth, School Library Journal,* June, 1990, pp. 121-22.

Dennis, Lisa, review of *The Great Big Scary Dog, School Library Journal,* May, 1994, p. 94.

Reeder, Stephanie Owen, review of *Dodger, Magpies,* March, 1991, p. 4.

Vasilakis, Nancy, review of *I Am Susannah, Horn Book,* September, 1989, pp. 628-29.

For More Information See

PERIODICALS

Horn Book, September, 1989, p. 628; April, 1991, p. 65; July, 1993, pp. 443, 496.

Publishers Weekly, April 11, 1994, p. 63.

School Library Journal, June, 1989, p. 108; September, 1993, p. 208.

Voice of Youth Advocates, October, 1989, p. 212; August, 1990, p. 160.*

* * *

GOSS, Clay(ton E.) 1946-

Personal

Born May 26, 1946, in Philadelphia, PA; son of Douglas P. (a counselor) and Alfreda (a teacher; maiden name, Ivey) Jackson; married Linda McNear (a teacher and performer), March 25, 1969; children: Aisha, Uhuru (daughters). *Education:* Howard University, B.F.A., 1972.

Career

Poet, playwright, and writer. Department of Recreation, Washington, DC, drama specialist, 1969; Howard University, Washington, DC, playwright in residence in drama department, 1970-73, playwright in residence at Institute for the Arts and Humanities, 1973-75. Instructor in poetry and development of Afro-American theater, Antioch College, Washington, DC, and Baltimore, MD, campuses, 1971-73. *Member:* Theatre Black, Kappa Alpha Psi.

Writings

FOR CHILDREN

Bill Pickett: Black Bulldogger (novel), illustrated by Chico Hall, Hill & Wang, 1970.

(With wife, Linda Goss) *The Baby Leopard: An African Folktale,* illustrated by Suzanne Bailey-Jones and Michael R. Jones, Bantam, 1989.

(With L. Goss) *It's Kwanzaa Time!,* Philomel, 1993.

PLAYS

Hip Rumpelstiltskin, produced in Washington, DC, 1969.

Ornette (three-act), produced in Washington, DC, at Howard University, 1970.

On Being Hit (one-act), produced in Washington, DC, at Howard University, 1970, produced as *Of Being Hit* in Brooklyn, NY, at Billie Holiday Theater, 1973.

Homecookin' (one-act), produced in Washington, DC, at Howard University, 1970.

Andrew (one-act), produced in Baltimore, MD, c. 1970, produced Off-Broadway at New York Shakespeare Festival Theatre, 1972.

Mars: Monument to the Last Black Eunuch, produced in Washington, DC, at Howard University, 1972.

Oursides (one-act), produced in New York City, 1972.

Spaces in Time, produced Off-Broadway by D. C. Black Repertory Company, 1972.
Homecookin': Five Plays, Howard University Press, 1974.

Also author of *Keys to the Kingdom.* Plays published in anthologies, including *Transition,* 1972; *Kuntu Drama,* 1974; and *The New Lafayette Theatre Presents: Six Black Playwrights,* 1974.

OTHER

Author of the television play *Billy McGhee,* for *The Place,* broadcast by WRC-TV (Washington, DC), 1974. Contributor to books, including *We Speak as Liberators: Young Black Poets,* 1970; *The Drama of Nommo,* 1972; and *The Sheet,* 1974. Contributor of short fiction, articles, and reviews to periodicals, including *Liberator, Reflect, Black Books Bulletin, Blackstage,* and *Black World.*

■ Sidelights

Clay Goss once commented: "What we must first do is to make our goals become our models instead of models becoming our goals. Then build from there."

■ For More Information See

PERIODICALS

Choice, January, 1976, p. 1444.
Grade Teacher, February, 1971, p. 147.
Jet, October 15, 1970.
Kirkus Reviews, October 1, 1970, p. 1096.
Library Journal, March 15, 1971, p. 1114; June 15, 1975, p. 1236.
Washington Post, March 21, 1971; March 1, 1973.*

* * *

GRAY, Les 1929-

■ Personal

Born August 20, 1929, in New York, NY; married Jacqueline Roberts (an administrative assistant), January 1, 1980; children: (previous marriage) Marcy, Debbie. *Education:* Philadelphia Museum School of Art, Certificate in Illustration, 1953. *Hobbies and other interests:* "Pre-Colombian art, reading; music: jazz, classical; Buster Keaton movies, gardening, t'ai chi."

■ Addresses

Home—491 Hill St., San Luis Obispo, CA 93405.

■ Career

Freelance illustrator, 1957—. Glass Craft Design, Philadelphia, PA, sand blasted designs for interior designers and architects, 1951-54; Fellman Associates Advertising, Philadelphia, designer and illustrator, 1954-55; *American Mercury* Magazine, Philadelphia, assistant art director, 1955-56; Philadelphia College of Art, Philadelphia, instructor in drawing and pictorial composition, 1961-63. *Military service:* 11th Airborne Division, 1946-48, served in Hokkaido, Japan, 1950-51, and Fort Campbell, Kentucky; became sergeant.

■ Awards, Honors

Silver medal, 1961, and Award of Excellence, 1969, both from Art Directors Club of Philadelphia; "Cover of the Year" awards, *Highlights for Children,* 1983, 1984, 1990, and 1993; Educational Press Association Award for Graphics of Children's Publications (cover illustration), 1990; honorable mention, Ozzie Award for Design Excellence, 1991; Neographics Silver Award (cover ilustration), 1993.

■ Writings

ILLUSTRATOR

The Mystery of Scull Cap Island, Knopf, 1958.
Princess Liliuokalani, Bobbs-Merrill, 1961.
Martha Washington, Bobbs-Merrill, 1961.
Patrick Henry, Bobbs-Merrill, 1961.
Yellow Silk for Mei Lee, Bobbs-Merrill, 1962.
Track the Grizzly Down, Morrow, 1962.
The Yellow Cat Screams, Morrow, 1962.
The Brownie Scout Handbook, Girl Scouts of America, 1963.
Fremont of the West, Viking, 1965.
The Word Machine, Viking, 1966.

LES GRAY

Joan Foster Munson, *The Giant Book of Giants,* Golden Press/Western Publishing, 1967.
Pauline Palmer Meek, *Back Yard Giant,* Western Publishing/Disney, 1968.
(With Judy Stang) *The Magic Realm of Fairy Tales,* Whitman/Western Publishing, 1968.
DeVere Ramsay, reteller, *Noah and the Ark,* Western Publishing, 1968.
Carlo Collodi, *Pinocchio,* Whitman/Western Publishing, 1968.
Eileen Daly, *Snoozeroo,* C. R. Gibson, 1968.
Norah Smaridge, *The Big Tidy-Up,* Golden Press/Western Publishing, 1970.
Happy Helper 1-2-3, Western Publishing, 1971.
Betty Ren Wright and Joanne Wylie, *Elephant's Birthday Party,* Golden Press/Western Publishing, 1971.
Famous Fairy Tales, Whitman/Western Publishing, 1971.
Mable Watts, reteller, *Little Red Riding Hood,* Little Golden Books/Western Publishing, 1972.
David Lee Harrison, *Piggy Wiglet and the Great Adventure,* Golden Press/Western Publishing, 1973.
The Great Gumshoe, Western Publishing, 1982.
Larry Dane Brimner, *Max and Felix,* Boyds Mills Press, 1993.
Judith Ross Enderle and Stephanie Gordon Tessler, *The Good-for-Something Dragon,* Boyds Mills Press, 1993.

Has also done illustrations for several children's magazines including: *Young People; High Call; Ranger Rick's; Today's Girl; Jack and Jill; Humpty Dumpty; Child Life; Children's Digest; Turtle;* and *Highlights for Children.*

Illustrator of various children's album covers, including *Peter Pan; Christmas Songs That Tickle the Funny Bone; Willy Wonka and the Chocolate Factory; The Golden World of Nursery Rhymes; Winnie-the-Pooh;* and *The Wizard of Oz.* Also collaborator on video production of *Max and Felix* for Boyds Mills Press/Piver Productions, 1993.

ILLUSTRATOR; SUPPLEMENTARY READERS

Ollie's Alligator, Macmillan, 1965.
Happy and Sad, Macmillan, 1970.
(With Marilyn Bass, Mary Val Marsh, Carroll Rinehart, Edith Savage, Ralph Beelke, and Ronald Silverman) *The Spectrum of Music,* Macmillan, 1974.
Fred the Frog, Lippincott, 1974.
Old Mr. Mack, Lippincott, 1974.
The Real Bandit, Lippincott, 1974.
Little Cub and the Bee's Nest, Lippincott, 1974.
An Apple, Lippincott, 1974.
Tip Top, Lippincott, 1974.
Drip Drop, Lippincott, 1974.
Martin Crumpet, Lippincott, 1974.
Mike and the Red Suspenders, Lippincott, 1974.
Greg and the Red Bike, Lippincott, 1974.
Ten Red Ants, Lippincott, 1974.
Sniff and Snuff, Lippincott, 1974.
Buttons the Clown, Lippincott, 1974.
The Old Merry-Go-Round, Lippincott, 1976.
The Nine Little Moppets, Lippincott, 1976.

Gray dressed Max in loud, mismatched clothing to highlight his energetic personality in Larry Dane Brimner's *Max and Felix.*

Sniff and Snuff Go Camping, Lippincott, 1976.
This and That, Lippincott, 1976.
(With Mitchell Sharmat and Marjorie Weinman Sharmat) *Kingdoms,* Holt, 1987.

Illustrator of other books in the J. B. Lippincott Reading Series, 1974-79, including: *Zoo Fun; More Zoo Fun;* and *Maybe It's Magic.* Also Illustrator of textbooks for Houghton Mifflin, Bobbs-Merrill, Harcourt Brace, D. C. Heath, J. B. Lippincott, Addison Wesley, Macmillan, McGraw-Hill, Harper & Row, Holt, Rinehart & Winston, Random House, Scribner, Zaner Bloser, Scott, Foresman, Prentice-Hall, Simon & Schuster, and Silver Burdett & Ginn, 1958-90.

AUTHOR AND ILLUSTRATOR WITH JANICE ROBINSON

The Fun and Care of a Puppy, Rainbow Educational Materials, Inc., 1974.
The Fun and Care of a Kitten, Rainbow Educational Materials, Inc., 1974.
The Fun and Care of a Gerbil, Rainbow Educational Materials, Inc., 1974.
The Fun of Training Your Dog, Rainbow Educational Materials, Inc., 1974.

Author/illustrator of wordless stories for *Highlights for Children,* 1992-93, including "A Day at the Beach," "The Monsters," "The Artist," "The Garden," and "The Tuba."

■ Work in Progress

Writing and illustrating a picture book called *The Circus-Horse Farmer.*

Sidelights

Les Gray told *SATA:* "My earliest recollection of drawing was at the age of four, sitting at the kitchen table in a house on the lower slopes of the Shawangunk Mountains. The street, Center Street, was the main access from the mountain to the small town of Ellenville, New York. Center Street also pointed the way to my grandfather's farm in the foothills of the Catskill Mountains on the opposite side of the valley. I spent summers there, exploring the fields and woods, watching trout under shady banks of streams and picking berries for huckleberry pies, expertly made by my grandmother.

"On occasion we visited my artist uncle, Milton Gray, in New York City. His roof-top studio on the East River was, to me, a place of wonder. The painters Robert Henri and George Bellows sponsored his first one-man show. And he participated in New York City's first 'Parisian Style' exhibition in Greenwich Village (on a wooden fence) in 1939. His influence, for me, was more spiritual than concrete. I saw him rarely and briefly. But, he did send me tubes of watercolors and notes of encouragement.

"An eventual move to New York City was a sharp contrast to the pine forests and rushing streams that had been my world. It was the beginning of many moves that I would make: Newburgh, New York, and graduation from high school; two years in Hokkaido, Japan, with the 11th Airborne Division; various states—Pennsylvania, Kentucky, Nevada, New Hampshire, and California—and towns and cities in each.

"As a result of the varied environments I experienced I have a wealth of images that I can call upon for my illustrations. I enjoy depicting situations in a humorous way. This allows me to emphasize individual characteristics and actions that I feel will be recognized and enjoyed by children and adults alike. I depicted Max in *Max and Felix* as a flamboyant character who had a zest for trying anything, even though his abilities never aligned with the results. His loud and mismatched clothing helped to convey his outgoing personality. I've known people like Max and I wanted to present him as a likable character with warmth and humor even though he is so silly.

"In another recent book, *The Good-for-Something Dragon,* Ashley, the baby dragon, is portrayed as a puppy-sized creature, one that the boy, James, could easily carry. I felt, as well, that children would identify Ashley as a pet they would want, especially since dragons are usually presented as monstrous. The adults were depicted as bulky, overbearing characters; formidable foes in James's quest to have Ashley accepted as his pet.

"My introduction to children's book illustration was through Henry C. Pitz, my instructor at the (then named) Philadelphia Museum School of Art. Mr. Pitz carried a rich tradition of illustration experience via a line extending from Howard Pyle through N. C. Wyeth and Thorton Oakley. He was an inspirational teacher of boundless energy who illustrated books at a prodigious rate as well as authoring books on the art and craft of illustration. He was a master of pen and ink.

"The field of children's books has changed since the enthusiastic lectures of Henry Pitz and my first book, *The Mystery of Skull Cap Island* for Alfred Knopf, in 1958. Not in underlying values, but more in the scope and diversity of market. Children's books were often looked upon as stepchildren of publishers, not the huge, competitive, and lucrative business of today. But still, it is an area of great dedication by publishers, authors, illustrators, and last, but not least, children's librarians. Children's books may well be the prime depositories of thought and points-of-view not tied to a commercial product presented for the sole purpose of exciting and fixating the attention of children.

"Regardless of technology, children's books still remain the most portable means of learning, imagination, and enjoyment for children."

For More Information See

PERIODICALS

Booklist, February 15, 1993.
Christian Science Monitor, October 7, 1993.
Kirkus Reviews, January 1, 1993.
Publishers Weekly, January 4, 1993.
School Library Journal, March, 1993.

* * *

GREENSTEIN, Elaine 1959-

Personal

Born May 8, 1959, in New York, NY; daughter of George (a baker) and Adele (a nurse; maiden name, Lilie) Greenstein. *Education:* Boston University, B.F.A., 1981; Pennsylvania State University, M.F.A., 1985. *Religion:* Jewish.

Addresses

Home—Wilmot Flat, NH.

Career

Bookmaker and author/illustrator. Formerly affiliated with a ceramics company. *Member:* Authors Guild, Authors League of America.

Awards, Honors

MacDowell fellow, 1983 and 1984; Virginia Center fellow, 1990.

Writings

(Self-illustrated) *Emily and the Crows,* Picture Book Studio, 1992.

(Self-illustrated) *Mrs. Rose's Garden,* Picture Book Studio, 1993.
(Illustrator) Candace Christiansen, *The Mitten Tree,* Philomel, 1995.
(Illustrator) Mark Karlins, *Mendel's Ladder,* Simon & Schuster, 1995.

■ Work in Progress

A book about hats and another about honey bees.

■ Sidelights

Although Elaine Greenstein was trained as a sculptor in college and graduate school, she found herself running the export division of a ceramics company and traveling around the world. As she wrote in her Picture Book Studio publicity release, Greenstein asked herself, "Who WAS this person carrying a briefcase?" She took some time to live at an artist's colony on a dairy farm and decided to make a change in her life. Fortunately for her young fans, Greenstein "changed from being a business person to a bookmaker."

Emily and the Crows, Greenstein's first book, shares an image that the artist enjoyed while living on the dairy farm: "a black-and-white-cow ... and a crow that sat most of the day on the cow's back." In Greenstein's tale, a little girl named Ivy is struck by the fact that Emily, a favorite cow, seems to prefer the company of crows to the other cows. In an initial attempt to understand this behavior, Ivy frightens away the birds. The clever girl perseveres, however, and imitates the crows so convincingly that they accept her as one of their own. Gathering with the crows around Emily, Ivy discovers that the cow is telling the crows wild and exciting tales of pigs with wings and mutant vegetables. Learning from Emily's example, Ivy delights her mother at bedtime by telling her a wild tale.

Diane Roback and Richard Donohue, writing in *Publishers Weekly,* noted that Greenstein uses a "unique watercolor-and-lithograph technique" and "renders highly textured, colorful images." Hazel Rochman commented in *Booklist* that *Emily and the Crows* "loses focus" after Ivy joins the crows, but added that the paintings are "bold and dramatic." Similarly, *School Library Journal* contributor Valerie F. Patterson decided that while the story is weak, Greenstein "is an illustrator with real talent."

■ Works Cited

"Elaine Greenstein" (publicity release), Picture Book Studio, c. 1992.
Patterson, Valerie F., review of *Emily and the Crows, School Library Journal,* January, 1993, p. 77.
Roback, Diane, and Richard Donohue, review of *Emily and the Crows, Publishers Weekly,* April 27, 1992, p. 267.
Rochman, Hazel, review of *Emily and the Crows, Booklist,* May 15, 1992, p. 1687.

■ For More Information See

PERIODICALS

Children's Book Watch, March, 1993, p. 2.
Horn Book Guide, fall, 1992, p. 232.

* * *

GREGORY, Valiska 1940-

■ Personal

Born November 3, 1940, in Chicago, IL; daughter of Andrej (a sign painter) and Stephania (a clerk; maiden name, Lascik) Valiska; married Marshall W. Gregory (a university professor), August 18, 1962; children: Melissa, Holly. *Education:* Indiana Central College, B.A. (cum laude), 1962; University of Chicago, M.A., 1966; postgraduate study at Vassar Institute of Publishing and Writing, 1984, and Simmons College Center for the Study of Children's Literature, 1986. *Politics:* Democrat.

■ Addresses

Home—5300 Grandview Dr., Indianapolis, IN 46208. *Office*—Butler University, Writer-in-Residence, 4600 Sunset Ave., Indianapolis, IN 46308. *Agent*—Dorothy Markinko, McIntosh & Otis, 310 Madison Ave., New York, NY 10017.

■ Career

White Oak Elementary School, Whiting, IN, music and drama teacher, 1962-64; Oak Lawn Memorial High School, Oak Lawn, IL, teacher, 1965-68; University of Wisconsin, Milwaukee, WI, lecturer in English, 1968-74; University of Indianapolis, Indianapolis, IN, adjunct professor of English, 1974-83; Butler University, Indianapolis, adjunct professor of English, 1983-85, fellow at Butler Writers' Studio and founding director of Butler University Midwinter Children's Literature Conference, 1989-92, Writer-in-Residence, 1993—. Speaker/workshop leader at schools, libraries, and conferences across the United States, 1983—. *Member:* Authors Guild, Authors League of America, American Association of University Women (Creative Writers president, 1984-86), Society of Children's Book Writers and Illustrators, National Book Critics Circle, Children's Reading Round Table, Society of Midland Authors.

■ Awards, Honors

Illinois Wesleyan University Poetry Award, 1982; Billee Murray Denny National Poetry Award honorable mention, Billee Murray Denny Poetry Foundation, 1982; Hudelson Award for Children's Fiction Work-in-Progress, 1982; Individual Artist Master Fellowship, Indiana Arts Commission and the National Endowment for the Arts, 1986, for artistic excellence and achievements; State Art Treasure, *Arts Indiana,* 1989, for achievement in poetry and children's fiction; Parents' Choice Award,

1992, for *Through the Mickle Woods;* Parents' Choice Honor Award, 1993, for *Babysitting for Benjamin.*

Sunny Side Up was a *Chickadee Magazine* Book of the Month, 1986; *Terribly Wonderful* was a *Grandparents Magazine* Best Book, 1986; *The Oatmeal Cookie Giant* and *Riddle Soup* were on the 1987 *Chicago Sun-Times* Best of the Best Books list; *Through the Mickle Woods* was named a "Pick of the List" by the American Booksellers Association, 1992; *Through the Mickle Woods* and *Happy Burpday, Maggie McDougal!* were on the State of Indiana Read-Aloud List, 1993.

■ Writings

FOR CHILDREN

Terribly Wonderful, illustrated by Jeni Bassett, Macmillan/Four Winds, 1986.
Sunny Side Up, illustrated by Bassett, Macmillan/Four Winds, 1986.
Riddle Soup, illustrated by Bassett, Macmillan/Four Winds, 1987.
The Oatmeal Cookie Giant, illustrated by Bassett, Macmillan/Four Winds, 1987.
Happy Burpday, Maggie McDougal!, illustrated by Pat Porter, Little, Brown, 1992.
Through the Mickle Woods, illustrated by Barry Moser, Little, Brown, 1992.
Babysitting for Benjamin, illustrated by Lynn Munsinger, Little, Brown, 1993.
Looking for Angels, illustrated by Leslie Baker, Simon & Schuster, 1995.
Stories from a Time Before, illustrated by Margot Tomes, Open Court, 1995.
Kate's Giants, illustrated by Virginia Austin, Candlewick Press/Walker Books, 1995.
When Stories Fell Like Shooting Stars, illustrated by Stephano Vitale, Simon & Schuster, 1996.

Contributor of stories and poems for children to *Cricket Magazine.*

OTHER

The Words Like Angels Come (poetry for adults), Juniper Press, 1987.

Also contributor of poetry and articles to periodicals, including *Publishers Weekly, Poetry Northeast, Spoon River,* and *Poet.* Contributor of children's book reviews to *Publishers Weekly.* Gregory's poetry and adult book manuscripts are kept with the Juniper Press collection in the Rare Book Room at the University of Wisconsin.

■ Work in Progress

Three picture books, *The Book Lady, Papa's Pancakes,* and *A Valentine for Norman Noggs;* two novels, *Grandpa's Shanty/Grandma's Loom* and *The Velcro Chicken.*

■ Sidelights

Although she's been writing since the mid-1980s, Valiska Gregory has recently come to be widely recognized as

VALISKA GREGORY

an up-and-coming star in the children's literature scene. Her books *Through the Mickle Woods* and *Babysitting for Benjamin* won Parents' Choice Awards in 1992 and 1993 respectively. Gregory gained her insights into the world of children's literature from a combination of practical and scholarly experience. "I received my M.A. degree from the University of Chicago on a Ford Foundation fellowship," she told *SATA,* "and I have taught every grade there is—from kindergarten children to seniors in college, with courses ranging from poetry and drama to music and American literature."

More than this, Gregory learned to love stories from an early age. "I was lucky enough to grow up in a Czech neighborhood in Chicago where money was scarce but children were treasured, and where, always, my father told us stories," Gregory told *SATA.* "My brothers and I ate them with our daily bread, swallowed them whole, and begged for more. My father shaped his tales as carefully as he painted my name on my lunch box in Gothic letters. The black ink seemed to appear like angels on the penciled lines, a dimness made clear. It is this clarity of vision I wish to offer children—stories told with humor, charm, and grace; stories that, like good soup, sustain the human spirit.

"I have always been passionate about words; I have always loved stories. Neither of my parents went beyond the eighth grade in school, but they believed in the power of education. When I was told at age four I'd have to wait until I was old enough to go to school to learn how to read, I convinced my parents to take me to see the school principal. I hinted that it was a matter of life and death: I simply *had* to learn to read, I told the principal, and to my delight, she let me start school a year earlier than the rules allowed. I have been happily reading and writing ever since.

"I became a writer, in part, because of my grandmother's loom. Grandma brought the metal parts of the loom in her trunk from Czechoslovakia, and my father, who was a young boy at the time, reconstructed the loom from old pieces of wood. When I was a child, one of my favorite places to play was in the basement, near the furnace, where the coal, like golden cobblestones, kept us warm. It was there that my father would tell me stories, and my grandmother, and then later my mother, would weave rugs made from strips of cloth cut from old clothes. Nothing was wasted.... As I played, I learned about making things. I learned that with discipline and love, things could be woven together—rugs could be made from rags, stories could be made from words, and lives could be crafted from threads of experience and thought. It came as no surprise that I would end up as a person who makes things—sometimes bread, sometimes quilts, sometimes stories and poems—and that I feel grateful to be doing work that I think is important and brings me great joy.

"I don't really choose the stories I write; they have a way of choosing me. I have long been fascinated by the creative process: how the experience we call life is woven into the pattern we call fiction. I try to save everything, the way some people save bits of string or pieces of cloth. This saving is important, because one never knows when a particular slant of light or glance of vermillion might be something from which a story grows.

"Had it not been for my bonny daughters, Mellie and Holly, and for their eighteen-pound lop-eared rabbit, I'm sure I would not have written *Babysitting for Benjamin.*" *Babysitting for Benjamin* is about Ralph and Frances, an old married mouse couple who decide to babysit a rabbit to put some zip back into their lives. They get more than they bargained for when Benjamin wreaks havoc upon their home. By the end of the story, however, Ralph and Frances arrive upon a happy solution to keeping their wits without having to lose Benjamin's frolicsome company. "This wholesome message," praised one *Kirkus Reviews* critic, "is appealing packaged with amusingly wry dialogue and disarming illustrations."

Babysitting for Benjamin, Gregory elaborated for *SATA,* "is a book about seeing things from another person's point of view, and though it has little to do with how the real life rabbit, Sebastian, terrorized our dog and chewed the vacuum cleaner hose, his toddler-like insouciance, his pocket-scientist curiosity, and his exuberance all made their way into the story. Sebastian was rowdy and rambunctious, just like the book's Benjamin, and, like Ralph and Frances, we felt privileged to watch our lively daughters as they became the extraordinary and civilized people they are."

Another one of Gregory's popular creations is *Happy Burpday, Maggie McDougal!,* in which Maggie faces the problem of getting her friend Bonkers a nice birthday present when she has no money. Cynthia, her snooty classmate, has spent tons of cash on a present, and Maggie is stumped at what to do until she finds some treasures in her grandmother's attic that Bonkers ends up liking more than Cynthia's gift. While *School Library Journal* contributor Maggie McEwen was uncomfortable with the coincidence that Maggie happens to find valuable issues of Bonkers' favorite comic book in the attic, she praised the "vivid images and neat turns of phrase"—especially the "delightfully funny" scenes portraying Ms. Chumley's efforts to teach Maggie's class—and concludes that the book is a "satisfying" work for "beginning chapter book readers."

Gregory told *SATA* about her source of inspiration for *Happy Burpday:* "I would not have written *Happy Burpday, Maggie McDougal!*—a book with a title only a second grader could love—had it not been that until I was eleven, my family lived in an apartment my father built from the attic of my grandparents' house. The walls were slanted like geometry triangles, and I lived in the middle of an enormous extended immigrant family. Like Maggie, I got to see my grandmother every day,

In this 1993 publication, a mouse couple run into trouble when they decide to babysit for a bouncy bunny.

To fulfill his queen's last wish, a king ventures into the woods and finds a wise bear with the power to heal his grief in Gregory's 1992 tale, *Through the Mickle Woods.* (Illustration by Barry Moser.)

and, like Gilbert and Sullivan's Major General, I lived surrounded by dozens of uncles and cousins and aunts. I had great fun with the classroom scenes because when I was fresh out of college I ended up unexpectedly teaching kindergarten, music, and drama, without any formal training at all. I was a lot like Ms. Chumley who is very enthusiastic, very dedicated, and very inexperienced, and I still draw on the wonderful things my students taught me every day as I write. Although none of the details of the published story are taken directly from my real life, there's also a hint in the book of the loving relationship that exists between my mother and her granddaughter Becky, and a whiff of the fun my brothers and I used to have making presents for all our many aunts and uncles at Christmas when we didn't have a penny in our pockets.

"*Through the Mickle Woods,* which won a Parents' Choice Award, is a book that means a great deal to me because the story was given as a gift. For three years my husband and I had experienced a series of tragedies that seemed unending. In that too short time, we experienced more grief—more illness, more pain, more deaths—than we thought, quite literally, we could endure. We needed healing. On Epiphany day, when tradition has it that the wise men brought their gifts to Bethlehem, I awakened with the first three pages of the book in my head. I knew that I needed to be patient until my heart and head had it written and then my pen could simply write it down."

Through the Mickle Woods is a much more serious work for Gregory. It tells of a king and his grief over his dying queen. Her last request to him is that he go into the "dark and mickle woods" and find the bear. When the king finds the bear, the animal turns out to be a wise creature whose stories about beauty and life eventually console the king. "The language and phrasing are as pleasing to the ear as the story is to the heart," declared *Horn Book* critic Elizabeth S. Watson.

"It took over a year for the rest of *Through the Mickle Woods* to come," Gregory continued to tell *SATA.* "Bits and pieces of it would appear whole and in order, like a photograph emerging in developing fluid. And when it was finished, I knew that none of the things we had experienced, no matter how hard, had been wasted. It was a story that wove together all I had learned about despair and the healing power of love."

Gregory had these closing thoughts: "If it is true that all of us write the stories of our own lives each day, as we live them, then books for children are important, because it is through books that children learn about the power of language, about joy and sorrow and laughter and action, about how they might weave together the disparate experiences and possibilities that will become the stories of their own lives."

■ Works Cited

Review of *Babysitting for Benjamin, Kirkus Reviews,* May 15, 1993, p. 660.

McEwen, Maggie, review of *Happy Burpday, Maggie McDougal!, School Library Journal,* June, 1992, p. 93.

Watson, Elizabeth S., review of *Through the Mickle Woods, Horn Book,* March/April, 1993, pp. 202-3.

■ For More Information See

PERIODICALS

Bulletin of the Center for Children's Books, September, 1992, p. 11.

Horn Book, September-October, 1993, pp. 585-86.

Kirkus Reviews, May 15, 1992, pp. 669-70.

Publishers Weekly, July 25, 1986, pp. 183-84.

School Library Journal, March, 1987; February, 1988.

H

HALE, Christy
See APOSTOLOU, Christine Hale

* * *

HALLOWELL, Tommy
See HILL, Thomas (Hallowell)

* * *

HAMILTON-PATERSON, James 1941-

JAMES HAMILTON-PATERSON

■ Personal

Born November 6, 1941, in London, England; son of John Hamilton-Paterson (a physician) and Ursula Im-Thurn (a physician). *Education:* Exeter College, Oxford, B.A., 1964, M.A., 1968; King's College, London, postgraduate study in education. *Hobbies and other interests:* Music, science.

■ Addresses

Agent—c/o John Johnson Ltd., Clerkenwell House, 45/47 Clerkenwell Green, London EC1R 0HT, England.

■ Career

Writer. Taught English in Tripoli, Libya, 1965-66; St. Stephen's Hospital, London, England, porter and operating room technician, 1966-68; free-lance journalist, including stints for the *Times Literary Supplement* and *New Statesman,* 1968-74. *Member:* Royal Geographic Society (fellow), Oriental Club (London).

■ Awards, Honors

Newdigate Prize for poetry, Oxford University, 1964; Whitbread Award for first novel and runner-up for book of year, both 1989, for *Gerontius;* Gold Medal, International Radio Festival of New York, 1990, for a radio play adapted from *Gerontius.*

■ Writings

FICTION

Flight Underground (juvenile), Faber, 1969.
The House in the Waves (juvenile), S. G. Phillips, 1970.
Hostage! (juvenile), Gollancz, 1978, Collins, 1980.
The View from Mount Dog (stories), Macmillan, 1986.
Gerontius, Macmillan (London), 1989, Macmillan (New York), 1990.
That Time in Malomba, Soho, 1990 (published in England as *The Bell-Boy,* Hutchinson, 1990).
Griefwork, J. Cape, 1993.
Ghosts of Manila, Farrar, Straus, 1994.

NONFICTION

A Very Personal War: The Story of Cornelius Hawkridge, Hodder & Stoughton, 1971, published as *The Greedy War,* McKay, 1972.

(With Carol Andrews) *Mummies: Death and Life in Ancient Egypt,* Collins, 1978, Viking, 1979.
Playing with Water: Passion and Solitude on a Philippine Island, New Amsterdam, 1987.
The Great Deep: The Sea and Its Threshold, Random House, 1992 (published in England as *Seven-Tenths: Meditations on the Sea and Its Thresholds,* Century Hutchinson, 1992).

OTHER

Option Three (poems), Gollancz, 1974.
Dutch Alps (poems), Redcliffe Poetry, 1984.

Hamilton-Paterson adapted *Gerontius* as a radio play for the British Broadcasting Corporation (BBC), 1990. Contributor of book reviews to *New Republic.*

■ Work in Progress

A nonfiction work and a novel.

■ Sidelights

Although he is best known for adult novels such as the Whitbread Award-winning *Gerontius* and nonfiction such as *Playing with Water,* British-born author James Hamilton-Paterson has also written books for younger readers. A regular traveler who divides his time between homes in Italy and the Philippines, Hamilton-Paterson has translated his rootlessness into works which often examine issues of alienation and communication. For instance, the juvenile novel *The House in the Waves* involves an emotionally disturbed boy who travels into the past, while *Hostage!* relates the harrowing kidnapping and maturation of a lonely, self-absorbed fifteen-year-old.

Hamilton-Paterson was born in London, the son of doctors, and considered music as a career before entering Oxford University, where he studied English. There he won the Newdigate Prize for poetry during his final year, but instead of attempting to parlay this early literary success into a career, he left the country to teach English. "My first job on leaving university was teaching in a government-run school in Libya," the author told Jean W. Ross in an interview for *Contemporary Authors.* "I wrote a novel while I was there, which I didn't publish; I was quite conscious that it was a trial run, as it were. I had been writing all the time, so I thought of myself then as a potential writer, at any rate." Hamilton-Paterson returned to England after a year and worked as an orderly in a London hospital.

"In 1968 I went up the Amazon for the first time," the author continued in his interview, "and as a result of that, and of traveling in South America and in Bolivia particularly, I came back and wrote a piece that I sent to the *New Statesman,* just on spec. They not only published it, but they asked me if I would like to join the staff, initially to fill in for people who were away on summer vacation. I did, and they asked me to stay on. That was my entree into journalism." Shortly after, Hamilton-Paterson's first book was published, a novel for children called *Flight Underground,* which was quickly followed by *The House in the Waves.*

Based in part on Hamilton-Paterson's experiences working at a London hospital, *The House in the Waves* is "the knowing story of a boy endowed with the sometime acuity/sometime remoteness of emotional disturbance," noted a *Kirkus Reviews* writer. Fourteen-year-old Martin has spent his life in and out of institutions with not much improvement, until a move to a seaside home takes him into the past. There, in the 1600s, Martin embarks upon an adventurous rescue which gives him some self-knowledge and confidence when he awakes in the present to find it all a dream. Some critics faulted the book for an abrupt transition from Martin's dream, as well as the dream's too-convenient interpretation by a sympathetic nurse. The *Kirkus Reviews* critic remarked, however, that "insights remain nevertheless and lend themselves to pondering," while a *Bulletin of the Center for Children's Books* writer called the book a "well-written" portrait of an emotionally disturbed youth that is both "sympathetic and convincing."

The maturation and growth of the protagonist in Hamilton-Paterson's *Hostage!* is less symbolic, as the kidnapping of fifteen-year-old Wayne transforms him from an overweight, irritable coward into a self-assured young man who refuses to look for easy answers. Set in a fictitious country in the Middle East, *Hostage!* contains "considerable political acuteness" while maintaining an "emphasis ... on personal experience," Margery Fisher wrote in *Growing Point.* Captured by mistake, Wayne comes to understand and identify with his captors, particularly their leader, Tewfiq. As his parents and the authorities attempt to rescue him, Wayne overcomes his captors' brutal treatment of him; his friendship with Tewfiq becomes "the core of this fine story," according to Marcus Crouch in the *Junior Bookshelf.* The result, writes the critic, is "a story which is as exciting as an old-fashioned 'reward' but which is also intelligent, topical, sharply observed and honest." *Times Literary Supplement* contributor David Rees concurred, remarking that *Hostage!* "is a well-written and moving story, quite unsentimental, and rich in its evocation of the background landscape in the desert."

Since *Hostage!,* Hamilton-Paterson has concentrated on works for adults that continue the themes—such as learning to grow and communicate—that are featured in his works for children. Although he has won considerable acclaim for his writing, the author prefers to shun the public spotlight, as he told Ross: "I really do still naively believe that a writer is what he writes and not who he is. That applies to any artist. That's almost an untenable position at this time. Nonetheless, I go on holding it."

■ Works Cited

Crouch, Marcus, review of *Hostage!, Junior Bookshelf,* October, 1978, p. 268.
Fisher, Margery, review of *Hostage!, Growing Point,* July, 1978, p. 3363.

Hamilton-Paterson, James, interview with Jean W. Ross in *Contemporary Authors,* Vol. 137, Gale, 1992, pp. 181-85.
Review of *The House in the Waves, Bulletin of the Center for Children's Books,* September, 1970, p. 9.
Review of *The House in the Waves, Kirkus Reviews,* April 15, 1970, pp. 464-465.
Rees, David, "Siege Mentalities," *Times Literary Supplement,* April 7, 1978, p. 379.

■ For More Information See

PERIODICALS

Los Angeles Times Book Review, June 2, 1991, p. 11.
New York Times Book Review, October 5, 1980, p. 30; April 29, 1990, pp. 25, 42-43; October 14, 1990, p. 7; June 30, 1991, p. 22.
Observer (London), January 21, 1990, p. 60.
Publishers Weekly, July 6, 1990, p. 58; September 21, 1990, pp. 56-57.
School Library Journal, August, 1980, p. 76.
Times (London), January 25, 1990.
Times Literary Supplement, July 2, 1970, p. 713; March 10, 1972, p. 264; February 28, 1975, p. 214; August 14, 1987, p. 883; March 24-30, 1989, p. 300; January 26-February 1, 1990, p. 87.
Vanity Fair, August, 1992, pp. 80-89.
Washington Post, October 26, 1990.
Washington Post Book World, May 5, 1991, pp. 3, 6.

* * *

HARLOW, Rosie 1961-

■ Personal

Born June 21, 1961, in Glasgow, Scotland; daughter of Christopher Geoffrey (a university professor and lecturer) and Margaret (a homemaker and part-time secretary; maiden name, Annan) Harlow; *Education:* University of Exeter, B.A., 1984; University of Durham, Post-Graduate Certificate in Education, 1985; University of Oxford, Certificate in Countryside Conservation, 1992. *Politics:* Green. *Religion:* Pantheistic. *Hobbies and other interests:* The great outdoors, wildlife, walking, mountaineering, windsurfing, sailing, traveling abroad, music, singing, literature, poetry.

■ Addresses

Home—12 Sunningwell Rd., Oxford OX1 45X, England.

■ Career

South Oxfordshire Countryside Education Trust, Oxford, England, teacher, 1985-87; Hill End Residential Environment Centre, Oxford County Council, Oxford, England, teacher, 1987-88; Sutton Courtenay Field Study Centre, Oxford County Council, Oxford, England, head of centre, 1989-93. *Member:* National Association of Field Study Organizers.

ROSIE HARLOW

■ Writings

(With Gareth Morgan) *175 Amazing Nature Experiments,* illustrated by Kuo Kang Chen and others, Random House, 1992.

"FUN WITH SCIENCE" SERIES; WITH MORGAN

Trees and Leaves, illustrated by David More and Liz Peperell, Warwick, 1991.
Energy and Growth, illustrated by Chen and Cecilia Fitzsimmons, Warwick, 1991.
Observing Minibeasts, illustrated by Chen and Oxford Illustrators, Warwick, 1991.
Cycles and Seasons, illustrated by Chen, Peperell, and Oxford Illustrators, Warwick, 1991.
Nature: Experiments, Tricks, Things to Make, Kingfisher Books, 1992.

"YOUNG DISCOVERER'S ENVIRONMENT" SERIES

Energy and Power, Kingfisher Books, 1995.
Nature in Danger, Kingfisher Books, 1995.
Pollution and Waste, Kingfisher Books, 1995.
Rubbish and Recycling, Kingfisher Books, 1995.

■ Sidelights

Rosie Harlow explained her love of nature to *SATA:* "Ever since childhood I have been fascinated by things in the natural world around me. Family holidays were always spent camping out in the wilds of Iceland, Scotland, Ireland, and Corsica. This allowed time and space for exploring, observing, and finding out the wonders of the natural world going on all around us.

"This is a legacy I have carried with me through my life, and I now find myself sharing it with today's children through my job as an environmental teacher at a field study center. I go out daily to an urban nature reserve owned by a Power Station. Here, groups of primary school children (age 4-11) come for a day visit or stay residentially up to a week. Through games, activities, and exploring, I can share with them my love, knowledge, and sense of caring for the natural world.

"Children have an innate sense of love and caring and it is up to us, their parents and teachers, to bring this out in them. If we cannot help our children to care for this world, what future does it have?

"*175 Amazing Nature Experiments* is a book to help children enjoy and find out more about the natural world around them. Only in this way will they learn to love and care for it."

■ For More Information See

PERIODICALS

Books for Young Children, summer, 1992, p. 17.
School Library Journal, June, 1992, p. 132.
Times Educational Supplement, May 1, 1992, p. 12.*

* * *

HARRIS, Rosemary (Jeanne) 1923-

■ Personal

Born February 20, 1923, in London, England; daughter of Arthur Travers (a British Royal Air Force marshal) and Barbara D. K. (Money) Harris. *Education:* Studied at Chelsea School of Art, London, and Courtauld Institute, London. *Politics:* Liberal. *Religion:* Church of England. *Hobbies and other interests:* Theatre, music, photography.

■ Addresses

Agent—A. P. Watt Ltd., 20 John St., London WC1N 2DR, England.

■ Career

Writer and critic; picture restorer. Reader for Metro-Goldwyn-Mayer, 1951-52; children's book reviewer, *Times* (London), 1970-73. *Member:* Society of Authors (deputy chairperson, 1987-90).

■ Awards, Honors

Carnegie Medal of Library Association (England) for outstanding children's book of 1968, American Library Association (ALA) Notable Book, *Horn Book* Honor List, and Book World's Children Spring Festival Honor Book, 1970, all for *The Moon in the Cloud;* Arts Council grant for research, 1971.

ROSEMARY HARRIS

■ Writings

FOR CHILDREN

The Moon in the Cloud (first book in trilogy), Faber, 1968, Macmillan (New York), 1969.
The Shadow on the Sun (second book in trilogy), Macmillan, 1970.
(Reteller) *The Child in the Bamboo Grove,* illustrated by Errol le Cain, Phillips, 1971.
The Seal-Singing, Macmillan, 1971.
The Bright and Morning Star (third book in trilogy), Macmillan, 1972.
The King's White Elephant, illustrated by le Cain, Faber, 1973.
(Reteller) *The Flying Ship,* illustrated by le Cain, Faber, 1975.
The Little Dog of Fo, illustrated by le Cain, Faber, 1976.
I Want to Be a Fish, Kestrel Books, 1977.
A Quest for Orion, Faber, 1978.
(Reteller) *Beauty and the Beast,* illustrated by le Cain, Doubleday, 1979.
Green Finger House, illustrated by Juan Wijngaard, Eel Pie, 1979.
Tower of the Stars, Faber, 1980.
(Reteller) *The Enchanted Horse,* Kestrel Books, 1981.
Janni's Stork, illustrated by Wijngaard, Blackie & Son, 1982.
Zed, Faber, 1982.
(Adapter) *Heidi,* Benn, 1983.
Summers of the Wild Rose, Faber, 1987.
Colm of the Islands, Walker Books, 1989.
Ticket to Freedom, Faber, 1991.
The Wildcat Strike, Hamish Hamilton, 1995.

Also author of television plays, *Peronik,* 1976, and *The Unknown Enchantment,* 1981. Several of the author's books have been translated into foreign languages.

FOR ADULTS

The Summer House, Hamish Hamilton, 1956.
Voyage to Cythera, Bodley Head, 1958.
Venus with Sparrows, Faber, 1961.
All My Enemies, Faber, 1967, Simon & Schuster, 1973.
The Nice Girl's Story, Faber, 1968, also published as *Nor Evil Dreams,* Simon & Schuster, 1973.
A Wicked Pack of Cards, Faber, 1969, Walker & Co., 1970.
The Double Snare, Faber, 1974, Simon & Schuster, 1975.
Three Candles for the Dark, Faber, 1976.

OTHER

Sea Magic and Other Stories of Enchantment, illustrated by le Cain, Macmillan, 1974 (expanded version published in England as *The Lotus and the Grail: Legends from East and West,* Faber, 1974).
(Editor) *Love and the Merry-Go-Round* (poetry anthology), illustrated by Pauline Baynes, Hamish Hamilton, 1988.

Contributor to *Young Winter's Tales #8,* edited by D. J. Denney, Macmillan (London), 1978.

■ Sidelights

Rosemary Harris is the author of historical romances for adults as well as novels and stories, often considered unusually sophisticated, for children and young adults. Insisting that young readers are capable of comprehending more than is usually expected of them, her works are known for their complex plots, undiluted presentations of good and evil, and intricate prose style. The daughter of a Royal Air Force pilot, Harris as a child moved frequently with her family around the British Isles. She cites her family's aristocratic, if not particularly wealthy, background with its tradition of military service to the Crown as an important influence on her development, along with the divorce of her parents and the onset of World War II during her adolescence. After receiving training in painting and sculpture at the Chelsea School of Art, Harris began a career as a picture restorer. Recovering from an accident which affected her eyesight inspired her to turn to writing, and though the results of those first attempts, a stage play, were never published, Harris felt "I had found what I was suited for at last," as she stated in an essay in *Something about the Author Autobiography Series* (*SAAS*).

Looking back on her long career, Harris also remarked in that *SAAS* sketch: "Writing as a career has brought ups and downs, pleasure and pain, and many fascinating contacts. Perhaps the most successful authors specialise—yet the variety of work is what stimulates me; from writing thrillers to texts of picture books, from TV stories for young children to TV plays for older ones. And from writing for teenagers to adult novels. I have worked as a critic for the *Times,* and my unassuaged desire for the stage has been partly met by the fun and privilege of working with teams of actors, some of whom are now household names. I am envious, though, of writers who really enjoy public speaking, and still more of those who do it well.... Why is it that all writers are expected to be natural talkers? It's so untrue. Or—come to that—ceaseless letter writers? One other lasting regret of mine is that I have not speeded up over the years, being by nature a plodder who rewrites every book at least three times, and avoids all unnecessary letter writing like the plague.

"Perhaps the most complex side of things for a woman writer is to get some balance into your life," Harris continued, "you must isolate yourself for periods to work properly, although paradoxically there is nothing more important to what you do than a good slice of extroverted living. The attempt to achieve both often produces a sense of mental squinting, not to mention exhaustion. The women writers I admire most are those like Susan Hill, Lisa St. Aubin de Teran, and Isabel Allende, who appear to have achieved a happy harmony."

Harris's books for adults have been described by Pamela Cleaver in *Twentieth-Century Romance and Historical Writers* as "modern gothics—intensely feminine stories of fear and romance. What makes them all the more frightening and claustrophobic is that the menace usually comes from someone who is beloved and should be above suspicion." "Harris's books are always a pleasure to read and deserve to be better known," Cleaver concluded. Harris is perhaps better known as the author of fantasy and adventure novels for young adults and longer, illustrated fairy tales for younger children. Her first attempt at young adult fiction, *The Moon in the Cloud,* won several prestigious awards upon publication and continues to be highly regarded. In a retrospective review written in 1992 of the trilogy that opens with *The Moon in the Cloud,* D. J. Stroud wrote in the *Junior Bookshelf:* "Twenty years ago saw the completion of a trilogy of outstanding books which are as delightful to read today as they were then, and which have since become classics in their own right."

The Moon in the Cloud sets an irreverent version of the biblical tale of Noah's ark in Egypt, where Reuben, a gentle and naive musician, is sent by Noah's lazy second son, Ham, to collect two sacred cats and two lions. Reuben is accompanied by his cat, dog, and camel, all of whom have distinct personalities and can talk. Together and apart, the four experience many comical and dangerous adventures. A critic for *Kirkus Reviews* dubbed this "a teasing, knockabout version" of the biblical tale and praised Harris's "wonderfully idiosyncratic creative energy." Many critics noted Harris's control of the novel's large cast of characters, numerous subplots, and detailed settings. Although Nancy J. Schmidt complained in an essay in her *Children's Fiction about Africa in English* that "Harris is writing more to be enjoyed than to re-create a historical period," thus introducing inaccuracies and improbabilities into her story, other critics praised the style with

Harris retells the story of the Flood in this suspenseful novel, focusing on how Noah overcomes the doubts of others to build his Ark.

which Harris relates her story, such as the *Times Literary Supplement* writer who declared: "The tale is told with humorous assurance, wit, and charm, in sparkling narrative."

At the conclusion of *The Moon in the Cloud,* Reuben and his wife, Thamar, take the evil Ham's place on the ark, and in the second novel of the trilogy, *The Shadow on the Sun,* they return to Egypt after the flood to the court of King Merenkere, becoming involved in the king's courtship of one of his courtier's daughters. A reviewer in the *Times Literary Supplement* commented: "It is ... an exciting, compelling story, full of tenderness and humour." Again, most critics emphasized the predominately humorous tone of the work, and while Michael Cart in *School Library Journal* complained about improbabilities in the plot, he also remarked: "The characterization is superb,... and the author's prose, a joy." Response was equally enthusiastic for the trilogy's concluding novel, *The Bright and Morning Star,* in which Thamar returns to the court of Merenkere seeking help for her deaf and troubled second son, Sadhi. The novel centers on various stories of the people and animals associated with Merenkere's court. A *Times Literary Supplement* contributor responded: "These entrancing stories, exotic and yet homely, humorous yet intensely dramatic, deserve to last long and bind many." Of the trilogy as a whole, *Children's Book Review* critic Eleanor von Schweinitz commented: "[Harris] has successfully combined the elements which characterise the best-seller: full-blooded plot, pace, action, romance, colourful settings and characters (including some splendid villains)—and served them up with a wit and elegance that lend her stories a unique and distinctive flavour."

Harris has also written several novels for young adults with contemporary settings. Her first, *The Seal-Singing,* is set on a remote island of Scotland, where the novel's three teenage characters become swept up in stories of the family's ancestry. Critics noted that the novel contained a compelling romance between two of the main characters, an account of the rescue and nursing back to health of a baby seal, and some supernatural elements. Virginia Haviland in *Horn Book* found this "a delightful reading experience for an able, sophisticated

In this sequel to *The Moon in the Cloud,* Reuben returns to the Black Land of Kemi after the Flood only to find it torn by political turmoil. (Cover illustration by Ant Parker.)

young person." Also set in the present is *Zed,* in which a young man recalls being held hostage, along with his father and his uncle, by Arab terrorists during his childhood. During their ordeal, Zed's father is revealed to be a shallow, cowardly sort, while his uncle behaves heroically. Critics noted Harris's emphasis on the humanity of the terrorists, citing the friendship that springs up between one of them and the narrator. Though a reviewer in the *Times Literary Supplement* felt that this element lacked credibility, it was nonetheless concluded that "on the whole *Zed* is a courageous, and largely successful, effort to face with honesty the many aspects of violence, including some which are necessary and healthy." Margery Fisher enthused in her review in *Growing Point:* "The tight but unconstricting shape of the novel, the firm direction of events and people, result in an outstanding piece of fiction."

Harris attempted futuristic fantasy in *A Quest for Orion,* an adventure story set in 1999 about a group of adolescents battling the repressive neo-Stalinist government that has conquered Western Europe. Critics noted

Now a prince, Reuben travels to Kemi to search for a cure for his disabled son, but is called upon to save the land again. (Cover illustration by Parker.)

that the author enriches the action of the plot by employing symbols from the legend of Charlemagne against an otherwise realistic backdrop of war-torn London. Others praised Harris's well-rounded characters. Peter Hunt in the *Times Literary Supplement* concluded: "Although not flawless, this book deserves a good deal of attention." The sequel to *A Quest for Orion, Tower of the Stars,* received mixed reviews. In this work, the defeated resistance forces rally and employ the magic embodied in the Charlemagne relics to defeat their oppressors. "Exciting and well told though the story is, it lacks real depth," commented Gillian Cross in the *Times Literary Supplement.* Similarly, M. Crouch in *Junior Bookshelf* concluded: "Harris' mastery of detail is impressive, and she handles her big scenes with tremendous gusto. It is a pity that the plot leans so heavily on leys, centres of power and other esoteric nonsense."

Harris has also written what many consider to be romances for young women. *Summers of the Wild Rose,* set in Innsbruck in 1937, combines elements of fairy tales with historical facts about Hitler and his persecution of the Jews in what critics agreed was basically a romance plot. Reviewer Crouch concluded: "While it is in essence a superior romance, it may also be seen as a social document." In Harris's *Ticket to Freedom,* set in contemporary England, a young woman with an abusive father and stepmother seems unable to accept help from social workers, teachers, psychiatrists, or her boyfriend. Critics praised the author's complex portrait of troubled adolescence. In *Books for Your Children,* T. Massey dubbed this "a fascinating character and a riveting read." Also for this age group is *Love and the Merry-Go-Round,* an anthology of poetry edited by Harris. Of the quality of the selection, which includes translations from numerous languages and focuses on the nineteenth and twentieth centuries, M. Hobbs remarked in a *Junior Bookshelf* review: "It is mind-stretching, thought-provoking and imaginatively arranged, following a pattern, humanly speaking, from youth to age." Fisher called it "a remarkable collection, not to be missed," in *Growing Point.*

Harris has published a number of picture books based on fairy tales and legends from different countries. While most were well received by critics, many reviewers cautioned readers that Harris's language is more complex and her stories longer than the ordinary picture-book audience can handle. Harris's first such effort, *The Child in the Bamboo Grove,* is based on a Japanese legend in which a poor bamboo cutter is rewarded for taking in an abandoned child who turns out to be the offspring of the sun. Although a reviewer for *Kirkus Reviews* faulted the author for a "remote tone, and unfocused viewpoint," Crouch averred in *Junior Bookshelf:* "The story is told with great beauty and in calm, timeless words." Harris's *The King's White Elephant* was described by Crouch as "a long-short story" set in ancient Persia. Although several critics found the work too sophisticated in tone for the picture-book audience, a critic in the *Times Literary Supplement* remarked: "A deceptive lightness of touch, com-

Eight-year-old Thomas's four days as a hostage to terrorists—a terrifying yet maturing experience—are recounted in this novel for young adults. (Cover illustration by Brian Grimwood.)

bined with the oblique humour and verbal wit which distinguish all her work, makes this a real delight."

Harris collected legends from all over the world for *The Lotus and the Grail: Legends from East and West,* published in an abridged version in the United States as *Sea Magic and Other Stories of Enchantment.* Fisher described Harris's role in *Growing Point* as "something more than re-telling. The author has taken a number of familiar tales and has turned them into what could be called reflective novellas." Critics noted with mixed feelings the author's attempts to reproduce the speech rhythms associated with the locale of each story. Nonetheless, E. Colwell in *Junior Bookshelf* called this "a highly individual and fascinating assembly" of stories. Harris's next picture book, *The Flying Ship,* is a Russian folk tale about a czar who offers his daughter to anyone who can collect her in a flying ship. Reviewer Hobbs enthused in *Junior Bookshelf:* "The delight of this amusingly-told story is increased a hundredfold by the clever setting," and Elizabeth Weir called this "a fresh approach to an old story," in her review in *School Librarian.*

Harris retold the story of *Beauty and the Beast* in picture-book format. Critics debated whether the author's prose is suitable for reading aloud, though Gabrielle Maunder in *School Librarian* dubbed it "a delightfully pretty book, and much to be recommended." Her next effort in this format, *Green Finger House,* in which a little girl creates a dream house in her fantasies as a way to escape a lonely stay with an aunt, was characterized by Maunder as "contrived with gentle simplicity." In *The Enchanted Horse,* set in India, an evil man sells his sons to the devil for a black opal. Reviewer Crouch praised this folk tale "told with great subtlety and beauty of language" in *Junior Bookshelf.* In *Janni's Stork,* set in Holland, a poor boy defies the village burgomaster to rescue and tend a wounded stork, which brings him good luck. Crouch remarked: "Miss Harris writes so eloquently and in such detail that her story hardly needs the addition of pictures." Harris's *Colm of the Islands* is an original fairy tale about a man who is helped by the wild animals he has long befriended when his beloved is stolen by giants. Fisher commented in *Growing Point:* "In this beautifully produced book artist and author are on equal terms, collaborating to produce enchantment in two media." Harris has also published an abridged version of *Heidi.*

A prolific and varied writer, Harris has produced everything from television plays and anthologies of poetry to science fiction novels for young adults and picture books for younger readers. Her interest in ancient legends and fairy tales has led her to exploit their symbols in her fantasy novels and to collect and retell lesser-known tales for her picture books. Harris's work has been praised in the highest terms for its sophisticated tone, erudite allusions, and well-paced plots. Her irreverent humor and ability to control numerous characters in several subplots simultaneously have also formed the basis for critical accolades.

■ Works Cited

Review of *The Bright and Morning Star, Times Literary Supplement,* July 14, 1972, p. 810.

Cart, Michael, review of *The Shadow on the Sun, School Library Journal,* November, 1970, p. 108.

Review of *The Child in the Bamboo Grove, Kirkus Reviews,* October 1, 1972, pp. 1144-45.

Cleaver, Pamela, essay on Rosemary Harris in *Twentieth-Century Romance and Historical Writers,* second edition, St. James Press, 1990, pp. 305-6.

Colwell, E., review of *The Lotus and the Grail, Junior Bookshelf,* August, 1974, pp. 229-30.

Cross, Gillian, "On the Astral Plain," *Times Literary Supplement,* March 28, 1981, p. 339.

Crouch, Marcus, review of *The Child in the Bamboo Grove, Junior Bookshelf,* December, 1971, pp. 377-78.

Crouch, Marcus, review of *The King's White Elephant, Junior Bookshelf,* February, 1974, pp. 23-24.

Crouch, Marcus, review of *Tower of the Stars, Junior Bookshelf,* April, 1981, p. 80.
Crouch, Marcus, review of *The Enchanted Horse, Junior Bookshelf,* December, 1981, p. 243.
Crouch, Marcus, review of *Janni's Stork, Junior Bookshelf,* April, 1983, pp. 67-68.
Crouch, Marcus, review of *Summers of the Wild Rose, Junior Bookshelf,* June, 1987, pp. 131-32.
Fisher, Margery, review of *The Lotus and the Grail, Growing Point,* July, 1974, p. 2422.
Fisher, Margery, review of *Zed, Growing Point,* March, 1983, pp. 4029-30.
Fisher, Margery, review of *Love and the Merry-Go-Round, Growing Point,* January, 1989, pp. 5106-7.
Fisher, Margery, review of *Colm of the Islands, Growing Point,* July, 1989, pp. 5181-82.
Harris, Rosemary, essay in *Something about the Author Autobiography Series,* Volume 7, Gale, 1989, pp. 75-89.
Haviland, Virginia, review of *The Seal-Singing, Horn Book,* February, 1972, p. 57.
Hobbs, M., review of *The Flying Ship, Junior Bookshelf,* June, 1975, pp. 175-76.
Hobbs, M., review of *Love and the Merry-Go-Round, Junior Bookshelf,* December, 1988, p. 303.
Hunt, Peter, "The Future Shook Us," *Times Literary Supplement,* September 29, 1978, p. 1089.
Review of *The King's White Elephant, Times Literary Supplement,* November 23, 1973, p. 1431.
Massey, T., review of *Ticket to Freedom, Books for Your Children,* Spring, 1992, p. 24.
Maunder, Gabrielle, review of *Beauty and the Beast, School Librarian,* June, 1980, p. 142.
Maunder, review of *Green Finger House, School Librarian,* December, 1980, p. 370.
Review of *The Moon in the Cloud, Kirkus Reviews,* January 1, 1970, p. 7.
Review of *The Moon in the Cloud, Times Literary Supplement,* December 5, 1968, p. 1367.
Schmidt, Nancy J., "Historical Fiction," in *Children's Fiction about Africa in English,* Conch Magazine Ltd., 1981, pp. 155-70.
Review of *The Shadow on the Sun, Times Literary Supplement,* July 2, 1970, p. 711.
Stroud, D. J., "Nile Trilogy," *Junior Bookshelf,* June, 1992, pp. 91-94.
von Schweinitz, Eleanor, review of *The Bright and Morning Star, Children's Book Review,* September, 1972, p. 114.
Weir, Elizabeth, review of *The Flying Ship, School Librarian,* December, 1975, p. 317.
Review of *Zed, Times Literary Supplement,* November 26, 1982, p. 1302.

■ For More Information See

BOOKS

Egoff, Sheila, A., *Thursday's Child: Trends and Patterns in Contemporary Children's Literature,* American Library Association, 1981, pp. 152-53.

PERIODICALS

Booklist, March 1, 1988, p. 1131.
Children's Book Review, spring, 1974, p. 11.
Children's Literature in Education, autumn, 1981, pp. 140-50.
Commonweal, November 19, 1971, pp. 179-82.
Growing Point, December, 1971, p. 1854; April, 1975, p. 2612; May, 1980, p. 3710; September, 1981, p. 3948; March, 1983, p. 4044.
Junior Bookshelf, February, 1992, p. 36.
Kirkus Reviews, May 1, 1980, p. 576.
Listener, December 8, 1988, p. 40.
New York Times Book Review, May 11, 1980, p. 25.
School Librarian, February, 1992, pp. 30-31.
School Library Journal, December, 1971, p. 64; August, 1984, pp. 83-84.
Times Educational Supplement, November 24, 1978, p. 50; March 20, 1987, p. 304; June 9, 1989, p. B12.
Times Literary Supplement, July 5, 1974, p. 716.

—Sketch by Mary Gillis

* * *

HAUTMAN, Pete(r Murray) 1952-
(Peter Murray)

■ Personal

Born September 29, 1952, in Berkeley, CA; son of Thomas Richard and Margaret Elaine (an artist; maiden name, Murray) Hautman; companion of Mary Louise Logue (a writer). *Education:* Attended Minneapolis College of Art and Design, 1970-72, and University of Minnesota, 1972-76.

■ Addresses

Home and office—4211 Pillsbury Ave., Minneapolis, MN 55409. *Agent*—Jonathon Lazear, Lazear Literary Agency, 400 First Ave. N., #416, Minneapolis, MN 55401.

■ Career

Writer. Has also worked in freelance marketing and design. *Member:* Mystery Writers of America.

■ Awards, Honors

Drawing Dead was selected as a *New York Times* Notable Book for 1993.

■ Writings

FOR ADULTS

Drawing Dead, Simon & Schuster, 1993.
Short Money, Simon & Schuster, 1995.

JUVENILE NONFICTION; UNDER NAME PETER MURRAY

Beavers, Child's World, 1992.
Black Widows, Child's World, 1992.
Dogs, Child's World, 1992.
Planet Earth, Child's World, 1992.
The Planets, Child's World, 1992.

Rhinos, Child's World, 1992.
Silly Science Tricks, Child's World, 1992.
Snakes, Child's World, 1992.
Spiders, Child's World, 1992.
The World's Greatest Chocolate Chip Cookies, illustrated by Anastasia Mitchell, Child's World, 1992.
The World's Greatest Paper Airplanes, illustrated by Mitchell, Child's World, 1992.
You Can Juggle, Child's World, 1992.
Your Bones: An Inside Look at Skeletons, Child's World, 1992.
The Amazon, Child's World, 1993.
Beetles, Child's World, 1993.
Chameleons, Child's World, 1993.
The Everglades, Child's World, 1993.
Frogs, Child's World, 1993.
Gorillas, Child's World, 1993.
Hummingbirds, Child's World, 1993.
Parrots, Child's World, 1993.
Porcupines, Child's World, 1993.
The Sahara, Child's World, 1993.
Saturn, Child's World, 1993.
Sea Otters, Child's World, 1993.
The Space Shuttle, Child's World, 1993.
Tarantulas, Child's World, 1993.
Silly Science Tricks with Professor Solomon Snickerdoodle, illustrated by Mitchell, Child's World, 1993.
Science Tricks with Air, Child's World, 1995.
Science Tricks with Light, Child's World, 1995.
Dirt, Wonderful Dirt!, illustrated by Penny Dann, Child's World, 1995.
Make a Kite!, illustrated by Dann, Child's World, 1995.
The Perfect Pizza, illustrated by Dann, Child's World, 1995.
Professor Solomon Snickerdoodle Looks at Water, illustrated by Mitchell, Child's World, 1995.

■ Work in Progress

Roo, for Simon & Schuster, 1996, and *The Mortal Nuts,* both novels for adults; *The Doors of Memory,* a young adult novel; *Perseverance: The Story of Thomas Alva Edison,* a biography for children; a sequel to *The Wind in the Willows* entitled *Beneath the Wild Wood;* a story for young children, *Rhino in My Bedroom,* and its sequel, *Gorillas in My Treehouse.*

■ Sidelights

Pete Hautman told *SATA:* "In 1992, I retired from a freelance marketing and design practice to devote myself full time to writing. It has turned out to be a happy decision. I never used to think of myself as a children's author, so it was with some trepidation that I undertook to author a series of books for Child's World. I found that the 'child's voice' came quite naturally to me, and that, for better or worse, the things that amused me thirty-five years ago *still* make me laugh.

"I live in a large house in south Minneapolis with mystery writer, poet, and children's author Mary Logue, and a cat named Ubik. We spend part of each summer at our second home, an old farmhouse in Stockholm, Wisconsin. Both Mary and I write every day, and we like it. We act as each other's editor, critic, and cheerleader."

PETE HAUTMAN

■ For More Information See

PERIODICALS

Booklist, March 15, 1993, p. 135.
Kirkus Reviews, August 15, 1993, p. 1018.
New York Times Book Review, November 7, 1993, p. 24; December 5, 1993, p. 56.
Publishers Weekly, August 30, 1993, p. 74.
School Library Journal, July, 1993, p. 77.
Wall Street Journal, November 22, 1993, p. A12.

* * *

HECKERT, Connie K(aye Delp) 1948-

■ Personal

Born November 5, 1948, in Jefferson, IA; daughter of Leland M. (a blacksmith/farmer) and LaVone J. (a homemaker) Delp; married John W. Heckert (an electrical engineer), June 20, 1970; children: Stephanie Gevone. *Education:* Career Academy, medical assistant certificate program, 1968; Augustana College (Rock Island, IL), B.A., 1976; University of Iowa, M.A., 1984. *Politics:* Republican. *Religion:* Lutheran. *Hobbies and other interests:* Reading, music, photography.

Connie K. Heckert with cat Benny, the model for her book, *Dribbles.*

Addresses

Home—16 Oakbrook Dr., Bettendorf, IA 52722.

Career

Iowa State University Veterinary Clinics, Ames, IA, medical records librarian, 1968-1973; freelance writer, 1972—; Peoria Engineering, East Moline, IL, proofreader, 1975; Illowa Health Systems Agency, Davenport, IA, assistant health planner, 1977-1978; Black Hawk College, Moline, IL, instructor, 1985; St. Ambrose University, Davenport, adjunct assistant professor of English, 1985-1993. Keynote speaker and teacher of numerous conferences and workshops. *Member:* National League of American Pen Women, Inc. (past president, Quad-Cities chapter), Society of Children's Book Writers and Illustrators, Children's Reading Roundtable of Chicago (associate).

Awards, Honors

Writer of the Year, Quad-Cities Writers Club, 1982; First place writing awards, Mississippi Valley Writers Conference, 1986, for nonfiction, juveniles, and novel categories; third place award in nonfiction, National League of American Pen Women, Inc., 1987, for *The Swedish Connections;* faculty development grant, St. Ambrose University, and state, regional, and national awards from respective branches of the National League of American Pen Women, Inc., 1987 and 1988, both for *To Keera with Love: Abortion, Adoption or Keeping the Baby;* Super Friend Award, Friends of Davenport Public Library, 1988, for fundraising and volunteer work; Certificate of Appreciation, Student Government Association, St. Ambrose University, 1988, for "commitment beyond the call of duty"; Historic Preservation Achievement Award, Scott County Historic Preservation Society, Inc., 1989, for publications emphasizing historical content.

Writings

FOR CHILDREN

Miss Rochelle and the Lost Bell, Quest Publishing (Rock Island, IL), 1985.

Dribbles, illustrated by Elizabeth Sayles, Clarion, 1993.

FOR ADULTS

Lyons: 150 Years North of the Big Tree, Lyons Business and Professional Association (Clinton, IA), 1985.

The Swedish Connections, Sutherland Publishing (Ft. Meyers, FL), 1986.

The First 100 Years: A Pictorial History of Lindsay Park Yacht Club, Lindsay Park Yacht Club (Davenport, IA), 1987.

(With Kayla M. Becker) *To Keera with Love: Abortion, Adoption or Keeping the Baby,* Sheed & Ward (Kansas City, MO), 1987.

(With Vernadine Berry) *Roots & Recipes: Six Generations of Heartland Cookery,* Pelican Publishing (Gretna, LA), 1995.

Contributor to numerous periodicals, including *Artsbeat, Quad-City Times, Area Business, Plus 60,* and *Daily Dispatch.* Frequently writes for *Des Moines Register.*

Work in Progress

The Day the Flood Came, a narrative poem; *In War, Flood or Fire,* a picture book; writing articles on assignment, giving speeches, working on a number of book projects, researching children's diabetes, researching life during the depression.

Sidelights

Connie K. Heckert told *SATA* that she worked as a veterinary medical records librarian in the late sixties and early seventies, but after she published her first piece in *ISU Veterinarian,* "the byline bug bit me, and I've been pursuing a writing career ever since.

"I've written a number of books for readers of various age levels, although *Dribbles* would certainly qualify as my greatest success. *Miss Rochelle and the Lost Bell* was based on a true experience at a children's literature festival and used the name of Miss Rochelle Murray, the head librarian at Davenport Public Library. *The Swedish Connections* was actually my master's degree essay. It told the story of hosting two Swedish exchange students. *To Keera with Love: Abortion, Adoption or Keeping the Baby,* in pre-publication stages, received a faculty development grant from St. Ambrose University, a Catholic liberal arts institution where I've taught. It

Siamese kittens Benny and Bing learn a lesson about friendship, aging, and loss in this gentle picture book. (Cover illustration by Elizabeth Sayles.)

was coauthored with a teen, Kayla Becker, who released her baby for adoption and told of her agonizing decision-making process. Two pictorial histories were commissioned works; one is about a town that was annexed to Clinton, Iowa, the other about a yacht club. My husband, John, helped with sizing photographs.

"Currently, my picture books—my passion—are based on personal experiences. Dribbles was the kitten John and I selected from a litter when we were first married. When we moved into student housing, his parents kept her until John's mother died and his father and Dribbles moved in with us and three other cats: Gracie, Bing, and Benny. Four months later, Dribbles died. I wrote the story while grieving the loss of my mother-in-law, so the book is a memorial to my in-laws and will always be terribly special.

"Other children's books, works-in-progress, that I care most about are based on personal experience. *The Day the Flood Came* is a narrative poem using details from June 1990 when Duck Creek overflowed its banks and invaded our home. We had six feet of water in our basement! Another book, *In War, Flood or Fire,* is a father-daughter story set on an Iowa farm. I can relate to the setting because of my Iowa farming background, but the rest of the story is complete fiction.

"As a writer, I've always admired those writers who are interested in writing for readers of all ages. E. B. White, C. S. Lewis, and popular children's author Jane Yolen are examples. I love to collect children's picture books—the beautiful hardcover editions—and I read everything by Jane Yolen I can find. One public library is next to my daughter's preschool center, and I frequently stop to raid the 'New Books' shelf. It's a good way to see what publishers are offering and helps give me ideas for classes and new projects. I'm constantly studying the work of other favorite authors: Nancy White Carlstrom, Eve Bunting, Eileen Christelow, Mary Downing Hahn, Mem Fox, W. Nikola-Lisa, and Patricia MacLachlan. I also subscribe to *Publishers Weekly* and receive newsletters from two professional organizations: the Children's Reading Roundtable of Chicago and Society of Book Writers and Illustrators.

"When I visit schools and libraries to talk to children about writing, I try to share the passion I have for writing and describe how many drafts some of the seven- or eight-page stories have gone through. It took two years to write *Dribbles,* and I've been working on *The Day the Flood Came* for more than three years. Writing is often lonely, hard work, but I can't imagine any other life."

■ For More Information See

PERIODICALS

Publishers Weekly, August 9, 1993, p. 478.
School Library Journal, November, 1993, p. 82.

* * *

HELYAR, Jane Penelope Josephine 1933- (Josephine Poole)

■ Personal

Born February 12, 1933, in London, England; daughter of Charles Graham (a managing director of an engineering firm) and Astrid (an artist; maiden name, Walford) Cumpston; married Timothy Ruscombe Poole (a driving instructor), July 14, 1956 (divorced 1974); married second husband, Vincent J. H. Helyar (a farmer), August 29, 1975; children: (first marriage) Theodora Mary, Emily Josephine, Katherine Virginia, Isabel Beatrice; (second marriage) Charlotte Mary, Vincent Graham. *Education:* Attended schools in Cumberland and London, England. *Religion:* Roman Catholic. *Hobbies and other interests:* Painting, sculpture, music, gardening, books, poetry.

■ Addresses

Home—Poundisford Lodge, Poundisford, Taunton, Somerset TA3 7AE, England. *Agent*—Gina Pollinger, Murray Pollinger Literary Agents, 222 Old Brompton Rd., London SWS OBZ, England.

■ Career

Solicitor's secretary in London, 1951-54; secretary, British Broadcasting Corp. (BBC) Features Department, 1954-56; freelance writer, 1956—.

■ Writings

FOR YOUNG ADULTS; UNDER PSEUDONYM JOSEPHINE POOLE

A Dream in the House, Hutchinson, 1961.
Moon Eyes, Hutchinson, 1965, Little, Brown, 1967.
Catch as Catch Can, Hutchinson, 1969, Harper, 1970.
The Visitor, Harper, 1972, published in England as *Billy Buck,* Hutchinson, 1972.
Touch and Go, Harper, 1976.

JANE PENELOPE JOSEPHINE HELYAR

When Fishes Flew, Benn, 1978.
The Open Grave, Benn, 1979.
The Forbidden Room, Benn, 1979.
Hannah Chance, Hutchinson, 1980.
Diamond Jack, Methuen, 1983.
Three for Luck, Hutchinson, 1985.
Wildlife Tales, Hutchinson, 1986.
The Loving Ghosts, Hutchinson, 1988.
Puss in Boots, Hutchinson, 1988, Barron's, 1988.
The Sleeping Beauty, Hutchinson, 1988, Barron's, 1989.
Angel, Hutchinson, 1989, Red Fox, 1991.
This Is Me Speaking, Hutchinson, 1990, Red Fox, 1991.
(Reteller) *Snow White,* Knopf, 1991.
Paul Loves Amy Loves Christo, Hutchinson, 1992.
Scared to Death, Hutchinson, 1994.
Pinocchio, Macdonald Children's Books, 1994.

FOR ADULTS; UNDER PSEUDONYM JOSEPHINE POOLE

The Lilywhite Boys, Hart-Davis, 1968.
Yokeham, J. Murray, 1970.
The Country Diary Companion, Webb & Bower, 1984.

OTHER; UNDER PSEUDONYM JOSEPHINE POOLE

Author of television scripts for *West Country Tales,* British Broadcasting Corp. (BBC-TV), 1975-82: "The Harbourer," 1975; "The Sabbatical," 1981; "The Breakdown," 1981; "Miss Constantine," 1982; "The Animal Lover," 1982; "Ring a Ring a Rosie," 1982; "With Love, Belinda," 1982; "The Wit to Woo," 1982; and "Fox, Buzzard," and "Dartmoor Pony," for the *Three in the Wild* series, BBC-TV, 1984.

Kate's loneliness is eased by the appearance of a mysterious aunt until Rhoda's visit turns threatening, endangering Kate and her little brother Thomas. (Cover illustration by Trina Schart Hyman.)

■ Sidelights

Jane Penelope Josephine Helyar, who writes under the name of Josephine Poole, has a simple dictum for success in young adult fiction. "I enjoy writing for children," she commented in *Twentieth Century Children's Writers.* "I hope this makes the books enjoyable." But Helyar's writings are anything but simply enjoyable. Blending the supernatural and the menace of evil with a bucolic countryside, she has created a body of work from *Moon Eyes* to *The Loving Ghosts* that have kept children turning pages and leaving lights on at night. Her favorite theme is the strength of goodness over evil, and this she works out in mysteries, suspense thrillers, and more recently, retellings of traditional fairy tales. What sets Helyar's writings apart from others is her deeply defined sense of place and depth of characterization.

Such realism is a natural outgrowth of Helyar's technique. "Inspiration for my children's books begins with my own childhood," she reported in *Something about the Author Autobiography Series* (*SAAS*). That inspiration, Helyar wrote, involves "a close—sometimes too close—family life, side by side with fear; of the dark, of the huge old house where we lived with its woods, attics, and imagined ghosts, of my mother's bad health, and of the war, which though remote, colored everything."

Born in 1933, Helyar was, like an entire generation in England and other parts of the world, deeply affected by the Second World War. Her first years spent in London in the midst of a secure and prosperous family, Helyar was displaced by the war, sent with her sisters and mother to the safety of the moors in the north of England near the Lake District. Her father remained in London while the four daughters and mother took up residence with an aunt in a draughty old house that became the setting for more than one of Helyar's later novels. The family soon settled in their own cottage and the world of nature was opened to her. Evenings were spent telling stories and painting pictures. Helyar's mother was herself an accomplished painter and a successful children's book illustrator, as well as a natural actress who brought books alive for her children. The notion of storytelling was thus early ingrained in Helyar. Occasional visits from her father reunited the family and punctuated a life lived close to the rhythm of nature. Largely schooled at home by governesses up to this point, Helyar and her sister were sent as weekly boarders to a nearby school.

After the war, the family took up life again in London and Helyar completed her schooling. "Writing mattered more than anything to me," she wrote in *SAAS.* "It was flowery—words, a marvelous cornucopia of words!" But she was engaged in more than flowery poetry; in her final year of high school, she wrote a play performed by fellow students. Upon graduation, she spent some months in Portugal, visiting her grandfather, and felt out of the social scene. "One of my worst afternoons was a swimming party," she recalled for *SAAS.* "I hate bathing suits, I can hardly swim, and I sat in acute misery while my bronzed 'friends' plunged in and out of the waves." Helyar then took an au pair job in Belgium where she learned French and gained self-assurance. She did not want to go to university for fear of losing her originality, and upon returning to London, took a secretarial course and thereafter worked in a solicitor's office. During this time, she followed her mother's lead and became a Roman Catholic, had an impossible romance in Rome, and then took up a new job in the features department of the British Broadcasting Corporation where she worked for some of the most original producers in radio.

Helyar's life took a momentous turn when she married Timothy Poole and became a mother. Cut off from creative outlets in outside work, Helyar began writing, a life-long ambition. Her first book, *A Dream in the House,* was accepted by Hutchinson and came out when she was in the hospital giving birth to her third child. The family left the suburbs of South London for the rural charms of Taunton in Somerset, yet Helyar was far from happy. Reeling from postnatal depression, she took comfort once again in writing, publishing *Moon Eyes* in 1965. Drawing deeply on the old house where she had lived during the war, the book is full of elements of Gothic horror and suspense with the interplay of good and evil that would be a hallmark of Helyar's work. "The writing is smooth and graphic," noted Ruth Hill Viguers in *Horn Book.* "The book should find an appreciative audience among children just leaving the fairytale age but still looking for tales of the supernatural." A reviewer in the *Times Literary Supplement* agreed: "No pandering to the young reader, in fact, either in the excellent writing or the events of the story, and this makes it a good book as well as a most unusual one."

Helyar next tried adult fiction with *The Lilywhite Boys* and *Yokeham,* but returned to young adult titles with the 1969 work *Catch as Catch Can,* which marked a turning point in Helyar's writing career. Helyar incorporated a realistic combination of characters that made most other juvenile mysteries "look like comic strips," according to a critic for *Kirkus Reviews.* With this book she came into her own as a writer of juvenile mysteries and suspense thrillers. The story of cousins who witness a suicidal leap from a train, the novel takes the youthful protagonists into the world of smuggling. "There is a certain compelling quality about the writing and the mounting tension of the plot holds one's interest with a kind of mesmerized horror," wrote Elizabeth Bewick in *School Librarian.* Helyar's next book, *The Visitor,* combined elements of black magic with Gothic romance to create a typical English village seething with grudges and revenge. The sinister character of Mr. Bogle, a tutor come to work with a boy recovering from an illness, becomes the devil himself. There is interplay between Christian and pagan here, the upper classes and laborers. But it is the suspense that holds the reader. "Josephine Poole knows how to use words and holds you by a skillful juggling of chilling detail and panoramic impression," wrote a reviewer in the *Times Literary Supplement,* and C. S. Hannabus, writing in *Children's Book Review,* noted that this book works because of "its frightening suggestion that gullible people can beget a panic more terrifying than any monster."

Despite the success with her writing, Helyar had not yet found herself. Her marriage with Timothy Poole looked good on the surface, but was not working. Helyar met and fell in love with a local farmer, Vincent Helyar, and in 1975 they were married. She had two more children with Helyar, found real domestic happiness and companionship, and her writing blossomed. There followed a torrent of writing, both in novel form and for television. *Touch and Go* is a mystery in the fashion of Agatha Christie with two youths in over their heads with the crooks hot on their heels. It is, as Anne Carter stated in the *Times Literary Supplement,* "a thriller of more than ordinary pace and excitement," and Zena Sutherland, writing in *Bulletin of the Center for Children's Books,* agreed: "The characterization is adequate, the dialogue unusually good, the plot tight, and the suspense delightfully unbearable." Mary M. Burns, in *Horn Book,* commented particularly on the "superb descriptive writing, and the evocative characterization." Helyar continued her children's thrillers with *Hannah Chance, Diamond Jack,* and *Three for Luck,* and began writing for television in 1975. "I have contributed several plays to the television series *West Country Tales,*" she reported in *SAAS.* "Of these, 'The Harbourer' and 'Miss Constantine' are the ones I like the best."

Helyar's 1986 *Wildlife Tales* marked something of a change for her writing. This set of short stories were told from the point of view of various animals. "Closely observed," wrote Naomi Lewis in the *London Observer,* "this book of stories earns a sure place in the genre." Other more recent detours from thrillers are retellings of classic fairy takes, such as her 1991 *Snow White,* which Linda Boyles, writing in *School Library Journal,* found "lyrical and dramatic with a stronger sense of character and setting than is usually found in other versions of the tale."

Helyar continues to write a wide variety of children's books and lives with her husband in Poundisford. "It is a very old house," Helyar noted in *SAAS,* "and Vincent's family has lived here for hundreds of years.... For me it has always been places, particularly houses, that are the catalysts that crystallise my ideas into books." And it is also Helyar's attic full of memories that give inspiration to her works. The author once described her literary aspirations and methods for *SATA:* "I've wanted to write books for as long as I can remember. Although my children's books are set in a place recently visited, the real inspiration for them comes from my own childhood." She continued, "I tried to remember the kind of book that gripped me most as a child, the kind of situations I found most tense, and put them in."

■ Works Cited

Bewick, Elizabeth, review of *Catch as Catch Can, School Librarian,* March, 1970, p. 85.

Boyles, Linda, review of *Snow White, School Library Journal,* January, 1992, p. 106.

Burns, Mary M., review of *Touch and Go, Horn Book,* February, 1977, pp. 60-61.

Carter, Anne, review of *Touch and Go, Times Literary Supplement,* December 10, 1976, p. 1548.

Review of *Catch as Catch Can, Kirkus Reviews,* October 1, 1970, p. 1097.

Hannabus, C. S., review of *The Visitor, Children's Book Review,* February, 1973, p. 14.

Lewis, Naomi, review of *Wildlife Tales, London Observer,* December 14, 1988, p. 21.

Review of *Moon Eyes, Times Literary Supplement,* December 9, 1965, p. 1133.

Poole, Josephine, essay in *Something about the Author Autobiography Series,* Volume 2, Gale, 1986.

Poole, Josephine, *Twentieth-Century Children's Writers,* fourth edition, St. James Press, 1995.

Sutherland, Zena, review of *Touch and Go, Bulletin of the Center for Children's Books,* September, 1976, pp. 15-16.

Viguers, Ruth Hill, review of *Moon Eyes, Horn Book,* April, 1967, p. 203.

Review of *The Visitor, Times Literary Supplement,* November 3, 1972, p. 1325.

■ For More Information See

PERIODICALS

Bulletin of the Center for Children's Books, March, 1973; January, 1992.
Horn Book, February, 1973; February, 1987; August, 1988; March, 1992.
School Library Journal, December, 1976.
Times Educational Supplement, July 4, 1986; January 3, 1992; May 28, 1993.
Times Literary Supplement, February 6, 1969; December 4, 1969; July 7, 1978.

* * *

HESLEWOOD, Juliet 1951-

■ Personal

Born March 17, 1951, in Leeds, England; daughter of Reginald and Doreen Oscar Heslewood. *Education:* University of London, B.A., 1978. *Politics:* "Green." *Religion:* Church of England. *Hobbies and other interests:* Walking, travel, music, sculpture and painting, history.

■ Addresses

Office—La Teuliere, Gagnac sur Cere, 46 130 Bretenoux, France.

JULIET HESLEWOOD

■ Career

Writer and translator.

■ Writings

JUVENILE

Tales of Sea and Shore (legends and folktales), illustrated by Karen Berry, Oxford University Press, 1983.
Earth, Air, Fire and Water (legends and folktales), illustrated by Jane Lydbury and others, Oxford University Press, 1985.
Introducing Picasso, Little, Brown/Belitha Press, 1993.
The History of Western Painting, Belitha Press, 1993.
(Translator) *The Valleys of the Lot and Cele,* Les Editions du Laquet, 1993.
The History of Western Sculpture, Belitha Press, 1994.
Tales of Two Rivers, the Dordogne and the Lot, Les Editions du Laquet, 1994.
(Translator) *The Segala,* Les Editions du Laquet, 1994.
(Translator) *The Causse,* Les Editions du Laquet, 1995.
The Magic Sandals of Hualachi (an Inca myth), Barefoot Books, 1995.

OTHER

Author of *Maui Plays with Death* (adapted from a Polynesian myth), BBC Radio for Schools; *A Travelling Actress,* BBC Radio 3, produced by Jane Morgan, starring Dame Judi Dench. Translator of various commercial and medical articles and advertising pieces.

■ Work in Progress

Friendly Earth, folktales about nature and the need to respect it; further titles for Les Editions du Laquet; radio plays; a novel.

■ Sidelights

Juliet Heslewood has brought many little-known folktales to the attention of young readers and has made Western art more accessible to children. Heslewood began to establish a reputation for clear, vibrant prose and careful scholarship with the publication of her first book, *Tales of Sea and Shore.* This work presents tales from Brazil, Japan, Polynesia, and England and features mermaids, sea serpents, and dragons along with the humans who are surprised to meet these creatures. A discussion of sources is included. A *Bulletin of the Center for Children's Books* critic praised the retellings in this book as "strong" and appreciated the text's "color and vitality." Linda Polomski in *School Library Journal* wrote that the plots are "fast paced and exciting."

Earth, Air, Fire and Water is a collection of twenty-four folktales from the Americas, Polynesia, New Zealand, Australia, Africa, the Far East, and Europe. The stories, which are grouped by subject according to the four elements, are accompanied by black-and-white woodcuts. An appendix, which reveals sources and explains Heslewood's methodology, is included. "Considering

In this collection of stories from around the world, Heslewood examines different myths about the four elements. (Cover illustration by Jane Lydbury.)

the diversity of the material," Betsy Hearne wrote in a review in the *Bulletin for the Center for Children's Books,* "these read fairly smoothly." A reviewer for *Kirkus Reviews* noted that Heslewood's "clear, inviting prose" illuminates the "storylines" and "underlying symbolism." According to Barbara Chatton in *School Library Journal,* the work is "an excellent resource" of stories for "use in thematic units and story programs."

Heslewood's art surveys, *The History of Western Painting* and *The History of Western Sculpture,* as well as *Introducing Picasso,* are informed by her education in art at the University of London. They are especially designed for young readers. Heslewood told *SATA* that, because she was introduced to art as a child, she would enjoy communicating "art to children." Heslewood added that she lives in France "in a lovely wooden house on a hill" and has created a book about the local fairytales she has discovered.

■ Works Cited

Chatton, Barbara, review of *Earth, Air, Fire and Water, School Library Journal,* June, 1989, p. 119.

Review of *Earth, Air, Fire and Water, Kirkus Reviews,* May 1, 1989, p. 693.

Hearne, Betsy, review of *Earth, Air, Fire and Water, Bulletin of the Center for Children's Books,* July, 1989, p. 277.

Polomski, Linda, review of *Tales of Sea and Shore, School Library Journal,* October, 1985, p. 172.

Review of *Tales of Sea and Shore, Bulletin of the Center for Children's Books,* May, 1985, p. 166.

■ For More Information See

PERIODICALS

Booklist, August, 1989, p. 1978.

Junior Bookshelf, February, 1995, p. 37.

School Library Journal, May, 1994, p. 34.

* * *

HEST, Amy 1950-

■ Personal

Born April 28, 1950, in New York, NY; daughter of Seymour Cye (a businessman) and Thelma (a teacher; maiden name, Goldberg) Levine; married Lionel Hest (a lawyer), May 19, 1977; children: Sam, Kate. *Education:* Hunter College of the City University of New York, B.A., 1971; C. W. Post College of Long Island University, M.L.S., 1972.

■ Addresses

Home—450 West End Ave., New York, NY 10024.

■ Career

New York Public Library, New York City, children's librarian, 1972-75; Viking Press, Inc., New York City,

AMY HEST

assistant editor, 1977; full-time writer, 1977—. *Member:* Society of Children's Book Writers and Illustrators.

■ Awards, Honors

Parents' Choice Award, 1984, for *The Crack-of-Dawn Walkers;* Christopher Award, 1987, for *The Purple Coat; Pete and Lily* was selected one of the Child Study Association of America's Children's Books of the Year, 1987, an American Library Association Notable Children's Book, and a *Booklist* Editor's Choice.

■ Writings

FOR CHILDREN

Maybe Next Year ..., Beech Tree/Morrow, 1982.
The Crack-of-Dawn Walkers, illustrated by Amy Schwartz, Macmillan/Puffin, 1984.
Pete and Lily, Beech Tree/Morrow, 1986.
The Purple Coat, illustrated by Amy Schwartz, Four Winds/Aladdin, 1986.
The Mommy Exchange, illustrated by DyAnne DiSalvo-Ryan, Four Winds/Macmillan, 1988.
Getting Rid of Krista, illustrated by Jacqueline Rogers, Morrow, 1988.
The Midnight Eaters, illustrated by Karen Gundersheimer, Aladdin Books, 1989.
Travel Tips from Harry: A Guide to Family Vacations in the Sun, illustrated by Sue Truesdell, Morrow, 1989.
Where in the World Is the Perfect Family?, Clarion/Puffin, 1989.
The Best-Ever Good-Bye Party, illustrated by DyAnne DiSalvo-Ryan, Morrow, 1989.
The Ring and the Window Seat, illustrated by Deborah Haeffele, Scholastic, 1990.
Fancy Aunt Jess, illustrated by Amy Schwartz, Morrow, 1990.
A Sort-Of Sailor, illustrated by Lizzy Rockwell, Four Winds, 1990.
Love You, Soldier, Four Winds/Puffin, 1991.
Pajama Party, illustrated by Irene Trivas, Beech Tree/Morrow, 1992.
The Go-Between, illustrated by DyAnne DiSalvo-Ryan, Four Winds/Macmillan, 1992.
Nana's Birthday Party, illustrated by Amy Schwartz, Morrow, 1993.
Weekend Girl, illustrated by Harvey Stevenson, Morrow, 1993.
Nannies for Hire, illustrated by Irene Trivas, Morrow, 1994.
Ruby's Storm, illustrated by Nancy Cote, Four Winds/Macmillan, 1994.
Rosie's Fishing Trip, illustrated by Paul Howard, Candlewick, 1994.
How to Get Famous in Brooklyn, illustrated by Linda Dalal Sawaya, Four Winds/Macmillan, 1994.
The Private Notebook of Katie Roberts, Age 11 (sequel to *Love You, Soldier*), illustrated by Sonja Lamut, Candlewick, 1995.
In the Rain with Baby Duck, illustrated by Jill Barton, Candlewick, 1995.
Party on Ice, illustrated by Trivas, Morrow, 1995.

■ Adaptations

The Purple Coat was featured on "The Reading Rainbow," 1988.

■ Sidelights

Amy Hest is known for her sensitive and insightful depictions of family relationships. Many of her books focus on children and their grandparents, although parents, annoying siblings, and fabulous aunts also make frequent appearances. Many of the stories are set in New York City and illustrate how love and support of family and friends can get us through both trying times and the ordinary ups and downs of everyday existence.

Hest grew up in a small suburban community about an hour's drive from New York City. As a child, her favorite things to do were biking, reading, and spying. "I spied on everyone, and still do," Hest said in a Four Winds Press publicity release. "All writers, I suspect, are excellent spies. At least they ought to be. My parents took me to the city quite often, and by the time I was seven, I was certain of one thing, that I would one day live there. Many years later, after graduating from library school, I moved to the Upper West Side of Manhattan, and I live here still, with my husband and two children, Sam and Kate."

Hest often uses her children's names for the main characters in her books. *Maybe Next Year,* Hest's first published book, features a twelve-year-old named Kate who lives with her grandmother on the Upper West Side of New York City. Two major events unfold in Kate's life during the course of the story, and she must sort out her feelings about both. First, Mr. Schumacher, a widower friend of her grandmother's, moves in to share their apartment. Kate also has to decide whether she is ready and willing to audition for the National Ballet Summer School, as her best friend, Peter, feels she should.

In *The Crack-of-Dawn-Walkers,* Hest again portrays a young girl's relationship with a grandparent. Every other Sunday, Sadie gets to go with Grandfather on his traditional morning walk. On the other Sundays, her little brother gets to spend time alone with Grandfather. Millie Hawk Daniel, writing for *The New York Times Book Review,* praised Hest's combination of the two themes, "the validity of intergenerational camaraderie and the understanding that each child needs his or her own private time with a grandparent."

Children and their grandparents are the primary focus in five more of Hest's books. In a story that Ellen Feldman of *The New York Times Book Review* called a "triumph of imagination, resourcefulness and hope," *The Purple Coat* tells how Gabrielle and her mother go on their annual trip to Grampa's tailor shop so that Gabby can get a new coat. Up until now, Grampa's always made Gabby a navy blue coat with "two rows of buttons and a half belt in the back"—just the way Mama likes it. This time, Gabby wants a purple coat,

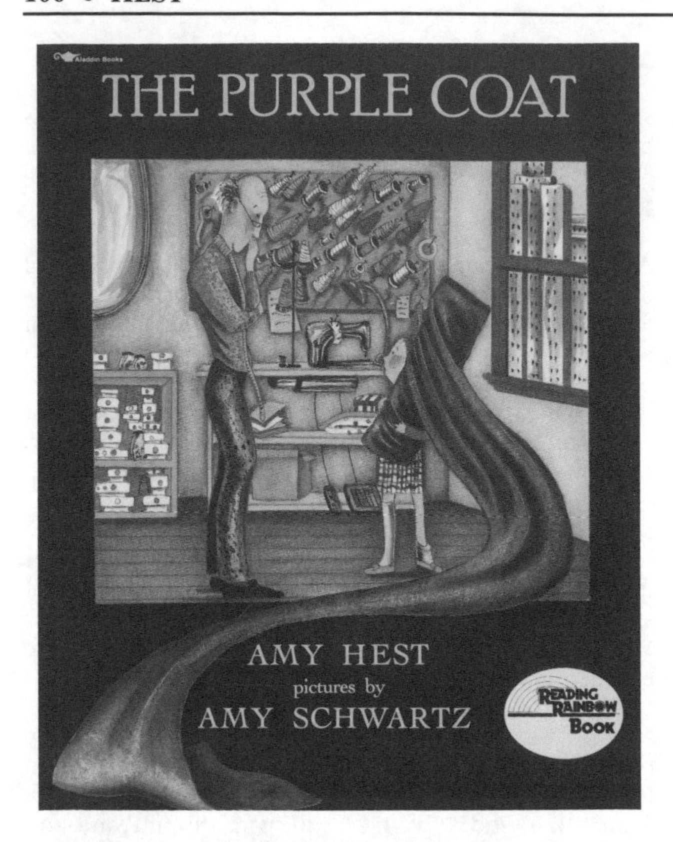

Gabrielle's wish to have something different than the usual navy blue coat is fulfilled in a special way by her tailor grandfather. (Cover illustration by Amy Schwartz.)

but Mama says no. Fashioning an imaginative reversible coat, Grampa manages to please them all.

A young girl's relationship with her grandmother is explored in *The Midnight Eaters* and *The Go-Between.* In the first book, Samantha Bluestein and her ill-but-recovering Nana share a bedroom, a cold midnight snack and some warm conversation in what Heide Piehler of *School Library Journal* called an adept portrayal of "the special love and understanding between generations." *The Go-Between* is also the story of granddaughter-grandmother roommates. Lexi and Gran share a room and enjoy looking out the window at the bustling New York City street below. There, they spy Murray Singer, who runs the newsstand and used to be a good friend of Gran's. Lexi plays matchmaker until she fears that Gran's budding romance with Murray may change their cherished relationship. All ends happily, however, in this story that, as a *Publishers Weekly* reviewer noted, "blends nostalgia and contemporary family dynamics."

New York City plays a large part in two more of Hest's books about grandparents. In *The Weekend Girl,* Sophie's parents take a "private, no-kid" vacation, leaving Sophie and her dog to spend the weekend with Gram and Grampa. Although Sophie is sad to be without her parents, she enjoys her grandparents' special surprise of a picnic and concert in Central Park. The city streets and a brewing storm are the background against which Ruby must make her way to keep a checkers date with Grandpa in *Ruby's Storm.* This book not only explores the intergenerational relationship, but also conveys what Joyce Richards called in *School Library Journal* the "allegorical message that nurturing family relationships often means weathering storms along the way."

It's aunts who provide nurturing family relationships in two of Hest's other books, *Fancy Aunt Jess* and *The Ring and the Window Seat.* The title character of *Fancy Aunt Jess* has luxurious blond hair, dresses stylishly, and loves to host her niece Becky at sleepovers in her Brooklyn apartment. Whenever anyone questions Jess about her unmarried status, she replies that she is waiting for someone special, someone who will give her goose bumps. Goose bumps appear when she meets the father of Becky's new friend. Eleanor K. MacDonald wrote in the *School Library Journal* that this story of a special friendship would "appeal to any child who has pondered the mysteries of adult romance."

Another aunt is featured in Hest's *The Ring and the Window Seat,* a "low-key introduction to the subject" of the Holocaust, according to Leone McDermott in *Booklist.* In this graceful tale, Annie's Aunt Stella recalls a birthday she had many years ago. Stella had been saving her money to buy a beautiful golden ring, but one day, a carpenter knocked on her door, asking for work. As he was building a window seat for Stella, he told her how he needed the work so he could earn money to send for his daughter, who was hiding from the Nazis. After she heard this, Stella silently slipped her ring money into the carpenter's bag. A few weeks later, she unexpectedly received a gift of a golden ring from the carpenter's

Grandmother isn't so fragile that she can't join Samantha in a midnight trip to the kitchen, where they eat sundaes and share family memories. (Cover illustration by Karen Gundersheimer.)

The three friends from *Pajama Party* return in this story of how Casey, Kate, and Jenny try to babysit Jenny's new sister. (Cover illustration by Irene Trivas.)

daughter. Now, Stella passes the ring on to Annie as a special birthday surprise.

The focus shifts from relatives to friends and their relationships in Hest's story, *Pete and Lily.* These two twelve-year-olds girls, who live in the same apartment building in New York, form an "Anti-Romance Mission" when Pete's (whose real name is Patricia) mother and Lily's father begin dating. Cynthia Percak Infantino praised the book's "convincing portrait of adolescent jealousy" in *School Library Journal,* noting that it also shows the "need to let go of the past and adapt to life's changes." *Getting Rid of Krista* also deals with the themes of jealousy and adaptation. When eight-year-old Gillie's father loses his job, her big sister Krista has to come back home from college. Gillie wants her self-centered, preening sister out of the house as soon as possible. With the help of her best friend and a coincidental meeting with a famous Broadway producer, Gillie gets her wish.

In all of Hest's books, an underlying theme is the incredible variety of family relationships that exist in our society. Large families, small families, single-parent families, families with step-parents and step-siblings, are all seen as having their own special charm, as well as their own special difficulties. Another type of special family arrangement is depicted in *Where in the World Is the Perfect Family?,* in which complicated problems face eleven-year-old Cornie Blume. Cornie is adjusting well to the joint-custody arrangement of her divorced parents, shuttling between the East and West sides of New York. But then Cornie's father announces that his new wife is about to have a baby, and her mother starts talking about moving to California. Roger Sutton noted in the *Bulletin of the Center for Children's Books* that these complications give the story "texture" and that "Cornie's a likable, one-of-us heroine whom readers will enjoy."

The problems in *The Mommy Exchange* are not quite as complex; however, they do demonstrate that differences in families have their good and bad points. The story compares and contrasts two families who live in the same apartment building. Jessica lives upstairs with her parents and her twin siblings; Jason lives downstairs, in peace and quiet with just his mother and father. The two friends envy each other's lives, so they decide to make a weekend switch. After they each experience how the other one lives, they discover the blessings their own environments have to offer. Hest continues Jessica and Jason's friendship in *The Best-Ever Good-Bye Party,* as the two adapt to the fact that Jason is moving away. Jason seems to be looking forward to the move, which hurts Jessica's feelings, and the two fight the day before the move. However, at the good-bye party arranged by Jessica's mother, the two realize that they're still the best friends they were before.

Best friends take the stage in another of Hest's two-book series, *Pajama Party* and *Nannies for Hire.* The main characters in both these books are three best friends, eight-year-old Casey and her pals Jenny and Kate. In *Pajama Party,* the girls decide to have their own pajama party when they are excluded from Casey's thirteen-year-old sister's party. Although Kate gets homesick and doesn't make it through her first night away from home, all ends happily when the girls are reunited in the morning with special breakfast treats. In what Hanna B. Zeiger, writing in *Horn Book,* calls "a warm-hearted tale of friendship," the three best friends in *Nannies for Hire* get together to baby-sit—for a small fee—for Jenny's new baby sister. Things don't go quite as smoothly as the girls had planned, and at the end of the day the girls have a much greater understanding of why Jenny's mother has been so tired and frazzled.

Before Hest began writing children's books, she worked for several years as a children's librarian, and then in the children's book departments of several major publishing houses. "All my life, though, I secretly wanted to write children's books," she wrote in her publicity release. "'What? You?' This nasty little voice in the back of my head simply laughed at me. 'What in the world would someone like YOU have to say? Don't you get it, Amy, you're the least exciting person in the universe! Go away and let the writers do the writing!'

"It took me a long time—and I won't tell you how many years—to smash that voice to smithereens ... but smash it I did, and I'm not a bit sorry. Having done that, I was able to get on with it, with the writing. Amazing! I

DID find something to write about, and every single day I find something more."

Works Cited

Daniel, Millie Hawk, review of *The Crack-of-Dawn-Walkers, The New York Times Book Review,* May 13, 1984, pp. 20-21.

Feldman, Ellen, review of *The Purple Coat, The New York Times Book Review,* November 9, 1986, p. 60.

Review of *The Go-Between, Publishers Weekly,* April 13, 1992, pp. 57-58.

Hest, Amy, *Amy Hest* (publicity release), Four Winds, 1993.

Infantino, Cynthia Percak, review of *Pete and Lily, School Library Journal,* August, 1986, p. 92.

MacDonald, Eleanor K., review of *Fancy Aunt Jess, School Library Journal,* June, 1990, p. 100.

McDermott, Leone, review of *The Ring and the Window Seat, Booklist,* January 15, 1991, p. 1063.

Piehler, Heide, review of *The Midnight Eaters, School Library Journal,* October, 1989, p. 86.

Richards, Joyce, review of *Ruby's Storm, School Library Journal,* April, 1994, p. 106.

Sutton, Roger, review of *Where in the World Is the Perfect Family?, Bulletin of the Center for Children's Books,* November, 1989, pp. 59-60.

Zeiger, Hanna B., review of *Nannies for Hire, Horn Book,* June, 1994, pp. 339-40.

For More Information See

PERIODICALS

Booklist, April 15, 1984, p. 1190; March 15, 1986, p. 1084; March 1, 1988, p. 1181; September 1, 1989, p. 72; February 1, 1990, p. 1091; September 15, 1991, p. 151; February 1, 1992, p. 1040; March 1, 1992, p. 1279; January, 1993, p. 810; May 1, 1993, p. 1603; August, 1993, p. 2060; January 15, 1994, p. 871; March 1, 1994, p. 1270.

Bulletin of the Center for Children's Books, February, 1983, p. 109; April, 1984, p. 148; April, 1986, p. 149; May, 1988, p. 179; March, 1990, p. 163; September, 1991, p. 11; March, 1992, p. 182; July, 1992, p. 263; April, 1993, p. 251; October, 1993, p. 46.

Childhood Education, winter, 1990, p. 116; summer, 1993, p. 209.

Children's Book Review Service, May, 1984, p. 101; July, 1986, p. 146; spring, 1988, p. 131; December, 1989, p. 39; spring, 1990, p. 135; October, 1991, p. 19; June, 1994, p. 122.

Emergency Librarian, January, 1992, p. 52; March, 1993, p. 50.

Growing Point, January, 1990, p. 5269.

Horn Book, June, 1984, p. 319; September, 1986, p. 589; July, 1988, p. 494; September, 1989, p. 611; March, 1990, p. 189; September, 1991, p. 591; July, 1992, p. 448; May, 1994, p. 339.

Horn Book Guide, July, 1989, p. 44; January, 1990, p. 213; spring, 1992, p. 59; fall, 1992, p. 233; fall, 1993, p. 286.

Junior Bookshelf, December, 1989, p. 238.

Kirkus Review, July 1, 1989, p. 990; August 1, 1989, p. 1158; March 1, 1990, p. 342; August 1, 1991, p. 1011; February 1, 1992, p. 184; July 15, 1993, p. 934; February 15, 1994, p. 226.

Parents Magazine, November, 1984, p. 53.

Publishers Weekly, November 5, 1982, p. 70; February 24, 1984, p. 140; May 30, 1986, p. 67; April 8, 1988, p. 94; July 28, 1989, p. 219; March 15, 1991, p. 59; March 30, 1992, p. 105; April 13, 1992, p. 57; February 8, 1993, p. 88; July 28, 1993, p. 77; December 6, 1993, p. 72.

School Library Journal, November, 1982, p. 86; August, 1984, p. 60; August, 1988, p. 95; October, 1988, p. 121; August, 1989, p. 122; December, 1990, p. 79; August, 1991, p. 166; April, 1992, p. 92, 93; August, 1993, p. 145; October, 1993, p. 100; May, 1994, p. 339; February, 1995, p. 74.

Smithsonian, November, 1992, p. 202; November, 1993, p. 182.

* * *

HILL, Thomas (Hallowell) 1960-
(Tommy Hallowell)

Personal

Born December 8, 1960, in Boston, MA; son of Thomas Dana and Carol (Hallowell) Hill; married Alison Friesinger, September 20, 1986; children: Thomas Dietrich, Frederica Van Horne. *Education:* Harvard University, A.B., 1983.

Addresses

Home—New York, NY. *Office*—Nickelodeon, 1515 Broadway, New York, NY 10036.

Career

Freelance writer, 1984-89; Nickelodeon, New York City, copywriter, editorial director, and associate creative director for on-air promotion, 1989—.

Awards, Honors

Outstanding Book Award (young adults category), University of Iowa, 1987, for *Varsity Coach: Fourth and Goal.*

Writings

(With Steve Slavkin) *Salute Your Shorts: Life at Summer Camp,* Workman Publishing, 1986.

(With wife, Alison Hill) *Otherwise Engaged; or, How to Survive the Happiest Time of Your Life,* Warner Books, 1988.

What to Expect When Your Wife Is Expanding: A Reassuring Month-by-Month Guide for the Father-to-Be, Whether He Wants Advice or Not, Andrews & McMeel, 1993.

THOMAS HILL

(With Donna Friedman) *Pat the Stimpy* (based on the Nickelodeon television series *Ren & Stimpy*), Grosset & Dunlap, 1993.

Also author of episodes of the Nickelodeon television series *Salute Your Shorts* and *The Adventures of Pete and Pete.*

"ALDEN ALL STARS" SERIES; UNDER PSEUDONYM TOMMY HALLOWELL

Duel on the Diamond, Puffin, 1990.
Jester in the Backcourt, Puffin, 1990.
Last Chance Quarterback, Puffin, 1990.
Shot from Midfield, Puffin, 1990.

OTHER; UNDER PSEUDONYM TOMMY HALLOWELL

Varsity Coach: Fourth and Goal, Bantam, 1986.
Varsity Coach: Out of Bounds, Bantam, 1987.

■ Sidelights

Thomas Hill's novels for young teens, written under the pseudonym Tommy Hallowell, highlight the drama and moral dilemmas that arise on juvenile sports teams. Critics praise the author's rendering of sports plays and strategies as authentic and exciting, often recommending Hallowell's titles for reluctant readers. Hallowell's contributions to the *Varsity Coach* series, including *Fourth and Goal* and *Out of Bounds,* center on a high school football team. In *Fourth and Goal,* the fact that the Kenmore Kings are playing better under the leadership of the team's new coach is the only good thing happening to halfback Craig Bower. His parents seem headed for a divorce, and his own troubled emotions, mixed with his perfectionism, combine to cause problems with his girlfriend. While noting the conventional plot and cast of characters, many critics found something to praise about Hallowell's first juvenile fiction effort. Todd Morning wrote in *School Library Journal* that "the simplistic approach never gets in the way of the action," making the book "enjoyable" for sports fans. A *Publishers Weekly* critic similarly observed that *Fourth and Goal* "isn't the most riveting of fiction, but it is refreshingly unaffected."

In the "Alden All Stars" series, Hallowell features a group of sports-loving young adolescents as they face various challenges on and off the playing field. *Jester in the Backcourt* centers on Nick, whose antics during basketball practice and during actual games disguise his real athletic ability. When Nick becomes too serious and intense, however, he must learn to balance the competitive and fun-loving sides of himself, with the coach's help. *School Library Journal* contributor Morning remarked: "The book is full of fast-paced accounts of the action." *School Library Journal* critic Tom S. Hurlburt reacted similarly to Hallowell's *Last Chance Quarterback.* Of this novel about a young football player facing stiff competition for the first time as he enters the seventh grade, Hurlburt remarked: "Hallowell gives sports fans what they want—fast-paced football," and praised the accuracy of the author's portrayal of the game.

In Hallowell's *Duel on the Diamond,* also in the "Alden All Stars" series, the plot centers on the rivalry that develops between baseball teammates Dennis and Duane. As the feud between the boys heats up, the team begins to lose games and morale falters until the two decide to reconcile their differences for the sake of the team. In a *Los Angeles Times Book Review* critique, Bob Sipchen noted the author's unaffected inclusion of multi-racial characters, female team members, and up-to-date slang that "the hardball hard core will relish." A *Publishers Weekly* reviewer felt that "Hallowell's fast-paced story is sure to be a hit with young readers," while a *Kirkus Reviews* critic enthused: "Like others in this new series, *Duel* features a straightforward plot, simple problem-solving, and plenty of exciting, realistic sports action."

Hill told *SATA:* "Though I was born in Boston, I grew up in Ithaca, New York. When I was young I enjoyed any and all sports, and was a big fan of [quarterback] Fran Tarkenton of the Giants, then Vikings. My first published work was a letter to *Football Digest* magazine. I played a little bit of everything, got cut from the eighth-grade basketball team, played football (weakly) on the ninth-grade team, but found that tennis was my best hope to earn a varsity letter. I made the conference all-star team my junior year in high school, was captain my senior year, and taught tennis during the summers at a camp in Maine during my college years.

"I read voraciously in my youth. Matt Christopher's sports books are surely the most direct influence on Tommy Hallowell, but other writers for kids I admired included C. S. Lewis, Laura Ingalls Wilder, Donald Sobol, and E. B. White. Other writers I read and still admire include humorists Mark Twain, James Thurber, Robert Benchley, and Stephen Leacock, along with cartoonist-writers Walt Kelly ('Pogo'), George Herriman ('Krazy Kat'), and Ernie Bushmiller ('Nancy').

"Today, I work primarily as a writer for cable TV's Nickelodeon. As Associate Creative Director for On-Air Promotion I write commercials and short form interstitial material for Nick Jr., Nickelodeon, and especially, Nick at Nite. It's a chance to write humor for TV, try new things, and communicate with a large, loyal audience about a channel they care about. I have also written episodes for the TV shows *Salute Your Shorts* and *The Adventures of Pete and Pete.* Most recently, I have been working on bringing my TV and publishing experiences together to help create a series of Nick at Nite books. I do expect to write more Tommy Hallowell books, but for the moment, other projects take my time.

"My photograph represents a childhood dream come true. We were filming a Nickelodeon commercial with a baseball theme—at Yankee Stadium, no less—and I wheedled my way into the role of catcher. For a few moments, it was 1973 and I was Thurman Munson."

■ Works Cited

Review of *Duel on the Diamond, Kirkus Reviews,* February 15, 1991, p. 248.

Review of *Duel on the Diamond, Publishers Weekly,* March 30, 1990, p. 63.

Hurlburt, Tom S., review of *Last Chance Quarterback, School Library Journal,* January, 1992, p. 109.

Morning, Todd, review of *Varsity Coach: Fourth and Goal, School Library Journal,* March, 1987, p. 160.

Morning, Todd, review of *Jester in the Backcourt, School Library Journal,* January, 1992, p. 109.

Sipchen, Bob, "For the Young, the Old Ballgame," *Los Angeles Times Book Review,* August 26, 1990, p. 8.

Review of *Varsity Coach: Fourth and Goal, Publishers Weekly,* October 31, 1986, p. 73.

■ For More Information See

PERIODICALS

Publishers Weekly, May 16, 1986, p. 75.

Voice of Youth Advocates, June, 1987, p. 88.

* * *

HOLMAN, Felice 1919-

■ Personal

Born October 24, 1919, in New York, NY; daughter of Jac C. (an engineering consultant) and Celia (an artist; maiden name, Hotchner) Holman; married Herbert Valen (a writer for the *New Yorker*), April 13, 1941; children: Nanine Elisabeth. *Education:* Syracuse University, B.A., 1941.

■ Addresses

Home—Del Mar, CA. *Office*—c/o Atheneum Publishers, 866 3rd Ave., New York, NY 10022.

■ Career

Poet and writer of books for children and young adults, 1960—. Worked as an advertising copywriter in New York City, 1944-50. *Wartime service:* Office of War Information, c. 1941-44.

■ Awards, Honors

Austrian Book Prize, Lewis Carroll Shelf Award, best book for young adults citation, and American Library Association (ALA) notable book citation, all 1978, all for *Slake's Limbo;* ALA notable book citation, 1979, for *The Murderer;* best book for young adults citation, 1985, for *The Wild Children;* Child Study Association Book Award, 1991, for *Secret City, U.S.A.* In 1994 *Slake's Limbo* was named by the ALA as one of the "101 Best Books for Young Adults" written since 1966.

■ Writings

Elisabeth, the Birdwatcher, illustrated by Erik Blegvad, Macmillan, 1963.

Elisabeth, the Treasure Hunter, illustrated by Blegvad, Macmillan, 1964.

Silently, the Cat and Miss Theodosia, illustrations by Harvey Dinnerstein, Macmillan, 1965.

Victoria's Castle, illustrated by Lilian Hoban, Norton, 1966.

Elisabeth and the Marsh Mystery, illustrated by Blegvad, Macmillan, 1966.

Professor Diggin's Dragons, illustrated by Ib Ohlsson, Macmillan, 1966.

FELICE HOLMAN

The Witch on the Corner, illustrated by Arnold Lobel, Norton, 1966.
The Cricket Winter, illustrated by Ralph Pinto, Norton, 1967.
The Blackmail Machine, illustrated by Victoria DeLarrea, Macmillan, 1968.
A Year to Grow, illustrated by Emily Arnold McCully, Norton, 1968.
At the Top of My Voice and Other Poems, illustrated by Edward Gorey, Norton, 1969.
The Holiday Rat and the Utmost Mouse, illustrated by Wallace Tripp, Grosset, 1969.
Solomon's Search, illustrated by Mischa Richter, Grosset, 1970.
The Future of Hooper Toote, illustrated by Gahan Wilson, Scribner, 1972.
I Hear You Smiling and Other Poems, illustrated by Laszlo Kubinyi, Scribner, 1973.
The Escape of the Giant Hogstalk, illustrated by Ben Shecter, Scribner, 1974.
Slake's Limbo, Scribner, 1974.
(With daughter, Nanine Valen) *The Drac: French Tales of Dragons and Demons,* illustrated by Stephen Walker, Scribner, 1975.
The Murderer, Scribner, 1978.
The Wild Children, Scribner, 1983.
The Song in My Head, illustrated by Jim Spanfeller, Scribner, 1985.
Terrible Jane, illustrated by Irene Trivas, Scribner, 1987.
Secret City, U.S.A., Scribner, 1990.

■ Adaptations

Elisabeth and the Marsh Mystery was adapted into a film for schools and libraries; *Slake's Limbo* was adapted into the television movie *The Runaway,* broadcast by PBS-TV, and has also been optioned for film; an abridged version of *The Wild Children* was published by Reader's Digest in English and in translation worldwide.

■ Work in Progress

Real, for Atheneum.

■ Sidelights

Felice Holman is a well-respected children's book author, poet, and young adult novelist. Holman's works often display a deep concern for social issues. Critics note the author's ability to combine a humorous, lighthearted touch with themes of child homelessness, ethnic prejudice, loneliness, and concern for the environment. While Holman has at times been faulted for resolving her characters' dilemmas too happily, she has more frequently been praised for the strength of her characterizations and the depth of her insight into the problems of her characters. Early in her career, Holman received the following accolade from *Publishers Weekly:* "Felice Holman is a very satisfying writer. With her you know ... that you have nothing to worry about."

Holman was born in New York City in 1919, into a family who enjoyed telling tales and stories. In a pivotal memory of her childhood, she is standing at the banister on the second floor of her home listening to the seemingly carefree laughter of her parents and other adult relatives below. Holman attributes the strength of this memory to the longstanding tradition of storytelling in her family, which boosted spirits despite the hard times brought on by the Depression in the 1930s. The author wrote in an essay she contributed to *Something about the Author Autobiography Series* (*SAAS*): "There was a joyous and liberating quality to this disregard for the details which hemmed in most people's lives—the freedom to invent facts. After spending my childhood at the banister, listening, I grew up to channel the family trait into writing." Holman added: "In writing, an author is perhaps trying to create enchanted places—places that live inside the covers of a book and stay there, quiescent, waiting for someone to open the cover. I could not draw those places and people, nor write the music for an opera, but I did find a way to make secret worlds: I wrote about them."

Holman began writing poetry at an early age, and her work was first published before she entered college. Growing up in Flushing, New York, she describes her childhood as a happy and busy time. She was sent to a private boarding school at the age of fifteen in the hope that there she would outgrow her lingering shyness. Although Holman remembers her time at the school as lonely and dull in the extreme, her experiences there formed the background for her first young adult novel, *A Year to Grow.* The future author later studied journalism and English literature at Syracuse University, and married one of her fellow students, Herbert Valen: "I didn't know it then, but I was ensuring that I would be laughing the rest of my life," Holman wrote in *SAAS.* The young couple lived in New York City, but later moved to Westport, Connecticut, where they spent the majority of their married life. There Holman wrote the bulk of her numerous books, enjoyed birdwatching and refurbishing antique dollhouses, and raised her daughter, Nanine.

Experiences with her daughter and neighborhood led to Holman's first books, *Elisabeth, the Birdwatcher* and *Elisabeth, the Treasure Hunter,* which are simple mysteries for first readers centered on a young girl and her father. A third book in the series, *Elisabeth and the Marsh Mystery,* is considered by critics to be a lightly humorous yet environmentally responsible tale about the attempts of Elisabeth, her father, and their friends to discover the identity of a bird in the nearby marsh. *Bulletin of the Center for Children's Books* critic Zena Sutherland called this "good science, good nature study, [and an] utterly satisfying story." Between publication of the first two Elisabeth books and the third, Holman published *Silently, the Cat and Miss Theodosia,* a humorous morality tale about an elderly woman who travels around at night performing good deeds, and the cat who advises her with blinks of her eyes.

Inspired by her daughter's own outdoor adventures, Holman's story has Elizabeth and her father searching for treasure by following clues in nature. (Cover illustration by Erik Blegvad.)

Holman followed these books with works containing more fantastic elements. In *The Witch on the Corner,* a woman is called a witch for so long she becomes convinced she is one, but comically, discovers she cannot perform any feats of magic. Though Lavinia Russ in *Publishers Weekly* found Holman's main character more "pathetic" than humorous, a *Times Literary Supplement* critic dubbed this story "neat and very funny." Similarly, in *Professor Diggin's Dragons,* an elderly professor is forced to take a leave of absence because he has admitted to a belief in dragons. He and five children go on a field trip together where each, with the help of the professor, learns how to face his or her own personal dragon. Sutherland in *Bulletin of the Center for Children's Books* found this story "charming rather than [sinister]." Though *Kirkus Reviews* felt the book was merely "wellbred, rather constrained entertainment for quiet children," Ethel L. Heins in *Horn Book* praised the story as "original, smoothly written with easy, unforced humor."

Another venture into fantasy is Holman's *Victoria's Castle,* which concerns a lonely little girl whose imaginary playmates are ignored by her parents until the day one of them turns out to be real. Ruth Hill Viguers in *Horn Book* hailed the book's "natural, engaging humor" as well as the "very funny" twist ending. Holman's next book, *The Cricket Winter,* is a gentle story of a friendship between a boy and a cricket; a *New York Times Book Review* writer dubbed the work "near perfect fantasy." In recounting the poetic qualities of the story, a *Publishers Weekly* reviewer concluded: "Like all truly rare books, it belongs to everyone."

Holman branched out into realistic fiction with *A Year to Grow;* the work was warmly received for its perceptive portrait of a year in the life of Julia, a shy young girl at boarding school. "Her growth is so humanly true," wrote Dorothy M. Broderick in the *New York Times Book Review,* "that more than one perceptive reader will be filled with the warming feeling of self-recognition." Sutherland in *Bulletin of the Center for Children's Books* remarked that, because the plot contains so little action, the book's appeal lies "wholly in the felicity and percipience of the author's treatment of girlhood observed." On a more fantastic note is *The Blackmail Machine,* a "rollicking tale of a trip in a tree house," according to *Publishers Weekly.* In this story, four children rescue the eccentric Miss Shrubb, who has been evicted from her home in the marsh, and fly her away in their tree house, proclaiming they will not come down until certain wrongs have been righted by the adults below. Sutherland in *Bulletin of the Center for Children's Books* commented: "The message is stirring, [and] the style and dialogue are excellent." Also for middle graders is *The Holiday Rat and the Utmost Mouse,* two stories about heroic rodents. "All the characters are believable, [and] the stories are well-written," remarked Sybilla A. Cook in *Library Journal.*

A summer outing to the seashore turns into an imaginative adventure for five boys and girls in *Professor Diggins' Dragons.* (Illustration by Ib Ohlsson.)

Holman's next picture book, *Solomon's Search,* received mixed reviews for its depiction of animals joining hands and encircling the globe in their search for world peacc. This was followed by a middle grade novel entitled *The Future of Hooper Toote,* a fantasy about a boy whose feet never touch the ground but rather float a few inches above it, sometimes causing him to fly up to the ceiling. Sutherland praised the book as "a lively and very funny story" which is "filled with action and palatable nonsense." As Robert Berkvist similarly concluded in the *New York Times Book Review:* "Miss Holman tells Hooper's story with gentle good humor and a keen eye for the absurdities of the rules we live by."

Holman's *Slake's Limbo* is one of her most popular and highly acclaimed works to date, a young adult novel that relates the experiences of Aremis Slake in his determination to survive by moving from his abusive aunt's home to a cave under the subway in New York City. Early reviews of the work highlighted Holman's lyric prose and the powerful imagery of Aremis's descent and final rise from the subway. *Bulletin of the Center for Children's Books* writer Sutherland dubbed this "a remarkably taut and convincing account of resourcefulness and tenacity." Upon the novel's publication in Great Britain, *Junior Bookshelf* reviewer D. A. Young commented that while the book contains familiar myths of quest and "ordeal by descent and return, ... the young reader will enjoy a story which fascinates by its strangeness and its portrayal of a survivor." And over a decade after *Slake's Limbo* first appeared, Sondra Gordon Langford remarked in *Horn Book* that the book "can be read as a paean to the indomitable human desire to live, to find and choose elements that will enhance one's surroundings, to conquer misfortune, and to make something of oneself."

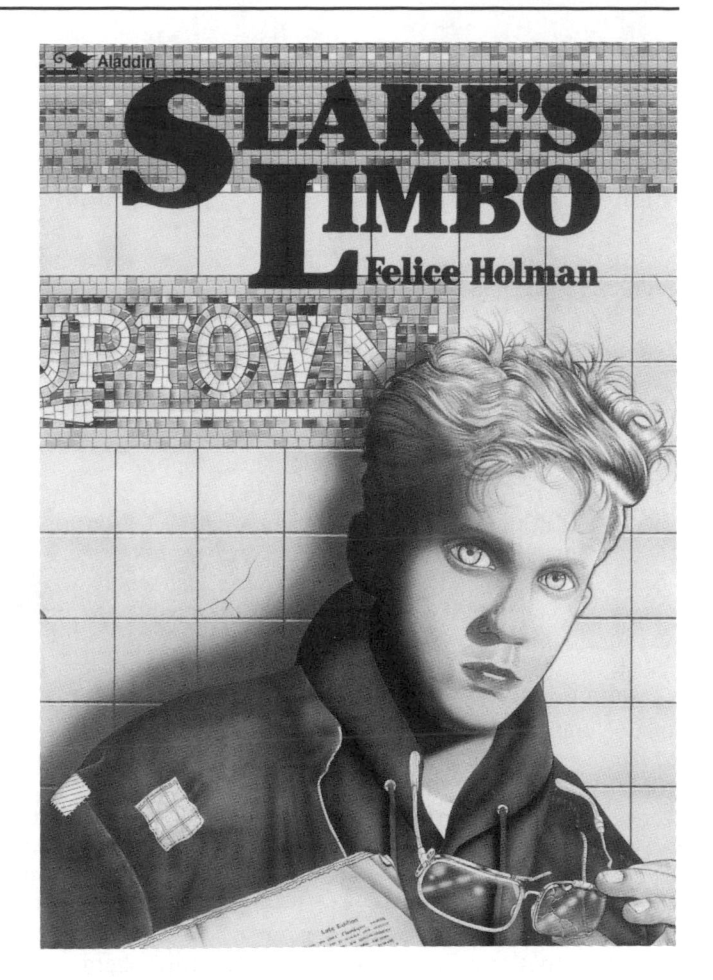

In this groundbreaking novel, an abused and tormented boy tries to escape his problems by running away to New York City's subway system, fending for himself in its tunnels. (Cover illustration by Jon Weiman.)

Holman's next publication, *The Escape of the Giant Hogstalk,* is a humorous adventure tale mixed with fantasy of the type of *The Future of Hooper Toote.* In this story, two boys with an interest in science find an unusual plant in Russia and bring home its seeds to England. The plant grows extremely quickly and escapes the garden to cause all sorts of trouble "described with a merry wit and a light touch," according to *Publishers Weekly. Junior Bookshelf* critic Young commented: "Nine-year-olds will certainly find it a great laugh." After teaming up with her daughter, Nanine Valen, for *The Drac,* a collection of French legends of strange and frightening creatures, Holman turned to the serious subject of prejudice in a story set in an mining town in Pennsylvania in the 1930s. In *The Murderer,* the narrative centers on Hershy Marks, a Jewish boy, during the year leading up to his bar mitzvah, and offers a series of vignettes depicting his humorous or frightening encounters with various members of the community. Patricia Manning in *School Library Journal* commented: "Carefully thought-out and written, this tale is as good as a drink of seltzer on a hot day."

Holman returned to the subject of abandoned and neglected young people in *The Wild Children,* a historical novel set in Russia after the revolution of 1917. The book centers on Alex, whose family disappears one night, leaving him to roam the streets along with thousands of other children, stealing and hiding from the government. "Both grim and dramatic" according to Sutherland of the *Bulletin of the Center for Children's Books,* this "touching story" resolves hopefully, with Alex and his friends leaving Russia for Finland in quest of a better life. Carolyn Noah of *School Library Journal* remarked that while "the book's resolution is a little too pat to be completely convincing ... the strength of the human spirit shines through as a powerful beacon of optimism."

Critical response was similar to *Secret City, U.S.A.,* in which Holman depicts Benno and Moon, two children from the inner city slums who one day discover an abandoned house in a deserted part of the city and decide to take it over for themselves and other children who need a place of refuge. "The author paints an uncompromising picture of the misery and squalor of our cities and sends an unmistakable cry for help," decreed Ethel R. Twichell in *Horn Book.* Other reviewers faulted the novel's ending as unrealistically upbeat but Barbara Chatton of *School Library Journal* nevertheless found it "hugely satisfying." "The story is carefully plotted and the characters fully realized, and there is plenty of action and suspense," concluded Tom Pearson in *Voice of Youth Advocates.*

Holman has also been recognized for her collections of poetry, in addition to the poetic sensibilities she brings to her fiction. *At the Top of My Voice and Other Poems,* for instance, contains verses characterized by "exuberance" and "delicate, quick movement" according to the *New York Times Book Review.* Other critics highlighted the author's wit and the beauty of the book's nature poems. In 1973, Holman published *I Hear You Smiling,* a collection of poems *Publishers Weekly* dubbed "direct, uncontrived, and articulate." *The Song in My Head,* Holman's third collection of poetry, was published in 1985, with reviewers like *School Library Journal* contributor Kathleen D. Whalin praising the author's genuine insight into the world of children that "obviously comes from the heart." Holman has also published *Terrible Jane,* a story in verse about a troublemaking little girl.

Inspired by the example of her parents, who were active and attending classes well into their eighties, Holman continues to write and research. She and her husband now live in Del Mar, California, where they enjoy frequent visits from their two grandsons. As the author once commented, "It is very exciting for me to see their reactions to the books for younger children which I wrote long before they were born—indeed, when their mother was a child. I wonder what else I could have done, all that time ago, that would interest them as much now?... Their pleasure tells me that other children have pleasure from the work, too. That's the real reward."

■ Works Cited

Review of *At the Top of My Voice, New York Times Book Review,* May 2, 1976, p. 42.

Berkvist, Robert, "Tripping the Quite Fantastic," *New York Times Book Review,* July 16, 1972, p. 8.

Review of *The Blackmail Machine, Publishers Weekly,* February 5, 1968, p. 66.

Broderick, Dorothy M., review of *A Year to Grow, New York Times Book Review,* November 3, 1968, p. 40.

Chatton, Barbara, review of *Secret City, U.S.A., School Library Journal,* April, 1990, pp. 140, 142.

Cook, Sybilla A., review of *The Holiday Rat and the Utmost Mouse, Library Journal,* March 15, 1970, p. 1195.

Review of *The Cricket Winter, New York Times Book Review,* November 5, 1967, p. 66.

Review of *The Cricket Winter, Publishers Weekly,* November 27, 1967, p. 43.

Review of *The Escape of the Giant Hogstalk, Publishers Weekly,* April 15, 1974, p. 52.

Heins, Ethel L., review of *Professor Diggin's Dragons, Horn Book,* October, 1966, p. 569.

Holman, Felice, essay in *Something about the Author Autobiography Series,* Volume 17, Gale, 1994.

Review of *I Hear You Smiling, Publishers Weekly,* September 10, 1973, p. 53.

Langford, Sondra Gordon, "A Second Look: *Slake's Limbo,*" *Horn Book,* November-December, 1987, pp. 778-79.

Manning, Patricia, review of *The Murderer, School Library Journal,* December, 1978, pp. 52-53.

Noah, Carolyn, "Tightrope Walking: Children on Their Own," *School Library Journal,* April, 1992, p. 42.

Pearson, Tom, review of *Secret City, U.S.A., Voice of Youth Advocates,* June, 1990, p. 104.

Review of *Professor Diggin's Dragons, Kirkus Reviews,* June 1, 1966, pp. 538-39.

Russ, Lavinia, review of *The Witch on the Corner, Publishers Weekly,* October 24, 1966, p. 51.

Sutherland, Zena, review of *Elisabeth and the Marsh Mystery, Bulletin of the Center for Children's Books,* July-August, 1966, pp. 179-80.

Sutherland, Zena, review of *Professor Diggin's Dragons, Bulletin of the Center for Children's Books,* December, 1966, p. 59.

Sutherland, Zena, review of *The Blackmail Machine, Bulletin of the Center for Children's Books,* April, 1968, p. 129.

Sutherland, Zena, review of *A Year to Grow, Bulletin of the Center for Children's Books,* March, 1969, p. 112.

Sutherland, Zena, review of *The Future of Hooper Toote, Bulletin of the Center for Children's Books,* July-August, 1972, p. 171.

Sutherland, Zena, review of *Slake's Limbo, Bulletin of the Center for Children's Books,* April, 1975, p. 131.

Sutherland, Zena, review of *The Wild Children, Bulletin of the Center for Children's Books,* December, 1983, p. 69.

Twichell, Ethel R., review of *Secret City, U.S.A., Horn Book,* May, 1990, p. 335.

Viguers, Ruth Hill, review of *Victoria's Castle, Horn Book,* August, 1966, p. 426.

Whalin, Kathleen D., review of *The Song in My Head, School Library Journal,* September, 1985, pp. 134-35.

Review of *The Witch on the Corner, Times Literary Supplement,* November 30, 1967, p. 1133.

Review of *A Year to Grow, Publishers Weekly,* September 30, 1968, p. 61.

Young, D. A., review of *The Escape of the Giant Hogstalk, Junior Bookshelf,* October, 1978, p. 255.

Young, D. A., review of *Slake's Limbo, Junior Bookshelf,* December, 1980, pp. 307-8.

■ For More Information See

PERIODICALS

Bulletin of the Center for Children's Books, December, 1965, pp. 63-64; March, 1971, p. 108; October, 1974, pp. 28-29; October, 1985, pp. 28-29; December, 1987, pp. 65-66.

Horn Book, April, 1968, p. 173; December, 1975, p. 590; August, 1976, pp. 417-18; February, 1979, pp. 61-62; December, 1983, pp. 716-17.

Kirkus Reviews, March 1, 1966, p. 244; December 1, 1969, p. 1256.

New York Times Book Review, May 24, 1970, p. 42; November 16, 1975, pp. 29, 38; January 21, 1979, p. 31.
Publishers Weekly, August 2, 1985, p. 69; March 16, 1990, p. 70.
School Library Journal, November, 1983, p. 94; April, 1992, p. 44.
Times Literary Supplement, October 3, 1968, p. 1112.
Voice of Youth Advocates, April, 1984, p. 30.

—*Sketch by Mary Gillis*

* * *

HUCK, Charlotte 1922-

■ Personal

Born October 6, 1922, in Evanston, IL; daughter of Carl M. (a wholesale jeweler) and Mildred (a homemaker; maiden name, Bridges) Huck. *Education:* Attended Wellesley College, 1940-41; Northwestern University, B.S., 1944, M.A., 1951, Ph.D., 1955. *Religion:* Episcopal. *Hobbies and other interests:* Gardening, quilting, genealogy, reading.

■ Addresses

Home—706 West Fern Ave., Redlands, CA 92373.

■ Career

Price School, LaDue City, MO, middle grade teacher, 1944-45; Halsey School, Lake Forest, IL, middle grade teacher, 1945-46; Joseph Sears School, Kenilworth, IL, primary teacher, 1946-51; Northwestern University, Evanston, IL, instructor, 1951-55; Ohio State University, Columbus, assistant professor, 1955-59, associate professor, 1959-62, professor, 1962-86, professor emeritus, 1986—. University of Denver, visiting professor, summer, 1964; University of Hawaii, visiting professor, summer, 1965; Senior Warden, St. Stephen's Episcopal Church, 1986-87; member, Redlands YWCA's board of directors, 1993-94; member, Redlands Day Nursery's board of directors, 1994—. *Member:* National Council of Teachers of English (chair, elementary section, 1967-69; president, 1975-76), American Library Association (chair, May Hill Arbuthnot Lecture Committee, 1973-74), Caldecott Committee (chair, 1980-81), Friends of Smiley Library.

■ Awards, Honors

Distinguished Teaching Award, Ohio State University, 1972; Landau Award, 1979; Distinguished Service Award, NCTE, 1987; Reading Hall of Fame, 1988; Arbuthnot Award, IRA, 1988; inducted into Hall of Fame, Ohio State University College of Education, 1990; Arbuthnot Honor Lecture, American Library Association, 1992.

CHARLOTTE HUCK

■ Writings

(With Susan Hepler and Janet Hickman) *Children's Literature in the Elementary School* (textbook), 4th edition, Holt, 1987, 5th edition, Harcourt, 1993.
(Reteller) *Princess Furball* (folktale), illustrated by Anita Lobel, Greenwillow, 1989.
(Editor) *Secret Places* (poetry), illustrated by Lindsay Barrett George, Greenwillow, 1993.

Princess Furball has been published in Japan and France. Founder of *The WEB* (Wonderfully Exciting Books), an Ohio State University quarterly which focuses on the use of children's literature in the classroom.

■ Work in Progress

A retelling of the folktale "Toads and Diamonds," expected 1995.

■ Sidelights

In the words of Ilene Cooper and Denise Wilms in *Booklist, Children's Literature in the Elementary School* is a "trustworthy standby." This textbook was in its fourth printing before Charlotte Huck, the respected expert on children's literature, began to make her mark as a children's book writer.

In Huck's retelling of a traditional fairy tale, a princess is sold to an ogre by her cruel father but uses her wits to escape and marry the man of her choice. (Cover illustration by Anita Lobel.)

Huck explained to *SATA* how she wrote both *Children's Literature in the Elementary School* and *Princess Furball,* her first children's book. "After completing my Ph.D. at Northwestern University, I began teaching at Ohio State. I stayed through one very hot August in order to teach my first class in children's literature. From that single course, we developed a program that offered specialization in children's literature at both the M.A. and Ph.D. levels. I wrote a textbook with Janet Hickman and Susan Hepler called *Children's Literature in the Elementary School,* which is now in its fifth edition. With graduate students and teachers we started a review quarterly titled *The WEB* (Wonderfully Exciting Books) which focused on the classroom uses of children's literature, and we began a yearly conference on children's literature which currently attracts over two thousand participants."

Huck, busy with academic life, finally found the opportunity to write *Princess Furball.* She related to *SATA:* "When I retired from Ohio State, I moved to Redlands, California, where my twin sister's children lived. Now I had the time to fulfill one of my secret desires; to retell my favorite fairy tale. I had wondered why no one had made a picture book of this gutsy variant of 'Cinderella.' In researching the story, I found my answer. The Grimm version had incest in it, but others did not. So I retold *Princess Furball* and Anita Lobel created stunning pictures for it."

Princess Furball tells the story of a princess whose father has betrothed her to an ogre in exchange for fifty wagons of silver. The Princess refuses to marry until she receives one dress of gold, one of silver, and one made of starlight. Finally, she demands a coat made of one thousand furs. When she receives these gifts from her father, she runs away instead of marrying the ogre. Princess Furball is found in the forest by men of another kingdom, and she goes to work in the king's kitchen. Like Cinderella, however, she gets attention from the prince at a ball when she wears her gown of gold. Wearing her two other dresses, she attends two more balls. The prince places a ring on her finger before she disappears at the third ball, and thus he is able to identify her even when he sees her in her rags. According to Linda Boyles in *School Library Journal,* this retelling is "smooth and graceful." Boyles describes Furball as "a strong female character ... she is resourceful and charming throughout" and relies "on her own abilities."

Huck told *SATA* how *Secret Places,* a collection of poems, developed. "All children have secret places that are special to them. At our summer cabin in Northern Wisconsin I had two—one down by the lake where I went when I had been scolded or I was angry, and one that was almost a little room in the pines where my twin and I played house. I decided to gather together a collection of poems about the various secret places of children."

The nineteen poems in *Secret Places* are, in the opinion of Kathleen Whalin, a reviewer in *School Library Journal,* "strong and sure." They include the writings of Byrd Baylor, Gwendolyn Brooks, Rose Burgunder, Elizabeth Coatsworth, Rachel Field, Aileen Fisher, Karla Kuskin, Myra Cohn Livingston, David McCord, A. A. Milne, and Nancy Dingman Watson. Whalin concludes that this anthology "should be welcomed universally."

Huck believes that it is important to read books aloud to children. "I still have wonderful memories of both my mother and father reading aloud to my twin sister and me," she recalled to *SATA.* "It was only natural that when I became a teacher I read aloud not once but several times a day to my students. I also gave them time each day to read books of their own choosing. For only as children hear stories lovingly read aloud and have time to read themselves, do they develop a love of reading."

Pleased with her new writing career, Huck told *SATA,* "the transition from writing about children's literature to creating books for children has been exciting, indeed. I feel fortunate that my life's work has been involved with a field that brings so much joy and satisfaction to all."

■ Works Cited

Boyles, Linda, review of *Princess Furball, School Library Journal,* September, 1989, p. 240.

Cooper, Ilene, and Denise Wilms, review of *Children's Literature in the Elementary School, Booklist,* May 15, 1990, p. 1811.
Whalin, Kathleen, review of *Secret Places, School Library Journal,* August, 1993, p. 175.

■ For More Information See

PERIODICALS

Booklist, April 1, 1987, p. 1212; October 1, 1993, p. 348.
Bulletin of the Center for Children's Books, October, 1989, p. 35.
Publishers Weekly, March 7, 1994, p. 73.

J

JAMES, Ann 1952-

■ Personal

Born December 6, 1952, in Melbourne, Australia; daughter of Bernard M. S. and Joan E. (Currie) James; companion of Ann Haddon. *Education:* Higher Diploma in Teaching.

■ Addresses

Home—300 Beaconsfield Parade, Middle Park, 3206, Victoria, Australia. *Office*—Books Illustrated, 15 Graham St., Albert Park, 3206, Victoria, Australia.

■ Career

Teacher at Doveton High School and Ringwood High School, 1974-77; Ministry of Education's Publication Branch, art and design department, Victoria, Australia, designer and illustrator, 1978-88; freelance illustrator for various Australian publishing houses, 1981—; Books Illustrated Gallery, Victoria, co-director, 1988—. Director of Nutcote Trust. *Member:* Society of Children's Book Writers International, Australian Society of Authors, Society of Book Illustrators (coordinator).

■ Awards, Honors

Australian Children's Book Council Book Award, Young Readers, for *Bernice Knows Best;* Best Books for Babies shortlist, United Kingdom, for *One Day, A Very First Dictionary;* Australian Children's Book Council Award shortlist, for *A Pet for Mrs. Arbuckle, Penny Pollard's Diary, Penny Pollard's Letters, Looking Out for Sampson, Wiggy and Boa, First at Last,* and *Dog In, Cat Out.*

■ Writings

SELF-ILLUSTRATED

The ABC of What You Can Be, Sugar and Snails Press, 1984.

One Day, A Very First Dictionary, Oxford University Press, 1989.

Finding Jack, Oxford University Press, 1992.

(With Ann Haddon) *Books Illustrated,* Ashton Scholastic, 1994.

ILLUSTRATOR

Gwenda Smyth, *A Pet for Mrs. Arbuckle,* Thomas Nelson, 1981.

Jenny Wagner, *Jo Jo and Mike,* Thomas Nelson, 1982.

Max Dann, *Bernice Knows Best,* Oxford University Press, 1983.

Robin Klein, *Penny Pollard's Diary,* Oxford University Press, 1983.

Klein, *Snakes and Ladders,* Dent, 1984.

Where's My Shoe, Longman Cheshire, 1984.

Klein, *Penny Pollard's Letters,* Oxford University Press, 1984.

Klein, *Penny Pollard in Print,* Oxford University Press, 1986.

Dangers and Disasters, Methuen, 1986.

Libby Hathorn, *Looking Out for Sampson,* Oxford University Press, 1987.

Hazel Edwards, *Sportsmad,* Bookshelf, 1987.

Klein, *Penny Pollard's Passport,* Oxford University Press, 1988.

Anna Fienberg, *Wiggy and Boa,* Dent, 1988.

Smyth, *A Hobby for Mrs. Arbuckle,* Viking Kestrel, 1989.

Netti Hilton, *Prince Lachlan,* Omnibus Books, 1989.

Klein, *Penny Pollard's Guide to Modern Manners,* Oxford University Press, 1989.

Julia MacClelland, *First at Last,* Oxford University Press, 1990.

Pippa MacPherson, *Beryl and Bertha at the Beach,* Oxford University Press, 1990.

Judith Worthy, *Amy the Indefatigable Autograph Hunter,* Angus & Robertson, 1990.

Mike Dumbleton, *Dial-a-Croc,* Omnibus Books, 1991.

Gillian Rubinstein, *Dog In, Cat Out,* Omnibus Books, 1991.

Kathleen Hill, *The Ding Dong Daily,* Heinemann, 1991.

Hill, *The Ding Dong Daily Extra,* Heinemann, 1992.

Ann James's pictures enliven this tale of the business partnership between a girl and a reptile in Mike Dumbleton's *Dial-a-Croc.*

Rod Quantock, *The Backsack Bulletin,* Mammoth Australia, 1992.
Margaret Clarke, *Ripper and Fang,* Omnibus Books, 1992.
Errol Broome, *Tangles,* Little Ark, 1993.
Roger Vaughn Carr, *The Butterfly,* Ashton Scholastic, 1994.
Broome, *Rockhopper,* Little Ark, 1994.
Jessica Joan, Reed, 1994.
Wendy Orr, *Snap,* Reed, 1994.

■ Sidelights

Ann James told *SATA:* "I've always liked to draw from my memory—from my head as we said when we were kids. It surprises me what comes out. But quite often, for illustration, I need to draw or paint things I don't know much about, like motorbikes or aardvarks, so I need to hunt these things out—pore over photos, devour books, scan the horizons. People and animals are the things I know best, and their expressions and moods interest me a lot.

"I like to do most things quickly and my illustrations reflect this. I use materials that allow a spontaneous approach and have a life of their own. I like surprises, and happy accidents are welcome. Since I am a bit of a perfectionist each piece of finished artwork has a long history—lots of preparatory drawings and self-rejected attempts. My photocopier is one of my handiest tools. It saves me from hours of tedious copying and redrawing.

"Other people's work is a great inspiration to me, and I have collected quite a library of illustrated books. Ann Haddon and I set up a gallery called Books Illustrated so that other people could have the opportunity to see the original artwork for children's books. We gather these from all over and have lots of exhibitions and visitors; many come to participate in our classes and workshops. We have a bookshop too, so I'm a bit of a jack-of-all-trades."

* * *

JASSEM, Kate
See OPPENHEIM, Joanne

* * *

JOHNSON, Eric W(arner) 1918-1994

OBITUARY NOTICE—See index for *SATA* sketch: Born March 22, 1918, in Philadelphia, PA; died of head injuries suffered after a fall, August 4, 1994, in Philadelphia, PA. Educator and author. A prolific writer of books for young people and adults, Johnson was a Quaker educator who began writing books as a means of providing his junior high school students with practical guidelines for improving their academic skills, as well as dealing with the social concerns of adolescence. Two of his most popular books for teens include *Improve Your Own Spelling* and *Love and Sex in Plain Language.* As a junior high school principal, Johnson observed parents and teachers seeking straightforward information about the transition from childhood to adolescence; he also noted that these same groups were asking for practical assistance relating to the nurturing of young adults. These observations led to the publication of such volumes as *How to Live through Junior High School, The Family Book about Sexuality,* and *Raising Children to Achieve.* Johnson authored more than fifty volumes, including text books, teacher education materials, and two stories for younger readers, *The Stolen Ruler* and *Escape into the Zoo.* Among his most recent books are *Humorous Stories about the Human Condition* and *Quaker Meeting: A Risky Business,* both published in 1991.

OBITUARIES AND OTHER SOURCES:

BOOKS

The Writers Directory: 1994-1996, St. James Press, 1993.

PERIODICALS

New York Times, August 9, 1994, p. B10.
Washington Post, August 10, 1994, p. B4.

* * *

JONES, Adrienne 1915-

■ Personal

Born July 28, 1915, in Atlanta, GA; daughter of Arthur Washington (a building-supply contractor) and Orianna (Mason) Applewhite; married Richard Morris Jones (an employee of North American Aviation), 1939; children: Gregory, Gwen. *Education:* Educated at Theosophical

ADRIENNE JONES

School of the Open Gate and public schools in Beverly Hills, CA; attended University of California, Los Angeles, 1958-59, and University of California, Irvine, 1972. *Politics:* Liberal democrat. *Religion:* Raised a Theosophist; later Episcopalian; more recently Unitarian-Universalist. *Hobbies and other interests:* Travel, books, music, beach-rambling, conservation activities, golf, conversation.

Addresses

Home—24491 Los Serranos Dr., Laguna Niguel, CA 92677.

Career

Freelance writer and novelist; has also worked as an office and managerial worker, cattle rancher, and with youth groups. Speaker at colleges, universities, conferences, schools, libraries, and writers groups. *Member:* PEN International, American Civil Liberties Union, Society of Children's Book Writers and Illustrators, Southern California Council on Literature for Children and Young People.

Awards, Honors

Outstanding Book Awards, University of California, Irvine, 1968, for *Sail, Calypso!,* 1972, for *Another Place, Another Spring,* 1975, for *So, Nothing Is Forever,* and 1979, for *The Hawks of Chelney;* Southern California Council on Children and Young People Awards for Best Book by a Southern California author, 1972, for *Another Place, Another Spring,* and 1975, for *So, Nothing Is Forever; The Hawks of Chelney* was named to the American Library Association's (ALA) Best Books for Young Adults List, 1979; Southern California Council on Literature for Children and Young People Award for a distinguished body of work, 1984; PEN International USA West Award, 1988, for *Street Family.*

Writings

FOR CHILDREN

Thunderbird Pass, Lippincott, 1952.
Where Eagles Fly, Putnam, 1957.
Ride the Far Wind, Little, Brown, 1964.
Wild Voyageur: Story of a Canada Goose, Little, Brown, 1966.
Sail, Calypso!, illustrated by Adolph LeMoult, Little, Brown, 1968.
Another Place, Another Spring, Houghton, 1971.
Hawk (short story), Bank Street College of Education, 1972.
My Name Is Gnorr with an Unsilent G (short story), Bank Street College of Education, 1972.
Old Witch Hannifin and Her Shoonaget (short story), Bank Street College of Education, 1972.
Niki and Albert and the Seventh Street Raiders (short story), Bank Street College of Education, 1972.
Who Needs a Hand to Hold? (short story), Bank Street College of Education, 1973.
The Mural Master, illustrated by David Omar White, Houghton, 1974.
So, Nothing Is Forever, illustrated by Richard Cuffari, Houghton, 1974.
The Hawks of Chelney, drawings by Stephen Gammell, Harper, 1977.
The Beckoner, Harper, 1980.
Whistle Down a Dark Lane, Harper, 1982.
A Matter of Spunk, Harper, 1983.
Street Family, Harper, 1987.
Long Time Passing, Harper, 1990.

Jones's books have been published in Germany, Austria, Denmark, the Netherlands, Italy, and Japan.

Work in Progress

A series of six illustrated books (beginning with *Friends for All Time* and *What's Going On Here?*) for readers in middle school.

Sidelights

As a successful writer of books for children and young adults, Adrienne Jones has always drawn on her own experience to provide the substance of her fiction. "The advice 'Write about what you know, what is familiar to you' is incorrect if viewed in the narrow sense," Jones wrote in her *Something about the Author Autobiography Series* (*SAAS*) entry. "After all, there are great stories of pure fantasy! But if the advice is taken to mean 'write of what is inside you, what is especially and uniquely you,' then *that* is supremely good counsel, and wc should heed it."

Jones was born in Atlanta, Georgia, in 1915. As Theosophists, the members of her family were vegetarians and stressed their individual responsibilities within the religious community. Jones's memories of early childhood are filled with images of nature, particularly impressions of the lush Blue Ridge Mountains where her family vacationed. At times throughout her life, the desire to be surrounded by nature drove Jones to seek high adventure and its accompanying sense of fulfillment. This romance with the outdoors remained constant and later inspired some of her books.

When Jones was six, her parents separated. Her mother moved Jones and her older sister, Doris, to Southern California. There, they took up residence at Krotona, which Jones described as a "Theosophical colony tucked into the hills above Hollywood." The colony was situated on the grounds of a mansion which had been divided into apartments, and Jones was delighted to learn that the famous comedian Charlie Chaplin was a close neighbor.

She and Doris attended the Theosophical School of the Open Gate on the colony grounds, where Jones received her first encouragement as an aspiring writer. Jones's teacher was so impressed by some verses the young Southerner had written that she had them printed in the school newspaper. As a result, the idea of becoming a writer was born in Jones as a "glorious dream." Later, the events of life at Krotona provided the material for the novel, *A Matter of Spunk.*

With the dutiful support of the author's father, whose construction-supply business prospered in Atlanta until the Great Depression, the three were able to purchase a house on the fringes of Beverly Hills. The children entered public school, and while their education in literature and natural science was advanced, they knew little arithmetic. Through the aid of a special "adjustment" classroom and teacher, the girls learned math quickly and just as quickly adjusted to life outside the Theosophical community. Both girls did well in school, but by the time of Jones's graduation from high school, her father's business had failed. Even with scholarships, Jones could not afford college.

In the midst of the Depression all three women had to work to keep their home and put food on the table. Despite the routine hardship, Jones recalled her mother laughing and saying: "'We can do without some of the minor necessities, but we can't do without a few frills.'" "So," Jones added in *SAAS,* "we had an occasional splurge with Albert Sheetz Ice Cream and homemade cookies. For entertainment, there was always our Atwater Kent radio. Favorite programs: 'The Blue Monday Jamboree' and President Roosevelt's reassuring 'Fireside Chats.'"

It was during this period that Jones rediscovered her childhood passion for the outdoors. During a trip to the San Gabriel Mountains, Jones was captivated by the "sagey smells lower down, the woodsy canyons, the streams, the echoes from hillside to hillside of happy laughter." Feeling a compulsion to spend further time outdoors, Jones joined the Sierra Club, which created the opportunity for extended outings in California's rugged environment.

According to Jones, her life changed as the result of her involvement with the Sierra Club; she met her future husband, Dick Jones, an avid rock-climber and national-class gymnast. Together they made both the ascent and descent of the sheer east face of Mt. Whitney, the highest mountain in the conterminous forty-eight states. Jones also came to appreciate the desert, which had once clashed in her mind with her beloved pine forests of Georgia, on its own terms. Jones felt that she belonged somewhere. At last the Western outdoor scene claimed her heart.

Ten years after she was married, and following the tumultuous years of the Second World War, Jones began her first novel, *Thunderbird Pass.* When the manuscript was rejected by a few publishers, Jones shelved the project. After some time, however, her husband ran across the manuscript and urged her to submit it to another publisher. The book was accepted and published by the J. B. Lippincott Company in 1952.

After so many years of struggle in the urban setting of Southern California, Jones and her family were eager to try another way of living. With her sister's family, Jones and her husband bought a two hundred-acre ranch on the Klamath River in Northern California. In a situation reminiscent of Jones's childhood, Dick remained at his job in Southern California to provide funds for the ranch. Expecting the ranch to become self-sufficient, Jones planned only a two-month separation from her husband. The ranch, however, required increasing infusions of cash, prolonging their separation. To help meet costs, Jones took a job and managed to write her second book, *Where Eagles Fly,* but expenses at the ranch continued to mount. When Dick became seriously ill, the family was reunited in Southern California. The ranch was sold, and Jones eventually began to write full time.

In her first critically recognized work, *Sail, Calypso!,* Jones developed the relationship between two boys as they spend the summer repairing a derelict sailboat. Clay, the son of African-American migrant workers, has been released from his summer chores to recover from a severe case of pneumonia. Confronted by empty summer days, Clay is overjoyed when he finds an abandoned boat which he might spend the summer repairing. He is dismayed, however, to find that another boy, Paul, who is white and lives with his neglectful father, has also claimed the boat and is equally desperate for the opportunity to repair it. Reluctantly the boys agree to work together, and over the course of their labor become close friends. Even as they ultimately lose the ship they

When two boys find an abandoned boat on the beach, they must overcome their differences and their selfishness to make it sail again. (Cover illustration by Adolph LeMoult.)

have made seaworthy, Clay and Paul realize that their friendship will endure. The relationship between the boys is "beautifully portrayed against a background of realistic sailing lore," wrote Ruth P. Bull and Betsy Hearne in a *Booklist* review. With similar praise for the book, a *Horn Book* reviewer said: "The quiet, introspective account of the boys' attitudes and behavior builds up to a thunderous climax." A reviewer in the *Bulletin of the Center for Children's Books* also appreciated the story and approved of Jones's writing, which he described as "deft."

With the novel *Another Place, Another Spring,* Jones again explored the relationship between a pair of protagonists. As the result of her father's participation in the Decembrist Revolt of 1825, Elena, a young member of the Russian nobility, and her maid, Marya, are exiled to Siberia. In mid-journey, however, it is revealed that the officer charged with their escort is leading them out of Russia, to a proposed reunion with Elena's father. After a flight fraught with suspense, Elena dies and Marya escapes to America, where she must adjust to life at Fort Ross, a small Russian town on California's north coast. The depiction of Russian society, monarchy, and prison camps, as well as an evocation of the landscape, all contribute to the success of the book. Despite some predictability, the novel has "strength in its intense narrative and vivid characterization," noted a *Publishers Weekly* reviewer.

In the award-winning novel, *The Hawks of Chelney,* Jones wrote about alienation and redemption. Siri, born to older parents in an isolated fishing village, is fascinated by birds, and whiles away entire days tracking their movements. Of particular interest to him is an osprey which has nested in the cliffs near the village. Before long, however, the villagers begin to associate poor fishing with the presence of the fish hawk, which is declared an agent of Satan by the village leaders. Siri's communion with birds places him in danger and ultimately forces him from the village to the rookery where the osprey nests. Siri then sprouts a coat of down, feels his bones grow lighter, and finds protrusions rising from his shoulder blades; he is becoming the bird he adores. This transformation is halted when Siri finds Thea, the sole survivor of a ship wreck. The outcasts eventually fall in love and are again menaced by the villagers. At the tale's conclusion Siri and Thea have disappeared, and it is unclear whether they have been murdered by the desperate villagers, or have actually become the sea birds that haunt the lonely community. In a review in the *Times Literary Supplement,* Sarah Hayes called *The Hawks of Chelney* "a novel of somber brilliance" and credited the work for raising fundamental questions about "nature, society, power, and human need," without directly broaching those issues. Virginia Haviland, in a *Horn Book* review, found the characters compelling enough for her to become engaged in their struggle to survive and praised Jones's ability to evoke a "haunting atmosphere and a sense of the wild terrain." Zena Sutherland, in *Bulletin of the Center for Children's Books,* asserted, "this is a book written by a craftsman: style, setting, story line, and characters are in complete harmony."

Jones's most clearly autobiographical works are *Whistle Down a Dark Lane* and *A Matter of Spunk.* Both examine material that refers directly to Jones's early childhood. *Whistle Down a Dark Lane* opens shortly after the First World War, in Georgia, where six-year-old Margery Standfield and her older sister Blainey must deal with their parents' increasingly tense relationship. While on vacation in the Blue Ridge Mountains, the girls' mother insists that she and their father sleep apart to avert another complicated, and potentially life-threatening, pregnancy. Thus begins an irrevocable falling-out, during which the mother struggles toward greater independence. Among other things, she learns to drive a car, becomes interested in the Suffrage Movement, and saves the life of an African-American acquaintance during an encounter with the Ku Klux Klan. In addition to witnessing, and struggling with, the distance opening between her parents, Margery confronts her own nascent sexuality. "Mother and daughter, in their separate ways, grope for emotional maturity in an era when women's roles are changing dramatically," pointed out Bill Erbes in a *Voice of Youth Advocates* review. "Jones's style matches in its quality the integrity of characterization [and] the understanding of relationships between siblings and between men and women of that time...," praised Lilian L. Shapiro in a *School Library Journal* review. A critic in *Kirkus Reviews* offered a different point of view, describing the book as "too weighty and wordy" and of "limited depth."

A Matter of Spunk rejoins Margery, Blainey, and their mother in a Theosophist colony outside Los Angeles. Here Margery encounters a varied cast of classmates, including a young movie star and a female bully who is eventually crippled by polio. The novel follows the Standfield women as they leave the colony and begin life as a truly independent family. In a review in *Horn Book,* reviewer Mary M. Burns asserted that *A Matter of Spunk* "is not dependent upon its predecessor [*Whistle Down a Dark Lane*] and imperceptibly integrates an adult perspective with a child's view." What emerges is a "portrait of an unforgettable, close-knit, family," Burns added.

Jones's more recent novels have dealt with some contemporary social issues familiar to young people. In *Street Family* Jones brings together a varied cast of homeless wanderers who regularly take shelter beneath a Los Angeles freeway overpass. Joshua and Chancy, both of whom have fled abusive living situations, are the youngest of the group, which also includes an alcoholic veteran and an irascible bag lady. Despite the seeming hopelessness of the situation, Chancy is determined to find a home where she and her companions can live in relative security. After narrowly escaping the violent hazards of the streets, Chancy and Joshua find shelter, and along with it, a sense of optimism about the future.

In an article written by Patty Campbell in the *Wilson Library Bulletin,* the research Jones undertook before writing *Street Family* is described. To form a clearer picture of life on the street, Jones interviewed Matt Lyons, a former employee of the Inner City Law Center in Los Angeles who tried living on the street to gain an appreciation of the lives of the people he helped daily. Lyons's experiment only lasted a week before he was so sick that he had to return home. Jones also relied on the expertise of the director of the Midnight Mission who told her that children on the street are especially vulnerable because they often are not old enough to be admitted to public shelters. "Careful research, empathy with human suffering, and a knack for good storytelling are the ingredients Adrienne Jones uses to make *Street Family* a vivid and interesting tale," Campbell concludes. Offering another point of view, a *Kirkus Reviews* critic considered the book "more convincing in its details than in its plot" but conceded that the work as a whole is "well-written and powerful."

Another work with a contemporary setting, *Long Time Passing,* examines the social upheavals of the 1960s as personified in the character of Jonas. When Jonas's mother dies in an automobile accident in 1969, his father, a marine about to be shipped out to Vietnam, sends him to live with his aunt in California. There Jonas is quickly swept up in the fervor of the anti-war movement and must confront his loyalty to his father and his values or the moral justification he perceives in protesting the war. The issue is complicated by Jonas's affection for Auleen, who is committed to the anti-war cause. Jonas's hesitation evaporates, however, when his father is reported missing in action. Jonas enlists and serves his time in Vietnam, only to return home emotionally scarred and without his father (who was actually killed in combat). Years later Jonas and Auleen meet again and consider the possibility of reconciliation and a future together. "The political and social realities are just as important to the plot as the bittersweet love interest," Syrul Lurie wrote in a *Voice of Youth Advocates* review. Candy Dawson Boyd supplied similar praise in the *Los Angeles Times Book Review,* noting that Jones provides her characters with "conflicts galore—and adroitly ties up all the loose threads by book's end."

Reflecting on her choice to become a writer, Jones once told *SATA:* "My endeavor is to learn and understand the feelings and reasons behind the human act, the human mind and heart. In my writing the effort is to portray the brotherhood and friendship that is found in its most vital and active form in the world of the young, yet to understand, and reveal the personal tragedies and failures which are so much a part of life. I have chosen to write mainly for young people, as this is the nearest one can come to touching the future."

■ Works Cited

Review of *Another Place, Another Spring, Publishers Weekly,* November 22, 1971, p. 41.

Boyd, Candy Dawson, review of *Long Time Passing, Los Angeles Times Book Review,* June 30, 1991, p. 13.

Bull, Ruth P. and Betsy Hearne, review of *Sail, Calypso!, Booklist,* October 15, 1968, p. 248.

Burns, Mary M., review of *A Matter of Spunk, Horn Book,* October, 1983, p. 584.

Campbell, Patty, "The Young Adult Perplex," *Wilson Library Bulletin,* April, 1987, pp. 50-51.

Erbes, Bill, review of *Whistle Down a Dark Lane, Voice of Youth Advocates,* April, 1983, p. 38.

Haviland, Virginia, review of *The Hawks of Chelney, Horn Book,* June, 1978, p. 283.

Hayes, Sarah, "The Twists of Time," *Times Literary Supplement,* December 14, 1979, p. 122.

Jones, Adrienne, essay in *Something about the Author Autobiography Series,* Volume 10, Gale, 1990, pp. 135-50.

Lurie, Syrul, review of *Long Time Passing, Voice of Youth Advocates,* December, 1990, p. 284.

Review of *Sail, Calypso!, Bulletin of the Center for Children's Books,* June, 1969, pp. 159-60.

Review of *Sail, Calypso!, Horn Book,* October, 1968.

Shapiro, Lillian L., review of *Whistle Down a Dark Lane, School Library Journal,* October, 1982, p. 162.

Review of *Street Family, Kirkus Reviews,* August 15, 1987, pp. 1241-42.

Sutherland, Zena, review of *The Hawks of Chelney, Bulletin of the Center for Children's Books,* November, 1978, p. 45.
Review of *Whistle Down a Dark Lane, Kirkus Reviews,* August 1, 1982, p. 872.

■ For More Information See

PERIODICALS

Washington Post Book World, May 14, 1978, p. G4.
Bulletin of the Center for Children's Books, December, 1983, p. 70; June, 1987, p. 190; October, 1990, p. 32.
Horn Book, February, 1972, p. 57; June, 1974, p. 283; April, 1980, p. 177; September, 1987, p. 618.
Kirkus Reviews, September 1, 1983, p. 175.
School Library Journal, April, 1978, p. 94; September, 1983, p. 136; September, 1987, p. 196.
Times Literary Supplement, June 6, 1968, p. 591.
Voice of Youth Advocates, February, 1984, p. 338; June, 1987, p. 79.

K

KAHN, Joan 1914-1994

OBITUARY NOTICE—See index for *SATA* sketch: Born April 13, 1914, in New York, NY; died following a brief illness, October 11, 1994, in Manhattan, NY. Editor and author. A leading editor of mystery and suspense anthologies, Kahn was also the author of numerous books, including the children's stories *Ladies and Gentlemen, Said the Ringmaster* and *Hi, Jock, Run around the Block,* the novels *To Meet Miss Long* and *Open House,* and a collection of short fiction entitled *Ready or Not: Here Come Fourteen Frightening Stories.* In 1945, Kahn began a thirty-four-year career at Harper & Row as an editor of nonfiction art, history, theater, and travel books. Bringing to public attention the works of authors such as Dorothy L. Sayers, Patricia Highsmith, and Tony Hillerman, Kahn developed a reputation for excellence among readers and writers of suspense fiction. She later left Harper & Row to serve as an editor for Ticknor & Fields, Dutton, and St. Martin's Press, before retiring in 1989. Honored twice by the Mystery Writers of America, Kahn received the 1985 Ellery Queen Award for lifetime service to the mystery industry and, upon retirement, an Edgar Allan Poe Award.

OBITUARIES AND OTHER SOURCES:

BOOKS

Authors of Books for Young People, 3rd edition, Scarecrow, 1990.

PERIODICALS

Chicago Tribune, October 16, 1994, Section 2, p. 6.
New York Times, October 13, 1994, p. B15.

* * *

KARR, Kathleen 1946-

■ Personal

Born April 21, 1946, in Allentown, PA; daughter of Stephen (a mechanical engineer) and Elizabeth (a home-

KATHLEEN KARR

maker; maiden name, Szoka) Csere; married Lawrence F. Karr (a physicist and computer consultant), July 13, 1968; children: Suzanne, Daniel. *Education:* Catholic University of America, B.A, 1968; Providence College, M.A., 1971; further study at Corcoran School of Art, 1972.

■ Addresses

Home—Washington, DC. *Agent*—Renee Cho, McIntosh & Otis, 310 Madison Ave., Suite 607, New York, NY 10017.

Career

Writer. Barrington High School, Barrington, RI, English and speech teacher, 1968-69; curator, Rhode Island Historical Society Film Archives, 1970-71; American Film Institute, Washington, DC, archives assistant, 1971-72, member of catalog staff, 1972; Washington Circle Theatre Corporation, Washington, DC, general manager, 1973-78; Circle/Showcase Theatres, Washington, DC, advertising director, 1979-83, director of public relations, 1984-88; Circle Management Company/Circle Releasing, Washington, DC, member of public relations staff, 1988-93. Assistant professor at George Washington University, summer, 1979, and 1980-81. Lecturer or instructor in film and communications at various institutions, including Providence College, 1969-70, University of Rhode Island, 1971, University of Maryland, 1972, Catholic University of America, 1973-77, New Line Presentations Lecture Bureau, 1974-76, American Film Institute, 1979-80, and Trinity College, 1985-86; lecturer at film and writing conferences, 1973-89. Juror, American Film Festival, 1971, and Rosebud Awards, 1991. *Member:* Washington Romance Writers (member of board of directors, 1985-86; president, 1986-87).

Awards, Honors

Golden Medallion Award for best inspirational novel, Romance Writers of America, 1986, for *From This Day Forward;* finalist, outstanding emerging artist, Washington D.C. Mayor's Arts Awards, 1986; "100 Books for Reading and Sharing" citation, New York Public Library, 1990, for *It Ain't Always Easy;* Parents' Choice Story Book citation, 1992, for *Oh, Those Harper Girls!*

Writings

FICTION FOR CHILDREN

It Ain't Always Easy, Farrar, Straus, 1990.
Oh, Those Harper Girls!; or, Young and Dangerous, Farrar, Straus, 1992.
Gideon and the Mummy Professor, Farrar, Straus, 1993.
The Cave, Farrar, Straus, 1994.
In the Kaiser's Clutch, Farrar, Straus, 1995.

Some of Karr's novels have been translated into French and Italian.

ROMANCE NOVELS FOR ADULTS

Light of My Heart, Zondervan, 1984.
From This Day Forward, Zondervan, 1985.
Chessie's King, Zondervan, 1986.
Destiny's Dreamers Book I: Gone West, Barbour, 1993.
Destiny's Dreamers Book II: The Promised Land, Barbour, 1993.

OTHER

(Editor) *The American Film Heritage: Views from the American Film Institute Collection,* Acropolis Press, 1972.

Also author of various short films, including *The Elegant Mr. Brown and I* (and director), 1969; *Mayor Tom Bradley,* 1973; *Profile: Tom Bradley,* 1974; and *No Smoking, Spitting or Molesting,* 1976. Contributor to numerous journals, including *Film Society Review, Film News, Journal of Popular Film, Providence Journal,* and *Rhode Island History;* contributor to texts, including *Cartoon: A Celebration of American Comic Art,* 1975, and *Magill's Survey of Cinema,* annual editions. Contributing editor, *Media and Methods,* 1970-72; editor, *ASFE News,* March, 1976; member of advisory board, *Children's Literature,* 1994—.

Work in Progress

A series of four books with a western theme for HarperCollins, for publication in fall, 1995.

Sidelights

Kathleen Karr's historical novels for young teens are noted for their humorous and suspenseful plots and boldly-drawn characters. Besides their settings of New York City and the American West in the late 1800s, Karr's works also feature sympathetic portrayals of the pains of growing up. In her first children's book, *It Ain't Always Easy,* two New York City orphans, eleven-year-old Jack and eight-year-old Mandy, are trying to get out west in the hope of finding a family to take care of them. Despite the odds against them, their determination to stay together stands them in good stead, and after many adventures they manage to find a home and family. While acknowledging the entertaining aspect of the children's adventures, some critics found the events and dialogue unrealistic; Gail Richmond pointed out in *School Library Journal* that Jack's character is "too good to be true, and loses some credibility as a result." The book "is nonetheless powerful," a *Publishers Weekly* writer concluded, "and the spirit and perseverance of the protagonists are uplifting." Other critics cited authentic period details and well-rounded characterizations in praising the book; as *Horn Book* writer Elizabeth S. Watson observed, even "lesser characters are three-dimensional," making for "an extremely appealing" story.

Karr utilizes the setting of the nineteenth-century American West to a more comic effect in *Oh, Those Harper Girls!; or, Young and Dangerous.* In this novel, the six daughters of a hapless father try a number of foolhardy and illegal schemes to save their west Texas homestead from bankruptcy and eventually land on the New York stage reenacting their famous escapades. Centered on the youngest daughter, Lily, the brains behind the girls' schemes, the story also comments on the restricted roles available to women in the nineteenth century. *Booklist* contributor Mary Romano Marks commented favorably on this aspect of Karr's work, adding: "The girls' hilarious escapades and good-natured sibling rivalry make the novel an enjoyable read." "Characterization is quite strong," Rita Soltan likewise remarked in *School Library Journal* review, dubbing *Oh, Those Harper Girls!* "fast paced and satisfying." A *Kirkus Reviews* writer called the novel "a happy, rip-roaring adventure, capped by a whirlwind of marriages, family reunions, and wishes fulfilled."

Critics characterized Karr's next effort, *Gideon and the Mummy Professor,* set on the Mississippi River in 1855, as a picaresque melodrama. In this work, twelve-year-old Gideon and his father, "the professor," are travelling vaudeville performers. When George, their four-thousand-year-old mummy, reveals a valuable emerald hidden in his wrappings, several thieves chase them all the way to New Orleans. While Beth Tegart in *School Library Journal* found the plot, studded with references to Victorian and Creole life, "too convoluted for most readers," other critics believed Gideon's adventures would appeal to young teens. *Horn Book* contributor Watson found that the "carefully chosen description ... heightens understanding without burdening the story." Betsy Hearne, writing in *Bulletin of the Center for Children's Books,* proclaimed: "This is one of those great reads that combines picaresque adventure, humorous incident, quirky characters, eerie elements, and a style in charge of it all." As a *Kirkus Reviews* writer summarized: "Once again, Karr comes up with an evocative vocabulary and a nonstop adventure."

Karr tells a rollicking adventure of the Old West as six sisters use a number of schemes to make their fortunes. (Cover illustration by Ellen Eagle.)

Karr came into the twentieth century with *The Cave,* which is set in the drought-burdened South Dakota of the Depression. The lack of rain poses many difficulties for young Christine, for it has threatened the livelihood of her family's farm and aggravated her younger brother Michael's asthma. Her father is considering moving the family to California when Christine unearths a cave in the foothills near the farm, complete with crystals, stalactites—and water. Although she wants to stay on the farm, Christine tries to keep her discovery from her father, for she fears in rescuing the farm he will destroy the cave's beauty. With numerous period details, "Karr excels in re-creating time and place," Cindy Darling Codell noted in *School Library Journal.* In addition, the critic wrote, the ecological conflict enhances the "sweet, well-crafted story of a family forced to be tough by the extremities of nature." Comparing the book to the children's classic *Caddie Woodlawn, Booklist* critic Mary Harris Veeder observed that "Karr creates an active and believable girl in the throes of both physical and emotional change" and praised the author's child's-eye view of the era. As a *Kirkus Reviews* writer concluded: "Fine period detail and masterful writing grace Karr's story of quiet courage during hard times."

Karr told *SATA:* "I began writing fiction on a dare from my husband. Tired of hearing me complain about not being able to find a 'good read,' he suggested I write a book myself. I sold my third attempt, entering the world of women's fiction. My children were responsible for finding my true calling, however. They asked me to write a book for them. I did (*It Ain't Always Easy*) and discovered I loved writing children's novels.

"After a number of years working in the 'real' worlds of motion pictures and education, I find it a pleasure to be able to create my own worlds in fiction. To watch a character come alive—become real flesh and blood and take the reins of a story in hand—is an exhilarating experience. It's also hard work.

"As for my penchant for historical settings, well, I've discovered that I feel quite comfortable in the nineteenth century. It's a challenge to try to recreate a specific time and place, with its specific language patterns. Short of inventing a time machine, this is my way of reentering the past and attempting to show my readers that while events may change, the nature of human beings is fairly constant. Courage and common decency against difficult odds have always existed."

■ Works Cited

Review of *The Cave, Kirkus Reviews,* July 15, 1994.

Codell, Cindy Darling, review of *The Cave, School Library Journal,* September, 1994.

Review of *Gideon and the Mummy Professor, Kirkus Reviews,* May 15, 1993, p. 663.

Hearne, Betsy, review of *Gideon and the Mummy Professor, Bulletin of the Center for Children's Books,* September, 1993, pp. 12-13.

Review of *It Ain't Always Easy, Publishers Weekly,* September 28, 1990, p. 103.

Marks, Mary Romano, review of *Oh, Those Harper Girls!, Booklist,* April 15, 1992, p. 1523.
Review of *Oh, Those Harper Girls!, Kirkus Reviews,* April 15, 1992, p. 539.
Richmond, Gail, review of *It Ain't Always Easy, School Library Journal,* December, 1990, p. 104.
Soltan, Rita, review of *Oh, Those Harper Girls!, School Library Journal,* May, 1992, p. 133.
Tegart, Beth, review of *Gideon and the Mummy Professor, School Library Journal,* June, 1993, p. 107.
Veeder, Mary Harris, review of *The Cave, Booklist,* September 15, 1994.
Watson, Elizabeth S., review of *It Ain't Always Easy, Horn Book,* March, 1991, pp. 199-200.
Watson, Elizabeth S., review of *Gideon and the Mummy Professor, Horn Book,* September-October, 1993, p. 599.

■ For More Information See

PERIODICALS

Bulletin of the Center for Children's Books, February, 1991, p. 143; July-August, 1992, p. 297.
Horn Book, May-June, 1992, p. 341.
Publishers Weekly, March 23, 1992, p. 73.
Voice of Youth Advocates, April, 1985, p. 44; February, 1991, p. 352; June, 1992, p. 96; December, 1994, pp. 275-76.

* * *

KEIR, Christine
See POPESCU, Christine

* * *

KELLER, Charles 1942-

■ Personal

Born March 30, 1942, in New York, NY.

■ Addresses

Home—162 19th St., Union City, NJ 07087.

■ Career

Writer. Author of the syndicated newspaper column, "Corn on the Cob."

■ Writings

COMPILER

Ballpoint Bananas, and Other Jokes for Kids, illustrated by David Barrios, Prentice-Hall, 1973.
Too Funny for Words: Gesture Jokes for Children, Prentice-Hall, 1973.
Laugh Lines, Prentice-Hall, 1974.
(With Richard Baker) *The Star-Spangled Banana, and Other Revolutionary Riddles,* illustrated by Tomie de Paola, Prentice-Hall, 1974.

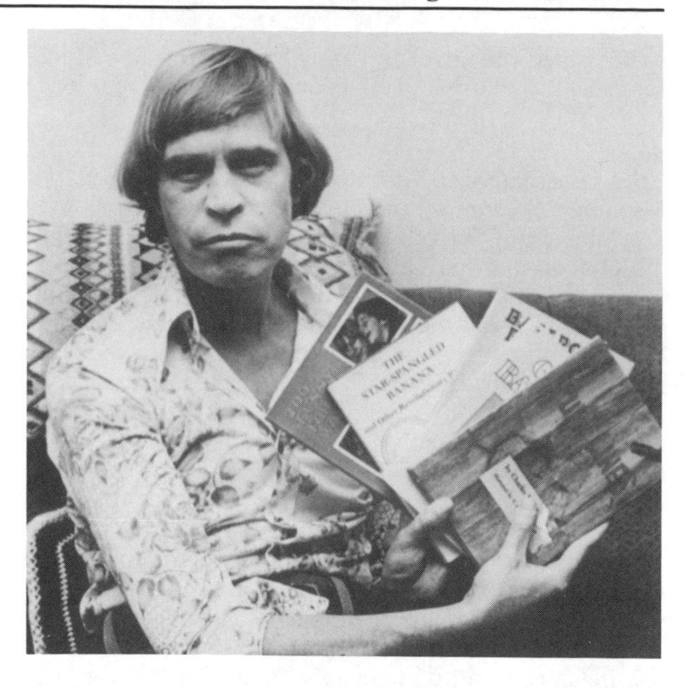

CHARLES KELLER

Going Bananas, illustrated by Roger B. Wilson, Prentice-Hall, 1975.
Punch Lines, Prentice-Hall, 1975.
Daffynitions, illustrated by F. A. Fitzgerald, Prentice-Hall, 1976.
Glory, Glory, How Peculiar, illustrated by Lady McCrady, Prentice-Hall, 1976.
(With Linda Glovach) *The Little Witch Presents a Monster Joke Book,* Prentice-Hall, 1977.
Giggle Puss: Pet Jokes for Kids, illustrated by Paul Coker, Prentice-Hall, 1977.
Llama Beans, Prentice-Hall, 1977.
More Ballpoint Bananas, illustrated by Leonard Shortall, Prentice-Hall, 1977.
The Nutty Joke Book, Prentice-Hall, 1978.
Laughing: A Historical Collection of American Humor, Prentice-Hall, 1978.
School Daze, illustrated by Sam Q. Weissman, Prentice-Hall, 1978.
The Wizard of Gauze, and Other Gags for Kids, Prentice-Hall, 1979.
The Best of Rube Goldberg, Prentice-Hall, 1979.
Still Going Bananas, Prentice-Hall, 1980.
News Breaks, Prentice-Hall, 1980.
Growing up Laughing: Humorists Look at American Youth, Prentice-Hall, 1981.
What's the Score? Sports Jokes, Prentice-Hall, 1981.
Smokey the Shark, and Other Fishy Tales, illustrated by Lee Lorenz, Prentice-Hall, 1981.
Ohm on the Range: Robot and Computer Jokes, Prentice-Hall, 1982.
Oh, Brother! Family Jokes, Prentice-Hall, 1982.
Alexander the Grape: Fruit and Vegetable Jokes, illustrated by Gregory Filling, Prentice-Hall, 1982.
Remember the a la Mode! Riddles and Puns, illustrated by Lorenz, Prentice-Hall, 1983.
Norma Lee I Don't Knock on Doors: Knock, Knock Jokes, Prentice-Hall, 1983.

What's Up, Doc? Doctor and Dentist Jokes, Prentice-Hall, 1984.
Grime Doesn't Pay: Law and Order Jokes, Prentice-Hall, 1984.
Astronuts: Space Jokes and Riddles, illustrated by Art Cummings, Prentice-Hall, 1985.
Swine Lake: Music and Dance Riddles, illustrated by Filling, Prentice-Hall, 1986.
Waiter, There's a Fly in My Soup! Restaurant Jokes, illustrated by Lorenz, Prentice-Hall, 1986.
Count Draculations! Monster Riddles, illustrated by Edward Frascino, Prentice-Hall, 1986.
Colossal Fossils: Dinosaur Riddles, illustrated by Leonard Kessler, Prentice-Hall, 1987.
It's Raining Cats and Dogs: Cat and Dog Jokes, illustrated by Robert Quackenbush, Pippin, 1988.
King Henry the Ape: Animal Jokes, illustrated by Frascino, Pippin, 1989.
Driving Me Crazy: Fun-on-Wheels Jokes, illustrated by Lorenz, Pippin, 1989.
Tongue Twisters, illustrated by Ron Fritz, Simon & Schuster, 1989.
Belly Laughs: Food Jokes and Riddles, illustrated by Fritz, Simon & Schuster, 1990.
Take Me to Your Liter: Science and Math Jokes, illustrated by Filling, Pippin, 1991.
Planet of the Grapes: Show Biz Jokes and Riddles, illustrated by Mischa Richter, Pippin, 1992.
Lend Me Your Ears: Telephone Jokes, illustrated by Kessler, Pippin, 1994.

Also compiler of *The Silly Song Book.*

The amazing reptiles of prehistoric days provide the subject for this collection of riddles. (Cover illustration by Leonard Kessler.)

Sidelights

Charles Keller has published many collections of humorous plays on words, from riddles and puns to silly songs and tongue twisters. As a *Publishers Weekly* reviewer of *Alexander the Grape* commented, Keller's collections of "batty humor are popular with boys and girls whose ambition is to shine as the life of the party." *School Library Journal* contributor Sandra Olmstead explained: "Keller captures the silly, groanable humor that young readers love to read and repeat." Keller's selections of humorous essays, short stories, and poetry from throughout American history have also been highly praised for introducing classic writers and traditional favorites to young adult audiences in a palatable format.

From the publication of Keller's first anthology of jokes, critics remarked on the likelihood of children's appreciation of them as they go through what some considered an inevitable joke-telling phase. Regarding *Ballpoint Bananas, and Other Jokes for Kids,* a collection of riddles, knock-knock jokes, and nonsense rhymes, a *Publishers Weekly* critic commented that "most children should find [these jokes] irresistible." Another of Keller's early works, *The Star-Spangled Banana, and Other Revolutionary Riddles,* takes its inspiration from the impending bicentennial celebration of the American revolution. Anita Silvey wrote in *Horn Book* that Keller's collection "should cause groans and laughter about everything from the signing of the Declaration of Independence to Paul Revere's ride."

Other early Keller collections include *Daffynitions,* a collection of puns for children, and *Glory, Glory, How Peculiar,* a compilation of parodic lyrics set to well-known melodies. Though Marjorie Lewis indicated in her *School Library Journal* review that such songs were probably "more fun to learn from friends," *Bulletin of the Center for Children's Books* reviewer Zena Sutherland wrote that the selections "have the sort of humor that is especially popular for group singing." Keller returned to joke anthologies with the publication of *Giggle Puss,* a collection of jokes about pets. Margaret Blue, writing in *School Library Journal,* commented that while some of the selections are familiar, "many are fresh, funny, and typical of kids' humor."

By drawing on centuries of adult humor writers in *Laughing,* "Charles Keller," *New York Times Book Review* contributor Peter Andrews stated, "has put together a really first-rate collection of American humor." The book is organized chronologically, drawing the reader through American history by way of contemporary humorous lyrics, essays, and short stories. "Each section is an engrossing reminder of critical issues," remarked a *Publishers Weekly* writer. Although the historical, adult origin of the material may prove interesting to students of cultural history, Andrews indicated the work's intended audience when he concluded: "I particularly like this collection because Mr. Keller has included stories he thinks kids will really enjoy, not those he thinks are good for them." Critical reaction was equally positive for a similar anthology, *Growing up Laughing,* in which Keller collects stories, poems, and cartoons whose shared theme is the difficulties of growing up. Originally written for an older audience, Sutherland noted, nevertheless most selections "should be enjoyed by older children and young adults." In *Voice of Youth Advocates,* Beverly V. Page wrote: "This book is highly recommended for young people who read for the sheer enjoyment of spending happy hours with a gay, rollicking, happy book."

In his subsequent publications, Keller returned to the simple format he had favored earlier of placing jokes, riddles, puns, and other short humorous pieces in thematic collections. *School Daze* features jokes and cartoons about school; *Smokey the Shark, and Other Fishy Tales* collects jokes about fish; *Alexander the Grape* features punning jokes about fruits and vegetables; and *Astronuts* contains a series of space jokes and riddles. Of *It's Raining Cats and Dogs,* an anthology of jokes about common pets, Betsy Hearne wrote in *Bulletin of the Center for Children's Books:* "Keller runs the gamut here from clever to just plain silly." "They're silly, they're challenging, and they're fun," Joan McGrath similarly commented in *School Library Journal* about Keller's *Tongue Twisters.* A *Junior Bookshelf* writer added: "Charles Keller's collection of tongue twisters is an agreeable reminder that words can be fun." And *School Library Journal* contributor Eva Elisabeth Von Ancken dubbed Keller's *Belly Laughs,* a collection of jokes and riddles about food, an "outstanding joke book" with many "fresh and funny" items.

Keller supplies enough food jokes to satisfy any kid's appetite in this collection. (Cover illustration by Ron Fritz.)

Works Cited

Review of *Alexander the Grape, Publishers Weekly,* April 2, 1982, p. 79.

Andrews, Peter, "Funny Books," *New York Times Book Review,* November 13, 1977, p. 34.

Review of *Ballpoint Bananas, and Other Jokes for Kids, Publishers Weekly,* February 19, 1973, p. 79.

Blue, Margaret, review of *Giggle Puss, School Library Journal,* February, 1978, p. 47.

Hearne, Betsy, review of *It's Raining Cats and Dogs, Bulletin of the Center for Children's Books,* November, 1988, p. 76.

Review of *Laughing, Publishers Weekly,* September 12, 1977, p. 132.

Lewis, Marjorie, review of *Glory, Glory, How Peculiar, School Library Journal,* February, 1977, p. 56.

McGrath, Joan, review of *Tongue Twisters, School Library Journal,* June, 1989, p. 119.

Olmstead, Sandra, review of *It's Raining Cats and Dogs, School Library Journal,* February, 1989, p. 78.

Page, Beverly V., review of *Growing up Laughing, Voice of Youth Advocates,* June, 1982, p. 34.

Silvey, Anita, review of *The Star-Spangled Banana, Horn Book,* October, 1974, pp. 151-152.

Sutherland, Zena, review of *Glory, Glory, How Peculiar, Bulletin of the Center for Children's Books,* April, 1977, p. 127.

Sutherland, Zena, review of *Growing up Laughing, Bulletin of the Center for Children's Books,* January, 1982, p. 87.

Review of *Tongue Twisters, Junior Bookshelf,* October, 1991, p. 205.

Von Ancken, Eva Elisabeth, review of *Belly Laughs, School Library Journal,* January, 1991, p. 86.

For More Information See

PERIODICALS

Bulletin of the Center for Children's Books, July, 1979, p. 193; May, 1989, p. 227.

New York Times Book Review, May 1, 1977, p. 34.

Publishers Weekly, September 25, 1981, p. 92.

School Library Journal, September, 1975, p. 85; September, 1976, p. 119; September, 1981, p. 124; September, 1985, p. 134; December, 1992, pp. 95-97.

KERSHEN, (L.) Michael 1982-

■ Personal

Born January 17, 1982, in Norman, OK; son of Drew L. (a law professor) and Kathleen J. (an elementary school teacher; maiden name, Colgrove). *Education:* Attends Whittier Middle Public School (Norman, OK). *Religion:* Roman Catholic. *Hobbies and other interests:* Sports (especially soccer), reading, geography, computers.

■ Addresses

Home—726 Hardin Dr., Norman, OK 73072.

■ Career

Student.

■ Awards, Honors

Finalist, Oklahoma Center for the Book Award, 1993, for *Why Buffalo Roam.*

■ Writings

Why Buffalo Roam, afterword by Drew L. Kershen, illustrated by Monica Hansen, Stemmer House (Owings Mills, MD), 1993.

■ Sidelights

Why Buffalo Roam, Michael Kershen's first book, grew out of a two-week unit on Native American peoples taught at the author's elementary school. In 1991 Kershen's third-grade class studied the Comanche tribe, a Plains Indian culture centered on the buffalo and the horse. Kershen drew on his knowledge of the Comanche to create *Why Buffalo Roam,* the story of Whitewolf, a warrior whose people are suffering from a severe famine. Whitewolf asks the Spirit for help and learns he must sacrifice what is most dear to him in order to get his wish.

Seeing in the story echoes of the Biblical story of Abraham and Isaac, Kershen's father was so impressed he decided to commission illustrations for the work as a reward for his son's efforts.

This decision eventually led to the discovery of art student Monica Hansen, who was assigned to illustrate the story for a class project at Bacone College in Muskogee, Oklahoma. Hansen's interest in the work stemmed in part from her Indian heritage, and spurred her to produce a series of illustrations inspired by Kershen's words. When Kershen's father saw the result, he decided his son's story might be publishable with Hansen's illustrations attached. After a year of rejections, an editor at Stemmer House responded positively, and shortly thereafter *Why Buffalo Roam* was published. That same year the book was a finalist for the Oklahoma Center for the Book Award.

MICHAEL KERSHEN

Michael Kershen told *SATA:* "At present, my biggest interest is soccer. I'm on a Norman Celtic Classic Soccer team that plays in a central Oklahoma conference. My team also travels to tournaments. I intend to play soccer for many more years. I went to two World Cup soccer games last summer.

"I have had fun this past year as a published author. I have signed books for many young people and their parents. One grandmother liked my book so much that she made a beautiful stuffed buffalo toy as a gift for me. Many people have told me how much they like my book. I feel proud when I hear these nice words. I am pleased that my book has brought joy to many readers."

■ For More Information See

PERIODICALS

Norman Transcript (Oklahoma), August 20, 1993.

* * *

KINDL, Patrice 1951-

■ Personal

Born October 16, 1951, in Alplaus, NY; daughter of Fred Henry (a mechanical engineer) and Catherine (a homemaker; maiden name, Quinlan) Kindl; married Paul Fredrick Roediger (a mechanical designer), October 16, 1976; children: Alexander. *Education:* Attended Webster College, 1969-70. *Politics:* Democrat. *Religion:* None. *Hobbies and other interests:* Raising monkeys.

Addresses

Home—37 Lakehill Rd., Ballston Lake, NY 12019.

Career

Writer. Works with Helping Hands, a program which raises and trains monkeys to aid the disabled. *Member:* Society of Children's Book Writers and Illustrators.

Awards, Honors

Golden Kite honor book for fiction, 1993, American Library Association notable book and book for reluctant readers, *School Library Journal* best book, *Bulletin of the Center for Children's Books* blue ribbon, and New York Public Library listing as a book for the teenage years, all for *Owl in Love;* Kindl was selected as one of the top ten new fantasy authors for 1994 by the Crawford Award judges.

Writings

Owl in Love (young adult fantasy), Houghton, 1993.

Work in Progress

Woman in the Walls, a young adult fantasy work.

Sidelights

Patrice Kindl told *SATA:* "When I was three years old my family moved to a Victorian house on a hill. To me it was a small country in itself. It had a cupola full of sunlight and dead flies, enormous attics suitable for imprisoning mad relatives, a butler's pantry, a grand staircase for grand entrances, and a secret, winding stair in a closet. There were miles of corridors and empty rooms, and the cellars were as dark and deep as the Minotaur's maze.

PATRICE KINDL

"In short, the house gave me a taste for the Gothic. We lived there for five years. When I was eight we moved to a brand-new split level. I spent the next decade sulking.

"The new house did have a forest behind it, and in the forest was a half-built log cabin. It had no door, windows, or roof, but it was some consolation for my lost kingdom. I spent hours at a time there reading, drawing, writing poetry, and eating too many apples.

"I got to have a dog in the new house, too. I had to share her with my three older sisters, but being the soul of tact, she managed to make us all feel loved. I also was allowed a series of mice, hamsters, and guinea pigs. I wanted a kangaroo.

"I never learned to like the house, though. It had no wasted space; the basement was a rec room and workshop. No one would dream of keeping a Minotaur there.

"Now that I am grown up I write for children because I am still that child, fond of reading, animals, and solitude. I wouldn't know how to write a book for grown-ups. I wouldn't know what to say.

"My life is nearly perfect now. I have a nice husband and a nice teen-aged son. I can read as much as I want to and call it research. People pay me money for the things that I write—sometimes, anyway. And I am surrounded by animals. We have two Capuchin monkeys, a dog, a cat, and a goldfish. The monkeys aren't pets; monkeys make terrible pets. They are better described as full-time obsessions. We are raising them to become aids to quadriplegics as part of a program called Helping Hands.

"The only thing wrong is the house. It's a nice Dutch Colonial in a pleasant neighborhood with an excellent school system. But as soon as my son goes off to college, I'm going house hunting. I'm looking for a house built during the reign of Queen Victoria, a house on a hill.

"I need someplace to put the Minotaur, if I ever get one."

For More Information See

PERIODICALS

Bulletin of the Center for Children's Books, October, 1993.
Kirkus Reviews, October 1, 1993, p. 1276.
Publishers Weekly, September 6, 1993.
School Library Journal, August, 1993.

KINSEY, Helen 1948-

■ Personal

Born September 14, 1948, in Barton, VT; daughter of Frederick (a farmer) and Louise (a child day-care provider; maiden name, Rowell) Kinsey. *Education:* University of Vermont, B.S., 1970. *Religion:* Presbyterian. *Hobbies and other interests:* Genealogy, quilting, camping.

■ Addresses

Home—18 Slim Brown Rd., Milton, VT 05468.

■ Career

Medical technician in Burlington, VT, 1970—. Trustee and vice-president, John W. Simpson Memorial Library, Burlington, VT. *Member:* American Society for Microbiology, New England Historical Genealogy Society, Genealogy Society of Vermont.

■ Writings

(With sister, Natalie Kinsey-Warnock) *The Bear That Heard Crying,* Cobblehill Books, 1993.

■ Sidelights

Helen Kinsey told *SATA* how she came upon the idea for the book she wrote with her sister, *The Bear That Heard Crying.* "For about twenty years one of my favorite, and most time-consuming, hobbies has been genealogy research on my ancestors and helping others with their genealogy. This is an endless endeavor, and I have discovered several interesting family stories, one of which was the basis for *The Bear That Heard Crying.* Some experiences of several Scottish ancestor families may eventually evolve into a book. Working in a hospital and genealogy both provide many additions to my collection of unusual names, several of which my sister has used in her books."

Kinsey, who lives in Vermont, also told *SATA* that "two cats allow me to share their home, and they provide entertainment and company."

* * *

KNIGHT, Joan (M.)

■ Personal

Born in Washington, D.C.; daughter of Donald Brehaut (a member of the Foreign Service) and Elinor (a homemaker; maiden name, Glidden) MacPhail; children: Elizabeth, Sophie. *Education:* Smith College, B.A., 1964. *Hobbies and other interests:* Painting, traveling.

■ Addresses

Home and office—1049 Park Ave., New York, NY 10028.

■ Career

Children's book author, editor, and translator. World Publishing Co., New York City, editorial assistant for children's books, 1964-68; William Collins, New York City, editor of children's books, 1978-80; Philomel Books, New York City, editor of children's books, 1980-83. Also translator (English to French and French to English) of children's and adult books, and freelance editor of children's books for such companies as Rizzoli International Publications and the Sierra Club. *Member:* Authors Guild, Authors League of America, Smithsonian Institution, Frick Museum, Metropolitan Museum, Brussels Griffon Club.

■ Awards, Honors

Children's Choice Award, 1986, for *Journey to Japan;* Parents' Choice Honor Award for Story, 1990, for *Tickle-Toe Rhymes.*

■ Writings

Journey to Egypt, illustrated by Piero Ventura, Viking, 1986.
Journey to Japan, illustrated by Kinuko Craft, Viking, 1986.
The Baby Who Would Not Come Down, illustrated by Debrah Santini, Picture Book Studio, 1989.
Tickle-Toe Rhymes, illustrated by John Wallner, Orchard Books, 1989.
Opal in the Closet, illustrated by Pau Estrada, Picture Book Studio, 1992.

JOAN KNIGHT

Bon Appetit, Bertie!, illustrated by Penny Dann, Dorling Kindersley, 1993.

Charlotte in Giverny: Letters from a Very Special Year (1892-1893), illustrated by Rosemary Fox, Rizzoli International Publications, 1995.

■ Sidelights

Joan Knight told *SATA:* "My growing-up years were fragmented. My father's career as a Foreign Service officer took us to Paris when I was ten years old. Shortly after our arrival, we all came down with hepatitis—as a result of having been inoculated with a tainted serum before we left Washington. My mother died six months later and, of course, nothing was ever the same again. Then, because of my father's career, we moved from one place to another. I went to a French school in Paris, the Lycee de Carthage in Tunisia, and the International School in Geneva, all within a short period of time. My childhood memories are especially meaningful to me because of these experiences. I write children's books because of them. Through my writing, I am able to stay in touch with the child I was."

Knight is the author of several picture books, both fiction and nonfiction, for preschool and early elementary age children. Her stories have been singled out for their lighthearted humor featuring improbable, but entertaining, scenarios. Knight's facility with language, showcased in her rhyming texts and the ease with which she incorporates information about other cultures and places into story lines and nonfiction passages, has also brought approving comments from the critics.

Knight's first two books, *Journey to Egypt* and *Journey to Japan,* are part of a pop-up series featuring various countries around the world. *Journey to Egypt* highlights the country's ancient past, including its spectacular tombs of the pharaohs. *Journey to Japan* offers a view of this small country that focuses on aspects of contemporary life there, including the bullet train, the high-tech robotics industry, and Tokyo's crowded skyline. Critics praised both books for their pleasant presentation of interesting information about the culture and history of each country. Eldon Younce in *School Library Journal* commented: "There is a great deal of well written information packed into a very few pages in these pop-up books."

In *Tickle-Toe Rhymes,* Knight invented more than a dozen simple counting rhymes for preschool children. Each short poem features a different animal in a humorous situation that inspires counting from one to five. Though Lauralyn Persson in *School Library Journal* praised some of the rhymes for their "infectious rhythm and interesting yet comprehensible language," she added that the same could not be said for all of Knight's poems in the book. On the other hand, a critic for *Kirkus Reviews* applauded the work as a whole, concluding: "Lots of variety here, lots of fun, and plenty of entrancing details to discover on rereading."

The adventures of Bernie and the Bonfig family in a Paris hotel provide a fun and interesting introduction to French in this picture book. (Cover illustration by Penny Dann.)

The Baby Who Would Not Come Down, Knight's next effort, is a picture book for the early grades that critics noted contains a lesson about how to treat babies. The story centers on a baby newly home from the hospital who is jostled, tickled, and thrown up into the air by family members once too often and decides to float up to the ceiling, safely out of reach. The baby finally comes down when its family realizes, as Sam Swope put it in the *New York Times Book Review,* that "babies aren't toys, they're people" who should be treated with respect. Although Swope was ultimately disappointed in what he perceived as a failure on the part of the author to follow through on her fantastic premise in favor of promoting the story's message, Anna Biagioni Hart, writing in *School Library Journal,* dubbed *The Baby Who Would Not Come Down* "a sophisticated lark" for children in the early grades, "who should enjoy the fun, much of which will float right over the heads of preschoolers."

Opal in the Closet, another preschool title, offers insight into the effect a new baby has on another young member of the family. In this story, a little girl begins startling, and annoying, the adult members of her household by jumping out at them unexpectedly from various hiding places after a new baby is brought home from the hospital. *School Library Journal* contributor Martha Topol remarked that "the spare, rhyming text hops right along with" Opal as she wreaks havoc among the adults in her efforts to capture some of their attention. A

Publishers Weekly reviewer commented approvingly: "Knight's straightforward, rhyming text focuses on the fun, not the lesson to be learned," and called the result "a sure child-pleaser."

Critics noted that *Bon Appetit, Bertie!*, Knight's next picture book, combines an entertaining story with an introduction to French culture and language. The story centers on Bertie, whose family has won free tickets for a trip to Paris. Bertie uses a map to direct the family from the airport to the hotel, but once there, disappears into the hotel's kitchen in his quest for food. The rest of the family frantically searches for him, enlisting the help of gendarmes, hotel staff, and people on the street, all of whom join the family in enjoying the feast Bertie has accidentally ordered—dinner for twenty-two instead of dinner for Room 22—once he is found. Critics generally agreed with *Booklist* writer Carolyn Phelan, who found *Bon Appetit, Bertie!* "well suited to children learning French in the primary grades." A reviewer for *Publishers Weekly* enthused: "Young readers can't help but appreciate this antic, ultimately effective introduction to another language and culture."

■ Works Cited

Review of *Bon Appetit, Bertie!*, *Publishers Weekly*, May 17, 1993, p. 79.

Hart, Anna Biagioni, review of *The Baby Who Would Not Come Down*, *School Library Journal*, January, 1990, pp. 84-85.

Review of *Opal in the Closet*, *Publishers Weekly*, November 30, 1992, pp. 54-55.

Persson, Lauralyn, review of *Tickle-Toe Rhymes*, *School Library Journal*, July, 1989, p. 67.

Phelan, Carolyn, review of *Bon Appetit, Bertie!*, *Booklist*, May 15, 1993, pp. 1695-96.

Swope, Sam, review of *The Baby Who Would Not Come Down*, *New York Times Book Review*, May 6, 1990.

Review of *Tickle-Toe Rhymes*, *Kirkus Reviews*, January 1, 1989, p. 50.

Topol, Martha, review of *Opal in the Closet*, *School Library Journal*, May, 1993, p. 87.

Younce, Eldon, review of *Journey to Egypt* and *Journey to Japan*, *School Library Journal*, February, 1987, p. 80.

■ For More Information See

PERIODICALS

Children's Book Review Service, August, 1993, p. 159.

Horn Book Guide, fall, 1994, p. 263.

Publishers Weekly, September 26, 1986, pp. 77-78.

School Library Journal, September, 1989, p. 165; July, 1993, p. 62.*

KOFFINKE, Carol 1949-

■ Personal

Born September 21, 1949, in Titusville, PA; daughter of Harry (an engineer) and Shirley (a jewelry retailer; maiden name, LaPenotiere) Graves; married Steve Jordan, August 15, 1973 (divorced August, 1978); married Richard Koffinke, Jr. (an engineer), March 23, 1979; children: (first marriage) Julie Jordan; (second marriage) Richard Koffinke III. *Education:* Western Maryland College, B.S., 1971; Boston University, M.Ed., 1975. *Hobbies and other interests:* Music, skiing, racquetball.

■ Addresses

Home—203 Briarcliff Lane, Bel Air, MD 21014. *Office*—P.O. Box 1607, Bel Air, MD 21014-7607.

■ Career

New Beginnings at Hidden Brook, Bel Air, MD, chief operating officer, 1988—. Writer; lecturer on addictions, co-dependency, and parenting. Consultant, Office of Education and Training of Addiction Services for Maryland; advisory board member, Essex Community College and Harford Council of Community Services. *Member:* National Association of Alcohol and Drug Abuse Counselors, National Council on Alcohol and Drug Dependence.

CAROL KOFFINKE

Awards, Honors

Certificate of Appreciation, Council on Child Abuse and Neglect, 1992.

Writings

I'll Never Do That to My Kids, Deaconess Press, 1991.
(With daughter, Julie Jordan) *Mom, You Don't Understand,* Deaconess Press, 1993.

Also a contributing author to *Treating the Chemically Dependent and Their Families,* edited by Daley and Raskin, Sage Publications, 1989.

Work in Progress

A novel which "addresses how the aging process presents the best opportunity to find one's true self," to be completed in 1995.

Sidelights

Carol Koffinke told *SATA:* "I began writing because I felt that I had learned so much from working with the chemically dependent and their families that I needed to share on a large scale. Both of my books are devoted to developing strong, healthy, loving families. The first is devoted to guiding parents who did not have the opportunity to experience a healthy parenting model to find their way to healthier parenting, the key to which is better self-awareness so that old traps don't ensnare.

"The second, co-written with my fifteen-year-old daughter, addresses many issues that arise in the life of a teenage girl. Many of these issues are confusing to both teen and parent. *Mom, You Don't Understand* attempts to make sense out of these issues. It provides a vicarious catharsis for both teens and mothers in a format where the teen indulges in her feelings about the issue, followed by the mother's perspective and feelings, and finally pulls the two together in a suggestion for resolution. This book has been selected for publication in China.

"I am forty-four years old and have sought creative expression from the time I was a child. I have dabbled in painting, music, and theater. To have found my creative niche, writing, is like being reborn."

* * *

KRAY, Robert Clement 1930-

Personal

Born September 10, 1930, in Wanamie, PA; son of Clement (a state claim settlement agent) and Ethel (a homemaker; maiden name, Rule) Kray; married Jacqueline D. Mahoney (a homemaker), June 17, 1955; children: Robert Clement, Jr., Bruce G. *Education:* Philadelphia University of the Arts, diploma, 1953. *Hobbies and other interests:* Fishing, birding, photography.

Addresses

Home and office—5002 Nuangola Rd., Nuangola Boro, Mountaintop, PA 18707. *Agent*—Carol Bancroft, 7 Ivy Hill Rd., Ridgefield, CT 06877.

Career

Wildlife artist. Member of art staff, Eureka Printing Company, PA, 1955-74; Luzerne County Community College, Nanticoke, PA, full-time art instructor, 1975-86. *Exhibitions:* Has exhibited in juried shows in New York City, Minnesota, Oklahoma, Maryland, Texas, Colorado, Kansas, and at the Cleveland Museum of Natural History, Cleveland, OH. Has also exhibited at the University of Minnesota, McBride Gallery, MD, and Academy of Natural Sciences, Philadelphia, PA. *Member:* Society of Animal Artists, Inc., Pennsylvania Outdoor Writers and Artists Association.

Awards, Honors

Award of Excellence, Society of Animal Artists, 1984; Merit Award of Excellence, Cleveland Museum of Natural History, 1984; Artist of the Year, Wyoming Valley Chapter, Ducks Unlimited, 1989; Top 20, Federal Duck Stamp Contest, 1991; Artist of the Year, Tunkhannock Chapter, Ducks Unlimited, 1993; Third Place, Federal Duck Stamp Competition, 1993; Winner, Pennsylvania Trout and Salmon Stamp Contest, 1994.

ROBERT CLEMENT KRAY

Illustrator

"OUR LIVING WORLD" SERIES

Jenny Tesar, *Mammals,* Blackbirch Press, 1993.
Tesar, *Spiders,* Blackbirch Press, 1993.
Edward R. Ricciuti, *Crustaceans,* Blackbirch Press, 1994.

OTHER

Animals Can Be Almost Human, Reader's Digest, 1979.

Works have been published by the Winchester-Western Arms Corp., Franklin Mint/World Wildlife Fund, Ideals Publishing, Bobbs-Merrill, Donald Art, National Wildlife Federation, Portraits of Nature, Applejack Publishing, Streamside Publishing, and Wilderness Editions (1994 Trout Stamp). Contributor of illustrations to periodicals, including *Outdoor Life, Sports Afield, Reader's Digest, Highlights for Children, Organic Gardening and Farming,* and *Prevention.*

Work in Progress

Wildlife paintings; ideas for federal duck stamps.

L

SIGMUND A. LAVINE

LAVINE, Sigmund A(rnold) 1908-

■ Personal

Born March 18, 1908, in Boston, MA; son of Phillip Henry and Etta (Bramson) Lavine; married Gertrude Kramer (a teacher), December 17, 1937; children: Maxine P. Lavine Rosenberg, Jerrold N. *Education:* Boston University, B.J., 1930, M.Ed., 1931. *Hobbies and other interests:* Collecting Gilbert and Sullivan memorabilia, raising tropical fish, showing dogs, greenhouse gardening.

■ Addresses

Home—9 Magnolia Rd., Milton, MA 02186.

■ Career

Free-lance author and book critic, 1926-35; *Boston Transcript,* Boston, MA, literary critic, 1926-34; Associated Press, Boston, correspondent, 1926-31; *Boston Post,* Boston, feature writer, 1930-31; U.S. Indian Service, Belcourt, ND, teacher, 1931-34; *Boston Herald-American,* Boston, literary critic and columnist, 1934-80; *Worcester Telegram,* Worcester, MA, critic, 1956-73; Dennis C. Haley School, Roslindale, MA, assistant administrative principal, 1963-80. Trustee, Milton (MA) Public Library, 1970. *Member:* Massachusetts School Master's Club, Boston Athenaeum, Phi Gamma Mu.

■ Awards, Honors

Joint Committee of the National Science Teachers Association and the Children's Book Council named several titles "outstanding science books for children"; Schoolman's Medal, Freedom Fountain at Valley Forge, 1973; New Jersey Institute of Technology citation, 1983, for *Wonders of Sheep. Strange Travelers* was a Junior Literary Guild selection.

■ Writings

"WONDERS OF" SERIES; PUBLISHED BY DODD

Wonders of the Aquarium, 1957.
Wonders of the Hive, 1958.
Wonders of the Ant Hill, 1960.
Wonders of the Wasps' Nest, 1961.
Wonders of Animal Disguises, 1962.
Wonders of the Beetle World, 1962.
Wonders of Animal Architecture, 1964.
Wonders of the Spider World, 1966.
Wonders of the World of Bats, 1969.
Wonders of the Fly World, 1970.
Wonders of the Owl World, 1971.
Wonders of the Hawk World, 1972.
(With Brigid Casey) *Wonders of the World of Horses,* 1972.

Wonders of the Eagle World, 1974.
Wonders of the Cactus World, 1974.
(With Vincent Scuro) *Wonders of the Bison World,* 1975.
Wonders of Herbs, 1976.
Wonders of Terrariums, illustrated by Jane O'Regan, 1977.
Wonders of Marsupials, 1978.
(With Scuro) *Wonders of Donkeys,* 1978.
Wonders of Camels, 1979.
Wonders of Mice, 1979.
(With Scuro) *Wonders of Elephants,* 1979.
(With Casey) *Wonders of Ponies,* 1980.
(With Scuro) *Wonders of Goats,* 1980.
(With Scuro) *Wonders of Pigs,* 1981.
Wonders of Flightless Birds, 1981.
Wonders of Peacocks, 1982.
Wonders of Rhinos, 1982.
(With Scuro) *Wonders of Mules,* 1982.
Wonders of Hippos, 1983.
(With Casey) *Wonders of Draft Horses,* 1983.
(With Scuro) *Wonders of Sheep,* 1983.
(With Scuro) *Wonders of Turkeys,* 1984.
Wonders of Coyotes, 1984.
Wonders of Woodchucks, 1984.
Wonders of Badgers, 1985.
Wonders of Giraffes, 1986.
Wonders of Foxes, 1986.
Wonders of Tigers, 1987.

OTHER

Wandering Minstrels We: The Story of Gilbert and Sullivan, Dodd, 1954.
Steinmetz, Maker of Lightening, Dodd, 1956.
Strange Partners, Little, Brown, 1959 (published in England as *Animal Partners,* Phoenix House, 1959).
Kettering, Master Inventor, Dodd, 1960.
Strange Travelers, Little, Brown, 1961.
Famous Industrialists, Dodd, 1962.
Allan Pinkerton, America's First Private Eye, Dodd, 1963.
Famous Merchants, Dodd, 1965.
(With Mart Casey and Rosemary Casey) *Water since the World Began,* Dodd, 1965.
Handmade in America: The Colonial Craftsmen, Dodd, 1966.
Famous American Architects, Dodd, 1967.
Handmade in England, Dodd, 1968.
Evangeline Booth: Daughter of Salvation, Dodd, 1970.
The Horses the Indians Rode, Dodd, 1974.
Indian Corn and Other Gifts, Dodd, 1974.
The Games the Indians Played, Dodd, 1974.
The Ghosts the Indians Feared, illustrated by O'Regan, Dodd, 1975.
The Houses the Indians Built, Dodd, 1975.
A Beginner's Book of Vegetable Gardening, illustrated by O'Regan, Dodd, 1977.

Contributor of book reviews to several newspapers. Member of editorial board, *World in Books.* Various works by Lavine have been selected for overseas translation by the U.S. Information Agency.

Lavine looks at the amazing structures animals and insects can create in this installment of the "Wonders of" series. (Cover illustration by Margaret Cosgrove.)

Work in Progress

Books on frontier folklore and rediscovered species.

Sidelights

Sigmund A. Lavine has devoted his writing career to informing and educating young people. The diverse works of this prolific writer range from a biography of Salvation Army chief Evangeline Booth to the "Wonders of" animal information series. Several of Lavine's books have been selected as "outstanding science books for children" by the Joint Committee of the National Science Teachers Association and the Children's Book Council, while his "Wonders of" series is widely known as one "that continually provides informative and entertainingly written books," according to Ilene Cooper in *Booklist.*

As Lavine once told *SATA,* one of his ambitions was "to spend all my time digging out little-known facts about people and animals." As a young man, however, "I was determined to become an actor. This was only natural as my parents were members of John Craig's famous stock company. However, persuaded by stars, bit players, and stagehands to 'get an education' I enrolled in college in Boston."

Lavine's years at Boston University were filled with working on school newspapers and magazines as well as acting and stage-managing in productions of Shakespeare and Gilbert and Sullivan, the latter of whom became the subjects of his first book, *Wandering Minstrels We.* "Then came the Great Depression and, as there was no demand for either actors or journalists, I returned to the classroom." After earning his education degree, Lavine travelled to North Dakota, where he taught in a Government Indian school. In addition, he was "learning to speak both Sioux and Cree, and learning to talk in sign language. I was invited to tribal ceremonies throughout the Northwest and Canada."

After returning to his home in Boston, Lavine taught and worked as an assistant principal in the city's schools. "As soon as I became accustomed to the feel of concrete rather than prairie under my feet, I began to transcribe the field notes I had accumulated while observing wildlife in North Dakota, and continued my study of scientific literature dealing with natural history. In time, out of this research came my nature books."

The lives of the Native Americans among whom he had taught provided the subject for many of Lavine's historical books. For example, *Indian Corn and Other Gifts* is a survey of food plants native to North America. Among others, Lavine discusses corn, beans, squash, and peanuts, all of which were unknown in Europe until the discovery and exploration of the New World. Throughout the book, Lavine combines facts about these plants and their use with Native American legends concerning the planting, harvesting, and preparation of food. In a *Publishers Weekly* review, Jean Mercier found the book "absorbing" and praised the inclusion of quotes from journals of the time that "enliven" the work. *The Houses the Indians Built* and *The Games the Indians Played* present other aspects of Native American life. In the former, Lavine discusses the many different types of homes that were developed throughout North America in response to changing demands of climate and culture. *Booklist* writer Judy Goldberger, while objecting to the use of the term "red men," found the book "intelligently done." *The Games the Indians Played* describes the origins and rules of many games played by Native Americans, and, like its two predecessors, includes some of the Native American lore surrounding the games. Although she described Lavine's writing here as "so direct and crisp as to be to almost terse," Zena Sutherland in *Bulletin of the Center for Children's Books* found the material "fascinating."

Lavine examines the work of America's settlers—specifically, the careful production of craft items—in *Handmade in America: The Colonial Craftsmen.* The book includes chapters on the practices of woodworking, glassmaking, pottery, and metalworking, as well as biographical sketches of some of the most recognized craftsmen of the period, including Paul Revere. *Horn Book* reviewer Helen B. Crawshaw described the book as "crammed" with information, and concluded that the book is a "valuable source" of material on the subject. In the *New York Times Book Review,* Edwin Tunis likewise declared *Handmade in America* a "pleasantly chatty survey of the early professional craftsman."

Lavine introduces readers to other important aspects of American history in his volumes of "famous biographies." In *Famous American Architects,* for instance, Lavine's overview includes brief biographies, including analyses of styles and major works, of several architects, ranging from Charles Bulfinch to Marcel Breuer. A similar approach is taken in *Famous Merchants,* which familiarizes students with the histories of such well-known American business leaders as "Diamond Jim" Brady, J. C. Penney, Howard Johnson, and Elizabeth Arden. Like its predecessor, *Famous Merchants* provides readers with information not readily found elsewhere, and contains "interesting material," as Alibeth Howell notes in *Library Journal.*

A more specific biography, *Evangeline Booth: Daughter of Salvation,* makes an account of the life of Evangeline Booth, daughter of William Booth, the founder of the Salvation Army. Lavine credits Evangeline with expanding the global influence of the Salvation Army, often against the will of her father and brother. Lavine also establishes how vital Booth's charisma and skill at preaching were to the success of her mission. A *Kirkus Reviews* writer found the subject worthwhile and the book informative, and observed that the story "moves rapidly and enthusiastically." While noting that the book might have "limited" appeal, Sharon K. Ryan pronounced the work "objective, thoroughly researched, and well-written" in her *Library Journal* review.

Lavine ventured into the "how-to" category of writing with *A Beginner's Book of Vegetable Gardening.* Here, Lavine provides readers with the basics of laying out, planting, and maintaining a vegetable garden. Photographs provide illustrations of both healthy and sick plants for reference, and charts and a table provide relevant data, such as the region and climate preferences of plants. In a *Publishers Weekly* review, Mercier remarked that the book stands out for its "straightforward and concise approach," and added that beginning gardeners of any age may find it useful. The book has the potential to increase a child's awareness of the world outside, wrote Ellen Rodman in the *New York Times Book Review,* calling the volume an "encouraging and mature guide."

Lavine's interest in gardening found its way into his "Wonders of" series with the title *Wonders of Terrariums.* Here Lavine provides a historical introduction to the art of indoor gardening, followed by practical advice on assembling a terrarium. He covers different plant types, and describes the methods for creating different environments, from lush to arid. Reviewer Sutherland in the *Bulletin of the Center for Children's Books* called the book "lucid and comprehensive." While Barbara C. Campbell in *School Library Journal* considered the text "overly wordy" and the illustrations inadequate, a *Booklist* reviewer speculated that Lavine's "experience and enthusiasm will undoubtedly help the novice and create new fans."

Lavine has contributed many other books to the long-running "Wonders of" series, for which he is perhaps best known. Each volume provides a general overview of its subject, distinguished by historical as well as scientific perspectives. In *Wonders of Pigs* Lavine and co-author Vincent Scuro subject the domestic pig to a thorough examination. The pig's evolutionary history is presented, along with pig folklore and documentation of the uses of nearly every part of the pig in agriculture and manufacturing. Special attention is given to American species of pigs, and their importance as a source of food is emphasized. *Horn Book* reviewer Karen Jameyson credited Lavine's "straight forward yet conversational" writing style, and noted the book's abundance of material. Other volumes in the series have also been praised for their usefulness to students; Mary Lathrope, writing in *Booklist,* found that *Wonders of Giraffes* "provides solid, well-rounded coverage," while an *Appraisal* critic called *Wonders of Donkeys* "a fascinating introduction" that contains "careful research."

It is the interesting historical details, however, that make Lavine's "Wonders of" books stand out. In *Wonders of Rhinos,* for instance, Lavine explores the wealth of folklore that has grown up around the rhino, describes each of the five extant species of rhinoceros, and provides a general introduction to rhino behavior. *School Library Journal* contributor Andrea Antico declared the book an "excellent choice" for students interested in specific information about rhinos, one that "will invite browsers as well as young researchers." Cooper offered a similar assessment in her *Booklist* review, calling the book a "solid, serviceable guide" to the rhino. *Wonders of Giraffes* will be "relished by report-writer and zoo enthusiast alike," a *Kirkus Reviews* writer similarly noted. And the survey of fox folklore and history in *Wonders of Foxes* "helps to make this book more than just another nature study," Cynthia M. Sturgis wrote in *School Library Journal.* With its "appealing" topic, Margaret A. Bush concluded in *Horn Book,* "the attractive, well-constructed book stands among the best of the many the author has done in this long series."

"With my wife ... I live in a house filled with books, fish-tanks, historical china, art glass, the largest privately owned collection of Gilbert and Sullivan material in America," Lavine told *SATA.* "For relaxation, we attend country auctions, go 'antiquing' or browse in bookstalls, but our greatest pleasure is truck gardening on a piece of rocky New Hampshire land."

Lavine has introduced children to all sorts of interesting facts and folklore about nature through his work, including this book, *Wonders of Badgers.*

Works Cited

Antico, Andrea, review of *Wonders of Rhinos, School Library Journal,* April, 1983, pp. 114-115.
Bush, Margaret A., review of *Wonders of Foxes, Horn Book,* March/April, 1987, p. 222.
Campbell, Barbara C., review of *Wonders of Terrariums, School Library Journal,* February, 1978, p. 59.
Cooper, Ilene, review of *Wonders of Rhinos, Booklist,* March 15, 1983, pp. 970-71.
Cooper, Ilene, review of *Wonders of Hippos, Booklist,* March 15, 1984, p. 1061.
Crawshaw, Helen B., review of *Handmade in America, Horn Book,* August, 1966, p. 447.
Review of *Evangeline Booth, Kirkus Reviews,* February 15, 1970, pp. 183-84.
Goldberger, Judy, review of *The Houses the Indians Built, Booklist,* September 15, 1975, p. 166.
Howell, Alibeth, review of *Famous Merchants, Library Journal,* June 15, 1965, p. 2896.
Jameyson, Karen, review of *Wonders of Pigs, Horn Book,* December, 1981, p. 678.
Lathrope, Mary, review of *Wonders of Giraffes, Booklist,* June 1, 1986, pp. 1461-62.
Mercier, Jean, review of *Indian Corn and Other Gifts, Publishers Weekly,* January 28, 1974, p. 300.
Mercier, Jean, review of *A Beginner's Book of Vegetable Gardening, Publishers Weekly,* July 11, 1977, p. 81.
Rodman, Ellen, review of *A Beginner's Book of Vegetable Gardening, New York Times Book Review,* November 13, 1977, p. 58.
Ryan, Sharon K., review of *Evangeline Booth, Library Journal,* October 15, 1970, p. 3638.
Sturgis, Cynthia M., review of *Wonders of Foxes, School Library Journal,* March, 1987, p. 160.
Sutherland, Zena, review of *The Games the Indians Played, Bulletin of the Center for Children's Books,* October, 1974, p. 31.
Sutherland, Zena, review of *Wonders of Terrariums, Bulletin of the Center for Children's Books,* July-August, 1978, p. 180.
Tunis, Edwin, review of *Handmade in America, New York Times Book Review,* July 3, 1966, p. 14.
Review of *Wonders of Donkeys, Appraisal,* winter, 1980, p. 35.
Review of *Wonders of Giraffes, Kirkus Reviews,* May 1, 1986, p. 722.
Review of *Wonders of Terrariums, Booklist,* March 1, 1978, p. 1108.

For More Information See

BOOKS

Children's Literature Review, Volume 35, Gale, 1995.

PERIODICALS

Booklist, November 1, 1965, p. 269.
Bulletin of the Center for Children's Books, November, 1974, pp. 46-47.
Kirkus Reviews, October 15, 1972, p. 1197; January 15, 1974, p. 58.
Library Journal, July, 1967, p. 2689; November 15, 1972, p. 3806.
New Yorker, December 4, 1971, p. 202.
Publishers Weekly, October 3, 1966, p. 85.
School Library Journal, September, 1977, p. 146; November, 1980, p. 76; May, 1988, pp. 105-106.

* * *

LEE, Mary Price 1934-

Personal

Born July 10, 1934, in Philadelphia, PA; daughter of Llewellyn and Elise (Mirkil) Price; married Richard S. Lee (a copywriter), May 12, 1956; children: Richard, Barbara, Monica. *Education:* University of Pennsylvania, B.A., 1956, M.S. (education), 1967.

Addresses

Home—6317 Fairfield Dr., Flourtown, PA 19031.

Career

Author of young adult books. Worked as a teacher for a short period; employed in public relations department at Westminster Press, Philadelphia, PA, 1973-74. Has tutored foreign students in English. *Member:* Children's Reading Roundtable, Philadelphia Athenaeum, Phi Beta Kappa.

Awards, Honors

Last Names First: And Some First Names Too was a Junior Literary Guild selection; *Careers for Women in Politics* was selected as one of the New York Public Library's Best Books for the Teen Age, 1990.

Writings

WITH HUSBAND, RICHARD S. LEE

Opportunities in Animal and Pet Care Careers, VGM Career Horizons, 1984, revised edition, 1993.
Exploring Careers in Robotics, Rosen Publishing, 1984, revised edition, 1986.
Last Names First: And Some First Names Too, illustrated by Debra Weber, Westminster, 1985.
Exploring Careers in the Restaurant Industry, Rosen Publishing, 1988, revised edition, 1989.
Coping with Money, Rosen Publishing, 1988.
Careers for Women in Politics, Rosen Publishing, 1989.
Coping through Effective Time Management, Rosen Publishing, 1991.
Careers in Firefighting, Rosen Publishing, 1993.
Drugs and the Media, Rosen Publishing, 1993.
Caffeine and Nicotine, Rosen Publishing, 1994.
Drugs and Codependency, Rosen Publishing, 1995.

OTHER

Grown-up Activities for Young People, Exposition Press, 1971.
Money and Kids: How to Earn It, Save It, and Spend It, illustrated by James Stewart, Westminster, 1973.
Ms. Veterinarian, Westminster, 1976.

The Team That Runs Your Hospital, Westminster, 1980.

Your Name: All about It, illustrated by Lee DeGroot, Westminster, 1980.

A Future in Pediatrics: Medical and Non-Medical Careers in Child Health Care, Messner, 1982.

Exploring Careers in Research and Development in Industry, Rosen Publishing, 1983.

Also columnist, *Chestnut Hill Local,* 1970-72; contributing editor, *Today's Girl,* 1972-73; contributor to *Philadelphia Magazine* and *Philadelphia Inquirer.*

■ Sidelights

Mary Price Lee once commented that she began writing for the young adult audience with the inspiration of her teenage children, who "serve both as guinea pigs and critics." As her children grew up, however, Lee's work found its basis more in research than in personal experience. "With the world changing so rapidly, young peoples' career books serve their purpose best if they're as up-to-date as the publishing process allows. So I will cite references from daily newspapers as readily as from dusty historical tomes," Lee commented. With a determination to entertain as well as inform her readers, the author attempts to supply the needs of young people for information about careers and personal choices. She often collaborates with her husband, Richard S. Lee; each contributes chapters to the work in progress and edits the other's writing "with sometimes painful honesty," said Lee, "but the results are worth it." She more recently told *SATA,* "Reflecting over almost thirty years of writing: 'once a writer—always a writer.' It has always been rewarding, but it has never been easy."

MARY PRICE AND RICHARD S. LEE

Lee's early publications include *Money and Kids: How to Earn It, Save It, and Spend It* and *Ms. Veterinarian.* In the first title, the author suggests ways that children can earn money, various ways to save it, including budgeting, and advice on spending money wisely. Although a contributor in *Kirkus Reviews* criticized the volume for lacking an overall philosophy or principle guiding its advice, a *Publishers Weekly* reviewer dubbed *Money and Kids* "a down-to-earth, no-nonsense discussion." In *Ms. Veterinarian,* the author provides an overview of careers available in animal medicine, educational requirements, opportunities available for women in the field, and personality traits required for success in the job. While a critic in *Kirkus Reviews* found "the feminist angle" of the book "muddy," with contradictory statements about women's capabilities and aptitude made in various sections of the work, *School Library Journal* reviewer Joan Scherer Brewer recommended the book for career guidance collections, stating that despite its title, male adolescents would find the book as helpful as females.

Like *Ms. Veterinarian, The Team That Runs Your Hospital* and *A Future in Pediatrics: Medical and Non-Medical Careers in Child Health Care* offer career advice to young people seeking information about jobs in the medical field. Lee provides a "chatty survey of hospital personnel and procedures" in *The Team That Runs Your Hospital,* according to Zena Sutherland, writing in the *Bulletin of the Center for Children's Books.* Critics noted that a large number of medical-related careers are introduced through the experiences of three fictionalized young patients. *A Future in Pediatrics* offers young adults the opportunity to explore more than thirty specialty careers in the field of children's medical care. *School Library Journal* contributor Joyce Baker praised the book for its "humor and insight," which might inspire young people to pursue this career, and Sutherland, in her review of the work, dubbed it "a most useful overview."

Lee's *Exploring Careers in Research and Development in Industry* offers information and advice to young people interested in careers that require an engineering or other science-related education. Sally Estes called this work "a cogent overview" in her *Booklist* review. In *Opportunities in Animal and Pet Care Careers,* co-written with her husband, Lee provides information on educational requirements, pay, and future opportunities for a number of careers working with or caring for animals. The book begins with "a concise history of the movement toward animal protection," according to Stephanie Zvirin, who reviewed the work in *Booklist.* Lee also teamed up with her husband for *Careers in Firefighting,* which outlines the skills and aptitudes necessary for success in the field, along with details on education, training, and opportunities for women. Diane P. Tuccillo asserted in *School Library Journal* that the book is "a timely and dynamic occupational guide."

Works Cited

Baker, Joyce, review of *A Future in Pediatrics: Medical and Non-Medical Careers in Child Health Care, School Library Journal,* April, 1983, p. 125.

Brewer, Joan Scherer, review of *Ms. Veterinarian, School Library Journal,* September, 1976, p. 135.

Estes, Sally, review of *Exploring Careers in Research and Development in Industry, Booklist,* June 15, 1983, p. 1331.

Review of *Money and Kids: How to Earn It, Save It, and Spend It, Publishers Weekly,* August 13, 1973, p. 55.

Review of *Money and Kids: How to Earn It, Save It, and Spend It, Kirkus Reviews,* November 1, 1973, pp. 1207-8.

Review of *Ms. Veterinarian, Kirkus Reviews,* November 1, 1976, p. 1178.

Sutherland, Zena, review of *The Team That Runs Your Hospital, Bulletin of the Center for Children's Books,* June, 1981, pp. 197-98.

Sutherland, Zena, review of *A Future in Pediatrics: Medical and Non-Medical Careers in Child Health Care, Bulletin of the Center for Children's Books,* December, 1982, p. 72.

Tuccillo, Diane P., review of *Careers in Firefighting, School Library Journal,* June, 1993, p. 138.

Zvirin, Stephanie, review of *Opportunities in Animal and Pet Care Careers, Booklist,* August, 1984, p. 1607.

For More Information See

PERIODICALS

Booklist, October 15, 1976, p. 314; May 15, 1993, pp. 1685-86.

School Library Journal, January, 1981, pp. 62-63.

Voice of Youth Advocates, April, 1984, p. 42.

* * *

LEE, Richard S. 1927-

Personal

Born June 17, 1927, in Philadelphia, PA; son of Manning (a magazine and book illustrator) and Eunice Celeste (an author and founding art director for *Jack and Jill;* maiden name, Sandoval) Lee; married Mary Lys Price (an author), May 12, 1956; children: Richard, Barbara, Monica. *Education:* College of William and Mary, A.B., 1951. *Hobbies and other interests:* Collector cars, reading, jazz, sailing, acting.

Addresses

Home—6317 Fairfield Dr., Flourtown, PA 19031.

Career

Advertising and sales promotion writer, senior writer, and creative director for advertising agencies in Philadelphia, PA, for more than thirty years; freelance writer. *Military service:* U.S. Army, 1945-47; served at Fort Knox, KY, and in Tokyo, Japan; became second lieutenant.

Awards, Honors

Last Names First: And Some First Names Too was a Junior Literary Guild selection; *Careers for Women in Politics* was selected as one of the New York Public Library's Best Books for the Teen Age, 1990.

Writings

WITH WIFE, MARY PRICE LEE

Opportunities in Animal and Pet Care Careers, VGM Career Horizons, 1984, revised edition, 1993.

Exploring Careers in Robotics, Rosen Publishing, 1984, revised edition, 1986.

Last Names First: And Some First Names Too, illustrated by Debra Weber, Westminster, 1985.

Exploring Careers in the Restaurant Industry, Rosen Publishing, 1988, revised edition, 1989.

Coping with Money, Rosen Publishing, 1988.

Careers for Women in Politics, Rosen Publishing, 1989.

Coping through Effective Time Management, Rosen Publishing, 1991.

Careers in Firefighting, Rosen Publishing, 1993.

Drugs and the Media, Rosen Publishing, 1993.

Caffeine and Nicotine, Rosen Publishing, 1994.

Drugs and Codependency, Rosen Publishing, 1995.

OTHER

Also contributor to regional newspapers and magazines; contributor and editor of regional and national auto enthusiast publications, including *Continental Comments,* 1961-64; editor of wife Mary Price Lee's first eight books for young readers, 1973-83.

Sidelights

Richard S. Lee told *SATA:* "My primary career has been advertising and promotion—more than thirty years of writing on virtually any subject, not with TV commercials, but to impart useful information to product buyers and users. During this time, of course, I did other writing, as a restaurant reviewer, managing editor of a national auto enthusiasts' publication (*Continental Comments,* published by the Lincoln Continental Owners' Club), and occasional freelance newspaper articles.

"When my wife, Mary Price Lee, began to write nonfiction for young people, I became editor-without-portfolio. That experience led to collaboration on the last eleven of her twenty titles. This collaboration is a cross-pollination in which whoever has the time does the needed research, then writes a draft chapter to be edited by the other (with no holds barred!) and in turn polished by the original writer. So adroit have we become at this that, even during book preparation, we can lose sight of exactly who wrote what parts!

"Although writing coping and career books for young adults is not our major income (our promotional work, now under my wife's direction, keeps us in dancing slippers), it is infinitely rewarding to know that we are helping young people decide on their careers and cope with life's problems. We feel we perform a genuine service, especially to kids who come from broken homes or otherwise lack family-based direction. The recent 'Drug Abuse Prevention Library' volumes we have done for The Rosen Publishing Group are especially rewarding in that respect.

"As to career books, my natural curiosity—a major survival skill in advertising—pays off here as well. We take on subjects we know little about. We research each career in great detail. More to the point, we present it to young people, warts and all. We have to be dead-honest about prospects and prerequisites. Firefighting, for instance, is the riskiest career of all. We have to say so. You can't kid a kid!

"Speaking of kids, we are now entering the lion's den of children's fiction. Many ideas, but as yet, no acceptances."

* * *

LEE, Robert E(dwin) 1918-1994

OBITUARY NOTICE—See index for *SATA* sketch: Born October 15, 1918, in Elyria, OH; died of cancer, July 8, 1994, in Los Angeles, CA. Playwright and educator. With longtime collaborator Jerome Lawrence, Lee wrote many successful plays, including the Broadway hit *Auntie Mame* and its musical adaptation, *Mame,* both of which were later made into popular feature films. The partnership began in 1942 when Lee, who was overseeing radio ads for a New York City advertising agency, met Lawrence, a writer for CBS radio. During the next five decades, the duo wrote thirty-nine plays, including fourteen Broadway productions. Two of their most enduring plays are *Inherit the Wind,* based on the Scopes "Monkey" trial of 1929, and *The Night Thoreau Spent in Jail,* which focuses on civil disobedience. These works, as well as their 1978 play *First Monday in October*—about the first woman member of the United States Supreme Court—were also adapted for film. Becoming an adjunct professor at the University of California, Los Angeles, in 1967, Lee taught aspiring actors, playwrights, and screenwriters. It was his conviction that the role of a theater artist is to explore political, psychological, and philosophical issues through drama. Plays should enlighten audiences while also entertaining them, he believed. The honors Lee received during his career include a 1948 Peabody award for radio programming, the *Variety* New York Drama Critics Poll in 1955 and the British Drama Critics award for best foreign play in 1960, both for *Inherit the Wind,* and Tony awards in 1955 and 1966. In 1988 Lee received the Best Comedy/Drama Special award by the National Television Academy for the television adaptation of *Inherit the Wind,* and he was recognized with a Lifetime Achievement Award at the William Inge Festival. Lee was named to the American Theatre Hall of Fame in 1990. Among his later works is the 1990 play *Whisper in the Mind,* written with Lawrence and Norman Cousins.

OBITUARIES AND OTHER SOURCES:

BOOKS

Who's Who in America, 47th edition, Marquis, 1992.

PERIODICALS

Los Angeles Times, July 10, 1994, p. A24.
Times (London), July 20, 1994, p. 19.

* * *

LEVY, Robert 1945-

■ Personal

Born July 11, 1945, in Mussoorie, IN; son of Walter and Grete (maiden name, Losch) Levy; married Ilsa Karger (a teacher). *Education:* University of Tampa, B.A., 1968; Hunter College of New York, M.A., 1974; Brooklyn College, advanced certificate in education, 1977.

■ Addresses

Agent—Louise Quayle, c/o Macintosh and Otis, 310 Madison Ave., New York, NY 10017.

■ Career

New York Board of Education, New York City, teacher and computer coordinator, 1968—.

■ Awards, Honors

Texas Lone Star Reading List, for *Escape from Exile,* 1995.

■ Writings

FANTASY ADVENTURE NOVELS FOR YOUNG ADULTS

Escape from Exile, Houghton, 1993.
Clan of the Shape-Changers, Houghton, 1994.
The Misfit Apprentice, Houghton, 1995.

■ Work in Progress

A fantasy adventure novel for young children entitled *Magic Key.*

■ Sidelights

Robert Levy told *SATA* that he has been "in love with fantasy ever since reading J. R. R. Tolkien's *The Hobbit* and *The Lord of the Rings.*" Making up his own worlds and telling his own stories fostered his talent for writing: "When my nieces were little, I made up stories for them about Martha Tooth Faerie and Horace the Belly Button Monster. By imagining that I'm just telling a longer story to them or to the sixth grade students I teach, I sit in front of my Mac and wait. If I'm lucky, a character pops into my head and tells me his or her adventure. All I do is write what I'm told."

In Robert Levy's second novel about the world of Enstor, Susan and her wolf have only their clan magic and the help of a small boy to fight against the forces of evil. (Cover illustration by N. Taylor Blanchard.)

The protagonists in *Escape from Exile* and *Clan of the Shape-Changers,* the author's first two books, communicate with and depend on animals. The story in *Escape from Exile* begins as Daniel Taylor works his way home through a blizzard. When a bolt of lightning hits the thirteen-year-old, he is knocked unconscious and wakes to find himself in a world destroyed by civil war. He soon finds that his survival depends on the help of the feline animals—the "samkits"—that have befriended him. Mentally communicating with Daniel, the samkits manage to get him to help them as well and save Queen Lauren from Resson, the evil man who keeps her from her throne. In the end, Daniel again loses consciousness and wakes to find himself near home. Li Stark concluded in *School Library Journal* that the "story is well paced, with some nice touches of humor." A *Publishers Weekly* reviewer noted that *Escape from Exile* is a "well-founded fantasy with abundant action."

In *Clan of the Shape-Changers* sixteen-year-old Susan has the ability to change her shape to that of an animal. When Ometerer, the ruler of Reune, begins searching for those with green eyes and the shape-changing power, Susan and her wolf, Farrun, flee her village. As she travels, Susan rescues a twelve-year-old boy who, unlike Susan, can't control his power to change his shape. Together they challenge Ometerer's plans by attempting to save the people of their green-eyed clan. Noting the book's "solid premise" and "exciting action," *Voice of Youth Advocates* reviewer Wendy E. Betts commented that *Clan of the Shape-Changers* is "an improvement over Levy's first book." Susan L. Rogers wrote in *School Library Journal* that "there is much more to be explained about this interesting planet and its inhabitants." In the opinion of *Booklist* contributor Chris Sherman, the "suspense" in *Clan of the Shape-Changers* "builds steadily to a dangerous climax that will satisfy fantasy and adventure lovers."

More recently, Levy has written a companion book to *Clan of the Shape-Changers* entitled *The Misfit Apprentice.* This third novel follows the adventures of Maria, a magician's apprentice who, because she is unable to control her magic, must seek her fortune in some other line of work. During her ensuing travels, Maria meets a mute boy named Tristan, who leads her on a journey to steal magical scrolls from a nearby country. In this and Levy's earlier novels, the author demonstrates a strong affection for fantasy and adventure stories and for the characters who inhabit his imaginative lands. As he explained to *SATA,* the "values I hold—people having a sense of honor, caring for the land they live on and the animals they share the land with—appear in my characters and help them come alive in my own mind."

■ Works Cited

Betts, Wendy E., review of *Clan of the Shape-Changers, Voice of Youth Advocates,* June, 1994, pp. 99-100.

Review of *Escape from Exile, Publishers Weekly,* April 12, 1993, p. 64.

Rogers, Susan L., review of *Clan of the Shape-Changers, School Library Journal,* May, 1994, p. 128.

Sherman, Chris, review of *Clan of the Shape-Changers, Booklist,* April 1, 1994, p. 1436.

Stark, Li, review of *Escape from Exile, School Library Journal,* May, 1993, p. 106.

■ For More Information See

PERIODICALS

Horn Book Guide, fall, 1993, p. 301.

Kirkus Reviews, March 15, 1994, p. 398.

Voice of Youth Advocates, August, 1993, pp. 166-67.

* * *

LINNEA, Sharon 1956-

■ Personal

Born August 15, 1956, in Elmhurst, IL; daughter of William Diderichsen (a minister) and Marilynn Joyce (a teacher/speaker; maiden name, Carlson) Webber; married Robert Owens Scott (a writer/producer); children: Jonathan Brendan Scott. *Education:* Attended Wheaton College, 1974-76; New York University, B.A., 1978.

SHARON LINNEA

Hobbies and other interests: Latching rugs, public speaking.

Addresses

Office—Imagining Things Enterprises, 43 West 16th St., Suite 7G, New York, NY 10011. *Agent*—Susan Cohen, Writers House, 21 West 26th St., New York, NY 10010.

Career

William Morrow and Co., New York City, editor, 1977-78; Taplinger and Associates, New York City, editor, 1978-80; Ziff Davis, *Flying Magazine,* New York City, staff writer, 1982-83; Scholastic Inc., *Scholastic Voice,* New York City, staff writer, 1983-85; Guideposts Associates, *Guideposts Magazine,* New York City, staff writer, 1985-91, contributing editor, 1991—. Vice President, Imagining Things Enterprises, New York City; producer of film, *Knowing Lisa,* 1991; speaker and leader of workshops. *Member:* Society of Children's Book Writers and Illustrators, New York Arts Group.

Awards, Honors

Best Book of 1993 citations, *Jewish World, Dayton Jewish Chronicle,* and *The Speaker,* all for *Raoul Wallenberg: The Man Who Stopped Death;* Silver Award, Worldfest/Houston (film festival), for *Knowing Lisa.*

Writings

"Romeo and Juliet" by William Shakespeare (study guide), Barrons, 1984.

"Hedda Gabbler" and "A Doll's House" by Henrik Ibsen (study guide), Barrons, 1985.

Raoul Wallenberg: The Man Who Stopped Death, Jewish Publication Society, 1993.

PLAYS

Clown of God (musical; based on the book by Tomie de Paola), produced in New York, 1977.

A Matter of Time, produced in New York, 1981.

Tales from the Vermont Woods, produced in New York, 1982.

OTHER

Also author of *The Singer,* a musical based on the book by Calvin Miller, 1978, and screenplays *Missouri, Ma Cheri* and *Tomorrow Is My Dancing Day.* Ghostwriter for *A Rustle of Angels,* Zondervan, 1994. Ghostwriter of articles for *Reader's Digest* and *Guideposts Magazine,* and author of articles for *Scholastic Voice* and *Seventeen.* Also profile biographer, World of Heroes School Curriculum, and freelancer for Marvel Comics, Children's Television Workshop, and Hallmark Hall of Fame.

Work in Progress

American Princess, a historical novel set in Hawaii, 1880-99; autobiography of Tom Veres, Raoul Wallenberg's photographer; *These Violent Delights,* a murder mystery.

Sidelights

Sharon Linnea told *SATA:* "I grew up in a home where storytelling—both written and oral—was deemed an important activity. The importance of this was brought home to me again last year when I was the profile biographer of the World of Heroes School Curriculum, writing biographies of twelve 'ordinary' people who changed the world. It included such diverse people as Harriet Tubman, Mahatma Gandhi, Eleanor Roosevelt, Mother Teresa, the Dalai Lama and Martin Luther King, Jr. As I did my research, it was fascinating to see common threads emerge in these lives separated by countries, cultures, and even centuries.

"For example, they all loved to read. Most of them had a strong faith, which translated into a keen sense of justice. They had each been through difficult personal times, but had come out the other side stronger for having triumphed. Perhaps most telling: they each had heroes. Someone they had read or heard about as a child, someone who had seen a wrong in the world and had successfully fought to right it.

"A recent Gallup poll found that fifty-one percent of American teenagers have no one they admire and would like to be like. No heroes. No one to prove it can be done. Where will our heroes come from? That, to me, emphasizes the crucial role of storytelling. It is an oh-so-necessary link in the cycle. That's part of the reason I felt compelled to tell the story of Raoul Wallenberg, the young Swedish architect who saved the lives of one hundred thousand Hungarian Jews at the end of World War II. I feel that storytelling—both biography and fiction—is a noble profession that both holds a mirror up to how things are, and shows how things can be."

■ For More Information See

PERIODICALS

Booklist, June 1 & 15, 1993, p. 1823.
Horn Book, September, 1993, p. 622.
Kliatt, September, 1993, p. 29.
Kirkus Reviews, June 15, 1993, p. 787.
School Library Journal, October, 1993, p. 163.
Voice of Youth Advocates, October, 1993, pp. 247-48.

* * *

LOURIE, Peter (King) 1952-

■ Personal

Born February 3, 1952, in Ann Arbor, MI; son of Donold King (a lawyer and writer) and Nancy Groves (maiden name, Clement; present surname, Stout) Lourie; married Melissa Stern (an actress and producer), May 2, 1988; children: Suzanna, Walker. *Education:* New York University, B.A., 1975; University of Maine at Orono, M.A., 1978; attended Cuernavaca Language School, 1978; Columbia University, M.F.A., 1989.

■ Addresses

Agent—Susan Ramer, Don Congdon Associates, 156 5th Ave., Suite 625, New York, NY 10010.

■ Career

Nairobi National Museum, Nairobi, Kenya, Africa, assistant to Margaret Leakey at Centre for Prehistory, 1971; American Museum of Natural History, New York City, guide in Hall of the American Indian, 1971; British Museum, London, assistant to curator of Greek coins, 1974; Colegio Americano, Quito, Ecuador, instructor in English as a second language, 1979-80; Dutchess Community College, Poughkeepsie, NY, adjunct lecturer in English composition and literature, 1984-89; Masters School, Dobbs Ferry, CT, writing teacher and director of Dobbs Writers Conference, 1989-91; University of Vermont, Burlington, instructor in travel writing, 1992, director of summer writing program, 1994-95. *Member:* Authors Guild, Authors League of America.

■ Awards, Honors

Magazine Merit Award, Honor Certificate for nonfiction, Society of Children's Book Writers, 1990; *Yukon River: An Adventure to the Gold Fields of the Klondike* was named a Best Book for the Teen Age by the New York Public Library, 1993; *Everglades* was named a Notable Book in the Social Studies by the Children's Book Council, 1995.

■ Writings

Sweat of the Sun, Tears of the Moon: A Chronicle of an Incan Treasure, Atheneum, 1991.
Amazon: A Young Reader's Look at the Last Frontier, illustrated by Marcos Santilli, Caroline House, 1991.
(And illustrator) *Hudson River: An Adventure from the Mountains to the Sea,* Caroline House, 1992.
(And illustrator) *Yukon River: An Adventure to the Gold Fields of the Klondike,* Caroline House, 1992.
Everglades: Buffalo Tiger and the River of Grass, Boyds Mills Press, 1994.
River of Mountains: A Canoe Journey Down the Hudson, Syracuse University Press, 1995.

Also author of a weekly column for the *Putnam County News and Recorder,* 1985-87. Contributor to magazines, including *Highlights for Children, Parenting, Diversion, Treasure, South American Explorer,* and *American Photographer.*

■ Sidelights

Peter Lourie's nonfiction books, based on his travels and his training as an anthropologist, often highlight his concern for the environment. His first book, *Sweat of the Sun, Tears of the Moon: A Chronicle of an Incan Treasure,* recounts the author's adventures in Ecuador, where as a graduate student he became involved in searching for treasure hidden by the Incas from the invading conquistadors centuries before. According to John Maxwell Hamilton, writing in the *New York Times Book Review,* the author "captures the discomfort, dreams, and despair of treasure hunting," but the reviewer found fault with Lourie's prose, which he dubbed "often purple." Others found much to praise in the author's first publication: "[Lourie's] journal is a captivating, if meandering adventure," commented a *Publishers Weekly* reviewer, and a *Kirkus Reviews* contributor called *Sweat of the Sun* "lots of fun."

For his next publication, *Amazon: A Young Reader's Look at the Last Frontier,* Lourie travelled through the heart of the Amazon basin, describing for his readers the clash between the traditional hunting and gathering culture and those who burn the ancient rain forest in order to farm the land. "The entire book creates an indelible picture of this endangered system," observed Frances E. Millhouser in *School Library Journal.* In addition, *Bulletin of the Center for Children's Books* contributor Roger Sutton praised the "you-are-there immediacy" of the publication, and Mary Harris Veeder, writing in the *Chicago Tribune,* singled out Lourie's "winningly direct prose." Although a *Publishers Weekly* contributor claimed the work "lacks immediacy and focus," several critics praised Lourie's efforts to deal with the environmental destruction in that area without lecturing to his audience.

In *Hudson River: An Adventure from the Mountains to the Sea,* Lourie's next publication, the author describes another trip taken down a river in a canoe. In this work,

Lourie recounts the history of and the current conditions along the more than three hundred miles of the Hudson River. Though in her *School Library Journal* critique Kate Hegarty Bouman found the author's photographs of his journey more impressive than his narrative account, Karen Hutt wrote in *Booklist* that "his straightforward account will appeal to canoe enthusiasts and to readers with a particular interest" in the history of the Hudson River. Lourie has also published *Yukon River: An Adventure to the Gold Fields of the Klondike,* an account of a nearly five-hundred-mile canoe trip the author took in an effort to duplicate the path of the turn-of-the-century gold prospectors in the Klondike. A *Kirkus Reviews* writer called *Yukon River* "powerful and beautifully presented." The author's most recent publications include *Everglades: Buffalo Tiger and the River of Grass* and *River of Mountains: A Canoe Journey Down the Hudson.*

■ Works Cited

Review of *Amazon: A Young Reader's Look at the Last Frontier, Publishers Weekly,* August 30, 1991, p. 86.

Bouman, Kate Hegarty, review of *Hudson River: An Adventure from the Mountains to the Sea, School Library Journal,* June, 1992, pp. 109-10.

Hamilton, John Maxwell, review of *Sweat of the Sun, Tears of the Moon: A Chronicle of an Incan Treasure, New York Times Book Review,* June 9, 1991, p. 48.

Hutt, Karen, review of *Hudson River: An Adventure from the Mountains to the Sea, Booklist,* April 1, 1992, p. 1442.

Millhouser, Frances E., review of *Amazon: A Young Reader's Look at the Last Frontier, School Library Journal,* January, 1992, p. 130.

Sutton, Roger, review of *Amazon: A Young Reader's Look at the Last Frontier, Bulletin of the Center for Children's Books,* November, 1991, pp. 68-69.

Review of *Sweat of the Sun, Tears of the Moon: A Chronicle of an Incan Treasure, Kirkus Reviews,* February 1, 1991, p. 157.

Review of *Sweat of the Sun, Tears of the Moon: A Chronicle of an Incan Treasure, Publishers Weekly,* February 1, 1991, p. 75.

Veeder, Mary Harris, review of *Amazon: A Young Reader's Look at the Last Frontier, Chicago Tribune,* October 13, 1991, Section 14, p. 6.

Review of *Yukon River: An Adventure to the Gold Fields of the Klondike, Kirkus Reviews,* August 1, 1992, p. 997.

* * *

LUCHT, Irmgard 1937-

■ Personal

Born May 10, 1937, in Bonn, Germany; daughter of Ernst (a university professor) and Charlotte (a kindergarten teacher; maiden name, Sellentin) Brandenburg; married Gerhard Lucht, August 2, 1961; children: Jan, Anne. *Education:* Attended Cologne Graphic Art School, 1958-61. *Religion:* Protestant. *Hobbies and other interests:* Reading, playing the guitar, cycling.

■ Addresses

Home—Ludwig-Thomastr. 77, D-85540 Haar, Federal Republic of Germany.

■ Career

Worked as a kindergarten teacher, Frankfurt/Main, 1956-57, and as a practical trainee in the costume department of Stadt. Buhnen, Frankfurt, 1957-58; painter and illustrator, 1961—.

■ Awards, Honors

Best Picture Book of the Year, Bologna Book Fair, 1971, for *Alle meine Blaetter;* German Children's Literature Prize honor list, 1977, for *Die Voegel Uhr,* 1979, for *Die Baum Uhr,* 1983, for *Die Wiesen Uhr,* 1988, for *Die Wald Uhr;* Austrian Children and Young Adult Books honor book, Austrian Encouragement Prize for Children and Young Adult Books, both 1979, both for *Die Baum Uhr;* Bratislava Biannual Award for Illustrations plaque, 1983, for *Die Wiesen Uhr;* Luchspreis, from *Zeit* and Radio Bremen, 1987, for *Die Wald Uhr;* German Children's Literature Prize, 1990, for *Wie kommt der Wald ins Buch?; Die gruene Uhr* was on the Premio

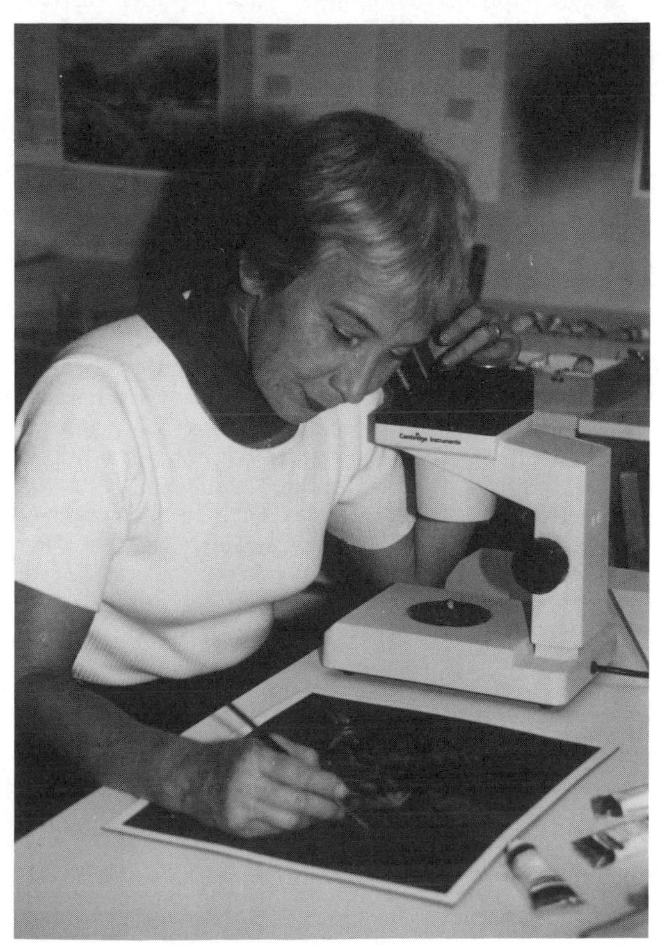

IRMGARD LUCHT

Europeo di Letteratura Giovanile honor list, received a German Gartenbau-Gesellschaft prize, and was named among the fifty best picture books in Germany.

Writings

(Illustrator with Josef Guggenmos) *Wonder-fish from the Sea,* adapted by Alvin Tresselt, Parents' Magazine Press, 1971 (originally published as *Alle meine Blaetter,* Middlehauve, 1970), published as *Sea-Change,* Macdonald, 1971.
(Illustrator) Ernest Benn, *Die Voegel auf den Stangen,* Ellermann, 1972 (translated into English as *The King's Tune*).
(Illustrator) Christa Spangenberg, *The Green Clock,* Blackie, 1983 (originally published as *Die gruene Uhr,* Ellermann, 1974).
The Bird Clock, Blackie, 1976 (originally published as *Die Voegel Uhr,* Ellermann, 1976).
The Tree Calendar, A. and C. Black, 1983 (originally published as *Die Baum Uhr,* Ellermann, 1978).
The Meadow Year, A. and C. Black, 1983 (originally published as *Die Wiesen Uhr,* Ellermann, 1982).
The Forest Calendar, A. and C. Black, 1988 (originally published as *Die Wald Uhr,* Ellermann, 1987).
Wie kommt der Wald ins Buch?, Ellermann, 1989.
In This Night, translated by Frank Jacoby-Nelson and adapted by Elizabeth Hollow, Hyperion, 1993 (originally published as *In dieser Nacht . . . ,* Ravensburger Buchverlag, 1992).
The Red Poppy, translated by Frank Jacoby-Nelson, Hyperion, 1995 (originally published as *Roter Mohn,* Ravensburger Buchverlag, 1994).

Lucht's *The Green Clock* and *The Bird Clock* have been translated into approximately a dozen languages.

Sidelights

Irmgard Lucht has written highly praised picture books that celebrate and teach young people about the beauty and complexity of nature. Her prose has garnered praise for its quiet lyricism, and the illustrations that accompany her narratives have also garnered enthusiastic praise for their brilliant colors, accurate details, and powerful beauty. However, Lucht told *SATA:* "If an 'illustrator' is supposed to be someone who illustrates texts, then that is not what I am. For me, pictures do not materialize out of words but have other roots. They arise from unknown sources like dreams—or they are triggered off by external impressions.

"During my years of training in Cologne, my sole aim was to learn the language of colors and shapes in order to be able to express myself and communicate. I did not give a thought to making books. Then I was married and had children and I did no painting for seven years—Jan and Anne were more important to me. Then it suddenly came to the surface again—like an underground water course which has at last found the way out. In just a few weeks, an extensive picture cycle came into being, and probably due to my situation in life at that time, my first children's book emerged from these pictures: *Alle meine Blaetter* ('All My Leaves,' 1970)."

Alle meine Blaetter appeared in the English translation entitled *Sea-Change.* In this fantasy, the leaves on the trees are depicted as jealous of the freedom of the birds. The autumn wind sets them free and they fall into the sea where they become beautiful fish and are captured by a fisherman. Kevin Crossley-Holland commented in the *Spectator* that *Alle meine Blaetter* "treads very delicately the tightrope between seen and imagined." A reviewer added in the *Times Literary Supplement,* "This is a book where text and pictures really complement each other."

"The 'Clock-books' are widely published and translated into up to thirteen languages," Lucht told *SATA.* "The first, *The Green Clock,* put me on the path which I followed with curiosity and joy. I began to discover nature and from book to book became increasingly interested in the subject—and with every step my amazement grew. It is this amazement that I would like to convey in words and pictures."

Various birds are viewed in their habitats during each month of the year in Lucht's *Die Voegel Uhr,* translated as *The Bird Clock.* The book was recommended as "an attractive introduction to bird-watching for children" by a *Junior Bookshelf* reviewer, who praised Lucht's accuracy. *The Meadow Year,* a translation of *Die Wiesen Uhr,* shares the same format. In *The Meadow Year,* Lucht surveys the changes each month brings to the animal and plant life commonly found in a meadow. Naomi Lewis described this effort in the *Times Educational Supplement* as "exquisitely illustrated (in both line and colour), with informing readable text." In her review in *Growing Point,* Margery Fisher also singled out Lucht's illustrations, "which delight the eye and exemplify seasonal change admirably." Other titles, such as *The Green Clock* and *The Tree Calendar,* originally published as *Die gruene Uhr* and *Die Baum Uhr* respectively, also garnered positive critical responses for their thorough and detailed approaches to their subjects. *Die Wald Uhr* (*The Forest Calendar*) is detailed and informative but still attractive to very young children due to its full-page "woodland illustrations," according to Lewis in a review published in the *Observer.*

Lucht has also written and illustrated *In dieser Nacht . . . ,* which was translated in English as *In This Night.* In this work, the author portrays the natural world at night, just as winter is turning into spring. A critic for *Publishers Weekly,* who dubbed the illustraitons "stunning," commented that the "ethereal quality of Lucht's rhapsodic narrative makes one want to read it in a whisper." Although in her *School Library Journal* review Ruth K. MacDonald found this "little more than a coffee-table book," Stephanie Zvirin in *Booklist* called Lucht's illustrations "luminous and expansive," recommending the book as "a perfect bedtime companion."

Through her paintings of nature's nighttime activities, Lucht tells the story of the coming of spring. (Illustration by the author from *In This Night . . .*)

"My children were and still are very close to me," Lucht later remarked to *SATA,* "and they helped me to find access to the child in myself. Perhaps for that reason a further eight children's books followed the first one over the years, although the work on books was interspersed now and again by longer periods of 'free painting.'

■ Works Cited

Review of *The Bird Clock, Junior Bookshelf,* August, 1976, pp. 206-7.

Crossley-Holland, Kevin, review of *Sea-Change, Spectator,* November 13, 1971.

Fisher, Margery, review of *The Meadow Year, Growing Point,* May, 1983, p. 4085.

Review of *In This Night, Publishers Weekly,* March 15, 1993, p. 85.

Lewis, Naomi, "Looks Natural," *Times Educational Supplement,* December 23, 1983, p. 23.

Lewis, Naomi, review of *The Forest Calendar, Observer,* August 7, 1988, p. 42.

MacDonald, Ruth K., review of *In This Night, School Library Journal,* August, 1993, pp. 147-48.

Review of *Sea-Change, Times Literary Supplement,* July 2, 1971, p. 771.

Zvirin, Stephanie, review of *In This Night, Booklist,* May 1, 1993, p. 1596.

■ For More Information See

PERIODICALS

Junior Bookshelf, August, 1983, p. 162; October, 1988, pp. 242-43.
Times Educational Supplement, March 11, 1983, p. 40.

M

ROSS MARTIN MADSEN

MADSEN, Ross Martin 1946-

■ Personal

Born July 8, 1946, in Gunnison, UT; son of Martin Christian (a mechanic) and Lois Mary (a homemaker; maiden name, Andrus) Madsen; married Eleanor Ellice Chambers (a homemaker), July 25, 1969. *Education:* University of Utah, B.A., 1970, M.Ed., 1975. *Politics:* Moderate. *Religion:* Church of Jesus Christ of Latter-day Saints (Mormon).

■ Addresses

Home—3136 Mark Ave., West Valley, UT 84119.

■ Career

Granite School District, social studies teacher, 1970—, and Granger Community School, teacher, 1976—, both Salt Lake City, UT. Has also been a lay minister in the Church of Jesus Christ of Latter-day Saints.

■ Writings

Perrywinkle and the Book of Magic Spells, illustrated by Dirk Zimmer, Dial, 1986.
Stewart Stork, illustrated by Megan Halsey, Dial, 1994.

■ Work in Progress

Perrywinkle and Mixed Magic, Dial Books; *Friends Don't Let Friends Eat Mice,* a picture book; *I'm Not Afraid of ABC,* a picture book; *Winston and the Dream Maker Machine,* a middle grade novel.

■ Sidelights

Ross Martin Madsen told *SATA:* "'I can write something this good.' It was a statement of fact made after a summer's worth of bedtime reading to my then young children. The problem was the reaction my comment brought from my wife. 'Why don't you do it?'

"I was trapped; corralled by my own smugness. I soon learned writing for publication is no easy task. It requires dedication, persistence, some talent, and a lot of luck. With the daily burden of earning a living for a family of five, creativity and energy are often drained into avenues other than writing. Gratefully, there has been enough inspiration, effort, and good fortune to produce two easy-to-read books already published while a third waits final revision. Don't misunderstand me, I enjoy teaching high school social studies, but my real love is writing."

For More Information See

PERIODICALS

Booklist, April 15, 1986, p. 1229; December 1, 1993, p. 702.
Horn Book Guide, spring, 1994, p. 62.
Kirkus Reviews, April 15, 1986, p. 639.
Publishers Weekly, June 27, 1986, p. 88; February 12, 1988, p. 89.
Reading Teacher, October, 1986, p. 96.
School Library Journal, May, 1986, p. 113; September, 1993, p. 215.*

* * *

MAGUIRE, Jessie
See SMITH, Sherwood

* * *

MAJOR, Kevin (Gerald) 1949-

Personal

Born September 12, 1949, in Stephenville, Newfoundland, Canada; son of Edward (a fisherman and boiler-room worker) and Jessie (Headge) Major; married Anne Crawford (a librarian), July 3, 1982; children: Luke, Duncan. *Education:* Memorial University of Newfoundland, B.Sc., 1973. *Religion:* Anglican.

Addresses

Home—Box 85, Eastport, Newfoundland, Canada A0G 1Z0. *Agent*—Nancy Colbert, 303 Davenport Rd., Toronto, Ontario, Canada M5R 1K5.

Career

Teacher in Roberts Arm, Newfoundland, 1971-72, and Carbonear, Newfoundland, 1973; Eastport Central High School, Eastport, Newfoundland, teacher of special education and biology, 1974-76; substitute teacher, beginning 1976. Freelance writer, 1976—. *Member:* Writers Union of Canada.

Awards, Honors

Canada Council Children's Literature Prize, Canadian Library Association Book of the Year Award, and Ruth Schwartz Children's Book Award, Ruth Schwartz Charitable Foundation-Ontario Arts Council, all 1979, and Hans Christian Andersen Honor List citation, International Board on Books for Young People, and *School Library Journal* Best Books of the Year citation, both 1980, all for *Hold Fast;* Canadian Young Adult Book Award, Young Adult Caucus of the Saskatchewan Library Association, and *School Library Journal* Best Books of the Year citation, both 1981, both for *Far from Shore;* Canadian Library Association Book of the Year runner-up, and Canadian Young Adult Book Award runner-up, both 1990, both for *Blood Red Ochre;* Brimer

KEVIN MAJOR

Award, Nova Scotia Library Association, Canadian Library Association Book of the Year Award, and Canadian Young Adult Book Award runnerup, all 1992, all for *Eating between the Lines;* Vicky Metcalf Award, Canadian Author Association, 1992.

Writings

YOUNG ADULT NOVELS

Hold Fast, Clarke, Irwin, 1978, Delacorte, 1980.
Far from Shore, Clarke, Irwin, 1980, Delacorte, 1981.
Thirty-six Exposures, Delacorte, 1984.
Dear Bruce Springsteen, Delacorte, 1987.
Blood Red Ochre, Delacorte, 1989.
Eating between the Lines, Doubleday, 1991.
Diana: My Autobiography, Doubleday, 1993.

OTHER

(Editor and contributor of illustrations) *Doryloads: Newfoundland Writings and Art,* Breakwater Books, 1974.

(With James A. Tuck) *Terra Nova National Park: Human History Study,* Parks Canada, 1983.

Major's works have been translated into French, German, Spanish, Hebrew, and Danish.

In his controversial first novel, Major portrays the conflicts of an orphaned teen who must leave his Newfoundland fishing village to live in the city with a strict uncle. (Cover illustration by Michael Dudash.)

■ Sidelights

Kevin Major is "among the best Canadian writers of his generation," according to John Moss in *A Reader's Guide to the Canadian Novel,* adding that the author "has established himself as a figure of singular importance in our literature." Often dealing with problems encountered by youth in the author's native province of Newfoundland, Major's groundbreaking novels are known for their frank portrayals of teenage language and sexuality—for which they have sometimes been banned from school libraries and classrooms. "Sex and strong language play no greater or no lesser a part in my work than they do in real life," Major stated in *School Libraries in Canada.* "The truth is both are preoccupations of adolescents as is their family life, school, their relationships with their friends. So why the great fear?"

Major related his start in writing to *Books in Canada* interviewer Sherie Posesorski: "As a substitute teacher, I saw that young people were voraciously reading the new genre of American realistic young adult fiction by Judy Blume, Robert Cormier, and S. E. Hinton.... I saw that there were no comparable stories for a similar age group situated in Newfoundland, so I decided to write a story about young people growing up in the outports, dramatizing situations that would be relevant to their lives." As the author once explained, "I wanted to capture the Newfoundland way of life, its way of speaking and manner of dealing with people, and I wanted to convey some of my pride in our traditions—fishing, hunting, and the general closeness to nature." As these traditions are challenged by modern trends, Major told Posesorski, "the young are caught between the old traditional values of Newfoundland outport society and the onslaught of American popular culture." This conflict plays a part in Major's first novel, *Hold Fast,* in which an orphaned teen is uprooted from his fishing village to live with his uncle's family in the city. Michael's attempts to adjust to the loss of his parents and a new way of life lead to conflict and rebellion.

Hold Fast brought Major instant attention. "*Hold Fast* is a landmark in Canadian writing for young people," Irma McDonough commented in *In Review,* praising the work as "a stunningly perceptive novel of family life in the outport and the city ..., and of one young person at the centre of it." In a distinctly Newfoundland voice, fourteen-year-old Michael relates his experiences as he is excluded at school because of his accent, contends with his tyrannical, materialistic uncle, and eventually steals a car and runs away. Michael's delinquent behavior has drawn fire from some critics, as has the profanity he often uses to describe it. But while Michael's story has "the egotistical, raw, first-person narrative" characteristic of the young adult genre, explained *Horn Book* critic Sarah Ellis, *Hold Fast* stands out because he tells it "in a language rich with thc history and identity of his people." Other reviewers have drawn favorable comparisons between Michael and two "delinquent" literary predecessors: Mark Twain's Huckleberry Finn and J. D. Salinger's Holden Caulfield. "The values emphasized here are some of the most significant and universal," Gary H. Paterson concluded in *Canadian Children's Literature:* "pride in oneself and one's heritage, courage to express and hold to one's opinions, the necessity to find a balance between emotion and reason and to cultivate a fine sensitivity for others and absolute honesty in assessing social relations."

After producing a first-person narrative for *Hold Fast,* Major experimented with a different writing style for his next work. In a *Contemporary Authors* interview with Jean W. Ross, Major declared: "One of the things I am interested in doing is trying to tell stories in different ways. I think a lot of books for young people are very similar in that they are told through the first person. There are not many chances taken in narrative form." *Far from Shore* uses five characters' points of view in depicting a family in crisis. After sixteen-year-old Chris's father loses his job and turns to alcohol, family tensions lead Chris to flunk out of school and become involved with a bad crowd. With his parents and sister too absorbed in their own troubles to deal with his, Chris's misbehavior escalates until he is arrested for an act of vandalism he was too drunk to even remember. Family conflicts are related by Chris, his parents, his sister, and the pastor who gives Chris a second chance after his arrest. While Janet Lunn found this multiple narrative "awkward and often confusing," she added in her *Books in Canada* review that Major's attempt to show five points of view "provides a richness and a roundness not often found in books about kids in high school."

Other critics have considered Major's narrative technique to be a success. In *Canadian Children's Literature,* Muriel Whitaker observed that "the strength of *Far from Shore* lies in the author's ability to present each of the major characters sympathetically in spite of their shortcomings. Through the device of interior monologue, actions and attitudes are provided with an emotional frame of reference that makes them comprehensible." As Ann Johnston explained in her *Maclean's* review, in this "brilliant" narration the characters "pass their story along like a hot potato, contradicting, misunderstanding and forgiving, until voices reverberate from the four corners of the house." And while Major's use of strong language has again drawn fire from some reviewers, others such as McDonough found it in keeping with the characters: "Major's strength lies in his absolute concentration on the story. He is psychologically and emotionally true to Chris and his destiny, and we believe him." *Far from Shore,* the critic concluded, "is a satisfying literary experience that once again reveals Major's uncommon artistic integrity."

Told from five points of view, this novel focuses on fifteen-year-old Chris and the family problems brought on by his father's layoff. (Cover illustration by Fran Stiles.)

Major employs a more radical narrative structure in *Thirty-six Exposures,* a story about the difficult senior year of a high school student with interests in poetry and photography. "Each of the 36 chapters in the book offers a snapshot," *Quill and Quire* writer Paul Kropp explained, "marvellous in its detail but not connected to the others." "The story is episodic, at times to a fault (perhaps an attempt to unfold it like frames from a roll of film)," Sally Estes likewise noted in *Booklist.* Nevertheless, she called the book "compelling." Other reviewers believed the novel is less successful than its predecessors. Ellen M. Fecher, writing in *School Library Journal,* saw "a coldness in the development of the characters that leaves readers detached," but she also noted "strengths" in the "fast-paced" plot. An episodic nature also distinguishes *Dear Bruce Springsteen,* which is told through the letters of a Newfoundland teen to the rock star of the title. His parents' divorce has left fourteen-year-old Terry facing the awkwardness of adolescence alone, and so he confides his feelings to his idol. While *School Library Journal* contributor Jack Forman felt the episodic format produces a "skeleton rather than telling the tale," he added that the "short, easy-to-read format . . . will attract many young readers."

Major again experiments with form in *Blood Red Ochre,* branching out into the supernatural in dealing with European settlers' destruction of Native American tribes. A third-person, past-tense narrative of a modern high school student and a first-person, present-tense account of a nineteenth-century young man of the Beothuk tribe alternate until, mysteriously, the two protagonists meet. As fifteen-year-old David learns more about the customs of the extinct Newfoundland tribe from young Dauoodaset's narrative, he is driven to survey the island where a Beothuk skeleton was uncovered. There Nancy, a fellow student, declares that she is Shanawdithit, Dauoodaset's lost love, and precipitates a vision of the tribe's destruction by white settlers. Some critics remarked that the complex structure of the novel could confuse readers. *School Library Journal* contributor Yvonne A. Frey wrote that while the book contains "good detail on Indian life and customs," it leaves the reader with "questions unresolved."

Ellis, however, believed that "Major achieves a remarkable balance between the two narratives, each with its own weight and energy." The difference in narrative style heightens the contrast between the two characters and their two lifestyles, helping to create the ending in which "the issue of responsibility is unresolved." As Catherine Simpson explained in *Canadian Children's Literature,* this lack of resolution is appropriate for the book's subject: "In the end, we are left, like David, baffled by this tragedy in our history, 'trying to make sense of it,' knowing that our attempt, like David's, to atone for the violence of our forebears comes too late to make any difference to the vanished Beothuk." In this manner, the critic concluded, "*Blood Red Ochre* adds a dark urgency to the universal, timely, and complex problem of the relationship between the native and immigrant peoples of North America."

Major continues to experiment with form in his books, even as he takes a more humorous approach. *Eating between the Lines,* for example, "is a quite successful blending of realistic fiction and fantasy into a delightful comedy," Betty M. Brett stated in *Canadian Children's Literature.* Young Jackson narrates as he has difficulty in school, has problems with girls, and watches his parents head towards divorce. But Jackson's story takes a fantastic turn when he discovers a magical talisman that transports him into the pages of the books he reads. As Jackson participates in the stories of Ulysses, Romeo and Juliet, and Huckleberry Finn—books that, like Major's own, have been banned on occasion—the author touches on the issue of censoring books for children. The result, while "immensely entertaining," also contains "a serious message about the importance of allowing children and young adults to experience literature in all its richness," Virginia Beaton remarked in *Books in Canada.*

Major combines contemporary school life with fantasy in this powerful work that examines the history and extinction of the Beothuk tribe.

Major tries an even more different approach in his next novel, focusing for the first time on the life and problems of a teenage girl. In *Diana: My Autobiography,* Major alternates the written "memoir" of his royalty-obsessed protagonist with her everyday observations on school, romance, and the British royal family. Diana's humorous escapades contrast with the self-conscious, "elevated" language of her autobiography, making these sections "unintentionally hilarious," according to Anne Louise Mahoney in *Quill and Quire.* As a result, while Diana is not as "introspective" as Major's previous heroes, this "character with a difference" has a "freshness and strong sense of self [that] will appeal to readers with a sense of humour." *Books in Canada* critic Pat Barclay similarly praised Major's success in creating a believable character, concluding: "This is a funny, clever story, enhanced by Major's ear for dialogue and his sly digs at Diana's novel-writing dad."

Major "continues to be one of our strongest and most technically innovative writers for young adults," Ellis asserted in her *Horn Book* article. In his interview with Ross, however, the author expressed dissatisfaction with the way his works are categorized: "I've never really been content with the term 'young adult book,' which is usually how they're labeled, because it tends to place a limit on the readership, on the kind of audience the labelers think the books would appeal to." As he further explained to Posesorski: "I write about young people, not exclusively for them. I would hope that my books have an interest for adults. Adults with teenage children have told me that they enjoy the books in themselves and for the insights they give them into their children's thinking. A good novel, whether it is about someone five or 55, should be able to stand on its own."

■ Works Cited

Barclay, Pat, "Roads to Maturity," *Books in Canada,* October, 1993, p. 58.

Beaton, Virginia, "Onward and Upward," *Books in Canada,* December, 1991, p. 39.

Brett, Betty M., "Breaking the Vacuum: Children's Books from Newfoundland," *Canadian Children's Literature,* Number 66, 1992, p. 54.

Ellis, Sarah, review of *Hold Fast, Horn Book,* February, 1984, p. 99-103.

Ellis, Sarah, review of *Blood Red Ochre, Horn Book,* September/October, 1989, pp. 659-61.

Estes, Sally, review of *Thirty-six Exposures, Booklist,* November 1, 1984, p. 361.

Fecher, Ellen M., review of *Thirty-six Exposures, School Library Journal,* February, 1985, p. 85-86.

Forman, Jack, review of *Dear Bruce Springsteen, School Library Journal,* May, 1988, p. 110.

Frey, Yvonne A., review of *Blood Red Ochre, School Library Journal,* April, 1989, p. 119.

Johnston, Ann, "Tales to Keep the Nightlights Burning," *Maclean's,* December 15, 1980, pp. 52, 54, 56-58.

Kropp, Paul, "Growing Up Is Hard to Do: Leaving the Boy Behind," *Quill and Quire,* November, 1984, p. 18.

Lunn, Janet, "Huck Finn in Newfoundland," *Books in Canada,* December, 1980, pp. 21-23.
Mahoney, Anne Louise, review of *Diana: My Autobiography, Quill and Quire,* April, 1993, p. 31.
Major, Kevin, "Challenged Materials: An Author's Perspective," *School Libraries in Canada,* spring, 1984, pp. 15-16.
Major, Kevin, interview with Sherie Posesorski, *Books in Canada,* December, 1984, pp. 24-25.
Major, Kevin, interview with Jean W. Ross in *Contemporary Authors New Revision Series,* Volume 21, Gale, 1988, pp. 263-66.
McDonough, Irma, review of *Hold Fast, In Review: Canadian Books for Children,* summer, 1978, p. 70.
McDonough, Irma, review of *Far from Shore, In Review: Canadian Books for Children,* February, 1981, pp. 42-43.
Moss, John, "Kevin Major," *A Reader's Guide to the Canadian Novel,* McClelland & Stewart, 1981, p. 340.
Paterson, Gary H., "Learning to Hold Fast," *Canadian Children's Literature,* Number 14, 1979, pp. 81-83.
Simpson, Catherine, "Beothuk Darkness," *Canadian Children's Literature,* Number 61, 1991, pp. 59-60.
Whitaker, Muriel, "Getting Loused Up in Newfoundland," *Canadian Children's Literature,* Number 22, 1981, pp. 50-53.

■ For More Information See

BOOKS

Children's Literature Review, Volume 11, Gale, 1986, pp. 123-33.
Contemporary Literary Criticism, Volume 26, Gale, 1983.
Dictionary of Literary Biography, Volume 60: *Canadian Writers since 1960, Second Series,* Gale, 1987.
Gallo, Donald R., editor and compiler, *Speaking for Ourselves,* National Council of Teachers of English, 1990, pp. 133-34.
Twentieth-Century Children's Writers, 4th edition, St. James Press, 1995.

PERIODICALS

Atlantic Insight, November, 1984.
Best Sellers, January, 1982, p. 403; February, 1985, p. 439.
Bulletin of the Center for Children's Books, March, 1985, p. 131; May, 1988, p. 183; April, 1989, p. 200.
Canadian Children's Literature, Number 66, 1992, pp. 23-34.
Children's Literature Association Quarterly, fall, 1985, pp. 140-41.
Emergency Librarian, January-February, 1992, pp. 26, 66-70; September, 1992, p. 37.
Globe and Mail (Toronto), March 26, 1988; March 11, 1989.
Maclean's, December 17, 1979.
Ottawa Journal, June 19, 1979.
Quill and Quire, November, 1980.
Saturday Night, October, 1978, pp. 14-15.
Toronto Sun, June 29, 1978.
Voice of Youth Advocates, February, 1985, p. 329; June, 1989, p. 104.
World of Children's Books, fall, 1978, pp. 56-59; Volume 6, 1981, pp. 29-30.*

—*Sketch by Diane Telgen*

* * *

MANN, Josephine
See PULLEIN-THOMPSON, Josephine

* * *

MARCUS, Paul 1953-

■ Personal

Born February 26, 1953, in New York, NY; married Irene Wineman (a child psychoanalyst), 1980; children: Raphael, Gabriela. *Education:* Adelphi University, B.A. (magna cum laude), 1974; New School for Social Research, M.A., 1976; University of London, Ph.D. (clinical psychology), 1980; trained in psychoanalysis at the New York Freudian Society and the National Psychological Association for Psychoanalysis.

■ Addresses

Home—115 Wooleys Ln., Great Neck, NY 11023. *Office*—114-06 Queens Blvd., Forest Hills, NY 11375.

■ Career

Psychoanalyst/psychologist, private practice, 1980—. Has taught psychology at the University of London, City University of New York, and New York Universi-

PAUL MARCUS

ty. *Member:* National Psychological Association for Psychoanalysis, American Psychological Association.

Awards, Honors

New York Society of Clinical Psychologists Holocaust Book Award, 1990, for *Healing Their Wounds: Psychotherapy with Holocaust Survivors and Their Families; Scary Night Visitors: A Story for Children with Bedtime Fears* was chosen as a main selection by *Psychotherapy Book News,* 1991.

Writings

(Editor with Steven A. Luel) *Psychoanalytic Reflections on the Holocaust: Selected Essays,* KTAV and University of Denver, 1984.

(Editor with Alan Rosenberg) *Healing Their Wounds: Psychotherapy with Holocaust Survivors and Their Families,* Praeger, 1989.

(With wife, Irene Wineman Marcus) *Scary Night Visitors: A Story for Children with Bedtime Fears,* Magination Press, 1990.

(With I. W. Marcus) *Into the Great Forest: A Story for Children Away from Parents for the First Time,* Magination Press, 1992.

(With Rosenberg) *Autonomy in the Nazi Concentration Camps and Mass Society: A Reevaluation of the Work of Bruno Bettelheim,* Praeger, 1995.

(Editor with Rosenberg) *Psychoanalytic Versions of the Human Condition and Clinical Practice,* New York University Press, 1995.

Work in Progress

The Queen and the Mouse, a children's book about oppositional children; a children's book on toilet training.

Sidelights

Paul Marcus told *SATA:* "As a psychoanalyst, I have always felt that a psychoanalytic perspective can offer a most evocative and illuminating framework for young children as they begin to try and make sense of their often chaotic and frightening inner worlds. [The books I've written with my wife] have attempted to use psychoanalytic insight to make contact with the underlying anxieties and fears that most normal children have, help them to understand them, and then finally, suggest some possible solutions that will foster a sense of mastery. Of course, the trick is to not be didactic and boring, but rather like the great classic fairy tales, to inspire the child's curiosity and passion so that she identifies with the characters. Above all else, one needs to tell a compelling story that makes the child want to turn the page.

"In my view, following [French author and philosopher Jean-Paul] Sartre, 'all books are attempts to improve one's biography,' and for me and my wife/coauthor, this has meant trying our best to understand our own children and raise saner and kinder kids."

For More Information See

PERIODICALS

Choice, July, 1992, p. 1641.

Readings: A Journal of Reviews and Commentary in Mental Health, September, 1990, p. 31.

Religious Studies Review, July, 1990, p. 209.*

* * *

MARTIN, Linda 1961-

Personal

Born October 10, 1961, in Colorado Springs, CO; daughter of Alvin (a reverend) and Juanita (a television producer) Martin; married Robert Johnston (divorced, 1985); children: Alex. *Education:* Attended University of Southern Colorado, 1979-80; Blair Business College, A.A., 1983. *Religion:* "Life!" *Hobbies and other interests:* Reading, crossword puzzles, meditation, old books, clothing, photos, and museum-haunting.

Addresses

Home and office—2914 W. Bijou Street #C, Colorado Springs, CO 80904.

LINDA MARTIN

Career

The Colorado College, Colorado Springs, clerk, 1986-89; Department of Social Services, Colorado Springs, clerk, 1989-1994; freelance illustrator/artist, 1980—. Owner of African doll and art business called "MAKI;" volunteer for the Kennedy Center's "Imagination Celebration" (an annual celebration of the arts.) *Member:* Colorado Springs Art Guild, Art Students League.

Writings

(Illustrator) *Fast Forward USA,* Oxford University Press, 1990.
(And illustrator) *When Dinosaurs Go Visiting,* Chronicle Books, 1993.

Work in Progress

Currently working on other picture books and getting ready for a one-woman show of more serious art pieces.

Sidelights

Linda Martin told *SATA:* "I have never been bored. I am interested in anything and everything and have a zest for trying new things. This has led to my experiencing a variety of jobs, including dance instructor, wallpaper hanger, cement layer, barbed-wire stringer, hotel maid, bill collector, and department store cashier!

"With the added enthusiasm of my ten-year-old son, Alex, there is never a dull moment in our house. I think that being open to so many different things has provided me with enough fodder to write stories and illustrate them for a long, long time. My life's philosophy is simple: ENJOY THE RIDE!"

For More Information See

PERIODICALS

Horn Book Guide, spring, 1994, p. 44.
Publishers Weekly, September 13, 1993, p. 126.
School Library Journal, March, 1994, p. 205.

* * *

McCANTS, William D. 1961-

Personal

Born August 9, 1961, in Long Beach, CA; son of John G. (an adult school principal) and Gwen (an art teacher; maiden name, Parks) McCants; married Anne Elizabeth (an assistant professor of economic history at Massachusetts Institute of Technology; maiden name, Conger), June 30, 1984; children: Thomas Edward. *Education:* University of California at Los Angeles, B.A., 1983; San Francisco State University, teaching credential (English and social studies), 1987; Harvard University, M.A., 1994; *Politics:* "Never." *Hobbies and other interests:* "Sailing, have traveled to forty-two states, speaking to students about writing, stand-up comedy."

Addresses

Office—Green Hall #115, 350 Memorial Dr., Cambridge, MA 02139.

Career

South Gate Middle School, Los Angeles Unified School District, Los Angeles, CA, teacher of history and English, 1987-91; Massachusetts Institute of Technology, Cambridge, associate housemaster, 1992—; Lexington High School, Lexington, MA, psychology instructor, 1993—. *Member:* American Psychological Association, Phi Beta Kappa.

Writings

Anything Can Happen in High School (and It Usually Does), Harcourt, 1993.
Much Ado about Prom Night, Harcourt, 1995.

Sidelights

William D. McCants told *SATA:* "When you are the sixth of eleven children (six girls and five boys), and you and your siblings must make do with four bedrooms, three pets, two bathrooms, and a single phone line, humor is a useful survival tool. On many occasions I escaped moral peril by disarming my parents and/or belligerent siblings with an impromptu stand-up comedy routine.

"My teachers in grade school helped me to channel my slightly skewed world view into my creative writing as

WILLIAM D. McCANTS

well, and by high school I was contributing satirical pieces to a very popular underground newspaper. Later, as a secondary schoolteacher in South-Central Los Angeles, I discovered that laughter helped me reach even the most reluctant learners, and this led me to wonder if I could reach them in print also.

"*Anything Can Happen in High School (and It Usually Does)* came out of this effort. When *School Library Journal* called my first novel 'a tongue-in-cheek, irreverent look at today's teens [and] a fun, hip read' and *Voice of Youth Advocates* praised it for 'sprightly dialogue and plausible plot twists [that] will keep them reading,' I knew I was on the right track.

"I currently teach psychology to high school students in Lexington, Massachusetts. I love how frank, creative, and funny teenagers can be, and I encourage them to write and speak from the heart. Some of their current concerns, like student free speech rights, sex education, and, above all, getting a decent date, inform the plot of my second novel, *Much Ado about Prom Night.*"

■ For More Information See

PERIODICALS

Booklist, October 1, 1993.
Bulletin of the Center for Children's Books, December, 1993, p. 128.
Children's Book Review Service, November, 1993, p. 35.
Kliatt, January, 1994, p. 10.
School Library Journal, October, 1993, p. 152.
Voice of Youth Advocates, December, 1993, p. 296.

* * *

McCOY, Karen Kawamoto 1953-

■ Personal

Born October 2, 1953, in Twin Falls, ID; daughter of George J. (a restaurant owner) and Florence F. (a homemaker; maiden name, Otsuki) Kawamoto; married Edward L. McCoy (a university professor); children: Kevin. *Education:* Oregon State University, B.S., 1978. *Hobbies and other interests:* Reading, drawing, hiking, cross-country skiing.

■ Addresses

Office—2632 Monterey, Wooster, OH 44691. *Agent*—Pema Browne Ltd., Pine Rd., HCR Box 104B, Neversink, NY 12765.

■ Career

Oregon State University Bookstore, Corvallis, sales clerk, 1979-84; Ohio Agricultural and Research Development Center, Wooster, OH, research technician in agronomy department, 1994—. Free-lance writer of children's books and magazine articles, 1984—. *Member:* Society of Children's Book Writers and Illustrators.

KAREN KAWAMOTO McCOY

■ Writings

A Tale of Two Tengu, illustrated by Koen Fossey, Whitman, 1993.

Contributor to *Children's Digest.*

■ Work in Progress

Another picture book that takes place during the author's grandmother's time; research on early Japanese settlers in the United States.

■ Sidelights

Karen Kawamoto McCoy told *SATA:* "As a third-generation Japanese American growing up in Twin Falls, Idaho, I heard many tales of the old country from my grandparents. About three years ago, I began compiling a collection of these folktales. That's where the idea of my first book, *A Tale of Two Tengu,* originated."

■ For More Information See

PERIODICALS

Booklist, January 1, 1994.
Children's Book Review, winter, 1994.

Kirkus Reviews, September 1, 1993, p. 1148.
Publishers Weekly, September 6, 1993, p. 97.
School Library Journal, January, 1994, p. 108.

* * *

McCURDY, Michael (Charles) 1942-

■ Personal

Born February 17, 1942, in New York, NY; son of Charles Errett (an artist) and Beatrice (Beatson) McCurdy; married Deborah Lamb (a social worker), September 7, 1968; children: Heather, Mark. *Education:* Attended School of the Museum of Fine Arts, Boston, 1960-66; Tufts University, B.F.A., 1964, M.F.A., 1971. *Politics:* Democrat. *Religion:* Episcopalian. *Hobbies and other interests:* Playing piano, reading history and biography, hiking.

■ Addresses

Home and office—66 Lake Buel Rd., Great Barrington, MA 01230.

■ Career

Artist and illustrator, 1965—; lecturer. Former director, Penmaen Press, Lincoln and Great Barrington, MA. School of the Museum of Fine Arts, Boston, MA, instructor in drawing, 1966-67; Impressions Workshop, Boston, designer and printer, 1970; Concord Academy, Concord, MA, instructor in printmaking, 1972-75; Wellesley College, Wellesley, MA, instructor in fine printing, 1976. *Exhibitions:* Work shown in one-man exhibitions, "Michael McCurdy and Penmaen Press," Boston Athenaeum, MA, 1976; Berkshire Museum, Pittsfield, MA, February-March, 1988; University of Missouri Library, April, 1988; Simon's Rock of Bard College, MA, November, 1988; Chartwell's Bookstore, New York City, 1990; Wells Gallery, Lenox, MA, 1991; Northfield-Mt. Hermon School, MA, 1991; St. Botolph Club, Boston, 1993. Work also exhibited in group shows. *Member:* Society of Printers (director of publications, 1978), St. Botolph Club (Boston).

■ Awards, Honors

Traveling Scholarship, Museum School, Boston, MA, 1966; Design Award, New England Book Show, 1982, for *World Alone;* Bronze Medal, International Book Show in Leipzig, Germany, 1983; Best Illustrated Children's Books of the Year citation, *New York Times,* 1986, for *The Owl-Scatterer;* Fellow, Simon's Rock of Bard College, Great Barrington, MA, 1987; McCurdy's Penmaen Press has received grants from the National Endowment for the Arts and the Massachusetts Council on the Arts and Humanities.

MICHAEL McCURDY

■ Writings

FOR CHILDREN; SELF-ILLUSTRATED

The Devils Who Learned to Be Good, Joy Street Books, 1987.

Hannah's Farm: The Seasons on an Early American Homestead, Holiday House, 1988.

The Old Man and the Fiddle, Putnam, 1992.

(Editor) Frederick Douglass, *Escape from Slavery: the Boyhood of Frederick Douglass in His Own Words* (nonfiction), Knopf, 1994.

FOR CHILDREN; ILLUSTRATOR

Isaac Asimov, *Please Explain,* Houghton, 1973.

Linda Grant De Pauw, *Founding Mothers: Women in America in the Revolutionary Era* (nonfiction), Houghton, 1975.

B. A. King, *The Very Best Christmas Tree,* Godine, 1984.

Howard Norman, *The Owl-Scatterer,* Atlantic Monthly Press, 1986.

King, *The Christmas Junk Box,* Godine, 1987.

Norman, reteller, *How Glooskap Outwits the Ice Giants and Other Tales of the Maritime Indians,* Little, Brown, 1989.

Louisa May Alcott, *An Old-Fashioned Thanksgiving,* Holiday House, 1989.

Mary Pope Osborne, *American Tall Tales,* Knopf, 1991.

X. J. Kennedy, *The Beasts of Bethlehem* (poems), McElderry Books, 1992.

Diana Appelbaum, *Giants in the Land* (nonfiction), Houghton, 1993.

Lillian Schlissel, *The Way West: Based on Diaries of Mrs. Amelia Stewart Knight* (adaptation), Simon & Schuster, 1993.
Donald Hall, *Lucy's Christmas,* Harcourt, 1994.
Hall, *Lucy's Summer,* Harcourt, 1995.
Neil Philip, editor, *Singing America,* Viking, 1995.
Abraham Lincoln, *The Gettysburg Address,* Houghton, 1995.

FOR ADULTS; SELF-ILLUSTRATED

(With George Selleck) *Dove at the Windows: Last Letters of Four Quaker Martyrs,* Penmaen Press, 1973.
(Compiler and editor with Michael Peich) *The First Ten: A Penmaen Press Bibliography,* Penmaen Press, 1978.
Toward the Light: Wood Engravings by Michael McCurdy, Porcupine's Quill, 1982.
The Illustrated Harvard: Harvard University in Wood Engravings and Words, Globe Pequot, 1986.
McCurdy's World: Prints and Drawings by Michael McCurdy, Capra Press, 1992.

FOR ADULTS; ILLUSTRATOR

The Brick Moon, Imprint Society, 1971.
Amauskeeg Falls, Barre, 1971.
This Quiet Place, Little, Brown, 1971.
Narrative of Alvar Nunez Cabeza de Vaca, Imprint Society, 1972.
Madam Knight, Godine, 1972.
William Ferguson, *Light of Paradise* (poetry), Penmaen Press, 1973.
Kennedy, *Celebrations after the Death of John Brennan* (poetry), Penmaen Press, 1974.
Richard Eberhart, *Poems to Poets,* Penmaen Press, 1975.
Pardee Lowe Jr., translator, *King Harald and the Icelanders,* Penmaen Press, 1979.
John Gilgun, *Everything That Has Been Shall Be Again: The Reincarnation Fables of John Gilgun,* Bieler, 1981.
Kennedy, editor, *Tygers of Wrath: Poems of Hate, Anger, and Invective,* University of Georgia Press, 1981.
Vicente Aleixandre, *Mundo a solas/World Alone* (bilingual edition), translations by Lewis Hyde and David Unger, Penmaen Press, 1982.
Margaret Atwood, *Encounters with the Element Man,* W. B. Ewert, 1982.
Philip Dacey, *Gerard Manley Hopkins Meets Walt Whitman in Heaven and Other Poems,* Penmaen Press, 1982.
May Sarton, *A Winter Garland: New Poems,* W. B. Ewert, 1982.
Susan Efird, *The Eye of Heaven: A Narrative Poem,* Abattoir Editions, University of Nebraska at Omaha, 1982.
William Edgar Stafford, *Listening Deep: Poems,* Penmaen Press, 1984.
Weldon Kees, *Two Prose Sketches,* Aralia Press, 1984.
Chet Raymo, *The Soul of the Night: An Astronomical Pilgrimage,* Prentice-Hall, 1985.
Jean Giono, *The Man Who Planted Trees,* Chelsea Green Publishing, 1985.
Henry David Thoreau, *The Winged Life: The Poetic Voice of Henry David Thoreau,* edited with commentaries by Robert Bly, Yolla Bolly Press, 1986.
Mary W. Freeman, *The Revolt of Mother,* Redpath Press, 1987.
Eva A. Wilbur-Cruce, *A Beautiful, Cruel Country,* University of Arizona Press, 1987.
Somerset Maugham, *The Three Fat Women of Antibes,* Redpath Press, 1987.
Charles Dickens, *A Christmas Carol: Bah! Humbug!,* Redpath Press, 1987.
John Muir, *My First Summer in the Sierra,* Yolla Bolly Press, 1988.
Muir, *The Yosemite,* Sierra Books, 1988.
Muir, *Travels in Alaska,* Sierra Books, 1988.
Scott Hastings, *Goodbye Highland Yankee,* Chelsea Green Publishing, 1988.
Villy Sorenson, *Downfall of the Gods,* University of Nebraska Press, 1988.
Richard Nunley, editor, *The Berkshire Reader: Writings from New England's Secluded Paradise,* Berkshire House, 1992.
David Mamet, *American Buffalo,* Arion Press, 1992.
Edward Abbey, *Earth Apples,* St. Martin's, 1994.

OTHER

Designer of jacket and cover art for various book publishers and magazines; designed poster for 1988

In this adaptation of a Russian folktale, an old soldier outwits and eventually tames a passel of devils. (Cover illustration by the author.)

production of David Mamet's Broadway play, *Speed the Plow.* Commissions include a print for the Lincoln Conservation Commission, Lincoln, MA; a print for the Art Society of the Cleveland Museum of Natural History, Cleveland, OH; and presentation prints for the Albany and Rochester (NY) Print Clubs.

■ Work in Progress

Illustrations for Ann Whitford Paul's *The Seasons Sewn: A Year in Patchwork,* for Harcourt, 1996, editor Neil Philip's *American Fairy Tales,* for Hyperion, 1996, and David Mamet's *Passover,* for St. Martin's.

■ Sidelights

During a time when mass production dominates the publishing industry, Michael McCurdy's efforts to preserve the art of engraving and to hand-craft books have provided book lovers with numerous treasures. While his woodcuts have enhanced the beauty of books published by major companies, McCurdy's small press, Penmaen Books, has produced exquisitely illustrated and bound editions of contemporary works. From writing the text and engraving the illustrations to setting type and binding, Michael McCurdy once told *SATA,* his "preoccupation is with the entire book."

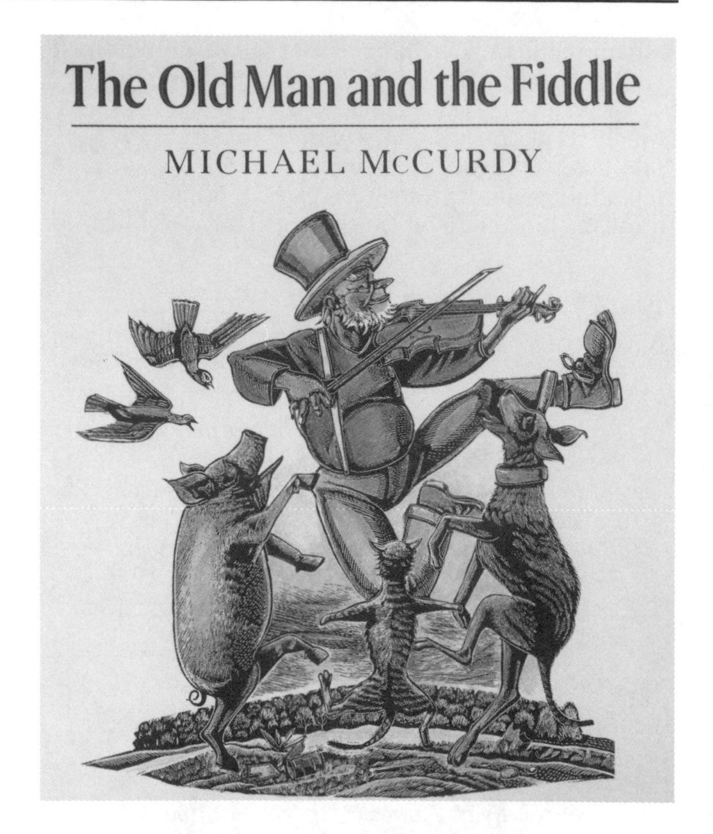

McCurdy's own woodcuts distinguish this tale of a selfish old man whose violin-playing leads him into trouble.

McCurdy, whose grandmother and father were artists, first became interested in wood engraving as a student at the School of the Museum of Fine Arts in Boston. The artist explained his attraction to wood engraving in a 1982 introduction to a collection of his work, *Toward the Light: Wood Engravings by Michael McCurdy,* "The wood engraving is an honest medium. It's straightforward and there is no room for error, no room for cover-up. A cut is made, and it stays.... I've always had a feeling that this is another reason wood engraving is not enormously popular as a technique among artists. It can't hide one's weaker moments." In an *American Artist* article that discusses the origin's of McCurdy's work, Eunice Agar notes that McCurdy laid the groundwork for his career as a student in the Boston area. He crafted his first book (a copy of the Book of Genesis) during that time. Also, as a student of X. J. Kennedy at Tufts, McCurdy realized his interest in contemporary literature. After working as an art instructor at the Concord Academy and Wellesley College, he began to devote himself full-time to engraving, bookmaking, and his press. As Agar writes, McCurdy "took the name for his press from Gerard Manley Hopkins's poem, 'Penmaen Pool.' Penmaen is a town in Wales and also the Welsh word for land's end."

While McCurdy did not publish books specifically for children at Penmaen, the quality of Penmaen work characterizes his fiction and nonfiction children's books published by other companies. One example is *Founding Mothers: Women in America in the Revolutionary Era.* Written by Linda Grant De Pauw with wood engravings by McCurdy, this work, according to a reviewer for *Horn Book,* "stands as a prototype of what can be done to make nonfiction appealing." The text, which tells of the lives of the women of the 1776 Revolution generation, is enhanced by McCurdy's engravings, which are "expertly drafted" and "stand as introduction to the bold, heavy typeface."

The Devils Who Learned to Be Good exemplifies McCurdy's work as a writer and illustrator of children's fiction. McCurdy, who traveled to Russia in 1969, based *The Devils Who Learned to Be Good* on a traditional Russian story. After serving in the army for thirty-five years, an old soldier returns home with nothing but two loaves of bread. He gives one loaf to a beggar, who rewards him with a magic set of playing cards that never let its owner lose a game, and he offers the second to another beggar, who gives the soldier a flour sack that will envelope anything the bearer wishes to control. The soldier uses his magic objects to roust devils from the tsar's palace; they play cards with the soldier, lose all their pilfered gold and silver to him, learn to be good, and practice community service throughout the countryside (despite some occasional lapses into deviltry). *New York Times Book Review* contributor Barbara Thompson praises McCurdy's "witty retelling" and "striking" engravings, which a *Publishers Weekly* critic notes "capture the somber intensity of the countryside." "With its lively pace and ingenious central character and an ending as logical as it is unexpected," Mary M. Burns concludes in *Horn Book,* "the book will become a staple in the storyteller's repertoire."

Describing another example of McCurdy's fiction for children, *The Old Man and the Fiddle, School Library Journal* critic Patricia Dooley writes that McCurdy's illustrations are "subtly colored," "stylishly homespun," and "superb." In this tale, an old fiddler annoys his neighbors with his music and refuses to make repairs on his crumbling house. The neighbors try to persuade the old man to stop playing the fiddle and tend to his home. The fiddler doesn't listen and keeps on playing until a flood carries him away. As one critic notes in *Kirkus Reviews,* on the final page the fiddler is shown "fiddling from 'beyond the next hill' (apparently the next life)." A *Publishers Weekly* reviewer concludes that while the "artwork ... shines more brightly than the story, the overall spirit never flags."

While McCurdy no longer works as a publisher, he continues to live in Great Barrington, Massachusetts, where he writes, designs, and illustrates books for children and adults alike.

■ Works Cited

Agar, Eunice, "Michael McCurdy's Penmaen Press," *American Artist,* August, 1984, pp. 42-46, 86-87.

Burns, Mary M., review of *The Devils Who Learned to Be Good, Horn Book,* January/February, 1988, p. 77.

Review of *The Devils Who Learned to Be Good, Publishers Weekly,* November 13, 1987, p. 70.

Dooley, Patricia, review of *The Old Man and the Fiddle, School Library Journal,* August, 1992, p. 143.

Review of *Founding Mothers: Women in America in the Revolutionary Era, Horn Book,* February, 1976.

McCurdy, Michael, *Toward the Light: Wood Engravings by Michael McCurdy,* Porcupine's Quill, 1982.

Review of *The Old Man and the Fiddle, Publishers Weekly,* June 8, 1992, p. 62.

Review of *The Old Man and the Fiddle, Kirkus Reviews,* June 15, 1992, p. 781.

Thompson, Barbara, review of *The Devils Who Learned to Be Good, New York Times Book Review,* December 13, 1987, p. 37.

■ For More Information See

PERIODICALS

Booklist, November 15, 1987, p. 570; November 15, 1988, p. 581.

Bulletin of the Center for Children's Books, January, 1988, p. 96.

New York Times Book Review, November 9, 1986; February 26, 1989, p. 22.

School Library Journal, January, 1988, p. 73; February, 1989, p. 74.

McGREGOR, Barbara 1959-

■ Personal

Born July 14, 1959, in Elizabeth, NJ; daughter of Edward N. and Mary C. McGregor. *Education:* Attended Union College, 1977-78; Kean College, B.A., 1982. *Religion:* Catholic. *Hobbies and other interests:* Illustrating cards, painting on objects, swimming.

■ Addresses

Home and office—413 West Sixth Ave., Roselle, NJ 07203.

■ Career

Illustrator, 1985—.

■ Illustrator

Lisa Westberg Peters, *Purple Delicious Blackberry Jam,* Arcade Publishing, 1992.

Robin Gorman Newman, *How to Meet a Mensch in New York,* City & Co., 1994.

■ Work in Progress

Illustrations for various magazines.

■ Sidelights

Barbara McGregor told *SATA:* "I have been drawing non-stop ever since I can remember. My mother used to bring home stacks of used paper from the office for my four sisters and I to draw on.

"After receiving a B.A. in Art Education, I became a fashion illustrator in New York City. I moved on to editorial and children's illustration because I wanted to put my ideas into the drawings. I can't imagine ever doing anything else."

* * *

MERRILL, Jean (Fairbanks) 1923-

■ Personal

Born January 27, 1923, in Rochester, NY; daughter of Earl Dwight and Elsie Almetta (Fairbanks) Merrill. *Education:* Allegheny College, B.A., 1944; Wellesley College, M.A., 1945. *Politics:* Independent. *Hobbies and other interests:* Reading, art, theater, mycology (the study of fungi).

■ Addresses

Home—Angel's Ark, 29 South Main St., Randolph, VT 05060; and Box 212B, R.R., Chelsea, VT 05038 (summer). *Agent*—Dorothy Markinko, McIntosh & Otis, 310 Madison Ave., New York, NY 10017.

JEAN MERRILL

Career

Scholastic Magazines, Inc., New York City, assistant feature editor, 1945-46, feature editor, 1946-49, associate editor of *Literary Cavalcade,* 1950-51, editor, 1956-57; Bank Street College of Education, Publications Division, New York City, associate editor, 1965-66, consultant, 1967-71; writer for young people. Faculty member of workshops for librarians at Drake University, 1969, and in Hutchinson, KS, 1969. *Member:* Authors Guild, Authors League of America, Society of Children's Book Writers and Illustrators, American Civil Liberties Union, War Resisters League, North American Mycological Association, Nature Conservancy, Fulbright Association, League of Vermont Writers, Vermont Council on the Arts, Vermont Institute of Natural Science, Vermont Natural Resources Council, Phi Beta Kappa.

Awards, Honors

Outstanding Alumni Achievement Award, Allegheny College, 1944; Fulbright research grant, University of Madras, 1952-53; Fund for the Republic Award, 1956, for one-hour television drama, *The Claws in the Cat's Paw;* Lewis Carroll Shelf Award, 1963, for *The Superlative Horse,* and 1965, for *The Pushcart War;* Boys' Clubs of America Award, 1965, for *The Pushcart War;* Dorothy Canfield Fisher Memorial Children's Book Award, 1975-76, and Sequoyah Award, 1977, both for *The Toothpaste Millionaire.* Several of Merrill's books have been Junior Literary Guild selections.

Writings

FOR CHILDREN; ILLUSTRATED BY RONNI SOLBERT

Henry, the Hand-Painted Mouse, Coward, 1951.
The Woover, Coward, 1952.
Boxes, Coward, 1953.
The Tree House of Jimmy Domino, Walck, 1955.
The Travels of Marco, Knopf, 1955.
A Song for Gar, Whittlesey House, 1955.
The Very Nice Things, Harper, 1959.
Blue's Broken Heart, Whittlesey House, 1960.
Emily Emerson's Moon (verse), Little, Brown, 1960.
Shan's Lucky Knife: A Burmese Folk Tale, W. R. Scott, 1960.
The Superlative Horse: A Tale of Ancient China, W. R. Scott, 1961.
High, Wide & Handsome and Their Three Tall Tales, W. R. Scott, 1964.
The Pushcart War, W. R. Scott, 1964.
The Elephant Who Liked to Smash Small Cars, Pantheon, 1967.
Red Riding, Pantheon, 1967.
The Black Sheep, Pantheon, 1969.
Mary, Come Running, McCall Publishing, 1970.

OTHER

Tell about the Cowbarn, Daddy, illustrated by Lili Wronker, W. R. Scott, 1963.
(Editor with Solbert and author of introduction) Issa Kobayashi, *A Few Flies and I,* translated by R. H. Blyth and Nobuyuki Yuasa, Pantheon, 1969.
Here I Come—Ready Or Not!, illustrated by Frances Scott, A. Whitman, 1970.
How Many Kids Are Hiding on My Block?, illustrated by Scott, A. Whitman, 1971.
Please, Don't Eat My Cabin, illustrated by Scott, A. Whitman, 1971.
The Second Greatest Clown in the World, Houghton, 1971.
The Jackpot, Houghton, 1971.
(Contributor) *Isn't That What Friends Are For?,* (includes one-act play "Tightrope Act"), edited by Bank Street College of Education, Houghton, 1972.
The Toothpaste Millionaire, illustrated by Jan Palmer, Houghton, 1972.
The Bumper Sticker Book, illustrated by Scott, A. Whitman, 1973.
Maria's House, illustrated by Scott, Atheneum, 1976.
(Adapter) *The Girl Who Loved Caterpillars: A Twelfth-Century Tale from Japan,* illustrated by Floyd Cooper, Philomel, 1992.

Also author of television drama, *The Claws in the Cat's Paw,* 1956. Associate editor and contributor, "Bank Street Readers" series, Macmillan, 1964-65; contributor to "Adult Reader" series, R & D Corporation, 1968, and to anthologies in the "Discoveries" series, Houghton, 1973. Contributor of short stories, articles, and reviews to various publications.

Adaptations

The Toothpaste Millionaire aired as an ABC-TV *Afternoon Special* in 1974; *The Superlative Horse* aired on the NBC-TV series *Vegetable Soup* and is available as a film from Phoenix Films. *A Song for Gar* was performed as a children's opera in San Diego, CA, 1970, and was adapted by William J. Adams for Readers Theatre; *Mary, Come Running* provided the libretto for a chamber opera by Gwyneth Walker which was first produced in Randolph, VT, 1983. *The Pushcart War* has been broadcast on radio in New York, Boston, MA, and Denmark, and on television in England; stage versions have been performed in Boston, 1978, and Seattle, WA, 1981; a script adaptation by Gregory A. Falls is available from Anchorage Press. *The Elephant Who Liked to Smash Small Cars* aired on the radio in 1971. Recordings of *The Travels of Marco, Red Riding,* and *The Elephant Who Liked to Smash Small Cars* have been produced by Random House. *Mary, Come Running* is available as a "talking book," while *The Pushcart War* and *The Toothpaste Millionaire* are available as "talking books" and in Braille.

Sidelights

"Jean Merrill has earned her solid reputation as a children's writer by the consistently fine quality of her books," Betty Boegehold comments in *Twentieth-Century Children's Writers.* The author is best known for her 1964 book *The Pushcart War,* which tells the story of how the drivers of little pushcarts withstand the bullying attacks of powerful truckers and keep their space on city streets. This "struggle of the small and weak against the strong and mighty" is typical of Merrill's work, according to Boegehold, and is enhanced by the author's mastery of "the subtle art of 'immediacy'—the reader is there and the adventure is happening to him or her."

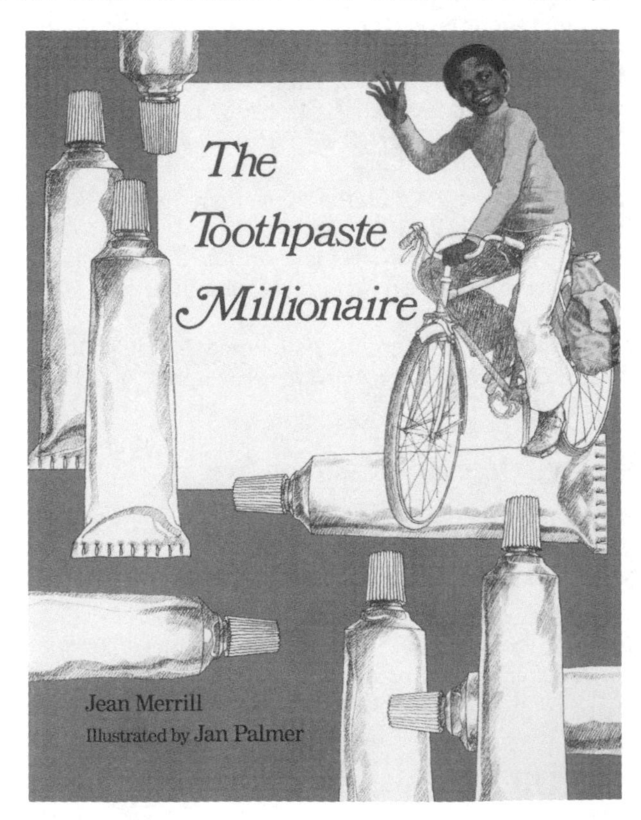

Rufus Mayflower sets out to make toothpaste at a reasonable price, becoming a millionaire—and teaching readers about business and math—in the process. (Cover illustration by Jan Palmer.)

Merrill's verse story *Emily Emerson's Moon,* for instance, has "wholly natural" relationships "that give the book ... special charm," a *Horn Book* reviewer comments. In addition, the story "is intriguingly told with ... catchy rhyme and rhythm," Joan Beck writes in the *Chicago Sunday Tribune. Maria's House,* the story of a poor girl who feels ashamed to draw her home for art class, similarly demonstrates how the author "has a rare gift for creating real characters and letting them develop," David K. Willis says in the *Christian Science Monitor.* The book "ends as the triumph of honesty over deceit, of love over selfishness," and is "so good, so universal in theme, that [it appeals] to the best in all of us."

Merrill's books also contain moral and informative elements in addition to realistic characters. *The Toothpaste Millionaire,* which relates how young Rufus Mayflower creates a big business from his homemade toothpaste, explains such business terms as cost and profit. But these concepts are "tucked so expertly and unobtrusively into the story that they only heighten the reader's enjoyment," Jennifer Farley Smith remarks in the *Christian Science Monitor. The Black Sheep* similarly brings a delicate touch to the tale of how a maverick sheep teaches his herd to accept individuals and their differences. According to Natalie Babbitt in a *New York Times Book Review* article, Merrill's story is "a satisfying sandwich in which the peanut butter, sticky and nourishing, slides down with ease due to a judicious use of jelly."

But it is *The Pushcart War,* with its spirited band of cart owners battling big-business truckers, that is "often considered a modern classic," as E. Wendy Saul comments in *School Library Journal.* Presented in the form of a scholarly study, *The Pushcart War* is "one of those rarities—a book that is both humorous and downright funny," a *Horn Book* reviewer states. The war for street space escalates as truckers run over pushcarts and cart owners puncture truck tires. "It's a delightful notion, and an utterly captivating book," Alberta Eiseman writes in the *New York Times Book Review.* The critic adds, "It's rare indeed to find a book for young people with both a point of view and a sense of the ridiculous." "This semi-recognized classic is one of the funniest and most satisfying triumphs of small-and-clever I know," *Washington Post Book World* contributor Noel Perrin claims. "It can be read in [many] different ways, and they are all funny."

"I grew up on an apple and dairy farm on the shores of Lake Ontario in Webster, New York," Merrill once commented, "and most of my waking hours, when I was not in school, were spent out-of-doors: building huts,

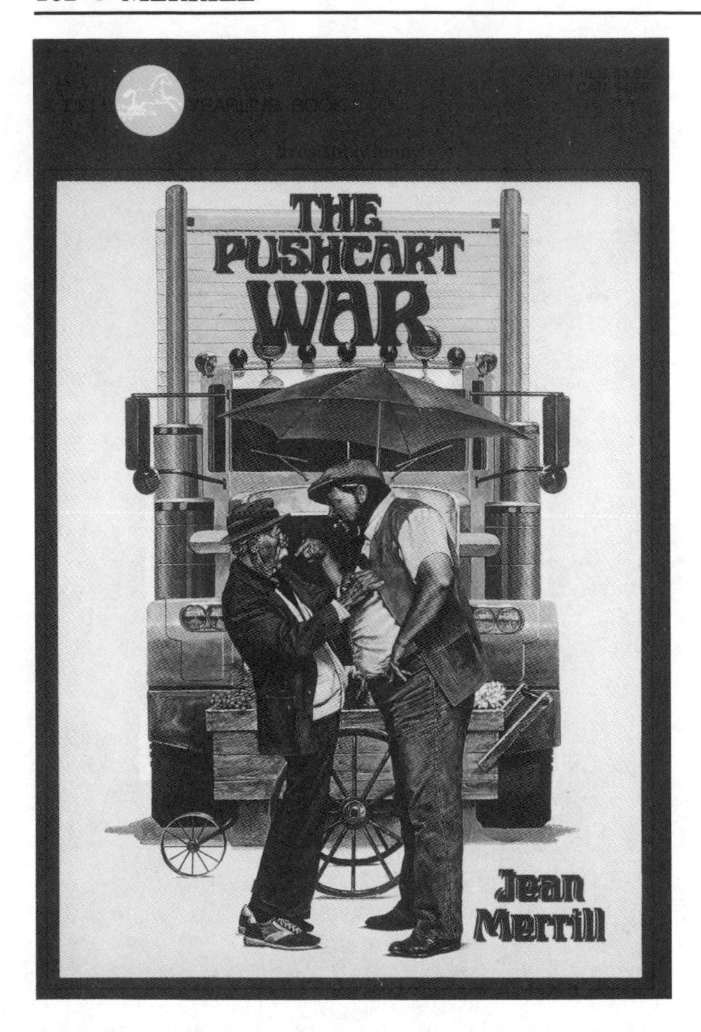

The ages-old conflict between big and little is hilariously portrayed in Merrill's classic tale of street warfare in New York City. (Cover illustration by Carl Cassler.)

dams, rafts, forts, making barrel-stave skis, inner-tube guns, roller-skate scooters, bows and arrows, collecting wild flowers and fossil rocks, swimming, tobogganing, climbing silos, riding hay wagons, tumbling in haylofts.

"Dolls, toys and games that came in boxes to be played on boards with set rules bored me swiftly. The only thing that could detain me indoors was a book—though a book could also be carried up into a tree, out to a meadow, down by the lakeside."

A child with similarly unconventional interests enlivens Merrill's 1992 adaptation *The Girl Who Loved Caterpillars.* Taken from a fragment of an ancient Japanese tale, Merrill's story follows the life of Izumi, a privileged inspector's daughter who spends more time outdoors studying nature than she does in acquiring the "womanly" arts that might gain her a place at court. Instead of making up her face to fit the latest fashion and learning poetry and musical instruments, Izumi plays with the common boys who bring her the caterpillars she loves to examine. The story ends as a young nobleman who has been courting Izumi concludes he cannot live in her world. "The retelling of this curious fragment is graceful and competent," Kate McClelland observes in *School Library Journal,* while a *Kirkus Reviews* critic calls Merrill's work "dignified and energetic, with touches of humor." *Booklist* contributor Ilene Cooper praises the author's portrayal of "a strong girl with ideas of her own," concluding that it is "a timeless story."

Merrill remarked to *SATA,* "My interest in writing children's books may have derived from the great impact certain books had on me as a child, and perhaps a wish to recreate the quality of that experience. Certainly, one of the satisfactions of writing for children is the intensity of caring young readers lavish on the books they like."

■ Works Cited

Babbitt, Natalie, review of *The Black Sheep, New York Times Book Review,* October 26, 1969, p. 42.

Beck, Joan, review of *Emily Emerson's Moon, Chicago Sunday Tribune,* November 6, 1960, p. 12.

Boegehold, Betty, *Twentieth-Century Children's Writers,* 3rd edition, St. James Press, 1989, pp. 677-79.

Cooper, Ilene, review of *The Girl Who Loved Caterpillars, Booklist,* September 1, 1992, p. 54.

Eiseman, Alberta, review of *The Pushcart War, New York Times Book Review,* July 12, 1964, p. 18.

Review of *Emily Emerson's Moon, Horn Book,* October, 1960, p. 399.

Review of *The Girl Who Loved Caterpillars, Kirkus Reviews,* September 15, 1992, p. 1191.

McClelland, Kate, review of *The Girl Who Loved Caterpillars, School Library Journal,* September, 1992.

Perrin, Noel, "The Harder They Fall," *Washington Post Book World,* January 14, 1990, p. 11.

Review of *The Pushcart War, Horn Book,* August, 1964, p. 378.

Saul, E. Wendy, "We Gather Together," *School Library Journal,* April, 1983, p. 30.

Smith, Jennifer Farley, review of *The Toothpaste Millionaire, Christian Science Monitor,* July 3, 1974, p. 7.

Willis, David K., "Reviewer's Choice: Maria's House," *Christian Science Monitor,* November 6, 1974, p. 11.

■ For More Information See

PERIODICALS

Bulletin of the Center for Children's Books, November, 1992, p. 82.

New Yorker, November 23, 1992, p. 79.

Saturday Review, November 7, 1964; January 24, 1970.

Times Literary Supplement, November 23, 1973.

* * *

MICHEL, Francois 1948-

■ Personal

Born May 7, 1948; son of Bertrand (a professor) and Marie-Therese Michel; married Francoise Moreau, September 4, 1969; children: Nicolas, Thomas, Marie, Clement. *Education:* Universite d'Orsay, received degree in geology. *Religion:* Catholic.

Addresses

Home—26 rue Marie-laure, 92160 Antony, France. *Agent*—c/o Bayard Editions, 22 cours Albert 1er, 75008 Paris, France.

Career

Secondary school teacher in Antony, France, 1968—.

Writings

FOR CHILDREN; IN ENGLISH TRANSLATION

(With Yves Larvor) *The Restless Earth: Secrets of Earthquakes, Volcanoes, and Continental Drift in Three-Dimensional Moving Pictures* (pop-up book), Penguin, 1990 (originally published as *La terre qui bouge,* Bayard, 1989).

Water (pop-up book), illustrated by Larvor, Lothrop, 1993 (originally published as *L'eau,* 1991).

IN FRENCH

Roches et paysages, BRGM, 1986.
Dans le secret des roches, Bayard, 1989.
Les cotes de France, BRGM, 1991.

For More Information See

PERIODICALS

Bulletin of the Center for Children's Books, June, 1993, p. 324.
Publishers Weekly, May 3, 1993, p. 311.
School Library Journal, January, 1991, p. 104; April, 1993, p. 137.
Washington Post Book World, May 9, 1993.

* * *

MICUCCI, Charles (Patrick, Jr.) 1959-

Personal

Surname is pronounced "Mee-*koo*-chee"; born October 25, 1959, in Camp Lejeune, NC; son of Charles P. (in U.S. Marine Corps) and Jeanne (a secretary; maiden name, Findley) Micucci. *Education:* Attended Northern Illinois University, New York University, and School for the Visual Arts.

Addresses

c/o Orchard Books, 95 Madison Ave., New York, NY 10016.

Career

Writer and illustrator.

Writings

SELF-ILLUSTRATED

A Little Night Music, Morrow, 1989.
The Life and Times of the Apple, Orchard Books, 1992.
The Cabbie Who Stole New York City, Bantam, 1992.
The Life and Times of the Honeybee, Ticknor & Fields, 1995.

ILLUSTRATOR

Alfred Tennyson, *The Brook,* Orchard Books, 1994.

Sidelights

Charles Micucci's first book for children, *A Little Night Music,* describes the adventures of a musical house cat whose nocturnal violin playing stirs several other animals—a trio of mice, a pair of cardinals, and the family dog—into a joyous frenzy of dancing. Patricia Pearl commented in *School Library Journal,* "The text is simple and poetic as it tells of paws tapping, singing, twirling, whisking, and prancing ... with grace and energy." A *Publishers Weekly* reviewer described Micucci's watercolor illustrations as "warmly lyrical."

Micucci followed *A Little Night Music* with *The Life and Times of the Apple,* a picture book which examines the growth cycle, uses, varieties, and history of the popular fruit. As part of his research for the book, the author planted twenty-three apple seeds and kept them in his apartment; two were eventually transplanted successfully in New York City's Central Park. Critical response to *The Life and Times of the Apple* was positive. A contributor to *Kirkus Reviews* remarked that "Micucci's lucid text flows logically from one topic to another," and in *Horn Book,* Carolyn K. Jenks asserted that the

In this self-illustrated work, Charles Micucci presents information about the life, cultivation, and folklore behind a favorite fruit.

"watercolor-and-pencil illustrations are simple and clear, providing superb information."

■ Works Cited

Jenks, Carolyn K., review of *The Life and Times of the Apple, Horn Book,* May/June, 1992, pp. 356-57.
Review of *The Life and Times of the Apple, Kirkus Reviews,* January 15, 1992, p. 118.
Review of *A Little Night Music, Publishers Weekly,* March 10, 1989, p. 88.
Pearl, Patricia, review of *A Little Night Music, School Library Journal,* July, 1989, p. 73.

■ For More Information See

PERIODICALS

Publishers Weekly, January 13, 1992, p. 57.
School Library Journal, March, 1992, p. 232; April, 1995, p. 126.

* * *

MORI, Kyoko 1957-

■ Personal

Born March 9, 1957, in Kobe, Japan; emigrated to the United States, 1977; naturalized U.S. citizen, 1984; daughter of Hiroshi (an engineer) and Takako (a homemaker; maiden name, Nagai) Mori; married Charles Brock (an elementary school teacher), March 17, 1984. *Education:* Rockford College, B.A., 1979; University of Wisconsin—Milwaukee, M.A., 1981, Ph.D., 1984. *Politics:* Democrat, feminist. *Hobbies and other interests:* Fiber arts (knitting, spinning, weaving), running, bird-watching.

■ Addresses

Office—106-A South Broadway, De Pere, WI 54115. *Agent*—Ann Rittenberg, 14 Montgomery Pl., Brooklyn, NY 11215.

■ Career

Saint Norbert College, De Pere, WI, associate professor of English and writer in residence, 1985—; writer. *Member:* Modern Language Association of America, Associated Writing Programs.

■ Awards, Honors

Editors' Prize, *Missouri Review,* 1992, for the poem "Fallout"; American Library Association Best Book for Young Adults, *New York Times* Notable Book, *Publishers Weekly* Editors' Choice, Council of Wisconsin Writers Best Novel, and Elizabeth Burr award for best children's book of the year from the Wisconsin Library Association, all 1993, all for *Shizuko's Daughter.*

KYOKO MORI

■ Writings

Shizuko's Daughter (young adult novel), Holt, 1993.
Fallout (poems), Tia Chucha Press, 1994.
The Dream of Water: A Memoir (adult nonfiction), Holt, 1995.
One Bird, Holt, 1995.

Also contributor of short stories, many of which were revised for use in *Shizuko's Daughter,* to *Maryland Review, South-East Review, Crosscurrents, Prairie Schooner, Kenyon Review—New Series,* and *Apalachee Quarterly.*

■ Work in Progress

A collection of poems.

■ Sidelights

Like the Polish novelist, Joseph Conrad, or the Czech-born playwright, Tom Stoppard, Kyoko Mori mastered the English language as a teen and writes in it with a depth and feeling few native speakers ever achieve. Her first novel, *Shizuko's Daughter,* was a distillation of years of experience and revision, and when it was finally published in 1993 it won critical praise, literary awards, and a wide readership with both teens and adult readers. Liz Rosenberg, writing in the *New York Times Book Review,* called *Shizuko's Daughter* a "jewel of a book. One of those rarities that shine out only a few times in a generation."

Despite the praise, Mori—a creative writing teacher at the University of Wisconsin—is typically understated about her success. "I never set out to write a young adult novel," she told *SATA* in an interview. "I don't write with a specific audience in mind. Mostly, I write the stories and poems I want to tell and hear." Mori began the novel with a short story, which became the book's epilogue. "The stories were part of my dissertation," she told *SATA.* As such, Mori instilled them with her own personal aesthetic: "What I like to do in writing is to get to the edge of saying it all and then hold back. I like to let the images speak and to be understated." It is precisely this understatement in a book about a mother's suicide and how her daughter copes with it that sets Mori's writing apart.

Born in Kobe, Japan, Mori grew up in a secure middle-class family, living mostly in the suburbs, with mountains and woods in sight. "Kobe is a very beautiful, sophisticated city," Mori told *SATA,* "but it is also close to nature. You can get to walking paths within twenty minutes." But there was little walking for Mori at first. Born with both hips displaced, she spent the first year and a half of life in leg harnesses to correct the dislocation. "There was a story in my family that I learned to talk before I walked. I guess I still like to talk," she joked. She and her younger brother and mother would spend summers with her maternal grandparents in the country, and it was her grandfather, a former teacher, who made her first understand the discipline of writing. "He would write in a journal every day," Mori recalled. "And even if we kids were pestering him for a walk, he would say that he had to finish the journal entry first."

Writing and reading were also important activities at home. Mori's mother, an amateur artist and needlepoint worker, instilled a love of books in both her children. "Before I could even write," Mori told *SATA,* "my mother bought a science notebook—it had lines in the bottom half and the top half was blank. My mother and I eventually filled several of these notebooks with our stories. After I learned enough symbols and characters in school, I would write down the stories and she would draw the pictures. They were mostly adventure stories, about girls going to faraway, magical places with their cats or dolls and coming back victorious and rich." Not much of a television watcher, Mori focussed on reading instead: the traditional sampling of international fairy tales as well as Japanese folk tales. "I especially liked Bible stories we would get at Sunday school," she said. "What I recall is not so much the lesson of the parables, but the flannel board and stick-on characters used to tell the stories as well as the emotions evoked in the story. How hungry that person must have been, or whatever. I continue to be fascinated by the irrelevant."

But Mori's youth was not only a bookish one. Her disability at birth did not keep her from becoming a successful athlete, both in track and volleyball. "But I never really liked my early schooling," she recalled. "I was rebellious, always having to stand in the back of class as punishment." It was the relationship between mother and daughter that was special for Mori. "She would let me stay home from school," Mori told *SATA,* "and we would go to exhibitions and look at the paintings together. My father and I were never close—he was distant and had a bad temper. But my mother and I were real friends."

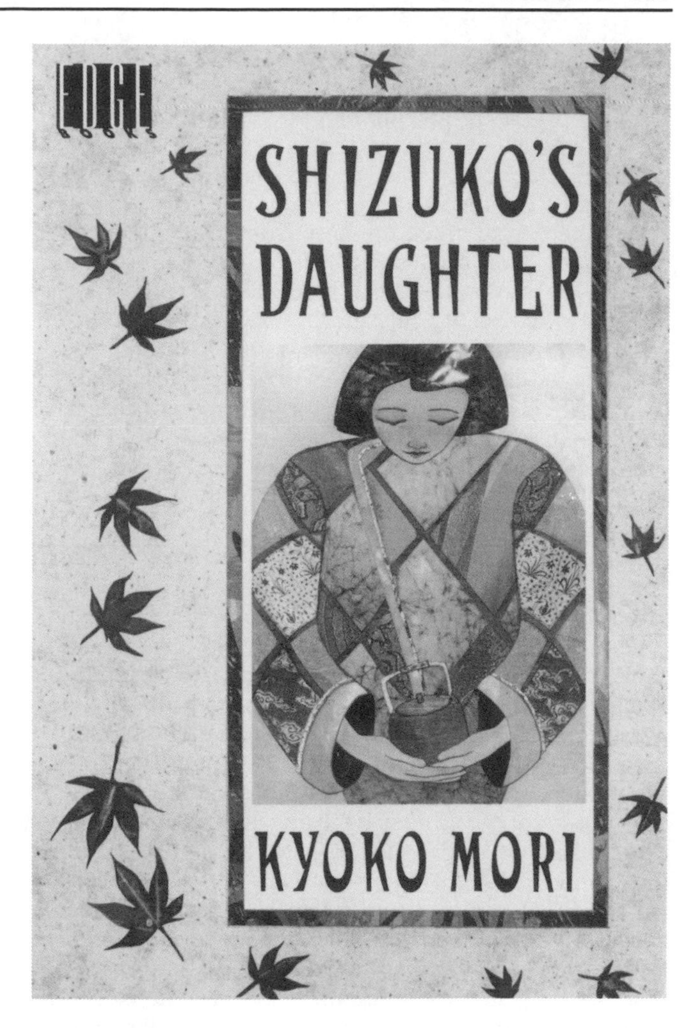

In her first novel, Mori tells the story of a lonely Japanese girl determined to grow up happy and strong in memory of the mother she lost. (Cover illustration by Mary Jo Mazzella.)

Mori's world was turned upside down with the suicide of her mother in 1969. "I guess I blamed everybody for her death, for not seeing the emotional pain she was in. I blamed my father and myself especially." It is this real-life suicide which forms the core of Mori's novel, *Shizuko's Daughter.* While that book minutely examines the aftermath of the tragedy from several points of view over a seven-year period, Mori's personal reaction was to get on with her life as well as possible. "I began to like school after my mother's death. I changed schools, from a public one to a private, and I felt more freedom and appreciation from teachers and students. Also, I wasn't too eager to be at home anymore. My father remarried, and my stepmother and I did not get along."

Mori not only excelled in athletics throughout junior high and high school, but she also did well in writing.

She began her own tentative poems and began writing stories, "sorts of warped fairy tales," as she described them to *SATA.* In her junior year of high school, Mori travelled to Mesa, Arizona, as an exchange student. "It was a revelation for me. For the first time in my life I was away from the social constrictions of my society. In Japan there is so much pressure from family. You can't do this or that because it will bring shame to your family. In Arizona I felt real freedom. But I also saw that the myth of equality in America is exactly that. There were lots of Mormons in my school in Mesa, and I saw that they were restricted, too. They couldn't smoke, drink coffee, or go out with non-Mormons because of their religion. But still I began to see that in many important ways life in America was more open than in Japan."

Returning to Japan, Mori decided to focus on English as a major. Finishing high school, she went on to two years of college. "I knew I wanted to write by then," she told *SATA.* "After my year in the United States, I began to think of English as my writing language. So much of Japanese aesthetics is involved in not saying what you want to. To talk about yourself in Japanese is considered rude. So English became a much better language for me as a writer; I could get close to what I wanted directly to say, but also be oblique by using nuance and suggestion." More and more she began to think of returning to the United States. "My friends in Japan started to change. All the girls I had been friends with suddenly began to wind down their independent lives, to prepare themselves for being good wives. I knew that wasn't for me." In 1977 she won a scholarship to attend Rockford College near Chicago and finished her undergraduate degree there. She went on to the University of Wisconsin—Milwaukee to complete graduate studies in 1984; she married that same year. Job possibilities opened in several places across the country, but Mori finally chose a small Catholic college in Wisconsin, where she still teaches.

It was while writing her doctoral dissertation that Mori first began the stories that would ultimately become *Shizuko's Daughter.* "I wanted to write a group of related stories," Mori told *SATA.* "As time went by, I began to see the stories as very connected and my agent wanted to market them. I went back to poetry and stopped thinking about them; I had worked through what I needed to with them." The stories made the rounds of publishers for a couple of years until an editor at Henry Holt saw the possibility for a young adult title in them. "I re-sequenced the material into chronological order," Mori explained, "and wrote new material. This rewriting forced me to be more honest with myself. My tendency as a writer is to rely on eloquence rather than plot. The rewrites on *Shizuko's Daughter* helped me to develop my skills in plotting and to be more true to the story."

The story, in this case, is simple yet tragic. In the opening pages of *Shizuko's Daughter* we meet the mother, Shizuko, just as she is about to kill herself. She leaves a note for her twelve-year-old daughter that is both explanation and mystery: "People will tell you that I've done this because I did not love you. Don't listen to them. When you grow up to be a strong woman, you will know that this was for the best." Returning from her music lesson, Yuki, the daughter, is the one to discover her dead mother. The rest of the insightful novel is told in episodic format over seven years time, with Yuki facing various challenges from the remarriage of her father, to dealing with her grandparents, school friends, and her own conscience and sense of loss and guilt. All this is told with a fine sense of detail accompanied by searing emotional probes. "Like the best realistic Japanese fiction," Rosenberg wrote, "[Mori's] prose blends bluntness and delicate restraint." Betsy Hearne, writing in the *Bulletin of the Center for Children's Books,* felt that this was "a first novel that truly bridges the interests of young adults and adults." For Hearne, *Shizuko's Daughter* was not only a coming of age novel, but one that went far beyond that through its portrayal of a Japanese family from multiple viewpoints. "Readers will be moved beyond cultural boundaries by the author's ability to render nuances of childhood with an immediacy devoid of nostalgia," Hearne reported. A reviewer in *Publishers Weekly* similarly said that the story is "quietly moving ... [and] an emotionally and

In this memoir the author relates her own struggles to deal with her mother's suicide, leave her lonely family life behind, and adjust to a new country.

culturally rich tale tracing the evolution of despair and hope."

"I wasn't going for conscious effect with *Shizuko's Daughter,*" Mori told *SATA.* "The simple message is that you've got to let go of things, of people, of emotional guilt. But I don't think of the big picture first. I work moment by moment, scene by scene. So it's not as if I consciously think of theme when beginning a work of art. I think we all bring good intentions to such work and they show through. I think of concrete events and of characters, not about what it all means." With the young adult novel she is currently working on, however, Mori is much more conscious of technique. "I still don't think about category when I write," Mori explained, "and I'm not constantly thinking about what makes a novel [suitable for teens]. But I am really emphasizing plot, which is something new from me. I'm learning all the time, especially about using plot as a guide and not as a constriction."

Unlike many writers, Mori is a lover of revision. "Sometimes, facing a blank sheet of paper in the morning, I go into a panic. But when I have some pages of writing that need revising, there is a calmness that comes over me. I like to write well. That is the craft aspect of writing. And that is something I am in control of. The quality of thoughts you have from one instant to the next or the moods and people that may influence you—over these you have little control. But with writing, you can go back and fix something you don't like. You have the power to make a sentence sound exactly as you want it to. I think I enjoy revising the most of all aspects of writing." Mori is also a steady worker, not one to wait for the muse. "I have a studio for writing," she told *SATA.* "I go there three times a week during the school year and almost every weekday during the summers. I sit there and write or revise for five to seven hours a day. I believe in discipline. Though I love to write and need to write, it's also hard work." It's exactly the hard work that is hidden in Mori's seamless prose. A recent collection of poems as well as an adult memoir of Mori's return to Japan have garnered further critical attention for her. With *The Dream of Water,* Mori goes back to her homeland for a visit in an attempt to put the past to rest. A reviewer for *Publishers Weekly* called the book a "beautifully written, troubling memoir." "I don't think I ever want to go back to Japan to live," Mori told *SATA.* "I feel mostly American in outlook. The fact that I am Japanese by birth is only one of many factors that go to make up who I am. It is far from determining."

Mori carries this same philosophy with her when discussing the effects of her works. "Several women told me that they read *Shizuko's Daughter* with their daughters and they cried, and that has meant a lot to me," she said in her *SATA* interview. "I like affecting my readers, touching them and making them look at their lives. But I do not want to be the whole influence. I want to be only one part of a constellation of ideas that touches and affects a person."

In the end, Mori's desires for her writing are as understated as her prose and life style: "I hope to evoke rather than prescribe. To create, through feelings and concrete details, a life. To put something out there between past and present that presents images, characters, and events that seem real to the reader."

■ Works Cited

Review of *The Dream of Water, Publishers Weekly,* November 7, 1994, p. 54.

Hearne, Betsy, review of *Shizuko's Daughter, Bulletin of the Center for Children's Books,* May, 1993, p. 291.

Mori, Kyoko, *Shizuko's Daughter,* Holt, 1993.

Mori, Kyoko, in a telephone interview conducted by J. Sydney Jones for *Something about the Author,* November 26, 1994.

Rosenberg, Liz, review of *Shizuko's Daughter, New York Times Book Review,* August 22, 1993, p. 19.

Review of *Shizuko's Daughter, Publishers Weekly,* January 25, 1993, p. 87.

■ For More Information See

PERIODICALS

English Journal, September, 1994, p. 87.

Horn Book, September-October, 1994, p. 603.

Voice of Youth Advocates, October, 1993, p. 217.

Wilson Library Bulletin, January, 1994, p. 117.

* * *

MURRAY, Peter
See HAUTMAN, Pete(r Murray)

N

DAVID NEEL

NEEL, David 1960-

Personal

Born in 1960; son of Dave Neel, Sr. *Education:* Attended Mount Royal College, 1978-80, and University of Kansas, 1980-82.

Addresses

c/o Publicity Director, University of Washington, University of Washington Press, P.O. Box 50096, Seattle, WA 98145-5096.

Career

Professional photographer and artist. *Exhibitions:* "Our Chiefs and Elders: Photographs by David Need, Kwagiutl," University of British Columbia Museum of Anthropology, 1990-91; "To Speak for Ourselves: Portraits of Chiefs and Elders by David Neel," National Archives of Canada, Ottawa, Ontario, 1991; "Spirit of the Earth," Vancouver Museum, Vancouver, British Columbia, 1993; "Photographs of Native Leaders and Related Works," Canadian Museum of Contemporary Photography, Ottawa, 1993.

Awards, Honors

Mungo Martin Memorial Award, 1988; Canada Council Project Grant, 1988; Canada Council Explorations Grant, 1991; Artist Assistance Grant, Ministry of Municipal Affairs, 1991; Community Scholar Grant, Smithsonian Institution, 1992.

Writings

Our Chiefs and Elders: Words and Photographs of Native Leaders, University of Washington Press, 1992.

Contributor to books, including *Gatherings: The En'owkin Journal of First North American Peoples, Volume 3,* Theytus Books, 1991; *Partial Recall: Photographs of Native North Americans,* edited by Lucy Lippard, New Press, 1992; *Indigena: Contemporary Native Perspective,* edited by Gerald McMaster and Lee-Ann Martin, Douglas & McIntyre, 1992; *Blood of the Land: The Government and Corporate War Against First Nations,* by Rex Wyler, New Society Publishers, 1992; *A*

Circle of Nations, edited by John Gattuso, Beyond Words Publishing, 1993.

Sidelights

David Neel told *SATA:* "I am a professional photographer as well as a hereditary Kwagiutl artist. I work in a number of mediums, including wood sculpture, photography, printmaking, and painting. I specialize in traditional masks about contemporary history and photography of people for commercial, editorial, documentary, and fine art use. I am also a writer and lecturer.

"I draw on my Kwagiutl heritage for my artistic direction. I inherited my name Tlat'lala'wis' from my father, Dave Neel, Sr., in addition to a rich artistic heritage. My father, a Fort Rupert (Tsaxis) Kwagiutl, was taught to carve by his mother, Ellen Neel, and her uncle, Mungo Martin. Ellen received her instruction in carving and design from her maternal grandfather, Charlie James. I use the work of my ancestors as the starting point for my own interpretation of carving and design.

"I returned to Vancouver in 1986 after studying and working in photography in the United States for six years. After studying in Kansas, I moved to Dallas, Texas, and had the opportunity to work with some of the country's top photographers. My images appear in magazines and posters, as well as in museums and galleries in the United States and Canada. Influenced by the 'concerned photographers' such as W. Eugene Smith and Henri Cartier-Bresson, I use my photography, sculpture, serigraphs, and writing to comment on today's issues."*

* * *

NEWMAN, Jerry 1935-

Personal

Born February 17, 1935, in Montreal, PQ, Canada; son of Leon (an embroiderer) and Ann (a housewife; maiden name, Dubin) Newman; married Frances Korn (a painter; divorced); married Margaret Reid (a teacher), August 14, 1992; children: Rafael, Adam, Zoe. *Education:* Concordia University, OISE; University of Toronto—MacMaster Medical School, M.D.; University of Toronto—Princeton, Ph.D., 1994. *Politics:* Socialist.

Addresses

Home—64-12110 Bath Rd., Richmond, BC, Canada VGU 2A6. *Office*—Creative Writing Department, University of British Columbia, Vancouver, BC, Canada V6T 1Z1.

Career

University of British Columbia, Vancouver, Canada, associate professor, 1971—.

Writings

Green Earrings and a Felt Hat, illustrated by Margaret Hewitt, Holt, 1993.
Sudden Proclamations, Cocanadada Press, 1993.

Also author of *We Always Take Care of Our Own,* McClelland & Stewart; and *A Russian Novel,* New Press.

For More Information See

PERIODICALS

Horn Book Guide, fall, 1993, p. 289.
Kirkus Reviews, May 1, 1993, p. 602.
School Library Journal, August, 1993, p. 148.
Western American Literature, November, 1993, p. 281.*

* * *

NG, Franklin

Personal

Born in Honolulu, HI. *Education:* Johns Hopkins University, B.A., 1968; Harvard University, M.A., 1970; University of Chicago, M.A., Ph.D., 1975.

Addresses

Office—Department of Anthropology, California State University at Fresno, Fresno, CA 93740-0016.

Career

California State University at Fresno, Fresno, CA, Department of Anthropology, began as assistant professor, became professor, 1978—. California State University, Ethnic Studies program coordinator, 1975-78, Asian American Studies program coordinator, 1975—. Instructor at Roosevelt High School, Honolulu, HI, summer, 1969, and Roosevelt University, Chicago, IL, summer, 1974. Georgetown University and Center for Strategic and International Studies, Washington, DC, researcher, summers, 1970, 1971, and 1972. Adviser, Chinese Students' club, 1975-81, and Scion (Japanese American Students club), 1975-77; adviser to annual *Amerasia Week,* 1975—; occasional adviser for the Chinese Overseas Students Association and Southeast Asian Students Club. Member of the board of directors, Central California (Golden Valley) Girl Scout Council, 1987-88; member of the Asian/Pacific American Advisory Group to California State Department of Education Superintendent Bill Honig, 1989—; member of the board of scholars, Japanese-American National Museum, Los Angeles. *Member:* American Historical Association, Organization of American Historians, Association for Asian Studies, Association for Asian American Studies, Society for Historians of American Foreign Relations, Chinese Historical Society of America, Japanese American Citizens League (Fresno chapter vice president for social activities; chairman of scholarship committee; board of directors 1981—), Asian Pacific

American Advocates for California, (Fresno chapter vice-president, 1984-86).

Awards, Honors

Summer grants, Center for Strategic and International Studies and Georgetown University, 1970, 1971, and 1972; Ford Foundation Fellowship, University of Chicago, 1970-73; Meritorious Performance and Professional Promise Award, CSUF, 1986; research grants from Chao Suet Foundation of San Francisco, 1991, East Asian National Resource Center, Stanford University, 1992, and School of Social Sciences, CSUF, 1992.

Writings

Chinese Americans Struggle for Equality (young adult), Rourke Publishing Group, 1992.

Also editor of *Encyclopedia of Asian Americans, New Visions in Asian American Studies: Diversity, Community, Power;* and (with Robert Kim and others) *Notable Asian Americans: A Biographical Dictionary.* Member of the editorial board, *Bridge Magazine,* 1979-1981; book review editor, *Journal of American-East Asian Relations,* 1993—. Contributor of numerous articles and reviews to anthologies. Referee, University of Hawaii Press, University of Washington Press, Harper and Row, D.C. Heath, Oxford University Press, *Journal of American History, Journal of American Ethnic History, Medical Anthropology Quarterly.**

* * *

NOLL, Sally 1946-

Personal

Born September 24, 1946, in Englewood, New Jersey; daughter of William (an architectural historian) and Margaret (a homemaker and sculptor; maiden name, Post) Pierson; married Christopher Noll (an architect), June 20, 1976 (divorced, 1994); children: Kate, Victoria. *Education:* Boston University School of Fine and Applied Arts, B.F.A., 1971. *Politics:* Democrat. *Religion:* Christian. *Hobbies and other interests:* Traveling.

Addresses

Home and office—3005 Claremont Ave., Berkeley, CA 94705.

Career

Writer and illustrator. Has also worked as a card designer at the Museum of Modern Art and Cartier; book layout and jacket designer, 101 Productions; freelance needlepoint designer. *Member:* Authors Guild, Authors League of America.

SALLY NOLL

Writings

SELF-ILLUSTRATED

Off and Counting, Greenwillow, 1984.
Jiggle Wiggle Prance, Greenwillow, 1987.
Watch Where You Go, Greenwillow, 1990.
That Bothered Kate, Greenwillow, 1991.
I Have a Loose Tooth, Greenwillow, 1992.
Lucky Morning, Greenwillow, 1994.

ILLUSTRATOR

Miela Ford, *Sunflower,* Greenwillow, 1995.

Sidelights

Sally Noll told *SATA* that her interest in art began when she was a small child in Williamstown, Massachusetts. "For a spacey child like me, that peaceful rural setting in which I had free rein was perfect. It was my most inspirational teacher. I spent timeless hours exploring the woods in back of my house, and behind the woods was a pasture. Alongside that pasture was the Clark Art Institute with its famous collection of Renoirs and other Impressionists. I visited it often with my father, a professor at Williams College. I loved to look at pictures in art books and, in my own mind, I was an artist; I drew and used watercolors from the time I was three or four." Noll's interest in art was nurtured by a high school art teacher, and she went on to earn a degree in graphic design at Boston University's School of Fine and Applied Arts.

"For several years," Noll said, "I did freelance design work, designing anything from flat graphic business

Noll's animated illustrations use animals to show young children the meaning of action verbs.

cards to ornate dining room rugs." She was married and living in the south of France when she began to think of writing and illustrating books for children. Upon her return to the United States, she "silkscreened a card of a cartwheeling Santa, which the Museum of Modern Art included in its Christmas offerings." Two years later, "Susan Hirschman saw a reissued box of my first Cartwheeling Santa design at the MoMa gift shop. She wrote me a letter asking me if I would consider illustrating and writing books for children, and needless to say, I have that letter framed in my office. Right now I am working on my seventh book for Greenwillow."

Off and Counting, Noll's first effort, is a "perfectly nice counting book," according to a reviewer for the *Bulletin of the Center for Children's Books,* A wind-up frog counts various toys, including a castle, rocking horses, dolls, tigers, and stuffed zebras, as he hops around the toy store. A contributor in *Publishers Weekly* asserted that if *Off and Counting* is an indication of Noll's future work, this book "will be remembered as the foundation of a remarkable career." Stephanie Shauck, a reviewer for *School Library Journal,* commented that "Noll's idea is original and the execution visually pleasing."

Jiggle Wiggle Prance features large illustrations of animals in motion and text that boldly highlights the verbs that describe each movement. A lion jumps, a dog and mouse race, a bear skips, and a crocodile skates. *Horn Book* reviewer Ann A. Flowers appreciated the "[b]rilliant, flat paintings" and the book's "crackling energy." A *Junior Bookshelf* critic praised the illustrations and concluded that Noll is "clearly ... someone to be reckoned with." Lisa Castillo wrote in *School Library Journal* that *Jiggle Wiggle Prance* "is as much fun to look at as it is to listen to."

According to Noll, *Watch Where You Go* was inspired by her memories of a trip to Kenya and Tanzania. In this "book of bright visual puzzles," as Virginia E. Jeschelnig called it in *School Library Journal,* a mouse rushes home through the jungle. Accompanied by a worried dragonfly, he runs over a lion's mane (thinking it is golden grass) and climbs up a tree that is actually an elephant's trunk. In the same manner, the mouse unknowingly creeps over a hippopotamus, a monkey, a snake, and a crocodile. According to one *Horn Book* critic, children will "immediately apprehend the joke" and enjoy the book.

Noll states that her daughters, Kate and Tory, "have been constant inspirations" for her work. *That Bothered Kate,* in the words of a *Horn Book* reviewer, "captures the universal dilemma of a younger sibling" who imitates her older sister. It aggravates Kate when Tory copies everything she does and when a neighbor says that they look like twins. Surprisingly enough, it annoys Kate even more when Tory finds a friend her own age and stops following Kate around. The situation is resolved when Kate and Tory's mother explains that Tory's behavior is all a part of growing up. Virginia Opocensky asserted in *School Library Journal* that this book is "as charming and on target" as Noll's earlier works.

As in *That Bothered Kate,* Noll uses gouache and colored pencil illustrations to depict an aspect of growing up in *I Have a Loose Tooth.* Noll explained to *SATA* that *I Have a Loose Tooth* is about her daughter "Tory and her frustrating quest to get adequate acknowledgment for her first loose tooth." In the book, everyone is busy preparing for Nanny's birthday party, and no one understands Molly when she tries to tell them her tooth is loose. Finally, she writes a message on her Grandmother's birthday card and is acknowledged by her family. A reviewer in *Publishers Weekly* concluded that "this is a winning choice for beginning readers."

Noll continues to write and illustrate books as well as travel. "I keep my heart and mind open at all times," she told *SATA*. "The sensory treats of foreign lands still keep my yearning to travel alive. I now relish taking my children and seeing them marvel at new things, but it is the culture and traditions of other lives and other times that help me look more deeply into my own."

■ Works Cited

Castillo, Lisa, review of *Jiggle Wiggle Prance, School Library Journal,* August, 1987, p. 72.

Flowers, Ann A., review of *Jiggle Wiggle Prance, Horn Book,* July/August, 1987, pp. 455-56.

Review of *I Have a Loose Tooth, Publishers Weekly,* July 27, 1992, p. 62.

Jeschelnig, Virginia E., review of *Watch Where You Go, School Library Journal,* April, 1990, p. 94.

Review of *Jiggle Wiggle Prance, Junior Bookshelf,* October, 1987, pp. 212-13.

Review of *Off and Counting, Bulletin of the Center for Children's Books,* November, 1984.

Review of *Off and Counting, Publishers Weekly,* March 9, 1984, p. 113.

Opocensky, Virginia, review of *That Bothered Kate, School Library Journal,* October, 1991, p. 102.

Shauck, Stephanie, review of *Off and Counting, School Library Journal,* May, 1984, pp. 68-69.

Review of *That Bothered Kate, Horn Book,* November/December, 1991, p. 730.

Review of *Watch Where You Go, Horn Book,* May/June 1990, p. 327.

■ For More Information See

PERIODICALS

Junior Bookshelf, February, 1985, p. 17.

Kirkus Reviews, August 1, 1992, p. 998.

School Library Journal, September, 1992, p. 208.

O

ELIZABETH ONEAL

ONEAL, Elizabeth 1934-
(Zibby Oneal)

■ Personal

Born March 17, 1934, in Omaha, NE; daughter of James D. (a thoracic surgeon) and Mary Elizabeth (Dowling) Bisgard; married Robert Moore Oneal (a plastic surgeon), December 27, 1955; children: Elizabeth, Michael. *Education:* Attended Stanford University, 1952-55; University of Michigan, B.A., 1970. *Politics:* Democrat. *Religion:* Episcopalian.

■ Addresses

Home and office—501 Onondaga St., Ann Arbor, MI 48104. *Agent*—Marilyn Marlow, Curtis Brown Ltd., 575 Madison Ave., New York, NY 10022.

■ Career

University of Michigan, Ann Arbor, lecturer in English, 1976-85. Member of board of trustees, Greenhills School, Ann Arbor, 1975-79. *Member:* PEN, Authors Guild, Authors League of America.

■ Awards, Honors

Friends of American Writers Award, 1972, for *War Work;* "Notable Book" citations and "Best Books for Young Adults" citations, American Library Association, 1980, for *The Language of Goldfish,* 1982, for *A Formal Feeling,* and 1985, for *In Summer Light;* "Best Books of the Year" citation, *New York Times,* 1982, and Christopher Award, 1983, both for *A Formal Feeling; Boston Globe/Horn Book* Award, 1986, for *In Summer Light.*

■ Writings

FOR CHILDREN; UNDER NAME ZIBBY ONEAL

War Work, illustrated by George Porter, Viking, 1971.

The Improbable Adventures of Marvelous O'Hara Soapstone, illustrated by Paul Galdone, Viking, 1972.

Turtle and Snail, illustrated by Margot Tomes, Lippincott, 1979.

The Language of Goldfish (young adult novel), Viking, 1980.

A Formal Feeling (young adult novel), Viking, 1982.

Maude and Walter (short story picture book), illustrated by Maxie Chambliss, Lippincott, 1985.

In Summer Light (young adult novel), Viking, 1985.

Grandma Moses: Painter of Rural America (biography), Puffin, 1986.

A Long Way to Go: A Story of Women's Right to Vote, illustrated by Michael Dooling, Viking, 1990.

Carrie has a loving family, talent, and intelligence, yet still has trouble adjusting to change and coping with feelings of suicide. (Cover illustration by Neil Waldman.)

Oneal's manuscripts are available at the Kerlan Collection, University of Minnesota.

■ Work in Progress

Another young adult novel; a novel for younger children.

■ Sidelights

Elizabeth Oneal, who writes under the first name Zibby, is best known as the author of acclaimed young adult novels that, according to Wendy Smith in *Publishers Weekly,* "exhibit a depth and complexity rare in any kind of fiction." Oneal's *The Language of Goldfish, A Formal Feeling,* and *In Summer Light* have been widely praised for their sensitive and perceptive portrayals of the complex emotions and problems of adolescents. Featuring teenage female protagonists, Oneal's stories deal with a variety of conflicts—puberty, sexual awareness, self-perception problems, the death of a parent—that her characters resolve on their way toward adulthood and independence. Throughout, Oneal focuses on the inner strength of her characters, which allows them to move forward with their lives. "I feel a responsibility to make children understand that adolescence is a self-absorbed world ... but it's not a place you can stay forever," she told Smith. "The movement away and out into the world, into concern for other people, has to happen; you aren't an adult until you make that move. Sure, explore your feelings, because if you're hung up on your problems you're never going to be able to move on. So work that out, but then get out into the world."

Oneal's early desire to become a writer began with her family, who considered books, as Oneal noted in the *Sixth Book of Junior Authors and Illustrators,* "as necessary to life as food.... There were toppling stacks of books on every flat surface in the house." Both of her parents regularly read to her and encouraged her early efforts at story writing. "I told myself stories all the time," she added. "When I was old enough I began to write them down.... I don't believe my parents ever worried. They let me alone to pursue my singleminded path without much comment." Growing up, she was also interested in painting, an activity she partook in with her father, a thoracic surgeon. While she harbored early aspirations to become a painter or even a surgeon, writing and stories remained her primary interest. "I don't recall when I didn't want to be a writer," Oneal said in a 1982 Viking Press promotional release. "It has seemed to me the best and most exciting thing a person can do, for as long as I can remember."

After attending Stanford University, where Oneal took creative writing classes, the author married plastic surgeon Robert Moore Oneal in 1955. "It was only after I'd married, had two children, and had begun to write stories for them that I discovered what I both like and could do," she commented in her Viking promotional release. "The first books came out of these stories created expressly for them." Her first book was published in 1971: *War Work,* a suspense story about three young children on the trail of espionage activities in a Midwestern town during World War II. She followed this work with two picture books for children, *The Improbable Adventures of Marvelous O'Hara Soapstone* and *Turtle and Snail.* Oneal turned to writing for adolescents after her own children began to grow up.

Oneal's first young adult novel, *The Language of Goldfish,* was widely acclaimed for its delicate handling of difficult subject matter. The novel deals with the attempted suicide and mental illness of Carrie Stokes, a thirteen-year-old girl who is terrified both of herself and of other people. "In a perceptive novel which avoids cliches and exaggeration," noted Christine McDonnell in *Horn Book,* "evocative images create a sense of Carrie's inner experiences: the gaps in her consciousness, her whirling terror, and her longing for a safe place—a place like the island in the goldfish pond, a sanctuary of childhood." The novel has been singled out by many critics for its technical merits, including rich characterization and an effective prose style. "The people and events in Carrie's life are a bit flat and a bit hazy around the edges, which is entirely how she perceives them," noted Joyce Milton in the *New York Times Book Review.* "In contrast, [Carrie's] inner turmoil—even during her dizzy spells when reality 'slips sideways'—is conveyed in language that is poetic and precise." Linda R. Silver praised *The Language of Goldfish* in *School Library Journal* for being "a serious but not dismal book, enlivened by flashes of humor, [which] draws out readers' empathetic response and enlarges understanding."

The title of Oneal's second young adult novel, *A Formal Feeling,* is taken from a line of Emily Dickinson's poetry: "After great pain, a formal feeling comes." The novel deals with sixteen-year-old Anne Cameron, who is struggling with the recent death of her mother and the remarriage of her father. The novel charts Anne's deep feelings for her dead mother and her attempts to reconcile both her mother's strengths and weaknesses—without feeling a sense of betrayal. Again, Oneal has been praised by critics for her technically accomplished and insightful depiction of the world of adolescents. In *Booklist,* Stephanie Zvirin remarked that while "Oneal's pacing is slow and deliberate and her style highly descriptive," the novel also contains "great emotional intensity, and Oneal ... captures Anne's conflicting feelings with subtlety and perception." Calling the novel "clearly one of the best young adult books of the year," *ALAN Review* contributor Robert C. Small described *A Formal Feeling* as "thoughtful and insightful," and praised Oneal's writing as "both natural and beautifully controlled."

Stuck with her famous painter father for the summer, Kate finds romance and learns to establish her own identity and emerge from her father's shadow. (Cover illustration by Bob Dacey.)

In Summer Light, Oneal's third novel, deals with seventeen-year-old Kate Brewer, who is struggling with the stifling perceptions she carries of both her parents and herself. In the shadow of her father, a successful artist, Kate strives to discover her own identity and form a relationship with a young graduate student named Ian. Trev Jones observed in *School Library Journal,* "It's hard to say which is more impressive in this literate, complex story: Oneal's use of language, imagery and color or the development of her finely drawn characters." Oneal "uses an elegant dazzle of images to illuminate Kate's Oedipal conflict, while neatly sidestepping the boggy self-pity of so much adolescent fiction," noted *New York Times Book Review* contributor Michele Landsberg. "Through Kate's rapt perceptions of light and color, both the prose and her character gain depth." The novel, which received the *Boston Globe/Horn Book* Award in 1986, arose from Oneal's interest in fairy tales and in William Shakespeare's play *The Tempest.* As Oneal described in *Horn Book,* "I wanted to write about a powerful, arrogant, magical father and about his daughter's involvement with him. I wanted to talk about how a girl begins to move away from this intense childhood involvement; about how it is when, like Miranda in *The Tempest,* she is able to gaze for the first time on a man besides her father."

In addition to her young adult novels and earlier books, Oneal has written a picture book collection of stories entitled *Maude and Walter,* a biography of the American rural painter Grandma Moses, and a historical story about the fight for women's suffrage, *A Long Way to Go: A Story of Women's Right to Vote.* Today she continues to find inspiration from writing for young adults. "Adolescents are on the brink of becoming what they will be as adults and their problems and perplexities are a rich source for fiction," she stated in *Twentieth-Century Children's Writers.* "How a young person negotiates this brief passage between childhood and the adult world is a subject that I find of continuing interest." Oneal lives in Ann Arbor, Michigan, where she has taught writing at the University of Michigan. She enjoys the mix between her own writing and teaching young people and is enlightened by her discussions with students where, as she notes in *Sixth Book of Junior Authors,* "we talk and talk about writing books." Oneal adds, "Sometimes in the midst of these discussions I find myself thinking about how almost sinfully lucky it is to be able to spend a life engrossed in the occupation one loves best."

■ Works Cited

Chevalier, Tracy, editor, *Twentieth-Century Children's Writers,* 3rd edition, St. James Press, 1989.
Holtze, Sally Holmes editor, *Sixth Book of Junior Authors and Illustrators,* H. W. Wilson, 1989, pp. 210-12.
Jones, Trev, review of *In Summer Light, School Library Journal,* October, 1985, p. 186.
Landsberg, Michele, review of *In Summer Light, New York Times Book Review,* November 24, 1985, p. 21.
McDonnell, Christine, review of *The Language of Goldfish, Horn Book,* August, 1980, p. 416.
Milton, Joyce, review of *The Language of Goldfish, New York Times Book Review,* April 27, 1980, pp. 52, 65.
Oneal, Zibby, *Zibby Oneal* (promotional piece), Viking Press, 1982.
Oneal, Zibby, "In Summer Light," *Horn Book,* January-February, 1987, pp. 32-34.
Silver, Linda R., review of *The Language of Goldfish, School Library Journal,* February, 1980, p. 70.
Small, Robert C., review of *A Formal Feeling, ALAN Review,* winter, 1983, p. 23.
Smith, Wendy, "Working Together," *Publishers Weekly,* February 21, 1986, pp. 97-98.
Zvirin, Stephanie, review of *A Formal Feeling, Booklist,* October 1, 1982, p. 199.

■ For More Information See

BOOKS

Children's Literature Review, Volume 13, Gale, 1987, pp. 153-60.
Contemporary Literary Criticism, Volume 30, Gale, 1984.

PERIODICALS

Best Sellers, April, 1980, p. 39.
Booklist, October 15, 1985, p. 330.
Bulletin of the Center for Children's Books, January, 1972, p. 77; October, 1986, p. 34.
Entertainment Weekly, May 25, 1990, p. 83.
Globe and Mail (Toronto), February 8, 1986.
Horn Book, April, 1983, pp. 173-74.
Kirkus Reviews, October 1, 1972, p. 1145; December 15, 1985, p. 1398; September 1, 1985, pp. 914-15.
New Statesman, October 10, 1986.
New York Times Book Review, November 14, 1982, p. 48.
Publishers Weekly, May 28, 1979, p. 57; August 2, 1985, p. 69.
School Library Journal, December, 1985, p. 110.
Times Literary Supplement, October 30, 1987.
Voice of Youth Advocates, August, 1980, p. 35.
Washington Post Book World, October 10, 1982.

* * *

ONEAL, Zibby
See ONEAL, Elizabeth

OPPENHEIM, Joanne 1934-
(Jane Fleischer, Kate Jassem)

■ Personal

Born May 11, 1934, in Middletown, NY; daughter of Abe P. (an electrical engineer) and Helen (Jassem) Fleischer; married Stephen Oppenheim (a lawyer), June 27, 1954; children: James, Anthony, Stephanie. *Education:* Attended University of Miami, FL, 1951-52; Sarah Lawrence College, B.A., 1960; Bank Street College of Education, M.S., 1980. *Hobbies and other interests:* Community theater.

■ Addresses

Home—P.O. Box 29, Monticello, NY 12701. *Office*—Oppenheim Toy Portfolio, 40 East 9th St., New York, NY 10003. *Agent*—(children's books) Toni Mendez, 141 East 56th St., New York, NY 10022; (adult books) Jim Levine, James Levine Communications Inc., c/o FWI, 330 7th Ave., 14th Fl., New York, NY, 10001.

■ Career

Substitute and full-time elementary school teacher in Monticello, NY, 1960-80; Bank Street College of Education, New York City, associate editor in publications department, 1980-92; *Oppenheim Toy Portfolio* (maga-

JOANNE OPPENHEIM

zine), New York City, president, 1989—. Member of board of directors, U.S.A. Toy Library, 1993—.

■ Awards, Honors

Outstanding Teachers of America award, 1973; Children's Choice citation, International Reading Association, 1980, for *Mrs. Peloki's Snake,* and 1981, for *Mrs. Peloki's Class Play;* Ruth Schwartz Children's Book Award, Ontario Arts Council, 1987, and Outstanding Science Book citation, both for *Have You Seen Birds?;* various book club selections, for books including *James Will Never Die, The Storybook Prince,* and *Choosing Books for Kids.*

■ Writings

FOR CHILDREN

Have You Seen Trees?, illustrated by Irwin Rosenhouse, Young Scott Books, 1967, illustrated by Jean and Mou-sien Tseng, Scholastic, 1995.
Have You Seen Birds?, illustrated by Julio de Diego, Young Scott Books, 1968, illustrated by Barbara Reid, Scholastic, 1986.
Have You Seen Roads?, Young Scott Books, 1969.
Have You Seen Boats?, Young Scott Books, 1971.
On the Other Side of the River, illustrated by Aliki, F. Watts, 1972.
Have You Seen Houses?, Young Scott Books, 1973.
Sequoyah, Cherokee Hero, illustrated by Bert Dodson, Troll, 1979.
Osceola, Seminole Warrior, illustrated by Bill Ternay, Troll, 1979.
Black Hawk, Frontier Warrior, illustrated by Hal Frenck, Troll, 1979.
(Under pseudonym Jane Fleischer) *Tecumseh, Shawnee War Chief,* illustrated by Frenck, Troll, 1979.
(Under pseudonym Jane Fleischer) *Sitting Bull, Warrior of the Sioux,* illustrated by Dodson, Troll, 1979.
(Under pseudonym Jane Fleischer) *Pontiac, Chief of the Ottawas,* illustrated by Robert Baxter, Troll, 1979.
(Under pseudonym Kate Jassem) *Chief Joseph, Leader of Destiny,* illustrated by Baxter, Troll, 1979.
(Under pseudonym Kate Jassem) *Pocahontas, Girl of Jamestown,* illustrated by Allan Eitzen, Troll, 1979.
(Under pseudonym Kate Jassem) *Sacajawea, Wilderness Guide,* illustrated by Jan Palmer, Troll, 1979.
(Under pseudonym Kate Jassem) *Squanto, the Pilgrim Adventure,* illustrated by Baxter, Troll, 1979.
Mrs. Peloki's Snake, illustrated by Joyce Audy dos Santos, Dodd, 1980.
James Will Never Die, illustrated by True Kelly, Dodd, 1982.
Mrs. Peloki's Class Play, illustrated by dos Santos, Dodd, 1984.
Barron's Bunny Activity Books, Barron's, 1985.
KidSpeak about Computers, Ballantine, 1985.
You Can't Catch Me!, illustrated by Andrew Shachat, Houghton, 1986.
(With Betty Boegehold and William H. Hooks) *Read-a-Rebus: Tales and Rhymes in Words and Pictures,* illustrated by Lynn Munsinger, Random House, 1986.
The Storybook Prince, illustrated by Rosanne Litzinger, Harcourt, 1987.
Mrs. Peloki's Substitute, illustrated by Joyce Audy Zarins, Dodd, 1987.
Left and Right, illustrated by Litzinger, Harcourt, 1989.
"Not Now!" Said the Cow, illustrated by Chris Demarest, Bantam, 1989.
Could It Be?, illustrated by S. D. Schindler, Bantam, 1990.
Wake up, Baby!, illustrated by Lynn Sweat, Bantam, 1990.
Follow That Fish, illustrated by Devis Grebu, Bantam, 1990.
Eency Weency Spider, illustrated by Schindler, Bantam, 1991.
The Donkey's Tale, illustrated by Demarest, Bantam, 1991.
Rooter Remembers: A Bank Street Book about Values, illustrated by Munsinger, Viking, 1991.
(With Barbara Brenner and Hooks) *No Way, Slippery Slick!: A Child's First Book about Drugs,* illustrated by Joan Auclair, HarperCollins, 1991.
Show-and-Tell Frog, illustrated by Kate Duke, Bantam, 1992.
(With Hooks and Brenner) *How Do You Make a Bubble?,* illustrated by Doug Cushman, Bantam, 1992.
(Adaptor) *One Gift Deserves Another,* illustrated by Bo Zaunders, Dutton, 1992.
Row, Row, Row Your Boat, illustrated by Kevin O'Malley, Bantam, 1993.
Do You Like Cats?, illustrated by Carol Newsom, Bantam, 1993.
(Reteller) *The Christmas Witch,* illustrated by Annie Mitra, Bantam, 1993.
"Uh-Oh!" Cawed the Crow, illustrated by Demarest, Bantam, 1993.
Oceanarium, illustrated by Alan Gutierrez, Bantam, 1994.
Floratorium, illustrated by Schindler, Bantam, 1994.
Money, Atheneum, 1995.
Have You Seen Bugs?, Scholastic (Canada), 1995.

OTHER

Kids and Play (adult), Ballantine, 1984.
(With Boegehold and Brenner) *Raising a Confident Child,* Pantheon, 1984.
(With Boegehold and Brenner) *Choosing Books for Kids,* Ballantine, 1986.
Buy Me! Buy Me! The Bank Street Guide to Choosing Toys for Children, Pantheon, 1987.
The Elementary School Handbook: Making the Most of Your Child's Education, Pantheon, 1989.
(With daughter, Stephanie Oppenheim) *The Best Toys, Books and Videos for Kids: The 1994 Guide to 1000+ Kid-Tested, Classic and New Products for Ages 0-10,* Harper, 1993, 1995 edition, 1994.

Also author of six activity books for children on maps, time, money, communications, and safety. Contributor to "Bank Street Readers" basal series, Macmillan, 1965. Contributor of articles to magazines, including *Family Circle, Parent and Child,* and *Working Mother.*

In this award-winning book, Oppenheim teaches children about birds using poetry that is filled with playful alliteration and repetition. (Cover illustration by Barbara Reid.)

Sidelights

Ten years as an elementary school teacher and another twelve as a senior editor of the Bank Street College of Education's publication department supply the experience behind Joanne Oppenheim's entertaining and educational books for children. From her first books, which provide new looks at everyday things, to her retellings of traditional tales, Oppenheim is known for works that appeal to children with their pleasing rhymes and sense of humor. Her realistic stories have also been praised for creating characters and situations with which young readers will identify.

Oppenheim's first books in the "Have You Seen?" series combine fanciful verse with illustrations that use unusual perspectives to give children new looks at ordinary items such as roads, trees, birds, boats, and houses. In *Have You Seen Trees?,* Oppenheim's "pleasant, read-aloud rhythms" and "touch of humor" distinguish it from other science books, according to *New York Times Book Review* writer Alice Fleming. Similarly, George A. Woods notes in *New York Times Book Review* that "the rhythm of Joanne Oppenheim's descriptive verse text" in *Have You Seen Roads?* will "transport" the reader, while a *Kirkus Reviews* critic writes that the rhymes in *Have You Seen Boats?* "titillate, educate, [and] play with the mind's ear." Although the series doesn't provide information directly, as a *Junior Bookshelf* reviewer observes, the aim "seems mainly to put their subjects in an environmental context and this is well done in an easy unforced style." "Oppenheim's poetry is magical," states Susan Perren in a *Quill & Quire* review of the 1986 edition of *Have You Seen Birds?,* and she praises the author's "use of alliteration and repetition. Her poetry swoops and rolls, pecks and hoots, bringing the birds alive on the page."

Oppenheim brings her classroom experiences to life in her books about elementary teacher Mrs. Peloki. In *Mrs. Peloki's Snake,* the discovery of a reptile in the boys' bathroom prompts a classroom uproar. This "sprightly

An annoying little fly teases a cow, a bear, and others in Oppenheim's playful rhyming story, published in 1986. (Cover illustration by Andrew Shachat.)

tale of reptilian high jinks [is] nicely tuned to the first-grade funny bone," Kristi L. Thomas comments in *School Library Journal.* The trials of staging a production of "Cinderella" form *Mrs. Peloki's Class Play,* which *School Library Journal* contributor Catherine Wood calls "true to life," with "class members' personalities and humor [that] emerge on almost every page." Ilene Cooper likewise praises Oppenheim in *Booklist* for her "real grasp of second graders and their habits." Another "realistic rendition of a day in second grade" is found in *Mrs. Peloki's Substitute,* according to a *Kirkus Reviews* writer, who says the book "has enough humor and verisimilitude to entertain children." In this episode, after their cherished teacher leaves class sick, the students try to misdirect her unfortunate replacement to avoid a spelling test. While some critics fault the book for potentially inspiring misbehavior, *Bulletin of the Center for Children's Books* writer Zena Sutherland finds the story "nicely appropriate" in length and vocabulary, adding that most young readers "will enjoy a story about a familiar situation."

Another situation familiar to many children—sibling rivalry—is portrayed in *James Will Never Die.* Young Tony can never beat his older brother in their imaginary games, for James always manages to turn everything Tony thinks of into a victory. Tony's efforts to finally best his brother make for a "zippy story of sibling rivalry and affection," a *Publishers Weekly* critic notes. Barbara McGinn likewise finds the brothers' adventures "refreshingly imaginative," even though they all involve someone dying, adding in *School Library Journal* that despite this negative aspect the book is "otherwise fast-moving [and] well-written." Another book about troublesome brothers is *Left and Right,* in which two cobbler brothers learn that they make better teammates than rivals. "Invitingly told in a rhythmic rhyme," according to *Booklist* reviewer Beth Herbert, the book explains concepts of left and right as well as cooperation, and "entices with its amusing insights on siblings."

A catchy refrain distinguishes *You Can't Catch Me!,* in which an annoying insect bothers every animal on the farm without fear: "'No matter how hard you try try try you can't catch me!' called the pesky black fly." Oppenheim's rhymes "are deft and simple," remarks a *Kirkus Reviews* writer, who adds that the story "has the rolling accumulative power of an old tale like *The Gingerbread Boy.*" Betsy Hearne similarly observes in *Bulletin of the Center for Children's Books:* "It's rare to find contemporary verse with a true nursery rhyme ring, but this has it." Another rhyming story with an old-time air is *The Storybook Prince,* which tells of the efforts of a royal household to get the Prince to sleep. "The couplets frolic along," Susan Powers comments in *School Library Journal,* making this "a book for those [who] really enjoy clever word romps."

More recently, Oppenheim has turned to familiar songs and fairy tales and updated them for today's children. Based on a story by the Brothers Grimm, *One Gift Deserves Another* relates how two brothers are rewarded by their king for their gifts. The poor brother, who unselfishly gives the king the giant turnip from his garden, is given wealth, while his greedy rich brother, in exchange for a calculated gift of money and jewels, is given the king's most treasured possession—the turnip. Karen K. Radtke praises Oppenheim's retelling, noting in *School Library Journal* that by eliminating several adult elements from the original Grimm Brothers tale, the author "has distilled the remaining premise into an enjoyable story for children." "Oppenheim's lively retelling ... captures its delicious ironies while lining out its tasty moral," a *Publishers Weekly* critic likewise states. And Kathryn Jennings also has praise for Oppenheim's "upbeat version" in *Bulletin of the Center for Children's Books,* concluding that "this has the humor of a 'Fractured Fairytales' episode and could become a storyhour favorite."

■ Works Cited

Cooper, Ilene, review of *Mrs. Peloki's Class Play, Booklist,* September 1, 1984, p. 70.

Fleming, Alice, "First Steps in Science," *New York Times Book Review,* May 7, 1967, p. 49.

Review of *Have You Seen Boats?, Kirkus Reviews,* August 1, 1971, p. 804.

Review of *Have You Seen Roads?* and *Have You Seen Houses?, Junior Bookshelf,* December, 1977, p. 339.

Hearne, Betsy, review of *You Can't Catch Me!, Bulletin of the Center for Children's Books,* September, 1986, p. 15.

Herbert, Beth, review of *Left and Right, Booklist,* November 1, 1989, p. 556.
Review of *James Will Never Die, Publishers Weekly,* October 22, 1982, p. 56.
Jennings, Kathryn, review of *One Gift Deserves Another, Bulletin of the Center for Children's Books,* September, 1992, p. 11.
McGinn, Barbara, review of *James Will Never Die, School Library Journal,* February, 1983, p. 70.
Review of *Mrs. Peloki's Substitute, Kirkus Reviews,* January 15, 1987, p. 136.
Review of *One Gift Deserves Another, Publishers Weekly,* October 5, 1992, p. 69.
Oppenheim, Joanne, *You Can't Catch Me!,* Houghton, 1986.
Perren, Susan, "Picture-book Plums for Christmas Gift-giving," *Quill & Quire,* December, 1986, p. 16.
Powers, Susan, review of *The Storybook Prince, School Library Journal,* April, 1987, pp. 87-88.
Radtke, Karen K., review of *One Gift Deserves Another, School Library Journal,* February, 1993, p. 83.
Sutherland, Zena, review of *Mrs. Peloki's Substitute, Bulletin of the Center for Children's Books,* June, 1987, p. 193.
Thomas, Kristi L., review of *Mrs. Peloki's Snake, School Library Journal,* October, 1980, p. 138.
Wood, Catherine, review of *Mrs. Peloki's Class Play, School Library Journal,* October, 1984, p. 150.
Woods, George A., review of *Have You Seen Roads?, New York Times Book Review,* October 5, 1969, p. 34.
Review of *You Can't Catch Me!, Kirkus Reviews,* July 15, 1986, p. 1121.

■ For More Information See

PERIODICALS

Bulletin of the Center for Children's Books, July, 1973, p. 174; November, 1984.
Christian Science Monitor, May 1, 1987, p. B7.
Kirkus Reviews, September 1, 1980, p. 1159; December 15, 1986, p. 1858.
Publishers Weekly, August 24, 1984, p. 79.
School Library Journal, August, 1980, pp. 63-64; June-July, 1987, p. 88; August, 1987, p. 72; December, 1989, p. 87; June, 1991, p. 87; April, 1995, pp. 126, 128.

—Sketch by Diane Telgen

P

PANIK, Sharon 1952-

■ Personal

Born May 29, 1952 in Detroit, MI; daughter of Robert and Phyllis L. McClain; married Steven Panik (a park ranger), May 25, 1974; children: Todd. *Education:* Central Michigan University, B.S., 1973; University of Northern Colorado, M.A., 1978.

■ Addresses

Office—1209 Parkwood Dr., Fort Collins, CO 80525.

■ Career

Poudre R-1, Fort Collins, CO, teacher, primary grades, 1974—. *Member:* International Reading Association, Society of Children's Book Writers and Illustrators, National Education Society, Colorado Council of the International Reading Association (membership director).

■ Awards, Honors

Parents' Choice Gold Award, paperback of the year, 1992, for *A Quetzalcoatl Tale of the Ball Game.*

■ Writings

"QUETZALCOATL" SERIES; WITH MARILYN PARKE

A Quetzalcoatl Tale of Corn, illustrated by Lynn Castle, Fearon Teacher Aids, 1992.

A Quetzalcoatl Tale of the Ball Game, illustrated by Castle, Fearon Teacher Aids, 1992.

A Quetzalcoatl Tale of Chocolate, illustrated by Castle, Fearon Teacher Aids, 1994.

■ Work in Progress

With Parke, *A Quetzalcoatl Tale of Colored Corn; A Quetzalcoatl Tale about the Rainforest.*

■ Sidelights

Sharon Panik told *SATA:* "I had never considered becoming an author, but when I could not provide readable material to my first graders about Mexico, I started to do some research. The lesson I prepared for my class grew into a new career—the coauthor of a series of folktales about Quetzalcoatl (pronounced 'Ketz-al-co-atl'), a mythological pre-Columbian character."

■ For More Information See

PERIODICALS

Reading Teacher, November, 1993, p. 250.

* * *

PAPE, Donna (Lugg) 1930-

■ Personal

Surname pronounced "Poppy"; born June 21, 1930, in Sheboygan, WI; daughter of Arthur Phillip and Ruth (Fenninger) Lugg; married William Pape (a carpet mechanic), June 16, 1951; children: Dianc Ruth, Janice Lynn, Jean Carol. *Hobbies and other interests:* Music, art.

■ Addresses

Home—1734 South 15th St., Sheboygan, WI 53081.

■ Career

Photojournalist, 1959-1965; free-lance writer, 1960—. Speaker and workshop leader at writers' conferences, educators' and library meetings, and at schools; has written verse for juvenile and adult greeting card companies. *Member:* Society of Children's Book Writers and Illustrators, National Writers Club, Wisconsin Regional Writers' Association, Sheboygan Country

DONNA PAPE

Writers' Club, Children's Reading Round Table of Chicago.

Awards, Honors

First prize, Wisconsin Regional Writers' Association juvenile writing contest, 1964; "Children's Choices for 1982" citation, for *The Mouse at the Show.*

Writings

PICTURE BOOKS

The Best Surprise of All, Whitman, 1961.
Splish, Splash, Splush, Whitman, 1962.
Tony Zebra and the Lost Zoo, Whitman, 1963.
I Play in the Snow, Whitman, 1967.
Mary Lou, the Kangaroo, E. M. Hale, 1968.
The Seal Who Wanted to Ski, E. M. Hale, 1968.
Bumper Bear's Bus, Whitman, 1968.
My Fish Got Away!, illustrated by Don Silverstein, L. W. Singer, 1969.
Leo Lion Looks at Books, illustrated by Tom Eaton, Garrard, 1972.
Mrs. Twitter the Animal Sitter, illustrated by Dora Leder, Garrard, 1972.
Mr. Mogg in the Log, illustrated by Mimi Korach, Garrard, 1972.
Count on Leo Lion, illustrated by Eaton, Garrard, 1973.
The Sleep-Leaping Kangaroo, illustrated by Eaton, Garrard, 1973.
Handy Hands, Standard Publishing, 1973.
A Gerbil for a Friend, illustrated by Diane Martin, Prentice-Hall, 1973.
A Special Way to Travel, Standard Publishing, 1973.
A Bone for Breakfast, illustrated by Bill Morrison, Garrard, 1974.
Promises Are Special Words, Moody, 1974.
Taffy Finds a Halloween Witch, illustrated by Carol Nicklaus, Garrard, 1975.
The Big White Thing, illustrated by Morrison, Garrard, 1975.
A Very Special Birthday, Moody, 1975.
Snowman for Sale, illustrated by Raymond Burns, Garrard, 1977.
Where Is My Little Joey?, illustrated by Eaton, Garrard, 1978.
The Peek-a-Boo Book, Golden Press, 1978.
Doghouse for Sale, illustrated by Eaton, Garrard, 1979.
The Snoino Mystery, illustrated by William Hutchinson, Garrard, 1980.
(With Leonard Kessler) *Play Ball, Joey Kangaroo,* illustrated by Eaton, Garrard, 1980.
The Mouse at the Show, illustrated by Gail Gibbons, Elsevier-Nelson, 1981.

In *The Mouse at the Show,* a 1982 Children's Choice book, a little mouse finds a polite solution to her height problem. (Illustration by Gail Gibbons.)

Jack Jump under the Candlestick, illustrated by Irene Trivas, Albert Whitman, 1982.
Big Words for Little People, Standard Publishing, 1985.
The Book of Foolish Machinery, illustrated by Fredric Winkowski, Scholastic, 1988.
Who Will Read to Me?, Houghton, 1991.
Let's Jump, Houghton, 1991.
The Little Bird, Dandelion Press, in press.
Mrs. Brown Becomes Busy, Dandelion Press, in press.

PUZZLE AND ACTIVITY BOOKS

(With Jeanette Grote) *Crossword and Activity Book,* Whitman, 1970.
(With daughter, Jan Pape, and Grote) *Puzzles and Silly Riddles,* Scholastic, 1973.
(With Grote) *Puzzling Pastimes,* Xerox Education Publications, 1973.
(With Grote) *Puzzle Panic,* Scholastic, 1976.
(With Grote) *Fun Puzzles for One,* Xerox Education Publications, 1976.
(With Grote and Carol Karle) *Puzzle Party,* Reader's Digest Press, 1977.
(With Grote) *Pack of Puzzles,* Scholastic, 1978.
(With Grote) *All Kinds of Puzzles,* Scholastic, 1978.
(With Grote) *A Turn for the Words,* Grosset & Dunlap, 1979.
(With Grote) *Puzzle Parade,* Xerox Education Publications, 1979.
(With Karle and Virginia Mueller) *Bible Activities for Kids,* Books 1-6, Bethany House, 1980-82.
(With Grote) *Ring-a-Riddle,* Xerox Education Publications, 1981.
(With Grote) *Puzzles and Mazes,* Scholastic, 1981.
(With Mueller and Karle) *Texas Puzzle Book,* Eakin Publications, 1981.
(With Mueller and Karle) *Arkansas Puzzle Book,* Rose Publishing, 1984.
(With Mueller and Karle) *Think-Pink Solve and Search Puzzles,* Xerox Education Publications, 1983.
(With Mueller and Karle) *Wisconsin Puzzle Book,* Bess Press, 1984.
(With Mueller and Karle) *Hawaii Puzzle Book,* Bess Press, 1984.
(With Mueller and Karle) *California Puzzle Book,* Bess Press, 1985.
(With Mueller and Karle) *Tennessee Puzzle Book,* Winston-Derek, 1985.
(With Mueller and Karle) *Country Music Puzzle Book,* Winston-Derek, 1985.
(With Mueller and Karle) *Vermont Puzzle Book,* Countryman Press, 1987.

"PAPE SERIES OF SPEECH IMPROVEMENT AND READING"; ILLUSTRATED BY LOLA EDICK FRANK

The Three Thinkers of Thay-lee, Oddo, 1968.
Professor Fred and the Fid-Fuddlephone, Oddo, 1968.
Scientist Sam, Oddo, 1968.
The Resting Ruler, Oddo, 1968.
Liz Dearly's Silly Glasses, Oddo, 1968.
Shoemaker Fooze, Oddo, 1968.

OTHER

Contributor to speech therapy workbooks for Word-Making Productions, and to *Parades,* a reader for Houghton, 1986; writer of stories for Whithaven Game Co. Contributor to periodicals, including *Humpty Dumpty, Jack and Jill, Ranger Rick,* and *Highlights.*

■ Adaptations

A Gerbil for a Friend is available in Braille; *The Sleep-Leaping Kangaroo* and *Count on Leo Lion* are available in paperback with cassette recordings from Coronet Instructional Media.

■ Sidelights

Donna Pape once told *SATA:* "I became interested in writing picture books when my children were younger. I wrote sound-saturated material for the Sheboygan Public School speech therapy department which led to writing more material of this nature for publishing. Originally intended for speech therapy, the Pape Series is now also used widely as supplementary reading material providing a phonics drill.

"Some of my ideas come from experiences with friends and family. Other ideas come through 'brain-storming' with other writing friends. A few of the stories in the Pape Reading Series were written by preparing a word list and then using my imagination to create an alliteration-filled rhymed story. Newspaper items often provide story ideas."

■ For More Information See

PERIODICALS

School Library Journal, March, 1975, p. 86; December, 1975, p. 65; September, 1979, p. 119; November, 1982, p. 71.
Washington Post Book World, October 28, 1979, p. 12.

* * *

PARKE, Marilyn 1928-

■ Personal

Born June 5, 1928, in Libby, MT; daughter of Walter (a lumberman) and Alma M. (a homemaker) Neils; married Robert V. Parke (a botany professor), August 25, 1951; children: Robert, Richard, Gayle Crawford, Lynn Castle. *Education:* University of Montana, B.A., 1950; University of Washington, teaching certificate, 1951; Colorado State University, M.Ed., 1973. *Hobbies and other interests:* Gardening, cooking, active sports, reading, and traveling in Latin America.

■ Addresses

Office—1209 Parkwood Dr., Fort Collins, CO 80525.

MARILYN PARKE

Career

Teacher-Poudre R-1, Fort Collins, CO, chapter I teacher, 1973—. *Member:* International Reading Association, Society of Children's Book Writers and Illustrators, National Education Association, Colorado Council of the International Reading Association.

Awards, Honors

Paperback of the year, Parent's Choice Gold Award, 1992, for *A Quetzalcoatl Tale of the Ball Game.*

Writings

"QUETZALCOATL" SERIES; WITH SHARON PANIK

A Quetzalcoatl Tale of Corn, illustrated by daughter, Lynn Castle, Fearon Teacher Aids, 1992.
A Quetzalcoatl Tale of the Ball Game, illustrated by Castle, Fearon Teacher Aids, 1992.
A Quetzalcoatl Tale of Chocolate, illustrated by Castle, Fearon Teacher Aids, 1994.

Work in Progress

With Panik, *A Quetzalcoatl Tale of Colored Cotton, A Quetzalcoatl Tale about the Rain Forest.*

Sidelights

Marilyn Parke told *SATA:* "My daughter, Lynn Parke Castle, is the artist for our series of books. I have the good fortune to have nine grandchildren, including two sets of twins."

For More Information See

PERIODICALS

Reading Teacher, November, 1993, p. 250.

* * *

PERCY, Charles Henry
See SMITH, Dorothy Gladys

* * *

PETERS, Julie Anne 1952-

Personal

Born January 16, 1952, in Jamestown, NY; *Education:* Colorado Women's College, Denver, B.A., 1974; Metropolitan State College of Denver, B.S. (summa cum laude), 1985; University of Colorado, Denver, M.B.A., 1989. *Hobbies and other interests:* Cross-stitching, reading, traveling, two-stepping, taking long walks, animal rights, singing, cooking.

Addresses

Home—14 Twilight Dr., Lakewood, CO 80215.

Career

Tracom Corporation, Denver, CO, secretary, research assistant, and computer programmer, 1975-84; Electronic Data Systems, Denver, CO, computer systems designer, 1985-88; Jefferson County School District, Lakewood, CO, educational assistant, 1990-94. Has also taught elementary school. *Member:* Society of Children's Book Writers and Illustrators, Rocky Mountain Headache Foundation, Denver Zoological Society, Denver Museum of Natural History, Cat Care Society, Project Angel Heart, Denver Women's Chorus.

Writings

The Stinky Sneakers Contest, illustrated by Cat Bowman Smith, Little, Brown, 1992.
Risky Friends, Willowisp Press, 1993.
B. J.'s Billion-Dollar Bet, illustrated by Cynthia Fisher, Little, Brown, 1994.

Also author of numerous articles for juvenile, young adult, and adult periodicals, including *World of Busines$ Kids, Wee Wisdom, Hopscotch, Career Woman,* and *Good Housekeeping.* Contributing editor for *IEA News.*

Work in Progress

An adult mystery series; a middle grade novel with a spelling bee at the story core for Little, Brown, 1996; a middle grade novel, entitled *Revenge of the Snob Squad,* about four misfits who avenge their prosecutors (a

JULIE ANNE PETERS

comedy); a chapbook about appreciating different kinds of "smarts," a sequel to *The Stinky Sneakers Contest.*

■ Sidelights

"About five years ago, after discovering a surprising aptitude for technical writing, I began work on a young adult novel," Julie Anne Peters told *SATA.* "It never saw the light of publication, but it did illuminate hopes for a career in writing. Since I had no formal training, my first two years were devoted to developing skills, learning the craft, and educating myself in the field of children's literature. During that time, I sold a number of short stories, nonfiction articles, and educational activities to children's periodicals. Then my first two books were accepted almost simultaneously—great cause for celebration."

Peters' first book, *The Stinky Sneakers Contest,* is based on a combination of a real-life experience and a "grungy" shoe contest that was held out east. "Reading about the contest reminded me of my own childhood humiliation of perpetually smelly feet," Peters told *SATA.* The plot moves far beyond the title and presents a tale of a friendship in jeopardy because of cheating. The story depicts familiar themes of winning, losing, and honesty, as Earl and Damian compete in the Feetfirst shoe company's smelly sneakers contest. An *Instructor* reviewer commented, "This pleasant, easy-to-read chapter book about two African-American boys will stimulate reflection on what it takes to be a winner." Lynnea McBurney, a reviewer for *School Library Journal,* also stated, "On the whole, this is a nicely written, humorous story. It is short enough for those just getting into transitional readers, yet there is enough here for enjoyment and food for thought."

Peters' second book, *Risky Friends,* explores the issue of choosing friends while confronting the reality of single-parent households. Two best friends, Kacie and Vicky, are at risk of losing their friendship over Kacie's newfound companion, Skye, who wins Kacie's attention by buying her gifts. "As a kid, I always envied people with more money than me—thinking wealth solved the world's problems," Peters said. "That misperception, along with the inevitable growing pains accompanying young adulthood, are the themes explored in *Risky Friends.*" Sister Bernadette Marie Ondus stated in *Kliatt:* "The younger set, girls primarily, will enjoy this story since they will be able to identify closely with the characters."

■ Works Cited

McBurney, Lynnea, review of *The Stinky Sneakers Contest, School Library Journal,* March, 1993, p. 184.

Ondus, Sister Bernadette Marie, review of *Risky Friends, Kliatt,* November, 1993, p. 10.

Review of *The Stinky Sneakers Contest, Instructor,* February, 1993, p. 5.

■ For More Information See

PERIODICALS

Booklist, February 15, 1993, p. 1068.

Books for Young People, June 1, 1994, p. 779.

Horn Book, September/October, 1994.

Kirkus Reviews, December 15, 1992, p. 1576.

* * *

POOLE, Josephine
See HELYAR, Jane Penelope Josephine

* * *

POPESCU, Christine 1930-
(Christine Pullein-Thompson; Christine Keir, a pseudonym)

■ Personal

Born October 1, 1930, in Wimbledon, Surrey, England; daughter of Harry James (an army officer, later secretary to Headmasters' Conference) and Joanna (an author; maiden name, Cannan) Pullein-Thompson; married Julien John Hunter Popescu (an author and journalist), 1954; children: Philip Hunter, Charlotte Vivien, Mark Cannan, Lucy Joanna. *Education:* Attended English schools. *Religion:* Church of England.

CHRISTINE POPESCU

Addresses

Home—The Old Parsonage, Mellis Eye, Suffolk, IP23 8EE, England. *Agent*—Jennifer Luithlen, 88 Homfield Rd., Leicester LE2 1SB, England.

Career

Writer. Grove Riding Schools, Ltd., Peppard and Oxford, England, director, 1945-55.

Writings

(Under pseudonym Christine Keir) *The Impossible Horse,* illustrated by Maurice Tulloch, Evans Brothers, 1957, published under name Christine Pullein-Thompson, Granada, 1972.

(Under pseudonym Christine Keir) *Riding,* illustrated by Glenn Steward, Granada, 1983.

JUVENILE FICTION; UNDER NAME CHRISTINE PULLEIN-THOMPSON

(With sisters, Diana and Josephine Pullein-Thompson) *It Began with Picotee,* illustrated by Rosemary Robinson, A. & C. Black, 1946.

We Rode to the Sea, illustrated by Mil Brown, Collins, 1948.

We Hunted Hounds, illustrated by Marcia Lane Foster, Collins, 1949.

I Carried the Horn, illustrated by Charlotte Hough, Collins, 1951.

Goodbye to Hounds, illustrated by Hough, Collins, 1952, Armada, 1965.

Riders from Afar, illustrated by Hough, Collins, 1954.

Phantom Horse, illustrated by Sheila Rose, Collins, 1955.

A Day to Go Hunting, illustrated by Rose, Collins, 1956.

The First Rosette, illustrated by Rose, Burke, 1956.

Stolen Ponies, illustrated by Rose, Collins, 1957.

The Second Mount, illustrated by Rose, Burke, 1957.

Three to Ride, illustrated by Rose, Burke, 1958.

The Lost Pony (also see below), illustrated by Rose, Burke, 1959.

Ride by Night, illustrated by Rose, Collins, 1960.

The Horse Sale, illustrated by Rose, Collins, 1960.

Giles and the Elephant, illustrated by Dorothy Clark, Burke, 1960.

For Want of a Saddle, illustrated by Anne Bullen, Burke, 1961, Granada, 1972.

The Empty Field, illustrated by Bullen, Burke, 1961, revised edition, Goodchild, 1986.

Giles and the Greyhound, illustrated by Clark, Burke, 1961.

The Open Gate, illustrated by Barbara Crocker, Burke, 1962, revised edition, Goodchild, 1986.

Bandits in the Hills, illustrated by Janet Duchesne, Hamish Hamilton, 1962.

The Gipsy Children, illustrated by Duchesne, Hamish Hamilton, 1962.
Giles and the Canal, illustrated by Clark, Burke, 1962.
Homeless Katie, illustrated by Prudence Seward, Hamish Hamilton, 1963.
The Doping Affair, illustrated by Enid Ash, Burke, 1963, published as *The Pony Dopers,* Atlantic, 1968.
The Eastmans in Brittany, illustrated by Clark, Burke, 1964.
(With others) *Triple Adventure* (includes *The Lost Pony*), Burke, 1964.
Granny Comes to Stay, illustrated by Christine Marsh, Hamish Hamilton, 1964.
No One at Home, illustrated by C. R. Evans, Hamish Hamilton, 1964.
The Eastmans Move House, illustrated by Susan Broadley, Burke, 1964.
The Boys from the Cafe, illustrated by Mary Russon, Hamish Hamilton, 1965.
The Eastmans Find a Boy, illustrated by Joan Calvert, Burke, 1966.
The Stolen Car, illustrated by Elisabeth Grant, Hamish Hamilton, 1966.
Little Black Pony, illustrated by Lynette Hemmant, Hamish Hamilton, 1966.
A Day to Remember, illustrated by Hemmant, Hamish Hamilton, 1966.
The Lost Cow, illustrated by Hemmant, Hamish Hamilton, 1966.
Robbers in the Night, illustrated by Andrew Sier, Hamish Hamilton, 1967.
Room to Let, illustrated by Hemmant, Hamish Hamilton, 1968.
Dog in a Pram, illustrated by Seward, Hamish Hamilton, 1969.
Nigel Eats His Words, illustrated by Clark, Burke, 1969.
Phantom Horse Comes Home, Collins, 1970.
Riders on the March, Armada, 1970.
They Rode to Victory, Armada, 1972.
Phantom Horse Goes to Ireland, Collins, 1972.
I Rode a Winner, Armada, 1973, Scholastic, 1978.
(With Diana and Josephine Pullein-Thompson) *Black Beauty's Clan,* Brockhampton Press, 1975, McGraw, 1980.
Mystery at Black Pony Inn, illustrated by Gareth Floyd, Pan Books, 1976.
Strange Riders at Black Pony Inn, illustrated by Floyd, Pan Books, 1976.
Pony Patrol SOS, Dragon Books, 1977, Simon & Schuster, 1991.
Prince at Black Pony Inn, illustrated by Floyd, Pan Books, 1978.
Secrets at Black Pony Inn, illustrated by Floyd, Pan Books, 1978.
(With Diana and Josephine Pullein-Thompson) *Black Beauty's Family,* illustrated by Grant, Hodder & Stoughton, 1978, McGraw, 1980.
Pony Patrol, Severn House, 1979, Simon & Schuster, 1991.
Black Velvet, illustrated by Grant, Hodder & Stoughton, 1979.
Pony Patrol Fights Back, Severn House, 1979, Simon & Schuster, 1992.
Phantom Horse in Danger, Severn House, 1980.
Ride by Night, Armada, 1980.
Riders on the March, Severn House, 1980.
Pony Patrol and the Mystery Horse, Severn House, 1981, Simon & Schuster, 1992.
Phantom Horse Goes to Scotland, Severn House, 1981.
Father Unknown, Dobson, 1982.
(With Diana and Josephine Pullein-Thompson) *Black Beauty's Family Two,* Beaver, 1982.
Ponies in the Park, illustrated by Tony Morris, Beaver, 1982.
Ponies in the Forest, Severn House, 1983.
Ponies in the Blizzard, Beaver, 1984.
Wait for Me, Phantom Horse, Severn House, 1985.
A Home for Jessie, illustrated by Sheila Ratcliffe, Goodchild, 1986.
Please Save Jessie, illustrated by Ratcliffe, Goodchild, 1987.
Stay at Home Ben, illustrated by Kate Rodgers, Hamish Hamilton, 1987.
Careless Ben, illustrated by Rodgers, Hamish Hamilton, 1988.
The Road through the Hills, illustrated by Gavin Rowe, Hodder & Stoughton, 1988.
The Big Storm, illustrated by Lesley Smith, Hodder & Stoughton, 1988.
Candy Goes to the Gymkhana, Ladybird, 1989.
Candy Stops a Train, Paperbird, 1989.
Smoke in the Hills, Hodder & Stoughton, 1989.
Good Deeds at Black Pony Inn, Ravette, 1989.
Catastrophe at Black Pony Inn, Ravette, 1989.
Across the Frontier, Andersen, 1990.
Runaway Ben, Hamish Hamilton, 1990.
The Long Search, Andersen, 1991, Bradbury Press, 1993.
I Want That Pony, Simon & Schuster, 1993.
A Pony in Distress, Cavalier, 1994.
The Best Pony for Me, Macdonalds, 1995.
Horse Haven, Cavalier, 1995.

OTHER; UNDER NAME CHRISTINE PULLEIN-THOMPSON

(Editor) *The First Pony Scrapbook,* Pan Books, 1972.
(Editor) *The Second Pony Scrapbook,* Pan Books, 1973.
The Follyfoot Horse and Pony Quiz Book, illustrated by David McKee, Pan Books, 1974.
A Pony to Love, illustrated by Claude Kailer and others, Pan Books, 1974.
Good Riding, illustrated by Christine Bousfield, Armada, 1975.
Riding for Fun, illustrated by Bousfield, Armada, 1976.
(Editor) *Christine Pullein-Thompson's Book of Pony Stories,* illustrated by Floyd, Pan Books, 1976.
(Editor) *The Second Book of Pony Stories,* illustrated by Ron Stenberg, Pan Books, 1977.
(Editor) *Pony Parade,* Granada, 1978.
Improve Your Riding, illustrated by Bousfield, Collins, 1979.
(Selector) *Horse and Pony Stories,* research by Charlotte Fyfe, illustrated by Victor Ambrus, Kingfisher, 1992, published as *Horse Stories,* 1994.

Pullein-Thompson's works have been translated into eleven languages.

■ Work in Progress

A childhood memoir, in collaboration with sisters Diana and Josephine; *Havoc at Horse Haven,* a sequel to *Horse Haven.*

■ Sidelights

British children's author Christine Popescu comes from a writing family. Her mother, who wrote as Joanna Cannan, her sisters, Josephine and Diana Pullein-Thompson, and her brother, Denis Cannan, are all authors, too. "Why do I write? Well, my mother wrote," Popescu once told *SATA.* "In fact, when I was a child growing up in a Georgian Dower House, we all wrote endlessly—plays, poems, articles, and stories for our family magazine. It seemed quite natural." Popescu wrote her first book, *It Began with Picotee,* with her sisters when she was only fifteen. Since then, she has written more than eighty books for children as Christine Pullein-Thompson, many of which are about ponies. "Her books demonstrate a consistency and professionalism not always found in children's books," Linda Yeatman states in *Twentieth-Century Children's Writers,* and as a result "she has been rewarded by steady sales and continuity in print which few authors can match."

"I grew up in the country with ponies, so they were what I wrote about," Popescu explained to *SATA.* As an adult, she was the director of a riding school in England, and several of her books are based on her experiences there. Not only did she write her first book in collaboration with her sisters Josephine and Diana, the trio also produced *Black Beauty's Clan* and *Black Beauty's Family,* story collections that follow Anna Sewell's 1877 classic *Black Beauty* by following the lives of the descendents of Sewell's downtrodden horse. The authors "invoke the spirit and intention of Anna Sewell" by using the horse's point of view to narrate their tales, according to *Growing Point* reviewer Margery Fisher. While *School Library Journal* contributor Wendy Delett finds the narrations do "a fairly good job of continuing the technique of horse-as-author," she feels that the stories "do not measure up to the much stronger original" due to some overly human observations. But *Junior Bookshelf* writer D. A. Young believes that the horses' observations "paint an interesting picture of the social conditions of the time," while Fisher finds the period detail interesting. She concludes in another *Growing Point* review that that the authors "use the animal autobiography confidently and without self-consciousness."

Not all of Popescu's books are about ponies, however. "The twenty or so books I have written for younger children with hardly a pony to be seen come mainly from life with my own family," she explained. "Some have been sparked off simply by a heading in a newspaper—something like, 'Small Boy Disappears,' or

Set in tumultuous eastern Europe at the time of communism's collapse, this novel tells of young Ion's struggle to be reunited with his unjustly imprisoned parents. (Cover illustration by Joe Baker.)

a piece on the plight of homeless children. Some have grown out of a visit to the seaside, or a holiday in Sicily." *Robbers in the Night,* for instance, tells of an immigrant family trying to survive in a basement apartment. Son Paul becomes involved with gang activities, leading to a conflict with the family. "This is a sensitive, even penetrating book, with much honest observation," writes a *Times Literary Supplement* critic, who adds that it is "above the usual level" of many children's books.

Travels to Eastern Europe inspired two of Popescu's more recent books, *Across the Frontier* and *The Long Search,* which are set in an unnamed Eastern European country. Both books follow ten-year-old Ion, who lives with his grandmother in a country that greatly resembles contemporary Romania; the fictional country of the stories is in the midst of political upheaval. In *Across the Frontier,* Ion has to make the difficult choice of whether to go live in safety in England with his uncle and cousins or stay with his ailing grandmother and face the uncertainty of living in a country in turmoil. *The Long Search* follows Ion as he tries to locate his parents, imprisoned ten years before for their opposition to the country's president. In another *Junior Bookshelf* review, Young describes the book as "a work of fiction, but the facts ring so true in our recent memories that it makes absorbing reading as history."

Popescu has traveled all over the world, but she resides in the English countryside, where she lives with her family and pets—including ponies. She feels that the writing gene is "embedded" in her family; however, she won't tell her children to be writers. "It is a difficult and a not particularly profitable profession," she told *SATA*. "Besides, I know if they have the gene, nothing will stop them writing in the end."

■ Works Cited

Delett, Wendy, review of *Black Beauty's Family, School Library Journal,* April, 1981, p. 130.
Fisher, Margery, review of *Black Beauty's Clan, Growing Point,* November, 1975, p. 2749.
Fisher, Margery, review of *Black Beauty's Family, Growing Point,* November, 1978, pp. 3407-8.
"Ganging-up on the Grown-ups," *Times Literary Supplement,* November 30, 1967, p. 1151.
Yeatman, Linda, "Christine Pullein-Thompson," *Twentieth-Century Children's Writers,* 3rd edition, St. James Press, 1987, p. 802.
Young, D. A., review of *Black Beauty's Family, Junior Bookshelf,* February, 1979, pp. 58-59.
Young, D. A., review of *The Long Search, Junior Bookshelf,* December, 1991, p. 267.

■ For More Information See

PERIODICALS

Bulletin of the Center for Children's Books, November, 1993, p. 96.
East Anglia Daily Times, November 19, 1994.
Growing Point, October, 1977, p. 3191; July, 1982, p. 3924; November, 1990, p. 5437; May, 1991, p. 5521; January, 1992, p. 5641.
Junior Bookshelf, October, 1990, p. 235.
Kirkus Reviews, November 1, 1993, p. 1396.
School Library Journal, December, 1993, p. 298.
Spectator, December 15, 1990, p. 40.
Times Educational Supplement, July 9, 1982, p. 26; April 7, 1989, p. B12.
Times Literary Supplement, October 3, 1968, p. 1121; October 16, 1969, p. 1201.
Voice of Youth Advocates, December, 1993, p. 298.
Weekend Telegraph, November 19, 1994.

* * *

PRATCHETT, Terry 1948-

■ Personal

Born April 28, 1948, in Beaconsfield, England; son of David (an engineer) and Eileen (a secretary; maiden name, Kearns) Pratchett; married; wife's name, Lyn; children: Rhianna.

TERRY PRATCHETT

■ Addresses

Agent—Colin Smythe, Ltd., P.O. Box 6, Gerrards Cross, Buckinghamshire SL9 8XA, England.

■ Career

Journalist in Buckinghamshire, Bristol, and Bath, England, 1965-80; Central Electricity Board, Western Region, press officer, 1980-87; novelist.

■ Awards, Honors

British Science Fiction Awards, 1989, for "Discworld" series, and 1990, for *Good Omens: The Nice and Accurate Predictions of Agnes Nutter, Witch;* Best Children's Book award, Writers' Guild of Great Britain, 1993, for *Johnny and the Dead;* British Book Award for Fantasy and Science Fiction of the Year, 1993.

■ Writings

"DISCWORLD" SERIES

The Colour of Magic, St. Martin's, 1983, new edition with foreword by Pratchett, Colin Smythe, 1988.
The Light Fantastic, Colin Smythe, 1986, Signet, 1988.
Equal Rites, Gollancz, 1986, Signet, 1988.
Mort, Gollancz, 1987, Signet, 1989.
Sourcery, Gollancz, 1988, Signet, 1989.
Wyrd Sisters, Gollancz, 1988, Roc, 1990.
Pyramids, Roc, 1989.
Eric, illustrated by Josh Kirby, Gollancz, 1989, published without illustrations, Gollancz, 1990.
Guards! Guards!, Gollancz, 1989, Roc, 1991.

Artist Stephen Player's rendition of Pratchett's "Discworld."

Moving Pictures, Gollancz, 1990, Roc, 1992.
Reaper Man, Gollancz, 1991, Roc, 1992.
Witches Abroad, Gollancz, 1991, Roc, 1993.
Small Gods, Gollancz, 1992, HarperCollins, 1994.
Lords and Ladies, Gollancz, 1992.
Men at Arms, Gollancz, 1993.
Soul Music, HarperCollins, 1994.
Interesting Times, Gollancz, 1994.
(With Stephen Briggs) *The Discworld Companion,* Gollancz, 1994.
Mort: A Discworld Big Comic (graphic novel), illustrated by Graham Higgins, Gollancz, 1994.
Soul Music, Gollancz, 1994.

"BROMELIAD" TRILOGY; JUVENILE FANTASY

Truckers, Doubleday, 1989.
Diggers, Doubleday, 1990.
Wings, Doubleday, 1990.

OTHER

The Carpet People (juvenile fantasy), Smythe, 1971, revised edition, Doubleday, 1992.
The Dark Side of the Sun (science fiction), St. Martin's, 1976.
Strata (science fiction), St. Martin's, 1981.
The Unadulterated Cat, illustrated by Gray Jolliffe, Gollancz, 1989.
(With Neil Gaiman) *Good Omens: The Nice and Accurate Predictions of Agnes Nutter, Witch,* Workman, 1990.
Only You Can Save Mankind (young adult), Doubleday, 1992.
Johnny and the Dead (juvenile), Doubleday, 1993.
(With Briggs) *The Streets of Ankh-Morpork,* Corgi, 1993.

Pratchett's novels have been published in eighteen languages.

■ Adaptations

The Colour of Magic was adapted as a four-part work by Scott Rockwell with illustrations by Steven Ross, Innovation Corporation, 1991, and published as a graphic novel, Corgi, 1992; *The Light Fantastic* was adapted as a four-part work by Rockwell with illustrations by Ross, Innovation Corporation, 1992, and published as a graphic novel, Corgi, 1993; the "Bromeliad" trilogy and the first six books of the "Discworld" series were released on audio-cassette by Corgi; an album, *Music from the Discworld* by Dave Greenslade, was released by Virgin Records, 1994; a video game, *Discworld,* was released by Sony/Psygnosis, 1994.

■ Work in Progress

A "Discworld" novel and map.

■ Sidelights

British author Terry Pratchett has penned numerous science fiction and fantasy novels and is known primarily for his "Discworld" series and his "Bromeliad" trilogy for children. Critic David V. Barrett stated in *New Statesman* that the novels of Discworld "are works of marvelous composition and rattling good stories." Discworld—as well as most of Pratchett's other works—also offers humorous parodies of other famous science fiction and fantasy writers, such as J. R. R. Tolkien or Larry Niven, and spoofs such modern trends as New Age philosophy and universal concerns like death. Nevertheless, "in among the slapstick and clever wordplay are serious concepts," as Barrett pointed out. In "genres assailed by shoddiness, mediocrity, and ... the endless series," asserted *Locus* critic Faren Miller in a review of *Witches Abroad,* "Pratchett is never shoddy, and under the laughter there's a far from mediocre mind at work."

Pratchett published his first work of fantasy, *The Carpet People,* in 1971. Aimed at young readers, the book describes a whole world set in a carpet, populated by creatures called deftmenes, mouls, and wights. The novel's protagonist, Snibril the Munrung, travels with his brother Glurk through the many Carpet regions—which are set off by different colors—to do battle against the evil concept of Fray. A *Times Literary Supplement* reviewer recommended *The Carpet People,* further noting that "the Tolkienian echoes may draw in some older readers."

Pratchett used the concept of a flat world when he embarked upon his first Discworld novel, *The Colour of Magic,* taking an approach more suitable to the fantasy genre than to science fiction. Discworld sits on the shoulders of four giant elephants, who in turn are resting on the back of a giant turtle as it swims through space. As W. D. Stevens reported in *Science Fiction and Fantasy Review,* Discworld is "populated with wizards, warriors, demons, dragons," and other fantastic attributes. The protagonist of *The Colour of Magic* is a hapless wizard named Rincewind. He teams up with a tourist from a remote portion of the disc. The result, according to Stevens, is "one of the funniest, and cleverest, [Sword and Sorcery] satires to be written."

Rincewind returns in Pratchett's second Discworld novel, *The Light Fantastic.* This time he must try to prevent Discworld from colliding with a red star that has recently appeared in its sky. The next book in the series, *Equal Rites,* puts the emphasis on the character of Granny Weatherwax, who also appears in *Wyrd Sisters,* this time accompanied by two fellow witches. In *Wyrd Sisters,* Granny and her companions form a trio of witches (reminiscent of those in William Shakespeare's play *Macbeth*) to foil the plot of the evil Lord Felmet and his wife, who have usurped the rightful king. This volume led Miller to declare: "Terry Pratchett continues to defy the odds. An open-ended series that just keeps getting better? Humorous fantasy with resources beyond puns, buffoonery, and generations of cardboard characters? Unheard of—until Pratchett."

In 1989, Pratchett published the first of his Bromeliad fantasy series for children. *Truckers* introduces young readers to the nomes, four-inch high people from another planet who have crashed on earth and who have made a new world for themselves under the floorboards of a department store. Some of the nomes, however, have lived on the outside; the fun begins when one of these, Masklin, meets with the nomes of the store. When they learn that their store is going out of business and will be torn down, they must cooperate with the outside nomes to find a new home and escape their old one in a human-sized truck. "A wild and hilarious chase sequence follows, with the baffled police doubting their sanity," observed a *Horn Book* reviewer. Elizabeth Ward summed up *Truckers* in the *Washington Post Book World* as "a delightful surprise" and a "benevolent little satire."

Diggers takes Masklin and his fellow nomes to their new home in an abandoned quarry. But problems ensue when humans attempt to reactivate the quarry. "In the book's funniest scene," according to Patrick Jones in *Voice of Youth Advocates,* "a group of nomes 'attacks' one of the humans, ties him to his desk chair, and stuffs a note in his hand proclaiming: 'leave us alone.'" "Satire and allegory abound," a *Horn Book* reviewer

In one of the many Discworld adventures, witches Granny Weatherwax, Magral Garlick, and Nanny Ogg must stop a fairy godmother war.

concluded of *Diggers,* but the critic also noted that the nomes' "trials and emotions are both moving and amusing." In *Wings* Masklin and his friends attempt to return to their home planet by placing the Thing—the "magic" box that in *Truckers* had warned them of the store's demise—aboard a communications satellite so that it can summon their old mother ship, which has been waiting for them throughout their earthly exile. Margaret A. Chang lauded this last book of the series in the *School Library Journal* as a "cheerful, unpretentious tale."

While Pratchett was working on the Bromeliad series, he continued to create new Discworld novels. *Pyramids,* which appeared in 1989, spoofs ancient Egypt, transparently labeled "Ankh-Morpork" by Pratchett. In *Pyramids* loyal Discworld fans meet Teppic, a teenager who is studying to become an assassin until a relative's death makes him Pharaoh. Other well-received Discworld books include *Witches Abroad,* which again features Granny Weatherwax and her witch companions. This time their mission is to stop the inevitable happy ending of a fairy tale because of the deeper disaster it will cause. A later Discworld novel is *Small Gods,* which Miller described in his *Locus* review of the work as "a book about tortoises, eagles, belief systems, conspiracies, religious bigotry, man's need for gods, and gods' even greater need for man."

Pratchett has continued to produce works outside of his two series, however. In 1992 Pratchett penned a young adult novel, *Only You Can Save Mankind,* which spoofs, among other things, the 1991 Persian Gulf War. In this fantasy tale, the computer game-playing protagonist, Johnny, is faced with a strange dilemma when the commander of the alien force he is about to destroy on-screen asks to surrender. Accepting his role as the Chosen One, the protector of the Scree Wee Empire, Johnny must rescue the aliens from the rest of the world's computer game players. *Only You Can Save Mankind* garnered strong reviews from critics for its blend of humor and suspense. A *Junior Bookshelf* contributor remarked that teenage readers "should thoroughly enjoy the teasing competence of Mr. Pratchett's high-tech conundrum, by turns comical, whimsical, and downright terrifying." Miller, in another *Locus* review, stated that the "serious message of this novel shows clearly, but it's delightfully packaged, with the typical Pratchett combination of wit and level-headed humanity."

A later work, *Johnny and the Dead,* finds the hero of *Only You Can Save Mankind* mixed up in another creepy yet humorous adventure. The residents of an old graveyard—the dead and buried residents, that is—take offense at the city council's plans to sell the cemetery to a corporation intent on replacing the gravesites with a new development. Enlisting the aid of Johnny as their spokesperson, the deceased try to sway public opinion against demolition of their "home." Marcus Crouch, reviewing *Johnny and the Dead* in *Junior Bookshelf,* remarked that the "story surprised with its depth and seriousness" and called it "a lovely, funny, witty, sometimes wise book, exciting and entertaining and always highly readable."

Works Cited

Barrett, David V., *New Statesman,* January 3, 1992, p. 33.
Review of *The Carpet People, Times Literary Supplement,* April 28, 1972, p. 475.
Chang, Margaret A., review of *Diggers, School Library Journal,* September, 1991, pp. 258-59.
Crouch, Marcus, review of *Johnny and the Dead, Junior Bookshelf,* August, 1993, p. 157.
Review of *Diggers, Horn Book,* May/June, 1991, p. 332.
Jones, Patrick, review of *Diggers, Voice of Youth Advocates,* February, 1991, p. 366.
Miller, Faren, review of *Wyrd Sisters, Locus,* January, 1989, p. 17.
Miller, Faren, review of *Witches Abroad, Locus,* October, 1991, pp. 15, 17.
Miller, Faren, review of *Small Gods, Locus,* June, 1992, p. 17.
Miller, Faren, review of *Only You Can Save Mankind, Locus,* September, 1992, p. 66.
Review of *Only You Can Save Mankind, Junior Bookshelf,* February, 1993, p. 33.
Stevens, W. D., review of *The Colour of Magic, Science Fiction and Fantasy Review,* March, 1984, p. 35.
Review of *Truckers, Horn Book,* March/April, 1990, p. 202.
Ward, Elizabeth, review of *Truckers, Washington Post Book World,* February 11, 1990, p. 6.

For More Information See

BOOKS

Twentieth-Century Science Fiction Writers, St. James, 1991.

PERIODICALS

Best Sellers, November, 1976, pp. 249-50.
Fantasy Review, November, 1986, pp. 31-32.
Locus, February, 1993, p. 58.
New Statesman, August 29, 1986, p. 26; January 29, 1988, p. 30.
New York Times Book Review, October 7, 1990, p. 27.
Science Fiction and Fantasy Book Review, April, 1982, p. 20.
Times (London), February 12, 1987; August 9, 1990; November 21, 1991, p. 16.
Washington Post, December 20, 1990.

* * *

PULLEIN-THOMPSON, Christine
See POPESCU, Christine

* * *

PULLEIN-THOMPSON, Diana
See FARR, Diana

PULLEIN-THOMPSON, Josephine (Josephine Mann)

Personal

Born in Wimbledon, Surrey, England; daughter of Harry James (an army officer, later secretary to Headmasters' Conference) and Joanna (a writer; maiden name, Cannan) Pullein-Thompson. *Education:* Attended Wychwood School. *Religion:* Anglican. *Hobbies and other interests:* Horseback riding, walking, reading, theater, travel.

Addresses

Home—16 Knivet Rd., London SW6 1JH, England.

Career

Writer. Former co-owner of two riding schools, competitor in horse shows and one-day horse events, and show judge of jumping and dressage events. *Member:* Society of Authors, Crime Writers Association, English Center of International PEN (general secretary, 1976-93; president, 1994), British Horse Society, Pony Club (visiting commissioner, 1960-68; district commissioner, 1970-76).

Awards, Honors

Ernest Benn Award, 1961, for *All Change;* member of the Order of the British Empire, 1984.

Writings

FOR CHILDREN

(With sisters, Christine and Diana Pullein-Thompson) *It Began with Picotee,* illustrated by Rosemary Robinson, A. & C. Black, 1946.
Six Ponies, illustrated by Anne Bullen, Collins, 1946.
I Had Two Ponies, illustrated by Bullen, Collins, 1947.
Plenty of Ponies, illustrated by Bullen, Collins, 1949.
Prince among Ponies, illustrated by Charlotte Hough, Collins, 1949.
Pony Club Team, illustrated by Sheila Rose, Collins, 1950.
The Radney Riding Club, Collins, 1951.
One Day Event, illustrated by Rose, Collins, 1954.
Show Jumping Secret, illustrated by Rose, Collins, 1955, Armada, 1981.
Patrick's Pony, illustrated by Geoffrey Whittam, Brockhampton Press, 1956.
Pony Club Camp, illustrated by Rose, Collins, 1957.
The Trick Jumpers, illustrated by Rose, Collins, 1958.
All Change, illustrated by Rose, Benn, 1961, published as *The Hidden Horse,* Armada, 1982.
Ponies in Colour, Studio, 1962.
How Horses Are Trained, Routledge & Kegan Paul, 1966.
Learn to Ride Well, Routledge & Kegan Paul, 1966.
(Editor) *Horses and Their Owners* (nonfiction), Nelson, 1970.
Race Horse Holiday, Collins, 1971.

JOSEPHINE PULLEIN-THOMPSON

(Editor) *Proud Riders: Horse and Pony Stories,* Brockhampton Press, 1973.
Ride Better and Better, Blackie, 1974.
(With Christine and Diana Pullein-Thompson) *Black Beauty's Clan,* Brockhampton Press, 1975, McGraw, 1980.
Star Riders of the Moor, illustrated by Elisabeth Grant, Hodder & Stoughton, 1976.
(With Christine and Diana Pullein-Thompson) *Black Beauty's Family,* Hodder & Stoughton, 1978, McGraw, 1980.
Ride to the Rescue, illustrated by Grant, Hodder & Stoughton, 1979.
Fear Treks the Moor, Hodder & Stoughton, 1979.
Black Nightshade, Hodder & Stoughton, 1980.
Ghost Horse on the Moor, illustrated by Eric Rowe, Hodder & Stoughton, 1980.
The No-Good Pony, Severn House, 1981.
Treasure on the Moor, illustrated by Jon Davis, Hodder & Stoughton, 1981.
The Prize Pony, Arrow, 1982.
(With Christine and Diana Pullein-Thompson) *Black Beauty's Family Two,* Beaver, 1982.
Pony Club Cup (also see below), Armada, 1983.
Pony Club Challenge (also see below), Armada, 1984.
Mystery on the Moor, illustrated by Chris Rothero, Hodder & Stoughton, 1984.
Save the Ponies!, Severn House, 1984.
Pony Club Trek (also see below), Armada, 1985.
Suspicion Stalks the Moor, illustrated by Glenn Steward, Hodder & Stoughton, 1986.
Black Swift, Cannongate Press, 1991.
A Job with Horses, J. A. Allen, 1994.
Pony Club Stories (contains *Pony Club Cup, Pony Club Challenge,* and *Pony Club Trek*), Reed, 1994.

OTHER

Gin and Murder (crime novel), Hammond, 1959, Linford Mystery Library, 1990.
They Died in the Spring (crime novel), Hammond, 1960, Linford Mystery Library, 1990.
Murder Strikes Pink (crime novel), Hammond, 1963, Linford Mystery Library, 1990.
(Under pseudonym Josephine Mann) *A Place with Two Faces,* Coronet, 1972, Pocket Books, 1974.

Also contributor to British horse journals.

■ Work in Progress

A childhood memoir, in collaboration with sisters Diana and Christine.

■ Sidelights

A veteran of various equestrian competitions, Josephine Pullein-Thompson draws from a lifetime of experience to create stories that children enjoy for their detailed portrayals of riding, raising, and showing horses. For instance, in collaboration with her sisters Christine and Diana, Pullein-Thompson has produced *Black Beauty's Clan* and *Black Beauty's Family,* two story compilations that follow Anna Sewell's 1877 classic *Black Beauty* by relating the adventures of various relatives of Sewell's long-suffering horse. By using the horse's point of view to narrate their tales, the Pullein-Thompsons "invoke the spirit and intention of Anna Sewell," according to *Growing Point* reviewer Margery Fisher. In addition, the observations of the horses "paint an interesting picture of the social conditions of the time," *Junior Bookshelf* writer D. A. Young notes. While *School Library Journal* contributor Wendy Delett finds the narrations do "a fairly good job of continuing the technique of horse-as-author," she feels that the stories "do not measure up to the much stronger original" due to some overly human observations. Fisher, however, finds the period detail introduced by the horses interesting, and concludes in another review that the authors "use the animal autobiography confidently and without self-consciousness."

Pullein-Thompson's individual efforts have ranged from tales of competition to nonfiction to stories of mystery and adventure, all involving horses. *The Prize Pony,* for example, shows Debbie's efforts to maintain and train the pony she has won in a story contest. The story is told "with the verve, authority and good sense which we expect" from the author, according to a *Growing Point* reviewer. In *Treasure on the Moor,* where a group of children search for hidden booty and try to save a farm, "the horse expertise is of course excellent," according to Dorothy Nimmo in *School Librarian,* making for "a rattling good yarn." Environmental concerns of a rabies epidemic and oil-polluted sea birds highlight *Mystery on the Moor,* whose plot "gallops—frequently literally—to an exciting conclusion," a *Junior Bookshelf* critic writes. With these popular combinations of horse lore and adventure, another *Junior Bookshelf* writer concludes, Pullein-Thompson "has delighted a generation of children with her books."

Pullein-Thompson more recently told *SATA*, "I am now attempting to write my childhood memoirs in conjunction with my sisters: identical twins Diana and Christine. As our first book [*It Began with Picotee*], written in committee when we were teenagers, was published in 1946 it seemed a good idea to produce another joint work for publication fifty years on.

"Our childhood was eccentric. There were writers on both sides of the family and our liberated novelist mother, who didn't believe in conventional education, provided ponies rather than lessons. We find writing about it rather a struggle, as we argue over chronology and half-remembered fact and strive to iron out the overlaps and yet allow all three voices to express their individual views."

■ Works Cited

Delett, Wendy, review of *Black Beauty's Family, School Library Journal,* April, 1981, p. 130.

Fisher, Margery, review of *Black Beauty's Clan, Growing Point,* November, 1975, p. 2749.

Fisher, Margery, review of *Black Beauty's Family, Growing Point,* November, 1978, pp. 3407-8.

Review of *Mystery on the Moor, Junior Bookshelf,* December, 1984, p. 267.

Nimmo, Dorothy, review of *Treasure on the Moor, School Librarian,* December, 1982, pp. 360, 362.

Review of *The Prize Pony, Growing Point,* July, 1982, p. 3934.

Review of *Treasure on the Moor, Junior Bookshelf,* October, 1982, p. 193.

Young, D. A., review of *Black Beauty's Family, Junior Bookshelf,* February, 1979, pp. 58-59.

■ For More Information See

PERIODICALS

Growing Point, July, 1983.

Junior Bookshelf, April, 1975, p. 129.

R

RANA, Indi
See RANA, Indira Higham

See RANA, Indira Higham

* * *

RANA, Indira Higham 1944-
(Indi Rana)

■ Personal

Born March 28, 1944, in Chhindwara, Madhya Pradesh, India; daughter of Harbans Singh Sachdev (a mining engineer) and Jeet Aurora Tara (a farmer); married John David Higham (a computer systems analyst), February 14, 1967 (divorced, 1975). *Education:* Delhi University, B.S., 1963, B.Ed., 1964; Briarcliff College, A.A., 1965; Stanford University, M.A., 1975. *Religion:* "All." *Hobbies and other interests:* Photography, theater, painting in oils and illustrations in gouache, yoga.

■ Addresses

Home—B/G-1 Rosewood Apartments, Mayur Vihar Ph I Ext II, New Delhi, India 110091. *Agent*—AP Watt, 20 John St., London WC1N 2DR, England.

■ Career

Harcourt Brace & World, New York City, art editor of school textbooks, 1965-66; Purnell and Sons, London, England, assistant to the editorial director and production manager, trade books, 1967-70; Paul Hamlyn Ltd., London, senior editor of children's trade books, 1970-71; Thomson Press Ltd., New Delhi, India, managing editor of children's trade books and *Target,* a children's magazine, 1976-80. Research and writing in cross-cultural issues, development education and communications, 1980—. *Member:* Authors Guild, Authors League of America, New Delhi Habitat Center, New Delhi Consumers' Forum.

INDIRA HIGHAM RANA

■ Writings

(With others) *The Human Adventure,* Addison-Wesley, 1975.
Beginners' Fun-to-Learn, Thomson Press, 1979.
(With others) *All Star Readers,* Harcourt, 1983.
Favourite Stories from Sri Lanka, Heinemann, 1983.
More Favourite Stories from Sri Lanka, Heinemann, 1983.
Monkey See, Monkey Do, Macmillan Educational, 1986.

The Devil on Auntie's Shoulder (novel for children), Hodder & Stoughton, 1986.

The Devil in the Dustbin (novel for children), illustrated by M. Padmanabhan, Hamish Hamilton, 1989, Holt, 1993.

The Roller Birds of Rampur (novel for children), Bodley Head, 1991, Rupa, 1994.

Also author of numerous film scripts and short stories.

■ Work in Progress

An adult novel, short stories, and a picture book for seven year olds.

■ Sidelights

Indira Higham Rana was born of Punjabi parents in a small district headquarters in the Central Provinces of India. Her books reflect her British upbringing, American education, and Indian heritage. Her most compelling subjects are the conflicts and confusions that arise between these three aspects. Rana's father was a mining engineer with a British firm. "Our homes were large and rambling British built bungalows on five acres and needed fourteen servants to maintain them," Rana recounted to *SATA*. "Our social life centered around the company club. There were mining disasters and hunting parties in which more was heard from tigers than seen or shot.

"I was sent to a public (meaning private) boarding school in the Himalayas as there were no good schools (by which was meant those that imparted education in English) apart from 'convents' run by nuns, in nearby towns.... Sanawar, which looks a little like Eton, was built by the British for the offspring of army personnel who could not afford to send their children home.

"I was a reclusive child in a jolly gung-ho highly structured environment—we wore dowdy uniforms, marched everywhere, and were incessantly drilled. My escape was books. Those to which we had access (since there was no Indian literature in English for Indian children at the time) were by British authors; generally escapist adventure fare. We identified with English heroines in environments which were not our own.

"I remember a time when I was thirteen, reading a book about an English child growing up in India. I hurtled through the pages with her, taking her point of view, as we do when we read fiction. Halfway through, the heroine thought something derogatory about the child of an Indian gardener. And I was astonished to find myself extremely angry that she thought so little of 'bloody Indians.' I saw then, for an instant, the split in my perceptions."

Rana won a scholarship to Briarcliff College in the United States, where she wrote for the school magazine and became interested in the seeming clash of cultures between East and West. After graduation, she obtained a position at Harcourt Brace and World publishers as an art editor for school textbooks. "I was terrified and delighted," she told *SATA*. "I wanted to belong to this city: the Center of the World. I wanted to be a New Yorker.... I loved my job, I loved the American work ethic." Rana met and married an Englishman, returned with him to London, and then moved to California when he got a job in what was to become Silicon Valley.

In 1976, her marriage ended and Rana returned to New Delhi. She began to work in children's publishing, a field in which she found herself "overproductive and ahead of the times" as her publisher told her when they parted company. However, she was responsible for a dramatic shift in perceptions on literature for Indian children in India, and her work has left an impact on other publishers. After seven years in India, she began to travel again and to write before she settled into work in India in rural education and communications. "I wrote the most incredible garbage," Rana confessed to *SATA*. "Reams of it. I began to realize I'd been mute most of my life—metaphorically without a voice. A real voice. A voice that, to use the jargon of transcendental psychology, '*comes from* self.' I had voices over the years with which I spoke, of course. Unconscious voices. The voices of others. Voices that actually 'spoke me.' Voices I *thought* came from me, but didn't.

"Then in 1986, my first novel for children, *The Devil on Auntie's Shoulder,* was published in London. It was based on the reactions of my Canadian nephews to me, an aunt from India, dressed in an alien garb, making them acutely uncomfortable with a part of their heritage that was not expressed adequately in their environment and set them off from their peers. It was the most difficult thing I'd ever done. But I'd found a true voice. It came out of dealing with my nephews' responses to me. I was moved, my perceptions deepened, I broke boundaries, I began to synthesize the western experience with the Indian."

The Devil on Auntie's Shoulder is the story of a young English boy's reactions when his aunt comes to visit from India. It is also concerned with universal myths of "devils" who are believed to cause problems and upheavals in each of our lives at one time or another. It is about "managing" these devils—not suppressing, killing, or hiding from them. In that, it is "philosophy" and "psychology" for the child, aligned to the roots of the Indian mind. The theme of devils was continued in Rana's next book, *The Devil in the Dustbin,* in which *brahmarakshasa,* an Indian tree-devil, inadvertently travels to England in a visitor's suitcase. There he befriends a schoolgirl named Ranjana and meets up with the few English fairy creatures left in the urban environment. A reviewer for *Junior Bookshelf* noted that the book was a cross-cultural fairy tale that would be a welcome read for those who "have not quite relinquished a belief in Father Christmas and the existence of invisible friends."

Rana's writings reflect her own continuing search for a definition of herself and her place in a world in which hierarchies of culture separate us, yet every day technology brings us closer to images from dominant cultures, overwhelming and marginalizing others. "All authors, no matter what language they write in, must, if they want to write with any quality, go through a search for self," Rana told *SATA*. "Those who write in the language of their forefathers have an easier time, for their search does not involve, in addition, the synthesis of a language, therefore a culture, of the mind which is almost diametrically opposed to the language of the heart. Those of us who write naturally in English, from choice or from circumstance, have a larger world to digest."

Rana's tumultuous journeys between East and West—physically, spiritually, and intellectually—are reflected in her novel *The Roller Birds of Rampur.* Roller birds are dull brown birds of India that reveal striking turquoise and ultramarine colors when they fly. *Roller Birds* concerns a young girl who is herself learning to "fly" in the world. Seventeen-year-old Sheila was born in India and brought up in London. When her English boyfriend ends the relationship because his parents don't approve of interracial dating, Sheila, anguished and confused, flies back to her grandfather's farm in India hoping to find safety and comfort. However, Sheila discovers that life in India is complicated as well, and there are no easy answers. Many of her acquaintances (especially the women) are caught between the old ways and the new.

Reviewer Celia F. Gibbs wrote in *School Librarian* that Rana "describes vividly the many contrasts between various classes, and between rural and urban life, in contemporary India." Much of the book focuses on conversations between Sheila and her grandfather, as he tries to explain in simple terms what being Indian is really about. Sheila, confronted with tragedy, tries to make sense of events and find her place in two worlds. What she learns, according to Hazel Moore in *Voice of Youth Advocates,* is that "a better world begins, not in revolutions, but with an understanding of one's personal responsibility."

Indi Rana admitted to *SATA* that the most difficult portions of *Roller Birds* were the "grandpa conversations." "Attempting to crystallize the concepts of dharma and karma, the pivot of Indian thought, for an adolescent seemed an insurmountable task," she said. "So much has been written, so many misconceptions.... I believe the strength of *Roller Birds* lies in this examination of values. Adolescence is the time for such an inquiry. And the inquiry is not restricted to 'immigrants' or 'Indians.' It is truly universal."

■ Works Cited

Review of *The Devil in the Dustbin, Junior Bookshelf,* April, 1990, p. 89.

Gibbs, Celia, review of *The Roller Birds of Rampur, School Librarian,* November, 1991, p. 154.

Moore, Hazel, review of *The Roller Birds of Rampur, Voice of Youth Advocates,* February, 1994, p. 372.

Seventeen-year-old Sheila rediscovers her rich heritage when she returns to India after growing up in England in Rana's 1991 novel.

■ For More Information See

PERIODICALS

Booklist, July, 1993, p. 1959.
Books for Keeps, May, 1992, p. 15.
Books for Your Children, autumn, 1991, p. 27; spring, 1993, p. 5.
Bulletin of the Center for Children's Books, May, 1993, p. 293.
Children's Book Review Service, June, 1993, p. 132.
Children's Bookwatch, November, 1993, p. 3.
Growing Point, September, 1991, p. 5565.
Horn Book Guide, fall, 1993, p. 312.
Junior Bookshelf, April, 1986, p. 71.
Kirkus Reviews, June 15, 1993, p. 790.
Publishers Weekly, June 14, 1993, p. 73.
Recent Children's Fiction, winter, 1991/92.
School Librarian, September, 1986, p. 254; May, 1990, p. 68.
School Library Journal, May, 1993, p. 127.
Teacher, January/February, 1992, p. 19.

Times Educational Supplement, June 8, 1990, p. B14.

* * *

REISBERG, Mira 1955-
(Veg Reisberg)

Personal

Born March 1, 1955, in Melbourne, Australia; daughter of Isaac (a mirror maker and storekeeper) and Lucy (resistance fighter, violinist, and storekeeper; maiden name, Silverberg) Reisberg. *Education:* Attended Preston Art Institute, 1972-73, and Seven Hills College of Art, 1978-79; Academy of Art College, San Francisco, B.F.A., 1986. *Politics:* "Leftist." *Religion:* "Jewish/Pagan." *Hobbies and other interests:* "Two cats: Guido and Possum, art and making art, film, music, travel, gardening, painting murals, empowering children, cooking, enjoying my five senses, graduate and enthusiast of Model Mugging, a self-defense course for women."

Addresses

Home—831 Hampshire St., San Francisco, CA 94110.

Career

Roxie Cinema, San Francisco, CA, box office and concession worker, 1982—; South of Market Cultural Center, San Francisco, graphic designer, 1988-90; Children's Book Press, San Francisco, book designer and illustrator, 1988—. Jewish Film Festival, San Francisco, window display artist, 1989—; Bay Area public school system, San Francisco, educational art consultant, 1989—. *Exhibitions:* "Auto Erartica," La Raza Graphics, San Francisco, CA, 1988; "Project Mission," Artists Television Access, San Francisco, 1990; "Translations by Three Artists/Illustrators," Olive Hyde Gallery, Fremont, CA, 1992; "Utopias in the Teen Age," Capp Street Project with A.W.O.L, San Francisco, 1993; "Under One Sky," Regional Center for the Arts, Walnut Creek, CA, 1994; "3 Strong Women," University of California, Berkeley Theatre, 1994. *Member:* Society for the Prevention of Cruelty to Animals (San Francisco chapter), A.W.O.L. (Artists and Writers Out Loud), Precita Eye's Muralists.

Awards, Honors

U.N.I.C.E.F. Ezra Keats Award citation and Reading Rainbow selection, both 1990, both for *Uncle Nacho's Hat; Baby Rattlesnake* was chosen as a "Sesame Street" read-along book.

Illustrator

(And designer) Roslyn Resnick-Perry, *Leaving for America,* Children's Book Press, 1992.

AS VEG REISBERG

Harriet Rohmer, adapter, *Uncle Nacho's Hat* (bilingual edition), Children's Book Press, 1988.

MIRA REISBERG

(And designer) Te Ata, teller, and Lynn Moroney, adapter, *Baby Rattlesnake,* Children's Book Press, 1989.

(And designer) Moroney, *Elinda Who Danced in the Sky,* Children's Book Press, 1990.

OTHER

Designer of books, including *Family Pictures* (with Armagh Cassil), 1990, *I Remember 121,* 1991, *Things I Like about Grandma,* 1992, and *This Land Is My Land,* 1993. Also creator of cover art for *I Have Something to Say about This Trouble,* written and illustrated by the children of the Tenderloin District, Glide Press, 1988.

Sidelights

Mira Reisberg told *SATA:* "I feel very connected to history, that my art and identity are directly related to these events. I was born March 1, 1955, in Melbourne, Australia. My twin sister Leonie came first and was a relatively easy birth while I was a breach and difficult. I got the nickname Veg when I was about four years old from some Italian kids next door. It's really a boring story. I finally outgrew it when I was thirty-five and felt ready to be an adult. I prefer my Yiddish name of Mira rather than the Anglicized Marilyn, as I only got called Marilyn when I was in trouble—which unfortunately was quite often. Mira or Mirala was definitely the sweeter name.

"My parents were Holocaust survivors who came to Australia after the war to a then-sparsely populated and very racist country. Growing up Jewish in the working class suburb of East Preston was alienating to say the least. Early on my mother gave Leonie and me art supplies saying, 'I can't give you a beautiful world but you can make one for yourselves.' Leonie and I drew in the closet, under the sheets, in the dark, on the walls, anywhere we could. She specialized in horses, and I did everything else. Making art has continued to be a magical thread through my life.

"Over the past twenty-odd years I have lived in Sydney, Melbourne, Adelaide, Brisbane, New Mexico, and San Francisco; in the bush, in the tropics, on the beach, and in the desert. I have traveled extensively throughout the east coast of Australia, as well as in New Zealand, Bali, Hong Kong, Europe, Mexico, and parts of America, having many adventures along the way. Since 1982, I have been based in San Francisco, in the sunny Mission District.

"I started illustrating children's books after Harriet Rohmer of Children's Book Press saw an exhibition of my paintings at La Raza Graphics in 1988. All the children's books I've illustrated and designed have had a great deal of personal meaning for me and hopefully will help empower children and contribute to the growing body of work against racism, sexism, and cultural alienation. My identity as an artist allows me a lot of freedom to be colorful, honest, outrageous, eccentric, intense, and very playful. I used to be ashamed of my sensitivity, my lack of perfection, my flaws, and my humanity. Now I see these things as great strengths. My work is a reflection of this, it connects me with life, with history and ideas, and with others in pursuit of these essential experiences."

* * *

REISBERG, Veg
See REISBERG, Mira

* * *

RICE, John F. 1958-

■ Personal

Born April 30, 1958, in Oneida, NY; son of Francis and Pauline (Magliocca) Rice. *Education:* Syracuse University, B.F.A., 1980. *Politics:* Democrat. *Religion:* Catholic. *Hobbies and other interests:* Fishing.

■ Addresses

Home and office—2032 Curting Ave., Bronx, NY 10461. *Agent*—Ivy League of Artists, 156 5th Ave., New York, NY 10010.

■ Career

Illustrator, New York City, 1980—. Has been commissioned to paint landscapes, seascapes, and sporting events, along with wood carvings of game fish and water fowl. Has donated paintings for fund raising.

■ Illustrator

(With Tom and Mimi Powers) Jack Myers, *Do Cats Really Have Nine Lives?: And Other Questions about Your World,* Bell Books, 1993.

Sneed B. Collard, *Sea Snakes,* Bell Books, 1993.

Illustrations have also appeared in *Field and Stream, Alaska Magazine, McClanes: Game Fish of North America, Sport Fishing Aquatic Resources Handbook,* and various textbooks.

■ Sidelights

John F. Rice told *SATA:* "I've always been interested in nature, science, and the outdoor sports—my work has always reflected these loves. As far as hobbies go, my greatest love is fishing—surf casting in particular—and much of my work reflects the love of the sea and its wildlife. Also, I've done many commissions of baseball players of the past and present. My medium is watercolor."

* * *

RICHEMONT, Enid 1940-

■ Personal

Born October 28, 1940, in Barry, Glamorgan, South Wales; daughter of Kenneth Herbert (a farmer) and Elizabeth Jane (a homemaker; maiden name, Lewis) Palmer; married David Arthur Richemont (a computer programmer); children: Jeremy David, Juliet (Polly) Sara. *Education:* National College of Art (Ireland), A.N.C.A. *Politics:* "Liberal pacifist." *Religion:* "No formal religion." *Hobbies and other interests:* Art, fashion, interior design.

■ Addresses

Home and office—48 Fortismere Ave., London N10 3BL England. *Agent*—Rosemary Bromley, Juvenilia Literary Agency, Avington Lodge, Avington, Winchester S021 1DB England.

■ Career

Writer. Rudolf Steiner School for Disturbed Children, West Dorking, England, teacher, 1960-62; toy designer and manufacturer for her own business, Cabbages Designs, 1975-85. Runs the local neighborhood watch she founded. *Member:* Society of Authors (London).

■ Writings

The Time Tree, Walker Books, 1989, Little, Brown, 1990.

The Glass Bird, Walker Books, 1990, Candlewick Press, 1993.

My Mother's Daughter, Hutchinson, 1990.

The Game, Walker Books, 1990.

ENID RICHEMONT

The Magic Skateboard, Walker Books, 1991, Candlewick Press, 1992.
Wolfsong, Walker Books, 1992.
Kachunka!, Walker Books, 1992.
Gemma and the Beetle People, Walker Books, 1994.
Twice Times Danger, Walker Books, 1995.

Also author of many short stories published in European magazines, 1960-63. *The Time Tree* has been translated into Danish.

■ Work in Progress

The Dog That Wasn't (tentative title), for Walker Books; developing a children's book set in the Chinese immigrant community in London.

■ Sidelights

Enid Richemont told *SATA:* "I was born and grew up in South Wales. My grandmother was bilingual, but I didn't pick up much Welsh because the grown-ups used it as a kind of secret code for discussing things you couldn't talk about in front of the children! My mother read to me a great deal when I was little, and I think it was from her that I developed my love of stories, poetry, and music. When I was eleven, I was crowned Bard of a youth 'Eisteddfod' (a Welsh festival of literature and music) for writing a long, patriotic poem, and given a miniature Bardic chair carved from a single piece of oak.

"At sixteen I won an art scholarship and went to study painting in Dublin, Ireland (I still retain very close connections with my Irish friends). Returning to Britain, I got a job—almost by accident!—in a Rudolf Steiner boarding school for mentally handicapped children, which made a point of employing only artists and musicians as teachers. After two years I left in search of the bright lights of London and took a series of temporary and often *very* odd jobs. One of these was working with a blind ex-sailor who was writing a first novel and needed his work read back to him and eventually typed. He was a darling, but he really couldn't write! After I'd finished, I still had a few days left on my typewriter hire, so, not to waste them, I wrote a short story, which was instantly accepted by a woman's magazine.

"I got myself an agent and sold a lot more stories, but still thought of myself as more of an artist than a writer. Then I got myself a husband, David, and two children: Jeremy and Juliet (who became known as Polly). Writing was replaced by clothes and toy making. Then as my children grew up, I began marketing some of the designs for toys that I'd made them, and this developed into a one-woman business: Cabbages Designs. I made cut-out Edwardian shops and screen-printed puppet

Richemont's first book originated as a story she made up for her daughter about two children who discover a tree with special powers. (Cover illustration by Jennifer Eachus.)

theatres, and a hanging playhouse called Roundhouse (named after a 'fringe' theatre in London).

"David's work took him to Paris, so we went to live there for a couple of years. My daughter's best friend, Justine, came over from London to stay with us. One hot summer afternoon I took the two girls for a very long walk by the river Seine. On the way back, they were tired and irritable, so to distract them, I began making up a story. When we got back to the flat, Justine asked me to write it down so that she could take it back home, and that was how *The Time Tree* came into being.

"From this point I started work on a collection of children's stories not originally written for publication, each one being a gift for a special child. Almost all of those stories have now grown into books, and three of them—*The Time Tree* (translated into Danish), *The Glass Bird* (German rights recently sold), and *The Magic Skateboard*—have been published in the United States.

"These days I'm a busy full-time author with ten children's and young adult books in print. Two adult novels are under consideration. When I'm working, I must look and sound a bit crazy (my two bossy cats are convinced I am). Curled up in a cavernous cane rocking chair, but using a word processor with the keyboard on my lap, I read aloud constantly from the screen, and have also been known to walk 'round the house acting out bits of the plot! The reading aloud bit is important—I need to hear the rhythm and the music of the words. It also does seem to show up any glaring mistakes.

"Whenever possible, I try to take manuscripts I'm working on into local schools. Children are my best and toughest critics, and I frequently edit according to the 'glaze factor' in their eyes! I would like to think of my work as reaching out particularly to children who feel isolated (I was a shy and quite isolated child myself). I hope, as well, that my stories are starting points for questionings, wonderings, and imaginings that will go on long after the book is finished.

"My latest novel, *Twice Times Danger*, is a thriller set in Cornwall (where my daughter—who is a print-maker—now lives). It's for nine to twelve year olds . . . . I still draw, paint, and make things, but wouldn't dream of trying to illustrate my own books. Instead, I look forward to the richness and variety of styles and interpretations offered by professional illustrators."

For More Information See

PERIODICALS

Booklist, August, 1990, p. 2179.
Call and Post (Cleveland, OH), April, 1993.
Junior Bookshelf, June, 1989, p. 135.
Minnesota Daily (Minneapolis), May 20, 1993.
New Advocate, fall, 1993.
Times Educational Supplement, May 12, 1989.

RIDDELL, Edwina 1955-

Personal

Born June 24, 1955, in Derby, England; daughter of John Michael (a draughtsman) and Edna Gwendoline (a housewife; maiden name, Poyser) Keene; married Warren Peter Riddell (a management consultant), October 12, 1984; children: Helen Elizabeth, Max. *Education:* Attended Derby and District College of Art & Technology, 1971-73; London College of Printing, B.A., 1976. *Hobbies and other interests:* Music (classical, opera, pop), travel, history, environmental concerns, alternative medicine/naturopathy.

Addresses

Home and office—The Gables, Thorpe by Water, Rutland, Leicesters LE159JQ, England. *Agent*—Frances Lincoln Publishers Ltd., 4, Torriano Mews, Torriano Avenue, London NW5, England.

Career

Quarto/QED Publishers, Soho, London, England, illustrator, 1979-81; freelance illustrator, 1981—.

Writings

SELF-ILLUSTRATED

100 First Words to Say with Your Baby, Barron's, 1988.
My First Animal Word Book, Barron's, 1989.
My First Home, Barron's, 1991.

EDWINA RIDDELL

My First Day at Preschool, Barron's, 1992.
My First Playgroup, Frances Lincoln, 1992.
My First Kindergarten, Angus & Robertson, 1993.
My First Ballet Class, Barron's, 1993.

ILLUSTRATOR

Clare Smallman, *Outside In,* Barron's, 1986.
Patricia Pearse, *See How You Grow,* Barron's, 1988.
Angela Royston, *The Senses,* Barron's, 1993.

■ Work in Progress

A board book for young children, for Frances Lincoln; a book to be included in the "Outside In" series for Barron's.

■ Sidelights

Edwina Riddell told *SATA:* "My illustrating career seems to be following my personal life. Before I had children, I worked on adult reference books, including some on health, pregnancy, and child development for such well-known authors as Dr. Miriam Stoppard and Sheila Kitzinger. The birth of my first child happened while I was working on a book about pregnancy. Subsequently, I illustrated books for children, with my two providing a useful reference.

"Recently I have become interested in environmental matters and natural medicine. Having suffered for the last few years from hayfever, asthma, doctors, the English climate, and the economic depression, I am now going to Bahrain, where I will continue illustrating. It's a great advantage being able to work anywhere your husband's job takes you.

"My books for young children are very simple and translate well into foreign languages. To date, there have been fourteen foreign editions of *100 First Words to Say with Your Baby,* although there isn't an Arabic version—yet!"

■ For More Information See

PERIODICALS

Childhood Education, fall, 1992, p. 46.
Growing Point, January, 1990, p. 5280.
Horn Book Guide, July, 1989, p. 40.
Junior Bookshelf, October, 1992, p. 200.
Magpies, March, 1993, p. 26.
School Librarian, August, 1992, p. 98.
School Library Journal, September, 1992, p. 210; February, 1993, p. 78.*

* * *

RIPLEY, Catherine 1957-

■ Personal

Born March 15, 1957, in Ottawa, Ontario, Canada; daughter of Herbert Sharples (a naval vice-admiral) and Betty Bachelier Graham (a homemaker; maiden name, Snook) Rayner; married Bruce Cornell Ripley (an entrepreneur), August 21, 1982; children: Thomas Owen, Phoebe Elizabeth, Robin Bachelier Sharples. *Education:* Trent University, B.A. (English; with honors), 1979. *Religion:* Anglican.

■ Addresses

Home—Manotick, Ontario, Canada. *Office*—c/o Publicity Director, Greey de Pencier Books, OWL Communications, 179 John St., Suite 500, Toronto, Ontario, Canada, M5T 3G5.

■ Career

Cricket Magazine, LaSalle, IL, 1979-81, began as editorial assistant, became associate editor; *Chickadee Magazine,* Toronto, Ontario, 1982-91, began as editorial assistant, became editor; Canadian Museum of Nature Publishing Division, Ottawa, Ontario, beginning 1992, currently managing editor of *Global Biodiversity* (quarterly journal). *Member:* Educational Press Association of America (regional representative, 1991-93), Canadian Children's Book Centre.

■ Writings

Night and Day, illustrated by Debi Perna and Brenda Clark, Golden Books, 1985.
The Polka Dot Door Activity Book, Stoddart, 1987.
(Compiler and editor) *Kitchen Fun,* Greey de Pencier, 1988, Joy Street Books, 1989.
(Compiler and editor) *Outdoor Fun,* Greey de Pencier, 1989, Joy Street Books, 1990.

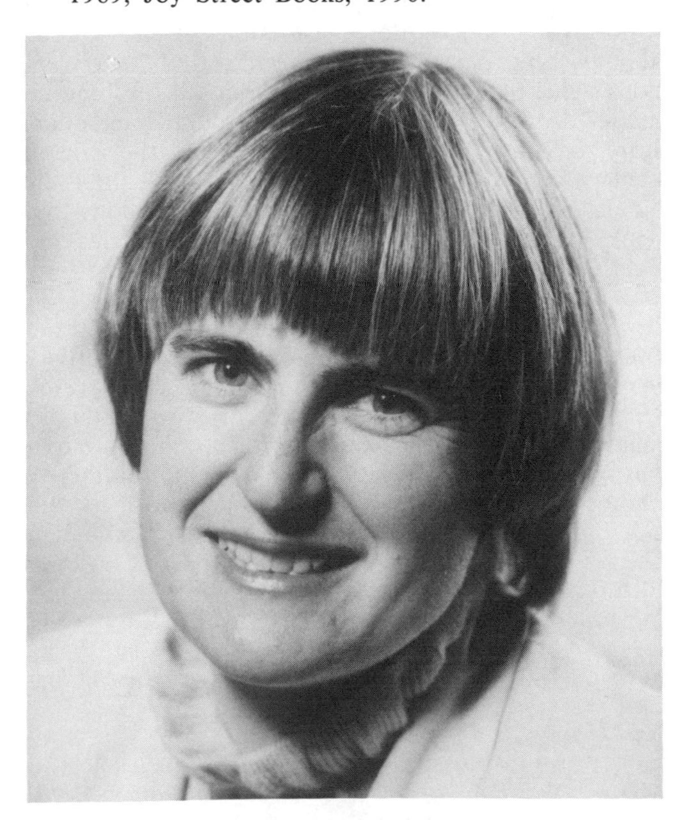

CATHERINE RIPLEY

(Compiler and editor) *Party Fun,* Greey de Pencier, 1989.

Two Dozen Dinosaurs: A First Book of Dinosaur Facts, Mysteries, Games and Fun, illustrated by Bo-Kim Louie, Greey de Pencier, 1991, Firefly, 1992.

Why Is Soap So Slippery? and Other Bathtime Questions ("Question and Answer Storybooks"), Greey de Pencier, 1995.

Do the Doors Open by Magic? and Other Supermarket Questions ("Question and Answer Storybooks"), Greey de Pencier, 1995.

■ Work in Progress

"Ideas and thoughts on nonfiction material for preschoolers; fun and exciting fiction for beginning-to-read readers; inklings for a junior novel."

■ Sidelights

Catherine Ripley told *SATA:* "Writing stories was always my favorite activity in elementary school and ever after! When, aged sixteen, I told my brother I wanted to be a writer, he said, 'Well, you better go into editing. Then you can edit on contract for half the year and write the other half, supported by your editorial earnings.' And that is about what I've done, except I have yet to take an entire six months off to devote to writing.

"I learned about editing with a sensitive pencil and about quality in stories from Marianne Carus, editor of *Cricket* magazine; I learned about writing for younger age groups by thinking in both words and pictures from Janis Nostbakken, editor of *Chickadee.* I also learned about writing to deadlines at *Chickadee* and the tremendous value in writing, writing, writing all the time no matter if it is a set of directions for a puzzle, an animal story, or a snappy verse. I learned about the pain of being edited from Annabel Slaight, president of the Young Naturalist Foundation, when she edited my first book; I learned to believe in my original thoughts and fight for them from Sheba Meland, my present editor."

It was Ripley's association with the editors of *OWL* and *Chickadee* that led to the publishing of several activity books for grades three to five, including *Kitchen Fun, Outdoor Fun,* and *Party Fun.* Activities in the books include cooking, science and art projects, family activities, games, and puzzles. The books contain attractive photos and include interesting additional information in side-bars, such as "Is a peanut a nut? No! . . . and it doesn't grow on a tree." As a result, *Horn Book* reviewer Elizabeth S. Watson calls *Kitchen Fun* "the perfect introduction to kitchen projects" while Amy Adler remarks in *School Library Journal* that "it's surprising how much fun is packed into so few pages" of *Outdoor Fun.*

Ripley also includes mazes, puzzles, and games in *Two Dozen Dinosaurs: A First Book of Dinosaur Facts, Mysteries, Games and Fun.* Geared toward youngsters who are old enough to be curious about dinosaurs but not old enough to read about them, the book teaches children facts about the creatures while leading them on fossil hunts, tracing, counting, and identifying adventures. Anne Gilmore writes in *Quill & Quire* that this book, targeted for grades one to three, "never underestimates the young child's ability or desire to learn real names and terms."

Writing for younger children is "challenging, fun, and oh so difficult," Ripley told *SATA.* "One of the great tricks is to spend a lot of time around the age group. The other is to think in both words and pictures, and then let the editor inside cut out most of the words to let the pictures tell the story. The final challenge is to make the few remaining words dance . . . sparkle . . . live forever!"

■ Works Cited

Adler, Amy, review of *Outdoor Fun, School Library Journal,* June, 1990, p. 130.

Gilmore, Anne, review of *Two Dozen Dinosaurs, Quill & Quire,* February, 1991, p. 24.

Ripley, Catherine, compiler and editor, *Kitchen Fun,* Joy Street Books, 1989.

Watson, Elizabeth S., review of *Kitchen Fun, Horn Book,* May, 1989, p. 388.

■ For More Information See

PERIODICALS

Booklist, August, 1989, p. 1979; March 15, 1990, p. 1458; May 15, 1991, p. 1808.

Bulletin of the Center for Children's Books, June, 1990, p. 251.

Canadian Children's Literature, Number 49, 1988, p. 85; Number 56, 1989, p. 96; Number 59, 1990, p. 91.

Horn Book, May, 1990, p. 356.

Quill & Quire, August, 1985, p. 36.

School Library Journal, May, 1989, pp. 98-99; May, 1992, p. 108.

* * *

ROBSON, Eric 1939-

■ Personal

Born October 27, 1939, in Haltwhistle, England; son of George W. R. (a factory worker) and Ethel C. (a homemaker; maiden name, Born) Robson. *Education:* Carlisle College of Art and Design, National Diploma. *Politics:* "Uncommitted."

■ Addresses

Home and office—72 North Ave., Southend-on-Sea, Essex, England SS2 5HU. *Agent*—Harry Lyon-Smith, Garden Studio, 23 Ganton St., London, England W1V 1LA.

■ Career

Ministry of Power, Sheffield Yorks, England, technical illustrator, 1960-63; Ministry of Education, Overseas Development Administration, Addis Ababa, Ethiopia, graphic artist, 1964-76; Natural History Museum, London, England, graphics officer, 1977-82; freelance illustrator, London, 1982-92; U.N.I.C.E.F., Addis Ababa, design consultant, 1992—. *Member:* Association of Illustrators, Ethiopian Wildlife and Natural History Society.

■ Writings

(With Christopher S. Clapham) *The Caves of Sof Omar,* Ethiopian Tourist Organization, 1967.

ILLUSTRATOR

Geoffrey Last and Richard Pankhurst, *A History of Ethiopia in Pictures,* Oxford University Press (Addis Ababa), 1969.
Tom Stacy, *The World of Animals,* Warwick Press, 1990.
Angela Royston, *The Goat,* Warwick Press, 1990.
Michael Chinery, *Ocean Animals,* Random House, 1991.
(With David Wright) Chinery, *Desert Animals,* Random House, 1991.
(With Bernard Long) Chinery, *Questions and Answers about Forest Animals,* Kingfisher Books, 1994.
(With Wayne Ford) Chinery, *Questions and Answers about Freshwater Animals,* Kingfisher Books, 1994.

Has also illustrated books, especially works on natural history, for Marshall Cavendish, Reader's Digest, Thomas Nelson, Longmans, BBC Publications, International Masters Publishers, and other publishing companies.

■ Work in Progress

Illustrating a set of collector's plates, "Wildlife Wonders of the World," for Danbury Mint, and a set of prints of the city of Addis Ababa.

■ Sidelights

Eric Robson told *SATA:* "Having long been interested in and influenced by the romantic writers, and in topics such as natural history and archaeology, I found myself at an early age traveling in some of the remoter 'foreign parts.'

"I crossed the Nubian Desert and followed the River Nile to Ethiopia at the age of twenty-four searching for Queen Hatshesut's long-lost land of Punt. In Ethiopia I worked for some twelve years producing textbooks and other educational materials. In 1965 I discovered, explored, and mapped the extensive caves of Sof Omar in southern Ethiopia, and crossed the Danakil Desert with the BBC-TV's 'Wildlife Safari' expedition in 1969.

"I left Ethiopia in 1976 and worked in the Natural History Museum in London for six years, after which I became a freelance (mainly natural history) illustrator. In 1976 I spent six months painting in India and Sri Lanka, subsequently having an exhibition of work in The Lyric, Hammersmith. In 1992 I again returned to Ethiopia to train Ethiopian counterparts in children's book design, illustration, and production in my former office in the Ministry of Education and have also been involved with the Wildlife Organization there."*

S

CRISTINA SALAT

SALAT, Cristina

■ Personal

Born in New York, NY. *Education:* Attended Southampton College of Long Island University.

■ Addresses

Home—P.O. Box 1519, Forestville, CA 95436. *Agent*—Bookstop Literary Agency/Kendra Marcus, 67 Meadow View Rd., Orinda, CA 94563.

■ Career

Author, editor, manuscript consultant, and creative living workshop facilitator, 1985—. *Member:* Society of Children's Book Writers and Illustrators, Native American Wordcraft Circle (mentor).

■ Writings

Alias Diamond Jones, Bantam, 1993.
Living in Secret, Bantam, 1993.
Defending the Dreamcatchers, Bantam, 1995.
Dancing Upside Down (novel), Simon & Schuster, 1996.

Also author of "50% Chance of Lightning," *Am I Blue,* HarperCollins, 1994. Contributor to anthologies, including *Sister/Stranger,* Sidewalk Revolution Press, 1993; and *Skin Deep—Colorism in America,* Crossing Press, 1994. Also contributor of adult fiction and nonfiction to periodicals, including *Popular Photography* and *Women's Voices.*

■ Work in Progress

Choosing Rabbit, the first title in the "Also Known as Anya" multi-racial children's book series; *The Creative Edge: From Starving Artist to Paid Bliss,* adult nonfiction; two picture books, *Peanuts Emergency* and *Step-Whales; Rising Signs,* a film novelization; a screenplay; and a collection of short stories.

■ Sidelights

Cristina Salat told *SATA:* "With twenty-seven boxes shipped UPS and a duffel bag full of dreams, I moved from New York to California in 1987 to leave the 9-5 publishing world and become a writer. I found a cheap room in a ramshackle house and a part-time newspaper job. The people in San Francisco were friendly and palm trees lined clean streets. It was the perfect place to begin a first novel. Because my new house was also home to three roommates, five dogs, one cat, and a baby, the rough draft of *Living in Secret* was scribbled in the relative quiet of fast food restaurants and Golden Gate Park. This book follows the adventures of Amelia, whose lesbian mom steals her from her father's custody. Being my first book, it is a special part of my life. Many part-time jobs later, I am blissfully living as a full-time writer/editor in a country home where the only noise I hear is my computer printing and cats chasing each other."

Critical reception of *Living in Secret* has been generally positive. In a *Booklist* review, for example, Emily Melton deemed the book to be "sensitive and empathetically written." *School Library Journal* critic Gerry Larson enjoyed the novel's main character, Amelia. While acknowledging that some of the story's themes—such as parental rights and same-sex relationships—were outside the experience of many young adult readers, Larson found *Living*'s young protagonist "a likable character." And in the *Bulletin of the Center for Children's Books,* Roger Sutton praised Salat's "firm focus on Amelia's feelings and perceptions."

In describing works to follow *Living in Secret,* Salat remarked to *SATA:* "I am just coming down from an intense period of research to complete *Defending the Dreamcatchers,* a young adult novel which explores homelessness, self-defense, pueblo life, and acting. Lately, my time is split between the whirlwind of book publicity and days alone, bundled in big sweaters and gloves, handwriting new projects in the chill of Northern California woods and beaches.

"Whether writer, gardener or business exec, everyone has a muse—that sassy, inquisitive (hopeful) inner voice. The more I've listened, the more I've enjoyed the company of mine. She continues to keep me honest."

■ Works Cited

Larson, Gerry, review of *Living in Secret, School Library Journal,* February, 1993, p. 94.

Melton, Emily, review of *Living in Secret, Booklist,* February 15, 1993, p. 1061.

Sutton, Roger, "The Big Picture," *Bulletin of the Center for Children's Books,* March, 1993, pp. 203-4.

■ For More Information See

PERIODICALS

Children's Book Review Service, March, 1993, p. 96.

Children's Book Watch, March, 1993, p. 5.

English Journal, April, 1993, p. 91.

Kirkus Reviews, February 1, 1993, p. 153.

Lamda Book Report, May, 1993, p. 45.

Los Angeles Times Book Review, June 20, 1993, p. 8.

Publishers Weekly, December 14, 1992, p. 57.

Voice of Youth Advocates, June, 1993, p. 94.

LINDA SAYLOR-MARCHANT

SAYLOR-MARCHANT, Linda 1963-

■ Personal

Born April 24, 1963, in Tallahassee, FL; daughter of Waymond (a teacher) and Violet (an office associate) Saylor; married Garth Marchant (a freelance reporter and lobbyist), October 8, 1987; children: Garth Jr., Aziza, Eleanor. *Education:* York College of the City University of New York, B.S.; University of Pittsburgh, M.L.S. *Politics:* Democrat. *Religion:* Baptist/Pentecostal. *Hobbies and other interests:* Creating organizations and services to help those in need, planning educational and recreational activities for the general public, traveling.

■ Addresses

Home—91-30 191st, Apt. 4-P, Hollis, NY 11423. *Office*—Baisley Park Library, 177-11 Sutphin Blvd., Jamaica, NY 11436.

■ Career

Queens Library, Queens, NY, began as page, became clerk and librarian, 1979-92, manager of the Baisley Park branch, 1992—. *Member:* American Library Association, Black Caucus, Arthur J. Pettiford American Legion Post 1947 (member of auxiliary board).

■ Writings

Hammer: 2 Legit 2 Quit, Dillon Press, 1992.

Work in Progress

Kings and Queens of Africa; The Ashanti Tribe of Ghana; From the Church to the Apollo (a biography of Thurman Ruth); and a biography of Clarence Thomas.

For More Information See

PERIODICALS

School Library Journal, February, 1993, pp. 99-100.

* * *

SCHICK, Eleanor 1942-

Personal

Born April 15, 1942, in New York, NY; daughter of William (a psychiatrist) and Bessie (a social worker; maiden name, Grossman) Schick; children: Laura, David. *Education:* Studied modern dance at the 92nd St. "Y" and with Martha Graham, Alvin Ailey, and others. *Religion:* Jewish/Episcopalian.

Addresses

Home—207 Aliso NE, Albuquerque, NM 87108.

Career

Author and illustrator of children's books. Writer in residence, Rio Grande Writing Project (a New Mexico site of The National Writing Project), 1986—; speaker at schools and universities. Former professional dancer and member of Juilliard Dance Theatre and Tamiris-Nagrin Dance Company; has lectured and taught dance at Hofstra College, Bryn Mawr College, and Connecticut College.

Writings

SELF-ILLUSTRATED, EXCEPT AS INDICATED

A Surprise in the Forest, Harper, 1964.
The Little School at Cottonwood Corners, Harper, 1965.
The Dancing School, Harper, 1966.
I'm Going to the Ocean!, Macmillan, 1966.
5A and 7B, Macmillan, 1967.
Katie Goes to Camp, Macmillan, 1968.
Jeanie Goes Riding, Macmillan, 1968.
City in the Summer, Macmillan, 1969.
Making Friends, Macmillan, 1969.
Peggy's New Brother, Macmillan, 1970.
City in the Winter, Macmillan, 1970.
Andy, Macmillan, 1971.
Student's Encounter Book for When a Jew Celebrates, Behrman House, 1973.
Peter and Mr. Brandon, illustrated by Donald Carrick, Macmillan, 1973.
City Green, Macmillan, 1974.
City Sun, Macmillan, 1974.
Neighborhood Knight, Greenwillow, 1976.
One Summer Night, Greenwillow, 1977.
Summer at Sea, Greenwillow, 1979.
Home Alone, Dial, 1980.
Rainy Sunday, Dial, 1981.
Joey on His Own, Dial, 1981.
A Piano for Julie, Greenwillow, 1983.
My Album, Greenwillow, 1984.
Art Lessons, Greenwillow, 1987.
I Have Another Language: The Language is Dance, Macmillan, 1992.
(With Luci Tapahanso) *Navajo ABC: A Dine Alphabet Book,* Macmillan, 1995.
My Navajo Sister, Macmillan, in press.

ILLUSTRATOR

Jan Wahl, *Christmas in the Forest,* Macmillan, 1967.
Jeanne Whitehouse Peterson, *Sometimes I Dream Horses,* Harper, 1987.
Sheldon Zimmerman, *The Family Prayerbook: Holidays and Festivals,* Rossel Books, 1988.
Zimmerman, *The Family Prayerbook: The Fall Holidays,* Rossel Books, 1989.
Zimmerman, *The Family Prayerbook: Shabbot,* Rossel Books, 1989.

Adaptations

City in the Winter and *City in the Summer* have been made into filmstrips.

Sidelights

Eleanor Schick is a prolific writer and illustrator of children's books who focuses on the everyday comings and goings, the first-time experiences, and the daily routines that make up a child's life. Through her books, children have been introduced to the schoolroom, to sleep-away camp, to the arrival of a new sibling, a first trip to the store, the responsibilities of being a latch-key kid, and other milestones. Schick's style, both in writing and in illustration, has often been described as simple and realistic, covering territory familiar to young readers. It is a child's private world that Schick is interested in creating in her books. "Children always excite me," she once commented. "They are always reachable. They are always responsive when an adult makes it clear to them that he or she is interested in listening to them speak, or write, about what really happens in their lives, and how they feel about it."

One of Schick's earliest books, *The Little School at Cottonwood Corners,* addresses preschoolers' curiosity about what really goes on in a classroom. Elegy Meadows, clutching her teddy bear and visitor's pass in hand, takes a tour of the little school. She gets a look at the various rooms and activities of the kindergarten classes, and that night she confides to her teddy bear that she might like to go to the little school, too. Praising the informative detail of Schick's drawings, *Horn Book* contributor Virginia Haviland calls the tale "refreshing real and childlike." Similarly, a *Bulletin for the Center of Children's Books* writer thinks *Katie Goes to Camp* is "just long enough, simple and realistic, low-keyed and pleasant" in relating how a young girl deals with homesickness during her first sleep-away camp. And

ELEANOR SCHICK

Jeanie Goes Riding "must strike a chord" in other young children awaiting their first trip on horseback, according to a *Times Literary Supplement* reviewer.

Many of Schick's books take place in an urban landscape, full of interesting buildings and peopled with characters of many races and cultures. Apartment dwellers may recognize the situation of Toby and Sandy in *5A and 7B;* each girl longs for a special friend, but the two only meet when a change in routine leads to a chance encounter. Although not dramatic, the story is "satisfying and useful," as Ruth P. Bull describes it in *Booklist,* especially for its "wonderfully detailed drawings." *City in the Summer* and *City in the Winter* both hinge on the effects of the weather on a young boy's daily existence: one tells of escaping the stifling heat of a city summer day with a trip to the beach at Coney Island; the other is the story of Jimmy's day with his grandmother when a blizzard forces the schools to close. Of the first, George A. Woods notes in the *New York Times Book Review* that it has the feel of a "documentary," making it "as if the city in summer had sat very still for its portrait." *City in the Winter* is "a most successful companion," Haviland observes, with the delicate drawings "just right for the little narrative."

The city serves as a setting for imaginative play in other books by Schick. When the other neighborhood children are too busy to play with him in the story *Andy,* the title character amuses himself around the city block by pretending to be a construction worker and cowboy, among other things. A *Booklist* reviewer praises the "simplicity and naturalness" with which Schick presents everyday play, as well as the "sharply detailed" drawings. Similarly, *Neighborhood Knight* is the tale of a young boy whose imagination turns his run-down apartment building into a castle, his mother into a queen, and his sister into a princess. His father, the king, has been "gone a long time." Schick told *SATA* that *Neighborhood Knight* is "truly about my son and is directly autobiographical." Jean Mercier describes the story and illustrations in her *Publishers Weekly* review as "fine representations of the small boy's private world," while a *School Library Journal* critic notes that the realistic drawings "run in pleasant counterpoint" to the boy's imaginings. And in 1974's *City Green,* a young girl named Laura expresses her feelings through a collection of brief poems and observations about the little things in life that affect her and her younger brother, David. Schick's poems have the "same gentle ambience" as her other stories, Nancy Rosenberg observes in the *New York Times Book Review,* with text and pictures that are "sedate and affectionate."

Many of Schick's books deal with contemporary issues of urban society. *Home Alone* is the story of a latch-key kid learning about independence and responsibility, as he must come home to an empty house when his mother gets a full-time job. In *Joey on His Own,* a young boy goes out to the store by himself for the first time when his mother, who must stay at home with his feverish sister, sends him out for bread. On his way to the store, the city streets and buildings appear larger, taller, and more menacing than they ever have before. But in the end, Joey navigates the sidewalks and the supermarket successfully. "The narrative subtly conveys Joey's apprehension," Kate M. Flanagan observes in *Horn Book,* adding that the "clean, uncluttered" pencil drawings contain "a surprising amount of detail." A reviewer for *Publishers Weekly* likewise declares that young readers "will feel they're living Joey's anxieties and his exhilaration at mission completed," while a *School Library Journal* critic hails Schick's drawings for using "perspective to canny advantage in reflecting Joey's shift in attitude."

In other works, Schick simply tells of how an ordinary, even dismal, situation can be lightened and brightened with a little creativity. In *One Summer Night,* Laura decides to play a record and dance instead of sleep, leading the entire neighborhood to dance along. Helen Gregory praises Schick's work in *School Library Journal* for combining "sensuous and dynamic" pictures with a "simple but enjoyable story," while in another *Publishers Weekly* review Mercier calls it "a lovely tale, with spirited pictures." Schick travels beyond the city for *Summer at the Sea,* where a young girl spends a happy, magical vacation before returning home. Containing a "real emotional weight," as one *Kirkus Reviews* critic states, this book will give children "a foretaste of what reading means not as a skill or a pastime but as total involvement." The story of how a girl enlivens a gray

Schick vividly describes an urban landscape in her self-illustrated book, *City in Summer,* which follows a day in the life of a boy named Jerry.

and dreary day, Schick's *Rainy Sunday* similarly demonstrates the power of the imagination. While a reviewer for the *Bulletin of the Center for Children's Books* finds the book has "little action" and "no humor," Holly Willett notes in *Horn Book* that the "family's positive approach to a potentially disappointing day" makes for a "pleasant and comforting" work. And Susan Bolotin of the *New York Times Book Review* states that this "quiet story" is made "brilliant" by Schick's use of colorful illustrations.

Schick's more recent works have communicated her love for the fine arts, introducing children to music, art, and dance. In *A Piano for Julie,* a young girl listens to her father play the piano at her grandmother's house and wishes to learn how to play herself. *School Library Journal* contributor Kathy Piehl praises the author's text for creating "a soft verbal melody," while a *Kirkus Reviews* writer hails Schick's gentle illustrations, calling the book "an exceptional here-and-now overall—with delicacy, involvement, and depth." *Art Lessons* similarly shows a young boy taking lessons in drawing from Adrianne, a neighboring artist. By showing the two talking about art, Schick takes a "provocative" approach in showing children how to draw through "ideas instead of technique," comments Diane Roback in *Publishers Weekly.* The way art can express emotion is also highlighted in *I Have Another Language: The Language Is Dance,* as a young girl prepares for her first dance recital. The girl's feelings before, during, and after her performance are "skillfully woven into her dance expression," Kay McPherson states in *School Library Journal.* The author, a former dancer herself, "conveys the joy a dancer feels at successfully celebrating her emotions," Maeve Visser Knoth concludes in *Horn Book,* and Schick's pencil illustrations, with their creative use of line, shading, and perspective, "create the excitement and tension of a new situation."

As Bolotin notes in the *New York Times Book Review,* Schick's work often "describes a child's emotional response to an all-too-real situation." Schick herself is pleased that writers are listening to children more than they used to. "We write with more sensitivity to what children really do think, and see, and feel," she once noted. "There is a true literature developing which speaks to children. It speaks to their thoughts, dreams, and yearnings. It addresses some of the experiences that they do have, which were not dealt with some fifteen or twenty years ago. I have witnessed, and surely been a part of, the development of 'children's books' from being vehicles or didactic adult teaching to a true

A young girl discovers the joys of dance in Schick's 1992 work. (Cover illustration by the author.)

literature which includes very deep and poetic expressions of childhood experience. This is very meaningful to me, and I feel deeply gratified to have been a part of this growth."

Works Cited

Review of *Andy, Booklist,* May 15, 1971, p. 800.

Bolotin, Susan, review of *Rainy Sunday, New York Times Book Review,* May 3, 1981, pp. 40-41.

Bull, Ruth P., review of *5A and 7B, Booklist,* May 15, 1967, pp. 997-98.

Flanagan, Kate M., review of *Joey on His Own, Horn Book,* August, 1982, p. 397.

Gregory, Helen, review of *One Summer Night, School Library Journal,* May, 1977, p. 55.

Haviland, Virginia, review of *The Little School at Cottonwood Corners, Horn Book,* October, 1965, p. 495.

Haviland, Virginia, review of *City in the Winter, Horn Book,* February, 1971, p. 44.

Review of *Jeanie Goes Riding, Times Literary Supplement,* December 4, 1969, p. 1392.

Review of *Joey on His Own, Publishers Weekly,* April 16, 1982, p. 71.

Review of *Joey on His Own, School Library Journal,* May, 1982, p. 80.

Review of *Katie Goes to Camp, Bulletin of the Center for Children's Books,* March, 1969, pp. 117-18.

Knoth, Maeve Visser, review of *I Have Another Language: The Language Is Dance, Horn Book,* July, 1992, pp. 446-47.

McPherson, Kay, review of *I Have Another Language: The Language Is Dance, School Library Journal,* July, 1992, p. 64.

Mercier, Jean, review of *Neighborhood Knight, Publishers Weekly,* March 1, 1976, p. 94.

Mercier, Jean, review of *One Summer Night, Publishers Weekly,* March 14, 1977, p. 95.

Review of *Neighborhood Knight, School Library Journal,* May, 1976, p. 75.

Review of *A Piano for Julie, Kirkus Reviews,* March 1, 1984, p. J9.

Piehl, Kathy, review of *A Piano for Julie, School Library Journal,* May, 1984, p. 72.

Review of *Rainy Sunday, Bulletin of the Center for Children's Books,* July, 1981, p. 217.

Roback, Diane, review of *Art Lessons, Publishers Weekly,* July 24, 1987, p. 186.

Rosenberg, Nancy, "A Tree Grows in Print," *New York Times Book Review,* May 5, 1974, p. 38.

Review of *Summer at the Sea, Kirkus Reviews,* April 1, 1979, p. 387.

Willett, Holly, review of *Rainy Sunday, Horn Book,* June, 1981, p. 297.

Woods, George A., review of *City in the Summer, New York Times Book Review,* June 29, 1969, p. 26.

For More Information See

PERIODICALS

Booklist, May 15, 1970, p. 1163; April 1, 1984, p. 1122; September 15, 1987, p. 153; May 1, 1992, p. 1610.

Bulletin of the Center for Children's Books, November, 1965, p. 49; October, 1970, p. 33; March, 1971, p. 114; June, 1982, p. 197.

Childhood Education, June, 1987, p. 364.

Christian Science Monitor, May 2, 1968, p. 83; November 12, 1970, p. 86; June 5, 1971, p. 21.

Horn Book, June, 1973, p. 261; June, 1976, p. 284; October, 1980, p. 516.

Kirkus Reviews, February 15, 1967, p. 194; March 15, 1970, p. 318; August 15, 1987.

Language Arts, March, 1982, p. 269; October, 1982, p. 746.

New York Times Book Review, October 26, 1969, p. 44.

Publishers Weekly, November 30, 1984, p 92; March 9, 1992, p. 57.

School Library Journal, December, 1984, p. 76; November, 1987, p. 96.

* * *

SCHRODER, Walter K. 1928-

Personal

Born March 30, 1928, in Pawtucket, RI; son of Walter E. and Emmy E. (Adam) Schroder; married Lora (a homemaker; maiden name, Shwaery), May 23, 1971; children: Leah. *Education:* Roger Williams College, B.S. (summa cum laude), 1975.

Career

U.S. Military Authority, Frankfurt, Germany, civilian office assistant and interpreter, 1946-48; building materials company for wholesale, clerk and salesperson, 1953-60; U.S. Federal Civil Service, military procurement, 1960-89; State of Rhode Island, Emergency Management Agency, training officer. 1992—. Has also designed and taught courses in military procurement; has given lectures describing life in Nazi Germany, and given tours of former Rhode Island Military Installations. Has taught speed courses in German with Berlitz. *Military service:* German army, Anti-aircraft, Luftwaffenhelfer, Germany, 1944-46; U.S. Army, interpreter and translator (in Germany), 1948-52; received the U.S. Navy Medal.

Writings

Stars and Swastikas: The Boy Who Wore Two Uniforms (autobiography), Archon Books, 1992.

Also author of *Defenses of Narragansett Bay in World War II,* a war history; and *Introduction to Government Procurement,* a textbook.

Work in Progress

Research, primarily on military and political subjects, using archives in Germany, the United States, and England.

Sidelights

Stars and Swastikas: The Boy Who Wore Two Uniforms is the autobiographical account of Walter K. Schroder's youth during World War II in Nazi Germany. Schroder explains his service in the German army, his time spent in a P.O.W. camp, his family's incarceration in Russian-occupied East Germany, and his eventual enlistment in the United States Army. Susan Ackler, a reviewer for *Voice of Youth Advocates,* commented, "This book will be good for mature students looking for the psychology of Hitler's followers or life in Germany from 1937-1950."

Works Cited

Ackler, Susan, review of *Stars and Swastikas: The Boy Who Wore Two Uniforms, Voice of Youth Advocates,* February, 1993, p. 376.

For More Information See

PERIODICALS

Kirkus Reviews, May 1, 1992.
Library Journal, June 1, 1992.

SERFOZO, Mary 1925-

Personal

Surname accented on second syllable; born February 21, 1925, in Seattle, WA; daughter of Patrick (an engineer) and Olive (Audett) Cannon; married John Serfozo, August 8, 1953; children: Stephen, David. *Education:* University of Washington, B.A. *Politics:* Independent. *Religion:* Catholic. *Hobbies and other interests:* Travel, swimming, reading, becoming computer literate.

Addresses

Home—California. *Office*—c/o Publicity Director, Margaret K. McElderry Books, 866 Third Ave., New York, NY 10022.

Career

Freelance author and copywriter. Has worked variously as an assistant editor of *Mademoiselle* magazine, a copywriter for a California advertising agency, and in publicity for Elizabeth Arden in New York City, Pan American Airways, and the Hawaiian sugar industry in Honolulu.

Awards, Honors

American Bookseller's Pick of the Lists and the Children's Choice Certificate of Excellence, for *Who Said Red?;* Parenting's Reading Magic Award, for *Who Wants One?* Several of Serfozo's book have been Junior Library Guild and Children's Book-of-the-Month Club selections.

Writings

Welcome, Roberto!/Bienvenido, Roberto!, photographs by husband, John Serfozo, Follett, 1969.
Who Said Red?, illustrated by Keiko Narahashi, Margaret K. McElderry, 1988.
Who Wants One?, illustrated by Narahashi, Margaret K. McElderry, 1989.
Rain Talk, illustrated by Narahashi, Margaret K. McElderry, 1990.
Dirty Kurt, illustrated by Nancy Poydar, Margaret K. McElderry, 1992.
Benjamin Bigfoot, illustrated by Jos. A. Smith, Margaret K. McElderry, 1993.
Joe Joe, illustrated by Nina S. Montezinos, Margaret K. McElderry, 1993.
There's a Square, Cartwheel Books, in press.
What's What, Margaret K. McElderry, in press.

Also author of two bilingual classroom packages.

Work in Progress

Working on several ideas for children's books.

■ Sidelights

Mary Serfozo was inspired to write her first published children's book when she observed a group of children listening to her local librarian sing and play the guitar. When it came time for the children to sing their line in every chorus, they "joined in so joyously," Serfozo told Diane Roback in *Publishers Weekly,* "I thought it would be fun in a read-aloud book to have a line that kids would know was coming up."

That observation led to *Who Said Red?,* a colorful tale of a young boy and his teasing older sister who repeatedly asks, "Did you say red?" Although the sister tempts him with "a green bean green," "a blue jean blue," and "lemonade and daisy yellow," it all comes back to the color of the little boy's kite—"cherry, berry, very red." Karen Leggett, writing in the *New York Times Book Review,* called the book "ripe ... with possibilities for playing, learning, reading and laughing. What more could you ask of any book?"

Young readers are taught about basic colors in Serfozo's 1992 easy reader. (Cover illustration by Keiko Narahashi.)

The brother and sister team featured in *Who Said Red?* return in *Who Wants One?,* as the imaginative older sister pulls an array of increasingly silly items out of a magic box and offers them to her younger brother. The little boy refuses each numbered offering with a firm, "NO, I WANT ONE!" until at the end, his sister presents him with one precious puppy. In her review in the *School Library Journal,* Luann Toth called the book a "magical presentation of the numbers from one to ten and back again." "This jaunty and original counting book is a standout," a *Publishers Weekly* critic similarly concluded.

MARY SERFOZO

Several of Serfozo's other books revolve around the start of school. The main character in *Dirty Kurt* can't seem to keep himself clean. No matter what he does, he is a "magnet for filth," as reviewer Laura Culberg noted in *School Library Journal.* When his mother expresses concern that the kids in his new school will think he's a "dirt ball with feet," Kurt solves the problem by going out to play bundled up in his raincoat. "Kids, just like dirt, will be drawn to Kurt," stated Culberg.

The problem for the main character in *Benjamin Bigfoot* is that he wants to wear his favorite footwear, his father's big shoes, to school. When Ben's mother takes him to meet the new teacher before school starts, he discovers that the big shoes are not exactly comfortable for climbing, sliding, or bike riding. Susan Hepler praised the book in the *School Library Journal,* noting how it "shows a five-year-old working through a situation on his own with the support of sympathetic adults."

Mary Serfozo told *SATA* that she became a "professional" writer in the third grade when she won ten dollars in a Christmas Seal essay contest, but "didn't get around to picture books until I was about ready to retire. I was writing advertising copy for the first time in a wordy career," she said, "and finding it quite illuminating. As with picture books, much of what I did involved choosing the right few words to go in a limited space and combine with art to make an impact. My boss was not impressed to learn of the parallel I saw between his target market and the average five-year-old, but it certainly exists. My picture book texts have been described as 'spare,' and I recognize this as a reflection of the discipline imposed by the column inch.

"I write picture books because I feel right at home with preschoolers who love the sound of words—like to roll them on their tongues and repeat them endlessly. I like rhymes and rhythms and exaggeration and humor. And I'm delighted to see my ideas come alive through the insight of an illustrator. I've been writing my entire life, and most of the time it has been rewarding. None of it has been this much fun."

■ Works Cited

Culberg, Laura, review of *Dirty Kurt, School Library Journal,* March, 1992, p. 224.
Hepler, Susan, review of *Benjamin Bigfoot, School Library Journal,* August, 1993, p. 151.
Leggett, Karen, review of *Who Said Red?, New York Times Book Review,* November 13, 1988, p. 63.
Roback, Diane, "Coming Attractions," *Publishers Weekly,* July 28, 1989, p. 136.
Serfozo, Mary, *Who Said Red?,* Margaret K. McElderry, 1988.
Toth, Luann, review of *Who Wants One?, School Library Journal,* December, 1989, p. 96.
Review of *Who Wants One?, Publishers Weekly,* July 14, 1989, p. 75.

■ For More Information See

PERIODICALS

Booklist, September 1, 1988, p. 84; November 1, 1989, p. 558; October 1, 1990, p. 340; February 1, 1992, p. 1042.
Growing Point, September, 1989, p. 5227.
Junior Bookshelf, June, 1989, p. 114.
Kirkus Reviews, August 15, 1989, p. 1256; October 1, 1990, p. 190; February 1, 1992, p. 190; March 1, 1993, p. 305.
Publishers Weekly, September 9, 1988, p. 130; July 27, 1990, p. 232; January 18, 1993, p. 471.
School Librarian, August, 1989, p. 101.
School Library Journal, January, 1989, p. 66; December, 1990, p. 87; January, 1994, p. 98.
Time, December 12, 1988, p. 87.

* * *

SEYMOUR, Tres 1966-

■ Personal

Given name pronounced "Trace"; born December 30, 1966, in Glasgow, KY; son of William R. (an executive) and Donna Faye (a teacher; maiden name, Locke) Seymour; married Amy T. Nemon (a park ranger), September 10, 1994. *Education:* Southern Methodist University, B.A. (English and journalism), 1989; University of Kentucky, M.S.L.S., 1991; attending University of Tennessee, 1993—. *Hobbies and other interests:* Reading, watching public television as well as science fiction shows, fencing, hiking, travel, playing music (dulcimer, banjo, fife, bodhran, celtic harp).

■ Addresses

Home—9764 Priceville Rd., Upton, KY 42784.

■ Career

Freelance writer. National Park Service, Mammoth Cave National Park, KY, seasonal park ranger, 1987—.

■ Awards, Honors

Life in the Desert was named an American Library Association Recommended Book for Reluctant Young Adult Readers, 1993; Notable Books of the Year citation, *New York Times,* and Best Books of the Year citation, *School Library Journal,* both 1993, for *Hunting the White Cow.*

■ Writings

Life in the Desert (novel), Orchard Books, 1992.
Pole Dog, illustrated by David Soman, Orchard Books, 1993.
Hunting the White Cow, illustrated by Wendy Anderson Halperin, Orchard Books, 1993.
I Love My Buzzard, illustrated by S. D. Schindler, Orchard Books, 1994.
The Smash-Up, Crash-Up Derby, illustrated by Schindler, Orchard Books, 1995.

TRES SEYMOUR

An emotionally troubled teen retreats into a world of fantasy in Seymour's successful first novel. (Cover illustration by Andrew Radcliffe.)

■ Work in Progress

Too Quiet for These Old Bones, illustrated by Paul Brett Johnson, for Orchard Books, 1996; *The Revelation of Saint Bruce,* a young adult novel; *Our Neighbor Is a Strange, Strange Man,* a picture book; *Made of Stone,* a poetry collection; *Stephen, King of the Dark,* a young adult novel.

■ Sidelights

Life in the Desert, Tres Seymour's well-received first novel, depicts the friendship between ninth-grader Rebecca Altsheler and her emotionally withdrawn classmate, Joseph Bell, who refers to himself as O. Z. As Rebecca earns O. Z.'s trust, she learns that he often retreats into his own fantasy world, the "Desert," where he finds solace from life's pressures, including his parents' unrealistic expectations of him. When Rebecca takes O. Z.'s journal to school, it is stolen by other students who use its contents to ridicule him. Shamed, O. Z. attempts suicide, with only Rebecca and O. Z.'s brother, Reuben, knowledgeable of his whereabouts.

Critics generally found *Life in the Desert* to be an affecting portrait of adolescent loneliness and alienation. "O. Z.'s feelings and needs are basic to us all," wrote Laura L. Lent in *Voice of Youth Advocates.* "At some point, the utter loneliness of O. Z. will be felt by the reading audience and will, no doubt, leave few eycs dry." Mary M. Burns, reviewing the work in *Horn Book,* deemed *Life in the Desert* "notable for its evocation of a unique personality through the eyes of a sympathetic observer." In *School Library Journal,* though, Jacqueline Rose stated that the author "conveys the pain experienced by a troubled teen.... However, like Rebecca, readers are ultimately kept in the dark as to what makes O. Z. tick." Conversely, *Booklist* reviewer Janice Del Negro observed that Seymour "realistically creates the environment that surrounds Rebecca and O. Z. and gently draws ... the reader into the fantasy world O. Z. has created."

Seymour followed *Life in the Desert* with several picture books, including the widely reviewed *Hunting the White Cow.* In this story, a young farm girl relates her family's efforts to recapture an elusive white cow that "went wild." After several messy, failed attempts to track the cow by the family's menfolk, the youngster manages to rope the animal, only to see it escape before she returns it to the farm, so that "now she, too, is part of the legend of the white cow," remarked *Horn Book* contributor Nancy Vasilakis. Critics were enthusiastic in their praise for *Hunting the White Cow.* In the *New York Times Book Review,* Kathleen Krull commended Seymour's "admirably terse and evocative" prose, and *School Library Journal* reviewer Trev Jones found the tale "spare and clean, accentuated with just the right amount of repetition and local color." "An *excellent* picture book," stated Daniel Menaker in the *New Yorker,* "with quiet humor and authority in the text."

Seymour told *SATA,* "When I rediscovered children's books as a college freshman, it was like meeting an old friend from whom I had drifted away and finding that we had more in common than we had ever imagined. The rediscovery began as a tickle in my mind, a memory of a book with a green cover, about some children and a coin, in our old public library in Morristown, Tennessee. I went back, so many years from the time I'd first read it and found the book by sight, having no idea of title or author. It was Edward Eager's *Half Magic.* Next I found again my favorite book of all time, Carol Kendall's under-recognized *The Gammage Cup.* My studies of Shakespeare, Faulkner, and their lofty ilk tumbled downhill from there. There was not time. I made weekly visits to what must be one of the best children's bookstores in the nation and came away laden with Nesbit, Alexander, LeGuin, Cooper, Babbit, Jacques, Ransome, Aiken, Christopher, Eddison, Tolkien, E. B. White, T. H. White—and so many others. I haven't stopped reading them yet.

"But to actually write—I have read biographies of writers who say that they've been writing since they were seven, or ten, or some such age, and knew what they wanted to do all along. I recall quite vividly that at the age of ten I told someone who suggested to me that I should be a writer that I *wouldn't* want to be, and I truly thought so. I have no notion why suddenly, as a young collegian, I should want to write books, nor yet why after several years thereafter of writing novels I should suddenly veer into the world of picture books, which I had never dreamed of writing. All of it—motivation, skill, inspiration—has just dropped into my lap. Where from?

"I think I know. As an avid reader, admirer, and student of the work of C. S. Lewis, I can hardly fail to perceive some divine assistance here. I don't want to sound like I think I am one of the *chosen* or anything; I only mean that I know this gift can't come from me, so I attribute it to God.

"For this reason I don't really worry about whether I'll have any more stories in me when I finish the one I'm working on now. They don't come from me to start with. People who know me often get frustrated when I'm not gushing with pride about a new book. They say, with hand gestures suggesting lifting, 'Aren't you excited?' Well, I suppose so. But why should I take overmuch pride in a book I write any more than a farmer should take overmuch pride in a good field of pumpkins? He may have done a good job of horticulture, but he didn't invent pumpkins.

"I don't, by the way, write for children. I write for me and for anyone enough like me that he or she enjoys my work. My goal has always been to someday write something that could affect another person the way *The Gammage Cup* affected me. If I've been able to do that, then I am grateful."

Works Cited

Burns, Mary M., review of *Life in the Desert, Horn Book,* January/February, 1993, p. 93.
Del Negro, Janice, review of *Life in the Desert, Booklist,* September 1, 1992, p. 49.
Jones, Trev, review of *Hunting the White Cow, School Library Journal,* December, 1993, pp. 93-94.
Krull, Kathleen, "Udder Voices, Udder Rooms," *New York Times Book Review,* November 14, 1993, p. 58.
Lent, Laura L., review of *Life in the Desert, Voice of Youth Advocates,* December, 1992, p. 286.
Menaker, Daniel, review of *Hunting the White Cow, New Yorker,* December 13, 1993, p. 117.
Rose, Jacqueline, review of *Life in the Desert, School Library Journal,* November, 1992, p. 124.
Vasilakis, Nancy, review of *Hunting the White Cow, Horn Book,* November, 1993, pp. 738-39.

For More Information See

PERIODICALS

Booklist, January 15, 1994, p. 939.
Bulletin of the Center for Children's Books, November, 1992, p. 87; October, 1993, p. 57; March, 1995, p. 249.
Horn Book, July/August, 1993, p. 449.
Kirkus Reviews, March 15, 1994, p. 403.
Publishers Weekly, September 14, 1992, p. 126; February 1, 1993, p. 93; July 19, 1993, p. 251.
School Library Journal, July, 1993, p. 71.
Tribune Books (Chicago), January 9, 1994, p. 6.

* * *

SIRACUSA, Catherine (Jane) 1947-

Personal

Born February 7, 1947, in Long Beach, CA; daughter of Louis Peter (an engineer/executive) and Bernadine (a housewife; maiden name, Tharp) Siracusa; married Sidney Levitt (an author/illustrator), August 4, 1979. *Education:* Hunter College of the City University of New York, B.F.A. (painting), 1968. *Hobbies and other interests:* Fashion, antiques, book collecting, reading, architecture.

Addresses

Home and office—112 West 74th St., New York, NY 10023. *Agent*—Joanna Lewis Cole Literary Agency, 404 Riverside Dr., New York, NY 10025.

Career

Author and illustrator of children's books, 1986—. *Harper's Bazaar,* New York City, editorial assistant, 1968-69; freelance illustrator, New York City, 1969-87. Montclair State University, Montclair, NJ, visiting specialist (editorial illustration), 1983-84. Society of Illustrators judge, "Illustrators 22," 1979. *Member:* Society of Children's Book Writers and Illustrators, Authors Guild, Authors League of America, National Writers Union, Graphic Artists Guild (board of directors, 1977-78).

Awards, Honors

Children's Choice Award, 1994, for *The Giant Zucchini.*

Writings

Bingo, the Best Dog in the World, illustrated by Sidney Levitt, HarperCollins, 1991.

SELF-ILLUSTRATED

No Mail for Mitchell, Random House, 1990.
The Giant Zucchini, Hyperion, 1993.
The Parrot Problem, Hyperion, 1994.
The Banana Split from Outer Space, Hyperion, 1995.
The Peanut-Butter Gang, Hyperion, 1996.

ILLUSTRATOR

Harriet Ziefert, *Mike and Tony, Best Friends,* Viking Penguin, 1987.
Ziefert, *Say Goodnight!,* Viking Penguin, 1987.
Margot Linn, *A Trip to the Doctor,* Harper & Row, 1988.
Linn, *A Trip to the Dentist,* Harper & Row, 1988.
Margo Mason, *Ready Alice?,* Bantam/Little Rooster, 1990.

CATHERINE SIRACUSA

Barbara Brenner, *Beef Stew,* Random House, 1990.

Also contributor of illustrations to books, including *Domestic Descendants* and *Aquatic Miniatures,* Time-Life, 1979; and *Potato Jokes* by Paul McMahon, Simon & Schuster, 1984; and to periodicals, including *Glamour* and *Seventeen.* Contributor of cartoons to anthologies, including *Cats, Cats, Cats,* edited by S. Gross, Harper, 1986; *Books, Books, Books,* edited by S. Gross and Jim Charlton, Harper, 1988; *Movies, Movies, Movies,* edited by S. Gross, Harper, 1989; *Mothers and Daughters,* edited by Liza Donnelly, Ballantine, 1993.

■ Sidelights

"I was born in Southern California," Catherine Siracusa told *SATA.* "Although I lived in other towns (Whittier and Downey), the old town of Huntington Beach was always my favorite place. My grandparents and many aunts, uncles, and cousins from both sides of my family lived there. My father's parents were from northern Italy, and my mother's parents were from Chanute, Kansas. They all ended up in Huntington Beach during the oil boom of the 1920s. It was wonderful for me that they lived a few blocks away from each other. I could have a nice piece of angelfood cake at the Tharp house, and after a short walk, a few anisette biscotti at the Siracusas'.

"As a young child I loved to draw and paint, and I loved books even before I could read. Many of my favorite books were written and illustrated by my cousin Leo Politi, my grandmother Caterina Siracusa's nephew. Her house was filled with all of his books, and many original drawing and paintings, including a large mural in her bedroom. I especially liked *Little Pancho, Pedro the Angel of Olvera Street,* and *Song of the Swallows* (which won the Caldecott Award in 1950). I remember meeting Leo at a book signing when I was five years old. It was very special to know the author of these books. Leo Politi's beautiful books inspired me to become an artist and an author.

"Once I learned to read, I wanted to read everything. In fact, it was difficult to get me to go to sleep at night. Some of my favorite books were *Charlotte's Web* by E. B. White and *The Little House on the Prairie* by Laura Ingalls Wilder. I especially loved Garth Williams' illustrations in these books. He is still one of my favorite illustrators. Another favorite book was *Half Magic* by Edward Eager, a very funny and clever story.

"In 1958, when I was eleven years old, my father, an oil tool company executive, was transferred from California to New York City. He worked in Rockefeller Center, and we lived in New Canaan and then Stamford, Connecticut. It was a big change for the whole family, but I really loved it. When I experienced my first snowfall, I was surprised to learn that snow was so cold and so wet. I also learned to ice skate on a frozen Connecticut pond.

"During junior high school and high school, my art teachers were always very encouraging and supportive. I was always drawing, and I loved to work in pen and ink and watercolor. When I lived in New Canaan, I took drawing lessons on Saturdays from a local artist. She gave the lessons in a barn near our house. I spent a lot of time learning the basics, sketching cones, cubes and spheres in charcoal. But I soon got to sketch the barn's residents: horses, a cow, some chickens, and two kangaroos. The kangaroos were former boxing stars in a circus.

"I fell in love with New York City when we moved from Manhattan from Connecticut in 1963. I finished my last year of high school in New York, and then I attended Hunter College (where I received a B.F.A. in painting in 1968). I still live in New York City and I still love it, too. After I graduated from Hunter College, I found a job as an editorial assistant at *Harper's Bazaar* magazine. I always liked fashion and fashion magazines. The magazine business was very exciting. My first illustration was published in *Harper's Bazaar,* a few months after I started working there. A short time later, I decided to leave my job and become a freelance illustrator. For many years my work appeared in the *New York Times, Harper's Bazaar, Glamour, Cosmopolitan, Mademoiselle, Seventeen,* and many other magazines and newspapers.

"In 1979, I married Sidney Levitt, an artist, author, and illustrator. I illustrated my first children's book, *Mike and Tony, Best Friends,* by Harriet Ziefert in 1986. I found it very challenging and interesting to illustrate this book. I loved creating the characters and their world. I decided I wanted to concentrate on doing

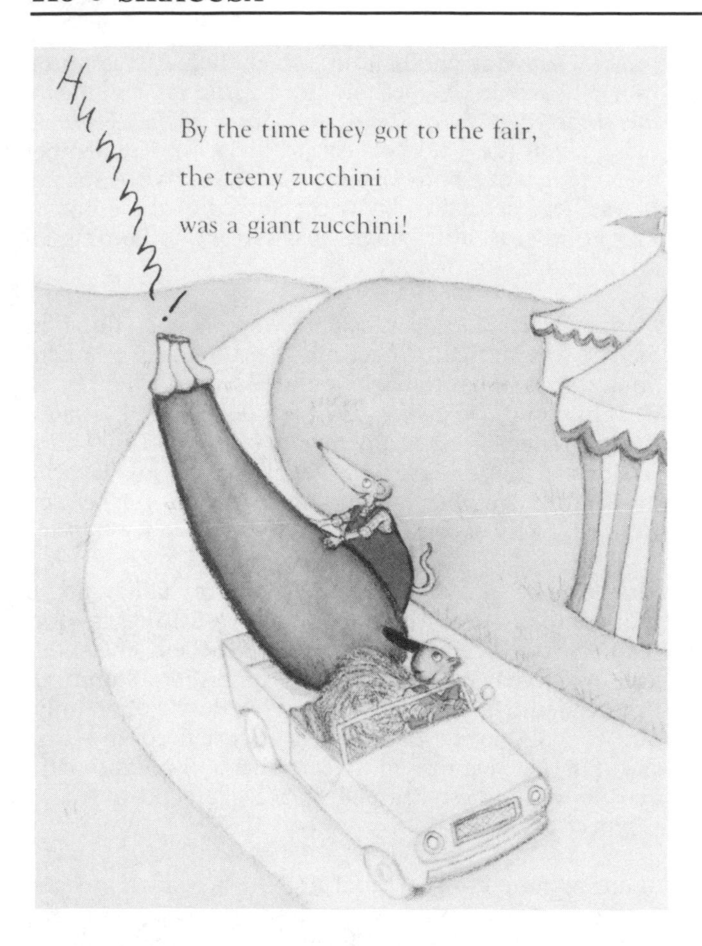

Robert Squirrel and Edgar Mouse raise a special zucchini that grows when they sing to it in Siracusa's Children's Choice book, *The Giant Zucchini.* (Illustration by the author.)

children's books. I illustrated four more books before I wrote my first story. When I illustrated *A Trip to the Doctor* and *A Trip to the Dentist,* two gate-fold picture books, I renewed an old friendship with Elizabeth Gordon who was a publisher there. When we were in college, she and I sold shoes at her uncle's store in New York City. She encouraged me to write my own stories as early readers.

"The first story I wrote was a Harper 'I-Can-Read' book called *Bingo, the Best Dog in the World.* It's the story of Sam, her little brother Stuart, their dog Bingo, and their adventures at the school dog show. My husband did the wonderful illustrations. It was our first collaboration. The first book that I wrote and illustrated was *No Mail for Mitchell,* a 'Step-into-Reading' book published by Random House. Mitchell is a mailman who doesn't get any mail. He's a dog, a 'mailhound' who wears shorts and kneesocks, and is very serious about his job. I loved illustrating this book because I love to draw animals and I love to write letters." Hazel Rochman, writing for *Booklist,* noted how the "brightly illustrated" book dramatizes "the pleasure of writing and reading personal letters" and conveys the message that "being able to read brings friendship and fun."

Siracusa was later reunited with her friend Elizabeth Gordon, who had moved to Hyperion Books for Children, where *The Giant Zucchini* was published. "This is the story of Edgar Mouse and Robert Squirrel," Siracusa told *SATA,* "two friends who try to grow a big squash so they can win first prize at the county fair. The odds are against them, and so is Humphrey Hog, a very nasty villain. Somehow they manage to win the prize with the help of a little magic and some songs. It was fun to write the songs, which I like to sing to the tune of 'Beautiful Dreamer' (with apologies to Stephen Foster). *The Giant Zucchini* is a fantasy, and I felt free to follow my imagination to wherever it would take me, in both the writing and the illustrations." Diane Roback and Richard Donahue called the book "laugh-out-loud funny" in *Publishers Weekly,* adding that "both text and pictures make this easy reader indeed a large-scale achievement."

The Giant Zucchini was followed by another easy reader, *The Parrot Problem.* "It's about Gina and a pizza-loving runaway parrot called Pepperoni," Siracusa explained to *SATA.* "Pepperoni causes a lot of trouble, as Gina and a lot of other people chase him all over town. *The Parrot Problem* is like a slapstick comedy. I was inspired by my sister Barbie and her parrot Winthrop. When I found out that Winthrop was crazy about pizza, I knew I could write a funny story. It was also fun to write about a pet who can talk back to you.

"My next book is *The Banana Split from Outer Space.* It is the story of two pigs, Stanley from Earth and Zelmo from Mars. They are both fantastic ice cream makers. This book combines a little science fiction with a lot of ice cream. I am looking forward to doing the pictures, and eating a lot of banana splits for reference. I am currently writing some new stories, too. I love to write and illustrate books that are fun for children to read. If I can introduce children to the joys of reading through my books, then I will be most gratified."

■ Works Cited

Roback, Diane, and Richard Donahue, review of *The Giant Zucchini, Publishers Weekly,* March 15, 1993, p. 88.

Rochman, Hazel, review of *No Mail for Mitchell, Booklist,* December 1, 1990, p. 754.

■ For More Information See

PERIODICALS

Booklist, May 15, 1993; July, 1993, p. 1981.

Horn Book Guide, July, 1990, p. 61; spring, 1992, p. 55; fall, 1993, p. 282.

Library Talk, January, 1992, p. 46.

Publishers Weekly, November 2, 1990, p. 73; July 5, 1991, p. 64.

School Library Journal, February, 1992, p. 78; August, 1993, p. 151; December, 1994, pp. 81, 87.

SMITH, Betty Sharon
See SMITH, Sharon

* * *

SMITH, Brenda 1946-

Personal

Born January 2, 1946, in Washington, DC; daughter of William E. (an architect) and Marjorie (a housewife; maiden name, Williams) Young; married Duane M. Smith (a senior computer consultant), August 4, 1978. *Education:* Ohio University, B.A. (cum laude), 1968, M.A., 1972; Ohio State University, postgraduate study, 1983. *Politics:* Democrat. *Religion:* Protestant.

Addresses

Home—3710 Harborough Dr., Gahanna, OH 43230. *Agent*—c/o Publicity Director, Lucent Books, Inc., P.O. Box 289011, San Diego, CA 92198-9011.

Career

Freelance author and editor of elementary and secondary social studies texts, 1991—. Lancaster, OH, middle school instructor, 1968-69; Reynoldsburg, OH, middle and high school instructor, 1970-71; Ohio statehouse, Columbus, OH, political speech writer, 1972-74; Josephinum College, public relations writer, 1976-78; Merrill Publishing, Columbus, editor, 1979-91, interim manager of social studies department, 1990. Delegate, United States-Russian Conference on Education, 1994. *Member:* National Council of Social Studies, Freelance Editorial Association, Association for Supervision and Curriculum Development, Ohio Council for Social Studies.

Writings

The Collapse of the Soviet Union, Lucent Books, 1994.
Egypt: Land of the Pharoahs, Lucent Books, 1995.

Project editor, *World History: The Human Experience,* 1992; and *Human Heritage: A World History,* 1985 and 1989 editions. Has also written narrative for two African-American and three American history textbooks. Has written chapters on world geography, economics, and world cultures.

Sidelights

Brenda Smith told *SATA:* "When I was in public school, I enjoyed learning and loved to read, especially about history. In fact, I became so entranced that I often wouldn't hear anything going on around me. I traveled to ancient Egypt or to whatever place and point in time I was reading about. I soon made up my mind to be a history teacher when I grew up. When I entered my first classroom, however, I knew it wasn't for me. That was a blow, and I didn't have any idea what to do next. In time, however, I began to write and edit social studies textbooks and library books for elementary and secondary students. The minute I started, I knew it *was* for me. Today I get to do what I always loved doing—read history and let it take me to faraway places and times. As a bonus, I get to write about it in such a way that the narrative will interest even those students who typically hate the subject. It's not a job—it's a privilege."

BRENDA SMITH

* * *

SMITH, Dodie
See SMITH, Dorothy Gladys

* * *

SMITH, Dorothy Gladys 1896-1990 (Dodie Smith; pseudonyms: C. L. Anthony, Charles Henry Percy)

Personal

Born May 3, 1896, in Whitefield, Lancashire, England; died November 24, 1990; daughter of Ernest Walter and Ella (Furber) Smith; married Alec Macbeth Beesley, 1939 (died, 1987). *Education:* Attended Manchester School and St. Paul's Girls' School, London; studied for the stage at Royal Academy of Dramatic Art, London.

DOROTHY GLADYS SMITH

Hobbies and other interests: Reading, music, dogs, donkeys.

Career

Actress, 1915-22; Heal & Son (furnishing company), London, England, buyer, 1923-32; full-time writer, 1932-90.

Writings

FOR CHILDREN; UNDER NAME DODIE SMITH

The Hundred and One Dalmatians, illustrations by Janet and Anne Grahame-Johnstone, Heinemann, 1956, Viking, 1957, reprinted with illustrations by Michael Dooling, Viking/Puffin Books, 1989.
The Starlight Barking: More about the Hundred and One Dalmatians, illustrations by J. and A. Grahame-Johnstone, Heinemann, 1967, Simon & Schuster, 1968.
The Midnight Kittens, illustrations by J. and A. Grahame-Johnstone, W. H. Allen, 1978.

NOVELS; UNDER NAME DODIE SMITH

I Capture the Castle, Atlantic/Little, Brown, 1948.
The New Moon with the Old, Atlantic/Little, Brown, 1963.
The Town in Bloom, Atlantic/Little, Brown, 1965.
It Ends with Revelations, Atlantic/Little, Brown, 1967.
A Tale of Two Families, Walker, 1970.
The Girl from the Candle-lit Bath, W. H. Allen, 1978.

AUTOBIOGRAPHIES; UNDER NAME DODIE SMITH

Look Back with Love: A Manchester Childhood, Heinemann, 1974.
Look Back with Mixed Feelings, W. H. Allen, 1978.
Look Back with Astonishment, W. H. Allen, 1979.
Look Back with Gratitude, Muller Blond & White, 1985.

PLAYS; UNDER PSEUDONYM C. L. ANTHONY

British Talent, first produced in London, 1924.
Autumn Crocus (three-act comedy; produced in London, 1931; produced on Broadway, 1932), Samuel French, 1931.
Service (three-act comedy; produced in London, 1932), Gollancz, 1932, acting edition, Samuel French, 1937.
Touch Wood (three-act comedy; produced in London, 1934), Samuel French, 1934.

PLAYS; UNDER NAME DODIE SMITH

Call It a Day (three-act comedy; produced in London, 1935; produced on Broadway, 1936), Samuel French, 1936, acting edition, 1937.
Bonnet over the Windmill (three-act comedy; produced in London, 1937), Heinemann, 1937.
(And co-director) *Dear Octopus* (three-act comedy; produced in London, 1938; produced on Broadway, 1939), Heinemann, 1938, acting edition, Samuel French, 1939.
Autumn Crocus, Service, and Touch Wood: Three Plays, Heinemann, 1939.
Lovers and Friends (three-act comedy; produced on Broadway), Samuel French, 1944.
Letter from Paris (three-act comedy adapted from Henry James's novel, *The Reverberator;* produced in London, 1952), Heinemann, 1954.
I Capture the Castle (two-act romantic comedy adapted by the author from her novel of the same title; produced in London, 1954), Samuel French, 1952.
These People, Those Books (three-act comedy), produced in Leeds, England, 1958.
Amateur Means Lover (three-act comedy; produced in Liverpool, England, 1961), Samuel French, 1962.

SCREENPLAYS

(With Frank Partos) *The Uninvited* (adapted from the novel by Dorothy Macardle), Paramount, 1944.
(With Lesser Samuels) *Darling, How Could You!* (adapted from *Alice-Sit-by-the-Fire* by James M. Barrie), Paramount, 1951.

Also author of screenplay "Schoolgirl Rebels" (under pseudonym Charles Henry Percy), 1915.

Adaptations

Autumn Crocus was filmed in England, 1934; *Call It a Day* was made into a movie by Warner Brothers, 1937; *Service* was filmed by Metro-Goldwyn-Mayer in 1944 as *Looking Forward; Dear Octopus* was filmed in England, 1945; *The Hundred and One Dalmatians* was made into the animated feature *One Hundred and One Dalmatians* by Walt Disney Productions, 1961.

Cruella De Vil is at her nastiest in Disney's *101 Dalmations,* adapted from Smith's popular story about greedy dognappers and brave puppies.

■ Sidelights

Although Dorothy Gladys Smith was primarily an author of works for adults, including plays, novels, and several autobiographies, she will most likely be remembered as the author of *The Hundred and One Dalmatians,* the children's story that Walt Disney Studios filmed as the animated *One Hundred and One Dalmatians.* Smith, better known as Dodie Smith, first gained recognition as a playwright, going by the pseudonym of C. L. Anthony until 1935, when she began to write under her own name. Her plays are generally light comedies about middle-class life that earned enough popular and critical praise in their time for *Dictionary of Literary Biography* contributor Martha Hadsel to call Smith "one of the few successful women dramatists in England and America during the first half of the twentieth century." Later in life Smith turned to fiction, penning the story about a pair of dalmatians who rescue their puppies from a terrible fate that became a classic children's story and film.

Smith credited her early family life as the greatest factor in determining her future career. "When I was eighteen months old," Smith once related, "my father died, and after that my mother and I lived with her family—my grandparents, three uncles and two aunts—in an old house with a garden sloping towards the Manchester Ship Canal. It was a stimulating household. Both my mother and grandmother wrote and composed. Almost everyone sang and played some musical instrument (we owned three pianos, a violin, a mandolin, a guitar and a banjo) and one uncle, an admirable amateur actor, was often to be heard rehearsing, preferably with me on hand to give him his cues. Although I had been taken to theatres long before I could read, it was this hearing of my uncle's parts which really aroused my interest in acting and in playwriting; the cues I gave got longer and longer and, by the age of nine, I had written a forty-page play. When I read this aloud to my mother she fell asleep—to awake and say apologetically, 'But darling, it was so dull.'"

Her mother's reaction did not discourage Smith in any way. Nevertheless, her original plan was to become an actress and not a playwright. After studying at the Royal Academy of Art, she performed professionally with some of her fellow students before becoming a member of the Portsmouth Repertory Theatre. During World War I, Smith went to France to help entertain the soldiers there, and she also played a role in a Zurich performance of John Galsworthy's *Pigeon.* But in 1923 the young actress decided to leave the theater and work as a buyer for Heal and Son, a furniture company where she was employed for the next eight years. Then, in 1931, Smith sold her play *Autumn Crocus* to one of her former stage directors. Although she had previously written a screenplay and a stage play, *Autumn Crocus* was the work that established her writing career, with productions in London and on Broadway. *Call It a Day* was the first play Smith wrote under her own name, as well as her most successful work, running for almost two hundred performances in New York City and for over five hundred performances in London.

As a full-time writer, Smith traveled to the United States in 1938 to help with a Broadway production of her *Dear Octopus,* and decided to remain in America, where she married her business manager, Alec Macbeth Beesley. During the next fifteen years, she lived mostly in California and did some writing for Paramount Studios. It was while she was living in Pennsylvania, however, that she published her first—and most popular—novel, *I Capture the Castle.* Smith later returned to England, where she continued to write plays and novels, and also began her first story for children, *The Hundred and One Dalmatians.* The owner of a number of pet dalmatians herself, it is not surprising that Smith chose the spotted dogs for her main characters. The novel opens as the happy family of Mr. and Mrs. Dearly, Pongo, Missis Pongo, and their fifteen puppies is suddenly disrupted by the evil furrier's wife, Cruella de Vil, who kidnaps the puppies in order to make a dalmatian-skin coat. Pongo and Missis's efforts to rescue their family result in "a fantasy of delightful horrors," according to a *Kirkus Reviews* writer.

Other reviewers praised Smith's treatment of her resourceful animal characters, as the Pongos use the "Twilight Barking" system of dog-to-dog communication to track their missing brood to Cruella's country estate, Hell Hall. *Library Journal* reviewer R. W. Stewart found that Smith's "skill in presenting dogdom" and the twilight barking "makes superb reading"; Aileen O'Brien Murphy similarly praised the "amusing and well-written story" in *Saturday Review* for obeying "the laws of good fantasy," as the Dearlys never quite realize that their pets have engineered the rescue. *New York Times Book Review* critic Ethna Sheehan, however, expressed doubts that children could see through the book's "witty sophistication to the fun and fantasy beneath." On the other hand, a *Publishers Weekly* writer found that Smith's "delicate wit" gives the story substance. As Polly Goodwin concluded in the *Chicago Sunday Tribune, The Hundred and One Dalmatians* is "full to overflowing" with the elements that make up "a good story—warmth and humor, imagination and suspense—and a fascinating array of characters, animal and human."

Smith's other children's books, while not as celebrated as her first, have also received their share of appreciation. *The Starlight Barking* continues the story of Pongo and Missis, as they wake one morning to discover that the entire world remains asleep—except for dogs, who are left to run the country and solve the problem. While Rachel R. Finne found that the lack of a villain makes the story less exciting than its predecessor, she added in the *New York Times Book Review* that "dog lovers nevertheless will enjoy this quietly imaginative adventure." Fans of cats will likewise enjoy *The Midnight Kittens,* in which orphaned twins Tom and Pam try to solve the ghostly comings and goings of kittens in their grandmother's garden. The story is "a thoroughly professional tale with pace, unity and an energetic belief in itself," a *New Statesman* critic commented, while a *Growing Point* reviewer similarly concluded that *The Midnight Kittens* is "a delightful mystery" that is "softly emotional and laced with surprise and humour."

The last years of Smith's life were spent working on her autobiography, the four volumes of which, entitled *Look Back with Love: A Manchester Childhood, Look Back with Mixed Feelings, Look Back with Astonishment,* and *Look Back with Gratitude,* relate her experiences from her childhood at the turn of the century, to her career as an aspiring actress and "flapper" in the 1920s, to the years she spent in the United States. Having made a successful career for herself as a writer in several genres, Smith nevertheless once stated: "I consider myself a lightweight author, but God knows I approach my work with as much seriousness as if it were Holy Writ."

■ Works Cited

Finne, Rachel R., review of *The Starlight Barking, New York Times Book Review,* May 5, 1968, p. 34.

Goodwin, Polly, review of *The Hundred and One Dalmatians, Chicago Sunday Tribune,* June 23, 1957, p. 5.

Hadsel, Martha, "Dodie Smith," *Dictionary of Literary Biography,* Volume 10: *Modern British Dramatists, 1900-1945,* Gale, 1982, pp. 158-62.

Review of *The Hundred and One Dalmatians, Kirkus Reviews,* February 1, 1957, p. 75.

Review of *The Hundred and One Dalmatians, Publishers Weekly,* November 28, 1966, p. 66.

Review of *The Midnight Kittens, New Statesman,* May 19, 1978, p. 683.

Review of *The Midnight Kittens, Growing Point,* March, 1981, p. 3851.

Murphy, Aileen O'Brien, review of *The Hundred and One Dalmatians, Saturday Review,* May 11, 1957, p. 56.

Sheehan, Ethna, "Kidnapped," *New York Times Book Review,* June 30, 1957, p. 18.

Stewart, R. W., review of *The Hundred and One Dalmatians, Library Journal,* July, 1957, p. 1802.

■ For More Information See

BOOKS

Smith, Dodie, *Look Back with Love: A Manchester Childhood,* Heinemann, 1974.

Smith, Dodie, *Look Back with Mixed Feelings,* W. H. Allen, 1978.

Smith, Dodie, *Look Back with Astonishment,* W. H. Allen, 1979.

Smith, Dodie, *Look Back with Gratitude,* Muller Blond & White, 1985.

PERIODICALS

New York Times Book Review, October 1, 1967, p. 48; July 26, 1970, p. 18.
Publishers Weekly, May 27, 1968, p. 58.
School Library Journal, January, 1987, p. 54.
Times Literary Supplement, December 31, 1971, p. 71; June 30, 1978, p. 733.
Washington Post Book World, August 18, 1968, p. 16; August 12, 1990, p. 9.

OBITUARIES:

PERIODICALS

Times (London), November 27, 1990.*

* * *

SMITH, Sharon 1943-
(Betty Sharon Smith)

■ Personal

Born May 1, 1943, in Shawnee, OK; daughter of Thomas J. (a builder) and Jewell L. (a homemaker; maiden name, Brown) Posey; married Al Smith, March 27, 1972 (divorced September, 1984); children: Keith Richard, David Randal, Katie Michelle, Ryan Michael. *Education:* Attended Oklahoma Baptist University, 1961-62; University of Oklahoma, B.A., 1964. *Politics:* Democrat. *Religion:* Unitarian. *Hobbies and other interests:* Gardening, history and government, movies, classical and country music, oldies, piano and guitar.

SHARON SMITH

■ Addresses

Home and office—16601 A Walker Rd., Shawnee, OK 74801.

■ Career

Shawnee News-Star, Shawnee, OK, reporter, 1961-62; State of Oklahoma, public relations graphic artist, 1965; *Edmond Sun,* Edmond, OK, editor, 1969-70; *El Reno Tribune,* El Reno, OK, reporter/photographer, 1970-72; U.S. Post Office, Oklahoma City, OK, clerk, 1981—; Oklahoma Postal Workers Union (AFL-CIO), president, 1993-95. *Member:* International Labor Communications Association, Authors Guild, Authors League of America, American Postal Workers Union, AFL-CIO, Oklahoma Postal Workers Union, Oklahoma Writers, Oklahoma Historical Society, Pottawatomie County Historical Society, Postal Press Association.

■ Awards, Honors

Editors award, column writing award, Oklahoma Press Association.

■ Writings

UNDER NAME BETTY SHARON SMITH

A Proofing Handbook, Oklahoma University Press, 1979.
(With Lawrence Clayton) *Coping with Sports Injuries,* Rosen, 1992.
Coping with School and a Job, Rosen, 1995.

■ Work in Progress

Ghost Offices and *Alpha to Omega: Oklahoma Post Office Stories,* 1995; research for *Violence in the Post Office—a History and Understanding.*

■ Sidelights

Sharon Smith told *SATA:* "Words are magic—and I have loved what they could do since I was old enough to put them on paper. I was not a good poet, but I created pictures with my words that wrapped all my emotions and visions into neat packages. As a seventh grader I helped edit my first newsletter, and my diaries and poetry notebooks were put aside. By the time I was a high school senior, I had done my first reporting on a real newspaper and discovered that doing feature stories was a real joy. Others read what I wrote with as much enthusiasm as I felt.

"Communication became a two-way street as I created venues for thought that reached everyone in some way: a humorous column made someone laugh, a theater or book review sent people to check for themselves, features on politicians and an interesting hobby or vocation helped readers know their neighbors in all walks of life and to look at them with new insights.

"My passion for life and all its quirks was being satisfied. Words could do magical things if put together in just the right way. News writing had to be concise and accurate and fictional or feature writing could be freer. Either way, years of reading everything from the ancient classics to modern writing had given me an instinct that improved my writing.

"After several years of doing layout and pasteup, proofreading, some technical and legal writing, and doing brochures for the state of Oklahoma, I went on to a completely different job. I spent a year with the post office before I discovered I had another passion—workers' rights. I began publishing and editing a local union newsletter and then writing monthly columns on labor issues for the state publication. Labor journalism is my new passion.

"To go back and trace the beginnings that made a difference, I'd remember the classics and especially the writings of Ray Bradbury and other science fiction imaginations. And I'd know why I get such a kick out of seeing my name in print! Thank you, God."

* * *

SMITH, Sherwood 1951-
(Nicholas Adams, Jessie Maguire, Robyn Tallis)

■ Personal

Born May 28, 1951, in Glendale, CA. *Education:* University of Southern California, B.A., 1973; University of California, Santa Barbara, M.A., 1977. *Hobbies and other interests:* Music, animals, children, nature, good tea, cozy firesides, and stimulating conversation.

■ Addresses

Agent—Valerie Smith, 1746 Rte 44-55, Modena, NY 12548.

■ Career

Writer. Taught elementary and high school for ten years. Has also tutored children with learning disabilities and critiqued manuscripts for beginning writers. *Member:* Science Fiction Writers of America, Mythopoeic Society, RWA, NINC.

■ Awards, Honors

Best writing contest winner, 1969, for the first draft of *Wren to the Rescue;* Best Books for Young Adult Readers, New York Public Library, 1993, for *Wren's Quest.*

■ Writings

YOUNG ADULT FANTASY

Wren to the Rescue, Harcourt, 1990.
Wren's Quest, Harcourt, 1993.
Wren's War, Harcourt Brace, 1995.

SCIENCE FICTION FOR ADULTS; WITH DAVE TROWBRIDGE

The Phoenix in Flight, Tor, 1993.
Ruler of Naught, Tor, 1993.
A Prison Unsought, Tor, 1994.
The Rifter's Covenant, Tor, 1995.

YOUNG ADULT SCIENCE FICTION; UNDER PSEUDONYM ROBYN TALLIS

Fire in the Sky, Ballantine, 1989.
The Giants of Elenna, Ballantine, 1989.
Rebel from Alphorion, Ballantine, 1989.
Visions from the Sea, Ballantine, 1989.

YOUNG ADULT; UNDER PSEUDONYM JESSE MAGUIRE

The Beginning, Ballantine, 1989.
Crossing Over, Ballantine, 1990.
Getting It Right, Ballantine, 1991.
Breaking the Rules, Ballantine, 1992.

YOUNG ADULT; UNDER PSEUDONYM NICHOLAS ADAMS

School Play, Harper, 1991.

OTHER

Also author of short stories collected in various horror, science fiction, and fantasy anthologies, including "Ghost Dancers" in *Things That Go Bump in the Night* and "Curing the Bozos" in *Bruce Coville's Book of Aliens.* Smith's works have been translated into Danish.

■ Work in Progress

With Dave Trowbridge, *The Thrones of Kronos, Exordium Book Five,* for Tor, 1996.

■ Sidelights

Sherwood Smith told *SATA:* "When I was five, I began making books out of paper towels. This went on for two years. At eight, I started writing stories about another world. Most of these got torn up soon after; it was easier to act out the stories with dolls. I began writing seriously again when I was eleven. By the time I was thirteen, I began submitting novels to publishers, at least one a year (when I'd finished typing it on my mother's ancient manual [typewriter], and had scraped up postage by baby-sitting). After some near misses, I stopped when I was twenty-one, figuring I needed to learn my craft better. College and jobs (from bartending to voice loops in Hollywood) and my own family intervened, until I began submitting again in the mid '80s, and these sold.

"As a child, I craved happy endings—this meant the child protagonists *could* always get back to Neverland . . . even stay. I also wanted *girls* to have adventures and fun. *Wren to the Rescue*—in which the princess is rescued by her best friend, a girl—was prompted by this wish. I try to write stories that I would have loved when I was a young reader. This meant adventurous stories with humor, mystery, magic, and joy—in worlds where an individual *can* make a difference."

Smith has written a number of science fiction and fantasy novels—for both teenage and adult readers—under a variety of pseudonyms. But Smith is becoming better known for the fantasy novels she writes under her own name for upper elementary age readers. These works, featuring Wren, an adventurous young orphan girl with magical powers, have garnered praise for their fast-paced plots and naturalistic treatment of supernatural elements. Lesa M. Holstine remarked in *Voice of Youth Advocates* that the "author is a welcome addition to the fantasy field." *Wren to the Rescue* introduces twelve-year-old Wren, a girl Holstine described as "a strong, likable heroine," her best friend Tess, who is revealed to be a princess in hiding, Tyron, a magician's apprentice, and Prince Connor, Tess's cousin. The novel opens in an orphanage, where the two girls live until the day Tess's identity is revealed and she, accompanied by Wren, goes to live in the palace. Soon thereafter, however, Tess is kidnapped by her evil uncle, and Wren,

In this sequel to *Wren to the Rescue,* Wren tries to find her parents, learns more about her magical powers, and gets involved in strange happenings in the kingdom of Cantirmoor. (Cover illustration by Dennis Nolan.)

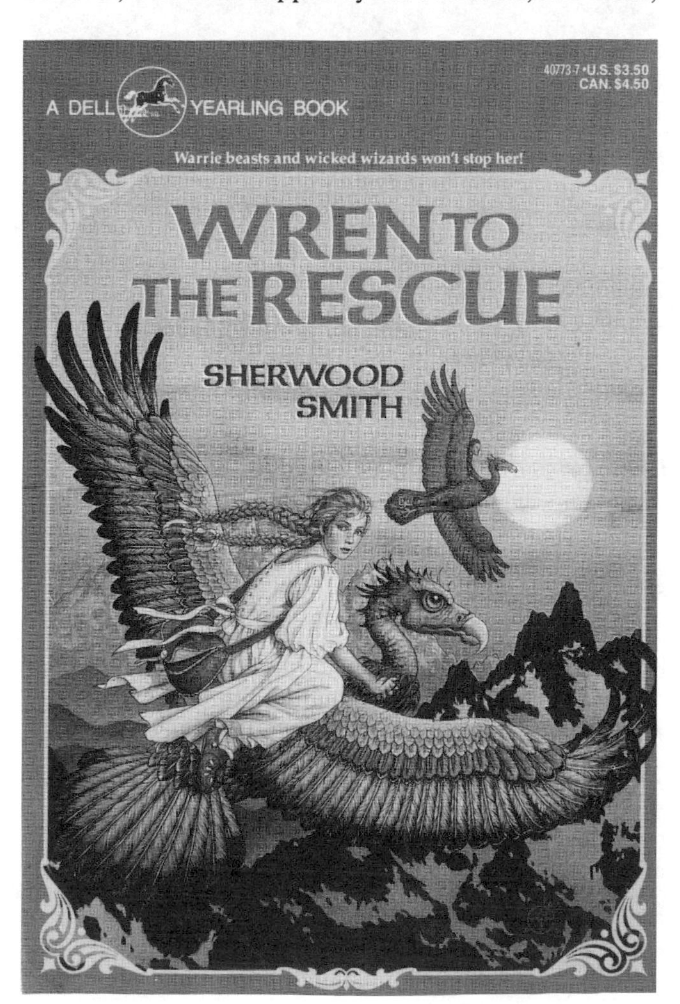

Sherwood Smith's first book introduces readers to the orphan named Wren and her daring adventure to rescue Princess Tess. (Cover illustration by Jody Lee.)

eventually joined by Tyron and Prince Connor, go in search of her friend. *School Library Journal* contributor Carol A. Edwards praised the fantasy world described in these children's adventures as "solidly constructed and divertingly revealed." Edwards, like some other reviewers, predicted a sequel to *Wren to the Rescue* and expressed the hope that subsequent titles would bring further character development as well as the answer to some of the many questions raised in the first volume. "Young fantasy lovers will enjoy the spunky heroine, the suspenseful plot, and some inventive magic," concluded *Horn Book* critic Ann A. Flowers.

Smith's sequel, *Wren's Quest,* employs many of the same elements reviewers appreciated in *Wren to the Rescue,* including an action-packed plot set in a well-realized fantasy world populated by interesting characters. In this story, Wren seeks clues to the identity of her parents and begins learning more about her magical powers with the help of Tyron, while Princess Tess becomes involved in the mysterious troubles that have been plaguing the palace court. Critical reaction to *Wren's Quest* was mixed. Patricia A. Dollisch, writing in *School Library Journal,* complained of shallow characterizations and an over-reliance on conventions of the genre, remarking: "With so much material to work with ... it is a shame that this book is such a humdrum effort." *Voice of Youth Advocates* reviewer Lucinda Deatsman, on the other hand, applauded the author's effective inclusion of magical elements, including commentary on the ethics of its use, and predicted that young readers would identify with Smith's characters, whom she described as "typical teenagers." Deatsman concluded by predicting that both *Wren to the Rescue* and *Wren's Quest* would "be popular with students and adults."

■ Works Cited

Deatsman, Lucinda, review of *Wren's Quest, Voice of Youth Advocates,* June, 1993, p. 105.
Dollisch, Patricia A., review of *Wren's Quest, School Library Journal,* June, 1993, pp. 110, 112.
Edwards, Carol A., review of *Wren to the Rescue, School Library Journal,* November, 1990, p. 140.
Flowers, Ann A., review of *Wren to the Rescue, Horn Book,* March/April, 1991, p. 202.
Holstine, Lesa M., review of *Wren to the Rescue, Voice of Youth Advocates,* December, 1990, p. 302.

■ For More Information See

PERIODICALS

Booklist, December 15, 1990, p. 857.
Horn Book, May/June, 1993, p. 348.
Kirkus Reviews, August 1, 1990, p. 1092.

* * *

SOUTH, Sheri Cobb 1959-

■ Personal

Born July 23, 1959, in Huntsville, AL; daughter of William Elbert (a NASA engineer) and Jayne (a homemaker; maiden name, Braswell) Cobb; married Mike South (a chemist) September 5, 1980; children: Jessamy, Trevor. *Education:* Wallace State Community College, A.A. (magna cum laude), 1980; University of South Alabama, B.A. (English; summa cum laude), 1992. *Religion:* Baptist.

■ Addresses

Home and office—Mobile, AL. *Agent*—Andrea Brown Literary Agency, P.O. Box 429, El Granada, CA 94018.

■ Career

J.C. Penney, Cullman, AL, sales clerk, 1978; Merrill's Photography, Cullman, photographer's assistant, 1980; police department, Livingston, AL, dispatcher, 1982; writer, lecturer, and speaker at schools. Judge for Mobile County School System, Alabama Penman Creative Writing Competition. *Member:* Romance Writers of America (president, Gulf Coast Chapter, 1993-94), Society of Children's Book Writers and Illustrators, Mortarboard, Phi Kappa Phi, Alpha Chi.

SHERI COBB SOUTH

■ Writings

Wrong-Way Romance, Bantam, 1991.
That Certain Feeling, Bantam, 1991.
The Cinderella Game, Bantam, 1992.
Don't Bet on Love, Bantam, 1994.
Blame It on Love, Bantam, 1995.

Contributor of short stories to *Teen* magazine; some of South's books have been translated into Polish and Chinese.

■ Work in Progress

Another novel, as yet untitled, for publication in 1996 by Bantam.

■ Sidelights

Sheri Cobb South told *SATA:* "I've always loved books, ever since I got my first library card at age three. By the time I was nine, I was writing truly awful poetry, and by age twelve I had moved on to novels, none of which (thankfully) ever made it past page three.

"Still, I always knew that someday I would write a *real* book. As my twenty-ninth birthday approached, I realized it was decision time. Was I going to spend the rest of my life saying 'someday' or was I going to sit down and *write*? Obviously, I chose to write. My goal was to become published by the time I turned thirty. I didn't quite make it, but I did sell my first novel, *Wrong-Way Romance,* four months before my thirty-first birthday.

"I never expected to write young adult; it just worked out that way, and I've been writing it ever since. The great thing about YA is that it lets me go back to high school and relive everything the way it should have been, rather than the way it actually was! Instead of addressing contemporary social issues, I tend to focus on the universal aspects of teen life: popularity, finding one's own identity, figuring out the opposite sex. These things haven't changed much since I was in high school, and I suspect they never will.

"Another reason I enjoy writing YA is that it lends itself so well to comedy. I love to watch old movies, especially musicals and romantic comedies, and I think that influence can be seen in my writing."

■ For More Information See

PERIODICALS

Teen, February, 1992.
Voice of Youth Advocates, June, 1992, p. 101.

* * *

SPOWART, Robin 1947-

■ Personal

Born August 14, 1947, in Martinez, CA; son of James Cambell (a worker at Shell Refinery) and Violet Louise (a homemaker and artist; maiden name, Bonin) Spowart; married Jeanne Modesitt (a children's book author), September 16, 1978. *Education:* Attended Ventura City College; University of California at Santa Cruz, B.A., 1981. *Politics:* Independent. *Hobbies and other interests:* Taking long walks in quiet places.

■ Addresses

Home—Northern California. *Agent*—Barbara Kouts, Box 558, Bellport, NY 11713.

■ Career

Commercial artist, 1975-85; children's book illustrator, 1985—. *Exhibitions:* Elizabeth Stone Gallery of Original Children's Book Art; Mazza Centennial Collection at the University of Findlay, Ohio; Dromkeen Collection of Australian Children's Literature. *Military Service:* U.S. Army. *Member:* Society of Children's Book Writers and Illustrators.

■ Awards, Honors

To Rabbittown, Vegetable Soup, and *Songs from Mother Goose* were named Junior Literary Guild Selections; *Latkes and Applesauce* and *Sometimes I Feel Like a Mouse* were chosen as American Booksellers' Pick of the Lists.

■ Illustrator

Clement Moore, *The Night Before Christmas,* Dodd, 1986.
Charlotte Zolotow, *A Rose, a Bridge, and a Wild Black Horse,* HarperCollins, 1987.
The Three Bears, Knopf, 1987.
Jeanne Modesitt, *Vegetable Soup,* Macmillan, 1988.
April Halprin Wayland, *To Rabbittown,* Scholastic, 1989.
Christine Barker Widman, *The Star Grazers,* HarperCollins, 1989.
Modesitt, *The Night Call,* Viking, 1989.
Nancy Larrick, compiler, *Songs from Mother Goose,* HarperCollins, 1989.
Fran Manushkin, *Latkes and Applesauce,* Scholastic, 1990.
Modesitt, compiler, *Songs of Chanukah,* Little, Brown, 1992.
Modesitt, *Sometimes I Feel Like a Mouse,* Scholastic, 1992.
Modesitt, *Mama, If You Had a Wish,* Green Tiger, 1993.
Modesitt, *Lunch with Milly,* Bridgewater, 1995.
Lynn Manuel, *The Night the Moon Blew Kisses,* Houghton, 1996.

ROBIN SPOWART

Spowart provided the softly colored illustrations for his wife Jeanne Modesitt's story, *Vegetable Soup,* which is about two rabbits who make new friends while gathering ingredients to make their dinner.

■ Sidelights

Robin Spowart told *SATA:* "I enjoyed drawing as a kid (what kid doesn't?), and much preferred it over any other type of school work (I was a pretty normal kid). Did I dream of being an artist when I 'grew up'? Nope. I knew I liked drawing, but the idea of being a professional artist never occurred to me. No one—no adults, as far as I can remember—ever encouraged me to continue to draw. If any kid artists are reading this, please allow me to say something VERY IMPORTANT: If you like drawing, keep at it—no matter what anyone else says (or does not say).

"I first considered the idea of illustrating children's books when I was in the U.S. Army, stationed in Germany. To relieve some of the monotony of army life, I had put together a couple of sketches I had drawn—sketches of imaginary places and people—and shown them to a German couple I had recently met. The couple liked my work and suggested I try my hand at children's book illustration. The seed was planted! After I was discharged from the army, I went to Ventura City College and took some art classes. I really enjoyed those classes, and my art instructors encouraged me to keep on doing my art! I'll never forget them for that. After Ventura College, I took on both art-related jobs (illustrating for newspapers, etc.) and non-art related jobs. Neither were satisfactory. I went back to school—this time the University of California at Santa Cruz (UCSC)—so that I could devote myself full time to art. While at UCSC, I did many 'fine art' paintings, that is, figure drawings, portraits, and landscape paintings. While doing such paintings had certain enjoyable aspects to them, it still wasn't right for me. I graduated from UCSC and began doing art work that was closer to my heart—imaginary images for greeting cards. This work proved to be satisfactory for me, at least for a while. Then it became boring, not challenging enough. And if that wasn't enough of a kick in the pants to get me to start something new, the fact that the greeting card companies stopped commissioning me to do work was! In my eyes, there was only one thing left for me to do—pursue my secret dream of illustrating children's books.

"The first book I illustrated was *The Night Before Christmas* by Clement Moore. (I had to pick a story that was in the public domain as I can't write worth a hill of beans and my wife, Jeanne Modesitt, wasn't writing at the time.) Seeing that it was the 'Year of the Teddy Bear,' Jeanne came up with the idea to illustrate all the characters in the book as teddy bears. We thought we had a sure seller on our hands. Wrong! Thirty publishers turned down the (very amateurish) dummy I had put together, saying that the teddy bear idea was 'cute,' but not right for their list. Boy, was I discouraged. But then, a miracle occurred. An editor from one house, who had seen the dummy, moved to another house, and decided that the second house would be the perfect publisher for the book. The lesson I learned from all this was: DON'T GIVE UP. No matter how many rejections you receive, keep at it until you drop.

"Getting a book to illustrate was never as hard as that first book. Publishers weren't breaking down my doors to get me to illustrate their manuscripts, but there was interest on their parts once they saw *The Night Before Christmas* and some other individual pieces of art I had put together for my portfolio. I have illustrated several books by my wife. These include *The Night Call, Vegetable Soup, Sometimes I Feel Like a Mouse, Songs of Chanukah, Mama, If You Had a Wish,* and *Lunch with Milly.* Jeanne and I work together very well. We're not envious or jealous of each other's work; on the contrary, we honor and respect each other's creative impulses.

"I seem to be drawn primarily to stories that have some sort of magical quality to them. However, I try not to make a rule of this. I'm open to illustrating all types of manuscripts. The only thing that matters is whether a particular story interests me. If it doesn't (no matter how good the story is), then it's best for me to turn the story down because it's agonizing (*and* boring *and* tedious) for me to work on something that my heart is not into.

"When I first started illustrating books, I had a lot of self-doubt. Can I *really* do this, I kept asking myself. I would rush through each one of my paintings just to see that, yes, I can do it! What an exhausting process that was! Today, I still have feelings of self-doubt when faced with a new story to illustrate, but I don't act on these feelings like I used to. As a result, the process of illustrating books is much more enjoyable to me (and much slower too!).

"Each story calls for its own medium. In illustrating books, I have used watercolor, acrylic, pastel pencil, and colored pencil. Sometimes it takes me a while to figure out which medium would be best suited for a particular story. For example, with *Lunch with Milly,* I tried acrylic, watercolor, and pastel pencil, but none of them seemed to fit the book just right. At last, I settled on colored pencil, which seem to be the perfect medium for this story (and my response to the story).

"The most important piece of advice I can give to aspiring artists is to follow your own inner guidance. This can be difficult at times, at least it is for me. Sometimes, when following my inner guidance on how to illustrate a particular story, I run into people who think the story should be illustrated altogether differently. Such disapproval can be a hard thing to face, but in the end, it hurts more to disobey one's own inner guidance than to receive disapproval. Surrender to the story—that's what I keep telling others, including myself."

■ For More Information See

PERIODICALS

Booklist, July 15, 1993.

Publishers Weekly, October 30, 1987, p. 67; January 29, 1988.

School Library Journal, October, 1987, p. 120; January, 1990.

* * *

STEIN, R. Conrad 1937-

■ Personal

Born April 22, 1937, in Chicago, IL; son of Konrad (a truck driver) and Mary (a factory worker; maiden name, Kariolich) Stein; married Deborah Kent (a writer), December, 1979; children: Janna. *Education:* University of Illinois, B.A., 1964; University of Guanajuato, Mexico, M.F.A. *Religion:* Catholic. *Politics:* "Varies from liberal to conservative."

■ Addresses

Home—5817 North Nina St., Chicago, IL 60631.

■ Career

Writer. Has also taught college-level creative writing. *Military service:* U.S. Marine Corps, 1955-58; became sergeant. *Member:* Society of Children's Book Writers and Illustrators.

R. CONRAD STEIN

Awards, Honors

Finalist, Western Writers of America Spur Award, 1992, for *Francisco de Coronado: Explorer of the Southwest.*

Writings

"OPEN DOOR BOOKS" SERIES

Steel Driving Man: The Legend of John Henry, illustrated by Darrell Wiskur, Children's Press, 1969.

(With Gail Hardin) *The Road from West Virginia,* Children's Press, 1970.

(With Adolphus Washington) *Hey, Taxi!,* A. Whitman, 1993.

(With Lillie D. Chaffin) *A World of Books,* Children's Press, 1970.

(With Joe C. "Lone Eagle" Vasquez) *My Tribe,* Children's Press, 1970.

(With Dave Stallworth) *Look to the Light Side,* Children's Press, 1970.

(With Herbert Hannahs) *People Are My Profession,* Children's Press, 1970.

(With Betsy Standerford) *No Hablo Ingles,* Children's Press, 1970.

"CORNERSTONES OF FREEDOM" SERIES

The Story of the Battle of the Bulge, illustrated by Lou Aronson, Children's Press, 1977.

The Story of D-Day, illustrated by Tom Dunnington, Children's Press, 1977, revised edition published as *D-Day,* 1993.

The Story of the Battle for Iwo Jima, illustrated by Len W. Meents, Children's Press, 1977.

The Story of the U.S.S. Arizona, illustrated by Dunnington, Children's Press, 1977, published as *The U.S.S. Arizona,* 1992.

The Story of the Homestead Act, illustrated by Cathy Koenig, Children's Press, 1978.

The Story of the Lewis and Clark Expedition, illustrated by Aronson, Children's Press, 1978.

The Story of the Golden Spike, illustrated by Dunnington, Children's Press, 1978.

The Story of Ellis Island, illustrated by Dunnington, Children's Press, 1979.

The Story of Arlington National Cemetery, illustrated by Richard Wahl, Children's Press, 1979.

The Story of the Smithsonian Institution, illustrated by Wahl, Children's Press, 1979.

The Story of the Clipper Ships, illustrated by Dunnington, Children's Press, 1981.

The Story of the Pullman Strike, illustrated by Meents, Children's Press, 1981.

The Story of the Gold at Sutter's Mill, illustrated by Aronson, Children's Press, 1981.

The Story of Marquette and Joliet, illustrated by Wahl, Children's Press, 1981.

The Story of the Pony Express, illustrated by Meents, Children's Press, 1981.

The Story of the Underground Railway, illustrated by Ralph Canaday, Children's Press, 1981.

The Story of the Flight at Kitty Hawk, illustrated by Meents, Children's Press, 1981.

The Story of the Panama Canal, illustrated by Keith Neely, Children's Press, 1982.

The Story of the Barbary Pirates, illustrated by Dunnington, Children's Press, 1982.

The Story of the Nineteenth Amendment, illustrated by Neely, Children's Press, 1982.

The Story of the New England Whalers, illustrated by Dunnington, Children's Press, 1982.

The Story of the Chicago Fire, illustrated by Wahl, Children's Press, 1982.

The Story of Wounded Knee, illustrated by David J. Catrow III, Children's Press, 1983.

The Story of the Little Bighorn, illustrated by Catrow, Children's Press, 1983.

The Story of the San Francisco Earthquake, illustrated by Nathan Greene, Children's Press, 1983.

The Story of Lexington and Concord, illustrated by Neely, Children's Press, 1983.

The Story of the Lafayette Escadrille, illustrated by Meents, Children's Press, 1983.

The Story of the Monitor and the Merrimac, illustrated by Neely, Children's Press, 1983.

The Story of Child Labor Laws, illustrated by Neely, Children's Press, 1984.

The Story of the Johnstown Flood, illustrated by Catrow, Children's Press, 1984.

The Story of the Boston Tea Party, illustrated by Neely, Children's Press, 1984.

The Story of the Oregon Trail, illustrated by Catrow, Children's Press, 1984, published as *The Oregon Trail,* 1994.

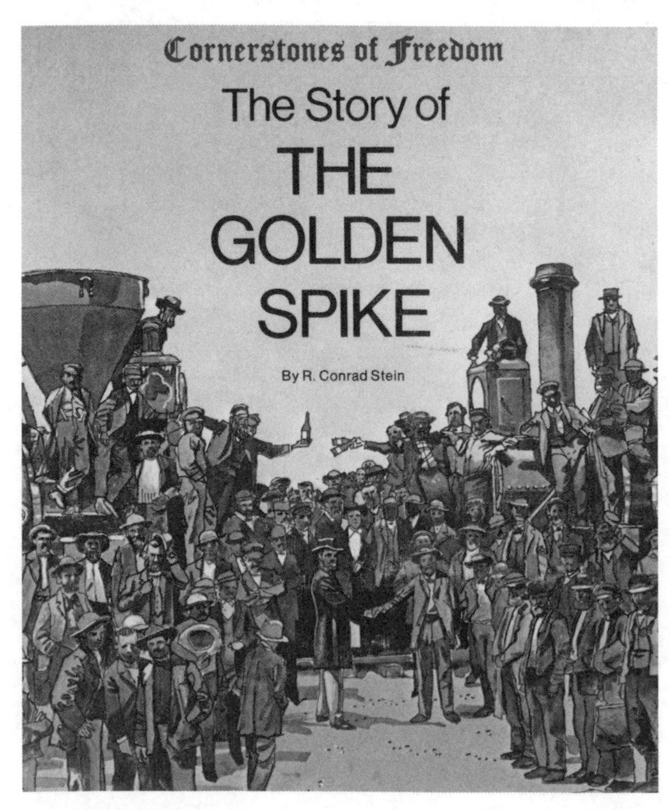

The story of the completion of the first transcontinental railroad is brought to life in Stein's 1978 book. (Cover illustration by Tom Dunnington.)

The Story of the Spirit of St. Louis, illustrated by Meents, Children's Press, 1984, published as *The Spirit of St. Louis,* 1994.
The Story of the Trail of Tears, illustrated by Catrow, Children's Press, 1985, revised edition published as *The Trail of Tears,* 1993.
The Story of Apollo 11, illustrated by Catrow, Children's Press, 1985, published as *Apollo 11,* 1992.
The Story of the Assassination of John F. Kennedy, illustrated by Neely, Children's Press, 1985, published as *The Assassination of John F. Kennedy,* 1992.
The Story of the Great Depression, illustrated by Greene, Children's Press, 1985, published as *The Great Depression,* 1993.
The Story of the Powers of Congress, illustrated by Neely, Children's Press, 1985.
The Story of the Powers of the President, illustrated by Neely, Children's Press, 1985.
The Story of the Erie Canal, illustrated by Neely, Children's Press, 1985.
The Story of Valley Forge, illustrated by Canaday, Children's Press, 1985, published as *Valley Forge,* 1994.
The Story of the Burning of Washington, illustrated by Wahl, Children's Press, 1985.
The Story of the United Nations, illustrated by Canaday, Children's Press, 1986, published as *The United Nations,* 1994.
The Story of the Montgomery Bus Boycott, illustrated by Greene, Children's Press, 1986, revised edition published as *The Montgomery Bus Boycott,* 1993.
The Story of Mississippi Steamboats, illustrated by Dunnington, Children's Press, 1987.
The Story of the Lone Star Republic, Children's Press, 1988.
The Story of the Powers of the Supreme Court, Children's Press, 1989.
The Bill of Rights, Children's Press, 1992.
Christopher Columbus, Children's Press, 1992.
Ellis Island, Children's Press, 1992.
The Manhattan Project, Children's Press, 1993.
The Hindenburg Disaster, Children's Press, 1993.
The Iran Hostage Crisis, Children's Press, 1994.
The Roaring Twenties, Children's Press, 1994.

"WORLD AT WAR" SERIES

Hiroshima, Children's Press, 1982.
Fall of Singapore, Children's Press, 1982.
Resistance Movements, Children's Press, 1982.
Dunkirk, Children's Press, 1982.
Siege of Leningrad, Children's Press, 1983.
Battle of Guadalcanal, Children's Press, 1983.
Road to Rome, Children's Press, 1984.
Nisei Regiment, Children's Press, 1985.
Hitler Youth, Children's Press, 1985.
Battle of Okinawa, Children's Press, 1985.
Invasion of Russia, Children's Press, 1985.
Warsaw Ghetto, Children's Press, 1985.
Auschwitz, Children's Press, 1986.
The Home Front, Children's Press, 1986.
The Holocaust, Children's Press, 1986.
Fighter Planes, Children's Press, 1986.

This 1989 book is part of Stein's "America the Beautiful" series.

Prisoners of War, Children's Press, 1987.
War Criminals, Children's Press, 1989.

"ENCHANTMENT OF THE WORLD" SERIES

Italy, Children's Press, 1984.
Mexico, Children's Press, 1984.
Kenya, Children's Press, 1985.
Hong Kong, Children's Press, 1985.
South Africa, Children's Press, 1986.
Greece, Children's Press, 1987.
The United States of America, Children's Press, 1994.

"AMERICA THE BEAUTIFUL" SERIES

America the Beautiful: Illinois, Children's Press, 1987.
America the Beautiful: Michigan, Children's Press, 1987.
America the Beautiful: Wisconsin, Children's Press, 1987.
America the Beautiful: New York, Children's Press, 1988.
America the Beautiful: New Mexico, Children's Press, 1988.
America the Beautiful: California, Children's Press, 1988.
America the Beautiful: Oregon, Children's Press, 1989.
America the Beautiful: Texas, Children's Press, 1989.
America the Beautiful: Indiana, Children's Press, 1990.
America the Beautiful: North Carolina, Children's Press, 1990.
America the Beautiful: Minnesota, Children's Press, 1991.

America the Beautiful: West Virginia, Children's Press, 1991.
America the Beautiful: Washington, Children's Press, 1992.

"SPORTS STARS" SERIES

Walter Payton: Record-Breaking Runner, Children's Press, 1987.
Don Shula: Football's Winningest Coach, Children's Press, 1994.
David Robinson (The Admiral), Children's Press, 1994.

"THE WORLD'S GREAT EXPLORERS" SERIES

Hernando Cortes, Children's Press, 1991.
Francisco de Coronado, Children's Press, 1992.

"AMERICAN WAR" SERIES

World War II in Europe: "America Goes to War", Enslow Publishers (Hillside, NJ), 1994.
World War II in the Pacific: Remember Pearl Harbor, Enslow Publishers, 1994.
The Korean War: "The Forgotten War," Enslow Publishers, 1994.

OTHER

Benjamin Franklin: Inventor, Statesman, and Patriot, illustrated by William Jacobson, Rand McNally, 1972.
Me and Dirty Arnie, Harcourt, 1982.
The Mexican Revolution, 1910-1920, New Discovery Books, 1994.

Work in Progress

A novel about a "fourteen-year-old American boy abandoned in the slums of Mexico City."

Sidelights

R. Conrad Stein told *SATA:* "I grew up in a no-frills, working class family. I guess today a sociologist would call my background 'culturally deprived,' but I have no regrets about my youth. I enlisted in the Marine Corps at age eighteen. In my neighborhood it was common in the 1950s for young men to enlist in the services. After the Marine Corps, I struggled through college and graduated with a degree in history. I then took a series of jobs, including stints as an industrial salesman and as a social worker. My main goal—my desire since I was twelve years old—was to be a writer. But as a young man I found it impossible to earn a living through writing.

"I achieved a break in 1966 when I sold a children's book to a textbook house. Then, thanks to my background as a history major in college, I began receiving assignments to write history books for young readers. Even though I still considered myself a fiction writer, I was thrilled to do the history assignments. I always tried to get the drama of history into my texts. I think any writer who fails to bring drama into a history book has failed at his craft. I now have published more than eighty books for young readers—most of them histories and biographies. Someday I wish to reestablish myself as a fiction writer, but I still find the field of history to be exciting."

For More Information See

PERIODICALS

Booklist, November 15, 1977, p. 556; February 15, 1982, p. 759; August, 1982, p. 1528; February 15, 1983, p. 780; August, 1983, p. 1468; January 15, 1984, p. 752; March 15, 1984, p. 1071; August, 1984, p. 1630; March 1, 1986, p. 1022; March 15, 1987, p. 1130; May 15, 1988, p. 1605; August, 1988, p. 1927; July, 1990, p. 2096; March 1, 1994, p. 1249.
Bulletin of the Center for Children's Books, November, 1982, p. 56; December, 1987, p. 57; July, 1988, p. 239.
Children's Book Review Service, August, 1982, p. 140.
Curriculum Review, December, 1982, p. 474.
Instructor, November, 1978, p. 136; November, 1979, p. 145.
Library Journal, June 15, 1970, p. 2310.
Library Talk, November, 1992, p. 48.
Reading Teacher, October, 1986, p. 107.
School Library Journal, February, 1978, p. 61; April, 1979, p. 63; March, 1982, p. 152; September, 1982, p. 128; November, 1982, p. 91; April, 1983, p. 119; September, 1983, p. 128; November, 1983, p. 83; April, 1984, p. 119; October, 1984, p. 162; May, 1985, p. 43; May, 1987, p. 104; February, 1988, p. 82; May, 1990, p. 114; January, 1993, p. 115; August, 1993, p. 184; March, 1994, p. 234; July, 1994, pp. 114, 126; August, 1994, p. 180.
Voice of Youth Advocates, August, 1994, p. 172.

* * *

STOVER, Jill (Griffin) 1958-

Personal

Born August 19, 1958, in Houston, TX; daughter of John (a physician) and Dodie Griffin; married Lanse Stover (an artist), December 18, 1983; children: Anna Stover, Clare Stover. *Education:* Austin College, B.A., 1980; attended University of Colorado at Boulder, 1981-82; Boston University, M.Ed., 1984. *Politics:* Democrat. *Religion:* Quaker.

Career

Teacher, storyteller, and author/illustrator of children's books. University of Massachusetts, Boston, MA, English as a second language instructor 1984-86; Endicott College, Beverly, MA, English as a second language instructor, 1989-91. Also supervises writing workshops. *Member:* Society of Children's Book Writers and Illustrators, Nature Conservancy, Audubon Society, Adirondack Mountain Club.

JILL STOVER

Awards, Honors

Best Children's Books of the Year list, *Smithsonian,* 1993, and Children's Choice Award (Texas), Harris County Public Library, 1994, both for *Alamo across Texas.*

Writings

FOR CHILDREN; SELF-ILLUSTRATED

Alamo across Texas, Lothrop, 1993.
Popsicle Pony, Lothrop, 1994.

Work in Progress

The Trailride, about riding across Texas as a young girl.

Sidelights

Jill Stover told *SATA:* "Kids often ask me, 'What's the best part about being an author and illustrator?' I always answer that, for me, it's getting to sit in my studio, alone, daydreaming of my Texas childhood and drawing the stories that come to mind. My studio walls are covered with photos, clippings, toys, and ceramic figurines that take me back to a time of magic, of growing up in Texas. Horses, longhorns, armadillos, alligators, cacti, banana trees, and colorful stucco buildings surround me in my small room. They're a small dose of Texas to get me through the long New England winter."

Stover's self-illustrated picture books have garnered praise for their engaging humor and brightly colored, childlike drawings. She made her writing debut with *Alamo across Texas,* an adventure story that offers the reader a tour of Texas, the nation's second largest state. The story centers on Alamo, an alligator whose river home dries up the year no rain falls. Alamo searches across Texas for a new home, trying out a swimming pool, a city fountain, and even the ocean before being floated back home by a flood. Although some critics, like *School Library Journal* reviewer Ann Welton, felt the story "lacks tension and is predictable," many also praised the author's artwork, which introduce the audience to creatures and landscapes commonly found in Texas. As one *Publishers Weekly* contributor noted, the illustrations "speak to their audience on a straightforward level."

Like her first book, Stover's second work, *Popsicle Pony,* is set in the Texas of the author's childhood. In this "nostalgic look at a time gone by," in the words of *School Library Journal* reviewer Lesley McKinstry, a little girl relates the story of what happens when Popsicle Pete goes to the hospital, leaving his stubborn horse, Chiefy, in her care. Every summer day, Popsicle Pete drove Chiefy around the town, selling popsicles and collecting treats for his pony along the way. While in the little girl's care, Chiefy won't go anywhere except the route he always travels with his owner, until the little girl figures out a way that both she and Chiefy can get what they want. Mary Harris Veeder singled out Stover's "carefully detailed depiction of the town" and lovable portrayal of Chiefy in her positive review of *Popsicle Pony* in *Booklist.*

Stover described her writing experience in her own words to *SATA.* "In March [1993], I went back to Texas to promote my newly published children's book, *Alamo across Texas.* Out of the studio ... on the road ... across Texas. Very like the hero of my book. The story tells of an alligator, Alamo, and his adventures when his river home dries up and all his pals hit the trail. He goes in search of a new home: to a cattle trough, the ocean, a swimming pool, a city fountain, and is finally washed home again in a great flood. His friends return, and all is well. Home is an exact combination of elements that makes life not only possible, but even marvelous. I moved to Massachusetts nine years ago and I love it, or I wouldn't stay here. But there's something in my chemistry that pulls me, like Alamo, home to the Lavaca River. That is where my myths were made.

"On my Texas trip I visited schools and had signings at bookstores cross the state. The major Texas newspapers all ran good articles on *Alamo* and me. Every bookstore I approached welcomed me. Owners were supportive, the experience enriching. People, people, people, excited about my book, excited for me. Pretty heady stuff after my isolation in the studio for so long. All of my artistic uncertainty and newcomer's insecurity vanished in the glory of a receptive public.

"As I presented *Alamo* to more and more schools, the book began to take on a life of its own. The audience filled in details that I never even knew were there. Kids in Texas know my characters well. Alligators, wild boars, armadillos, rattlesnakes, and longhorn cattle are no strangers to them. One four-year-old girl told me, 'I have a pet alligator at my house. It lives in the sewer.' I went to my young friend's house to see her alligator. She lives in a tiny shack next to a ditch full of trash, broken bottles, and sewage overflow. A full-grown alligator lives in the ditch. This young reader saw Alamo's river home in my book and made the connection between that pristine environment and her own back yard. Children see through magical eyes.

"At the schools I tried hard to look at each young face in my audience, to see myself, to experience the world of childhood again. They looked back at me, all kinds of kids, all colors of skin, so many languages, so many stories being formed. Such a vast audience. I tried to tell them that where they are in life is where it all starts, the world of dreams and stories. The world of books. The stuff that makes your grown-up years rich and deep. Important stuff happens when you're a kid. Their eyes shone at this idea. Really? they asked. I promise, I said.

"The pay isn't great for most children's book author/illustrators. I learned that a different payment comes from the contact with my audience. When I read my book to the children, there was a spark between us that ignited memories of my own magical childhood.

"As I drove the long stretches of road between cities, I watched the landscape roll by with such personal clarity,

Alamo the alligator searches for a new home in Texas in Stover's award-winning picture book. (Cover illustration by the author.)

as though I were alone in a treasure box. Patsy Cline or the Texas Tornadoes on the tape player, Bluebonnets and Indian paintbrushes whizzing by, a herd of longhorns all facing east, an armadillo too close to the road. Cacti just putting out new green, banana trees with huge purple flowers drooping down. Rivers and creeks deep dirty green, rimmed with elephant ears. When I arrive at the next stop, I am full of it all, and I tell the kids about it, and they nod yes, they will take care of it and remember it.

"Soon after I returned from Texas, I scheduled a reading at a local elementary school. An urban school. The neighborhood houses sit close together. These kids build snow caves and explore frozen mountains heaped along the busy streets. This is the magical world of my own northern-born children. But I was nervous. Would these Yankee children be able to relate to me? To my strange exotic tale of a faraway land filled with creatures they have never seen? To my relief, they laughed at the funny, odd animals. They marveled that an author would write about her own childhood memories. They watched, they listened, and together we found the common spark. New England kids, too, have their own stories, their own connections with the land, the water, and the people, that together provide the exact combination of elements that makes this place their home. They recognized that *Alamo* was a story of belonging, of struggling, of adventuring through unfamiliar territory. They brought their own lives to the book, and brought the book to life."

■ Works Cited

Review of *Alamo across Texas, Publishers Weekly,* February 8, 1993, p. 84.

McKinstry, Lesley, review of *Popsicle Pony, School Library Journal,* May, 1994, p. 105.

Veeder, Mary Harris, review of *Popsicle Pony, Booklist,* March 15, 1994, p. 1375.

Welton, Ann, review of *Alamo across Texas, School Library Journal,* June, 1993, p. 90.

■ For More Information See

PERIODICALS

Children's Book Review Service, April, 1993, p. 102; April, 1994, p. 102.

* * *

STOW, Jenny 1948-

■ Personal

Born March 8, 1948, in Manchester, England; daughter of Charles Kenneth and Irene (maiden name, Kirkham) Foster; married Barry Stow (an architect), July 21, 1973; children: Jack James. *Education:* Attended Manchester College of Art and Design, 1966-67; University of London, B.A., 1970; University College of Wales, Aberystwyth, P.G.C.E., 1971; University of Bristol, M.E.D., 1983; attended Chelsea School of Art, 1988-90.

JENNY STOW

Hobbies and other interests: Travel, living abroad (Africa, West Indies), music, opera.

■ Addresses

Home—90 Trentham St., Southfields, London SW18 5DJ, England. *Agent*—Eunice McMullen, 38 Clewer Hill Rd., Windsor, Berkshire SL4 4BW England.

■ Career

Teacher of special educational needs in London, England, 1971-72, Hampshire, England, 1973-75, and Bristol, England, 1975-82; primary school teacher, Botswana, South Africa, 1982-84; special needs teacher, London, 1987—; writer and illustrator.

■ Awards, Honors

The House That Jack Built was shortlisted for the Black-Eyed Susan Picture Book Award, 1993.

■ Writings

SELF-ILLUSTRATED

The House That Jack Built, Dial, 1992.
Growing Pains, Bridgewater Books, 1994.

ILLUSTRATOR

John Agard, *The Monster Who Hated Balloons,* Longman, 1994.
Agard, *The Monster Who Loved Toothbrushes,* Longman, 1994.
Agard, *The Monster Who Loved Cameras,* Longman, 1994.
Agard, *The Monster Who Loved Telephones,* Longman, 1994.

Has also illustrated books and book jackets for Longman and Macmillan; contributor of illustrations to periodical *Nuevo Estilo,* Madrid, Spain.

■ Sidelights

Jenny Stow told *SATA:* "After leaving school, I attended art college but got sidetracked into the teaching of children with special educational needs. It was while living in the Caribbean, based in Antigua (1987-88) that I returned to drawing and illustration.

"A previous trip to Pakistan had fired my imagination, as did the vivid colors of the West Indies and the luscious flora. In my latest book, *Growing Pains,* I am drawing upon my experience of living in Botswana (1982-85)—chiefly wildlife and flora. Travel is thus one of my chief sources of inspiration. Color and texture play an important part in my work."

■ For More Information See

PERIODICALS

Horn Book Guide, fall, 1992, p. 293.

T

TALLIS, Robyn
See SMITH, Sherwood

* * *

THOMPSON, K(athryn Carolyn) Dyble 1952-

■ Personal

Born April 2, 1952, in Milwaukee, WI; daughter of William J. (a welding engineer) and Ruth Kathleen (a legal secretary; maiden name, Sperberg) Dyble; married Michael D. Thompson, 1973 (divorced, 1975); children: Michael Glynn. *Education:* University of Wisconsin, Milwaukee, B.F.A. (with honors), 1979; studied drawing and painting at Atelier Prohl, 1990-91; attended Milwaukee Institute of Art and Design, 1989, and Fox Valley Technical Institute, 1992. *Hobbies and other interests:* Being a "screever" (a pavement artist).

■ Addresses

Home and office—3122 North Newhall St., Milwaukee, WI 53211.

■ Career

City of Milwaukee, City Clerk's Office, Milwaukee, WI, artist, 1979-81; Spectrumedia, Marcus Corporation, Milwaukee, art director, 1981-82; TSR, Inc. (manufacturer of games, books, toys, and leisure products), Lake Geneva, WI, designer, 1983-84; Creative Concepts, Inc., Milwaukee, art director, 1984-90; freelance illustrator, 1989—; City of Milwaukee Health Department, Milwaukee, graphic designer, 1992-93; Milwaukee Institute of Art and Design, Milwaukee, instructor in illustration media, 1993. Lecturer. *Exhibitions:* "People, Places & Designs," Wauwatosa Public Library Gallery, Wauwatosa, WI; "Classical Realism: The Tradition Continues," West Bend Gallery of Fine Arts, West Bend, WI; "Off the Top of Your Head," Government Center Gallery, Kettering, Ohio; "Mad Hatters on the Verge of a Nervous Breakdown," Metropolitan Gallery, Milwaukee; "Flesh Experts," Flesh Experts Studio, Milwaukee. *Member:* Society of Children's Book Writers and Illustrators, Illustrators and Designers of Milwaukee.

K. DYBLE THOMPSON

■ Writings

(And illustrator) *Undercover: A Collection of Little Known & Unrelated Facts about Milwaukee,* City of Milwaukee, 1981.

ILLUSTRATOR

James Edward McGoldrick, *Luther's English Connection,* Northwestern Publishing, 1979.

Debie Cotton, *Messy Marcy MacIntyre,* Gareth Stevens, 1991.

Isaac Asimov and Elizabeth Kaplan, *Henry Hudson, Arctic Explorer and North American Adventurer,* Gareth Stevens, 1992.

Alma Flor Ada, *My Name Is Maria Isabel,* Atheneum, 1993, published in Spanish as *Me Llamo Maria Isabel,* Atheneum, 1994.

Artwork included in *Design in the Visual Arts,* by Roy R. Behrens, Prentice-Hall, 1984, and *Illustration as Art,* by Behrens, Prentice-Hall, 1986. Contributor of illustrations to *Cricket, Ladybug,* and *North American Review.*

■ Work in Progress

Researching Mexican culture.

■ Sidelights

K. Dyble Thompson told *SATA,* "Although I received a bachelor's degree in fine arts, in drawing and painting, upon graduation I began working as a graphic designer. I pursued this career as a designer and art director for ten years before I started to illustrate. I found what I liked most as a designer was doing layouts and the drawing they involved. As an art director, I viewed many portfolios and worked with wonderful illustrators. I wanted to do more with my art and began taking night courses in drawing and painting, portraiture, and still life, which I found rewarding. When a colleague asked me to recommend some illustrators, I asked if I might also submit a proposal for the project and so launched my career as an illustrator.

"When I receive an assignment, I immediately work out a schedule: when pencil ideas are due, when final art is due, and leaving time for revisions by the art director and editor before the final due date. This kind of time framework keeps the anxieties and pressures of deadlines at bay for me. Then it's off to do research. I love spending time in libraries and bookstores, tracking down visual and text reference on the subjects. Often I need to take my own photo reference. For example, when working on *Henry Hudson, Arctic Explorer and North American Adventurer* there was very little pictorial reference on what Hudson looked like. The one image of him was a small woodcut portrait done sixty years after his death. In the book I illustrated there is a surprising resemblance between Henry Hudson and my brother John. I try to be as accurate as I can in regards to historical costumes and settings.

"My work is influenced by many artists, but two who have made a distinct impression on me are Jerry Pinkney and Gary Kelly. Each has made visits to Milwaukee to give talks. I find their love of drawing, commitment to excellence, and exquisite work inspirational."

TOBIAS, Tobi 1938-

■ Personal

Born September 12, 1938, in New York, NY; daughter of William S. (a doctor) and Esther (Meshel) Bernstein; married Irwin Tobias (a college professor), September 4, 1960; children: Anne, John. *Education:* Barnard College, B.A., 1959; New York University, M.A., 1962.

■ Addresses

Home—38 West 96th St., New York, NY 10025.

■ Career

Hudson Review, New York City, managing editor, 1959-60; freelance writer, 1960—; *Dance Magazine,* New York City, contributing editor, 1971-76, associate editor, 1976-83, senior editor, 1983—. Adjunct professor of dance criticism, Barnard College, 1977—; instructor of seminars in dance style and criticism.

■ Writings

FOR CHILDREN

Maria Tallchief, illustrated by Michael Hampshire, Crowell, 1970.

Marian Anderson, illustrated by Symeon Shimin, Crowell, 1972.

A Day Off, illustrated by Ray Cruz, Putnam, 1973.

Isamu Noguchi: The Life of a Sculptor, Crowell, 1974.

The Quitting Deal, illustrated by Trina Schart Hyman, Viking, 1975.

Arthur Mitchell, illustrated by Carole Byard, Crowell, 1975.

Moving Day, illustrated by William Pene du Bois, Knopf, 1976.

An Umbrella Named Umbrella, illustrated by Lady McCrady, Knopf, 1976.

Where Does It Come From? ("That's a Good Question" series), illustrated by Sharon Elzaurdia, Children's Press, 1977.

Liquid or Solid? ("That's a Good Question" series), illustrated by Gene Sharp, Children's Press, 1977.

Quiet or Noisy? ("That's a Good Question" series), illustrated by Elzaurdia, Children's Press, 1977.

Easy or Hard? ("That's a Good Question" series), illustrated by Sharp, Children's Press, 1977.

Chasing the Goblins Away, illustrated by Victor Ambrus, F. Warne, 1977.

Jane, Wishing, illustrated by Hyman, Viking, 1977.

Petey, illustrated by Shimin, Putnam, 1978.

At the Beach, illustrated by Gloria Singer, McKay, 1978.

How Your Mother and Father Met, and What Happened After, illustrated by Diane de Groat, McGraw-Hill, 1978.

The Man Who Played Accordion Music, illustrated by Nola Langner, Knopf, 1979.

How We Got Our First Cat, illustrated by Emily Arnold McCully, F. Watts, 1980.

The Dawdlewalk, illustrated by Jeanette Swofford, Carolrhoda, 1983.

Pot Luck, illustrated by Nola Langner Malone, Lothrop, 1993.

TRANSLATOR

Ole Hertz, *Tobias Catches Trout,* Carolrhoda, 1984.
Hertz, *Tobias Goes Ice Fishing,* Carolrhoda, 1984.
Hertz, *Tobias Goes Seal Hunting,* Carolrhoda, 1984.
Hertz, *Tobias Has a Birthday,* Carolrhoda, 1984.
Poupa Montaufier, *One Summer at Grandmother's House,* Carolrhoda, 1985.

OTHER

Also contributor to oral history program of the Dance Collection, Lincoln Center Library of the Performing Arts, and to "An Oral History of the Royal Danish Ballet and Its Bournonville Tradition." Contributor to "Dance in America" television series and to other television dance programs. Contributor of articles to periodicals, including the *New York Times.* Member of editorial staff, *The Compleat Parent,* 1967-68; member of editorial board, *Barnard Alumnae Magazine,* 1973-76; advisory editor, *Dance Scope,* 1973-78; contributing editor, *New York Dance,* 1975-77; dance critic, *Soho News,* 1979-81, and *New York Magazine,* 1980—.

■ Adaptations

Jane, Wishing was filmed as a CBS-TV production, 1982.

■ Sidelights

Tobi Tobias's many-faceted writing career encompasses journalism and criticism for a number of art and general interest publications, as well as picture books, fiction, and nonfiction for children. Her first book, published in 1970, was a biography of Maria Tallchief, the Native American ballerina who became one of the greatest dancers in American history. The book not only informs young readers of the facts of Tallchief's life, it also emphasizes the hard work and dedication it takes to be a successful artist.

These qualities are emphasized as well in Tobias' other biographies for young people about singer Marian Anderson and dancer Arthur Mitchell, both African Americans, and Japanese-American sculptor Isamu Noguchi. In her review of *Marian Anderson* for *School Library Journal,* Helen Wright stated that the book would "impress readers with [Anderson's] determination and pride." Of *Isamu Noguchi: The Life of a Sculptor,* a reviewer for the *Interracial Books for Children Bulletin* similarly noted that "Ms. Tobias stresses the hard work, risks, compromises and commitment required of all artists." The author's biography of dancer Arthur Mitchell not only recounts the prejudices he faced as a black man in the world of classical ballet, but also "notes the hard work and strong discipline required" for his success, as a *Booklist* critic stated.

Tobias showed another aspect of discipline in one of her most praised works, *The Quitting Deal,* a fictional account of a mother and daughter who are both trying to

A mother and daughter make a pact to stop their bad habits of smoking and thumb sucking in Tobias's 1975 story. (Cover illustration by Trina Schart Hyman.)

rid themselves of nasty habits. The mother wants to give up smoking, and her little girl wants to stop sucking her thumb. Together, they try a variety of methods to kick their habits, none of which are entirely successful. While Marge Blaine, a contributor to the *New York Times Book Review,* felt that the book was unsuccessful because the "characters are left with their nasty habits, and we feel let down," other critics praised Tobias's realistic portrayal of an everyday situation. *Bulletin of the Center for Children's Books* reviewer Zena Sutherland, for instance, called *The Quitting Deal* "an understanding, rueful, and realistic acceptance of people's hang-ups," and a *Publishers Weekly* reviewer observed that "without any kind of falsity or sentimentalizing Tobi Tobias explores real problems."

Other problems are also explored in Tobias's picture books for younger children. *Moving Day* relates the noise and bustle of a move with a "gentle, poetic text" that is "direct and childlike in word and tone," Mary Jane Anderson remarked in *Booklist.* Daydreams and family teasing make up the action in *Jane, Wishing,* which *New York Times Book Review* contributor Nancy Larrick judged to be a "sensitive and artistic" book. And *Petey* tells of the loss of a girl's beloved pet and how her family helps her to deal with it. Although the subject and style are nothing new, "the book still is one of the better stories about accepting death," Sutherland ob-

Rachel's grandmother tells her stories of growing up in Poland in this cross-generational tale by Tobias. (Cover illustration by Nola Langner Malone.)

served in another *Bulletin of the Center for Children's Books* article.

Challenges of a lighter nature are the subject of other Tobias picture books. *How We Got Our First Cat* describes how two children get their reluctant parents to adopt a stray cat. *Booklist* contributor Judith Goldberger praised the author's "bemused, low-key style" that makes the story "one readers will smile over." Similarly, *The Dawdlewalk* is a simple story in which a little boy and his mother walk to school. All along the way, the boy runs into distractions, and, despite his mother's reminders, stops to dawdle. At the end, the tables are turned as the young boy urges his mother to hurry when she stops to chat with a friend. This familiar situation is one that will "coax a rueful smile from boys and girls as they ponder the ways of parents," noted Jean Mercier in *Publishers Weekly.*

Another intergenerational relationship is portrayed in *Pot Luck,* where Rachel has a problem understanding why her grandmother ("Gram") is taking great pains shopping for food and preparing a meal for her friend Sophie after Gram has told her she is going to serve a pot luck meal of whatever can be scraped together in the house. As the day and the preparations progress, Gram tells Rachel stories about how she and Sophie grew up together and became special friends in Poland. After an evening of listening to the two older women share heartfelt reminiscences, Rachel once again asks why Gram didn't serve pot luck. Gram tells Rachel, "A woman like Sophie Paderewski, you don't feed last night's stew." The warm relationship between Rachel and her grandmother is "the book's most obvious and appealing draw," Ilene Cooper stated in *Booklist.* Cyrisse Jaffee, writing in *School Library Journal,* called it "a satisfying, flavorful story that will evoke many sweet memories."

Tobias's many interests, and her professional status as a journalist, critic, and college professor, keep her writing all the time. As she once told *SATA:* "I write because I can't imagine doing anything else. In my free time I pursue what interests me—dance, graphic arts, exploring New York, reading, asking questions and listening, really listening to the answers—and I find that, in the long run, it all goes into the work."

■ Works Cited

Anderson, Mary Jane, review of *Moving Day, Booklist,* June 1, 1976, p. 1410.

Review of *Arthur Mitchell, Booklist,* July 1, 1975, p. 1130.

Blaine, Marge, review of *The Quitting Deal, New York Times Book Review,* May 4, 1975, p. 40.

Cooper, Ilene, review of *Pot Luck, Booklist,* April 1, 1993, p. 1442.

Goldberger, Judith, review of *How We Got Our First Cat, Booklist,* January 15, 1981, p. 703.

Review of *Isamu Noguchi: The Life of a Sculptor, Interracial Books for Children Bulletin,* Volume 7, numbers 2-3, 1976, pp. 20-21.

Jaffee, Cyrisse, review of *Pot Luck, School Library Journal,* May, 1993, p. 92.

Larrick, Nancy, review of *Jane, Wishing, New York Times Book Review,* July 24, 1977, p. 18.

Mercier, Jean, review of *The Dawdlewalk, Publishers Weekly,* June 10, 1983, p. 65.

Review of *The Quitting Deal, Publishers Weekly,* June 2, 1975, p. 53.

Sutherland, Zena, review of *The Quitting Deal, Bulletin of the Center for Children's Books,* October, 1975, p. 36.

Sutherland, Zena, review of *Petey, Bulletin of the Center for Children's Books,* June, 1978, p. 168.

Tobias, Tobi, *Pot Luck,* Lothrop, 1993.

Wright, Helen, review of *Marian Anderson, School Library Journal,* April, 1973, p. 72.

■ For More Information See

BOOKS

Children's Literature Review, Volume 4, Gale, 1982, pp. 213-18.

PERIODICALS

Booklist, July 1, 1973, p. 950; July 1, 1978, p. 1682; September 15, 1985, p. 144; February 1, 1994, p. 1011.

Bulletin of the Center for Children's Books, December, 1975, p. 71; January, 1979, p. 91.

New York Times Book Review, October 23, 1977, p. 32.

Publishers Weekly, March 8, 1976, p. 66; September 18, 1978, p. 166; September 26, 1978, p. 32.
School Library Journal, December, 1977, pp. 35, 61; September, 1978, p. 126; October, 1983, p. 154.

* * *

TURK, Ruth 1917-

■ Personal

Education: M.A. in Education.

■ Addresses

Home—7320 Pine Park Dr. N., Lake Worth, FL 33467.

■ Career

Writer, lecturer. English teacher and guidance counselor in the New York school system for many years. *Member:* Society of Children's Book Writers and Illustrators, Florida Freelance Writers Association.

■ Writings

You're Getting Older, So What? (adult nonfiction), illustrated by John Livesay, Herald Publishing House, 1976.
More Than Friends (novel), Bantam, 1980.
Hillary for President (for children), Trillium Press, 1989.
They Reached for the Stars!, illustrated by Ned Tripp, Blue Bird Publishing, 1992.
"15" Is the Pits (young adult novel), New Win Publishing, 1993.
The Second Flowering (adult nonfiction), New Win Publishing, 1993.
Lillian Hellman: Rebel Playwright (young adult biography), Lerner Publications, 1995.
Noises in the Night, Armstrong Publishing, in press.
Edith Wharton: Beyond the Age of Innocence, Morgan Reynolds, in press.
Ray Charles: Genius of Soul (young adult biography), Lerner Publications, in press.
Rosalynn Carter: Steel Magnolia, F. Watts, in press.

Also author of poetry, stories, and articles that have appeared in a variety of national publications. Author of "Dear Ruth" weekly advice column for older people for nearly two decades.

■ Sidelights

Ruth Turk told *SATA:* "My first poem was accepted for publication in a leading newspaper when I was ten years old. From that day until the present, writing in some form is a daily part of my lifestyle. While writing in longhand may be considered 'archaic' in a computer age, there is also a compelling need to hold that pen in my hand in order to release that creative flow.

"After several decades of teaching in a public school system that absorbed most of my time and energy, I

RUTH TURK

realized there would have to be a time when I would write for *myself.* Correcting themes and encouraging my students was a rewarding experience while it lasted. I soon learned that the retirement phase of life was more 'refirement' than anything else. Two adult nonfiction books, *You're Getting Older, So What?* and *The Second Flowering,* pretty much sum up my attitude toward living in general. Today my writing continues to move in many directions—novels, picture books, articles on a variety of subjects, free verse and traditional poetry—as long as there are words, I continue to explore and use them. Travel and research play a vital role in the preparation of material—inspiration and dedication do the rest. Writing for and about young people also means never growing old!"

■ For More Information See

PERIODICALS

Publishers Weekly, June 27, 1980, p. 84.
School Library Journal, November, 1993, p. 126.

* * *

TYERS, Kathy 1952-

■ Personal

Born July 21, 1952, in Long Beach, CA; daughter of H. Chester (a dentist) and Barbara Louise (a musician;

maiden name, Putnam) Moore; married Mark J. Tyers (an educator), June 1, 1974; children: Matthew Benjamin. *Education:* Montana State University, B.S., 1974, elementary education certificate, 1977. *Religion:* Christian. *Hobbies and other interests:* Music (listening, performing, teaching), gardening (trees, herbs, vegetables), Tae Kwon Do, jogging, ice skating.

■ Addresses

Agent—Martha Millard, 204 Park Ave., Madison, NJ 07940.

■ Career

Montana State University, Bozeman, MT, immunobiology technician, 1974-1976; Christian Center School, Bozeman, primary grades teacher, 1977-1980; freelance writer, 1983—. Private flute teacher, 1969—; Bozeman Symphony Orchestra, flutist, 1970-77; folk musician (with husband), 1972—. Board member, Friends of KUSM Public TV, 1991. *Member:* Science Fiction and Fantasy Writers of America, Society of Children's Book Writers and Illustrators (newsletter editor for Big Sky Chapter, 1991-92), National Space Society, Montana Authors Coalition.

■ Writings

Firebird, Bantam/Spectra, 1987.
Fusion Fire, Bantam/Spectra, 1988.
Crystal Witness, Bantam/Spectra, 1989.
Shivering World, Bantam/Spectra, 1991.

KATHY TYERS

Exploring the Northern Rockies (travel), Companion Press, 1991.
Star Wars: The Truce at Bakura, Bantam/Spectra, 1994.
One Mind's Eye, Bantam/Spectra, in press.

■ Sidelights

Kathy Tyers told *SATA:* "My first drafts are essentially outlines with dialog. I can easily hear characters speak to each other. In later drafts, I lay down background, scenery, and motivations and stitch each element to every other throughout the narrative. Finally, I tighten it stylistically. I particularly check every verb to make sure it carries its load. I envy writers who can accomplish all that in one or two drafts!

"I had published three space adventure novels when my editor asked me to write a 'hard' science fiction book," Tyers continued. "In 'hard SF,' the plot must revolve around the solution of a scientific problem. Since I'd taken my first degree in microbiology, I designed *Shivering World* around genetic engineering and terraforming. Those fields are developing so quickly that current research already reads like science fiction, and microbiology plays a major part in both of them. In *Shivering World,* I also dealt with two major characters' spiritual struggles in a future where religion has traveled with humankind to the stars."

The main plot of *Shivering World* revolves around Graysha, a biologist who is dying from a genetic defect. She travels to a newly settled planet in the hope of finding a cure. There she learns that another scientist—her predecessor—was murdered, the planet is entering an Ice Age, the townspeople are trying to scare her off, and her mother is trying to stop the inhabitants' illegal genetic engineering, the only means by which Graysha can be cured. Carolyn Cushman, reviewing the work in *Locus,* remarked, "What follows mixes basic thriller elements with a little romance, and plenty of details on terraforming and microbiotics." "*Shivering World* combines several fascinating story lines into one very readable book," wrote Jennifer Langlois in *Voice of Youth Advocates.* However, she found the "overwhelming amount of scientific techniques and jargon" difficult to comprehend.

"My love of space adventure never died," Kathy Tyers admitted to *SATA.* "From the day I watched the third *Star Wars* movie [*Return of the Jedi*], I wished I could write a novel about Luke Skywalker, Han Solo, and Princess Leia, but that universe was closed to all writers except George Lucas and his staff. When my editor called in 1992 to invite me to participate in Bantam's new 'Star Wars' series, I was thrilled. *Star Wars: The Truce at Bakura* received national attention simply because it was set in the *Star Wars* universe, but I couldn't have written it if I hadn't already enjoyed the mythos."

The novel takes place where *Return of the Jedi* left off, shortly after Luke and the Rebel Alliance have defeated Darth Vader and the Emperor. A reptilian species called

Ssi-ruuk learn of the Emperor's death and attack Bakura, an Imperial planet, hoping to conquer it while the Empire's defenses are down. Leia goes to the planet as an ambassador and negotiates a truce so that Imperial and Rebel forces can unite to defend Bakura. *Voice of Youth Advocates* contributor Lisa Prolman stated that "Tyers delves into the psyches of her characters." Leia struggles to accept her parentage and her growing feelings for Han. Luke, in an attempt to fend off the solitude that accompanies being a Jedi, seeks to persuade Dev, a boy who strongly feels the force, into becoming a Jedi too. Prolman didn't find Tyers' writing style as suspenseful as that of Timothy Zahn's—another author of "Star Wars" books—but felt that "Tyers tells a well-paced story that is a good addition to the *Star Wars* saga."

"My favorite *Star Wars* character is Luke Skywalker," Tyers told *SATA*. "Han Solo shines as the self-centered rogue, but Luke—son of the villainous Darth Vader—yearns to remain virtuous. He must learn to wield great power wisely, or he'll become a force for death and inhumanity. I think it's sad that people hesitate to admire a man or a woman with deeply moral convictions and intentions. Perhaps we're so aware of the darkness inside us that it embarrasses us to look into the light. Awareness of our shortcomings is a tremendous starting point, but awareness alone doesn't overcome them.

"I write for the joy of character-, world-, and plot-building. Dorothy L. Sayers, one of my favorite mystery writers, wrote in [an] ... essay, 'Man is most godlike and most himself when he is occupied in creation.' I can't imagine any higher pleasure than watching a universe come to life."

■ Works Cited

Cushman, Carolyn, review of *Shivering World, Locus,* June, 1991, p. 27. Langlois, Jennifer, review of *Shivering World, Voice of Youth Advocates,* February, 1992, p. 387.

Prolman, Lisa, review of *Star Wars: The Truce at Bakura, Voice of Youth Advocates,* June, 1994, p. 101.

■ For More Information See

PERIODICALS

Booklist, June 15, 1991, p. 1937.
Kirkus Reviews, November 1, 1993, p. 1358.
Library Journal, May 15, 1987, p. 101.
Locus, July, 1991, p. 49.

V

JEAN VAN LEEUWEN

Van LEEUWEN, Jean 1937-

Personal

Surname pronounced "Van *Loo*-en"; born December 26, 1937, in Glen Ridge, NJ; daughter of Cornelius (a clergyman) and Dorothy (a teacher; maiden name, Charlton) Van Leeuwen; married Bruce David Gavril (a digital computer systems designer), July 7, 1968; children: David Andrew, Elizabeth Eva. *Education:* Syracuse University, B.A., 1959. *Hobbies and other interests:* Gardening, reading, travel, antiques, music.

Addresses

Home—7 Colony Row, Chappaqua, NY 10514.

Career

Began career working for *TV Guide;* Random House, Inc., New York City, assistant editor and then associate editor of juvenile books, 1963-68; Viking Press, Inc., New York City, associate editor of juvenile books, 1968-70; Dial Press, New York City, senior editor of juvenile books, 1971-73; currently full-time writer.

Awards, Honors

New Jersey Institute of Technology award, 1972, for *I Was a 98-Pound Duckling;* Art Books for Children award, 1974, for her adaptation of Hans Christian Andersen's *The Emperor's New Clothes;* New Jersey Institute of Technology award, 1975 and 1976, for *Too Hot for Ice Cream;* Ethical Culture School award, 1975, William Allen White award, 1978, and South Carolina Children's Book award, 1979, all for *The Great Christmas Kidnapping Caper; Seems Like This Road Goes on Forever* was named one of the best books of 1979, American Library Association (ALA), Young Adult Services Division; Massachusetts Honor Book Award, 1981, for *The Great Cheese Conspiracy;* American Booksellers Pick of the Lists, Parents' Choice Remarkable Books for Literature, both for *The Great Rescue Operation;* IRA Teachers' Choice, American Booksellers Pick of the Lists, *Parents'* Magazine: The Best in Kids' Entertainment, all for *Going West.*

More Tales of Oliver Pig, Amanda Pig and Her Big Brother Oliver, Tales of Amanda Pig, and *More Tales of Amanda Pig* all won the *Booklist* Children's Editors' Choice award; *More Tales of Oliver Pig, Amanda Pig and Her Big Brother Oliver,* and *More Tales of Amanda Pig* were noted on the American Booksellers Pick of the

Lists; *Amanda Pig and Her Big Brother Oliver, Benjy and the Power of Zingies,* and *Benjy in Business* were all listed as Child Study Association Children's Books of the Year; *Oliver, Amanda, and Grandmother Pig* and *Going West* were listed in New York Public Library: 100 Titles for Reading and Sharing; *Oliver, Amanda, and Grandmother Pig* and *Tales of Amanda Pig* received the Library of Congress Books of the Year award; *More Tales of Oliver Pig, Amanda Pig and Her Big Brother Oliver,* and *Tales of Amanda Pig* have all been named ALA Notable Books.

■ Writings

(Editor) *A Time of Growing,* Random House, 1967.
Timothy's Flower, illustrated by Moneta Barnett, Random House, 1967.
One Day in Summer, illustrated by Richard Fish, Random House, 1969.
The Great Cheese Conspiracy, Random House, 1969.
(Adaptor) Hans Christian Andersen, *The Emperor's New Clothes,* illustrated by Jack Delano and Irene Delano, Random House, 1971.
I Was a 98-Pound Duckling, Dial, 1972.
Too Hot for Ice Cream, illustrated by Martha Alexander, Dial, 1974.
The Great Christmas Kidnapping Caper, illustrated by Steven Kellogg, Dial, 1975.
Seems Like This Road Goes on Forever, Dial, 1979.
Tales of Oliver Pig, illustrated by Arnold Lobel, Dial, 1979.
More Tales of Oliver Pig, illustrated by Lobel, Dial, 1981.
The Great Rescue Operation, illustrated by Margot Apple, Dial, 1982.
Amanda Pig and Her Big Brother Oliver, illustrated by Ann Schweninger, Dial, 1982.
Benjy and the Power of Zingies, illustrated by Apple, Dial, 1982.
Benjy in Business, illustrated by Apple, Dial, 1983.
Tales of Amanda Pig, illustrated by Schweninger, Dial, 1983.
Benjy the Football Hero, illustrated by Gail Owens, Dial, 1985.
More Tales of Amanda Pig, illustrated by Schweninger, Dial, 1985.
Oliver, Amanda, and Grandmother Pig, illustrated by Schweninger, Dial, 1987.
Dear Mom, You're Ruining My Life, Dial, 1989.
Oliver and Amanda's Christmas, illustrated by Schweninger, Dial, 1989.
Oliver Pig at School, illustrated by Schweninger, Dial, 1990.
Amanda Pig on Her Own, illustrated by Schweninger, Dial, 1991.
Going West, illustrated by Thomas B. Allen, Dial, 1991.
The Great Summer Camp Catastrophe, illustrated by Diane deGroat, Dial, 1992.
Oliver and Amanda's Halloween, illustrated by Schweninger, Dial, 1992.
Emma Bean, illustrated by Juan Wijngaard, Dial, 1993.
Two Girls in Sister Dresses, illustrated by Linda Benson, Dial, 1994.
Bound for Oregon, Dial, 1994.
Across the Wide Dark Sea, illustrated by Allen, Dial, 1995.
Oliver and Amanda and the Big Snow, illustrated by Schweninger, Dial, 1995.

■ Sidelights

"I had a book-filled childhood," Jean Van Leeuwen wrote in her *Something about the Author Autobiography Series* (*SAAS*) entry. "It was not that my family was a particularly literary one. I was just irresistibly attracted to books. Any time, anywhere, I was likely to be found with a book in my hand. I read riding in the car, even though it made me dizzy. I read when the family went visiting, even though my mother said it was rude. I read late at night under the covers, by flashlight, when I was supposed to be asleep. And I would read almost anything, just as long as it had a story. What I liked best of all was to stretch out on my bed with a book, so far lost inside some other world that when I heard my mother's voice, summoning me to dinner, I would look around and blink, wondering where I was."

Van Leeuwen recalls her earliest childhood "as a secure, carefree time." The oldest of three children, she was raised in Rutherford, New Jersey, where her father was the minister of the Congregational church. The author recalls the main sources of any early unhappiness as stemming from her own shyness, especially when compared to her younger sister, "who not only had an outgoing personality, but was also pretty and annoyingly good all the time," and from the high expectations placed on her as a minister's daughter. These themes have appeared in Van Leeuwen's books for children. The feelings associated with competing with a younger sibling are treated in a lighthearted fashion in Van Leeuwen's book, *Two Girls in Sister Dresses,* and she addresses an adolescent girl's extreme reaction to repressive parenting by a minister father in the somber young adult novel, *Seems Like This Road Goes on Forever.*

After a tomboyish childhood and an adolescence spent "trying to be popular," Van Leeuwen entered Syracuse University, graduating with a bachelor's degree in journalism. A first job at *TV Guide,* while not the glamorous career she had envisioned at a women's magazine, inspired a move to New York City and gave her a start in publishing that eventually led to work as a children's book editor. Van Leeuwen rediscovered her childhood ambition to write while working as an editor and in 1967 joyfully saw the publication of her first book, *Timothy's Flower.*

Timothy's Flower, "based on a small boy whom I had observed in my New York City neighborhood," as Van Leeuwen recalled in her *SAAS* essay, was warmly received by critics. A reviewer for the *Bulletin of the Center for Children's Books* credited the "simple, unpretentious style" of the prose for the book's successful rendering of how a flower improves the life of a poor boy. Van Leeuwen's early works also include *A Time of*

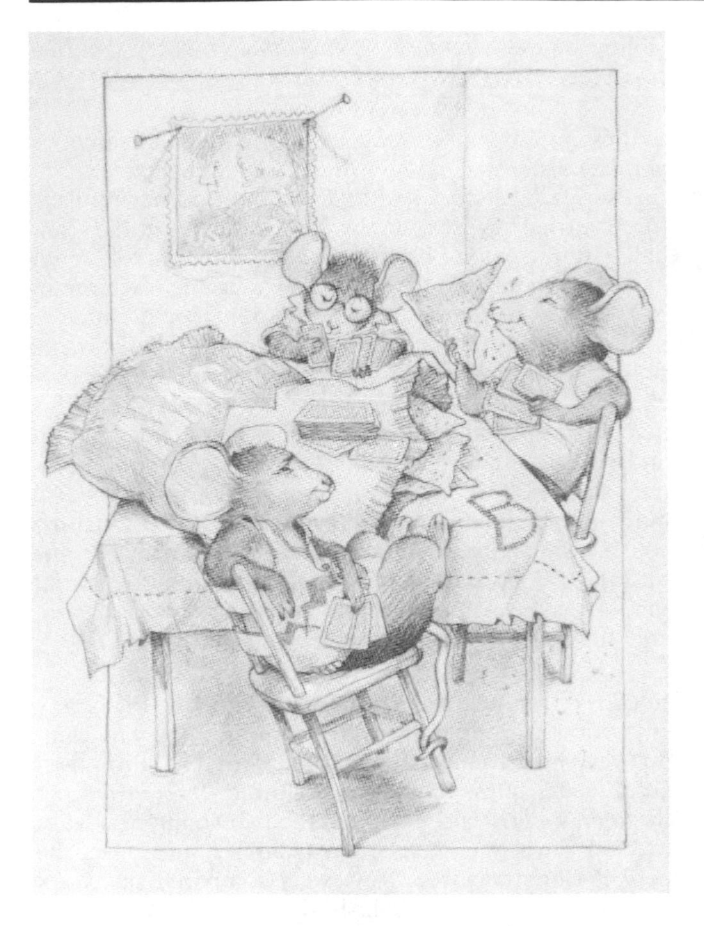

Raymond and Marvin the Magnificent set out to rescue their friend Fats from the wicked mouse-torturer Dr. Henry Simpson in Van Leeuwen's humorous adventure tale, *The Great Rescue Operation.* (Illustration by Margot Apple.)

Growing, an anthology of fictional reminiscences of adolescence by established authors, which she edited, and the picture book *One Day in Summer,* described by a *Bulletin of the Center for Children's Books* critic as a "quiet" story with possibly limited appeal due to the "static quality" of the plot.

During this time Van Leeuwen married Bruce Gavril, a computer systems designer who became her "technical consultant, a role which he has continued to play admirably through the years," as she said in her *SAAS* essay. Her husband was also the inspiration for the character Raymond in *The Great Cheese Conspiracy* and its sequels. Van Leeuwen describes Raymond as the one "with brains": "a thinker, problem solver, and saver of seemingly useless objects—just like Bruce." *The Great Cheese Conspiracy* features three mice—Raymond, Marvin, the brave but foolhardy leader of the gang, and Fats, whose laziness and passion for food often land him and his friends in trouble—in a story about the trio's efforts to rob a cheese store. Van Leeuwen's mouse books have typically received praise from critics. For example, one *Bulletin of the Center for Children's Books* reviewer, writing about *The Great Rescue Operation,* wrote that "[Marvin, Raymond, and Fats] are distinct—if exaggerated—personalities, the style is colorful and breezy, the plot—deliberately unrestrained—is nicely structured and paced."

In the first sequel to *The Great Cheese Conspiracy, The Great Christmas Kidnapping Caper,* the three mice move into a doll house in Macy's department store, where they are befriended by Mr. Dunderhoff, who annually plays Santa Claus. When Mr. Dunderhoff is abducted by the store's greedy competitor, the mice use all their ingenuity to rescue him. Jean Mercier described the result as "zestful and surprising" in her review in *Publishers Weekly;* a *Bulletin of the Center for Children's Books* critic commented that the "story has a happy blend of humor in dialogue, Christmas setting, local color, and silly situations." The trio are put to the test again in *The Great Rescue Operation,* in which Marvin and Raymond wake up one day to find that Fats has disappeared along with the doll carriage in which he likes to nap. The friends' attempts to rescue Fats from what they fear is a horrible fate at the hands of a scientist lead to "slapstick humor and nonstop action," according to Caroline S. Parr in the *School Library Journal.* Doris Orgel similarly described the story in her *New York Times Book Review* article as a "funny, lively and appealing book." The three mice again leave Macy's in *The Great Summer Camp Catastrophe,* in which they are inadvertently packed off with a box of cookies to summer camp in Vermont. "What will grab readers" observed Jacqueline Rose in the *School Library Journal,* "is the action-packed plot, with its series of near disasters."

In the early years of her marriage to Gavril, Van Leeuwen published her first young adult novel, *I Was a 98-Pound Duckling,* a comical account of a girl's thirteenth summer, when she and her best friend are consumed with thoughts of boys and dates and following the beauty regimen outlined in a teen magazine. Although several reviewers noted the lack of originality in the story's plot, a *Bulletin of the Center for Children's Books* contributor remarked: "Kathy tells her story . . . with such wry humor and candor that it gives a fresh vitality to a familiar pattern." In another *Publishers Weekly* review, Mercier declared: "This is a witty and charming book."

In the early 1970s Van Leeuwen left publishing to care for her two small children, but was determined to continue to write. Her first effort, *Too Hot for Ice Cream,* dubbed by Mercier as "a curiously charming book," tells the story of the everyday adventures of two sisters who spend a hot day in a city park when their father can't take them to the beach. A more far-reaching consequence of Van Leeuwen's decision to stay home to raise her children is the series of first-reader books filled with stories about Oliver and Amanda Pig, based on her experiences with her own children.

Tales of Oliver Pig, and the subsequent books in this series, have been warmly received for their gentle humor and loving portrayal of the everyday trials and joys of living with small children. Mary Gordon described the relationship between Amanda and Oliver Pig, which is

Upon her daughter's request, Van Leeuwen focused on little Amanda in her next story about the Pigs. (Cover illustration by Ann Schweninger.)

at the center of each of the books in this series, in the *New York Times Book Review:* "The younger Pigs are occasionally perfectly dreadful to each other. But remember, they are siblings, and one of the great values of these books is their ability to dramatize the ridiculous and trivial and sickeningly frequent fights that siblings engage in every day of their lives, and yet suggest the siblings' essential fondness for each other, their dependency, their mutual good will."

More Tales of Oliver Pig, the first sequel to Van Leeuwen's successful *Tales of Oliver Pig,* features stories about Oliver's first efforts at gardening, how he adjusts to being cared for by his grandmother, and his attempts to stall at bed-time. A *Bulletin of the Center for Children's Books* critic singled out the "gentle humor in the simple, fluent writing style" for praise in its review of this work. In response to her daughter's request, Van Leeuwen's next work in this series shifted the focus away from Oliver toward his younger sister, Amanda. The stories in *Amanda Pig and Her Big Brother Oliver* highlight Amanda's frustrations at being unable to do some of the things her big brother can do and her parents' sympathetic responses. "Never cloying, the humor is genuine, the incidents right on the younger-sibling mark," remarked a *School Library Journal* reviewer.

Critics noted that Amanda is more than an envious younger sister in *Tales of Amanda Pig,* the next work in this series. The stories in this volume find her refusing to eat a fried egg, scaring the clock-monster in the front hall with the help of her father, and switching roles with her sleepy mother at bed-time. Though a reviewer in *School Library Journal* found "the domestic drama . . . a bit dull this time out," a contributor to *Kirkus Reviews* praised "the same irreproachable, unforced child psychology, and if anything more sly by-play" in this installment. Amanda "maintains her pluck, imagination and vulnerability," according to a *School Library Journal* critic, in *More Tales of Amanda Pig,* in which she plays house with her brother, becomes jealous of visiting cousins, and gives her father her favorite toy for his birthday. *Horn Book* reviewer Karen Jameyson found the story to be as "comfortable as an easy chair, as warm and filling as a cup of cocoa."

In *Oliver, Amanda, and Grandmother Pig,* the Pig family enjoys a week-long visit by Grandmother Pig, who can't do everything younger adults can do but tells stories and gives good hugs. This was followed by *Oliver and Amanda's Christmas,* in which the two young pigs learn to keep Christmas secrets, bake cookies, and select the perfect Christmas tree. Reviewers compared this work favorably with earlier books in the series; Betsy Hearne, writing in *Bulletin of the Center for Children's Books,* described it to be "as comfortable as tradition."

Oliver and Amanda are starting to grow up in the next two works in this series. In *Oliver Pig at School,* Oliver experiences his first day of kindergarten, befriending a

Revisiting her popular character in *More Tales of Oliver Pig,* Van Leeuwen creates five new stories featuring the beloved Pig family. (Illustration by Arnold Lobel.)

scary classmate and making and eating a necklace in art class. Martha V. Parravano praised "the author's understanding of childhood experiences" in her review in *Horn Book.* In *Amanda Pig on Her Own,* Amanda learns to enjoy the adventures she can have when her big brother is away at school. Reviewing the work in *Bulletin of the Center for Children's Books,* Ruth Ann Smith particularly enjoyed Van Leeuwen's ability to "combine gentle humor with ingenuous dialogue."

Van Leeuwen has also written several chapter books for slightly older readers, featuring Benjy, a third-grade boy critics have described as a lovable academic and athletic underachiever. A reviewer commented in *Horn Book,* "Like Henry Huggins, Ellen Tebbits, and Ramona, Benjy is an engaging personality—one not quickly forgotten." In *Benjy and the Power of Zingies,* Benjy decides his only chance against the school bully who picks on him is to build up his body by eating Zingies breakfast cereal. A *Bulletin of the Center for Children's Books* critic praised the book's "light-hearted" and "often funny" treatment of life in the third grade. This was followed by *Benjy in Business,* in which Benjy attempts to earn enough money to buy a special baseball mitt he hopes will improve his game. "Benjy displays a sturdy tenacity that makes his extended effort credible and enjoyable," commented Carolyn Noah in the *School Library Journal.* Irene Cooper remarked in *Booklist* that some of the action in the third work in this series, *Benjy the Football Hero,* may be lost on readers not familiar with the rules of the game at the book's center, but the critic added "this has the same good humor and engaging characters of the other Benjy books." About the series as a whole, Robert E. Unsworth remarked in *School Library Journal* that "Van Leeuwen has a fine ability to see the humor in the tribulations of nine year olds and she writes about them with understanding."

Although she is best known for her picture books and simple stories for first readers, Van Leeuwen noted in her *SAAS* essay that she has always enjoyed writing for older children and adolescents. One of her first attempts for this age group, *Seems Like This Road Goes on Forever,* draws on the author's understanding of the kinds of expectations and pressures put on children of members of the clergy. Mary Alice, the daughter of an overly strict minister, retraces with the help of a psychologist the steps that brought her to a hospital bed with a broken leg, unable to communicate or think clearly about her recent past. Although a reviewer in *Bulletin of the Center for Children's Books* found this a "slow-paced" if "convincing account of an emotional breakdown," a *New York Times Book Review* contributor concluded that it "is finely written, though cheerless—which it must be, I suppose, in order to be told properly." In a more light-hearted vein, *Dear Mom, You're Ruining My Life* is a novel for upper elementary school grades inspired by Van Leeuwen's daughter Elizabeth. "As a sixth grader," the author wrote in her *SAAS* essay, "she was acutely embarrassed by everything about her family: our rusty old car, her father who actually insisted on *talking* to her friends, and especially me." A critic in *Kirkus Reviews* called the resulting portrait of life in the sixth grade "a genuinely funny look at a roller-coaster year."

Eleven-year-old Samantha is embarrassed by her height, her big feet, and her mother in this humorous look at growing up. (Cover illustration by Deborah Chabrian.)

Van Leeuwen credits her advancing age with her increased interest in the past. In her *SAAS* essay she states: "In my writing ... I find that I am starting to look backward. I have always been fascinated by history, not the history of big events and dates that I was taught in school, but of people and how they lived. I have written recently about my own childhood. I have ideas of writing about my family history, and perhaps, if I can find the right way to do it, about our country's history." Van Leeuwen's reminiscence of her childhood, *Two Girls in Sister Dresses,* evokes the author's feelings about her younger sister. The book was highly praised for its realistic yet sensitive portrayal of the relationship between sisters. Carolyn Phelan noted in her review in *Booklist* that *Two Girls in Sister Dresses* is written with Van Leeuwen's "accustomed simplicity and finesse." Also memorable for its nostalgic atmosphere is *Emma Bean,* which details the life of a homemade stuffed rabbit, a gift to Molly at birth from her grandmother. Critics noted similarities between *Emma Bean* and the children's classic, *The Velveteen Rabbit,* but Annie

In this work of historical fiction, Van Leeuwen uses a seven-year-old's point of view to describe the hardships of travelling to the American West in the 1800s. (Cover illustration by Thomas B. Allen.)

Ayres argued in her *Booklist* review that Van Leeuwen's "warmly sentimental book" is for those children not yet ready for the "more sophisticated and emotionally weighty themes" of the latter title.

Van Leeuwen has also produced two historical books for young readers: *Going West,* a fictional journal of seven-year-old Hannah as she and her family travel west by wagon in the days of the pioneers, and *Bound for Oregon,* based on the real-life journey of Mary Ellen Todd and her family on the Oregon trail in the 1850s. Although more serious than many of the works for which she is best known, these books have been praised for the author's signature emphasis on a warm and supportive family atmosphere. *Publishers Weekly*'s Diane Roback and Richard Donahue remarked of *Going West:* "Into a gentle text brimming with family warmth and love, Van Leeuwen ... packs a wealth of emotional moments."

Reviewers have consistently praised the warm yet realistic celebrations of family life found in Van Leeuwen's books, emphasizing her gentle humor and insightful portrayal of common childhood experiences. In a review of *Oliver, Amanda, and Grandmother Pig,* Jameyson concluded in *Horn Book:* "With perceptiveness and gentle humor Jean Van Leeuwen shapes even the most mundane subjects into pleasing, warm tales."

■ Works Cited

Review of *Amanda Pig and Her Big Brother Oliver, School Library Journal,* December, 1982, p. 75.

Ayres, Annie, review of *Emma Bean, Booklist,* July, 1993, p. 1977.

Review of *Benjy and the Power of Zingies, Bulletin of the Center for Children's Books,* March, 1983.

Review of *Benjy and the Power of Zingies, Horn Book,* April 1983, pp. 168-69.

Cooper, Irene, review of *Benjy the Football Hero, Booklist,* September 1, 1985, p. 72.
Review of *Dear Mom, You're Ruining My Life, Kirkus Reviews,* May 15, 1989, p. 772.
Gordon, Mary, "Pig Tales," *New York Times Book Review,* November 10, 1985.
Review of *The Great Christmas Kidnapping Caper, Bulletin of the Center for Children's Books,* November, 1975.
Review of *The Great Rescue Operation, Bulletin of the Center for Children's Books,* July-August, 1982.
Hearne, Betsy, review of *Oliver and Amanda's Christmas, Bulletin of the Center for Children's Books,* October, 1989, p. 47.
Review of *I Was a 98-Pound Duckling, Bulletin of the Center for Children's Books,* September, 1973, p. 19.
Jameyson, Karen, review of *More Tales of Amanda Pig, Horn Book,* March-April, 1986, pp. 199-200.
Jameyson, Karen, review of *Oliver, Amanda, and Grandmother Pig, Horn Book,* September, 1987, pp. 606-7.
Mercier, Jean, review of *I Was a 98-Pound Duckling, Publishers Weekly,* September 25, 1972.
Mercier, Jean, review of *Too Hot for Ice Cream, Publishers Weekly,* October 7, 1974, p. 63.
Mercier, Jean, review of *The Great Christmas Kidnapping Caper, Publishers Weekly,* September 8, 1975.
Review of *More Tales of Amanda Pig, School Library Journal,* December, 1985, p. 110.
Review of *More Tales of Oliver Pig, Bulletin of the Center for Children's Books,* July, 1981, p. 221.
Noah, Carolyn, review of *Benjy in Business, School Library Journal,* December, 1983, p. 70.
Review of *One Day in Summer, Bulletin of the Center for Children's Books,* July, 1969, p. 184.
Orgel, Doris, "Mice in Macy's," *New York Times Book Review,* April 25, 1982.
Parr, Caroline S., review of *The Great Rescue Operation, School Library Journal,* August, 1982, p. 123.
Parravano, Martha V., review of *Oliver Pig at School, Horn Book,* September-October, 1990, p. 599.
Phelan, Carolyn, review of *Two Girls in Sister Dresses, Booklist,* April 1, 1994, p. 1453.
Roback, Diane, and Richard Donahue, review of *Going West, Publishers Weekly,* December 13, 1991, p. 55.
Rose, Jacqueline, review of *The Great Summer Camp Catastrophe, School Library Journal,* April, 1992, p. 126.
Review of *Seems Like This Road Goes on Forever, Bulletin of the Center for Children's Books,* October, 1979.
Review of *Seems Like This Road Goes on Forever, New York Times Book Review,* November 11, 1979.
Smith, Ruth Ann, review of *Amanda Pig on Her Own, Bulletin of the Center for Children's Books,* March, 1991, pp. 180-81.
Review of *Tales of Amanda Pig, Kirkus Reviews,* September 1, 1983.
Review of *Tales of Amanda Pig, School Library Journal,* December, 1983, p. 80.
Review of *Timothy's Flower, Bulletin of the Center for Children's Books,* June, 1968, p. 166.
Unsworth, Robert E., review of *Benjy the Football Hero, School Library Journal,* May, 1985, p. 111.
Van Leeuwen, Jean, essay in *Something about the Author Autobiography Series,* Volume 8, Gale, 1989, pp. 317-30.

■ For More Information See

PERIODICALS

Booklist, May 1, 1992, p. 1603.
Book World, October 7, 1979.
Bulletin of the Center for Children's Books, February, 1968, p. 103; February, 1975, p. 100; January, 1986, p. 98; September, 1987; May, 1989, pp. 238-39; September, 1990, p. 18; November, 1994, p. 107.
Horn Book, February, 1975; December, 1979, p. 660; August, 1981, p. 419; June, 1982, p. 294; December, 1982, pp. 646-47; December, 1983, p. 713; February, 1984, pp. 48-49; November, 1989, p. 754; March-April, 1992, p. 199; April, 1995, p. 197.
Kirkus Reviews, October 1, 1967, p. 1202; April 15, 1969, p. 436; October 1, 1972, p. 1155; September 1, 1982, p. 997; December 1, 1982, p. 1293; June 1, 1992, p. 724; August 1, 1993, p. 1008.
New York Times Book Review, November 5, 1967; November 30, 1975, p. 26; June 24, 1979; May 3, 1981; November 13, 1983; May 19, 1985; January 10, 1988, p. 36.
Publishers Weekly, December 4, 1967, p. 44; September 3, 1982; August 14, 1987, p. 107; August 2, 1993, p. 79; April 25, 1994, p. 78; September 5, 1994, p. 112.
School Library Journal, October, 1975, p. 78; May, 1979, p. 76; December, 1979, p. 93; May, 1981, p. 80; January, 1983, p. 80; March, 1988, p. 177; June, 1989, pp. 109-10; October, 1989, p. 45; May, 1991, p. 85; March, 1992, p. 225; June, 1994.
Time, December 3, 1979, p. 100.
Times Educational Supplement, June 8, 1984.

—Sketch by Mary Gillis

W

DIANNE MARIE CATHERINE WALKER

WALKER, Dianne Marie Catherine 1950-
(Kate Walker)

■ Personal

Born January 10, 1950, in Newcastle, Australia; daughter of William Walter (a salesperson) and Eileen Maisie (a homemaker; maiden name, Appleyard) Sruhan; married Roger Edwin Walker (a mechanic), January 24, 1975 (divorced August 8, 1980); children: Josie. *Politics:* Independent. *Religion:* "Unaffiliated." *Hobbies and other interests:* Reading, gardening, film, Tai Chi.

■ Addresses

Home and office—14 Dent St., Islington, Newcastle, New South Wales 2296, Australia.

■ Career

Writer; writing teacher at workshops for teachers of primary and high school students, 1987—. Has worked variously as a waitress, cook, restaurant manager, clerk, cleaner, and offset printer.

■ Awards, Honors

Highly Commended, Picture Book Section, Australian Children's Book of the Year, 1981, for *Marty Moves to the Country;* Australian Children's Book of the Year, Honour Book, Junior Section, 1990, for *The Dragon of Mith;* Mary Grant Bruce award, 1991, for unpublished work, "Running away to Sea"; highly commended, Australian Human Rights Award, 1991, shortlisted in NSW Premier's Literary Award, 1991, South Australian Literary Award, 1991, Australian Children's Book of the Year Honour Book, Young Adult Section, 1991, Talking Book of the Year Award, 1992, and selected for all three of the American Library Association's 1994 Best Book Lists (Notable Books of the Year, Best Books for Young Adults, and Best Books for Reluctant Young Adult Readers), all for *Peter.* Recipient of grants from the Literature Board of the Australia Council and several awards for short stories.

■ Writings

PICTURE BOOKS

Marty Moves to the Country, illustrated by Bruce Treloar, Methuen, 1980.

The Frog Who Would Be King, illustrated by David Cox, Ashton/Bookshelf, 1989.

King Joe of Bogpeat Castle, illustrated by Chellew, Ashton/Bookshelf, 1989.

The First Easter Rabbit, illustrated by Marina McAllan, Martin Educational, 1989.

Our Excursion, illustrated by Cox, Ashton/Omnibus, 1994.

FOR CHILDREN

The Alien Challenger, illustrated by Peter Lewis, Methuen, 1983.
Suzie and the Pencil-Case Genie, illustrated by Trish Hill, Ashton/Bookshelf, 1988.
The Letters of Rosie O'Brien: A Convict in the Colony of New South Wales, 1804, illustrated by Paul Borg, Ashton/Bookshelf, 1988.
Tales from the Good Land, illustrated by Gillian Campbell, Ashton/Bookshelf, 1988.
Burying Aunt Renie, illustrated by Margie Chellew, Nelson, 1989.
The Dragon of Mith, illustrated by Laurie Sharpe, Allen & Unwin, 1989.

FOR YOUNG ADULTS

Peter, Ashton/Omnibus, 1991, Houghton, 1993.

NONFICTION

Writing Games, Kate Walker Ink, 1991.
Step By Step Stories, Kate Walker Ink, 1991.
Story Writing the Low Stress Way: A Manual for Primary and High School Teachers, Kate Walker Ink, 1992.
Creativity and Story Writing, Kate Walker Ink, 1993.
Story Writing: Teaching and Tapping Your Subconscious Mind (manual for adults), Kate Walker Ink, 1993.
Writing Enrichment, Kate Walker Ink, 1994.
Journal Writing, Kate Walker Ink, 1994.

OTHER

Contributor to numerous anthologies and magazines.

■ Sidelights

Kate Walker told *SATA:* "I began writing after a camper-van tour of Australia with my husband and daughter, during which I started making up bedtime stories for her. When I came home, I began writing them down and realized I loved it! That was it, I wanted to be a writer.

"I have breakfast, walk the dog, do some Tai Chi, read, and *then* finally start writing and work from nine in the morning till four in the afternoon. I write my stories in longhand first and will do another three or four drafts in longhand, literally cut-and-pasting the story with a pair of scissors and a role of sticky tape.

"After four drafts, it's a great mess of paper, written in various colored pens with lots of scratchings-out, and it is almost unreadable. At this point I key it into the computer, get a printout, and start over again—rewriting passages, sticking in new bits, cutting out old ones, until I've turned a neat manuscript into another multicolored mess. I go back to the computer and key in the changes, run off a clean printout, and begin all over again with my scissors, sticky tape, and colored pens. Some stories write themselves in six drafts. Others I chase and change and do battle with over a hundred drafts or more. And I always work on three stories at once so I can skip from one to the other.

Walker's award-winning young adult novel offers a candid exploration of sexuality and peer pressure among teens in Australia. (Cover illustration by Vivienne Goodman.)

"My main interest is people. The crazy things they do, their foolishness, their vulnerability, their great strength and courage, their determination to discover who and what they are. When I teach writing, I feel that's what I'm doing also, showing people a means by which they can take a small part of themselves and project it out and get a glimpse of themselves, maybe even of their spirit."

■ For More Information See

PERIODICALS

Booklist, October 15, 1988, p. 424; April 15, 1993, p. 1505; March 15, 1994, pp. 1355, 1359, 1361.
Horn Book, July, 1993, p. 467; September, 1993, p. 571.
Horn Book Guide, spring, 1994, p. 91.
Junior Bookshelf, October, 1982, p. 180.
School Library Journal, March, 1987, p. 168; September, 1987, p. 133; June, 1993, p. 132.
Times Literary Supplement, July 23, 1982, p. 792.
Voice of Youth Advocates, June, 1993, p. 96.

WALKER, Kate
See WALKER, Dianne Marie Catherine

* * *

WEBB, Lois Sinaiko 1922-

Personal

Born February 15, 1922, in Madison, WI; daughter of William (in business) and Pauline (in business; maiden name, Silverman) Sinaiko; married Preston Webb, March, 1969 (divorced, 1975); children: Josie Rosenberg Wilson, Richard Louis Rosenberg. *Education:* Attended University of Wisconsin. *Religion:* Jewish.

Addresses

Home—P.O. Box 784, Seabrook, TX 77586.

Career

Worked as an interior designer in Milwaukee, WI, for twenty-eight years; Webb's Cove (seafood restaurant), Seabrook, TX, owner, 1972-86; writer, 1988—. Has taught cooking classes in Changchun, China; also works as a restaurant and catering consultant. *Member:* International Association of Culinary Professionals, Hadassah.

Awards, Honors

International Designs award, American Institute of Interior Designers, 1962, for wall covering; 1994 Epicurean Night, Houston Chamber of Commerce.

Writings

(With Carole Lisa Albyn) *Multicultural Cookbook for Students,* Oryx Press, 1993.
Holidays of the World Cookbook for Students, Oryx Press, 1995.

Has also contributed articles in the *Houston Post, Cooking for Profit,* and *Restaurant Hospitality Magazine;* recipes published in *Bon Appetit.*

Sidelights

Lois Sinaiko Webb told *SATA* that she is currently giving cooking classes and demonstrations for clubs and organizations in the Houston, Texas, area.

* * *

WEIN, Elizabeth E(ve) 1964-

Personal

Surname is pronounced "Ween"; born October 2, 1964, in New York, NY; daughter of Norman Harts (an educational psychologist) and Carol Saylor (a social worker; maiden name, Flocken) Wein. *Education:* Yale University, B.A., 1986; University of Pennsylvania, M.A., 1989, Ph.D., 1994. *Politics:* Democrat. *Religion:* Protestant. *Hobbies and other interests:* English church bell ringing, travel.

Addresses

Home—103 Pine Ave., Box 692, Mt. Gretna, PA 17064.

Career

Church of St. Martin-in-the-Fields, Philadelphia, PA, English church bell ringer, 1987—; U.S. Postal Service, Washington, D.C., conference manager, 1993-94; Harrisburg Area Community College, Harrisburg, PA, adjunct faculty member of English department, 1994. Newsletter editor, North American Guild of Change Ringers, 1994. *Member:* Society of Children's Book Writers and Illustrators, Children's Literature Association, Science Fiction and Fantasy Writers of America, American Folklore Society.

Awards, Honors

Jacob K. Javits Fellow, 1988-92.

Writings

The Winter Prince, Atheneum, 1993.

Contributor to *Writers of the Future, Volume IX,* Bridge Publications, 1993, and *Not the Only One,* edited by Tony Grima, Alyson Press, 1995.

Work in Progress

Young adult novel, *The Oysterman's Opera,* to be completed in 1995.

ELIZABETH E. WEIN

■ Sidelights

Elizabeth E. Wein told *SATA:* "When I was seven, and living in Jamaica, my grandmother designed her own 'Book-of-the-Month-Club' service for me. Some of the books she sent me were not bookstore-new: she sent her own copy of *The Secret Garden,* and my aunt's copy of a wonderful French novel called *The Horse without a Head,* and my mother's old copies of *Henry Huggins* and *Ellen Tebbits.* But they were all books new to me. She sent *A Little Princess, The High King,* and every single one of the Laura Ingalls Wilder books. I don't remember graduating from picture books to chapter books, but I think it happened when I was seven. My grandmother sent me the best stories I'd ever read, and I knew that I was going to write books like these.

"I went around for twenty years after that telling people 'I'm going to be a writer' or 'I want to be a writer,' and it was one of the hardest transitions of my life to change that statement to 'I am a writer.' I have a very big ego, but a very low sense of self-esteem. Even having written and published a book, and a good one, has only barely given me the confidence to tell people that I really am a writer.

"I have terrible working habits. I have no self-discipline: if I don't have to get out of bed in the morning, I don't. I rarely make myself sit at a desk for a set period of time to work on a story, or research, or whatever I'm supposed to be doing. I write during commercials while watching TV, or while I'm sitting in a service station waiting for my car to be repaired, or while I'm eating lunch. When I began the final draft of *The Winter Prince,* I was working as a sales clerk in a bookstore. I wrote on discarded cash register receipts in between waiting on customers. Then I'd take these scraps home and copy them out on a single sheet, and marvel at how coherent my writing was.

"I am a literary snob. I was an English major in college and had a very classical background in Western literature. The writers I emulate are also literary snobs: Alan Garner, T. S. Eliot, James Joyce, Dorothy Sayers. Alan Garner, an English children's book writer, has had so great an influence on me that I can scarcely measure it. It's not just his exquisite style that I admire, or his thorough and complete immersion in all aspects of his subject, or his ability to paint a picture so chilling that I can't get to sleep at night for thinking about it, but also tiny aspects of his work, such as the perfectly chosen epigraph for a story, or a lyrically singsong list of chapter titles. Most of all it is the way he grounds his stories in landscapes that he knows and loves. That landscape is Cheshire, the English county south of Manchester. I used to live there also, and it's where I set *The Winter Prince.* I did so partly as a tribute to Alan Garner, but mostly because I know that landscape well, and Alan Garner taught me that nothing—*nothing*—is so important to your writing as a specific and concrete sense of place.

"There are messages in my writing, and morals, but I don't put them there on purpose. I write because I have a story to tell. I write for myself: *The Winter Prince* is what I was looking for to read when I was sixteen. Once when I was rereading it, I thought in astonishment, 'If I hadn't written this it would be my favorite book.' Immediately I chastised myself for my outrageous self-congratulation. But then the thought occurred to me: the book I write *should* be my favorite book. It's in my power to create exactly the characters I want to get to know, playing out exactly the plot I want to follow.

"This power amazes me. It's what keeps me going. Only recently have I become brave enough to write about my own family and my own experiences. Suddenly I realize that I can change the ending. I can repeat good times over and over. I can make bad times come out the way they should have: I can change destiny. Someone, somewhere, may be warned not to make the mistakes I made, through my manipulation. I can go back in time. I

Wein's first young adult book is a variation of Arthurian legend in which the author uses Welsh lore to tell of the struggle between King Artos's (Arthur's) children for the throne. (Cover illustration by Darrell K. Sweet.)

can rearrange things. I longed for magic when I was a child—other writers' books brought tantalizing, fleeting glimpses of glitter and glamour that might be mine. Through reading I could become enchanted, and the magic seemed real. Now, as a writer in my own right, it *is* real. I can *make* the worlds I wanted so much to be part of. I wished myself Aladdin, with a magician at my beck; instead I have become the magician.

"A fiction writer is by definition a liar. That's the paradox of my life: through fiction I can come at the truth."

■ For More Information See

PERIODICALS

Horn Book, March/April, 1994.
Kirkus Reviews, September 1, 1993.

* * *

WELSCH, Roger L(ee) 1936-

ROGER L. WELSCH

■ Personal

Born November 6, 1936, in Lincoln, NE; son of Christian (a stationary steam engineer) and Bertha (Flack) Welsch; married second wife, Linda Hotovy (an artist), April 25, 1981; children: (first marriage) Chris, Jennifer, Joyce; (second marriage) Antonia. *Education:* University of Nebraska, B.A., 1958, M.A., 1960; folklore studies at University of Colorado, 1962, and Indiana University, 1963 and 1964. *Politics:* Liberal. *Religion:* Native American Church. *Hobbies and other interests:* Tinkering with 1930s tractors.

■ Addresses

Home—Dannebrog, NE. *Agent*—Freya Manston, 145 West 58th St., New York, NY 10019.

■ Career

Dana College, Blair, NE, instructor in German, 1960-64; Nebraska Wesleyan University, Lincoln, assistant professor of folklore and German, 1964-73; University of Nebraska, teacher of folklore in Extension Division, 1966-88, member of English and anthropology faculties, 1973-88, adjunct professor, 1988—; *CBS News: Sunday Morning* essayist, 1988—; guest faculty member and lecturer at various universities. Formerly wrote and hosted *Hand-Me-Downs,* a series for Nebraska Educational Television, and *The Guinness Book of Sports* for ESPN. Smithsonian Institute Festival of American Folklife, field representative, 1974-77; National Endowment for the Arts Folk Arts panel, panelist and chair, 1977-81. *Member:* American Folklore Society (life member), Association of Living History, Farms and Agricultural Museum (member of board of directors), Nebraska State Historical Society, Phi Sigma Iota, Delta Phi Alpha.

■ Awards, Honors

Outstanding Young Faculty Award, Nebraska Wesleyan, 1967; Distinguished Teaching Award, University of Nebraska, 1977; Fling Fellowship, 1978; honorary Doctor of Humane Letters degree, Kearney State College, 1989; Nebraska Public Speaker of the Year, University of Nebraska Speech Honoraries, 1990; Nebraska Highway 58 renamed "Roger Welsch Avenue" by the governor of Nebraska and the State Highway Commission, 1990; Friend of Festivals Award, Nebraska Travel Industry, 1991; Distinguished Nebraskan, Washington, D.C., Nebraska Club, 1992; Ruth Etting Award for Contributions to Live Performance, 1993; Knights of Ak-Sar-Ben Contributions to Agriculture Award, 1993.

■ Writings

An Outline-Guide to Nebraska Folklore (syllabus), Extension Division, University of Nebraska, 1966.
A Treasury of Nebraska Pioneer Folklore, University of Nebraska Press, 1966.
Sod Walls: The Story of the Nebraska Sod House, Purcell Publications, 1968.
(Translator) Kaarle Krohn, *Folklore Methodology,* University of Texas Press, 1971.
Shingling the Fog and Other Plains Lies, Swallow Press, 1972.
Tall Tale Postcards: A Pictorial History, A. S. Barnes, 1976.
(Editor) *Germans and German-Russians in Nebraska,* University of Nebraska Center for Great Plains Studies, 1980.

Omaha Tribal Myths and Trickster Tales, Ohio University Press, 1981.
Mister, You Got Yourself a Horse: Tales of Old-Time Horse Trading, University of Nebraska Press, 1981.
Catfish at the Pump: Humor and the Frontier, Plains Heritage, 1982.
Inside Lincoln, Plains Heritage, 1984.
You Know You're a Nebraskan, Plains Heritage, 1985.
(Editor) P. M. Hannibal, *Beautiful Dannebrog,* Plains Heritage, 1986.
You Know You're a Husker, Plains Heritage, 1986.
Cather's Kitchens, University of Nebraska Press, 1987.
It's Not the End of the Earth but You Can See It from Here (fiction), Random House, 1990.
Touching the Fire: Buffalo Dancers, the Sky Bundle, and Other Tales (fiction), Villard Press, 1992.
Liars Too: The Legend Continues, Lee Book Publishers, 1993.
Uncle Smoke Stories: Four Nehawka Coyote Stories from the Big Belly Lodge (young adult), Knopf, 1994.

Contributor of book reviews to the *Los Angeles Times;* regular contributor to *Abstracts of Folklore Studies,* 1963—, and other folklore journals and regional magazines. Author of scripts for *Hand-Me-Downs,* a series for Nebraska Educational Television, and *The Guinness Book of Sports,* for ESPN. Author of recordings, "Songs for Today," Lutheran Records, 1963, and "Sweet Nebraska land," Folkways, 1965. Author of a twice monthly column in the *Nebraska Farmer,* a weekly column in twenty-one Nebraska newspapers; a monthly column, "Science Lite," in *Natural History* magazine; a quarterly column in *The Esquire Gentleman;* and book reviews published twice annually in *Successful Farming.*

Adaptations

Essays from *Touching the Fire: Buffalo Dancers, the Sky Bundle, and Other Tales* are slated to be presented on CBS.

Sidelights

Roger L. Welsch told *SATA:* "I am a Nebraskan, born, raised, and stayed. I was born in 1936 in Lincoln to Chris and Bertha Welsch, migrant farm workers and laborers. I report that only because I so profoundly admire the fact that from this background they not only gave me every ounce and inch of education I was willing to accept, but they themselves have throughout their own lives never missed a chance to learn, becoming the most learned and wise people I know.

"I, on the other hand, wasted a lot of people's time at Lincoln High School and the University of Nebraska. What I learned, I learned mostly by virtue of profoundly kind teachers like Paul Schach in languages and Robert Knoll in English and through my own pig-headedness. Told by my high school German teacher that I was one of those people who simply cannot learn language, I took enormous pride in returning to visit her during my senior year at the University to tell her that I was studying French, German, Icelandic, Old Norse, Hebrew, and Latin. Told by professors that I would never be a scholar, I began a ferocious program of research and publication, publishing extensively (including at this point sixteen books), and becoming a university faculty member and eventually a full professor with tenure—and a colleague of those very same professors.

Welsch created the fictional Nehawka tribe and its great storyteller Uncle Smoke to introduce young readers to the rich traditions of American Indians. (Cover illustration by Richard Mantel.)

"From a previous marriage I have three children—Chris, Jenny, and Joyce. I have been married to Linda Hotovy Welsch for thirteen years; we have a daughter, Antonia, age ten. Linda is my partner and editor as well as my wife; there is no doubt in my mind that she is in large part responsible for whatever I have accomplished during the last fourteen years of my life.

"I currently make a living at banquet speaking, writing a column ('Science Lite') for *Natural History* magazine, and writing and delivering essays entitled 'Postcards from Nebraska' on CBS's *Sunday Morning* with Charles Kuralt. Kuralt and I became friends almost twenty years ago when he was in Nebraska on a speaking engagement and asked someone if there was anything going on in the state that might make a good piece for his *On the Road* series. The person noted that there was a fruitcake in

Lincoln who admired and ate weeds, was running for the Weed Board on a pro-weed ticket, had been endorsed by Euell Gibbons, and was generally having a real good time running for office. That was me. Kuralt came to Lincoln and did an *On the Road* piece with me. We got along famously and over the years did six more *On the Roads* and a couple of small pieces for *Sunday Morning.* In 1988 Kuralt asked me to become a member of the *Sunday Morning* cast, an opportunity beyond my imagination, and I am now in my sixth year with that distinguished program. I have also written and hosted series for Nebraska Educational Television entitled *Hand-Me-Downs* and for ESPN, *The Guinness Book of Sports.*

"I love life at Primrose Farm, a tree farm, and Dannebrog. My current hobby is 1930s Allis Chalmers WC tractors, with which I tinker endlessly and contentedly. I am excited about my new careers of writing fiction . . . and television essays. (I just signed a new two-year contract with CBS.) In 1994 Knopf published *Uncle Smoke Stories,* my first effort for young readers; the book is an introduction to Native American culture and folklore.

"I am committed to my relationship of thirty years with the Omaha Indians and a more recent association with the Pawnee Tribe; these kind and wise people have given me spiritual direction, for which I am constantly grateful. My hope is to repay them some day for their kindness."

* * *

WEZYK, Joanna 1966-

■ Personal

Born January 19, 1966, in Krakow, Poland; daughter of Stanislaw (a professor of science) and Jolanta (a biochemist; maiden name, Halibozek) Wezyk. *Education:* Academy of Fine Arts (Krakow, Poland), M.F.A., 1989. *Religion:* Roman Catholic. *Hobbies and other interests:* Classical music (Mozart, Chopin), the history of art, hiking, skiing.

■ Addresses

Home—934 Kenneth Ave., Elizabeth, NJ 07202. *Agent*—Virginia Knowlton, Curtis Brown Ltd., 10 Astor Pl., New York, NY 10013.

■ Career

Free-lance artist in Krakow, Poland, New York City, and Washington, D.C. *Exhibitions:* Stamford Art Association, Stamford, CT; Polish and Slavic Center for the Arts, New York City; Schoenbouer Gallery, Annapolis, MD; Innercity Gallery, Providence, RI; Consulate General of the Republic of Poland, New York City; and Greenwich Library, Greenwich, CT (all 1993). *Member:* American Society of Writers and Illustrators, Knickerbocker Art Club, Stamford Art Association, American Center of Polish Culture, American-Polish Art Association, Artist Women Club.

■ Awards, Honors

Second prize, Krakow, Poland, for "Student Song Festival" (poster); third prize, Ministry of Culture, Poland, for "Illustration of Old Krakow"; honorable mention, Innercity Gallery, for "Summer 1993."

■ Illustrator

Elsa Okon Rael, *Marushka's Egg,* Four Winds Press, 1993.

Also author and illustrator of *Ptaki Samotraki* (for children), 1988, and graphic designer and illustrator for *Lemkowszczyzna Poems,* 1988. Illustrator of the cover for the Polish Cultural Foundation Guide, 1992. Contributor of illustrations to various publications, including *Drobiarstwo, Krag, Wierchy,* and *Ecological Club.*

■ Work in Progress

Illustrations and poster for concerts, for American Center of Polish Culture; research for a second volume to *Marushka's Egg,* as well as *Clever Manka, Christmas Eve, Belinda of Butterflies,* and many other books.

JOANNA WEZYK

Sidelights

Joanna Wezyk told *SATA:* "I was born and raised in Poland. I've always loved fairy tales, legends, and folk-stories. Ever since I was a little girl, I have lived in an imaginary world, full of fairies, witches, and other rather unreal creatures. Baba Yaga was one of my favorites. I used to spend hours painting and drawing her kingdom, especially her hut on two chicken legs. I guess I never grew up. I have never left Baba Yaga's world. I think my illustrations for *Marushka's Egg* show it. They were done with all my heart and love.

"I graduated from the Academy of Fine Arts in Krakow, Poland, where I specialized in painting and children's book illustrations. After five years of studying for my M.F.A. I came to America. I have always done my illustrations in the colors of the rainbow, very bright—full of golden and silver accents; when I was leaving Poland I couldn't get my artwork published the way I wanted. Thus began my artist career in the U.S.A. I found a wonderful agent and soon I was able to make my dream come true. Finally my illustrations had an audience—the best I could imagine—the children. Now my world full of Cinderellas, Thumbelinas, Don Quixotes, and dwarfs opened its doors for American children.

"One day (after I had already made illustrations for *Marushka's Egg*), I decided to give material shape to another dream of mine: a puppet show. I painted the scenery, changed my heroes into puppets, made costumes for the actors, and with author Elsa Rael I performed for children at the White House and many bookstores. I consider the 'White House Easter Egg Roll' my best show because I could introduce my Baba Yaga to thirty thousand kids from all over the world.

"I am also a painter, and have had exhibitions in the U.S.A. and Europe. I paint portraits of women with different kinds of ideas. But if you look closer, you find out that we and they have something in common. We're all dreamers ... just like me!"

For More Information See

PERIODICALS

Booklist, March 15, 1993.
Kirkus Reviews, February 1, 1993.
Manhattan Arts, September-October, 1992, p. 19.
Publishers Weekly, February 8, 1993, p. 86.

* * *

WIGGERS, Raymond 1952-

Personal

Born October 17, 1952, in Lake Forest, IL; son of Raymond P. (an advertising executive) and Irene Mary (a homemaker and editor; maiden name, Knapp) Wiggers. *Education:* Purdue University, B.S. *Politics:* "Waning." *Religion:* "Waxing."

Addresses

Home—1740 South Park Ave., Springfield, IL 62704. *Office*—Illinois State Museum, Spring & Edwards Sts., Springfield, IL 62706.

Career

Environmental protection geologist with the Illinois E.P.A., 1979-80; self-employed horticulturist, 1980-92; classical music announcer and program host for public radio, 1988-90; national park service ranger and environmental education specialist, 1992-93; Illinois State Museum, Springfield, IL, museum editor and curator of publications, 1993—. *Military service:* U.S. Navy, 1974-78; became full lieutenant. *Member:* Geological Society of America, New England Wildflower Society, Illinois Native Plant Society.

Writings

Picture Guide to Tree Leaves, F. Watts, 1991.
The Amateur Geologist: Explorations and Investigations, F. Watts, 1993.
The Plant Explorer's Guide to New England, Mountain Press, 1994.

Also author of numerous newspaper articles on horticultural topics.

Work in Progress

Currently researching two upcoming books on the natural history of the Great Lakes region.

Sidelights

Raymond Wiggers told *SATA,* "I am particularly interested in explaining fascinating aspects of geology and botany to children and to adults. Writing is my first and greatest love, and if I succeed in helping my readers understand the world about them a little more clearly, I feel I have accomplished something that is crucially important."

Wiggers' botanical and geological reference materials have drawn favorable reactions from commentators. *Picture Guide to Tree Leaves* received praise from Barbara B. Murphy, a critic for *School Library Journal.* Murphy commented: "the illustrations are very attractive" and "help readers recognize various kinds of North American trees." Carolyn Phelan, a reviewer for *Booklist,* stated that in *The Amateur Geologist* "Wiggers proves an enthusiastic and organized guide to the subject."

Wiggers said that *Picture Guide to Tree Leaves* is not only being used as a "guidebook and learning resource in our nation's most preeminent horticultural and botanical institutions" including, "the Missouri Botanical Garden in St. Louis and Chicago's Morton Arboretum," but is now issued in a paperback edition for students, librarians, and educators.

Works Cited

Murphy, Barbara B., review of *Picture Guide to Tree Leaves, School Library Journal,* July, 1991, p. 78.
Phelan, Carolyn, review of *The Amateur Geologist, Booklist,* January 15, 1994, p. 918.

For More Information See

PERIODICALS

Book Report, March, 1994, p. 54.
Library Talk, May, 1991, p. 35.
Science Books and Films, May, 1994, p. 108.*

* * *

WING, Natasha (Lazutin) 1960-

Personal

Born February 7, 1960, in Milford, CT; daughter of Alexander Paul (a salesman) and Paula (a bookkeeper; maiden name, Kimball) Lazutin; married Daniel Brian Wing (a civil engineer), January 16, 1988. *Education:* Attended Fairleigh Dickinson University; Arizona State University, B.S., 1982. *Hobbies and other interests:* Sabaka, a husky, and Toonces, a cat; also collects signed children's books and sterling silver snowflakes.

Addresses

Office—1955 Sycamore Ct., McKinleyville, CA 95521.

Career

Author. Worked for the *Arizona Republic/Phoenix Gazette,* 1982-88; MTC Associates (advertising agency), Arcata, CA, account representative, 1988-90; Write Ideas, McKinleyville, CA, owner and writer, 1990—. *Member:* Society of Children's Book Writers and Illustrators, Friends of the McKinleyville Library (president).

Writings

Hippity Hop, Frog on Top, illustrated by DeLoss McGraw, Simon & Schuster, 1994.
Jalapeno Bagels, Atheneum, 1996.

Sidelights

Natasha L. Wing told *SATA:* "I was at a Christmas fair in Phoenix when I picked up *Polar Express* and was captivated by its magic. That's when I decided I wanted to write children's books. I am intrigued by children's curiosity and openness to fantasy. I am also a believer in 1 + 1 = 3. When you put two things together, such as a story and illustrations, the result is greater than what you expected. That's what I find so exciting about picture books—and life!"

NATASHA WING

WOLKSTEIN, Diane 1942-

Personal

Born November 11, 1942, in New York, NY; daughter of Harry W. (a certified public accountant) and Ruth (Barenbaum) Wolkstein; married Benjamin Zucker (a gem merchant), September 7, 1969; children: Rachel Cloudstone. *Education:* Smith College, B.A., 1964; studied pantomime in Paris, 1964-65; Bank Street College of Education, M.A., 1967. *Religion:* Jewish. *Hobbies and other interests:* Travel, gardening in New York City.

Addresses

Home—10 Patchin Pl., New York, NY 10011.

Career

WNYC-Radio, New York City, hostess of weekly radio show "Stories from Many Lands with Diane Wolkstein," 1968-80; featured storyteller at numerous festivals and gatherings in the United States, Canada, and Europe. Bank Street College of Education, New York City, instructor in storytelling and children's literature, 1970—; teacher of mythology at Sarah Lawrence College, 1984, and New School for Social Research, 1989. Leader of storytelling workshops for librarians and teachers; has also recorded stories for Canadian Broadcasting Corporation (radio and television); featured on *Sunday Morning with Charles Kuralt,* 1992. Co-director, Cloudstone Productions, a multimedia publishing company.

Awards, Honors

New York Academy of Sciences Children's Science Book honorable mention, 1973, for *8,000 Stones: A Chinese Folktale;* Lithgow-Osborne fellowship, 1976, 1977; American Institute of Graphic Arts award, 1977, for *The Red Lion: A Persian Sufi Tale;* notable book citations, American Library Association, 1978, for *The Magic Orange Tree and Other Haitian Folk Tales,* and 1979, for *White Wave: A Tao Tale;* recipient of Marshall grant.

Writings

RETELLER OF FOLKTALES

8,000 Stones: A Chinese Folktale, illustrated by Ed Young, Doubleday, 1972.
The Cool Ride in the Sky, illustrated by Paul Galdone, Knopf, 1973.
Squirrel's Song: A Hopi-Indian Story, illustrated by Lillian Hoban, Knopf, 1975.
Lazy Stories, illustrated by James Marshall, Seabury, 1976.
The Red Lion: A Persian Sufi Tale, illustrated by Young, Crowell, 1977.

DIANE WOLKSTEIN

The Magic Orange Tree and Other Haitian Folk Tales, illustrated by Elsa Henriquez, Knopf, 1978.
White Wave: A Tao Tale, illustrated by Young, Crowell, 1979, revised edition, Harcourt, in press.
The Banza: A Haitian Folk Tale, illustrated by Marc Brown, Dial, 1980.
(With Samuel Noah Kramer) *Inanna, Queen of Heaven and Earth: Her Stories and Hymns from Sumer,* Harper, 1983.
The Magic Wings, illustrated by Robert Andrew Parker, Dutton, 1983.
The Legend of Sleepy Hollow (based on the story by Washington Irving), illustrated by R. W. Alley, Morrow, 1987.
The First Love Stories: From Isis and Osiris to Tristan and Iseult, HarperCollins, 1991.
Oom Razoom; or, Go I Know Not Where, Bring Back I Know Not What, illustrated by Dennis McDermott, Morrow, 1991.

OTHER

The Visit, illustrated by Lois Ehlert, Knopf, 1974.
Little Mouse's Painting, illustrated by Maryjane Begin, Morrow, 1991.
Abulafia: Part of My Heart, Dreamsongs, Cloudstone, 1991.
Step by Step, illustrated by Jos. A. Smith, Morrow, 1994.

Also author of audio recordings *Tales of the Hopi Indians,* 1972, *California Fairy Tales,* 1972, and *Eskimo Stories: Tales of Magic,* 1974, all for Spoken Arts; *The Cool Ride in the Sky,* Miller-Brody, 1975; *Hans Christian Andersen in Central Park,* Weston Woods, 1981; *Psyche and Eros,* 1984, *Romping,* 1985, *The Story of Joseph,* 1986, *The Epic of Inanna,* 1987, and *Tales from Estonia,* 1988, all for Cloudstone Productions; and *The Banza: A Haitian Folk Tale,* for Storytime. Author of video recording, *Inanna,* Cloudstone Productions, 1988. Contributor to periodicals, including *Horn Book, Wilson Library Bulletin, Parabola, Quadrant, Confrontation,* and *School Library Journal.*

Work in Progress

Esther's Story, a biblical adaptation, 1996, and *Sun Mother Wakes the World,* an aborigine tale, both for Morrow; *Bouki Dances the Kokioko: A Haitian Story* and *The Grass Slipper: A Chinese Cinderella,* both for Harcourt.

Sidelights

Known as the "official storyteller of New York City" for her weekly radio show and summer story sessions in Central Park, Diane Wolkstein "has worked hard to revitalize the art of storytelling," Donna Seaman remarked in *Booklist.* "Storytelling is immediate and intimate," Wolkstein noted in a 1983 *Horn Book* article, an experience where "the audience is as important as the storyteller." Before she begins a story, Wolkstein related, she often uses this type of introduction: "I hope you can all see and hear me, for what we are going to do is go on a journey together, and the way in which we go and what we see will depend as much on you as on me." By producing book versions of the stories she has learned, Wolkstein has brought many readers along on her voyages to other lands and cultures.

Born in New York City, Wolkstein wrote in a 1992 *Horn Book* article that "the seed for storytelling was planted in my childhood" in stories she heard from her mother and at the local synagogue. "The stories my mother told were pleasurable and reassuring; the stories of the rabbi were riveting. They posed questions and portended answers, and I was a young girl filled with questions, wonderings, ponderings." To fulfill her need to learn and tell stories, Wolkstein majored in drama at Smith College; she followed this with a year of pantomime study in Paris, learning from the renowned Marcel Marceau. In France she also worked in film dubbing and told Bible stories to a group of ten nine-year-olds. But upon returning to the United States, the author related, "I realized that what I cared about most was not the glitter of the sophisticated film or theater world but the storytelling I had done with ten children. That's what I wanted to continue."

Wolkstein studied for a master's degree in education at the noted Bank Street College in New York, thinking that as a teacher she could at least dramatize stories for her students. After graduating, however, she sought work as a storyteller, and proposed to New York City's parks department that they hire her to perform stories around the city. Although she was initially refused, she persisted and was hired as one of the country's first professional storytellers. She prepared with hours of memorizing and practicing before taking her stories to local schools, libraries, community centers, and hospitals, as well as to Central Park. With the start of her radio show the following year, Wolkstein's tales began reaching even more listeners, and she began training and practicing even more, taking lessons in elocution, dance, and voice, and studying with musicians from different cultures.

This collection of Haitian tales was a 1978 American Library Association notable book. (Cover illustration by Elsa Henriquez.)

In 1972, five years after she began her storytelling career, Wolkstein published her first folktale adaptation, *8,000 Stones: A Chinese Folktale.* This version of the story of a prince who solves the problem of how to weigh an elephant is "skillfully retold," according to a *Kirkus Reviews* writer. The author stayed closer to home to relate the African American tale *The Cool Ride in the Sky,* which was also popularized in the Nat King Cole song "Straighten up and Fly Right." On a hot day, a buzzard gets free meals by offering to take other animals flying on his back, whereupon he eats them. But a smart monkey outfoxes him, getting a cool ride and giving the other animals something to cheer about. "The written text, with its repetitions and long run-on sentences, begs to be read out loud," Margaret F. O'Connell observed in the *New York Times Book Review.* While a *Bulletin for the Center of Children's Books* critic believed the tale "loses some of its vitality in print," a *Kirkus Reviews* writer found that "the drama and humor of the situation" help make the book "a story hour success."

Reviewers have frequently noted Wolkstein's ability to produce texts that will allow readers to entertain their own audiences. Of the three tales in *Lazy Stories, School Library Journal* contributor Joan E. Bezrudczyk wrote that "the simple, direct language," along with useful storyteller's notes, makes them "well-suited for reading aloud." A *Publishers Weekly* critic concurred, noting that the tales from Mexico, Japan, and Laos "are all entertaining flights of fancy with the flavor of their locales preserved." *The Red Lion: A Tale of Ancient Persia* similarly brings the ancient Middle East kingdom to life with the story of how Prince Azgid overcomes his fear of lions to claim his throne. While *Wilson Library Bulletin* contributors Donnarae MacCann and Olga Richard felt the story loses a bit in the translation, needing "the larger context to amplify both its meaning and its poetry," Mary M. Burns praised Wolkstein's "flowing, rhythmic style." The critic concluded in *Horn Book* that "the tale is a superb addition to the storyteller's repertoire."

In bringing different folktales to her audiences, Wolkstein frequently travels around the world, getting tales direct from native storytellers. Seven visits to the Caribbean island nation of Haiti resulted in the collection *The Magic Orange Tree and Other Haitian Folk Tales* and the picture book *The Banza: A Haitian Folk*

Tale. "The spirit of Haiti comes alive" in the former, wrote Barbara Elleman in *Booklist,* with Wolkstein's notes helping to reveal the nature of the Haitian people. "The musical quality of the prose carries the narratives," observed Anne Hanst in *School Library Journal,* and Wolkstein even includes music to accompany each tale. Music also plays a role in *The Banza,* which tells of how Tiger's gift of a banjo, or banza, gives Goat the courage to face off ten strange, hungry tigers. "Told with rich economy, this brief tale is laced with action and humor," George Shannon commented in *School Library Journal,* and is "filled with many inner levels of meaning." "Wolkstein's airy, humorous version of the tale," concluded a *Publishers Weekly* critic, "will add laurels to her status as a folklorist."

Two retellings of Chinese folktales demonstrate the contrasting styles Wolkstein can use. *White Wave: A Tao Tale,* a delicate story about a poor farm boy who is visited during his life by a goddess that comes out of a moon snail, is told "with great skill and style," according to a *Bulletin of the Center for Children's Books* review by Zena Sutherland, with Wolkstein "suiting the fluent, subdued telling to the grace and tenderness of a gentle story." On the other hand, *The Magic Wings* is a humorous tale of the competition between several women, including a goose girl and a queen, to earn wings. "This sly bit of one-upmanship and comeuppance begs to be told aloud and dramatized," Ellen D. Warwick declared in *School Library Journal.* As a *Publishers Weekly* critic related, the audience participation Wolkstein encourages in this tale, as she does with other stories, "has earned her an enviable reputation."

In explaining the appeal of Wolkstein's retellings, several critics have remarked on the author's use of language and rhythm. For *Inanna: Queen of Heaven and Earth,* a scholarly reworking of several Sumerian myths, Wolkstein has used "prose which is mesmerizingly rhythmic and poetic" in producing "a considerable achievement of synthesis and condensation," Gregory Maguire wrote in *Horn Book.* The storyteller's reworking of Washington Irving's *The Legend of Sleepy Hollow* "has an effervescent flow that begs to be shared," Elleman stated in *Booklist,* making it appropriate for adults and children. And in *Oom Razoom; or, Go I Know Not Where, Bring Back I Know Not What,* a Russian story of a faithful couple's battle against a wicked king, the author "nicely hones her language to the spoken word," a *Kirkus Reviews* critic noted, "keeping the many events in this lengthy, complex tale moving briskly."

In addition to her folktale adaptations, Wolkstein has written original stories for children, including *Little Mouse's Painting,* which *School Library Journal* contributor Lisa Dennis termed "an appealing, insightful look at friendship and creativity," and *Step by Step,* another tale of camaraderie. No matter the source of her tale, however, it is the story that is of foremost importance. "Each time a storyteller tells an important story, she finds something new and interesting," Wolkstein wrote in her earlier *Horn Book* article; "what intrigues the storyteller almost always fascinates the listeners, for it

Wolkstein adapted the Haitian folk tale of the friendship between a tiger and a goat in this 1981 book. (Cover illustration by Marc Brown.)

permits them to be caught by *their* own personal interests." She further described this interactive process in her 1992 *Horn Book* piece: "Whether folk tale, myth, or dream—whatever the age for which it is intended—for me the telling of a story requires attention to many details. But once a story begins, and I am standing before the audience, I let the ingredients do their own mixing so I can participate in the alchemical heat which flows back and forth from teller to listener, creating the spirit of a new story."

■ Works Cited

Review of *The Banza: A Haitian Folk Tale, Publishers Weekly,* October 9, 1981, p. 67.

Bezrudczyk, Joan E., review of *Lazy Stories, School Library Journal,* September, 1976, p. 127.

Burns, Mary M., review of *The Red Lion: A Tale of Ancient Persia, Horn Book,* April, 1978, pp. 157-58.

Review of *The Cool Ride in the Sky, Kirkus Reviews,* July 1, 1973, pp. 682-83.

Review of *The Cool Ride in the Sky, Bulletin of the Center for Children's Books,* January, 1974, p. 88.

Dennis, Lisa, review of *Little Mouse's Painting, School Library Journal,* June, 1992, p. 105.

Review of *8,000 Stones: A Chinese Folktale, Kirkus Reviews,* June 1, 1973, p. 621.

Elleman, Barbara, review of *The Magic Orange Tree and Other Haitian Folk Tales, Booklist,* July 15, 1978, p. 1738.

Elleman, Barbara, review of *The Legend of Sleepy Hollow, Booklist,* October 15, 1987, p. 404.
Hanst, Anne, review of *The Magic Orange Tree and Other Haitian Folk Tales, School Library Journal,* April, 1979, pp. 64-65.
Review of *Lazy Stories, Publishers Weekly,* May 24, 1976, p. 60.
MacCann, Donnarae, and Olga Richard, "Picture Books for Children," *Wilson Library Bulletin,* February, 1978, p. 496.
Review of *The Magic Wings, Publishers Weekly,* November 4, 1983, p. 65.
Maguire, Gregory, review of *Inanna, Queen of Heaven and Earth, Horn Book,* December, 1983, p. 729.
O'Connell, Margaret F., review of *The Cool Ride in the Sky, New York Times Book Review,* September 30, 1973, p. 8.
Review of *Oom Razoom; or, Go I Know Not Where, Bring Back I Know Not What, Kirkus Reviews,* July 1, 1991, p. 862.
Seaman, Donna, review of *The First Love Stories: From Isis and Osiris to Tristan and Iseult, Booklist,* January 15, 1991, p. 999.
Shannon, George, review of *The Banza: A Haitian Folk Tale, School Library Journal,* December, 1981, p. 58.
Sutherland, Zena, review of *White Wave: A Tao Tale, Bulletin of the Center for Children's Books,* November, 1979, p. 64.
Warwick, Ellen D., review of *The Magic Wings, School Library Journal,* October, 1983, p. 154.
Wolkstein, Diane, and James Wiggins, "On Story and Storytelling: A Conversation," *Horn Book,* June, 1983, pp. 350-57.
Wolkstein, Diane, "Twenty-five Years of Storytelling: The Spirit of the Art," *Horn Book,* November/December, 1992, pp. 702-8.

■ For More Information See

PERIODICALS

Bulletin of the Center for Children's Books, April, 1977, p. 135; March, 1982, p. 140.
Horn Book, October, 1972, pp. 459-60; August, 1978, p. 406; February, 1984, p. 47.
Kirkus Reviews, March 15, 1977, p. 283.
New York Review of Books, October 13, 1983, p. 7.
New York Times, July 15, 1968, p. 34.
New York Times Book Review, March 23, 1980, p. 39; September 25, 1983, p. 31; February 17, 1991, p. 17.
Publishers Weekly, May 23, 1977, p. 246; April 27, 1992, pp. 267-68.
Saturday Review/World, December 4, 1973, p. 32.
School Library Journal, September, 1979, p. 124; November, 1987, p. 92; September, 1991, p. 249; August, 1994, p. 148.
Village Voice, November 22, 1983, p. 50.
Washington Post Book World, July 9, 1978, p. E4.

—Sketch by Diane Telgen

WUNSCH, Marjory 1942-

■ Personal

Born November 15, 1942 in Brooklyn, NY; daughter of Harry (a businessman) and Ruth (a school psychologist; maiden name, Cohen) Markel; married Carl Isaac Wunsch (a professor of physical oceanography), June 6, 1970; children: Jared, Hannah. *Education:* Cornell University, B.A., 1964; Harvard University, M.AT., 1965; Harvard University Graduate School of Design, M.Arch., 1974.

■ Addresses

Home and office—78 Washington Ave., Cambridge, MA 02140.

■ Career

Freelance illustrator and author of children's books, 1977—. *Exhibitions:* Society of Illustrators 10th Annual Exhibition, "The Original Art," 1990; "Women Illustrators in New England" Radcliffe College, 1991. *Member:* Society of Children's Book Writers and Illustrators, Graphic Artists Guild.

■ Awards, Honors

Ford Junior Fellowship, Boston Museum School, 1966.

MARJORY WUNSCH

■ Writings

SELF-ILLUSTRATED

Spaceship Number Four, Lothrop, 1992.
Aunt Belle's Beach, Lothrop, 1994.

ILLUSTRATOR

Sharla Gold and Michael Miswari Caspi, *The Answered Prayer and Other Yemenite Folktales,* Jewish Publication Society, 1990.
Sandi Barrett Ruch, *Junkyard Dog,* Orchard Books, 1990.

Has also done illustrations for *Harvard Magazine, Boston Globe,* and for textbooks published by D. C. Heath.

■ For More Information See

PERIODICALS

Horn Book Guide, spring, 1993, p. 51.
Library Talk, November, 1992, p. 16.
New York Times Book Review, November 22, 1992, p. 34.
Publishers Weekly, September 7, 1993, p. 62.
School Library Journal, December, 1992, p. 94; July, 1994, p. 92.